The End of the European E
1890 to the Present

SECOND EDITION

$0925XX

THE NORTON HISTORY OF MODERN EUROPE

General Editor: FELIX GILBERT, Institute for Advanced Study

The Foundations of Early Modern Europe, 1460–1559
EUGENE F. RICE, JR.

The Age of Religious Wars, 1559–1689, *2nd edition*
RICHARD S. DUNN

Kings and Philosophers, 1689–1789
LEONARD KRIEGER

The Age of Revolution and Reaction, *1789–1850, 2nd edition*
CHARLES BREUNIG

The Age of Nationalism and Reform, *1850–1890, 2nd edition*
NORMAN RICH

The End of the European Era, 1890 to the Present, *2nd edition*
FELIX GILBERT

The End of the European Era
1890 to the Present

SECOND EDITION

FELIX GILBERT
Institute for Advanced Study

W · W · NORTON & COMPANY · INC · NEW YORK

Grateful acknowledgment is made for permission to quote
from the following: Siegfried Sassoon, "Repression of War Ex-
perience," from *Collected Poems* by Siegfried Sassoon. Copy-
right 1918 by E. P. Dutton, Inc., renewed 1946 by Siegfried
Sassoon. Reprinted by permission of Viking Penguin, Inc. and
G. T. Sassoon; W. H. Auden: "Spain, 1937," from *The English
Auden: Poems, Essays, and Dramatic Writings, 1927–1939* by
W. H. Auden, edited by Edward Mendelson. Copyright 1940,
renewed 1968 by W. H. Auden. Reprinted by permission of
Random House, Inc. and Faber and Faber Ltd.

Copyright © 1979, 1970 by W. W. Norton & Company, Inc.

Library of Congress Cataloging in Publication Data
Gilbert, Felix, 1905–
    The end of the European era, 1890 to the present.
    (The Norton history of modern Europe)
    Bibliography: p.
    Includes index.
    1. Europe—Politics and government—20th century.
2. World politics—20th century.   I. Title.
D443.G473   1979   940.5   79–312
ISBN 0–393–05690–2
ISBN 0–393–09020–5 pbk.

Published simultaneously in Canada by
George J. McLeod Limited, Toronto.
PRINTED IN THE UNITED STATES OF AMERICA.
All Rights Reserved
Cartography by Harold K. Faye
Picture research by Liesel Bennett

1 2 3 4 5 6 7 8 9 0

Contents

Illustrations

Maps

PART I

EUROPE'S APOGEE

CHAPTER 1

The Beginning of a New Century

ONE AFTERNOON early in the twentieth century a member of the British aristocracy, a great landowner, stood with one of his guests on the terrace extending along the back of his large country house. In the valley at their feet lay farms, cottages, a railway, a coal mine, and streets dense with workers. Beyond this valley was a hill, with another large country house on top of it. Pointing to this house, the host said to his guest: "You see, there is no one between us and them."

This is a revealing story. In earlier centuries it may have been natural for great landowners to feel themselves far removed from the servants and agricultural laborers who lived and worked in their houses and on their estates, and to have considered them of no account. But in the twentieth century, as the monopoly of power slipped out of the hands of the landowning classes, and those living in the neighborhood were no longer as dependent, this undisguised feeling of superiority seems inappropriate and even perverse. At the same time, however, this story points up the reasons for social and political tensions and instability in the twentieth century; in times of great changes a ruling class has not only difficulty permitting others to participate in power, but still more, in recognizing that such a change is going on.

A RISING POPULATION

The story of our landowner is a striking example of the inability of the upper classes to realize one of the main changes in this period: the increasing role of the industrial urban population and the decline of the agrarian sector. Between 1871, when the unification of Germany altered the map of Europe and established a new balance of power, and 1914, when the outbreak of the First World War occurred and European political life was molded into new forms, the population of Europe rose by more than 150 million, and, if Russia is included, totaled almost 450 million people. In the first decade after 1870 this growth of population

3

Traffic on one of the main streets of Paris, the Boulevard des Italiens, in 1909, before the widespread use of the automobile.

was still slow and gradual; but it accelerated from the 1880's on. There was a close connection, of course, between industrialization and population growth, and therefore the population rise was greatest in Germany where, at that time, industrialization was achieving full speed. The German population grew between 1890 and 1910 from 49 to 65 million, or, by more than 25 per cent. The population of Great Britain, where industrialization had come earlier into full stride, amounted in 1914 to 42 million and had grown between 1890 and 1914 by 7.8 million, by a still considerable growth rate of 18 per cent. Even the countries of the Mediterranean area, which for a long time had lagged behind the northern European countries, began to grow with great speed: for instance, from 31 million in 1890, Italy had grown to 36 million in 1910. The two greatest contrasts were between Russia and France: Although exact statistics for Russia are not available, its population increased rapidly and it certainly was the most populous great European power; France, however, was the only European state whose population did not increase during this period. In discussing the developments of European foreign policy at this time it must be kept in mind that, while until 1914 no great frontier changes occurred with regard to the great European powers, their internal strength in relation to each other was in a state of flux.

Perhaps even more startling than increases in population was the migration which took place within the various European states. Before the Industrial Revolution economic life had been primarily agrarian, and agriculture remained the dominant occupation far into the twentieth century in eastern and southeastern Europe. In the two western European countries—England and France—in which industrialization had begun to develop at the end of the eighteenth century, the relation between the number of people occupied in industry and agriculture remained roughly the same from the middle of the nineteenth century until 1914; in England only 10 per cent of the population were engaged in agriculture. In France, where, even in the times of the first industrial revolution, agriculture had remained highly important, it continued to absorb 40 per cent of the population.

In Italy the greater part of the population were occupied in agriculture, but the percentage of those employed in industry and commerce grew steadily especially from the nineties on; by the turn of the century industry represented 20.2 per cent of the gross national product, eight years later 26.1 per cent. But the most striking change in social structure occurred in Germany. In the middle of the nineteenth century about 70 per cent of the German population had been engaged in agriculture. By the nineties this figure had been reduced to 35 per cent and continued to decline. These statistics are interesting from still another point of view: Despite the decrease of Germans employed in agriculture in percentages of the entire population, their absolute number did not decrease. This means that the population growth which took place in these decades was exclusively an increase in the industrial labor force. Although in other countries this development is less clear, it remains true that most of the population growth fed industrialization.

These demographic developments had one consequence which was noticeable without any study of statistical figures: the increase in the number and the size of big cities. Whereas in 1850 there had not been more than fourteen European cities with more than 200,000 inhabitants, this figure had risen to thirty-eight by 1910. In Great Britain and France, the rate of urban growth began to slow down by the end of the nineteenth century. Nevertheless, Greater London grew from 5 million inhabitants in 1880 to 7 million in 1914; Paris, from 2 million to almost 3 million. Cities in those countries which entered the industrial age in the fifty years before the First World War grew even more dramatically. Berlin, with about 500,000 inhabitants in 1866, had more than 2 million in 1914. Barcelona and Milan, the industrial capitals of Spain and Italy, both surpassed 500,000 by 1914. Most significant was the rise in population and the growth of urban settlements in the great coal- and iron-mining districts. In northern France, the city of Lille doubled its population between 1850 and 1914. By 1914 Lille had 200,000 inhabitants, and the

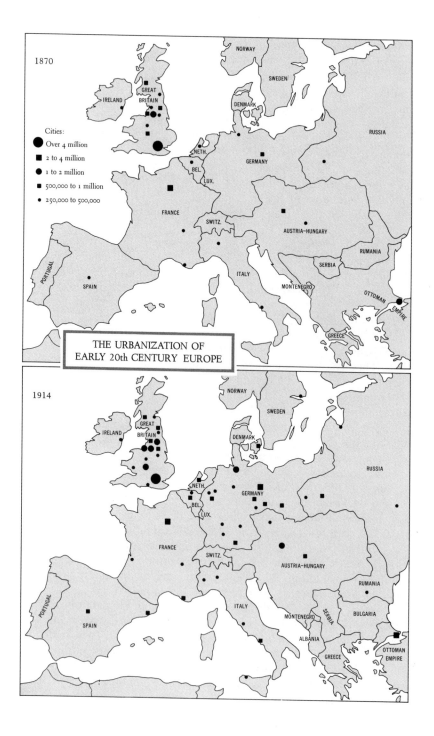

1870

NORWAY

SWEDEN

GREAT
BRITAIN

IRELAND

DENMARK

RUSSIA

Cities:

● Over 4 million

■ 2 to 4 million

● 1 to 2 million

■ 500,000 to 1 million

• 250,000 to 500,000

NETH.

GERMANY

BEL.

LUX.

FRANCE

SWITZ.

AUSTRIA-HUNGARY

RUMANIA

PORTUGAL

SPAIN

ITALY

SERBIA

MONTENEGRO

OTTOMAN
EMPIRE

GREECE

THE URBANIZATION OF
EARLY 20th CENTURY EUROPE

1914

NORWAY

SWEDEN

GREAT
BRITAIN

IRELAND

DENMARK

RUSSIA

NETH.

GERMANY

BEL.

LUX.

FRANCE

SWITZ.

AUSTRIA-HUNGARY

RUMANIA

PORTUGAL

SPAIN

ITALY

BULGARIA

MONTENEGRO

SERBIA

ALBANIA

OTTOMAN
EMPIRE

GREECE

population in neighboring cities so increased that northeastern France began to form one megalopolis. The same phenomenon could be observed in Germany in the Ruhr area, where, for example, Essen, Gelsenkirchen, Bochum, and Mülheim began to run into each other; and the same was happening in the coal-mining districts of upper Silesia around Kattowitz. Russia entered the industrialization race last. But there urban development was rapid. In 1863 Russia had only three cities with more than 100,000 inhabitants—St. Petersburg, Moscow, Kiev; forty years later there were more than fifteen. Around the coal and iron mines of the Donetz Basin and in the oil areas of the Caucasus densely populated districts developed.

INTELLECTUAL DISQUIET AND CULTURAL REVOLT

These shifts in the European social structure are easy to recognize at a later time after they have been reflected in events and can be elucidated with statistical data. But although the specific nature of the changes which occurred were not clearly grasped by contemporary Europeans, they were aware that developments were taking place which cast doubt on the validity of the assumptions and values which had dominated the nineteenth century. Their doubts grew slowly and gradually until, at the end of the century, particularly in the 1890's, movements in literature, art, and philosophy arose, in revolt against traditional attitudes and approaches. Sometimes explicitly, sometimes only implicitly, those classes of society which had been the supporters and protagonists of the established culture came under attack.

Perhaps the most striking indication of widespread intellectual uneasiness was the spread of criticism and demands for reform of those institutions which by their very nature acted as the defenders of the existing order: the churches. In the Catholic and Protestant churches single individuals—de Mun in France; the Catholic Bishop Ketteler and the Protestant court preacher Stoecker in Germany—organized movements which concentrated on the workers, recognizing that the disinterest, if not rejection of Christianity, on the workers' part was closely connected with the misery in which they lived. The most important document expressing the need for religion to take an interest in the situation of industrial workers was the encyclical of Pope Leo XIII: "Rerum Novarum," issued in 1891. The encyclical had a practical purpose: the approval and encouragement of the formation of Christian trade unions. But its theoretical assumptions are no less significant. Not unlike Karl Marx, the pope envisaged as the outcome of industrialization an increasing number of people living in dependence and misery, and an accumulation of wealth in the hands of a very few rich people. The Pope expressed the view that under these circumstances the state had the right to interfere, and to initiate social legislation to protect the workers against exploitation and ameliorate their economic condition. The encyclical was sharply critical of liberalism, in particular, of laissez faire economics, and the underlying assumption that a good society could be achieved by giving free play to the forces of the individual.

Criticism of those attitudes and values which had dominated the rise of the liberal bourgeoisie to influence and power, was also a feature of new movements in literature and art. The recognized leader of the modern drama was the Norwegian, Henrik Ibsen (1828–1906), whose perfectly constructed, provocative plays appeared in the eighties and nineties and were produced all over Europe; some of the greatest actors and actresses of the time—the Italian, Eleonora Duse and the Austrian, Josef Kainz—had their greatest triumphs in Ibsen's plays. In his dramas Ibsen attacked the many injustices in the social life of his time; the inferior and dependent position of women and the ruthlessness of men in the pursuit of social advance were favorite themes. But almost all of Ibsen's plays were also directed against what he considered a more basic and more general defect of his society: the hypocrisy of the bourgeois, who in order to preserve the outward appearance of respectability, built his life on lies, ruthlessly condemning those who had sinned against the accepted moral code and even destroying them.

Ibsen was the great model and teacher for two dramatists who, in Germany and England, dominated the stage from the nineties almost to the middle of the twentieth century: Gerhart Hauptmann (1862–1946) and George Bernard Shaw (1856–1950). Hauptmann gained his reputation in the nineties with a play called *The Weavers*. It presented the revolt of Silesian weavers in the first part of the nineteenth century against the introduction of machines and factories, and contained a strong revolutionary message directed against the bourgeoisie for disregarding the human misery which accompanied their chase after money. In Hauptmann's plays of this early period the chief themes are the contrasts between the ruling group and the poor, and the human tragedies resulting from the insistence on the preservation of conventional morality; Hauptmann was a socialist who agitated for the overthrow of the existing order. George Bernard Shaw was also a socialist, but a Fabian socialist, who believed in the possibility of establishing a better social order by reforms rather than by revolution. Shaw's plays were mostly comedies. At first he selected as themes certain features of modern society—for example, prostitution and militarism—and built the entire play around bitter satiric criticism of them. His later work was lighter, aimed at teasing the prejudices of the ruling classes. The earlier and later plays differed so much in their tone that Shaw himself called them, in a collected edition, "unpleasant and pleasant plays."

These modern playwrights abandoned the tradition of heroizing verse dramas; they were "naturalists." Their people spoke on the stage as they were assumed to speak in real life. This social realism had had its first triumphs in another literary genre—the novel. Emile Zola (1840–1902), the master of this technique continued to publish into the twentieth century, depicting the social changes brought about by industrialization. But the main focus of the younger novelists was given to the phenomenon of the decline of the ruling group; this decline was considered to be most strikingly reflected in the disintegration of the family as an institution—the tendency of later generations to enjoy wealth rather than to increase it, the accompanying decline in morals or acceptance of an aristocratic behavior by the bourgeoisie. At the end of the nineties Thomas Mann (1875–1955) wrote the novel *Buddenbrooks*, in which this process of bourgeois decline is pictured with the deepest psychological understanding; this novel has become the most famous example of many novels with the same theme. Hauptmann, Shaw, Mann, who in the last decade of the nineteenth century made names for themselves with works which outraged and shocked the ruling classes, were thirty years later almost classics; all three received the Nobel prize for literature before the end of the 1920's.

If the fame of these writers has grown in the course of the twentieth century, they were not the most widely known or appreciated literary figures in the 1890's or at the beginning of the twentieth century. These were the years of the "cult of decadence" and attention was focused on the representatives of this attitude. The writers and poets of this aestheticizing trend were no less antagonistic to conventional bourgeois morality than Hauptmann or Shaw, but if the latter had confidence in the coming of a freer life and society, the protagonists of aestheticism saw only decline as result of industrialization and of the emergence of the masses. Understanding for art and beauty had been lost; if it still existed it was the privileged possession of a selected few with finer perceptions and greater sensitivity than the average person. This view was most provokingly flaunted by Oscar Wilde (1854–1900); his comedies dominated the London theatre in the 1890's. There is irony in the fact that Wilde and his plays were the vogue, applauded by those whom, quite intentionally, he attacked and ridiculed. Actually, Wilde's own views, his disregard for moral considerations when and as long as actions resulted in new sensual experiences, is less reflected by these comedies than by his play *Salome* (1894) which Aubrey Beardsley (1872–1898) illustrated in a fitting identical spirit.

The fashionable admiration of decadence passed quickly, but a neoromantic trend remained strong in literature. Poets and writers believed that the cultural achievements of past aristocratic ages were greater than those of the modern world, and that in order to show the potentialities of life you must not depict the reality of the contemporary world but resuscitate the image of a better past. Many of these literary works were set to music because the connection of word and music heightened the feeling of being transposed to a more ideal world. The greatest masters of this neoromanticism were the Belgian, Maurice Maeterlinck (1874–1949), whose *Bluebird*, indicating the search for a never-attainable goal, became a symbol of the entire movement, and the Austrian, Hugo von Hofmannsthal (1874–1929), whose poems, published when he was nineteen, made him the embodiment of poetic youth all over Europe. It is characteristic that the main works of these two poets became operas: Maeterlinck's *Pelléas and Mélisande* became the most successful composition of the French composer, Claude Debussy (1862–1918); Hofmannsthal's evocation of the eighteenth-century Viennese aristocracy, *Der Rosenkavalier*, the masterwork of Richard Strauss (1864–1949).

Remote as these romantic evocations of a better past might appear from the modern industrial world, they had their impact on the political climate of the twentieth century; unintentionally they were an important ingredient in the ideology of the political groups and parties which opposed the trend towards progressivism and socialism and the nourished notions from which fascism and racism would spring. The neoromantic idealization of a past aristocratic age was not only linked to achievements in the cultural sphere; it was also viewed as tied to a heroic style of life which despised material comfort and was willing to lead a strenuous

Pablo Picasso, *The Blind Man's Meal.*

life in the service of higher ideals. The most eloquent preacher of this aspect of neoromanticism was the Italian writer and poet, Gabriele d'Annunzio (1863–1938). The unrealistic contents of his novels—presenting men ruthlessly but selflessly serving great causes, leading a life devoted to passion and beauty—are redeemed by sudden scenes of psychological insight and a rich and powerful language. Now half-forgotten, he was one of the most widely read and most influential writers at the end of the 1890's and the beginning of the twentieth century.

When d'Annunzio had his great successes, the philosopher, Friedrich Nietzsche (1844–1900), whose writings were disregarded and almost unknown when they appeared, had suddenly become a widely read and much-discussed author. D'Annunzio's heroes are echoes of Nietzsche's Superman; with d'Annunzio the process began in the course of which Nietzsche's Superman became the embodiment of a ruthless pursuit of power. Actually, the ideas which Nietzsche connected with this concept were much more sophisticated. He believed that Christian morality, with its praise of humility, was frustrating the development of man's powers and suffocating human creativity, and that not an idealized and invented picture of man, only a recognition of his natural instincts and drives, could constitute the basis of a true ethical code and of a new society of equality. His aim was not the creation of a world of men recklessly striving for power but a new ethics.

In Nietzsche's writing his criticism of modern morality and convention was expressed in a literary, almost poetic form. It constituted the immense importance of Sigmund Freud that he gave scientific proof to the notions which formed an element in the various literary and philosophical trends of the period: that man was oppressed by a conventional morality which had lost its original justification and was now becoming only frustrated and inhibited, and that this suppression of man's instincts was an element in the oppression and injustice of the social world. Of course, Freud's teaching began to exert influence only much later, but it is significant that the book which would make him most widely known, his *Interpretation of Dreams*, was a work of the last decade of the nineteenth century and appeared in the first year of the twentieth century.

Although the voices of those who, in either hopeful or fearful expectation, believed in the coming of a crisis which would result in the end of a period of civilization were strong, certainly not all, perhaps not even very many Europeans shared these feelings. Although the belief in progress, so strong in the eighteenth century and in most of the nineteenth century, had been shaken, it had not been extinguished; the conviction remained alive that, on the basis of the achievements of the past, in a continuous process, a better future could be attained. Such expectations received strength and confirmation from the discoveries of science which were steadily extended over all fields of human life. In celebration of the beginning of the new century H. G. Wells wrote a number of articles, then assembled in a book under the title *Anticipation of the Reaction of Mechanical and Scientific Progress upon Human Life and Thought.* Wells painted a glowing picture of the world which, on the basis of new discoveries and their industrial exploitation, lay before humanity in the twentieth century: better health, better living conditions, availability of goods from all parts of the globe, a regulation of economic life which would permit greater leisure and full employment. Wells certainly expressed the ideas of wide groups of the European middle classes about the outlook of the future more correctly than the poets and philosophers of cultural pessimism. There were not only those who felt threatened by the rise of the new industrial world, or those who aimed for a revolution because they felt suppressed and excluded, there were also those who looked to the coming of the twentieth century with pride and expectation.

THE SECOND INDUSTRIAL REVOLUTION AND THE GLOBAL DIMENSIONS OF EUROPEAN POLITICS

Hopes for a revolution, fears of cultural and social decline because of the emergence of a mass civilization, expectations for steady material progress—all these views became magnified and intensified by the developments in the economic sphere which occurred during the last decade of the nineteenth century. From the end of the Napoleonic era, one long deflationary trend, only briefly interrupted in the middle of the century, characterized European economic developments; but this changed by 1896. An increasing supply of money, stimulated by the discovery of large new gold fields in South Africa and the Klondike, allowed new investments and spurred industrial activities. A new development, which has been called the Second Industrial Revolution, began. The foundation for this "revolution" had been laid in the previous decades: the discovery of a new process to produce basic steel which possessed neither the hardness of pig-iron nor the corrosiveness of wrought iron. The advances then made propelled the development of two new industries: the electrical and chemical industries. These new industries brought about a startling transformation of the external conditions of life: lighting and heating, streetcars, subways, railroads—all made living and working in extensive urban centers possible and created the preconditions for the development of the large cities. But these innovations also affected the economy of the countryside, changing the forms of production and the marketing of agricultural products. The chemical industry completed this process through industrial manufacturing of fertilizers; the dyestuffs which it produced diminished the costs and enlarged the availability of textile and cleaning products; the development of synthetic fibers perfected the transition to mass production of clothing materials.

However, the influence which these new industries exerted on the process of manufacturing and their byproducts were as important as the new goods which they brought onto the market. First of all they were instrumental in opening new sources of energy and widening energy distribution. Power stations allowed a more rational and economic location of factories at points close to the needed mineral resources or to the market. Then, within the factory, electricity stimulated the creation and the use of precision instruments which accelerated and mechanized labor. Output would be increased by augmenting the number of workers without special training. Although the potential of oil as a source of energy had been known, the chemical industry converted it into a fuel, which from the first years of the twentieth century was increasingly used in warships and in ocean liners.

Advancements in the fields of steel production, electricity, and chemistry all contributed to the invention of what must be considered the most characteristic phenomenon of the second industrial revolution: the internal combustion engine. The automobile and, later, the airplane were the most dramatic evidence of the coming of a new age widely different from the world of the nineteenth century.

A crucial factor in the second industrial revolution was that it created the possibility of industrialization in countries which, because of a lack of coal and iron, had seemed destined to remain mainly agricultural. With the development of an electrical and chemical industry the possession of coal and iron resources became less of a necessity. Of course, although all European countries were now able to participate in industrialization, the extent and degree of their participation differed and depended on their geographical situation, their social and economic structure, and the extent and character of public education. In practice this new situation meant that Great Britain, which during a good part of the nineteenth century had possessed a monopoly on the European and almost on the world market, now began to meet stiff competition. The chief competitor was the newly unified Germany, with its rich deposits of coal and iron in the Ruhr and Silesia and its burgeoning electrical and chemical industries. The changed situation is reflected in the transition from free trade to protective tariffs to which, with the exception of Great Britain, all European countries became converted in the latter part of the nineteenth century. The various continental countries wanted to prevent that the advantages which Great Britain as a first-comer in the age of industrialization possessed, would slow down or impede the industrial development in their countries. Great Britain was now not only excluded from the German market but met competition from Germany, France, and other European countries on the world markets.

This new wave of protectionism meant that the second industrial revolution had repercussions on international relations and foreign policy. It

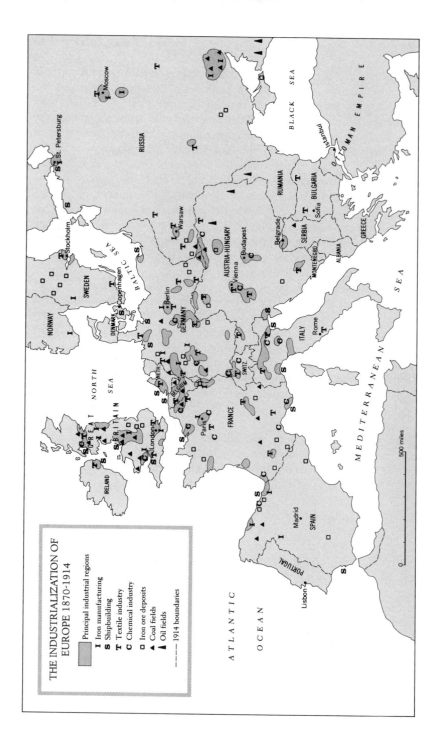

THE INDUSTRIALIZATION OF
EUROPE 1870-1914

Principal industrial regions

I Iron manufacturing
S Shipbuilding
T Textile industry
C Chemical industry
□ Iron ore deposits
▲ Coal fields
◀ Oil fields
---- 1914 boundaries

ATLANTIC OCEAN

IRELAND

GREAT BRITAIN

London

NORTH SEA

NORWAY

SWEDEN

Stockholm

Copenhagen
DENMARK

BALTIC SEA

St. Petersburg

RUSSIA

Moscow

Warsaw

Berlin
GERMANY

NETH.
BELGIUM

Paris

FRANCE

SWITZ.

AUSTRIA-HUNGARY

Vienna

Budapest

ITALY

Rome

MEDITERRANEAN SEA

500 miles

SPAIN

Madrid

PORTUGAL

Lisbon

RUMANIA

Belgrade
SERBIA
MONTENEGRO

BULGARIA

Sofia

ALBANIA

GREECE

BLACK SEA

Istanbul

OTTOMAN EMPIRE

stimulated interest in the regions that could supply raw materials for domestic industries. Indeed, during the last quarter of the nineties and the first fourteen years of the twentieth century more than eleven million square miles were added to the colonial possessions of the great European powers. These new colonial possessions lay in Africa and in southwest Asia. The islands in the South Pacific aroused the ambitions of France, Germany, and Great Britain; there European powers met a new rival in the United States. Yet, despite some diplomatic crises the wrangles ended with a peaceful division of the spoils among the competing powers. In Africa at the beginning of the twentieth century only Ethiopia, the Boer Republics, and Morocco—states that had a long history of independence —remained sovereign, and competition for control over these areas was sharp, lasting far into the twentieth century.

From the economic point of view the creation of a colonial empire was hardly more important than the domination of areas which—politically independent, or at least independent by standards of international law—could serve as markets for industrial products. Until the second industrial revolution these countries had been economically dominated by Great Britain. Now Germany entered a contest with Great Britain in South Africa; and British economic influence in China became disputed not only by the industrialized nations of Europe, but also by the United States and by a new industrial power, Japan. The greatest prize, however, which for economic and strategic reasons all the great powers tried to win, was the "sick man of Europe," the Ottoman Empire. Politically debilitated, it seemed unable to put up much resistance to economic penetration and control by a foreign power.

It is characteristic of the uncoordinated interaction of old and new in these decades, usually regarded as the highpoint of imperialism, that the old nationalistic contrasts and conflicts continued—but· in different forms and on an extended area.

THE STRUCTURE OF SOCIETY

Although the extension of European power and control over the entire globe appeared to be the most striking feature of the second industrial revolution, the home market remained for the industrialized countries of Europe more important than finding outlets for production beyond their frontiers. While within each European nation the nature of the problems involved in adjusting the new to the old or the old to the new varied, the process was crucially difficult in all of them. The anecdote with which this chapter began, about the inability or unwillingness of the aristocratic landowner to recognize the existence of a large working class, is an almost comical indication of the difficulties involved in becoming aware of the emergence of a new social structure. The industrial worker was the decisive new element in this structure, and the integration of the industrial labor force into the existing order the most crucial issue.

The Workers

Whereas in previous centuries a number of social groups—household servants, serfs and half-free peasants, craftsmen, artisans—had formed the weakest class of society, at the end of the nineteenth century, the industrial workers—the proletariat—were in the lowest, and most endangered position. During the early years of industrialization, the workers had experienced insecurity and misery. With the economic improvement of the late nineteenth century, wages began to rise, and the workers' living standards improved gradually. Nevertheless, better wages and the possibility of somewhat better food and clothing did not eliminate the hardships which formed part of the existence of the proletariat.

Industry, particularly as it developed in the first and second industrial revolutions, meant removal of work in the home to work in factories, and decline in small enterprises and rise in large enterprises employing more than fifty people. Factory workers, had to live close to their workplace and to each other, and the industrial centers, in which the workers lived, grew in an entirely unplanned way. Housing for the masses that streamed into these centers was controlled by private builders, speculators, or absentee landlords.

In Great Britain people continued to live in small one-family houses, but these small houses now accommodated numerous families and soon became overcrowded, unsanitary slums. In other countries workers were housed in apartment buildings four to six stories high, each floor containing five or six apartments. Built side by side with no intervening space, centered around small dark courtyards, these buildings had no gardens, no green areas, and were bounded by treeless streets.

The factories were generally large structures without adequate air or light. Working conditions began to improve after the first cruel years of the beginning of industrialization. Even at best, however, sanitary conditions in the factories were appalling, and little was done to ensure the safety of the workers from occupational hazards. Safety precautions, particularly in the coal mines, were neglected. In Russia, Italy, and Spain there were no laws against the employment of children or women, nor were their working conditions different from those of male adults. Economic crises, frequent dismissal of workers, and a considerable rate of unemployment were regarded as unavoidable. No provision was made for these recurring periods of hardship, and wages were so low that the workers were unable to accumulate savings to fall back on in these times. In the oil fields of the Caucasus, workers like the young Iosif Vissarionovich Dzhugashvili, who later would take the name of Josef Stalin (1879–1953), were imprisoned in barracks for eight hours during the night and

Working-class housing in the East End of London, 1912.

worked during the day under police supervision. The young Aneurin Bevan (1897–1960), after the Second World War one of the inspiring leaders of the British Labor party, grew up in the misery of a Welsh coal-mining village. One of his brothers was killed in what Bevan was always to regard as an avoidable mine accident, and his mother died of starvation. A picture of life in a worker's house, of the desperate struggles of mothers for food for their children, of the lack of medical care, of the men's escape into drunkenness, of the recruitment of teenagers to work in the mines is given by D. H. Lawrence in his novel *Sons and Lovers* (1913). This British writer, with his message of a free life, grew up amidst the collieries of a Midlands mining village.

People living under such conditions were naturally inclined to regard the world which permitted such misery with hostility. Realizing their economic and social weaknesses, many workers placed their hope in organizing themselves and formed trade unions in the expectation that unified action would improve their common lot. In the 1890's the trade-union movement began to make great strides; by 1905 the British unions, which had developed earlier than those on the Continent, had more than three million members; in Germany one and a half million workers were unionized; and in France, one million. These figures sound impressive; actually not even 25 per cent of the adult industrial workers in these countries belonged to unions. Nevertheless, the trade unions benefited the entire working population because employers were gradually forced to provide better conditions in order to keep their workers.

The main activities of the trade unions were directed toward improving the material situation of the workers by collective bargaining, by granting financial assistance to strikers when negotiations failed, and by collecting benefit funds with which the unemployed, the sick, and the aged could be supported. But unions also attempted to equip the workers for the struggle for social betterment: They organized training schools, set up educational courses, arranged holiday excursions. They made the lives of the workers more meaningful, liberating them from a sense of helpless isolation by providing a sense of community.

It was soon noticed that the trade unions exerted considerable influence on the minds of the workers. Ministers and priests became aware of the extent to which these organizations were successfully competing with the churches. The encyclical *Rerum Novarum*, in which Pope Leo XIII expressed approval of the attempts to form Christian trade unions, arose from this concern. Although the Catholic trade unions never were as powerful as the "free" trade unions, they became a significant political and social factor in Germany and Austria.

Yet the continued existence of trade unions was by no means secure. They had to fight for recognition, which was achieved only gradually: in Great Britain between 1870 and 1876; in France in 1884; in Germany after 1890. In some countries only local trade unions or trade unions for particular industrial activities were permitted. In Russia trade unions remained illegal until 1906. Few countries recognized the right of collective bargaining. Strikes and picketing were frequently prohibited. Since the activities by which the trade unions tried to improve the lot of their members met with limited success only, many workers came to feel that a real improvement of their situation required a change in the entire political system: action in the economic sphere had to be complemented by action in the political sphere. Many trade-union leaders shared this view and took a leading role in political movements that attempted to organize the workers for revolution.

The last quarter of the nineteenth century saw the formation in almost all European countries of political parties which called themselves socialist or social democratic. These parties shared the main tenets of the political creed which Karl Marx (1818–1883) had formulated. Before the First World War the most powerful socialist party was the German Social Democratic party. Its program, named after Erfurt, the town where it was adopted in 1891, was written with the cooperation of the aged Friedrich Engels (1820–1895), Marx's friend and collaborator. The Erfurt Program, subsequently the model for the programs of all the European socialist parties, was based on a few clear and simple tenets. Fundamental was the Marxist assumption that every society consisted of classes determined by economic interests, and every political struggle was actually a struggle between different economic classes. Thus, no improvement of the economic situation of the workers could be expected without a political revolution in which the workers would wrest power from the capitalist ruling group. By this transfer of power the means of production would fall into the hands of the proletariat; private property would be replaced by common possession of all goods; and the results of labor could be distributed to the benefit of all. Everyone would receive according to his needs.

Such possibilities were presented not as an unrealistic utopia but as the sequence of events which scientific investigation had proved to be necessary and inevitable. Because under capitalism wealth was becoming increasingly concentrated among fewer and fewer people, and more and more people were being pushed down into the proletariat, fewer people would have the means to buy goods and to stimulate the economy; consequently the economic crises which were considered to be inherent in the capitalist system would become progressively more frequent and severe. However, the Marxists urged the workers not to stand idly by waiting for the final crisis and the collapse of capitalism. The capitalists would defend themselves by force, so the workers had to strive for a position from which they could seize power. They were to work for a democratization of political life in capitalist society, in order to undermine the existing state and to defeat the last stand of capitalism. Since capitalism dominated the world, its overthrow presupposed an international revolution. In 1889 the socialist parties of all countries therefore formed an alliance, the International, and representatives from these parties met regularly. Although the decisions of the International were recommendations only and not binding on the individual socialist parties, the International did create the impression of a great supranational force working toward a single goal.

The socialist doctrine had obvious attractions for the workers who were outsiders in the prewar society. But the doctrine had inner contradictions: If society had to be entirely transformed, was it meaningful to work for its democratization? If the collapse of capitalism was historically inevitable, what justification was there for forming political parties and for undertaking a political struggle? These contradictions became the more puzzling because the actual political and economic situation in the prewar years did not develop according to the Marxian scheme. Economic crises did not become more frequent or more serious. Indeed, no serious economic crisis arose between 1890 and 1914; in general there was an upward trend in the standard of living on the Continent. By 1900 the wages of skilled workers were almost double those of unskilled workers, and the skilled workers were able to accumulate some reserves.

The growth of socialist parties and of trade unions led to the creation of large bureaucratic apparatuses. They employed numerous officers; they acquired publishing houses and newspapers; some of their leaders were elected to parliaments. Consequently, many party and trade-union offi-cers became more interested in keeping their organizations alive than in risking their existence by political action. Some socialists suggested that evolution rather than revolution was the way to socialism. Since the workers would slowly become a majority, it might be possible, they thought, to achieve the transition to socialism gradually, by a democratic process. The originator of this theory was a German socialist, Eduard Bernstein (1850–1932), who had been impressed by improvements in the situation of the working classes in Great Britain during the nineteenth century. Revisionism, as the movement was called, was particularly influ-ential in Great Britain and Germany, countries with highly developed industrial systems, where the workers received some of the benefits of economic progress. In Spain, France, and Russia, where industrialization was still in its infancy, and where the governments looked with disfavor upon demands of the workers that might retard the process of indus-trialization, socialists rejected the entire doctrine of Revisionism. In the meetings of the International, the views of the Revisionists were debated, but they never became official socialist doctrine. The demand for revolu-tion was maintained.

The Ruling Group in Europe

If the second industrial revolution brought into the political scene a new element which tended to oppose the existing political order, the established ruling group also had difficulty maintaining its position in an industrialized society or in adjusting to it. The European ruling group— to a lesser degree in Great Britain, still strongly in Central and Eastern Europe—carried the traces of the past: of its origin in an agrarian society, of feudal and hierarchical ideas.

Around the turn of the century, there were only two republics in Europe: France and Switzerland. The prevalent form of government was the monarchy. The degree to which monarchical rulers possessed actual political power varied. But whether or not they had sufficient power to exert real influence on state policy, the monarchs were justified in con-sidering themselves the most important persons in the European political arena. In each country the monarch was the apex of society, and the status of both individuals and groups was dependent on their relation-ship to the throne. Among themselves, royalty formed a kind of extended family, which seemed to tie European society together into one great unit.

Members of ruling dynasties could marry only members of other ruling dynasties, unless they were willing to relinquish their status and rights.

A royal jamboree. *King Edward VII of Great Britain and his son, later King George V, the German Emperor William II, the Spanish King Alfonso XIII, and their wives are easily recognizable.*

At the beginning of the twentieth century even the members of the British royal family, who with the ruling monarch's permission might marry commoners, were for the most part married to members of princely families. Religion somewhat separated the dynasties into two groups. Almost all of the Catholic princes were related to the Habsburgs and the Bourbons. The Protestant ruling families, into which the Eastern Orthodox rulers, particularly the Russian tsars, also tended to marry, were tied together through the numerous small German dynasties, which provided marriageable princes and princesses for almost any contingency. In the nineteenth century the remarkable fertility of the admirable couple Victoria and Albert had bound the Protestant rulers still more tightly together. Thus the British king, Edward VII, was the uncle both of the German emperor, William II, and of Alexandra, the wife of the Russian tsar, Nicholas II. The birthdays, weddings, and funerals of monarchs were not only state occasions but also family reunions. It was natural that at the wedding of the daughter of William II in 1912 the tsar and tsarina of Russia and the king and queen of England would come to Berlin, and that almost all of Europe's rulers would be present at the funeral of Queen Victoria in 1901, and of her son Edward VII in 1910.

After the death of Queen Victoria the oldest ruling monarch in Europe was the Emperor Francis Joseph of Austria-Hungary; born in 1830, he had ascended the throne in 1848. He was venerated as a kind of patriarch by all the rulers and his seventieth birthday in 1900, his eightieth in 1910, and the sixtieth jubilee of his reign in 1908 were all occasions for royal meetings. Visits among cousins were frequent. The German emperor often met with the tsar. Edward VII, in order to lose weight and to remain in shape for the gastronomic feasts which he loved, regularly visited the spa of Marienbad, and when he passed through Germany it

Reigning monarchs at the funeral of Edward VII in 1911: *From left to right, seated, are Alfonso XIII of Spain, George V of Great Britain, Frederick VIII of Denmark; standing are Haakon VII of Norway, Ferdinand I of Bulgaria, Manuel II of Portugal, who the year before had been forced from the throne, the German Emperor William II, George I of Greece, and Albert I of Belgium.*

would have been impolite for him not to arrange a meeting with his nephew, William II, though there was little love between them. On their travels the monarchs were accompanied by high officials, and, unavoidably, political subjects were discussed. Most of all, this network of princely relations and connections gave the monarchs a feeling of solidarity against the common danger of revolution, although, as the First World War would show, this feeling of standing together against a common danger did not guarantee peace.

The monarchs were also the leaders of the society in their respective countries. In holding court they reinforced a traditional hierarchy and determined its order by giving titles and decorations and by receiving or excluding people according to the standards of the crown. That the monarchy fulfilled the function of guaranteeing the existence of an established order was the view not only of its adherents but of the enemies of the existing system, the advocates of revolution, as well. For them the monarchs were an important target. Although in the first two decades of the twentieth century attacks on the lives of the princely heads of the state were fewer than in the 1870's and 1880's, the monarchs were still in the line of fire. In 1900, King Humbert of Italy was assassinated. In 1906, at the wedding of the king of Spain, an assassination attempt was made which claimed many victims although the king and his bride escaped. In 1908 the king of Portugal and his oldest son were killed. In June, 1914, a Serbian nationalist killed the heir to the Habsburg throne, the Archduke Francis Ferdinand. This assassination precipitated the outbreak of the First World War.

The existence of a monarchy presupposed the existence of a ruling group closely connected with the throne. In the eighteenth century the princes of continental Europe had become absolute by gaining direct control of the armed forces and by allying themselves with the landowning nobility. This alliance of the monarchs with the army and the landed aristocracy lasted into the twentieth century. Although by that time an elected parliament had become an influential factor in politics, the arbiter of social status remained the court, with its officialdom of ministers, chamberlains, masters of ceremonies—all nobles and mostly descendants of the oldest families. The monarchs kept up their special closeness to the army by insisting on a voice in the promotion of officers. Moreover, the monarchs stood in particularly intimate relation to certain regiments —the guard regiments. These were stationed in or near the palace or capital; in them the heirs of the throne and other princes received their military education. The officers of these regiments, almost exclusively the sons of aristocratic families, were among the few who were on familiar terms with members of the royal families. Thus, in the monarchy a landed aristocracy with military values and a military code of honor continued to set the social standard.

The eminence of a landed aristocracy, which had been justified by the economic and political conditions of previous centuries, seemed an anomaly in the twentieth century, when industry and commerce became dominating factors in economic life. The heads of the large banks, the owners and managers of the great industrial enterprises were the creators of the prosperity and power of a nation. But even in those countries in which industrialization was most advanced, agriculture retained an important place in the economy. In many parts of Europe the possessor of a large landed estate was still very wealthy. Although the Dohnas, an old noble family with vast estates in East Prussia, were not as rich as the Krupps, the great armament manufacturers of the Ruhr, they were still among the richest families of Germany. The estates of the Esterházy and Károlyi families in Hungary yielded incomes which permitted the owners to indulge themselves in every luxury resort of Europe. The fabulous wealth of the Russian aristocracy came from agriculture; a Prince Yussupov even as a teenager traveled in his special train through Europe. Moreover, many of the aristocrats had lands from which coal, the most precious raw material of the time, was mined. Lord Derby, of the Stanley family in England, the Princes Pless and Henckel-Donnersmarck in Germany, the Hohenlohes in Bohemia were landowners and industrialists at the same time. Moreover, in France, Italy, and Germany the cultivation of vineyards and the installation of breweries yielded the owners of landed estates an income often equal to that of the great bankers and captains of industry.

There remained tensions, however, between the industrial and agricultural sectors of European society. The less well-situated members of the nobility looked with envy and disdain on the increasing wealth of the bourgeoisie. The owners of smaller industrial enterprises usually retained many of the anti-aristocratic views of the early nineteenth century, when the bourgeoisie had been struggling against the Old Regime. Yet, between the upper strata of the landed aristocracy and the wealthiest members of the industrial and commercial society there were many links; gradually these two elements came to be joined together in a single ruling group. The monarchs furthered this process by receiving the important personages of the commercial and industrial world at court and giving them titles, enobling such bankers and industrialists as the Rothschilds, the Sassoons, and Ernest Cassel in Great Britain; the Krupps and the Siemenses in Germany; the Rothschilds and the Gutmanns in Austria; the Franchettis in Italy. The manner and the extent of the amalgamation into the ruling classes of these two—the old landed aristocracy and the new leaders of the commercial and industrial world—varied in the different European countries. But, generally, the business class became closely tied to the policies of the national government. Authoritarian concepts and aristocratic mores and interests pervaded the thinking and the aims of the owners and managers of industry. And the dominance among them of this point of view hardened the tensions and conflicts within an industrial society.

A preindustrial, antimodern element persisted in the European society of the early twentieth century. The code of honor of the nobility—its concern for rank and for gentlemanly behavior—the social preeminence of the military profession, and the prestige of the life of leisure, along with a certain contempt for money-making activities—all were characteristic of the period. Symbolic was the importance of the horse in this society. It would be reasonable to assume that in a technical and industrial age the horse, previously important for agriculture, transport, and war, would become obsolete. But horse racing remained the most elegant sport, its great events honored by the presence of royalty. Establishing a stable of race horses was the surest way for a wealthy man to advance into the upper strata of society. Admission to membership in the jockey clubs, founded for the promotion of horse racing, was a sign of having entered the Upper Ten Thousand, as the ruling group was called. In the armies the guard-cavalry regiments were the most elegant: the blue and red tunics and helmets with drooping horsehair plumes of the English Royal Horse Guards; the black caps with death's heads and fur-trimmed jackets of the Prussian "black" hussars; the light blue coats and the golden froggings of the Austrian imperial chasseurs—these were the uniforms of the cream of the European armies. In all Europe, cavalry regiments were maintained in a strength hardly compatible with the changes in warfare which the technical age required and strategic thinkers envisaged. Soon after the First World War had started, the uselessness of these trappings became obvious: colorful uniforms were replaced by drab gray, horses bred and trained for the cavalry were left behind, and cavalrymen had to fight as foot soldiers.

The Middle Classes

The social group usually considered to have been the driving force in the development of industrial society was the "middle classes." Before the second industrial revolution, this social group was usually united in aims, interests, and beliefs; the second industrial revolution, though chiefly the work of this social group, shattered its unity. Then term "middle classes" remains appropriate only if it is quite literally understood as comprising that part of the population which belonged neither to the upper strata of society nor to the proletariat.

The lack of coherence and of unity in this social group is reflected in its being frequently divided into an "upper middle class" and a "lower middle class." Before the second industrial revolution, the term "middle classes" was applied to a segment of society whose members possessed economic independence. Merchants, artisans, craftsmen, shop-owners— though they might differ in wealth—had a common bond of interests that distinguished them clearly from the other classes of society: they were urban, free, masters of their own business. Industrialization favored concentration and bigness in economic life. Some shop-owners or artisans succeeded in adjusting to the times: they developed their business or trade into a small factory or chain stores. Nevertheless, the small family-owned factory, in most countries, was soon changed into a joint-stock company or absorbed by larger companies working in the same field. Moreover, the income of a member of the managerial top echelon, of a director or manager of a large factory or bank, exceeded that of the owner of a small enterprise struggling to remain independent. Together with the best-paid members of the so-called free professions—doctors, lawyers, teachers—the high-level employees of the industrial concerns and of the banks now formed the upper bourgeoisie, and their ambition was to advance to the head of their enterprises and to rise into the ruling group.

Inside of one of the major department stores in London, Harrod's, in 1903; the escalator had been installed in 1898.

Not only had the economic gap widened immensely between the industrial entrepreneurs and managers, and the artisans, craftsmen and shop-owners, the latter group had to struggle for survival against competition from factory-produced goods and department stores. But they did not entirely disappear; over some shops, particularly those of wine merchants or butchers or greengrocers, signs still proclaimed ownership in the same family extending over centuries. One would find relatively prosperous shop-owners or artisans chiefly in small towns; in the big cities their existence became increasingly precarious. For a while it seemed that "tossed about between the hope of entering the ranks of the wealthy class, and the fear of being reduced to the state of proletarians or paupers," they would "finally disappear in the face of modern industry"—that had been the prognosis of Marx and Engels in the middle of the nineteenth century. But this view overestimated the rapidity and thoroughness with which modern industry would remove all remnants of preindustrial society. Further, industrialization itself led to the expansion of the lower middle classes.

Industrial life required in increasing numbers what came to be called "white-collar workers"; they were needed in commerce and factories, but also in public service in which the economic and demographic growth entailed an expanding bureaucracy; the number of post-office and railroad employees, police officers, and administrative officials rose steadily. Similarly the need grew for doctors, lawyers, and teachers. The increase in demand made these professions so attractive and rewarding that they quickly became overcrowded. As supply outraced demand, wide differences appeared in the financial position within the professional group. The great corporate and criminal lawyers and the renowned medical specialists had very high incomes and certainly belonged to the upper bourgeoisie; many lawyers and doctors, however, had to scrape by on meager earnings.

This emergence of a new lower middle class as a consequence of industrialization can be most clearly and strikingly observed in Germany, where industrialization advanced most suddenly and most rapidly. In 1914, at the time of the outbreak of the First World War, the number of industrial workers exceeded thirteen million, but the number of people who can be considered as belonging to the lower middle classes was almost half as large; among them there were two million white-collar employees and two million low- and middle-rank civil servants.

It is clear that the lower middle classes formed a heterogenous group, widely differing in occupation, income, and social status, easier to define in negative than positive terms. They were not workers; they had a higher income and, to a certain extent—through fixed salaries, pension rights, etc.—greater economic security. Moreover, they, or at least their children, had the possibility of social mobility.

Until far into the nineteenth century, men engaged in economic activities had no need for higher education. But the new industrial society

The middle classes reveling at the beach in the first summer of the twentieth century.

required highly trained specialists—economists, engineers, chemists—and gradually the educational system in all European countries began to change. There was an improvement in primary education, but the really significant changes took place in the secondary schools and the universities. Secondary schools introduced programs concentrating on natural sciences and modern languages. In the universities, which formerly had served to train a limited number of lawyers, doctors, teachers, and civil servants, emphasis began to shift away from a general education in arts and letters toward scientific training and technical instruction; technical colleges were founded which, like the universities, received the right to grant higher degrees. Philosophers and historians no longer dominated the universities, as they had in the early and middle decades of the nineteenth century; the admired leaders of academic life were the great scientific discoverers—men like Helmholtz, Pasteur, Lister.

The wealthy upper group of the leaders of industrial and commercial life was small and entry in their circle was difficult, yet not impossible. It could be gained through technical expertise—in chemistry and physics, in economics, in engineering. The best, almost the only, means for economic and social advancement was the possession of special knowledge and techniques for which the degree of a university or a technical college was prerequisite. This was the road on which middle-class parents wanted their sons to proceed. It was a difficult road, however, because it demanded some financial resources to send their sons to preparatory schools and to maintain them during their years of university study. Despite the value of the university degree, the number of those who enjoyed a higher education remained small; statistics from the year 1913 show that in the various countries of Europe before the First World War the number of university students among each *ten thousand* of the population ranged between seven and eleven.

Although, in practice the possibilities of upward mobility for the members of the lower middle classes were limited, the prevailing tendency was to emphasize their separation from the laboring classes. That was almost the only common bond or common attitude; otherwise little or nothing tied the members of the middle class together. Diversity in occupation, in financial resources, in social status was reinforced by a constant movement, some rising upward in the social scale, others heading down. Such a miscellaneous group could no longer have common political and economic goals; in the major countries of Europe, perhaps less in Great Britain than in the rest of Europe, the liberal parties, which in the earlier and middle decades of the nineteenth century had formed the political home of the middle classes, began to disintegrate into a variety of parties and splinter groups.

THE WANING OF POLITICAL CONSENSUS

The decline of liberalism was of importance not only for those who had believed in the liberal tenets; it implied a change in the climate of political thought. Certainly liberalism had never exerted an uncontested rule over the minds of the people of the nineteenth century, but the conservative attitude had been mainly defensive, insisting on the importance of traditional values and the maintenance of a hierarchical social order. Certain basic liberal ideas—the necessity of a constitution, the representation of the people by a legislative body, and a guarantee of fundamental individual rights—had been accepted also by the conservatives. The extent to which a basic liberal outlook had become an ingredient of all political thinking could still be seen at the end of the nineteenth and the beginning of the twentieth century when the condemnation of Captain Alfred Dreyfus in France in secret military court proceedings in the 1890's and, in the following decade, the execution of the anarchist Francisco Ferrer in Spain without sufficient proof of his participation in revolutionary activities aroused excitement and indignation all over the Western world.

A weakening of liberal beliefs did not yet find expression in direct doubts or in direct rejection of basic liberal tenets, but it became noticeable in hesitations and tensions about the consequences of liberalism for practical politics. We have mentioned already that, in the last quarter of the nineteenth century, in order to counter the advantages inherent in Britain's industrial headstart, the European powers converted to protectionism, and thereby began to abandon the liberal free-trade doctrine.

Another fundamental economic doctrine of liberalism was noninterference of the state in economic life, but here again the maintenance of a principle was in conflict with the situation and the interests existing in the new industrial society. There were humanitarian reasons which demanded government action for the maintenance of hygienic standards in factories, limitation of working hours, protection of women and children against exploitation—in short, an active role of the state in the regulation of industrial life. If such demands might appear to be in the interest of the workers, the industrial leaders were no less eager for government action: they endorsed protective tariffs, they wanted the state to prohibit strikes or at least to protect strike-breakers. The leaders of heavy industry were interested in government contracts for the production of guns and warships. Moreover, the great armament concerns—Krupp in Germany, Schneider-Creusot in France, Skoda in Austria—were anxious to sell their goods all over the world, and for this kind of business fre-

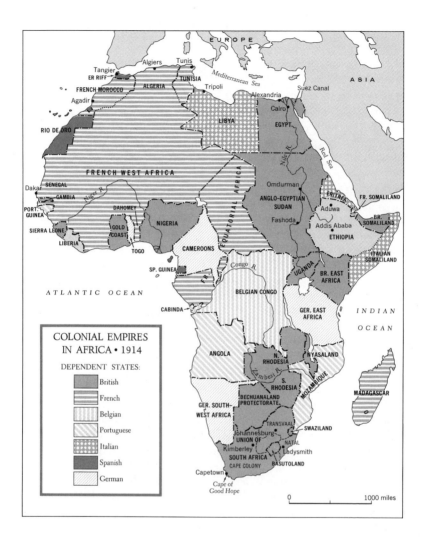

COLONIAL EMPIRES
IN AFRICA • 1914

DEPENDENT STATES:

- British
- French
- Belgian
- Portuguese
- Italian
- Spanish
- German

0   1000 miles

quently needed the support of their governments. The frontiers between economics and politics became increasingly blurred.

The main shock to the liberal tenets, however, was administered by the rise of socialism, with its rejection of a free competitive economy and its threat of revolution. If an underlying trend in the liberal age had been extension of suffrage and widening democratization, questions arose whether this kind of policy might not lead to the suppression of that right which formed the point of departure and the paramount aim of all liberal thought: freedom of the individual. Although the movements for removing inequalities in voting and for universal suffrage did not stop, they slowed down; and there was little inclination to limit the powers of the upper houses of parliaments, whose members generally gained their seats either by heredity or by weighted elections in which the wealthier classes preserved control. The march of democracy seemed to falter.

What changed the political climate at the end of the nineteenth century was not only the weakening of the hold of liberal ideas but even more the emergence of new ideas contradictory to basic liberal notions. It has been said that the liberals committed a fatal sin by accepting and promoting imperialism. Of course, the notion that industrialists and bankers had the right to pursue and to extend their business all over the globe corresponded to the liberal notions of free trade, but the form which this economic expansion took—colonialism and market control in less-developed countries—created a situation in which the Europeans became a superior class above the indigenous peoples whose fate they controlled. This, in itself, represented a violation of the liberal notion of equality, or equal dignity of rational man. It was unavoidable that a rationalization of this elitist attitude was undertaken. The crucial elements in this process of rationalization were Social Darwinism and racism. Darwin was interpreted to have suggested that it was not only natural but almost desirable that the stronger rules over the weaker. Racism provided justification for

The white rulers administer justice to their black subjects, the German Cameroons, 1911.

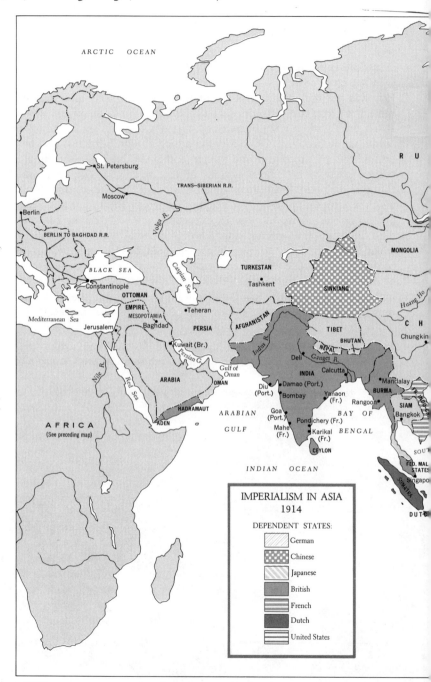

ARCTIC OCEAN

R U

St. Petersburg

TRANS–SIBERIAN R.R.

Moscow

Berlin

BERLIN TO BAGHDAD R.R.

MONGOLIA

Volga R.

BLACK SEA

Caspian Sea

TURKESTAN

Tashkent

SINKIANG

Huang Ho

Constantinople

OTTOMAN

EMPIRE

Mediterranean Sea

MESOPOTAMIA

Teheran

AFGHANISTAN

TIBET

C H

Jerusalem

Baghdad

PERSIA

Chungkin

BHUTAN

Kuwait (Br.)

Indus R.

NEPAL

Persian G.

Deli

Ganges R.

Calcutta

Nile R.

ARABIA

Gulf of Oman

OMAN

Diu (Port.)

Damao (Port.)

INDIA

Mandalay

Red Sea

Bombay

Yanaon (Fr.)

BURMA

Rangoon

HADRAMAUT

ARABIAN

Goa (Port.)

SIAM

AFRICA

ADEN

GULF

Pondichery (Fr.)

BAY OF

Bangkok

(See preceding map)

Mahe (Fr.)

Karikal (Fr.)

BENGAL

CEYLON

SOU

FED. MAL. STATES

Singapo

INDIAN OCEAN

SUMATRA

DUT

IMPERIALISM IN ASIA
1914

DEPENDENT STATES:

German

Chinese

Japanese

British

French

Dutch

United States

the rule of white Europeans over the black, brown, and yellow populations of the globe—the "lesser breeds" as Kipling defined them.

Such views served not only to exculpate imperialist expansion, they began to make an impact also in the domestic policy of the various European countries. Racism often took the form of anti-Semitism. And indeed, anti-Semitism, not as the social attitude of individuals but as a political movement, gained a certain mass appeal in these years. Racism also underlay the acceptance of the notion that birth or race made one segment of society superior to others; this view rationalized the exclusion of large groups—like the workers—from the right to participate in government. Differences in social status were believed to follow from natural selection, from having "better blood"; the existence of a ruling group, of an elite, in every society was not an accident, but a natural necessity.

These ideas were cultivated by small groups. As presented in the novels of Maurras and Barrès, two of the most widely read French writers of this time, for example, they seemed mainly to imply an aesthetic disdain of the mass culture of the big cities. Their emergence, however, was an ominous sign of the reawakening of an authoritarianism, no longer moderated by tradition and religion as in the age of absolutism, and of contempt for the life of individuals belonging to another race or a lower class who were judged to be of little value.

As racism developed and became wedded to nationalism, it endowed nationalism with an explosive and aggressive character. In the first half of the nineteenth century, the expression of nationalism and the demands of national unification were part of a broad liberal political program; it was assumed that, united by their belief in the same human values, the various nation states would live harmoniously together as one great family. But with the weakening of the faith in liberalism and democratization, nationalism served to emphasize what was unique and different in each nation.

The situation was paradoxical. Europe dominated the world more than ever before or ever after. But the forces which held European society together had become increasingly tenuous. The mass of the working population had no part in the government and believed in an internationalism encompassing the whole world and extinguishing all national boundaries. At the other end of the social hierarchy, royalty and aristocracy still formed a supranational element united by personal relationships and a common style of life. But the most important constituents in the social life of the period, the industrial and commercial groups, became more and more closely tied to the nation state and placed their hopes on its strength and on its support in the competition against others. This development formed the basis for the picture of the interconnection between domestic and foreign policy which Lenin presented in his famous pamphlet: "Imperialism, the Highest Stage of Capitalism." According to Lenin, the industrial and financial forces in each country were united in one large combine and the few men at its head determined the foreign policy of the nation. After the undiscovered and unexplored areas of the world had been divided among the great powers, a period of world wars was inevitable because the states would clash with one another in their efforts to increase their markets and stave off economic crises at home.

It was a picture which was widely overdrawn. Neither did Lenin's view of the relation of business and government—business as commanding the governments—correspond to reality; frequently it was the reverse: the government ordering business to make investments to justify political demands. Nor was the business of one country always opposed to the business of another country: the trend toward a supranational cooperation of economic corporations was already noticeable in the period before the First World War. But even if the clash among the European powers was not unavoidable, international tension and the possibility of war formed an integral element of the political atmosphere of Europe at the beginning of the twentieth century.

CHAPTER 2

The Great Powers, 1890-1914: The Parliamentary Governments

GENERALIZATIONS in history are dangerous. When closely examined, historical events and developments almost invariably reveal aspects which are individual and unique. For a true picture of the past, a grasp of the general pattern of development must be combined with an understanding of the individual features which in each country modified the pattern and gave to each nation's history its particular shape. Thus, after a broad survey of the factors determining the course of European history at the beginning of the twentieth century, we now turn our attention to the developments in the individual European nations. In their constitutional developments, the western European states differed decisively from those in central and eastern Europe. In western Europe, in Great Britain, France, Spain, and Italy, elected parliaments determined the character of the governments and the course of their policies.

GREAT BRITAIN

From the Victorian to the Edwardian Age

Of the great powers Great Britain had advanced furthest in democratic evolution and in industrialization. Having made progress while preserving continuity, Britain gave the impression of remarkable political and social stability. The "miracle of its constitution"—the British two-party system, British parliamentarism—seemed to offer an example of how the problems and tensions of the twentieth century could be overcome.

Yet at the close of the nineteenth century even in Britain one epoch seemed to come to an end and a new one to begin. Queen Victoria died in 1901. A famous cartoon by Max Beerbohm illustrates the difference between Victoria and her heir, King Edward VII (ruled 1901–1910). No more striking contrast can be imagined than that between the strict and dignified queen and her flamboyant son. Edward indulged in all the pleasures of a gilded society. He was devoted to beautiful women and good

A famous cartoon by Max Beerbohm, alluding to the strained relations between Queen Victoria and the Prince of Wales.

food. In his youth he gambled; in later years he played bridge from afternoon until late at night during his weekend visits to the country houses of the British rich. He had a stable of race horses, and he was also a motorist. When he died, the *Illustrated London News* praised him for his support of the motorcar industry: "When public opposition was at its height, when the outlook was dark indeed for the industry, when rumors and signs portended repressive legislation, His Majesty's accepted patronage of the then Automobile Club of Great Britain and Ireland—by which it became the Royal Automobile Club—came in the very nick of time." Together with his wife, Queen Alexandra, one of the great beauties of the age, the king was the recognized social leader of an ostentatiously opulent and luxurious society.

The sudden change from the dignified and aloof court of Victoria to the pleasure-loving and indulgent court of Edward VII had the effect not of impairing the position of the monarchy, but of strengthening it. During Victoria's reign the bourgeoisie through hard work—slowly and steadily—had transformed Great Britain into the leading industrial country of the world. By the turn of the century this work was done and its fruits could be enjoyed. Edward was the perfect representative of this stage of British economic development, and he was extremely popular.

With the wisdom of hindsight it is easy to see that the British economic position in the first decade of the twentieth century was not as brilliant as it appeared. In the last quarter of the nineteenth century the tempo of British economic development had slowed down. If there was no absolute decline, certainly growth decelerated. Between 1885 and 1913 the rate of increase in Britain's industrial production was 2.11 per cent, while Germany's increased by 4.5 per cent and that of the United States by 5.2 per cent. The actual output of steel, iron, and coal, the chief sources of Britain's strength as an industrial and commercial power, was still very high. But Great Britain was no longer the leading producer of these goods. By 1906 it had been overtaken by the United States in the production of steel, iron, and coal and by Germany in the production of steel. Similarly, in the development of innovations connected with electricity, the motorcar, and chemicals Britain lagged behind Germany and the United States. Besides, these two countries possessed more modern industrial equipment than Great Britain. Other aspects of economic life were more favorable. In the shipping industry, in textile production, and as a center of trade, Britain remained the leading power. Above all, during its period of economic growth, Britain had made immense investments in foreign countries, which now paid off and generated new investment possibilities. Thus, it was the world's greatest capital market. Its banks enjoyed enormous prestige. The gold standard and the pound were almost synonymous. But Britain did not produce as much as it imported, although the receipts from its foreign investments concealed this deficit in the balance of trade. The basis for the economic difficulties which it had to face after the First World War, and still more threateningly after the Second World War, had already been laid.

The golden glimmer of the Edwardian era was an evening glow, but few were aware of this. To most people, London was the capital of the world in the decades before the First World War, the embodiment of a luxurious style of life unequaled since the Roman Empire. The harmoniousness of the ruling group confirmed this impression of stable prosperity. Conflicts between the attitudes of a feudal and authoritarian military class and that of a bourgeois society did not exist in Great Britain. The British people had successfully fought against the standing army which they viewed as an instrument of princely absolutism and their insular position made conscription unnecessary. Moreover, the economic basis of a military caste— agriculture—had been almost eliminated. If in the first half of the nineteenth century the repeal of the corn laws and the establishment of free trade had signified the victory of the industrial and commercial classes over agricultural interests, this development was completed by the agricultural crisis of the 1880's. In a country unprotected by tariffs, competition against grain imported from Russia or America became impossible; the cultivation of grain was virtually abandoned and the soil was used for grazing, dairyfarming, or fruitfarming. But the landowners remained wealthy. Many found that their soil was rich in coal; industrial settlements sprang up on their land, and they drew large incomes from rents. Landowners frequently became involved in industrial and financial activities. The amalgamation of the rising classes of businessmen with the old aristocratic ruling group represented no problem in Britain: "While business men were becoming peers, peers were becoming business men, so that when the new rich reached the Upper House they found themselves on familiar ground."[1]

The Politics of the Ruling Class

Politics mirrored this homogeneity of the ruling class. Although strife between the Unionists, as the Conservatives were officially named, and the Liberals was quite vehement, the social composition of the leadership in each of the parties was very much alike. After William Gladstone's resignation in 1894 and the short-lived Liberal government under Lord Rosebery, the Conservatives held power for ten years, from 1895 to 1905: until 1902 the marquis of Salisbury (1830–1903) was prime minister; from 1902 to 1905 Salisbury's nephew Arthur Balfour (1848–1930). In both parties, descendants of the aristocratic families who had ruled Britain in previous centuries continued to be prominent. Salisbury and Balfour were Cecils; Greys and Ponsonbys were to be found on the councils of the Liberals. The leadership of both parties included aristocrats with industrial and financial connections, like the Liberal Rosebery, who was married to a Rothschild, and the Conservative earl of Derby, who had large coal-mine holdings. In both parties, businessmen played significant roles. Conservative and Liberal politicians enjoyed the same strictly classical education. Attendance at one of the great public schools—Eton, Harrow, Rugby—followed by Oxford or Cambridge was the usual background for a political career and almost a requirement for it; prominence in the debating society of one of the two universities marked a young man for political success. In this period, Oxford's Balliol College was the breeding ground of statesmen. Its master, Benjamin Jowett, the translator of Plato, attracted the most brilliant minds to his college and infused them with the idea that public service was the duty of the social elite.

Leaders of both parties were also knit together by strong common intellectual interests. Among the Liberals, John Morley (1838–1923) was an eminent literary historian; Richard Burdon Haldane (1856–1928) a distinguished student of German philosophy. The philosopher among the Conservatives was Arthur Balfour, who as a young man wrote the stimulating *Defence of Philosophical Doubt.* Balfour is the most puzzling and fascinat-

---

[1] Élie Halévy, A *History of the English People, Epilogue,* trans. by E. I. Watkin, Vol. II (London, 1934), p. 306.

ing figure among Britain's statemen of the early twentieth century. Although he never became prime minister again after 1905, he remained influential in the inner councils of the Conservative party. His mind was open to all that was new and modern in the social, literary, and artistic scene, and politics was only one of his many interests. He considered politics a game rather than an avocation and kept aloof from the enthusiasms and nationalist passions of the masses. Skeptical, ironical, and languidly elegant, he never lost the instincts of a member of the ruling class.

The British ruling class had no doubt of the nation's right to rule over other peoples, to maintain the empire, and to continue imperial expansion despite the increasing competition of other states. The most important leaders of both parties were conscious imperialists. The Conservative government of Salisbury used the occasion of Queen Victoria's Diamond Jubilee in 1897 to glorify Britain's world-spanning empire. But Liberals like Rosebery and Haldane were equally enthusiastic advocates of Britain's imperial role. Conservatives might be more concerned with maintaining their nation as the world's foremost power, while Liberals might emphasize its mission of guiding the colonial peoples to self-government and the other blessings of British society, but leaders of both parties were firmly resolved not to be content with what Britain possessed and to compete actively for the African and Asian lands which were up for grabs.

This was the time when the visionary dream of a British empire in Africa reaching from the Cape to Cairo made its impact on British policy. The first consequence was a serious clash between the British and the French. Seeking to enlarge their African holdings, the French had organized two expeditions, one starting from Ethiopia in the east and moving west, the other moving from Lake Chad to the east. They were to meet in the upper Nile Valley and there establish the French claim to this area, the possession of which would link French Somaliland in the east with the French colonies of Algeria in the north and Senegal in the west. This empire would cut straight across the continuous territory stretching from the Cape to Cairo which was sought by the British. Hence they quickly decided on countermeasures. They ordered General Herbert Kitchener (1850–1916) to move up the Nile into the Sudan, which, since the defeat of General Gordon in 1885, had remained in the control of the Mahdi. In 1898 the army of the Mahdi was overcome in two battles, at the Atbara River (April 8) and at Omdurman (September 2), and "the whole mass of the dervishes dissolved into fragments and into particles and streamed away into the fantastic mirages of the desert," according to a description of the battle of Omdurman by a participant, the young supernumerary Lieutenant Winston Churchill. Kitchener moved quickly ahead along the upper Nile, for the French expedition under Colonel Jean Baptiste Marchand, coming from the west, had reached Fashoda, in the southeastern Sudan, and had planted a French flag there on July 10, 1898. With a few of his troops Kitchener sailed up the Nile, arriving at Fashoda on September 18. He asked Marchand to withdraw; Marchand refused. Kitchener and Marchand conferred and agreed to await the decision of their home governments; then they drank whiskey and soda together. Public opinion in Great Britain was so enraged by the French audacity in placing obstacles in the path of the British imperial plans that even if the government had wanted to make concessions it could not have done so. The French were faced with the alternative of going to war against Great Britain or giving in. On November 3 the French government decided to surrender and ordered the unconditional evacuation of Fashoda.

The Labor Movement and Social Reform

The Diamond Jubilee of Queen Victoria in 1897 and Omdurman and Fashoda in 1898 represented the apex of British imperial power. Nevertheless, the coherence of society, the grasp of the ruling classes over the mass of the nation, was less firm and secure than one might have expected as a result of the unbroken success of British policy in the nineteenth century. Although Great Britain had passed the worst hardships and sufferings which accompanied industrialization in its early stages, misery among the masses of the working population was still great. The sacrifice of agriculture to industry, accelerated by a severe agricultural crisis in the 1880's, had forced small farmers and farm hands to migrate to the cities, thus increasing the number of unskilled workers. Housing conditions in the great industrial centers were bad. In the East End of London, families of eight or ten people often lived in one room.

From the middle of the 1890's to the outbreak of the First World War no severe economic crisis occurred in Great Britain. But wages, which had been steadily rising until the turn of the century, then began to stagnate—while prices increased. Moreover, the shadow of unemployment hovered perpetually over the industrial workers. At the end of their lives they were almost unavoidably dependent on charity and the very insufficient provisions of the Poor Law. The trade unions, which supplied almost the only protection the workers had, were handicapped by their limited financial means, and their rights were not clearly determined. Hence, a new, more militant spirit arose in the trade unions: the conviction grew that a change of the economic system to provide "collective ownership and control over production, distribution and exchange"[2] was necessary and that to effect this change labor had to enter the political arena as an independent force. The driving personality in the new movement was James Keir Hardie (1856–1915), a Scottish miner and trade-union organizer. Whereas previously trade-union men elected to Parliament had joined the Liberals, Keir Hardie and his friends had succeeded by 1900 in persuading the trade

[2] From the program issued at the foundation of the Independent Labor Party in Bradford in 1893.

unions to finance and to support at the forthcoming elections a slate of candidates who would represent the interests of the workers in Parliament. The Labor party, then called the Labor Representation Committee, had come into life.

This development was helped by a movement among middle-class British intellectuals whose social consciences were deeply stirred by the contrast between the wealth of the ruling group and the misery of the workers. Calling themselves Fabians after the Roman dictator Fabius, whom they admired because he had waited patiently for the right moment but then had struck hard, the influential members of this movement were rather disparate. Among them were reform-minded radicals like Annie Besant, successful literary figures like the novelist H. G. Wells, and George Bernard Shaw, at that time not yet a dramatist, but a music and literary critic, and scholars like the political scientist Graham Wallas. But the guiding spirit was that of a husband and wife whose closeness of aims is well testified by the fact that they are usually named together as "the Webbs." Sidney Webb (1859–1947) began as a civil servant, but soon decided to devote himself to the problems of industrial society. Beatrice Webb (1858–1943) was a woman of great beauty from a socially prominent family, and had a sensitive social conscience. From sporadic welfare activities, in which she had engaged as a young woman, she went forward to serious scientific study of social problems and became one of the great pioneers in the field of social reform in industrial society.

The Webb's house served as a kind of headquarters for intellectuals concerned with social questions. The Fabians began by publishing a series

Beatrice and Sidney Webb.

of studies on the problems of modern industrial life. The Webb's *History of Trade Unionism* (1897) is a classic. One of the Webb's most lasting achievements was the founding of the London School of Economics, later a division of the University of London, which has been particularly devoted to the investigation of political and social problems in the modern world. The Fabians believed that the march of modern society was irrevocably set toward greater democratization. But democratization could be complete only if it was economic as well as political. And economic democratization meant socialization: the public authorities—local, regional, or central—were to have the right to organize basic industries and to determine how capital income would be used. Fabianism was socialism, but not Marxism. It did not presuppose a revolution which would give all power to one class, the proletariat, and it did not advocate the end of the national state. The socialist transformation of society was to be brought about democratically, by the will of the people. The Fabians felt that their goals were in accordance with the British political tradition, constituting the natural destination toward which their nation's political life had been moving since the beginning of the nineteenth century.

For a while the Fabians tried to convince the leaders of the existing political parties that they ought to adopt the Fabian program. Sidney Webb, who disapproved of spending money on clothes or jewels, permitted Beatrice to buy a new dress if doing so might make political leaders willing to listen to the Fabian program. But when both Conservative and Liberal leaders proved unresponsive, some of the Fabians turned to the idea of establishing a third party, which would realize socialism in Britain. They joined forces with Keir Hardie's Labor Representation Committee, and their ideas soon began to dominate the young Labor party; the combination of intellectuals and trade unionists has remained a characteristic of the British Labor party. When in the 1920's the Labor party came to power, several of the Fabians received high government positions. So prominent had some of their leaders become that on the occasion of their fiftieth anniversary in 1933, George Bernard Shaw, the principal speaker, began by saying, "Ladies and Gentlemen," but then, looking to his right and left on the podium, where the early members of the Fabian movement were seated, he quickly added, "Oh, I see I have to say My Lords, Ladies and Gentlemen."

Both the Conservatives and the Liberals were aware that the founding of an independent Labor party was a threat to the two-party system. They recognized that they had to make a greater effort to satisfy the demands of the laboring classes. Ever since Disraeli had coined the slogan "Tory Democracy," a wing of the Conservative party had placed emphasis on social reform. This movement received new impetus when in 1886 Joseph Chamberlain (1836–1914), with a group of followers, broke with Gladstone and the Liberals and joined the Conservatives. Chamberlain, coming from industrial Birmingham, had made a name for himself as an advocate of radical reforms. As lord mayor of Birmingham he had introduced "municipal socialism"; he had improved public services and made them less expensive by placing streetcars, street lighting, and public utilities under the administration of the city government. Chamberlain had also modernized party politics by creating wards with party organizers who would get the masses to the polls. For a politician of this outlook "Conservative" seemed hardly the right label, and following his alliance with the Conservatives they were officially named "Unionists."

A similar tendency toward social reform could be observed in the Liberal party. Nonconformists and radicals had always formed a strong element in this party. Such Liberals felt that leaders like Rosebery and the imperialists did not represent the true Liberal tradition, and many thought they ought to oppose the imperial expansionism which oppressed other peoples. They believed that the Liberal party ought to concentrate on domestic problems and work toward the solution of the Irish question by seeking to obtain for Ireland its own government and parliament: home rule. The members of this group were sometimes called Little Englanders because of their doubts about the value of the empire. Their most respected leader, Sir Henry Campbell-Bannerman (1836–1908), had held high government office under Gladstone and was regarded as Gladstone's authentic heir, the man who would continue his reform policy. Among this group a new leader arose in a young lawyer and brilliant orator from Wales, David Lloyd George (1863–1945), whose political passion was fired by the misery which he saw among the Welsh mine workers.

Imperialism Versus Domestic Reform

The tensions between the imperialists and the domestic reformers were sharpened by Britain's conflict with the Boer republics in South Africa. In Salisbury's government Joseph Chamberlain had become secretary for the colonies. Partly because he saw little chance to move his Conservative colleagues toward social reform, and partly because of the demands of his office, Chamberlain turned his great energies to the realization of an empire extending from the Cape to Cairo. French ambitions for the upper Nile Valley had been thwarted at Fashoda, but Transvaal and the Orange Free State, the independent Boer republics in southern Africa, still remained a barrier to these plans. A conflict between these independent states and Great Britain seemed unavoidable; its outbreak was accelerated by the discovery of gold in the Transvaal. The Boers feared that the immigrants streaming to the Transvaal in search of quick riches would soon outnumber them, limiting Boer political influence, and—since most of the immigrants (known as Uitlanders) were British—that they might decide to make the Boer republics part of the British empire. There is no doubt that Cecil

Rhodes, the dominating figure in the British Cape Colony, aimed at an absorption of the Boer republics by the empire. He believed that the unrest created by the tension between Boers and Uitlanders might provide the opportune moment. In 1896 he organized an invasion by a small force of 470 men under the leadership of a Dr. Jameson, an adventurer. The expectation was that the march of this force into the interior of the Transvaal would give the signal for a rebellion in Johannesburg by the Uitlander against the Boers. But no such upheaval occurred; Jameson and his men were quickly defeated and surrendered to the Boers. Rhodes's responsibility for the raid was incontestable and he was forced to resign as prime minister of the Cape Colony. But the much-discussed question was whether Chamberlain, the British colonial secretary, had previous knowledge of the raid. The British government immediately declined all responsibility for the raid and a committee of the House of Commons gave Chamberlain a clean bill of health. But doubts about Chamberlain's role were never entirely removed and recent investigations have revealed that he knew much more about what was planned than he admitted at the time.

People outside England had no doubt that the Jameson Raid was a British defeat. The German emperor, William II, sent a telegram to the president of the Transvaal republic, Paul Kruger, congratulating him upon his success "in restoring peace and in maintaining the independence of the country against attacks from without." This message, which rubbed salt in Britain's wounds, may have been unwise politically, but in giving vent to his indignation about British ruthlessness, William expressed the feelings not only of the German nation but of all the European continent. The Jameson Raid and the telegram of the German emperor made war between the Boers and Great Britain almost certain. To the British, conquest of the Boer republics had become a matter of prestige. On the other hand, the raid confirmed the Boers in their fear of the influence of the immigrants, while at the same time the public acknowledgement of the Boers' right to independence encouraged them to resist the British. Hence, they continued their discriminatory policy against the Uitlanders, while the British took up the cause of these new immigrants and insisted that they should receive the right to vote. When negotiations proved fruitless, Britain sent troop reinforcements to the Cape Colony; and on the demand of the Boers for withdrawal of these troops, the British cut off all discussion. In October, 1899, war broke out between the Boer republics (Transvaal and the Orange Free State) on the one hand and the British on the other.

The Boer War followed a pattern common to many colonial wars. The resistance of the indigenous forces proved to be more effective than had been expected, and initially the British had severe losses. But when the full force of the British was brought into play, the difference in strength proved decisive. Where the Boer War differed from most other colonial engagements was in the severity of the reverses suffered by the invading British forces, which were first repulsed, then encircled at Ladysmith and Kimberley and there besieged. They were relieved only at the end of February, 1900, after large reinforcements from England had arrived and a change in command had taken place. The British offensive ended with the conquest and annexation of the Transvaal in September, 1900. But military action continued for another year and a half. The Boers engaged in guerilla warfare, and Kitchener, the British commander, proceeded against them ruthlessly, burning the farms of Boer guerillas and interning the women and children of Boer soldiers in specially constructed camps. Finally, on May 31, 1902, a peace treaty was signed in which the Boers acknowledged British sovereignty.

The Boer War was a terrible shock to the British people. Since the colonial army was not sufficiently large, troops had to be sent from England; 350,000 men were needed to subdue 60,000 Boers. In England families grew increasingly anxious over the fate of relatives and friends whose lives had been unexpectedly endangered by a colonial war. Moreover, all over Europe there was an outburst of fury against Great Britain. This sudden revelation of their unpopularity was a great surprise to the British, and although the European governments did not take any common action against them, they began to fear that their country might be confronted by a combination of all the continental powers. Thereafter British foreign policy gradually began to veer away from "splendid isolation" and into an acceptance of cooperation with other states. The Boer War had shown the obsoleteness and clumsiness of British military organization, and raised serious doubts about the aims of British policy and the efficiency of British political processes.

Was the imperial expansion worth the loss of life and the expenditure of money exacted by the Boer War? At first, the opponents of the policy which had led to war were shouted down and socially boycotted. But as the conflict dragged on, the politicians who had resisted the wave of imperialist enthusiasm—men like Campbell-Bannerman and Lloyd George—gained in political stature. They found increasing support for their arguments that attention should be focused upon domestic problems. Events confirmed the view that internal tensions were reaching a dangerous state. The newly militant trade unions had encountered fierce resistance by employers, and had retaliated with local strikes against the employment of "free," or nonunion, labor. The tenseness of this situation was aggravated by the Taff Vale decision (1901), which asserted that a trade union was financially liable for damage caused by all strikes in which its members took part. Indignation among the working population was immense because the decision underlined the precarious position of the trade unions and the helplessness of the working classes. The government also lost popularity as a result of the measures it instituted for reform in education. The need for such reform was generally recognized. Great Britain had only a limited number of elementary schools maintained by the state, that is, by the counties and towns. More than half of the children of England and Wales received their elementary education at voluntary schools which were unable to maintain reasonable standards. The Education Act of 1902 placed all these schools under county and town control so that they were forced to adhere to recognized standards; if necessary they would receive financial support from local taxes. The measure undoubtedly represented a great improvement in English education. But because it implied that tax money would be used to support Anglican and Roman Catholic schools, it aroused the vehement opposition of an important segment of the British population, the nonconformists.

The Triumph of the Liberal Party

The final cause for the end of ten years of Conservative rule was a split among the Conservatives themselves. Joseph Chamberlain had not abandoned his original radicalism when he turned from internal reforms to imperial expansion. On the contrary, he regarded a resolute imperial policy as a means for improving the lot of the masses. He believed that his country's continued economic prosperity depended on the expansion of opportunities to emigrate to the colonies. He advocated protective tariffs which would limit foreign competition in the British market, and by giving preferences to the British colonies, would tie the empire together as a great economic unit. To promote these aims Chamberlain organized the Tariff Reform League, and to devote himself to this campaign he left the government. In Prime Minister Balfour's view, British public opinion was not ready to accept protective tariffs. In a country dependent on the importation of agricultural goods the first result of protection would be an increase in the price of food, which would place another burden on the masses. Split over the tariff question, the Conservatives seemed to lack an economic policy, while the Liberals adhered to the hallowed tradition of free trade. Unable to control his own party, Balfour resigned in December, 1905, and the Liberals took over. Campbell-Bannerman became prime minister, not without the displeasure of the imperialist elements in his own party. But he reconciled them by giving them strong representation in the cabinet. Sir Edward Grey (1862–1933) became foreign secretary; Herbert Asquith (1852–1928), chancellor of the exchequer; and Haldane, secretary of state for war. The radical wing of the reformers was also well represented. Lloyd George became president of the Board of Trade, and John Burns (1858–1943), president of the Local Government Board. The new government was an incongruous mixture of imperialists and social reformers. But at this time Great Britain was still prosperous enough to attempt simultaneously to maintain a powerful position in foreign affairs and to undertake reforms at home. In the elections of January, 1906, the Liberals gained a sweeping victory, but it was a sign of the times that the new Labor party gained twenty-nine seats.

Ten years of Liberal rule followed the Conservative defeat of 1906. This decade saw the accomplishment of reforms which had a wide-ranging effect. The first years of the new government did not give the impression that the change of government was different from those of earlier years: namely that the outs were in and the ins were out. The Liberal government was chiefly occupied with redressing those measures of the Conservatives which had aroused passionate indignation, and with repairing defects in the machinery of government which recent events had revealed. By giving self-government to the Transvaal, the Liberal government contributed to healing the wounds of the Boer War. The Taff Vale decision was annulled; a Trades Disputes Act legalized peaceful picketing and relieved trade unions from liability for damages caused by their members. Haldane carried through an army reform which fully proved itself in the First World War. The army was divided into two parts, an expeditionary force ready for immediate action on the Continent and a territorial force into which were merged traditional organizations such as the volunteers and the yeomanry. Moreover, Haldane created a general staff as had existed in Prussia since the nineteenth century and was regarded to be responsible for German military superiority. Like other successful military reforms, these measures also resulted in financial economies.

Even so, the results of the first years of Liberal rule were somewhat meager. The reason was that many measures which the government advocated—among them change in the Education Act, which would have removed the objections of the nonconformists—were rejected by the House of Lords, controlled by the Conservatives. Moreover, Asquith, chancellor of the exchequer, pursued a traditional line in his financial policy and was disinclined to finance social experiments. This situation changed in 1908, when Asquith succeeded the dying Campbell-Bannerman as prime minister and Lloyd George took Asquith's place as chancellor of the exchequer.

A sudden acceleration in the policy of reform could be traced in part to this dynamic figure. Lloyd George was a Welshman of immense energy, of great ambition, impatient to get things done, and anxious always to be in the public eye. Moreover, he was the leader of the radicals in the Liberal party and he considered the success of the Labor party in the elections of 1906 as an indication that if the government remained relatively inactive a good part of the radical supporters of the Liberals would desert to Labor. Therefore, Lloyd George resolutely used the power of the purse for social reform. The most important feature of this reform was the National Insurance Act (1911), patterned after the social legislation which Bismarck had sponsored in Germany. Contributions made on a compulsory basis by workers, employers, and the state were to provide payments to workers in case of sickness and unemployment. Social reforms were to be paid for by means of a revised system of taxation which placed the chief burden for the expenses of the new programs on the wealthy classes. Thus Lloyd George's first budget, that of 1909, represented a radical departure. He raised the death duties, made a sharp distinction between earned and unearned income, and introduced a super-tax to be levied on the possessors of large incomes. He also increased the taxes on tobacco and liquor.

In present day terms, Lloyd George's proposals were moderate. The payments given to workers in case of sickness or disability were low, and the small unemployment benefits were granted for only a limited period, a maximum of fifteen weeks in any one year. On the other hand the supertax started only on a yearly income of over £ 5,000 (which might be compared to an income today of more than $100,000) and the general income tax for unearned income and for earned income above £ 2,000 was raised only from one shilling to one shilling two pence in the pound. Nevertheless, on a very small scale Lloyd George's budget incorporated all the essential features of the future British welfare state; in the benefits provided and in the methods of financing them the government of present-day Britain continues the policy initiated by Lloyd George in 1909.

Lloyd George emphasized the novel character of his budget by introducing it with a four-hour speech. Opposition formed at once. The Conservatives were particularly upset by a suggestion which later proved to be impractical and was abandoned—the taxing of increases in land value. Since much of the wealth of the British landowners came from estates having mineral resources like coal, this tax was regarded as a direct attack on the position of the propertied classes.

The Conservatives fought the budget vigorously, and when it reached the House of Lords it was rejected. Since the Liberals had been constantly balked in their legislative proposals by the House of Lords, they were deeply aroused by this further frustration of their plans, particularly since tradition had established that the handling of finance bills was primarily a function of the House of Commons. The rejection of the budget by the House of Lords was regarded as a breach of the constitution.

As a next step the Liberal government introduced the Parliament Bill, designed to eliminate the House of Lords as a partner equal to the House of Commons in the law-making process. If it passed, the House of Lords would be able only to delay legislation, not to veto it absolutely. The great problem which faced the Liberal government was how to persuade the House of Lords to agree to its own diminution of power. This issue began to become more important than the details of the budget.

The Liberals were not unhappy about this course of events. The struggle of the "people vs. the Lords" overshadowed their failure to have tackled crucial problems which they had been expected to solve.

First of all, there was the perennial problem of British policy: the Irish question. As long as Gladstone was the leader of the Liberal party, home rule for Ireland had been a cornerstone of the Liberal program. Still a good portion of the Liberals had great doubts about home rule and were disquieted about its likely effects on the contacts between Protestant Ulster and Catholic Ireland. Thus, when the Liberal government was formed in 1905, it stated that while home rule remained the aim of the party, nothing could be done beyond some preparatory measures in the immediate future. This dilatoriness soon created great dissatisfaction.

Another issue which had aroused increasing attention and unrest was the question of the vote for women. In Europe the advocates of women's right to vote were almost exclusively the socialist parties; because of the gap between the socialists and the ruling groups, socialist sponsorship condemned this demand to ineffectiveness. In Great Britain the situation was somewhat different. Since the Local Government Act of 1894, women had the right to vote in municipal and county elections; their exclusion from national elections seemed arbitrary. In England the fight for women's votes was therefore conducted not only by members of the Labor party, like their leader Keir Hardie, but also by women of the middle and upper classes. They presented their demands in the election meetings of the various parties and continued their propaganda by distribution of leaflets, street demonstrations, and petitions to Parliament. It is perhaps questionable whether the movement for women's right to vote would have made such an impact had it not been led originally by women of such boundless energy as Emmeline Pankhurst, and her daughters, Christabel and Sylvia. These women were later joined in the struggle by others as energetic and devoted to the cause: including Annie Kenney, Emmeline Pethick-Lawrence, Dame Ethel Smyth, and Lady Constance Lytton. As with the Irish question, the members of the Liberal government were disinclined to take a stand. In this situation the conflict over the role of the House of Lords occurred at an appropriate moment. It was not unwelcome to the Liberals to have the attention of the public directed to an issue which also demonstrated loyalty to liberal and radical principles but was of a less divisive nature. Lloyd George aimed at transforming the parliamentary controversies into a great constitutional conflict which could be represented as a fight of the people against the lords. In a number of speeches, and with great oratorical force, he castigated the unequal distribution of wealth in England due to "the fraud of the few and the folly of the many." Lloyd George was happily seconded by Winston Churchill, who in 1904, had moved from the Conservatives to the Liberals and in 1908 had been made president of the Board of Trade in the Liberal government. But the Conservatives fought back with equal vehemence, characterizing the Liberal proposal as a subversive attack on the entire English tradition.

Radicals of the Edwardian era. *Lloyd George and Churchill on the way to the House of Commons on Budget Day, 1910.*

The debate over the Parliament Bill was conducted with an animosity previously unknown in English political life. On one occasion Prime Minister Asquith was prevented from speaking in the House of Commons by a group of diehards shouting "traitor" and drowning his voice in hoots and jeers. The struggle lasted for over two years and ended only after two dissolutions of the House of Commons, new elections, and the threat that the government would create enough Liberal peers to get the proposal through the House of Lords. The final vote, on August 10, 1911, took place under immense excitement because the outcome seemed quite uncertain; the bill was passed only after thirty-seven Conservatives and thirteen bishops decided not to abstain and cast their votes with the government.

Intensification of Internal Conflicts:
Women's Rights and the Irish Question

Edward VII died on May 6, 1910, in the midst of the struggle over the Parliament Bill. With his death, British life seemed to lose some of its splendor. His son and successor, King George V (ruled 1910–1936), was a much less glamorous figure; in a sense his somberness corresponded to the dark and threatening atmosphere which prevailed in Great Britain in the two or three years before the outbreak of the First World War.

Even after passage of the Parliament Bill it became evident that the conflicts and problems which had existed before were still there and unsolved; moreover, the bitterness which the struggle had engendered gave a sharp edge to all political conflicts.

The campaign for women's right to vote had never entirely ceased; clashes with the police when women marchers entered areas in which demonstrations were forbidden, or disturbances in political meetings, had led to frequent court proceedings. When the court gave the accused the choice between fines and prison the suffragettes frequently chose the latter; there they went on hunger strikes to which the government replied with forced feeding. Pictures showing police roughness in handling women demonstrators or women prisoners resisting forced feeding caused outcries about police brutality. Ironically, as home secretary, Herbert Gladstone, the former prime minister's son, was responsible for the behavior of the police although himself in favor of women's right to vote. Yet, until 1911 the outbreaks of violence remained sporadic, because as long as the fight on the Parliament Bill continued the suffragettes hoped that frequent elections would finally result in a Parliament which would give them the vote. But when the struggle over the Parliament Bill had ended and

Suffragettes are arrested after a demonstration before Buckingham Palace.

Parliament showed no sign of widening the franchise, a systematic policy of militant demonstrations was adopted by the Women's Social and Political Union (WSPU), as the organization of the suffragettes was called. Targets of attack were no longer only the Parliament building or government offices; disturbances were extended to all spheres of life in the hopes of achieving the surrender of the ruling male politicians. For instance, on March 1, 1912, 150 well-dressed women marched along the main shopping streets in the center of London—Oxford and Regent Streets—and, with hammers concealed in their handbags, smashed the windows of the large department stores in the vicinity: Burberry, Liberty's, Marshall and Snelgrove. This was the beginning of a concerted campaign of destruction which included cutting telegraph wires, burning railroad cars, smashing exhibits in the Tower of London, slashing pictures in the National Gallery, and setting fire to private homes of prominent politicians. A tragic culmination was reached at the Epsom Derby on June 4, 1913, when one of the most active suffragettes, Emily Davison, threw herself in front of the king's horse, ending her life. Those who retrieved her body found a banner inscribed with VOTES FOR WOMEN sewn into her coat. Militant suffragette actions continued until the outbreak of the First World War, but it can be questioned whether they were not becoming counterproductive. People who might be neutral began to turn against the suffragettes, so that their demonstrations began to meet counterdemonstrations. Moreover, among the suffragettes themselves, opposition arose, and while Emmeline and Christabel Pankhurst—who were most insistent on continuing the violence—remained leaders at the core of the movement, several splinter groups pursuing a more conciliatory policy were formed. It is difficult to say whether, without the war, when women had to take over many of the jobs which men had done, the aims of the suffragettes would have been realized in the near future. However, it is quite clear that if the movement had not directed public attention to the question of the female franchise, the war would not have brought about female suffrage. Women received it in the Representation of the People Act of 1918.

The Irish question became urgent because of the intricacies of the English parliamentary situation. Gladstone's home rule proposals in the nineteenth century had always been wrecked by the resistance of the House of Lords. The Irish nationalists, therefore, under the leadership of Redmond, supported the Liberal government in its attempt to curtail the power of the House of Lords. The support of the Irish nationalists became crucial when, in the various elections held to clarify the trends of public opinion in the struggle over the Lords, the Liberals lost their majority and kept government control only with the help of the Irish nationalists. After the struggle was over the nationalists asked to receive their reward;

A violent protest. *The suffragette Emily Davison throwing herself in front of the king's horse at the Derby on June 4, 1913. At this time, action photographs were rare and usually obtained only by chance.*

a home rule bill was drafted by the government in 1912. But this proposal led to a critical situation because of changes in Ireland since the times of Gladstone's abortive home rule legislation. Although the Conservative government, which had followed Gladstone, opposed home rule, the Conservatives had been aware of the need to allay misery and discontent in Ireland. By a Land Purchase Act they had made it possible for the tenants on the large estates to become owners of the land which they cultivated, and a certain amount of self-administration on the local level was introduced.

These measures coincided with the beginning of the movement for an Irish cultural renaissance. The Irish people, now economically less oppressed and more conscious of their national identity, became increasingly resentful that almost all the high positions in the administration of Ireland were in the hands of Protestant Englishmen. Despite the improvements brought about by the Conservative government, the demand for home rule had gained in strength rather than diminished. Moreover, the stress on Irish-Catholic traditions made home rule less acceptable to the English Protestants in Ireland who were particularly strong in Ulster. "Home rule is Rome rule," was the Protestant slogan and they formed organizations of volunteers ready to resist the introduction of home rule.

One of their most influential and most passionate leaders was a prominent lawyer, one of the great orators of the time, Sir Edward Carson. What is astonishing is that the appeal for rebellion which Carson and other Ulstermen uttered was defended and encouraged by the leaders of the Conservative party in England. Clearly the Conservatives regarded home rule legislation as a way to get rid of the Liberal government.

The Asquith government tried to effect a compromise, according to which the status quo might be maintained in the northern Protestant section, and that part of the country excluded from home rule. But, since neither the Irish nationalists nor the Ulstermen were pleased with such a compromise, no agreement about the frontier to be drawn between home rule Ireland and Ulster could be reached. By the spring of 1914, the period of delay which the House of Lords was still able to interpose was over, the home rule bill had passed through all the parliamentary stages, and a most explosive situation had come about. Officers of a regiment stationed in Ulster, most of them Conservative, many of them descended from the Protestant Irish, demanded a pledge from the government that they would not be asked to coerce Ulster; otherwise they preferred to resign. Weapons to equip volunteer formations were landed in north and south of Ireland. Only the outbreak of the First World War prevented a test of the resolve and power of the government to carry through its Irish policy. In contrast to the question of the women's vote, however, the war did not bring about a solution to the Irish problem. Although in a patriotic outburst all the divided forces—Irish nationalists and Ulstermen—expressed their willingness to defend Great Britain against Germany, the conflict continued to smolder. It would explode two years later in an uprising known as the Easter Rebellion of 1916.

The Waning of Confidence

The violence that accompanied the suffragette cause and the agitation for home rule legislation occurred because these movements lay outside the traditional constitutional framework. In both movements one finds reflected the feeling that parliamentary institutions did not function properly under the pressures of the rapidly changing world of the twentieth century. The fight of the people against the Lords gave further impetus to the notion that the existing institutions were a hindrance to full democracy. In the years before the war the statistics of a contemporary bestseller were frequently quoted: In Great Britain, with a total population of 45 million people, 38 million had hardly more than half the national income, whereas 125,000 rich had more than a third. Although these figures were estimates and exaggerated, the popularity of this pamphlet revealed the growing resentment existing toward British class society. This view was particularly strong among the workers, and in the years before the outbreak of the First World War their discontent was well grounded. Prices had increased in consequence of the inflationary process which had been set in motion with the discovery of the South African gold fields. And although the wages of the workers had also increased, they had not risen enough to compensate for the rise in prices. Industrialists were hesitant to raise wages because of the competition of Germany and the United States on the world market. The impression of class rule, of suppression of workers by the rich, established ruling group, was also reinforced by a court decision that denied trade unions the right to collect political contributions. Consequently, the Labor party, which the trade unions saw as representing their interests, was weakened and unable to repeat in subsequent elections the success which it had had in the elections of 1906. Confidence in attaining better economic conditions by means of parliamentary action through the Labor party was shaken.

Disillusionment about the efficacy of the pressure exerted by their party led elements of the labor movement to look favorably upon other recipes for the ills of their economic situation. They became attracted by the idea, which reached Britain from the Continent, particularly from France, that "direct action"—strikes—was the appropriate weapon for workers seeking to improve their situation. Thus, economic and political motives lay behind a number of strikes in 1911 and 1912. The most notable were a seamen's strike, a general railway strike, a strike of the coal miners, and a strike of the dockers. Most of them were accompanied by violence, looting, and sabotage of the machinery in the factories. Frequently troops had to be used, since the police were not able to keep order. Some of the strikes were ended quickly by concessions on the part of the employers. The miners' strike resulted in the introduction of the Miners' Minimum Wage Act, which was a tacit admission by the government of the hardships faced by the mine workers. But some of the strikes simply collapsed, partly because the wage lag began to be made up and partly because the public, tired of economic unrest, began to turn sharply against the trade unions.

The attitude of the liberal government in these labor disputes was rather ambiguous. Whereas Lloyd George demonstrated his sympathy for the cause of the workers, others were more inclined to propose legislation which would forbid strikes in essential services like the railroads. There was also no agreement on the question of how far the government should go in fixing and enforcing minimum wages.

Irritation about the restlessness of the workers and hesitancy to spend money on social reforms was also increased by tension on the international scene. Churchill, who in the earlier years of the liberal government had been Lloyd George's strongest ally in supporting social reforms and the beginnings of a welfare policy, had become first lord of the admiralty. As such he favored the building of large warships, the so-called dreadnoughts. This brought him in conflict with Lloyd George. Asquith, the prime minister, succeeded in effecting a compromise and preventing a break-up of the government, but it was evident that the tension between the imperialists and the radical wing of the liberal government was again coming into the foreground. After the First World War, when the problems of government intervention in economic life and social reforms once more would dominate political discussion, the Liberal party would split and gradually become eliminated as decisive factor in British political life. But even before the war its failure to develop a clear, unified program caused cracks within the party that reflected larger uncertainties in the nation.

FRANCE
Social Basis of French Parliamentarianism

During the decade before the First World War France was the most democratic of the powers on the continent. France, too, had a parliamentary system. The head of the state, the president, had little power and the executive arm of the government, led by a prime minister, was dependent on the confidence of elected representatives—the Senate and the Chamber of Deputies. In a formal sense, France was even more democratic than Great Britain, for the French upper house, the Senate, was elected, whereas in Britain membership in the upper house was hereditary. However, the voting system by which French senators were chosen favored rural districts and the well-to-do, so the Senate functioned as a conservative counterweight to the more liberal Chamber of Deputies.

In contrast to the British system, French political life was not characterized by the dominance of a two-party system. The French parliament was composed of a large number of small parties; every government was a coalition, and governments changed frequently. In the twenty-four years between 1890 and 1914 there were forty-three governments and twenty-six prime ministers. Yet these statistics are deceptive; stability was greater than the figures imply. The multiplicity of French political parties was not a reflection of irreconcilable internal tensions. The French population was socially quite homogeneous. France was a country of small businessmen and farmers. Industrial enterprises were generally limited in size and frequently family owned. Until the First World War, more than half of the entire population was occupied in agriculture, which accounted even in 1890 for more than a third of the national income. The multifariousness of the political groupings was chiefly a reflection of tiny differences in economic interests and of variations stemming from local and regional particularities. Politicians moved easily from one party to the other. The center of the political spectrum formed the basis of almost all governments. A number of the same politicians were to be found in almost every cabinet, although they were usually assigned different ministries each time a change in government took place. The various governments differed mainly in whether the center ruled with support of the left or with support of the right.

Ironically, the strength of the center in French politics was an indication that France was lagging in the industrial race. France had entered the industrial age almost simultaneously with Great Britain. But after the spurt given by the French Revolution and Napoleon, the rate of industrial growth slowed down in the nineteenth century and France trailed far behind the United States and Germany. By its accumulated wealth the nation remained a great financial power. However, the French were inclined to invest their capital not in industrial enterprises, but—more cautiously— in public loans. In the market for government loans French banks played a particularly great role. The heavy industries were mainly centered in the northeast, where there were rich coal mines and a textile industry, and in Lorraine, which had valuable iron ore deposits. Thus the problems arising from modern industrialization were concentrated in relatively small areas and aroused little interest in the rest of the country. Health and safety precautions in industrial enterprises, particularly in the mines, were unsatisfactory. Trade unions had finally been legalized in 1884, but remained very much restricted in their activities. Membership in each union was limited to men who had the same trade or produced the same goods. Full-time, paid officials were not allowed in the unions, nor were civil servants permitted to form unions, and even the laborers of the Paris sewage system were defined as civil servants. Moreover, the activities of the unions remained confined to the study and defense of economic, industrial, commercial, and agricultural interests. They were not supposed to engage in politics.

France had an active Socialist party, but it was small and many of its deputies could not have been elected without support from the rural population. Thus the Socialists, despite theoretical radicalism, were inclined to be conciliatory in practice. Since the workers could not expect much from parliamentary action, theories which recommended direct action and emphasized the efficacy of purely economic weapons—such as strikes— were appealing. As the propagandist of the myth that the general strike was the proper instrument for the overthrow of capitalism, Georges Sorel became an influential figure among radical intellectuals through his book entitled *Reflections on Violence* (1908). His views increased the appeal of syndicalism, a revolutionary doctrine which preached direct action with the goal of building a new society through the cooperation of the trade unions of individual factories. Syndicalism was popular among workers in France and spread from there to Italy and Spain. Among the workers of these countries it was a serious competitor to Marxian socialism.

The Republican Regime vs. Monarchist Traditions

Because the progress of industrialization in France was slow, political life was not dominated by social conflicts. The main divisions were ideological: they concerned issues which the French Revolution had raised. It has been said that after the French Revolution there were two Frances, an aristocratic monarchical France and a republican France. Defeat in the Franco-Prussian War had strengthened the feeling of malaise about the unavoidable decline of the deeply divided nation. The republic, which had been born in the times of the heroic resistance at the end of the Franco-Prussian War, was now beset by scandals and corruption and appeared unable to give an impulse to a regeneration of power. The enemies of the republican and revolutionary tradition felt justified in their conviction that the democratic form of the French government was the reason for the decline of their nation's power and that what France needed was a more authoritarian regime. Moreover, the enemies of the republic were firmly entrenched in two institutions: the army and the Church.

In the last decade of the nineteenth century a crucial event brought about an open confrontation of the two Frances. The impact of the Dreyfus Affair on French thinking was so profound that it took decades to digest and absorb it. This is strikingly indicated by the role which the Affair played in the work of the great French novelists of the twentieth century. Roger Martin Du Gard inserted in his novel *Jean Barois* an almost stenographic report of some of the high points of the Affair. In *Remembrance of Things Past* by Marcel Proust the Affair serves to question the values of the brilliant society which the novel pictures. Anatole France in his *Penguin Island* pictured the Affair as an example of the eternal struggle between reason and human weakness.

The importance of the events beginning in 1894 became clear only slowly. On October 15, 1894, Alfred Dreyfus (1859–1935), a captain in the French general staff, was placed under arrest for high treason. After some weeks Dreyfus was found guilty at a secret military trial, and a few days later, on January 5, 1895, he was sentenced in a solemn ceremony in the courtyard of the general-staff building; he was deprived of his rank, his sword was broken, and he was sent for life to Devil's Island, in French Guiana. The trial had been full of legal irregularities. The main proof used against Dreyfus was a small piece of blue paper, which became famous as the *bordereau*. It had been found by a cleaning woman in the wastepaper basket of the German military attaché; it contained information about the French army; and handwriting experts maintained that it had been written by Dreyfus.

The Dreyfus Affair. *Above: Dreyfus leaving the court building after his trial.*

Right: Le Bordereau. *This famous document, on which the Dreyfus Affair turned, was given to the German military attaché.*

AFFAIRE DREYFUS,
Document No. 1.
Le Bordereau. Fragement)

A republican and a Jew, Dreyfus had been an outsider among the aristocratic and Catholic officers of the French general staff; his fellow officers were easily convinced, therefore, that if a traitor was among them, it could only be Dreyfus. He belonged to a wealthy Alsatian family, which made every effort to obtain a new trial. A few journalists and lawyers who opposed the military caste were active on Dreyfus' behalf. But for a long while no one could make headway.

In 1896 the counterespionage section of the French general staff received a new chief, Colonel Georges Picquart, who must be considered the true hero of the Dreyfus Affair. Picquart noticed that the removal of Dreyfus had not ended the leakage of military secrets. He also became aware that the handwriting of the *bordereau* was much more similar to that of Walsin Esterhazy, another member of the general staff, than to that of Dreyfus. Moreover, Esterhazy was in continuous financial difficulties. But when Picquart insisted on proceedings against Esterhazy, nobody in the general staff was willing to listen to him and he was transferred from Paris to Algiers. Before leaving Paris he confidentially informed a few people, among them the vice president of the Senate, Scheurer-Kestner, of his suspicions about Esterhazy. Now a number of influential voices joined the campaign for Dreyfus. In addition to Scheurer-Kestner, there were Georges Clemenceau (1841–1929), a journalist and politician; Anatole France; and others. Still, this was not a popular cause. The Socialist leader Jean Jaurès (1859–1914) was for a long time doubtful of Dreyfus' innocence, and when he finally became convinced that a miscarriage of justice had occurred, and was ready to take up the fight, he met reluctance and hesitation in his own party. The Socialist leaders doubted that their adherents, the workers, would perceive a connection between their own interests and the cause of a wealthy Jewish officer.

It is hard to say what would have happened if the army leaders had not got rattled and overplayed their hand. In order to quell once and for all the agitation for Dreyfus, they ordered a trial of Esterhazy, and he was acquitted. Picquart, one of the witnesses against Esterhazy, was arrested and imprisoned. This arbitrary procedure provoked one of the great political documents of modern times—*J'accuse* (1898). In this open letter addressed to the president of the republic, Emile Zola (1840–1902) stated the case against the army leaders briefly and concisely, singling out the responsible officers by name and devoting to each of them a single paragraph beginning *J'accuse.* The publication led to proceedings against Zola, and rightly expecting that he would be condemned, he fled to England, where he continued the fight. Zola's intervention represented the turning point in the Dreyfus Affair. Immense public interest had been aroused, and every step taken in the proceedings was carefully scrutinized. It emerged that in order to strengthen the case against Dreyfus, documents had been falsified. Colonel Hubert Henry who had done this falsification, committed suicide; Esterhazy fled to England. Under these circumstances the highest court of appeal on June 3, 1899, set aside the previous condemnation of Dreyfus and ordered a new trial. But the military were unwilling to accept the humiliation of the rehabilitation of Dreyfus. It was widely assumed that the officers were preparing a *coup d'état* to overthrow the republican regime.

This threat against the existing regime made all the adherents of the republic realize that they had to act and to act quickly. For the first time in European history Socialists declared their willingness to support a bourgeois government. On June 22, 1899, René Waldeck-Rousseau, a member of a well-known family that was both republican and Catholic, and a man who had proved himself an able administrator in previous governments, formed a coalition government reaching from the right of center to the left, with the suppressor of the Paris Commune of 1871, Gaston de Galliffet, as minister of war and the left-wing Socialist, Alexandre Millerand (1859–1943), as minister of commerce. When the new trial culminated in a grotesque verdict which confirmed Dreyfus' guilt while conceding him "extenuating circumstances," the Waldeck-Rousseau government was strong enough to pardon him.

In the course of the Affair the personal fate of Dreyfus became relatively insignificant. When Dreyfus accepted pardon from the Waldeck-Rousseau government, Charles Péguy, a young French writer, wrote: "We would have died for Dreyfus. Dreyfus did not die for Dreyfus."[3] In Péguy's opinion Dreyfus was no Dreyfusard; he should have continued to insist on his full rehabilitation because the fight had involved irreconcilable principles and ought therefore to have ended with the full victory of the right principles over the wrong ones—of the republican over the authoritarian ideas.

The Emergence of New Ideologies on the Right and on the Left

The obstinacy of the anti-Dreyfusards, which appeared to be stupid, if not downright criminal, becomes more comprehensible when the Affair is seen as a struggle for principles. The most influential advocate of a monarchical revival in France was Charles Maurras (1868–1952), who fought for his idea in a number of brilliantly written essays and articles, notably his *Enquête sur la monarchie* (1900). But Maurras' concept of monarchy had little to do with the institution as it had existed in France. In his view monarchy, army, and church were necessary because they formed and maintained discipline and order. Discipline and order were the conditions of national strength. National power and vitality depended on the completeness with which the individual was willing to identify and subordinate himself to the national organization of which he was part. Against the revolutionary doctrines of individual rights, Maurras set the idea of a hierarchically organized society. Therefore to him the question of Dreyfus' actual guilt or innocence was unimportant. The individual had to be sacrificed if his rehabilitation would damage the prestige of institutions— like the army—which were essential for the life of the nation. Similar views were championed by another great figure of that period, Maurice Barrès. He placed particular emphasis on the idea that every nation was a racial unit and that those of other races have no rights as citizens. One of Barrès' novels bears the characteristic title *Les Déracinés* (1897). Gifted as these writers were, they must be counted among the intellectual ancestors of all the antiliberal and antidemocratic movements of the twentieth century. Their intense nationalism and racism, their attacks against Jews as an alien internationally minded force, their praise of discipline and military values, their contempt for law and right in favor of strength and vitality contained the germs of Fascist philosophy.

The Dreyfus Affair gave to the republic and to the republicans a prestige which they had never possessed before. High courage had been necessary to defend Dreyfus, for the Affair had aroused violent emotions. If Zola had not

---

[3] Charles Péguy, "Notre Jeunesse," in *Oeuvres en prose 1909–1914* (Paris, 1957), p. 541.

fled to England he might have been assassinated. Scheurer-Kestner was beaten in the streets; Dreyfus' lawyer was shot at; stones were thrown at windows in the houses of Dreyfus supporters; and the police were very slow in protecting the Dreyfusards. But after the Affair was over, the individuals who had risked their careers and their lives for the sake of justice were highly esteemed. In the following decades most of those who played a leading role in French politics were men who had first attracted public attention as defenders of Dreyfus: Clemenceau, Briand, Millerand, Viviani, Caillaux, Blum.

As a result of the Dreyfus Affair the political right acquired an ideology; the left received a new sense of direction, becoming aware that the aims of the French Revolution had not been realized, that the social problems inherent in the rise of industrial society involved new tasks to which the structure of government must be adapted. It was characteristic that the history of the French Revolution, previously a rather neglected field of study, now became a topic of scholarly interest. Indicative was the establishment of a chair for the history of the French Revolution at the Sorbonne.

The Consolidation of the Republic

Obviously, progress toward a more democratic society could be achieved only if those institutions which had shown themselves open enemies of the government and obstructed its policy were deprived of power. The chief target was the army, which was now brought under civilian control: promotions to the rank of general in the army were taken out of the hands of a military council and placed in those of the minister of war, a civilian. He was inclined to favor those officers whom he considered to be reliable republicans. But while this measure did eliminate the danger of an antirepublican military coup, it also had the effect of splitting the officer corps into monarchist and republican groups. Moreover, the influence of political considerations did not always bring the most capable generals into the forefront; for instance, the selection of Maurice Gamelin (1872–1958), an officer popular among republican politicians but of moderate military gifts, as commander in chief at the beginning of the Second World War demonstrates the disadvantages of these political appointments.

The other force which had shown itself openly hostile to the republic was the Church, and the attempts at curbing its influence became the crucial issue in French politics in the first decade of the twentieth century. The problem had two aspects. One was the legal relationship between the Roman Catholic Church and the state; this was regulated by Napoleon's Concordat, according to which members of the secular clergy were paid by the state, and bishops were appointed by the Church from a list of names approved by the government. Another problem arose from the leading role which the Church had in education. A large number of French schools were controlled by Roman Catholic religious orders, which provided most of the teaching personnel. Even before the Dreyfus Affair the government had undertaken to build additional state schools and to increase their attractiveness by offering free primary education. The religious orders, however, continued to control a great many schools. After the Dreyfus Affair the government decided on a policy of reducing the number and influence of these schools. The means which the government used was a more rigid interpretation of the law regulating the existence of associations. Religious orders were declared to be associations; to exist legally, they had to obtain authorization, which required a legislative act. In 1902 Waldeck-Rousseau, whose policy had been to limit the influence of the Church on education, but who had not been anxious to eliminate all Catholic schools, resigned and was succeeded by Émile Combes (1835–1921), a fanatic anti-Catholic. Combes decided to refuse authorization to most of the religious orders. They had no choice but to leave France. The measures against the orders were vehemently denounced by the Church and the entire Catholic clergy, and provoked widespread demonstrations against the government all over France. The possibilities of a compromise between the anti-Catholic political powers and the Church began to disappear. In 1904 a law was passed that prohibited all teaching by religious orders. The relations between France and the Vatican were broken off and the Concordat was terminated. Diplomatic relations between France and the Holy See were restored only after the First World War, and then the religious orders were permitted to return.

The outcome of this conflict was the separation of church and state in 1906. The state guaranteed freedom of conscience but refused to pay the clergy. In France, where for centuries the Catholic Church and the state had been closely linked, this break between the two was revolutionary. Certain practical issues kept tensions alive until the First World War. The most difficult problem concerned the ownership of Church buildings. The state claimed them, but was willing to give them to private societies organized for this purpose, which might lease them to the Church. The Church, however, maintained that it must have the right of ownership. Because of the pressure of the Church, the private societies were not formed, and the state closed Church buildings, a step that resulted in excited demonstrations, with the police guarding Church doors. On Sundays Catholic worshipers knelt outside the closed churches, on the steps and in the streets, stopping all traffic.

Only slowly and gradually were compromises reached. In the long run, however, the situation created by the separation of Church and state did no serious damage to the Church. French Catholicism survived, and the hostility between Church and state died down. A man like Aristide Briand, who had guided the law of separation through the Chamber of Deputies and had been denounced by Catholics as an irresponsible revolutionary, would become in later years a leader respected by all groups.

The educational policy of the government could not be confined to eliminating the influence of the Church. The vacuum had to be filled, and the importance of infusing education with republican ideals was apparent. New schools had to be created; more teachers had to be trained, and they had to be guided by new educational ideas. The center from which the government's educational philosophy spread was the Ecole Normale Supérieure, which prepared the future professors of high schools and universities. It provided an anticlerical, secular education, inspired by a belief in human rights and scientific progress. Whether taught directly at the École Normale Supérieure or by professors trained there, school teachers became the protagonists of the spirit of the Third Republic. Many novels describe the situation in the villages where the aristocratic landowner and the priest represented the Old Regime, while the mayor and the school teacher embodied the spirit of the French Revolution.

The Rise of New Tensions

The governments that carried through the rehabilitation of Dreyfus and the separation of church and state—those of Waldeck-Rousseau and Combes—were broadly based left-center coalitions, and their measures were prepared by the *cartel des gauches*, a committee including representatives of all the center and leftist parties. But the years from 1906 to the outbreak of the First World War saw the break-up of the coalition and a sharp division of French political life into right and left. One reason for this split was that the French socialists—not unlike the British Labor party—wanted to be rewarded for their support of the government in the years of crisis by measures of social reform. Although France remained far behind Germany, Great Britain, and the United States in industrial activity, the economic upswing which had begun in 1896 had given a spur to the French economy. But this surge of industrialization revealed the retrograde and out-dated character of labor conditions and labor legislation: i.e., lack of security regulations in factories, long working hours, even for women and children, and no collective bargaining. Chances of effective parliamentary pressure were not good because only a quarter of the entire population was employed in industry. Consequently, the appeal of "direct action" by strike was great. And indeed, a variety of strikes followed upon each other. Among the most important was a miners' strike, which resulted from a mining disaster for which the workers held the mine owners responsible. The lack of firm wage scales and fixed terms of employment in public enterprises led first to a strike of the postal workers, and in 1911 to a strike of the railroad workers. Under Clemenceau, the government reacted with remarkable severity. In the miners' strike troops were sent in to protect strikebreakers. The postal strike was met with sharpening the law forbidding state employees to strike. In the case of the railroad strike, the trains were kept rolling by the government ordering military mobilization so that the railroad workers were conscripted as soldiers and forced to work under military command.

Why did the government proceed in such a repressive manner? There is a old proverb that "Frenchmen wear their hearts on the left and their pocketbooks on the right." The government was aware that if it extended its ideological struggle against the right into a costly policy of social reform it would lose much support. Moreover, memories of the Paris Commune of 1871 still haunted many Frenchmen, warning them against concession to radical workers. But a decisive reason was the situation in foreign policy: The struggle with Germany over Morocco had come to the fore in 1905, leading to a grave crisis in 1911, which was temporarily eased only after 1911. The government did not want the impression to spread that France was unable to act and to resist because of internal unrest.

Yet the external danger also had the effect of increasing the differences between left and right. The French military leaders, supported by the right, maintained that in order to compensate for Germany's greater strength and manpower it was necessary to extend conscription from two to three years. The left, particularly the socialists, of whom many were pacifists, opposed this measure on principle, and were especially incensed because the financing of the military service required higher taxes and diverted outlays that could be used for social reform to the military instead. At this time it became clear that the introduction of an income tax was a necessity. The left demanded that the burden of such a tax be distributed so that the rich would carry their appropriate share. Caillaux, the finance minister, indeed proposed a tax reform scheme which provided an income tax according to which income from property would be taxed at 4 per cent; profits from industry, commerce, and agriculture at 3.5 per cent; and wages and salaries at 3 per cent; moreover, he suggested a progressive surtax on higher incomes. These proposals encountered wide opposition for several reasons: their novelty; the fact that the rents, which would be taxed by the imposition of a tax on property, constituted a good part of the income of many Frenchmen; and opposition from the wealthier upper group, who used every possible means to defeat these proposals. Thus, the extension of conscription to three years was accepted, while the tax reform was defeated. The victory of the right seemed complete when in January, 1913, their chief leader, Raymond Poincaré (1860–1934), a successful lawyer from Lorraine, who had proved himself to be a good administrator, was elected president of the

The French Socialist leader Jean Jaurès speaking to a crowd in front of the banners and symbols of the French Revolution.

republic. Yet, as the elections to the Chamber in the following spring showed, a countertrend soon set in. Even after the consolidation of the republic achieved in the years of the Dreyfus Affair and the struggle with the Church, France seemed still to be a very unstable factor in European politics.

Foreign Policy

Actually France had succeeded in strengthening its position in the European balance of power. In the years of the Dreyfus Affair and the struggle over the separation of church and state the conduct of foreign policy had been almost independent of the domestic party struggles. From 1898 to 1905 the foreign ministry had been held by one man—Théophile Delcassé (1852–1923)—and France had a number of extremely capable ambassadors who remained at the same post for unusually long periods—Paul Cambon in London for over twenty years (1898–1920), Camille Barrere in Rome for more than twenty-five (1897–1924). Foreign policy was not subjected to pressure from economic interest groups because France was almost self-sufficient, at least more self-sufficient than any other industrial nation. This situation made for the ready acceptance of the protective tariffs which the agricultural interests desired. From 1892, when a new tariff was adopted, France was a highly protected country. Undoubtedly as a result of this protection, French agricultural prices were above those in the world market and agriculture remained highly profitable. France's export trade was not much affected by the adoption of a protective tariff because the exports were primarily luxury goods—wine, leatherware, textiles—and their sales suffered little from countermeasures by other countries.

France had already aquired an extended colonial empire and there was no pronounced economic interest in further colonial expansion. Although France did participate in the imperialist race of the 1890's, it quickly abandoned this policy after the setback at Fashoda. France retained, however, a serious concern in the countries on the North African shore across the Mediterranean: Tunisia and Morocco. This interest was political and strategic rather than economic, because in case of war the control of these countries by another power might make the transport of troops from Algeria to France impossible, and might even open France to an attack from the south. In the interest of securing domination in this area the French were willing to abandon other colonial claims. They conceded to the British their rights in Egypt and recognized the Italian demands on Tripoli. In compensation Great Britain and Italy acknowledged France's predominant interest in Morocco. Since neither of these states had claims on Morocco their concrete gains from these agreements were greater than those of France. But the ties with Great Britain and Italy gave France increased weight in Europe. This was the chief aim of French foreign policy: the nation was to become again a factor to be reckoned with in Europe. In the pursuit of this policy, financial strength was a precious asset. By means of loans France was able to establish close ties with Russia. French firms invested widely in Russian private industry, particularly in mining and metallurgy. Indeed, one third of all foreign investments in nongovernmental enterprises in Russia were of French origin. But the French banks also took up a substantial proportion of Russian government loans. At the time of the outbreak of the First World War almost half of the loans which the Russian government issued were held by foreigners and the French people held 80 per cent of this amount.

Thus France had again become powerful in European politics, a situation disadvantageous to Germany, which since the war of 1870–1871 had attempted to keep France isolated. Indicative of the tension between the two states is the fact that between 1871 and the outbreak of the First World War no official visit between French and German statesmen ever took place. Whether the maintenance of such a rigidly hostile posture was unavoidable, or whether after France had reasserted its position in Europe some gradual lessening of the tension could have been effected remains an open question. There were French financial circles interested in economic cooperation with Germany. Left-wing groups would have liked the government to spend less on defense and more on social reform. Moreover, the French Socialists were pacifists and their leader, Jean Jaurès, gave eloquent voice to their ideals. Yet, there was deep emotional resistance to any attempt at reconciliation with Germany. Throughout this period, on the Place de la Concorde in Paris, where each large French city was represented by a statue, the statue of Strasbourg remained veiled in black. The French did not envisage a war to reconquer Alsace-Lorraine, but there was strong feeling that as long as Germany held Alsace-Lorraine, cooperation between the two States was impossible. French foreign policy, it was felt, ought to hold the line against Germany. This indeed remained the prevailing tendency of that policy, and was probably the decisive factor why, after the war broke out, the deep cleavage which separated left from right did not prevent general support of the war effort. It is significant that Jaurès was assassinated by a nationalist on the day the war began because the murderer assumed that Jaurès was to make a speech opposing the war. Ironically the speech which Jaurès had prepared was intended to support the government in its resistance to the Germans.

THE MEDITERRANEAN POWERS

Rise of Industrial Activities in Feudal Societies

The constitutional arrangements in Spain and Italy were externally very similar to those of Great Britain. But below the surface the differences were great. In Spain and Italy the kings could exert some influence of their own by means of the army, commanded by generals conservative in outlook and bound by deep loyalty to the crown. Moreover, the political systems of Spain and Italy, despite two-chamber parliaments and the dependence of the governments on securing votes of confidence from these chambers, can only be characterized as pseudoparliamentary, as limited in their democratic components. Wide parts of the population, in both countries probably the majority, were unable to make their voices heard and remained outside the policy-making process—partly because of the low level of education; partly because of ruthlessly exerted pressure by local officials directed by the central government; and, in Italy, also because the pope had forbidden Catholics to participate in the political life of the Italian kingdom. The parliamentary form disguised the fact that both countries were ruled by a relatively small social group.

In both Italy and Spain the middle classes, the chief protagonists of liberalism, formed only a small section of the population; in Spain Catalonia almost alone possessed a middle class. Both countries were predominantly agricultural, and the rural areas, dominated and controlled by the owners of large landed estates, retained a feudal aspect. There were a few highly industrialized regions: in Italy, around Turin and Milan; in Spain, Barcelona and wide stretches of Catalonia around it in the northeast, Andalusia with its coal and zinc mines in the south, and the rich, foreign-owned copper mines of Riotinto in the southwest. Even in these districts industrial development was still embryonic, however, and the workers were subjected to all the hardships of the beginnings of industrialization. Wages were so low that not only the father of a family but the wife and the children had to work. Treated with ruthlessness and forming a small minority, the workers were receptive to ideas of revolutionary change, and this radical activism is indicated by the fact that a high proportion— almost one third of them—were members of labor organizations. Those who were organized were divided among various movements. Marxism, anarchism, and syndicalism all had adherents, and the radicalism of the workers was frequently expressed in violence. The rest of Europe regarded Italy and Spain as unstable and threatened by revolution.

Spain

In Spain the rule of a small group—great landowners allied to a few wealthy industrialists—behind a parliamentary façade had been secured by agreements made in the 1870's between the Conservative leader Antonio Canovas and the Liberal leader Mateo Sagasta. They arranged that each party would constitute a government for a number of years and then hand it over to the other party, which would arrange new elections. It was a foregone conclusion that these elections would produce the desired majority for the party in power. Suffrage was limited to the propertied classes, and in the rural areas the *cacique*, a government official, determined who should vote and how to vote. By the end of the century, discontent with the system was increasing. A group of young writers, known as the Generation of 1898, was particularly vocal in advocating political and social reforms. In an article which soon became famous one of the leaders of this group, Miguel de Unamuno (1864–1936), made a distinction between the political nation and the real nation, stating that the real nation was entirely unrepresented in politics.

Dissatisfaction increased with the defeat suffered by Spain in the Spanish-American War and the resultant loss of Cuba and the Philippines. In addition to being a national humiliation, the defeat created serious economic problems. Officials, military officers, priests, entire religious orders, had to be settled and reestablished after their return to Spain. Moreover, Cuba and the Philippines had absorbed a certain part of Spain's industrial production. Faced with a rising wave of discontent, the ruling group began to feel insecure. In both parties, the Liberals and the Conservatives, the feeling grew that revolution could be avoided only if broader groups of the population were drawn more closely to the state. A competition for the masses set in between the two parties, and the tacit understanding which had secured the tenures of successive Conservative and Liberal governments broke down. Among the Conservatives, the leader of a group urging an energetic policy of renovation and social reform was Antonio Maura (1853–1925), who was prime minister in 1903–1904 and returned to that office in 1907. But because Maura was not willing to observe any longer the agreed rules of the political game, unrest set in and a revolutionary outbreak, triggered by protests against the conscription of young workers for a campaign in Morocco, occurred in Barcelona.

During the so-called Tragic Week of Barcelona, in July, 1909, the masses seized the city, and their long-endured suppression and sufferings exploded in acts of violence. Twenty-two churches were destroyed and thirty-four convents burned to the ground. After the revolt had been defeated by military forces, the government carried out a number of executions; that of Francisco Ferrer, a well-known intellectual anarchist, aroused wide indignation because valid proofs of his role in the uprising were lacking. The entire revolt was a spontaneous outbreak of dissatisfaction rather than a well-planned conspiracy. The actions of the masses as well as the reaction of the government strongly revealed the violence underlying Spanish political life.

Moreover, the Tragic Week of Barcelona disclosed the two basic difficulties militating against effective opposition to the established order in Spain. One was the unavoidable connection of all reform movements with anticlericalism. As in France—and what had happened in France was highly influential in Spain—the extension of the state school system and restriction of the influence of the teaching orders became the most essential demand of the reformers. The anticlericalism of the intellectuals in the urban centers reinforced the bond between the Church and the conservative landowners, but the Church had strong supporters also among the masses, for the clergy and the numerous religious orders were frequently the refuge of the sons and daughters of the poor.

At the same time, reformers were handicapped by the fact that the most industrialized part of the country, and hence the center of liberal and progressive movements, was Catalonia, with its capital Barcelona. With some justification the Catalans were suspected by the rest of Spain of separatist tendencies, and for this reason the revolt of July, 1909, did not spread beyond Barcelona. It was difficult to organize a unified opposition on a national basis. Thus the regime was able to survive. Maura, the Conservative prime minister, was overthrown soon after the Tragic Week of Barcelona because his plans for social reform were believed to have seduced the revolutionaries to action. The Liberal leader, Jose Canalejas, who made an attempt to carry out an anticlerical program with the help of all the forces of the left, was assassinated in 1912. With the wisdom of hindsight it is not difficult to see that the alternatives in Spain were dictatorship and revolution.

Italy

The loss of Cuba and the Philippines exemplified Spain's decline as an imperial power. If it was still counted among the great powers this status had its basis in tradition rather than in the nation's actual strength. In contrast, Italy was a newcomer among the great powers and the recent struggles, through which unification had been achieved, left Italian political life strongly tinged with nationalism, which now manifested itself in the urge to demonstrate that Italy could be rightly counted among the great powers.

The Italian social structure showed the same sharp contrasts as that of Spain. In the south were large landed estates owned by an old nobility which was allied with the Church. Little industry existed in the south, and the percentage of the people going to school or receiving some technical training was smaller than in the rest of Italy. In the north, industry extended over a wider area than in Spain. Italy's performance as an industrial and military power was limited by the fact that its resources of pig iron and steel were insignificant. But in the north waterpower was abundant and permitted growth of electrical, textile, and chemical industries. Northern Italy played an active role from the outset in the development of the automobile industry; Fiat was established here in 1899. Indeed, the nerve center of Italian industrial life was in the triangle formed by Milan, Genoa, and Turin. This area had a large working population and prosperous middle class. In contrast, the primarily agrarian south was an area of great poverty. The situation of the peasants all over Italy, but particularly in the south, was very difficult. The Italian protective tariff of 1887, instead of promoting the cultivation of fruits and vegetables, had favored wheat production and by extensive farming maintained the latifundia and limited the need for agricultural workers or intensive cultivation of the land by peasant families. The difficulties of the situation were heightened by the rising birth rate of the peasants, particularly in the devoutly Catholic south. The Italian population increased in the first decade of the twentieth century by 3 million, from 33 million to 36 million, and although an industrialized country like Germany—which grew in the same decade from 56 to 65 million—could easily absorb this increase, an increase of nearly 10 per cent meant grave problems for a predominantly agrarian country like Italy. As a solution there was on the one hand emigration; the annual average rate of emigration in the years from 1900 to 1910 was around 600,000 people. On the other, many young peasants streamed from the rural areas to the industrial centers where their presence only augmented the number of unskilled workers and held wages down.

Italian national unification had primarily been the work of the middle class in northern and southern Italy. Although politically unified, the social differences between northern and central Italy and southern Italy, the Mezzogiorno, where a firmly entrenched feudal nobility remained all powerful, had never been bridged. Rising industrial activity intensified this regional contrast and contributed to the growth of a revolutionary-minded lower class. Marxist and Syndicalist ideas had a stronghold over the industrial workers, while discontent spread among the poor peasants and agricultural workers. In central Italy peasant farmers felt hemmed in by the sharecropping system, the *mezzadria*, which gave them seldom more than 30 per cent of the income from the harvest. The situation was even worse for the peasants in the south. Not only industrial but also agricultural strikes and occupation of land by agricultural workers and peasants happened frequently in this period. In the quarter of a century before the outbreak of the First World War, Italy was perhaps changing more rapidly than any other great European power.

The outstanding figure among Italian statesmen in the last decades of the nineteenth century was Francesco Crispi (1819–1901), one of the heroes of the *Risorgimento* period. Crispi decided to turn Italian energies to colonial expansion, a policy that corresponded with Italy's ambition to be a great power. Many Italians still lived under the rule of the Habsburg empire in South Tyrol, Gorizia, and Istria. Crispi, however, wanted to turn Italian nationalist ambitions away from these areas because he was anxious to avoid a clash with Austria-Hungary and its ally, Germany; the only support for Italy in an anti-Austrian policy could come from France, and such an alliance would be inferior in strength to the German-Austrian combination. Moreover, Italian colonial expansion might overcome the feeling that Italian policy had reached a dead end. Crispi decided to enter the race with the other great powers for the control of African areas which had not yet been subjected to European rule; because Italy had a small colonial possession along the Red Sea, he wanted to extend its rule in the area to neighboring Ethiopia. A first Italian advance from the Red Sea toward Ethiopia had suffered a setback at Dogali (1887). But then the Italians helped Menelik (1844–1913), one of the tribal chiefs, to make good his claim to the imperial throne. In return, so Crispi claimed, Menelik had recognized an Italian protectorate over Ethiopia. But neither Menelik nor the other Ethiopian tribal chiefs acknowledged this claim and there were frequent military encounters between Italian troops and local Ethiopian forces along the frontier between Eritrea and Ethiopia. In 1896, against the better judgment of his military advisers, Crispi ordered the advance into Ethiopia of the troops stationed in Eritrea. Crispi miscalculated his opponent's military strength. The Ethiopians were good warriors; they had received some training from French officers and had been equipped with guns by the French. At Adua, in difficult mountainous terrain, the Italian army of 20,000 men—half of them Italians, half of them natives—encountered a well-directed force of about 100,000 Ethiopians. The Italians were completely defeated; about 6,000 were killed, 2,000 wounded, and 2,000 taken prisoner. When the news of the defeat reached Rome, the Crispi government resigned amid immense public demonstrations demanding the immediate end of the African adventure. Crispi's successor, Antonio Rudinì (1839–1908), made peace with Menelik immediately, thus recognizing the independence of Ethiopia. Italy's status among the European states plunged. Instead of solidifying Italian national unity, the attempt to become a world power had only increased discontent, and the Ethiopian adventure was followed by years of unrest.

Moreover, the protective tariffs adopted by France had provoked Italian countermeasures and the ensuing tariff war diminished Italian exports and impeded industrial expansion by cutting off loans from French banks. Unemployment rose in the industrial areas, and in May, 1898, bread riots broke out in Milan, barricades were erected in the streets, and order was restored only after some fighting and a declaration of martial law. A general, Luigi Pelloux (1839–1924), became prime minister. He ruled by royal decree and tried to establish a military dictatorship. He was defeated in the elections of 1900, and a month later King Humbert, who had appointed Pelloux and had supported his dictatorial policy, was assassinated.

Thereafter, the situation quieted, the radical left had overplayed its hand. Railway strikes in 1902 and a general strike in 1904 aroused widespread indignation. They appeared inspired by political motives rather than by economic hardships, and were viewed as an attempt at revolution. In consequence, all the moderate forces drew more closely together; the threat of revolution even led to a softening of the hostility between the Italian state and Roman Catholicism. Pope Pius X now permitted Catholics to enter the party struggle because the safety of the society order was threatened. In the elections of October, 1904, the radical left suffered harsh defeat.

One of the reasons for greater calm in the domestic situation was the economic upswing which had taken place in Europe since 1896 and made itself felt in Italy in a quickening of the tempo of industrialization. It has been said that during the period from 1896 to 1914 Italy had its industrial revolution. In the 1890's the Banca d'Italia was founded and assumed the role of a central bank. It had the sole right for issuing currency and thus could control and regulate the money supply and provide money for industry. Newly established stability in the money market led immediately to the founding of a number of commercial banks, frequently with strong participation of foreign, particularly German, capital; they became active in the financing of industrial enterprises.

The political situation in Italy also took a turn toward stability. In 1903, Giovanni Giolitti (1842–1928) became prime minister. Giolitti came from the north and had started his career in the government service, but he was soon elected deputy and proved himself to be an unusually clever parliamentarian, whose tactical skill assured a remarkable degree of political stability. He considered the modernization of economic life as the primary task in the Italian situation. Giolitti was prime minister three times—from 1903–1905, 1906–1909, 1911–1914; even when out of office, he remained the dominant political figure. Under his influence, the government took an active part in promoting the process of industrialization. It ordered military equipment from Italian suppliers even if the price was higher and the quality lower. It started an ambitious program of railroad building after the railroads, previously privately owned, had been taken over by the state, and it gave direct subsidies to key enterprises like the merchant marine to stimulate the various activities involved in shipbuilding. Giolitti's policy of industrialization had remarkable results. In the twenty years before the outbreak of the First World War the share of industry in the national production increased from 20 to 25 per cent and the national income grew by approximately 50 per cent.

Giolitti was aware that economic progress demanded a favorable social climate. He initiated numerous measures of social reform. Trade unions were legalized and collective bargaining was promoted. Minimum standards for hygienic conditions in factories were set and working conditions for women and children were improved.

The beneficial effects of Giolitti's regime on Italian economic life were undeniable, but the means by which he carried out his policy were questionable, subjecting Giolitti to criticisms that he exerted a corrupting influence on Italian politics and that his regime was really a dictatorship. From the point of view of parliamentary support Giolitti was in a difficult situation. The traditional ruling group was opposed to his social policy and the socialists were disinclined to cooperate with a capitalist and monarchical government. In order to attain his aims Giolitti ruled with fluctuating majorities which he created by means of a political maneuver called *trasformismo*. Unlike other European countries where electoral districts were large and frequently sent two or three representatives to the national parliament, Italian electoral districts were small and elected only one deputy; consequently he was dependent for reelection on the good opinion of the inhabitants of his district rather than on his party. By granting a deputy special advantages for the district which he represented Giolitti got the vote of deputies who did not belong to the government party or who even belonged to parties opposed to the government. Ideals and principles became a façade behind which deputies bargained for political and material advantages. Giolitti's sacrifice of principles for tactical advantages emerged most starkly in his treatment of the Mezzogiorno. He did not extend his policy of economic and social reforms into the south; he made no attempt to institute agrarian reform there, to dissolve the latifundia and provide land for the numerous peasants living in abject poverty. This gained him the votes of the deputies of the south, but it also meant that the great landowners, allied with the Church, remained all powerful, and that in Sicily the Mafia—which, according to private and official investigations, had ordered and approved fraud, violence, and even murder—maintained its influence. Giolitti even made some concession to Church interests by facilitating religious education in those localities where parents demanded it. In practice, this meant that the schools in the south were controlled by priests, themselves only half-educated, and of no great help in educating others. The gap between the Italian north and the Italian south was considerably widened; whereas in parts of the north the illiteracy rate was reduced to 11 per cent, in the south it remained over 90 per cent. This policy actually damaged Giolitti's own economic aims: The great majority of the population of the south could not be employed in work which demanded even a minimum of skills; nor did they have the money to buy industrial goods. The internal market, which had an impact on the entire industrial development of Italy, was retarded by the south.

Giolitti's exclusive concern with material progress and the debasement of liberal and democratic values kept alive discontent with the existing system and alienated groups which ought to have been in sympathy with his general aims. The most devastating attack against Giolitti's regime was launched by a young Italian historian, Gaetano Salvemini. In a pamphlet ironically entitled *Il Ministro della Mala Vita* (The Minister for Misery) he formulated the program which Italian liberalism ought to adopt: partition of the latifundia, spread of secular education, honest elections.

Of course, Giolitti was aware of the need to secure a broader parliamentary base for his regime, and he had a left-center government in mind with Socialist participation. Many of his social measures were directed towards gaining the support of the trade unions, which exerted great power in the Socialist party; with their help Giolitti believed he would be able to overcome the traditional Marxist resistance against collaboration in a capitalist system. Giolitti thought he was so near to this goal that he proclaimed in parliament that the Socialists had "put Marx in the attic." He felt that this policy would be sealed by the government carrying an electoral reform through in 1912 which raised the number of voters from 3.5 to 8 million and made universal suffrage of males over thirty years old a reality. Only male illiterates who had done no military service (and women) were denied the right to vote.

But in the Socialist party the groups opposing the assumption of governmental responsibility proved stronger than once thought. The trade unions were competing in most northern provinces with the chambers of labor in which all the workers of a particular area were joined. These chambers of labor were radical and revolutionary in their outlook because their membership also included the badly paid workers of small industries and in some areas, like the Romagna, the agricultural workers, for whom nothing had been done by Giolitti's reforms. The reformist wing of the Socialist party had the upper hand only for a brief period. In general, the radical wing, which had anarchist tendencies and argued for revolutionary actions, strikes, and sabotage, set the tone. At the Party Congress of 1912, the radicals gained control. One of their leaders, Benito Mussolini, became editor of *Avanti*, the official paper of the Socialist party.

This triumph of the Socialist left over the Socialist right was also influenced by events in the area of diplomacy and war. The wounds inflicted to Italian self-esteem by the defeats of Dogali and Adua had never fully healed. These resentments found expression in a nationalist political movement organized by Enrico Corradini. Corradini ascribed these military humiliations to the lack of heroism inherent in democracy and parliamentary government. The powerful spokesman of this movement was Gabriele d'Annunzio, Italy's most famous writer, who proclaimed the need for one great man to rule the country. He found many adherents among the younger generation. Even if the nationalist movement remained numerically rather weak, a feeling that Italy had to assert itself as a great power was widespread. When the French began to claim Morocco, Italy began an economic penetration of Tripoli. The view that the conquest of Tripoli was necessary extended even into Socialist ranks; if Giolitti had wanted to refrain from this action he would hardly have been able to do so.

However, the great masses of the Socialist party were not willing to accept the view of their moderate leaders that the economic improvement which was expected to result from the creation of a colony in North Africa was worth a war. The majority of the Socialist party condemned the war as imperialist and felt hardened in the attitude of refusing cooperation with the capitalist government.

If Giolitti had hoped that by undertaking this war he would gain support on the right he was also disappointed. The nationalists considered the war chiefly as proof that movements and actions outside parliament were needed and could be effective. The election in 1913 based on the new law establishing universal suffrage did not create a secure parliamentary basis for a reform government but demonstrated the strength of radicalism on the left and on the right. When the First World War came the "liberal state was in a serious crisis."

CHAPTER 3

The Great Powers, 1890-1914: The Authoritarian Governments

THE COMMON ELEMENT in the governmental structure of the great powers of western Europe was the controlling power of the parliaments. The great powers of central and eastern Europe—Germany, Austria-Hungary and Russia—are distinguished from those of the West by the fact that their monarchs had strong policy-making influence, although the extent of their influence and the constitutional arrangements in these countries differed. Russia at the beginning of the twentieth century was an autocracy; the system of government in the various parts of the Habsburg monarchy varied; the German empire had a constitution, the rights of the citizens in Germany were legally secured, and elected representatives had a part, although not a decisive one, in the government.

GERMANY

Constitution and Social Structure

The authoritarian system of the German empire was primarily a product of its historical development in the preceding century. Because the unification of Germany had been accomplished by Prussia, the political structure of the German Reich bore a Prussian pattern.

Prussia had successfully withstood the middle-class revolution of the nineteenth century. Its constitution was highly authoritarian; the army was outside civilian control, under direct command of the king, and the Prussian parliament was elected by a method which guaranteed control to the great landowners from east of the Elbe, the *Junkers*.

The Prussian monarch and the Prussian leaders did not want to see their system of government submerged in a wider Reich. Hence, the German empire became not a unitary state but a federal state composed of twenty-five individual states. With the exception of three free cities, the rulers of these states were princes; the government of each of these states appointed a delegate to a federal council, the Bundesrat, which met in Berlin under the chairmanship of the delegate appointed by the Prussian king, who regularly designated the Prussian prime minister for this post. It was as president of this federation of princes that the king of Prussia held the title of German emperor. Since the number of votes which each state possessed within the council was determined by its geographical extent and the size of its population, the Bundesrat was dominated by Prussia.

The leaders of Prussian policy at the time of German unification had to take into account, however, that the chief resistance to unification had come from the princely rulers of the German states and the groups bound to them through interest or loyalty. The chief protagonists of unification had been the masses of the people, particularly the middle class. Thus, in order to check separatist tendencies which might come into the foreground in the Bundesrat, a parliament—the Reichstag—was created, with members elected on the basis of a most progressive voting system: universal suffrage of all males above twenty-five years of age.

Legislation for the Reich had to be passed by both the Bundesrat and the Reichstag. The areas over which the Reich could decide and legislate were strictly limited: foreign affairs, naval affairs, the mail and the telegraph, customs, colonies. And it had the right to establish common standards for the administration of justice and military affairs, although the armies remained under the control of the rulers of the individual states and were placed under a unified command only in wartime. The Reich was to receive a certain percentage of the taxes raised by the states, and it had the right to levy indirect taxes.

Although the tasks of the Reich were limited, they were extended enough to require governmental agencies, and the manner in which the federal administration was organized reinforced the dominating position of Prussia. The control and supervision of the federal administration was entrusted to the chairman of the Bundesrat, who was expected to explain and to defend new legislation in the Reichstag. Since this chairman was always the Prussian prime minister, he combined in his person two functions. As head of the federal administration he had the title of chancellor— *Reichskanzler*—and had under him a number of high officials, "secretaries," who administered the various areas under federal control: foreign affairs, naval affairs, colonies, and so on. As Prussian prime minister he directed Prussian policy and presided over the Prussian cabinet, composed of "ministers": of the interior, of war, of education, of finance, and so on. This arrangement gave the chancellor a remarkable amount of independence. He was appointed by the Prussian king and could be removed neither by the Bundesrat nor by the Reichstag. Despite the strength of his position, the chancellor could more easily prevent a new departure in politics than initiate one. He could frustrate measures of which he disapproved by playing against each other the Reich and Prussia, the Bundesrat and the Reichstag. But he had to maneuver carefully to move these different forces in the same direction. Thus, the complicated political structure of the Reich led to strange contradictions. It made it possible for Prussia to take the leading role without having to give up its system of government and its autonomy. But in providing guarantees against meddling in Prussian affairs, the constitution of the Reich also secured the other German states against interference in their systems of government. Hence, within the German empire great political diversity existed. In contrast to the conservative north, the southern German states—Bavaria, Württemberg, Baden—were liberal, even democratic, and they had parliamentary governments. The majority of the German population was Protestant but the Catholic minority was very considerable; in 1900 there were 35 million Protestants and 20 million Roman Catholics in Germany. Some of the German states were prevailingly Protestant; in others Catholicism had an important political influence.

The complex constitution doubtless required of the Reich's leaders great art in balancing the divergent forces which constituted the German empire. The unified Reich was Bismarck's creation and its constitution had been tailored to his forceful but prudent personality. He was also favored by the fact that in the first decade after unification, an equilibrium of social forces still existed: the conflict between the interests of agriculture and industry was still muted. But toward the close of the nineteenth century the conditions for a successful functioning of the German constitution began to disappear: Bismarck was dismissed in 1890, and the rapid and striking change in the German social structure upset the delicate balance of social forces. Germany had become a highly industrialized and commercial country.

At the outbreak of the First World War, Germany's merchant marine was the second largest in the world, surpassed only by that of Great Britain. By then, too, Germany was the third largest coal-producing power—behind the United States and only slightly behind Great Britain. Germany produced considerably more pig iron and steel than any other European power, Great Britain included, and almost half as much as the United States. Germany's rich mineral resources favored the development of an armament industry. Krupp, the leading German armament manufacturer, together with Skoda in Austria and the French firm of Schneider-Creusot, dominated the armament market of the world. The electrical and chemical industries also flourished. Some of the German dyestuffs and pharmaceuticals enjoyed a kind of monopoly on the world market. In contrast to the United States and the British empire, Germany produced much more than could be consumed on the domestic market. Between 1887 and 1912 the value of German exports increased 185 per cent. Germany's rise as an industrial world power thus involved a rapid penetration into foreign markets; until 1880 it had traded almost exclusively with other European countries; thereafter Germany began to exchange goods increasingly with other continents.

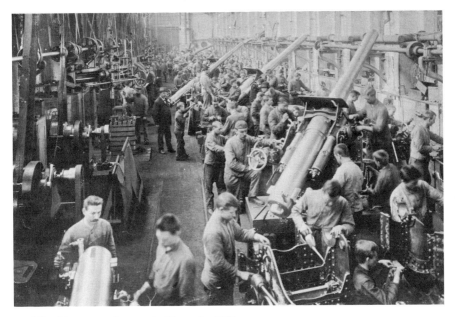
The Krupp gun factory in Essen in 1904.

The mineral resources on which industrial development was based could be found in almost every part of the nation. Most important was the Ruhr, where coal and iron were available. In the southwest, in the areas ceded by France in 1871, were iron and potash; in the east, Upper Silesia was rich in coal; and in central Germany, lignite deposits served the electrical and chemical industries. Thus the impact of industrialization was felt all over the country. Since industrial development in Germany started later than in Great Britain and in France, large capital investments were needed to facilitate competition with the more advanced nations. Such quantities of capital could be provided only by banks, not by the industrial entrepreneurs themselves or by private financiers. In German economic development banking and industrial enterprises became closely interconnected. This alliance promoted the formation of big companies possessing greater efficiency than smaller ones that produced the same goods. In some fields the large enterprises achieved a monopoly; in others a few big industrial companies banded together in cartel agreements that enabled them to fix prices and delimit markets. The members of a cartel could establish high price levels at home to maintain profits while they attempted to conquer foreign markets by "dumping" goods there at low prices. For this reason the German government not only permitted monopolies and cartels but even gave legal protection to cartel agreements; violators could be brought to court and punished.

Small and middle-sized economic enterprises did not entirely disappear from German economic life, but in Germany there was some truth in the picture, given by Lenin in his treatise on *Imperialism, the Highest Stage of Capitalism,* of the domination of a nation's economic life by a small group of financiers and industrialists.

The rapid development of Germany into a great economic power, and the accompanying rise in wealth in almost all groups of the population, had a dangerously intoxicating effect on the German upper and middle classes. Most of them succumbed to the fatal fascination of the idea of becoming a "world power": Germany ought to have a navy; it ought to have colonies; German passenger ships had to be the largest and fastest. German bankers and industrialists were convinced that wherever they found the opportunity for economic penetration—in Turkey, in China, or anywhere else—they ought to make use of it, regardless of the claims, rights, or interests of other nations. Since Germany was a latecomer on the world scene, they felt, it had to be pushy to gain its due "place in the sun," as William II characterized his realm's political ambitions.

Nevertheless, industrial development in Germany did not progress without conflicts. Wherever industrial and agrarian interests clashed, the *Junkers* were able to put up strong resistance for they dominated the political system of Germany's most powerful state. Moreover, the transition to industrialization was unavoidably accompanied by social tensions, and the gap between entrepreneur and workers was widened by the resentment which Bismarck's repressive antisocialist laws had created. After these laws had lapsed, and as a consequence of the rapid progress of industrialization, the socialists made great strides. The Social Democrats increased their number of deputies in the Reichstag from 35 in 1890 to 110 in 1911 and became the strongest political party. Although by then the Social Democratic party and the allied trade unions had become big bureaucracies inclined to move slowly and cautiously, the Marxian view of the need for a revolution remained dominant among the workers, especially since the government continued to proceed vigorously against all subversive agitation and propaganda.

After 1890 instability was further increased by the fact that the role which the constitution assigned to the emperor, but which actually had been filled by Bismarck, had fallen to a monarch who wanted to rule, but lacked the qualities necessary for doing so.

The Empire under William II

In the public mind, particularly in those countries which fought against Germany in the First World War, William II (ruled 1888–1918) is usually pictured as the prototype of the warlord—imperious, brutal, barbarian. Indeed, William did like to appear in full military panoply, preferably in the uniform of an officer of the cuirassier guards, in silvery, shining mail and a helmet crowned by a golden eagle. He talked to his ministers and to his people as an officer talks to his soldiers, giving them orders and commands. William felt himself the heir and successor of the absolutist Hohenzollern kings of the eighteenth century. He believed that his power came from God and considered himself, as he said in one of his bombastic speeches, "an instrument of God." Most of all, he felt obliged to maintain the Prussian military tradition. He was hardly aware that the army was no longer an army

Officers of the Death's-Head Hussars, one of Germany's most feudal regiments. *Prominent on the balcony are* (from left to right) *their commander Mackensen (an illegitimate Hohenzollern descendant); Emperor William II; the crown prince; two unknown officers; the emperor's daughter Victoria Luise, to later become the duchess of Brunswick; the crown princess, in a white cuirassier uniform; behind her, in a naval uniform, another son of the emperor, Prince Adalbert.*

of mercenaries, the personal property of the monarch, but was now based on general conscription. Addressing a Berlin regiment about the socialist opposition, he told the soldiers that they would have to shoot their fathers and mothers if he ordered them to do so. Because he disapproved of modern dances he forbade all men in uniform to dance the tango, when it became popular in 1913. Since the inner organization of the army, and the appointment of officers, were entirely outside of civilian control, William had some legal justification for believing he could demand absolute obedience.

Nevertheless, he wanted to be more than the preserver of an absolutist tradition. He wanted to be a modern monarch who would lead Germany into a new era of history. He surrounded himself not only with members of the Prussian aristocracy but also with industrialists and bankers. Albert Ballin, the leading spirit of the largest German shipping line, was his friend. Rhenish industrialists such as the Stumms and the Krupps were his favorites. Although in his youth William had participated in meetings of an anti-Semitic group, he was later inclined to favor wealthy Jews and to grant them titles, to the great disgust of the Prussian aristocracy. He was fascinated by discoveries in the natural sciences and delighted in bestowing decorations on outstanding scientists, and occasionally nobilitating them. He preached enthusiastically the need for making Germany a world power. William was a zealous reader of Mahan and accepted his view that sea power was the crucial factor in the struggle of nations and the competition for empire.

This combination of Prussian authoritarianism with faith in technological progress and capitalist expansion corresponded to the inclinations of the German bourgeoisie. In the earlier years of his reign William II was extremely popular. There is some justification for the brilliant satire of the German middle-class mind in Heinrich Mann's novel *The Patrioteer* (1918), in which the hero, a bourgeois parvenu, is depicted as modeling his life in every detail according to that of his ideal, the emperor.

But William II also had many opponents, and their number increased over the years. His adversaries and critics were to be found not only among the socialists, who condemned the entire regime, but also among those who knew him best. Some considered him to be the gravedigger of the German monarchy. They were aware of his superficiality; his various intellectual and aesthetic enthusiasms were short-lived and he was incapable of sustained effort and serious work. Nervous and restless, he traveled continually from one place to another and expected to be constantly entertained. And these entertainments were not very refined. Quite a public scandal developed when one of his chamberlains, elderly and fat, died of a heart attack while dancing before him in the costume of a ballet girl. Most of all, despite his martial appearance and powerful gestures, William II was weak, easily

Cartoon from *Simplicissimus*, satirizing William II's priorities: *"His Majesty has no time for Europe. His Majesty is designing a uniform for service chaplains."*

influenced by men with stronger wills, especially when they presented their ideas in amusing and flattering forms. A kind of Byzantine atmosphere permeated the court. Military men, industrialists, bankers, and courtiers could sway the emperor. In the first decade of his reign William's great favorite was Count Philipp Eulenburg (1847–1921); his homosexual inclinations, which were unknown to the emperor, led to a scandal that severely damaged the prestige of the court. In later years a powerful influence was the secretary of the navy, Admiral Alfred von Tirpitz (1849–1930), who kept alive William's interest in the building of a great navy.

Although he failed to provide unifying direction to the nation, William II was unwilling to concede to his chancellors that decisive influence which Bismarck had possessed. Each chancellor had to struggle against military, naval, and personal influences, and the course of German policy became erratic.

Of Bismarck's successors, the first, Count Leo von Caprivi (chancellor from 1890 to 1894) was a military man; the others were civil servants. Prince Chlodwig von Hohenlohe, (from 1894 to 1900) had been the administrative head of Alsace-Lorraine; Bernhard von Bülow (from 1900 to 1909) came from the diplomatic corps; Theobald von Bethmann-Hollweg (from 1909 to 1917) from the Prussian administration. The appointment of civil servants to high positions of political leadership emphasized the independence of the government from parliamentary influence. But as we have seen, although the role of the Reichstag was limited, its approval of new legislation and taxation was necessary. The Social Democrats, as opponents of the entire system, always voted against the government, which therefore had to seek support from the parties to the right of the socialists. And these were of greatly varying political shadings. The Conservatives spoke chiefly for the agrarian interests, while the Center party included members of every stratum of society since its unifying bond was religion: Roman Catholicism. The bourgeois world was represented by two groups: the National Liberals, who championed the interests of heavy industry; and the Progressives, supported by small entrepreneurs and white-collar workers, and retaining the nineteenth-century ideal of a liberal and democratic Germany.

Cooperation among parties of such varied interests was difficult to achieve. The government usually had the support of the Conservatives and the National Liberals, although their alliance—an alliance between agricultural and industrial interests—had not been easy to achieve. The crucial problem had been of an economic nature. There was the conflict between the landowner's demand for protective tariffs against American and Russian grain and the industrialist's desire for low food prices which would allow low wages and facilitate competition on the world market. At the beginning of the reign of William II, under Bismarck's successor, Caprivi, agricultural tariffs were lowered in the interest of industrial expansion. But the *Junkers* forced Caprivi's fall and the government changed its course and embarked on a policy of agricultural protection, buying the agreement of the National Liberals by concessions to industrial interests.

One of these concessions was the execution of a major program to build a fleet of battleships. The origin of the naval program has to be ascribed to William II's envy and admiration of Great Britain and to the influence of Admiral von Tirpitz on the emperor. But support for the program was not lacking. It provided heavy industry with a continuous flow of government orders; in the eyes of the industrialists this was an advantage which might outweigh the disadvantages of protective tariffs. Likewise the Conservatives considered protective tariffs a compensation for their abandonment of opposition to a large fleet.

The cooperation of industrial and agrarian leaders with the government served not only parliamentary purposes; it was also intended to defend and maintain the social order against the subversive Social Democratic movement. Schools (elementary schools as well as the *Gymnasium*, which was required for admission to the university) were state institutions and the teachers were commanded to fight Social Democratic ideas by emphasizing patriotism and Christian piety in their teaching. Moreover, attainment on any position of importance in the civil service was dependent on demonstrating full acceptance of "official" values. Although Jews were legally freed from all restrictions, they were not appointed to positions in the civil service. Civil servants sitting on the boards examining candidates for admission to the civil service gave much weight to the political reliability of the candidates. But the crucial factor in this process of selecting civil servants was the introduction of the reserve officer. It was almost impossible to become a member of the civil service without being a reserve officer. In Germany every male was obligated to two years of military service, but those who had received a higher education needed to serve only one year. To become a reserve officer after this one year was like becoming member in a club. The decision to make someone a reserve officer depended on the active officers of the regiment in which the potential reserve officer had served; these officers would accept only those who shared their standards of behavior. But to be a reserve officer had still wider implications; it was a virtual requirement to be counted as a member of court society and the higher social circles. Thus, influence in Germany, particularly in Prussia, depended on adjustment to the behavior and the values which dominated the higher civil service and the officers' corps of the army, groups in which the nobility played the decisive role. The feudal and militaristic values of the Prussian nobility remained powerful. In Germany, therefore, aristocratic values were not replaced by bourgeois values; instead, the German high bourgeoisie became feudalized.

The predominant tendency of this agrarian-industrial combination was maintenance of its ruling position, and defense of the status quo. A government relying mainly on these forces would not be inclined to undertake a policy of social change or reform. But since the combined forces of the Conservatives and National Liberals had no majority in the Reichstag, the government needed the backing of either the Center Party or the Progressives to pass any legislation. This support could usually be bought by some concession to the particular interests of one party or the other. The Center Party, in particular, was willing to vote with the government in return for obtaining positions for Catholics in the administration. But agreement on larger issues was almost impossible to achieve among Center and Progressives on one side and the Conservative–National Liberal bloc on the other; German domestic policy was singularly weak in creative legislation. The work on unification of the legal system which had begun under Bismarck was now complete. Germany had a uniform law code for the entire country.

Measures which could be justified by an appeal to nationalism had the best chance to find wide support among the bourgeois parties. The most important legislation in the period of William II is due to this fact. The strength of the army (officers and men) between 1890 and 1913 grew from 509,000 to 864,000, its expenses by the outbreak of the First World War had risen to 75 per cent of the budget of the Reich. The regular financial resources of the imperial government could not cover these costs. In

Prussia an income tax had been introduced in the early nineties. But the federal government remained dependent on indirect taxes and contributions from the individual states. However, in 1913 a finance bill was passed that instituted a capital levy that could be raised directly by the federal government. This was an important step in strengthening the position of the Reich in relation to the federal states.

A number of members of the high civil service held the view that a purely negative attitude to the demands of the Social Democrats and the trade unions for an improvement of the situation of the workers was dangerous because it might lead to a violent confrontation. Thus, they succeeded in passing legislation continuing the policy Bismarck had initiated. The social insurance system was extended to additional groups and payments to the elderly and invalids were increased. Working hours for women and children were strictly limited.

Although the German ruling group was not willing to permit a democratization of German political life, the administration was both efficient and anxious to show that it was concerned with the well-being of the citizens: the bureaucracy was incorrupt, the police, although perhaps overzealous, maintained order and peace. The government was not despotic. On the contrary, the Germans prided themselves on living in a society which was ruled according to law—in a *Rechtsstaat*. In court proceedings legal forms were strictly observed and the individual could

"The Lieutenant the Day before Yesterday, Yesterday and Today," a caricature from *Simplicissimus. The caption was presented in slang which is difficult to reproduce in English. The lieutenant says "Yesterday, gambled at the jockey club, improved my finances; then champagne nothing but champagne."*

be sure of having his rights carefully protected. There was no censorship. The satirical weekly *Simplicissimus*, which attacked the ruling group and the stereotype of the Prussian lieutenant in a witty but savage way, circulated freely and was widely read. If intellectual life in Berlin and in Prussia was stifled by the narrowness and the conservatism of the outlook of the Prussian ruling group, a livelier and freer intellectual climate could be found in other parts of Germany. The cultural life in Munich, the capital of Bavaria, stood in stark contrast to that of Berlin. Munich was the home of the leading German exponents of Expressionism, and of literary figures like the novelist Thomas Mann and the dramatist Frank Wedekind, who advocated a new, freer morality in his plays. If Berlin was the political capital, Munich was the center of modern movements in German art and literature.

Nevertheless, the existing system made any opposition to the prevailing militaristic tendencies futile. This was strikingly shown in 1913 when popular demonstrations took place in the Alsatian town of Zabern against the troops stationed there. In an arbitrary extension of their functions the military authorities placed the town under martial law. William II's response was to congratulate the officer responsible for his energetic behavior. All the protests of political moderates did not help. Yet the authoritarian behavior of the emperor in the Zabern affair increased and intensified doubts about the viability of continuing the kind of regime which existed in Germany. On the local level, particularly in municipal administrations, a collaboration between Socialists and Progressive bourgeois parties began to develop. The Catholic Center party started to activate the role of the Reichstag, and to prepare, in cooperation with the Progressives and Socialists, a transition to a parliamentary system. Whether without the war and defeat these tendencies could have won out over the coalescence of powerful economic interests and deeply ingrained traditions, which supported the existing authoritarian regime, is impossible to say.

The amalgamation of the outlook of the rich industrial and financial bourgeoisie with feudal military traditions had a dangerous effect on foreign policy. In Germany's struggle for a "place in the sun," the accent was very much on power politics. Wherever some acquisition of territory seemed possible—in Africa or China or the Pacific—Germany raised claims, and these widespread claims brought about conflicts of interest with almost all the other major European states. The influence of the Prussian Conservatives made it certain that Germany would remain the strongest military power in Europe. But the building of a first-rank navy, combined with the economic competition arising from Germany's growing industrial strength, complicated German relations with Great Britain, traditionally the strongest naval power. Moreover, in order not to endanger the alliance between agrarian and industrial interests, the government tended to yield to their pressures. Thus, for example, it supported the building of the Baghdad Railway in Turkey by German financial groups, thereby stepping into an area which previously Great Britain and Russia had regarded as exclusively theirs. Because of its ambitious rush into world politics Germany became exposed to pressure from all sides.

THE HABSBURG MONARCHY

Of the seven great European powers which existed at the turn of the century, Austria-Hungary alone failed to survive the First World War. Even before that conflict, the Habsburg monarchy, including the most different nationalities—Germans, Magyars, Slovaks, Croatians, Czechs, Rumanians, Italians, Poles—was an anachronism. Much of the time, despite feeble and inconsistent attempts at constitutional forms and parliamentarism, it was ruled dictatorially. The anachronistic nature of this monarchy gave to Austria-Hungary, and particularly to the Vienna of the prewar years, a peculiar attraction. Aristocratic and cosmopolitan Vienna seemed to preserve a refined cultural tradition which was disappearing in the rest of Europe. Vienna was the center of the music world, attracting the most famous singers to its opera, and the best orchestra conductors and composers. Johannes Brahms might be seen sitting next to the wife of Johann Strauss; and while Strauss was conducting his waltzes, Brahms wrote on Mrs. Strauss' fan: "Unfortunately not by Johannes Brahms." The best German actors and actresses performed in the Burgtheater. Vienna was the center of literary trends exploring the complexities of human psychology, and in the coffeehouses the representatives of this modern literary approach—Arthur Schnitzler and Hermann Bahr—might be found talking respectfully to a fragile youth, not yet twenty years old, who had just become famous as the author of a small volume of exquisite poems: Hugo von Hofmannsthal, later to write the libretto of Richard Strauss' *Rosenkavalier* (1911). And there were the elegant Baroque palaces, from which issued carriages drawn by beautiful horses taking their noble and wealthy owners—the Liechtensteins, the Esterházys, the Schwarzenbergs —to Vienna's famous park, the Prater. They all contributed to making the life of the Vienna court the most brilliant in Europe, and because of the scandals in which the wild young Habsburg archdukes became involved, it was also the most romantic.

Francis Joseph, the Last Emperor

The embodiment of this anachronism was Emperor Francis Joseph (ruled 1848–1916). In 1900, he had ruled for more than fifty years, and he would go on ruling into the First World War. Having lived through political and personal disasters—having been forced to abandon part of his heritage to Italy, having been pushed out of Germany, having lost his son by suicide and his wife by assassination—he still continued to get up every morning at five to begin the study of the files on his desk and went on to preside over his court, in which the most rigid Spanish etiquette was observed. It is typical of the strength as well as the weakness of this regime that when in June, 1914, Francis Joseph's nephew and presumptive heir, Francis Ferdinand, and his morganatic wife were assassinated at Sarajevo, the emperor's primary reaction was not sorrow about the death of a close relation, but relief that this event would avert the danger that the son of this misalliance might become ruler of Austria-Hungary. "A higher Power has restored the order that I was unhappily unable to maintain" were the words with which he reacted to the news from Sarajevo.

It is not difficult to see why this composite of different nationalities did not survive. Rather, it is difficult to explain why the Habsburg empire continued to exist as long as it did. One reason was that all the great European powers believed that the destruction of this empire would result in a frightening disturbance of the European balance of power. It was feared that if the Habsburg empire collapsed, its Slavic nationals—its Poles, Czechs, Slovaks, Serbs, and Croatians—would turn to Russia thereby allowing it to gain an overwhelmingly strong position in Europe. Moreover, the considerable influence of the Roman Catholic Church was exerted to maintain the Habsburg realm. The frontier between the Roman Catholic and the Eastern Orthodox churches ran through the empire, and the continuing strength of the Roman Catholic Habsburgs seemed to the Roman Church a better guarantee for maintaining its position than Slavic states oriented toward the Orthodox tsar.

Furthermore, Austria-Hungary was held together by economic forces. It was a geographic unit; the Danube, which formed the great link between northwestern and southeastern Europe, facilitated an exchange of goods among the regions of the empire. The economy was well balanced. Agricultural production was sufficient to provide food for the areas where natural resources—particularly coal in Bohemia and iron in Styria—stimulated industrial activity.

Despite this development of industry Austria-Hungary remained a predominantly agrarian state. The forms of land ownership forged a further bond within the empire. For the land was in the hands of the nobility. This was particularly true in Hungary, where in 1895, 4,000 landowners—0.16 per cent of all landowners—possessed 33 per cent of the total farming area. Of these, less than 150 owned more than half of this area. The wealthiest among them—the Károlyis and the Esterházys—had immense *latifundia*. On the other hand, there were 1,300,000 peasants with holdings of less than seven acres, hardly enough to squeeze out a livelihood, and in addition the rural population included 2,000,000 farmhands and itinerant farm workers

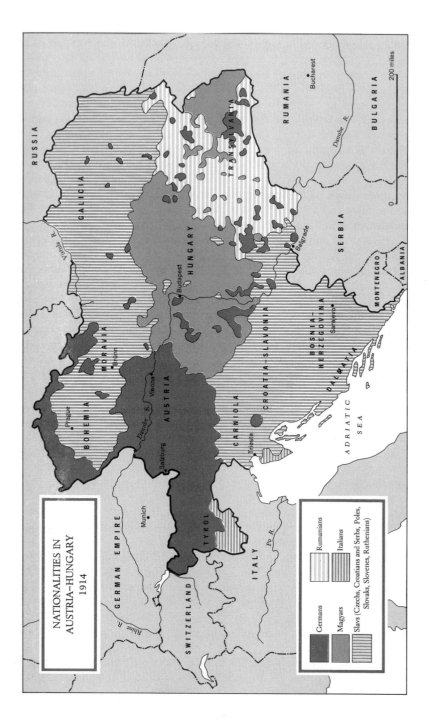

NATIONALITIES IN
AUSTRIA-HUNGARY
1914

Germans

Magyars

Slavs (Czechs, Croatians and Serbs, Poles,
Slovenes, Ruthenians)

Rumanians

Italians

200 miles

RUSSIA

GALICIA

Vistula R.

BOHEMIA

Prague

MORAVIA

Brünn

GERMAN EMPIRE

Munich

Rhine R.

Danube R.

Vienna

AUSTRIA

Salzburg

SWITZERLAND

TYROL

ITALY

Po R.

CARNIOLA

Trieste

Budapest

HUNGARY

TRANSYLVANIA

Danube R.

RUMANIA

Bucharest

BULGARIA

Belgrade

SERBIA

CROATIA-SLAVONIA

BOSNIA-
HERZEGOVINA

Sarajevo

DALMATIA

MONTENEGRO

ALBANIA

ADRIATIC
SEA

without any land of their own. In other parts of the Habsburg monarchy the social differences were not quite as deep, but the situation was not entirely dissimilar. There were extended *latifundia* also in Galicia and Bohemia. In Bohemia the great landlords were German while the bulk of the population was Czech. Serfdom had ended, but the prosperity of the aristocrats still depended on their keeping the masses of the agricultural population dependent so that they would have to work for the great landowners. Hence the great nobility, fearing economic change, gave firm support to the Habsburg monarchy. The close relationship maintained with the monarchy by the aristocracy from all parts of the empire can be seen in the diverse national origins of the men holding the most important position in the imperial government, that of foreign minister: Count Gustav Siegmund Kálnoky (in office from 1881 to 1895) was a Magyar; Count Goluchowski (1895 to 1906) was a Pole; Baron von Aehrenthal (1906 to 1912) was a Bohemian; Count Berchtold (1912 to 1915) was a German.

Finally, the most effective but also the most dangerous instrument in maintaining the coherence of the empire was the policy of playing one nationality out against the others.

The Dual Monarchy

The Habsburg empire was a Dual Monarchy. In one part—the empire of Austria—the Germans predominated; in the other—Hungary—the Magyars. These two parts had in common only the person of the emperor, foreign policy, customs policy, and the army. But Austria was not purely German, nor was Hungary purely Magyar, and the maintenance of German or Magyar rule over the subordinate nationalities became more difficult from decade to decade. The widening distribution of printed materials —newspapers and literary works—made the various nationalities conscious of their particular cultural heritage. Industrialization drew many peasants into the cities and gave them economic strength. Social tensions inherent in the general economic changes of this period were heightened by the resistance against German and Magyar rule. Both parts of the Austrian-Hungarian monarchy had constitutions but they were of a very different character.

The name Austria was used for reasons of convenience, because the German areas which had this name since the Middle Ages formed only a part of the non-Hungarian half of the dual monarchy. In addition to the German-speaking areas, this half comprised Poles and Ruthenians in Galicia; Czechs and Slovaks in Bohemia and Moravia; and Slovenes in Carniola. The great problem for the dual monarchy, and in a very acute form for its Austrian half, was created by the rise of nationalism. Order was difficult if not impossible to maintain if all these various nationalities remained dissatisfied and oppressed, but any concession to them aroused the resistance of the Germans, who were accustomed to be the ruling nationality and to serve as government officials in this entire part of the Habsburg Empire. Thus the constitution of Austria was very complicated. The Reichsrat (the parliament) had a voting system which favored the propertied classes, particularly the landowners, who were regarded as reliable support of the government. Moreover, each nation had a quota, a fixed number of deputies, so that all nationalities had a voice, but the quota of Germans was so large that they remained dominant. As could be expected, the other nationalities demanded a greater share. Moreover, the Germans were split into a liberal and a Conservative-Catholic group. Consequently each legislative proposal became the subject of endless bargaining.

A dramatic crisis occurred at the end of the nineties when the prime minister, Count Badeni, in an attempt to pacify the Czechs and gain their support, issued a series of decrees which ordered that in districts with a mixed German and Czech population, officials must be able to use both languages. The Germans were vehemently opposed because, while most Czechs knew German, most Germans did not know Czech and were therefore in danger of losing positions in the administration. Violent demonstrations arranged by German nationalists proclaiming German racial superiority took place in Vienna and most of the larger cities of German-speaking Austria. There were clashes between the army and demonstrators; under the pressure of this agitation Badeni was dismissed and his language decrees were withdrawn.

Not without awareness of the difficulties inherent in Austria's nationality problems the constitution provided that Cabinet and Crown had the power of temporary emergency legislation when the Reichstrat was not meeting, and during much of the following decade Austria was ruled on the basis of a rather doubtful application of this emergency provision. Since the eighteenth century Austria had been ruled almost uninterruptedly by bureaucrats who were highly competent in carrying out administrative tasks but administrative routine did not suffice for the needs of modern industrial society. The government gave cautious support to industrial development, especially by furthering the construction of railroads and making gradual progress in social legislation. But it was evident that, in order to keep pace with the developments in the other European countries, Austria needed economic and financial measures and reforms for which parliamentary approval was needed. Thus in 1907 the government gave in to the pressure of liberal and nationalistic forces and decreed the introduction of an electoral reform which, although maintaining quotas for the various nationality groups, provided universal male suffrage. The government believed that the main protagonists of nationalism were the middle classes in the towns, whereas workers and peasants to whom the vote was now given were loyal to the monarchy, or at least interested in maintaining the unity of a wide economic area. It is ironic that in the Habsburg monarchy, which in many respects must be regarded as a remnant of the Middle Ages and of absolutism, the Social Democrats supported the government; they too believed that the industrial development would suffer if the various nationalities became autonomous or even independent because then the middle classes would rule, hindering industrial development and preventing improvement of the workers' situation.

The combination of the interests of an aristocratic administration with far-reaching socialist reform ideas was one of the factors which gave the intellectual life of imperial Vienna its unique, free-wheeling character. However, the alliance of an aristocratic government with Social Democrats was too unnatural to create a stable situation. The electoral reform strengthened nationalities like the Slovenes and Ruthenians, who previously had played no role in the government, but now raised demands for autonomy and by means of violent demonstrations interrupted and obstructed work in the Reichsrat. In March, 1914 the government again dissolved the Reichsrat and returned to rule by means of emergency decrees. Pessimism about the future of the Habsburg monarchy was widespread.

In contrast to the Austrian part of the Habsburg monarchy, Hungary had a functioning parliamentary system, but voting was restricted in such a way that Magyars and great landowners could be assured of a majority. The ruling group, which through protective tariffs remained economically prosperous, began to consider its ties with the Habsburg monarchy—which required financial expenses for common obligations like defense and foreign policy—as a burden. The Independence party, which had existed since the revolution of 1848, began to again exert greater influence under the leadership of Franz Kossuth, son of the hero of the Hungarian revolt, Ludwig Kossuth. The demand of the party which caused a clash with the government in Vienna was the request to separate the Hungarian regiments from the rest of the army. The Hungarian government proposed that these regiments have their own insignia; and that the language of military command for them be Hungarian instead of German. When Emperor Francis Joseph rejected these demands, regarding them as direct interference with his powers, the Magyars refused to recognize the government which the emperor had appointed. This Magyar revolt was broken by the threat of the emperor to introduce universal suffrage, which would have destroyed both the Magyar domination and the power of the landowners. The Hungarian leaders realized that they had gone too far. Henceforth, the dominant figure in Hungarian politics, a man who also had an influential voice in the general affairs of the Habsburg empire, was Count Istvàn Tisza (1861–1918); he was a strong defender of Magyar superiority, but he knew that Magyar rule in Hungary was inextricably tied up with the maintenance of the empire as a whole and might suffer from changes or a general upheaval.

The crises in Austria and in Hungary revealed the lack of underlying principles in Habsburg policy. Sometimes the government would seem to favor the non-German or non-Magyar nationalities; sometimes it would rely exclusively on Germans or Magyars; sometimes it would exert power dictatorially; sometimes it played with democratic suggestions. Its only aim was to maintain the *status quo*.

It may be the inherent logic of a fundamentally illogical situation that some of the most energetic leaders in the Habsburg empire turned away from ideas of domestic change and reform and came to believe that the empire could best be maintained by a policy of expansion. Their hope was that the pride aroused by military successes might form a bond among the various nationalities. But Austria-Hungary was without access to an ocean; world politics, sea power, and colonies had no attraction. As in previous centuries, the Balkans were the crucial area for Habsburg foreign policy. Because of the relationship between some of the Balkan nations and the peoples in Austria-Hungary, the nationalism of the Balkan states created unrest and dissatisfaction among the minorities living in the Dual Monarchy; at the same time, the Austrian concern with the Balkans kept alive the tension with Russia, which had its own ambitions in this area.

RUSSIA

The Autocracy in Practice

Tense and unstable though the situation was in many European countries, the only state in which the tensions led to a full-scale revolution before the First World War was Russia. In its political development Russia was less advanced than any other European nation; at the end of the nineteenth century it was still ruled by an absolute monarch. Moreover, the man who held this formidable power was in character the most insignificant of all the monarchs of his time. The diary of Tsar Nicholas II (ruled 1894–1917), with its monotonous notices about the weather and visits of relations, even on days when the fate of his country and dynasty was being decided, gives the impression that for this monarch the world was confined to the precincts of his palaces. Like other weak and stupid men he clung with a desperate obstinacy to the few ideas with which he had been indoctrinated in his youth, and primary among these was the conviction that the absolute power which he had inherited should be left, intact and unlimited, to his son.

Nicholas was easily dominated by stronger personalities who shared this belief. In the first ten years of his reign he was under the influence of the procurator of the Holy Synod, Konstantin Pobedonostsev (1827–1907), who had been his tutor and who in his religious zeal expected that the

Left: An informal picture of the tsar and tsarina in hunting clothes. *Right:* Tsar Nicholas II and the tsarina in their coronation robes.

salvation of Russia would be achieved by shutting the nation off from all liberal Western ideas. In the tsar's later years he was dominated by his wife and the monk Rasputin. The tsarina believed that Rasputin possessed healing powers which could keep her hemophilic son alive. And since Rasputin's grasping and corrupting manners were generally resented and despised, the tsarina felt that he could be kept at court only if the tsar remained an autocrat. Thus, it was in the interest of both the tsarina and Rasputin to reinforce the tsar's absolutist notions. But since many ministers opposed Rasputin's political ideas and he was frequently able to force the dismissal of his opponents, Rasputin's presence at the court represented a serious political issue. In rejecting the attacks against Rasputin, the tsar and tsarina convinced themselves that their "friend" was a "holy man," through whom they heard the "voice of the people."

It was hardly feasible for one man to govern the immense Russian empire at the beginning of the twentieth century. The real ruler of Russia was a gigantic bureaucracy—slow, clumsy, uncontrolled, and corrupt. If administrators of talent and energy did emerge—as for instance, Count Sergei Witte (1849–1915), who was finance minister between 1892 and 1903, and, after the Revolution of 1905, Peter Stolypin (1863–1911), prime minister between 1906 and 1911—they soon found themselves entangled in bureaucratic intrigues. Furthermore, the tsar became distrustful of the new ideas advocated by such men, and saw in their popularity a threat to his power; thus, neither Witte nor Stolypin enjoyed the full support of the tsar and he was soon anxious to get rid of them.

The obvious weakness of an absolutist system in modern times was augmented by the tsar's personal defects.

The Drive Toward Industrialization

The problems which the Russian government faced were staggering. Russia was predominantly agricultural but after the Crimean War it had been realized that the nation would have to develop industries in order to remain a great power. It did possess the natural resources necessary for industrialization: coal and iron in the Donets Basin, oil in the Caucasus, cotton in Turkestan. But the obstacles to industrialization were also formidable. Before 1860 Moscow, St. Petersburg, and Kiev were the only great cities; Russia lacked the social strata which in other countries provided the capital and the skills needed for industrial development. Most of the capital therefore had to come from abroad. In 1900 more than 50 per cent of the capital of Russian industrial companies was foreign; about 90 per cent of the capital invested in mining and over 60 per cent of the capital in metal industries was foreign. The Royal Dutch Oil Company of Henri Deterding led in the exploitation of Caucasian oil; British capital played a major role in the development of the iron industry in the Ukraine.

A requisite for industrial development was the improvement of communications through the construction of a countrywide network of railroads. In the wide steppes of Russia, some of them hardly inhabited or explored, railroad construction was a complicated and difficult task which naturally fell to the state and gave the state a direct share in the development of the iron and coal industries. Thus the government was an important entrepreneur; the capital necessary for its enterprises was derived from loans and they again were largely taken up by foreign banks, particularly the French. Almost 50 per cent of all the interest paid on Russian state loans went out of Russia.

Obtaining the manpower needed for industrialization was difficult. One of the principal motives behind Alexander II's famous emancipation of the serfs in 1861 had been that of making it possible for peasants to emigrate to the urban areas to become industrial workers. But this purpose was partly defeated by details in the emancipation regulations. The former serfs had to pay for the land which had been granted to them. To fulfill this obligation, village committees, *mirs*, were formed; these undertook to make the payments, but they needed men to work the land and were unwilling to permit emigration to the cities. In order to move to the industrial centers the peasants either had to give up all claims to land or had to return for the harvest, spending only part of the year in the cities. Unable to work continuously in industry, they remained unskilled and had to take any job given to them. Their wages were extremely low; in 1880 Russian workers in Moscow received only 25 per cent as much as their British counterparts.

Workers' quarters, St. Petersburg.

The workers were housed in barracks, awakened by bells, marched to the factories, and marched back again after work, and then the gates of the barracks were closed. These conditions created unrest and dissatisfaction; when the workers returned to their villages and families they gave vent to their feelings and spread revolutionary propaganda among the rural population. Moreover, Russia's industrialization suffered from the ills common to the beginnings of industrialization in all countries: the absence of health and safety precautions in the factories, and of limitations on working hours, even for women and children. For instance, in the textile industries workers were expected to work twelve to fifteen hours a day. There was no collective bargaining and no right to strike. In addition, the change in Russian social life brought about by industrialization was deeply upsetting. With the sudden eruption of big cities, industrialization in Russia was not only an economic event but an emotional experience.

Russia was the home of many nationalities. The great masses of the population in the center of the country were Russians, but the situation in the outlying districts was very different. In the west the population was Polish; in the north the Finns had been annexed to Russia only in the early nineteenth century; in the Baltic states German nobles ruled as landowners over Estonians, Latvians, and Lithuanians. The Caucasus was populated by Georgians. Most of these national groups, particularly the Poles and the Finns but also the inhabitants of the Baltic states, had formed part of the European world at the time when Russia was still isolated. Hence they were very different from the Russians in their social structure and their intellectual outlook. They had old medieval towns and a middle class. They had been active in trade and industry; the manufacture of textiles, for example, had been carried on in Poland while Russia was still purely agrarian. They had old universities, and their intellectual life was oriented toward the West. The Poles were Catholics; the Finns and the Balts were Lutherans. Religious differences reinforced the tensions arising from differences of nationality. All these non-Russians, close to the West in their outlook, felt humiliated by the absence of institutions which the West possessed: constitutional government and self-administration. On the other hand, the Russian government feared that the granting of a constitution and of self-administration would increase the centrifugal tendencies in these areas, and was brutal enough to make various attempts at Russification, demanding the use of the Russian language and placing obstacles in the way of all those churches which were not Orthodox. Moreover, the great landowners were favored at the expense of the rest of the population. All of these policies only increased national feeling and social tension.

The Opposition

The usual outlets for political dissatisfaction, the usual means for testing the strength of opposition, were absent in Russia. Political parties were not permitted. Even associations like trade unions did not exist. A few professional organizations enjoyed approval, but even their meetings were supervised. There was rigorous censorship. Some critical views and plans for change and reform might be inserted in larger theoretical treatises, where they escaped the eyes of the censor, but political literature or even newspapers expressing criticism of the government had to be secretly printed and distributed. Frequently, such publications were the work of exiles and were smuggled over the frontiers.

Switzerland and Great Britain were the chief destinations of Russian political émigrées. *Iskra* ("The Spark"), the main organ of the Russian Social Democratic party, which was an underground organization, was edited and printed in Switzerland. The party's first congress, at Minsk in 1898, had resulted in the arrest of some of the leaders, and the next one, in 1903, was held first in Brussels and then in London; it was attended largely by exiles. One of the chief points of debate of the 1903 congress concerned the organization of the party: whether it should be limited to people who were active revolutionaries or should also admit those who were just sympathizers. Clearly, a small party could be directed and controlled from the outside, whereas a larger organization would be affected by the changing moods in Russia and would be less serviceable as an instrument for conspiratorial activities. The dispute also involved a broader issue. Would the overthrow of absolutism be immediately followed by a socialist state, or would socialism have to be preceded by a bourgeois liberal regime? The division on this point was the Russian version of the split in European socialism between the orthodox Marxists and the Revisionists.

The advocates of a small revolutionary party were led by Vladimir Ilich Lenin (1870–1924), a young émigré who had escaped from Siberia to Switzerland and had attracted attention by a number of brilliant articles in *Iskra*. In a vote which was of doubtful validity because a number of the principal members of the congress were absent, Lenin's faction won out, and thereafter it called itself the Bolsheviks ("majority group"). Lenin's leadership was soon bitterly attacked, and the control of the party came into the hands of his opponents, the Mensheviks ("minority group"); the Bolsheviks, led by Lenin, essentially became a socialist splinter faction. The policy of the Mensheviks, aiming at closer collaboration with other opposition elements, seemed much more realistic than that of the Bolsheviks because the workers were only a small part of the population. Dissatisfaction was not restricted to them; it was particularly strong among the peasantry. The Social Revolutionaries, who worked chiefly among the rural population, were almost more powerful than the Social Democrats. A successful revolution seemed more likely to come about through collaboration between peasants and workers than through the exclusive efforts of the proletariat on which Lenin wanted to rely.

All these opposition movements worked underground. The threat of punishment, usually exile to Siberia, hung over the heads of everyone involved. Violence was the only effective expression of dissatisfaction with the government. Attempts on the lives of high officials and of members of the ruling dynasty were frequent. To discover prohibited meetings, investigate forbidden activities, detect conspiracies, a large police force was a necessity. The police department was one of the most extended and most feared institutions of the Russian bureaucracy. The police were said to have spies in every block of houses. They infiltrated opposition groups, and the revolutionaries countered by offering themselves as spies to the police, in order to find out about police plans. In some cases it seems impossible to establish whether a man was a police spy or a genuine revolutionary. Typical of these enigmatic figures was Azev (1869–1918), an influential member of the Social Revolutionary party who was deeply involved in organizing the assassination of an uncle of the tsar, Grand Duke Sergius, the governor general of Moscow. Later it was revealed that Azev had been in the service of the police and participated in assassination attempts only in order to gain the full confidence of the revolutionaries.

When Prime Minister Stolypin, who had become unpopular with the reactionaries of the court, was assassinated in 1911, it was widely believed that the police had had some hand in the act. These rumors were characteristic of the atmosphere of suspicion and insecurity which permeated the entire Russian political scene.

Yet, if belonging to the Russian ruling group had dangers, there were also compensations. It has been said that anyone wanting to taste the full sweetness and pleasure of life at the end of the nineteenth century should have lived among the Russian nobility. In Russia at this time land ownership meant great wealth because recent innovations in transportation facilitated the export of Russian wheat to other European countries, and wheat prices were rising. The aristocrats lived in palaces in St. Petersburg and Moscow. During the year they moved from their great city palaces to their estates and to the Crimea; they traveled in private railroad cars to the Riviera, to Paris, and to London. A characteristic expression of the luxury of the Russian nobility was the popularity of the works of Fabergé: miniature sculptures constructed of precious jewels, which the members of the aristocracy found fashionable and amusing to give one another as Easter presents. From all over the world the Russian nobles imported the most famous singers and musicians for private entertainments. Some of them were remarkably sensitive to the current trends in art. Georges Braque and André Derain painted backdrops for the Russian ballet; a wealthy Russian assembled the most complete collection of early paintings by Pablo Picasso; Russian poets experimented in the most advanced literary forms.

If the Russian aristocrats appeared to indulge in senseless luxuries, one reason was that they too suffered from the distrust of the absolutist ruler and his bureaucrats, and were excluded from responsible participation in political life. Thus it should not be assumed that all the members of the Russian nobility were frivolous and unaware of the seriousness of their country's political situation. Tolstoi, with his radical ideas of returning to a life of pristine Christian virtues was one such exception. And Russian aristocrats were active in the *zemstvos*, regional councils established by Alexander II, which represested the nearest approach to local self-administration in Russia. Many tried to work in the *zemstvos* for improvements in the economic situation and attempted to extend the sphere of activities of the *zemstvos*, legally limited to local and charitable tasks, to political matters. But they were always rebuffed by the government.

The Russo-Japanese War

Resentment about the continued absolutism of the tsars permeated almost all strata of society, and though the opposition groups differed in their concrete aims, only a spark was needed to unite them in a general revolutionary explosion. This spark was provided by the Russian defeats in the Russo-Japanese War. The war started on February 8, 1904, with a surprise attack by Japanese torpedo boats against the Russian Far Eastern squadron anchored in the harbor of Port Arthur. But the attack had been preceded by negotiations in which the Japanese had shown their willingness to reach a peaceful solution if the Russians relinquished a Far Eastern policy which would prevent Japanese expansion on the Asian mainland. Responsible Russian statesmen had been inclined to give the Japanese assurances that a penetration into Manchuria and Korea which the Russians had started in the preceding years would remain limited. But a Russo-Japanese understanding was blocked by the tsar. Nicholas II, since his travels in the Far East in his youth, had had vague ideas about making Russia a great naval power by extending its boundaries to the Pacific. These ideas had been fed by William II, who liked to call himself Admiral of the Atlantic and to address the tsar as Admiral of the Pacific. And the tsar listened to military men and financial speculators who urged him to bring all of Korea under Russian control. Probably he was also dazzled by the thought that Russian expansion in the Far East would help silence critics of his absolutist regime.

So the Japanese struck. The defeat of the Russian land forces in the Battle of Mukden was a great surprise. Few had foreseen that a great European power could succumb to an Asiatic state. With the wisdom of hindsight, one can recognize the reasons for the Japanese victory. The Japanese had been prepared for the war, while the supplying and strengthening of Russian forces in the Far East had been slow and difficult because the trans-Siberian railway had only one track and did not yet extend to the Pacific. Before Russia could bring the full weight of its military forces into play, the Russians agreed to accept the mediation of President Theodore Roosevelt of the United States in arranging a peace with Japan. A treaty with the Japanese was signed on September 5, 1905 in Portsmouth, New Hampshire.

The Revolution of 1905

An early conclusion of peace had been forced upon Russia because of upheavals in the interior. The Russo-Japanese War placed an immense strain on the Russian system of transportation, and the provisioning of the great urban centers broke down. Bread prices soared and the wages of the workers proved insufficient. Spontaneous strikes broke out in many places. When on January 9, 1905, a procession of workers approached the Winter Palace of the tsar to submit to him their grievances, the way was blocked by troops, whose commander lost his head and fired on the masses. This Bloody Sunday set in motion the revolution. A general strike was declared in St. Petersburg, and most industrial centers followed suit. The workers combined into unions; the professional organizations which had been allowed a supervised existence now became politically active, electing new leaders and drawing up programs of political reform. The *zemstvos* formulated political demands. The general cry was for the creation of a parliamentary government based on universal suffrage.

Progress toward this goal was achieved in stages. In March the tsar was forced to declare that a consultative assembly would be established. In August he conceded that this assembly would be elected, but he insisted that suffrage would be limited and the power of this assembly, the Duma, would be purely deliberative. Then a new wave of strikes and revolutionary outbreaks occurred; in October, under the pressure of a breakdown of public order, with cities like St. Petersburg and Moscow in the hands of the workers, the tsar made a further concession: the Duma would be elected on the basis of a wide franchise and it would have legislative functions. Civil liberties would be guaranteed. The change in the political system was indicated by the appointment of a prime minister; this office was given to Count Witte. But revolutionary agitation among the workers continued and peasant unrest began to spread. In the southern parts of Russia peasants burned the houses of landowners and occupied the land. Under the threat of this peasant revolt the tsar, on Witte's advice, in December conceded universal and secret suffrage. But this was his last concession. Troops returning from the Far East bolstered the government; the leaders of the workers in St. Petersburg were arrested, and an insurrection of the workers in Moscow was defeated. Boris Pasternak's *Doctor Zhivago* (1957) contains a graphic description of the Cossacks riding down the masses in Moscow in the winter of 1905.

The Revolution of 1905 did not seal the fate of tsarism. It might be called a turning point which did not turn. A constitutional system was introduced. Although universal suffrage was not maintained and the voting structure favored the wealthier classes, large groups of the population were willing to cooperate with the government to make the constitution work. Moreover, the peasants were freed from making further payments for their land, and under Stolypin the dissolution of the *mirs* opened the way to an agricultural development based on private ownership; wealthy peasants— kulaks—began to appear. But the tsar, far from welcoming these developments, obstructed them in every way. In March, 1906, he dismissed Witte, whom he believed to have made unnecessary concessions; Stolypin, who came to office later in 1906, had lost the tsar's favor by the time he was assassinated in 1911. Whenever possible, Nicholas appointed reactionary ministers. He openly bestowed his favor on the most reactionary groups, among them the Black Hundreds, who with the support of the troops embarked on barbaric punitive actions against the peasants. The tsar also encouraged anti-Semitic pogroms. As before, the influence of the crown remained the chief target of all liberal forces.

Actually, the tsar might have utilized the revolution and its consequences to broaden the basis of support for his government. Through the summer of 1905, almost all social groups except for the extreme reactionaries had favored the revolutionary movement. This unified front broke down in the autumn, as agrarian unrest continued and the workers began to fight more openly for a socialist republic. Liberal aristocrats, professional groups, the middle classes—all were by then satisfied with the concessions made by the

"Bloody Sunday," January 9, 1905. *Demonstrators are fired on by troops outside the Winter Palace.*

tsar in the October decree. Revolutionary activity between October and December faltered because it began to lose general support and became restricted to workers and peasants. For a moderately liberal policy the tsar could have counted on the backing of a large segment of society.

Except for the Paris Commune of 1871, previous revolutions had been bourgeois in character. The Russian Revolution of 1905 can be regarded as the first socialist revolution. It showed the immense importance of the general strike as a political weapon. Moreover, it revealed new techniques for effecting a social revolution. For the first time workers' councils, composed of men elected by the workers of the various factories, exerted a directing influence upon events and in certain critical periods functioned as an effective government. The leading spirit of the workers' council in St. Petersburg was a young socialist writer named Leon Trotsky. Like Lenin, he realized that in revolutionary times these workers' councils could serve as the authority which could prevent chaos and at the same time keep power in the hands of the proletariat.

The Russian Revolution of 1905 had a great impact all over Europe. Fear of revolution became tangible in the political atmosphere; governments became more concerned about maintaining their authority and their prestige than they had ever been before. The result was an increase in tensions within the nations of Europe and also a more intensive pursuit of success in foreign policy. And the dangers and opportunities in the international arena were abruptly expanded, for the sudden revelation of Russia's weakness changed the entire European scene.

CHAPTER 4

The Quest for Hegemony and World Power

TWENTIETH-CENTURY DIPLOMACY

GREAT BRITAIN, France, Spain, Italy, Germany, Austria-Hungary, and Russia were great powers. This term was applied to them not only because of their territorial extent, economic strength, or size of population. The expression "great power" had a more particular, almost technical meaning. The world of states was seen as a hierarchy with the great powers at the summit. Their eminent role was reflected in diplomatic custom: only international meetings attended by all the great powers were called congresses; the highest rank in the diplomatic profession was that of ambassador, which applied only to diplomats of great powers who served at the court of another great power. These customs had been formed in previous centuries and continued to be maintained. It can hardly be said that Spain, which had rightly enjoyed the distinction of being a great power up to the end of the eighteenth century, pulled much weight in times when political power depended decisively on industrial capacities. Yet Spain remained among the great powers. Tradition was an important element in the conduct of diplomatic affairs, and diplomacy remained an aristocratic profession. In France, where after the establishment of the republic the aristocracy refrained from participation in the government or in politics, members of the nobility continued to pursue diplomatic careers. Because diplomats were accredited to the head· of the state and closely connected with the court, there was justification for the aristocratic monopoly in diplomacy. Furthermore, diplomacy was an expensive career and could be afforded only by those belonging to the wealthiest stratum of the nobility. Usually diplomats—as members of the landowning classes —were more closely connected with the agrarian part of economic life than with the industrial and commercial sectors.

This remoteness from the problems of modern industrial society strengthened the hold which tradition had not only on form and ceremony, but also on the ideas and assumptions of the men responsible for the conduct of foreign affairs. Most of the diplomats who advanced to high positions in the period before the First World War had received their training under the great masters of nineteenth-century diplomacy: Bismarck in Germany, Gorchakov in Russia, Disraeli in Great Britain, Cavour in Italy, and Andrássy in Austria-Hungary. Diplomats in the early twentieth century held firmly to the ideas which had dominated diplomatic thinking in the two previous centuries: balance of power and *raison d'état*. They believed in a "concert of Europe," which really meant that the smaller nations were coerced into carrying out what the great powers had agreed upon among themselves. Without openly acknowledging it, the great powers still assumed the right of intervention propounded a century earlier by Prince Metternich. They did not subscribe to the principle of national self-determination, for it threatened to lead to a disturbance of the balance of power.

The secretive manner in which diplomats of the old school used to handle affairs became more difficult to maintain in the face of a steadily increasing interest in foreign policy on the part of the general population. Popular concern was aroused for a number of reasons—some of a more intellectual, some of a more technological nature. The rise of nationalism throughout the nineteenth century implied the political participation of a wider population. Moreover, the masses not only wanted to be heard, they wanted their nation to excel. They regarded international politics as a competition in which their own country should come first. The feelings of national arrogance which are described by the word "jingoism" were a factor and force all over Europe. Jingoism probably entered the political vocabulary through the words of a song by the English songwriter G. W. Hunt, which was popular during the Russo-Turkish War (1877–1878): "We don't want to fight, but, by jingo, if we do,/ We've got the ships, we've got the men, we've got the money, too."

Jingoistic tendencies were nourished and strengthened by new means of communication. As illiteracy steadily decreased, a literature mainly produced for mass circulation and frequently directed towards flattering one's own nation and asserting its material interests began to develop and was made widely available in cheap paper editions and lending libraries. Newspapers gained in circulation and in influence. Both newspapers and the newer forms of communication—telegraph, telephone, photography—bridged distances and gave events in foreign and distant lands concreteness and immediacy. The popular media often placed special emphasis on the exploits of men of their audience's own nation. People followed breathlessly the expeditions into darkest Africa, full of pride if their own countrymen made new discoveries; the attempts to reach the North and South Poles became competitions of nation against nation. In the race to the North Pole the Americans Peary and Cook were pitted against the Norwegian Amundsen, and Amundsen made the race to the South Pole against the British explorer Scott. Scott's notes, found after his death in the Antarctic, give an affecting picture of the suffering and heroism involved in these enterprises in which scientific curiosity, romanticism, and national pride were strangely combined. Seeing the flag of his own nation implanted in the polar snow or flying among the palm trees of an island in the South Seas filled the common man with pride. The prestige of one's country became a popular concern, and diplomacy could not remain aloof from this national competitiveness. Even those diplomats who did not share these sentiments were aware that they could not ignore them. In the quest for national prestige, diplomats became anxious to achieve resounding successes without regard for the lasting hostility whih temporary triumphs might arouse.

It soon became obvious that the pressure which an aroused public opin ion might exert could be used for special purposes and interests. Active propaganda lobbies were set up, which used newspapers and pamphlets to draw attention to the causes they favored. Manufacturers and land owners formed societies to promote their particular interests and to obtain popular backing. But the preferred field of pressure by public opinion was foreign affairs. The most popular cry was for overseas expansion. In almost all countries, organizations for colonial propaganda were strongly supported by economic interests. Every great European state wanted to become a "world power." At the beginning of the twentieth century this phrase dazzled even cool and critical minds. This demand simultaneously reflected the heated climate of national competitiveness and the pressures of industrial and commercial interests. The age of nationalism was succeeded by the era of imperialism. The great powers, as we have mentioned, stood at the top of a hierarchy above the smaller, less powerful members of the European state system; and it was taken for granted that most of the rest of the globe—the "lesser breeds"—belonged to the European states. No fault was seen in depriving non-European peoples of their independence and of forcing them into a modern, European mold. Bound by the idea of their racial superiority and haunted by the fear that if they remained passive they might miss the last chance for participation in the division of the world, the European nations became less concerned with the questions of concrete advantages than with success and prestige. Spurred on by popular enthusiasm, diplomacy was driven by events rather than by rational calculations.

The freedom of action by statesmen and diplomats was further diminished by changes in the nature of the military organization. The military establishment had become an integral part of industrial society. The processes Alfred Nobel had invented for the development of explosives were applied to small caliber weapons, particularly machine guns, and to new models of heavy long-range artillery. On the sea ironclad ships replaced the older wooden vessels and increased in strength, size, and mobility. The new armaments could be produced on a sizable scale only in a country which had developed a modern industrial apparatus and possessed or could obtain the necessary raw materials. Moreover, speed in the mobilization of mass armies, on which military success was believed to depend, could be achieved only if there existed a well-developed railroad system.

Accordingly, the distinction between mobilization and war became increasingly difficult in the industrial age. Whereas in the preindustrial age a country could mobilize its troops, march them to the frontier, and stop them there, now mobilization and war became almost identical. For the mobilization and the deployment of mass armies a timetable had to be established well in advance, and once the military plans had been worked out, last-minute modifications could not be made without leading to chaos. In the crisis of 1914 almost all the European states were bound to military plans worked out many years before and to the arrangements with other powers which had been set up by their military staffs. But diplomats seemed to have been almost unaware of the extent to which military timetables encroached upon their freedom of action. In no country was diplomatic strategy and military planning completely coordinated. A gap had developed between the customs, traditions, and assumptions of the diplomats and the reality of the modern industrial world.

THE RIGIDIFICATION OF THE ALLIANCE SYSTEM

The year 1905 was crucial in the unfolding of a new European diplomacy: the events of that year decided that the European state system would be divided into two opposing blocs. Alliances between the great powers of Europe had been in existence since the nineteenth century. Primary among them was the Triple Alliance between Germany, Austria-Hungary, and Italy; this was followed in the nineties by the Russo-French alliance. But some flexibility, some room for maneuvering between alliances and powers had remained. Although after Bismarck's fall the Reinsurance Treaty, through which he had tried to maintain good relations with Russia, had not been renewed, collaboration between Germany and Russia, chiefly by means of an assumed friendship and an actual familial relationship between the tsar and William II, had not entirely ceased. Most important, Great Britain was not bound by any alliance.

The rigidification of the existing compacts in 1905 did not occur overnight. Great Britain had been surprised by the reaction which the Boer War had aroused on the Continent. The Boers clearly enjoyed the sympathy of the peoples on the Continent and English defeats were viewed with a certain glee. The Boer War had created a somewhat contradictory but nonetheless unfavorable image of Great Britain: ruthless in its pursuit of worldly treasures on the one hand, decadent on the other. To avoid a common stand of the great powers against them, and to reinforce the security of their empire, the English needed to abandon their policy of "spendid isolation" and seek the backing of a great continental power.

The most likely potential partner of Britain was Germany, which was stronger than Britain's closest continental neighbor, France. Moreover, the interests of Great Britain and Russia, France's ally, clashed in Persia, on the northern frontier of India, and in China. However, if Britain was unpopular in Germany, Germany was no less unpopular in Britain. Perhaps the German emperor seriously believed that Germany wanted nothing but its deserved "place in the sun." He had certainly convinced many of his subjects that this was the case. But, with possession spread out all over the globe, the British saw the German advances into Africa, China, and the South Seas as the actions of a spoiled and brutal young man who wanted to grab everything he could lay his hands on. In the eyes of the leaders of British policy, two actions of the German government posed a special danger: the construction of a powerful navy and the financing and building of the Baghdad railway. When the German naval program began, there was probably little awareness of what its later consequences would be. Because sea power was regarded as essential for effective participation in world politics the navy soon became popular among the German bourgeoisie; in contrast to the predominantly aristocratic officers of the army, naval officers came mainly from bourgeois families. The popular backing for the navy was efficiently promoted by the

The Baghdad Railroad. *German and Turkish officials celebrate the launching of the enterprise.*

secretary of the navy, Admiral von Tirpitz, who established a special office which edited pamphlets, helped to organize navy leagues, and arranged meetings where speakers discussed the importance of naval power: this office was the forerunner of all later propaganda ministries. In 1898 the Reichstag had sanctioned a navy bill which was a new departure for Germany in that it proposed not only cruisers which might defend the German coast but also battleships fit for combat on the open sea: the bill provided for the building of eleven battleships and five first-class cruisers by 1905. The German navy envisaged here was still rather small. However, two years later, in 1900, Tirpitz carried through the adoption of a second bill which would expand the building program, calling for the construction of thirty-eight battleships to be completed in twenty years. The anti-British tendency of this second bill was evident. Tirpitz' goal was a fleet of such strength that the British would hesitate to attack Germany.

Likewise, the German project for a railroad to Baghdad developed from innocuous beginnings into an enterprise with dangerous political consequences. The capital needed and the financial risks involved were so large that the Deutsche Bank, the German financial house interested in the undertaking obtained concessions for the project from the Turkish government in 1899 almost by default of other competitors. The leaders of the Deutsche Bank tried without success to obtain the cooperation of financiers of other countries for this enterprise. The only serious opponents of the project were the Russians. The French supported the Germans, and the British raised no objections; both Great Britain and France were anxious to bar Russian expansion in the Near East and to involve Germany in the preservation of Turkey. However, their attitude changed when, almost unavoidably, the construction of the railroad gave Germany economic and then political control in Turkey.

If these German enterprises lowered the attractiveness of an understanding with Germany, all such attempts were cut off by the attitude of the German political leaders. British feelers, particularly those of the colonial secretary, Joseph Chamberlain, received a very cool reception. The German statesmen in power, especially Chancellor Bernhard von Bülow (1849–1929) and his political advisor Friedrich von Holstein, felt sure that Britain could turn to no other power. Thus Germany could refuse to be satisfied with an agreement that merely delimited German and British colonial interests and wait until the time was ripe to demand a defensive alliance.

But the British government, having no intention of going that far, turned to France and the result was the Entente Cordiale, concluded on April 8, 1904. Formally, this treaty was an agreement on all the issues concerning colonies that had occasioned disputes between Great Britain and France; the chief points were that France abandoned all its claims in Egypt and Britain recognized that France had a dominating interest in Morocco and promised diplomatic support of French plans for achieving control of Morocco. The marquis of Lansdowne (1845–1927), the British foreign secretary who concluded this agreement, always maintained that the treaty had no aim except that of moderating the tensions which had arisen from colonial conflicts. But a year later what was a limited temporary agreement had become a close political partnership.

The developments which took place in 1905 were preceded by a change in the position of Russia. Throughout the nineteenth century the contrast between Great Britain and Russia had been a basic factor in European foreign policy; it was axiomatic that "bear and whale could never come together." Significantly, when the British government abandoned the policy of "splendid isolation" the first agreement it concluded was an alliance, which recognized Japan's special interest in Korea. But the primary British interest in this treaty was to strengthen the barrier against any further Russian advance in the Far East. When the Russo-Japanese War broke out two years later, the Russians feared that Great Britain might enter the war on the Japanese side—especially after an incident at Dogger Bank in the North Sea in which Russian ships sailing from the Baltic to the Far East had mistakenly fired on British trawlers. Consequently, the Russians began to set great store on a benevolent neutrality of Germany and began to seek German support. This situation appeared to the German statesmen an ideal opportunity to reassert German predominance on the Continent. They persuaded themselves that, because Russia, involved in the Far East, could not come to the assistance of France, this was the right moment to humiliate the French and show them that their Entente Cordiale with Great Britain was without value. They believed that German superiority and French helplessness would be strikingly demonstrated if they halted the French penetration into Morocco.

THE CRISES OF 1905–1914

The First Moroccan Crisis

The Germans opened their action against France by claiming that the arrangements about Morocco violated German interests. This was just a pretense; German economic activities hardly existed in Morocco, and indeed the German government had found it necessary to exert pressure on the Mannesmann Company, a metallurgical and mining company, to make investments in Morocco so that there could be some substance for the assertions concerning the violation of German interests.

The Moroccan crisis started when William II, on a Mediterranean trip in March, 1905, debarked briefly in Tangier and solemnly declared that the Germans were willing to maintain the independence and integrity of Morocco. German and French claims clearly confronted each other. France regarded Morocco as belonging to the French sphere of interest and planned to absorb the country; the Germans insisted that it was an independent and sovereign state in which all nations should have equal opportunities. From the point of view of international law the French were in a weak position. So they tried to come to some arrangement with Germany, indicating their willingness to make concessions in other colonial areas. The Germans countered by demanding an international conference. They were not interested in getting advantages to compensate for French rule in Morocco; rather they were concerned with demonstrating French political impotence. They refused to enter into any bilateral negotiations with France, and made it clear that they considered the French foreign minister Théophile Delcassé—whose policy had raised French prestige by establishing close connections first with Russia and then with Great Britain—so hostile to Germany that negotiations with him were purposeless. The situation became increasingly tense. Delcassé insisted that he had a commitment from Great Britain to support France in case of war, but the other French ministers rightly maintained that the close consultation to which Britain had agreed in the Entente Cordiale did not mean that it had any obligation to enter combat on the French side. France without Britain would not be able to hold out against Germany. These questions were thrashed out in a dramatic meeting of the French cabinet. On June 6, 1905, Delcassé resigned.

Germany had achieved a resounding diplomatic triumph. But the Germans did not know what to do with their victory. The French were now willing to agree to an international conference about Morocco but proposed that Germany and France should first work out a settlement between themselves, to be then ratified by the conference. For such a preliminary settlement the French were willing to pay a high price; for a free hand in Morocco they were prepared to make far-reaching concessions to Germany in other colonial disputes. But the German government still refused to enter into bilateral negotiations with France and demanded unconditional acceptance of the convocation of an international conference. This attitude was widely interpreted as a sign that Germany was not content with having shown its superior strength but was driving toward a war against France. Indeed, Count Alfred von Schlieffen (1833–1913), the chief of the German general staff, did want a preventive war, but there are no indications that either Chancellor Bülow or Holstein shared this view. It appears that after they had solemnly declared that the Moroccan problem ought to be submitted to an international conference they found it difficult to withdraw from this position; to make a prior settlement with France would have been to turn the conference into a farce. Furthermore the Germans believed that they would dominate the conference and that France would be unable to offer serious opposition to their demands.

The German statesmen had grounds for optimism. In Russian governing circles there was an increasing inclination to reestablish close relations with Germany, not only as a means of restraining Great Britain, but also because Wilhelminian Germany was the only state from which the Russians could expect sympathy and support for their attempts to maintain an autocratic system. Accordingly, negotiations toward an alliance treaty were conducted at a meeting in July, 1905 between Nicholas II and William II at Björkö on the Baltic coast. At a time when Russia was losing to Japan and was in the midst of revolutionary turmoil, William II had no great difficulty in persuading, almost forcing, his dispirited cousin to sign an alliance treaty, which, although discussed for months, had never been signed.

Just when Germany seemed at the high point of power, with Delcassé eliminated and Russia as an ally, things began to go wrong. The Russian statesmen were disgusted with their tsar's weakness in yielding to the German emperor's demands. They began to raise objections to the treaty and to delay its completion. After the peace treaty with Japan was signed in September, Russia had less need for German support. Moreover, a French loan helped to alleviate Russia's acute financial difficulties and increased the authority of the government. Under these circumstances the Russians had no reason any longer not to give diplomatic support to their French ally in the Moroccan crisis. Moreover, the British had begun to fear that the French might be forced to align themselves with Germany and Russia. The new British foreign secretary, Sir Edward Grey, a Liberal more inclined toward France than toward Germany, encouraged the French by permitting consultations between the French and British military staffs regarding common action in wartime, and promised the French support in the negotiations over Morocco. Thus, although the French in September, 1905, gave in and agreed to an international conference without prior accords with Germany, they could look forward to the conference with confidence.

In January, 1906, when the conference over Morocco convened in the Spanish city of Algeciras, it was not France but Germany that was in an almost isolated position. Characteristic of the polite, subtle, and indirect ways of the diplomacy of this period is the fact that there was no dramatic indictment of German policy. A test vote on a minor question revealed that Russia, France, Great Britain, Italy, even the United States, all sided with France; only Austria-Hungary voted with Germany. This was proof enough: if Germany decided to unleash a war against France it would now be opposed by almost every great power. Chancellor Bülow realized that Germany had to give in. The final agreement was couched in terms which concealed the German defeat. There was confirmation of the independence of Morocco and assurance of an economic open door for other powers. But the police in Morocco were put under the combined authority of France and Spain, and France was given control of the state bank, and thereby the finances, of Morocco. The conference had established that France would be the ruling power in Morocco.

The affair had been primarily a struggle among the European powers for hegemony, and the details of the regulations of the Moroccan situation were less significant than what the conference revealed about the diplomatic constellation in Europe: at Algeciras the powers which would confront one another in the First World War found themselves for the first time grouped in opposing camps.

The Moroccan crisis of 1905–1906 was followed by a chain of further crises and wars—the Bosnian crisis of 1908–1909, a second Moroccan crisis and the Tripolitan War between Italy and Turkey in 1911, the first Balkan War in 1912, the second Balkan War and the Liman von Sanders crisis in 1913—until, in the summer of 1914, tensions exploded into the First World War.

In the last years before the outbreak of the war the issue which sparked most of these crises was an old problem that had troubled European diplomacy since the eighteenth century, the fate of Europe's "sick man," Turkey. By the early twentieth century the Ottoman Empire extended into southeastern Europe over the northern coast of Africa and ruled over the Near East. The main source of unrest was in its European sector, in the Balkans. In the course of the gradual economic development of this area, which was accomplished largely with the help of foreign capital, the middle classes had become stronger; professional men—lawyers, doctors, teachers—were needed in increasing numbers. Rumanians, Serbs, Greeks, Bulgars, studied in foreign countries, particularly in Germany and France, and absorbed an almost religious faith in nationalism. Contact with the powerful national states of central and western Europe could only increase dissatisfaction with the situation at home, with the subjection of the Balkan peoples to the Ottoman Empire and the Habsburg monarchy. The demand for the elimination of Turkish rule in Europe became more general and more urgent. In earlier times the great powers had always been aware of a last recourse in case the illness of the "sick man" proved fatal—partition. But this means of escape from a clash among the European powers over the spoils of the Ottoman Empire was now barred, for Germany made the maintenance of the Ottoman Empire the cornerstone of its policy. Whereas in Bismarck's time Germany could act as a mediator between the two great powers which bordered the Balkan peninsula—Austria-Hungary and Russia—as they competed for influence there, now Germany itself had become an interested participant in the affairs of this area. This change in Germany's role constituted a new and dangerous element in the situation.

The Bosnian Crisis

After the humiliation suffered in the war against Japan, the Russian government was eager for a success in foreign policy. The Slavic brethren in the Balkans were popular with the Russian public, and Russian ruling circles believed that a policy favoring independence of the Balkan nations would strengthen the authority of the tsar and weaken the trends toward parliamentarianism and democratic government. Quick action seemed appropriate because in July, 1908, a revolution had taken place in the Ottoman Empire; the tyrannical Sultan Abdul-Hamid II had been forced to abdicate, and the Young Turks, advocates of modernization and parliamentary government, had come to power. Concessions from a Turkey strengthened by reforms would be difficult to obtain. Hence, in September, 1908, the Russian foreign minister, Alexander Izvolski (1856–1919), set out to visit the courts of the European great powers, hoping to obtain their permission to open the Dardanelles to Russian warships, a move which would strengthen Russian influence in Turkey and in the Balkans. Izvolski's first stop was at Buchlau, in Bohemia, where he met the Austrian foreign minister Aehrenthal. The exact nature of the exchange between Izvolski and Aehrenthal has never become entirely clear because the accounts of the two ministers diverge widely. However, there can be little doubt that Aehrenthal promised to raise no objections against the opening of the Dardanelles to Russian warships. As a *quid pro quo*, Izvolski agreed not to oppose Austrian annexation of the Turkish provinces of Bosnia and Herzegovina, which Austria-Hungary had occupied since the Congress of Berlin. Aehrenthal was a clever and ruthless diplomat and Izvolski was not his equal. For while Izvolski continued his round of visits to the European capitals, seeking to work out a general agreement on the opening of the Dardanelles, the Austrian government, on October 6, proclaimed the annexation of Bosnia and Herzogovina. One day earlier, in collusion with Austria, Bulgaria—hitherto under the sovereignty of the sultan—had declared its full independence. The crisis had come about before Izvolski could get agreement from the other great powers, and he had to return to St. Petersburg empty-handed. Austria-Hungary had strengthened its position in the Balkan area without the Russians' receiving any compensation. In order to reassert Russian influence in Balkan affairs, and also driven by passionate hatred of Aehrenthal, Izvolski tried in every way to prevent international recognition of Austria's annexation of Bosnia and Herzegovina. The Turks, under German pressure, accepted the annexation when they were offered financial compensation. The country which was most indignant over the Austrian action was Serbia. Because the peoples of Bosnia and Herzegovina were primarily South Slavs, the Serbs felt that they, not the Austrians, ought to rule these provinces. Thus the crisis dragged on. Encouraged by Russian backing, Serbia made military preparations, and Austria followed suit. Finally, in March, 1909, the German government sent a sharp note to Russia demanding that it abandon its support of Serbia and recognize Austria's annexation of Bosnia and Herzegovina. Still too weak to risk a war against the great European powers, Russia gave in. The crisis was over.

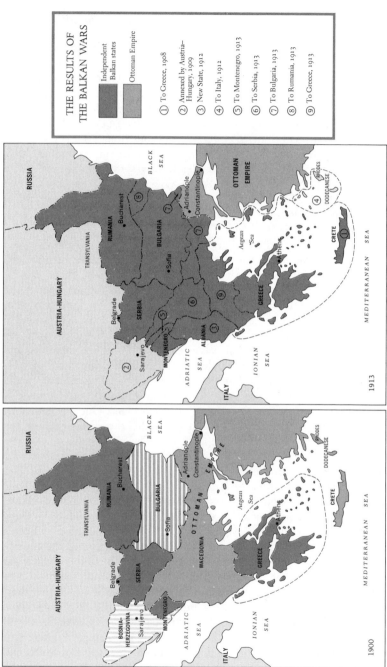

THE RESULTS OF
THE BALKAN WARS

Independent
Balkan states

Ottoman Empire

① To Greece, 1908
② Annexed by Austria–Hungary, 1909
③ New State, 1912
④ To Italy, 1912
⑤ To Montenegro, 1913
⑥ To Serbia, 1913
⑦ To Bulgaria, 1913
⑧ To Rumania, 1913
⑨ To Greece, 1913

1913

RUSSIA

BLACK SEA

TRANSYLVANIA

RUMANIA
• Bucharest ⑧

AUSTRIA-HUNGARY

BULGARIA
• Sofia

Adrianople
Constantinople ⑦

OTTOMAN EMPIRE

Belgrade

SERBIA
⑤

⑥

⑨

Aegean Sea

Athens

RHODES

DODECANESE ④

CRETE ①

MEDITERRANEAN SEA

② Sarajevo •

MONTENEGRO

ALBANIA ③

ADRIATIC SEA

IONIAN SEA

ITALY

1900

RUSSIA

BLACK SEA

TRANSYLVANIA

RUMANIA
• Bucharest

AUSTRIA-HUNGARY

BULGARIA
• Sofia

Adrianople
Constantinople

OTTOMAN EMPIRE

Belgrade

SERBIA

MACEDONIA

Aegean Sea

Athens

RHODES

DODECANESE

CRETE

GREECE

MEDITERRANEAN SEA

BOSNIA-
HERZEGOVINA
Sarajevo •

MONTENEGRO

ADRIATIC SEA

IONIAN SEA

ITALY

The Bosnian crisis has frequently been considered a rehearsal of the crisis which ended with the outbreak of the First World War. It is indeed true that Germany tried to repeat in 1914 what it had succeeded in doing in 1908–1909. But in 1914 Russia was not willing to back down.

In any case the Bosnian crisis made Germany and Russia direct opponents and ended all ideas of a German-Russian alliance. Germany's reaction was almost automatic; it tried to escape from isolation by moving closer to Great Britain. This shift in policy was connected with a change in the German government. Whereas Chancellor Bülow had been anti-British and chiefly interested in an alliance with Russia, Theobald von Bethmann-Hollweg (1856–1921), who succeeded Bülow in 1909, accepted Russian hostility as inevitable and directed his policy toward cooperation with Great Britain.

The Second Moroccan Crisis

Nevertheless, the German's first important move under the chancellorship of Bethmann-Hollweg could hardly be interpreted as a new departure in their foreign policy. The German government provoked another Moroccan crisis. Although the conference at Algeciras had recognized France's predominant interest in Morocco it had also acknowledged the independence of that state. When internal struggles broke out in Morocco the French intervened and began to take over the entire country. The Germans ostensibly did not want this to happen, at least not without receiving compensation. In order to force the French to negotiate, a German gunboat, on July 1, 1911, anchored in Agadir, a harbor on the Atlantic coast of Morocco. But the French were in a much stronger position than they had been in 1905 at the time of the first Moroccan crisis, when Russia was engaged in the Far East and the Entente Cordiale with Great Britain was still new and untried. The British gave the French strong support, their attitude being particularly evident in a speech, delivered by Lloyd George in Mansion House. He warned that Germany should not forget that Great Britain too had vital interests in Morocco and would not shy away from fighting for them: "National honor is no party question." Although the French government consented to negotiate with the Germans, it was not prepared to yield much; the French were tough, and negotiations dragged on until November. In the agreement which was finally signed, the French gained a free hand in Morocco and the Germans received part of the French Congo connecting the German Cameroons with the Congo River. This was not a brilliant outcome for Germany. The German foreign secretary, Alfred von Kiderlen-Waechter (1852–1912), who was praised by his friends as a second Bismarck and saw himself in this role, rationalized the 'meager results of his policy by maintaining that the purpose of the entire action had been not to make colonial gains, but to improve relations with France by removing the festering wound of Morocco with one sharp incision of the knife. Also, Germany would now be able to draw closer to Great Britain, which would no longer consider a German-British rapprochement incompatible with the Entente Cordiale. Whatever the actual aims of Kiderlen-Waechter's policy, the impression which the sudden appearance of a German warship in Moroccan waters made on other countries was not that of a country striving for appeasement. On the contrary, both statesmen and the general public chiefly remembered that since 1905 Germany had three times tried to get its way by sudden and brutal action: in Morocco in the summer of 1905; by the ultimatum to Russia in 1909; and finally, at Agadir.

Nevertheless, negotiations between Germany and Great Britain did finally take place. Frightened by the drift toward war which the Agadir crisis had indicated, the British government was also aware that military preparations in response to international tensions would diminish the financial resources available for its program of domestic reform. Hence, the British decided to probe German intentions once more; the secretary of state for war, Haldane, was sent to Berlin. The aim of his mission was to prevent the Germans from carrying out their plan for increased naval construction. Tirpitz had declared that three great battleships (dreadnoughts) would be built instead of the previously announced two. But Haldane did not obtain any modification of German naval plans. Actually, the German chancellor and the German foreign secretary, Bethmann-Hollweg and Kiderlen-Waechter, were willing to slow down the naval program and tried to keep negotiations going even after Haldane left Berlin. But Tirpitz, who entirely dominated William II, was able to prevent any concession. The naval race between Germany and Great Britain was not stopped.

Since 1905 British policies had lost much of their flexibility, and they gave the Germans some reason to distrust British intentions. After the agreement with France in 1904, Britain concluded an agreement with Russia in 1907. Like the Entente Cordiale this concerned colonial questions and settled the most urgent imperialist disputes between the two countries. Persia was divided: the north fell into the Russian sphere of influence, the south into the British sphere, and a neutral zone remained in the middle. Moreover, in the Agadir crisis Britain had not only given diplomatic support to France but agreed to military discussions, which resulted in an understanding between the French and British general staffs that in case of war a British expeditionary force would be sent to France; plans were made concerning transportation, troop-concentration areas, and command organization. While these arrangements did not constitute a definite military alliance and the political commitments between Great Britain and France did not go beyond close consultation, it was clear that the position of the European powers had become more rigid. Triple Entente as the some-

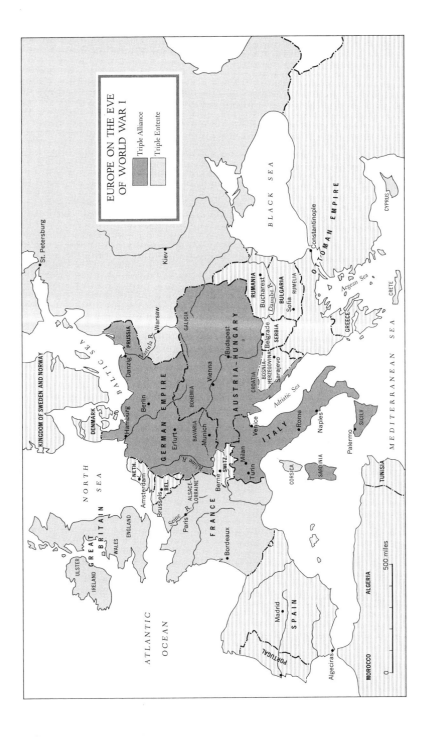

EUROPE ON THE EVE
OF WORLD WAR I

Triple Alliance
Triple Entente

ATLANTIC OCEAN

NORTH SEA

BALTIC SEA

KINGDOM OF SWEDEN AND NORWAY

St. Petersburg

Kiev

Vistula R.

Warsaw

PRUSSIA

Danzig

GERMAN EMPIRE

Berlin

Hamburg

DENMARK

NETH.

Amsterdam

BEL

Brussels

ALSACE-LORRAINE

Erfurt

BOHEMIA

BAVARIA

Munich

Rhine R.

SWITZ.

Berne

FRANCE

Seine R.

Paris

Bordeaux

GREAT BRITAIN

ULSTER

IRELAND

WALES

ENGLAND

GALICIA

Vienna

AUSTRIA-HUNGARY

Budapest

CROATIA

BOSNIA-HERZEGOVINA

Sarajevo

SERBIA

Belgrade

Venice

Adriatic Sea

ITALY

Milan

Turin

Genoa

Rome

Naples

Palermo

SICILY

SARDINIA

CORSICA

RUMANIA

Bucharest

Danube R.

BULGARIA

Sofia

RUMELIA

GREECE

Aegean Sea

CRETE

BLACK SEA

Constantinople

OTTOMAN EMPIRE

CYPRUS

MEDITERRANEAN SEA

SPAIN

Madrid

PORTUGAL

Algeciras

MOROCCO

ALGERIA

TUNISIA

500 miles

0

what loose combination of Great Britain, France, and Russia was called, confronted the Triple Alliance of Germany, Austria, and Italy.

War and Crisis in the Balkans

The possibility of avoiding war if tensions continued became increasingly less likely. After the Agadir crisis the focus of tension shifted to the East. From 1912 on the affairs of the Ottoman Empire and the national aspirations of the Balkan nations evoked one crisis after the other. The prelude was the war which began in September, 1911, between Turkey and Italy. All the great powers had recognized that Tripoli was in the ·Italian sphere of interest; when France finally absorbed Morocco, the Italian government decided to take action and proclaimed the annexation of Tripoli. Turkey answered with a declaration of war against Italy. The Italians won a quick victory, but in the meantime the Tripolitan War triggered action in the Balkans. Serbia and Bulgaria believed that if they did not take action before the end of Turkey's conflict with Italy, they might miss an opportunity for driving the Turks out of Europe. They succeeded in getting the support of Montenegro and Greece, and war against Turkey broke out in October, 1912. The Turkish troops in the Balkans were defeated in a number of battles in which the Bulgarian and Serbian soldiers proved themselves to be excellent warriors.

But a diplomatic settlement was much more difficult to achieve than military victory. There was dissension among the victors about the drawing of the frontiers after the war had assured the end of Turkish rule in Europe. The two areas about which disposition had to be made were Macedonia and Albania.

Bulgaria, Greece, and Serbia all demanded parts of Macedonia, and the claims of Greece and Bulgaria were particularly irreconcilable because both were anxious to control the northern coast of the Aegean Sea. The result was a second Balkan War, in which Greece, Serbia, Rumania, and Turkey rallied against Bulgaria. The outcome of this war determined that only a very small part of Macedonia fell to Bulgaria. Most of it was divided between Serbia and Greece, and the Turks regained Adrianople. The division of Macedonia among three powers remained a cause for tension and conflict among them almost until the end of the Second World War.

The Serbs were less successful in their demand for Albanian territory which would give them a direct access to the Adriatic Sea. The great powers, meeting with the Balkan nations and Turkey in London, forced Serbia and Montenegro to accept the creation of an independent Albania. Serbia remained cut off from the Adriatic.

In the meetings in London, Russia had backed the claims of Serbia whereas Austria-Hungary advocated those of Bulgaria, and together with Italy, sharply opposed the Serbian demand for access to the Adriatic Sea. To underline the seriousness with which they looked upon the situation, both—Russia and Austria-Hungary—made some military preparations. Great Britain and Germany cooperated to obtain a peaceful solution of the conflict. Nevertheless, the Balkan wars accumulated new explosive material which the compromise worked out by the great powers in London concealed rather than eliminated. Turkey, in need of military reorganization, called in a German general, Otto Liman von Sanders, but this move evoked violent Russian protests because it appeared to be a further step in the establishment of German control over Turkey. Both Russia and Austria indicated that in the negotiations about the final settlement of the Balkan wars they should have received stronger support from their respective friends, Great Britain and Germany. Consequently, in both Britain and Germany the government leaders felt that their alliances might be endangered if in the next emergency they did not give stronger support to their allies. But the most dangerous consequence of the Balkan wars was that all the resentment of Serbian nationalism was now focused on the Habsburg monarchy. The Serbs had considered the Austrian annexation of Bosnia and Herzegovina in 1908 as a blow to Serbia's aspirations to become the home of all South Slavs. Now in 1913, Austria-Hungary had again been the chief obstacle to Serbia's ambitions and had deprived it of the fruits of victory: access to the Adriatic Sea. To the nationalistic Serbs the Habsburg monarchy was an old evil monster which prevented their nation from becoming a great and powerful state. On June 28, 1914,

A German military maneuver in 1913. *Note the use of cavalry which proved almost useless in the real war.*

a young Serbian nationalist, Gavrilo Princip, assassinated the heir of the Habsburg monarchy, the Archduke Francis Ferdinand, and his wife at Sarajevo.

THE OUTBREAK OF THE FIRST WORLD WAR

The events of the five weeks between the assassination of the Archduke Francis Ferdinand and the outbreak of the First World War have been more carefully investigated than almost any others in world history. An endless number of books and articles have reviewed and probed all aspects of the question of responsibility for the outbreak of the war: whether the Serbian government had knowledge of the plans for the assassination of the archduke; whether Germany encouraged Austria-Hungary to take action against Serbia and deliberately instigated a general war in 1914; whether France believed this crisis would be a favorable opportunity for starting a war in order to regain Alsace-Lorraine, and therefore stiffened the attitude of its Russian ally; whether military requirements restricted and eliminated the freedom of decision of the political leaders; and whether British policy was mistaken in not taking a clear stand.

Most of the facts bearing on these questions have been clarified. The responsible leaders of the Serbian government did not know about the plans for the attempt on the life of the archduke. On the other hand, the assassination was the work not of an individual, but of a group of Bosnian and Serbian nationalists who were encouraged and promoted by a Serbian secret society, the Black Hand, in which the chief of the intelligence department of the Serbian general staff was a leading figure. However, when in an ultimatum of July 23, 1914 the Austrian government accused Serbian government officials of being involved in the plot, it had no proof, based its accusation on falsified documents, and did not mention the Black Hand, specifying only individuals and organizations that in truth had nothing to do with the assassination. Thus, the assassination was consciously used by the Austrian government for the purposes of power politics: to remove the threat which Serbia represented to the existence of the Habsburg monarchy. Further proof that this was Austria's intention is the fact that although the Serbian government accepted almost all the demands of the exceedingly harsh and humiliating ultimatum, the Austrian minister in Belgrade, acting on instructions given to him before he had received the Serbian note, declared the Serbian answer unsatisfactory and left Belgrade, making war between the two states inevitable.

However, without the certainty of German backing, the Austrian leaders would not have embarked on the war against Serbia. Actually, Austrian governmental circles were divided in their views on the course to follow; influential men, notably the Hungarian prime minister, Tisza, were opposed

The Murder at Sarajevo. *Archduke Francis Ferdinand on his visit to Bosnia a few hours before his assassination. Right. The police seizing the assassin, Princip.*

to any action which might lead to war. However, the German government urged the Austrians to resolute action against Serbia, and Tisza's hesitations were overcome when he was given proof that Germany desired Austria to proceed against Serbia and had promised support if other powers became involved in the conflict.

The Germans encouraged Austria because they regarded the death of the heir of the Habsburg throne as a danger signal foreshadowing a possible collapse of the Habsburg monarchy, which would leave Germany without allies. The Germans hoped that a successful show of strength against Serbia might revitalize the Habsburg monarchy. Since the assassination of the archduke and his wife had aroused general indignation and widespread sympathy for the Austrian emperor, there seemed to be a chance that the war between Austria and Serbia might remain localized. However, from the outset the Germans were aware that the Austrian action against Serbia ran the risk of a general war in which Russia, France, and Great Britain might be allied against Germany and Austria, and the justifiable indictment against the German leaders might be made that they willingly accepted this risk. Their attitude was the result of a variety of circumstances. A predominant part of the German ruling group was obsessed by the idea that the future belonged to the great world powers and that Germany would become a world power only through a war which would show it to be equal to the strongest and which would gain for the German people and for German economic expansion a broader territorial basis than it possessed. And if war were long delayed, Germany's chances for ascending to the small circle of world powers might be missed forever. Once Russia, with its large population and great mineral resources, became fully developed, it would tower over all its neighbors and Germany's opportunities for development would disappear. From a purely military point of view, too, time seemed to be running against Germany. In a few years Russia's recovery from losses and defeat and France's three-year conscription law would tilt the military balance against Germany. Historical speculations, economic expansionism, military calculations reinforced one another to create a climate in which war became acceptable. Such considerations guidèd the policy of the German government. Chancellor Bethmann-Hollweg was an earnest and responsible man inclined to pessimism and he was aware that the consequences of a world war were unforeseeable. Yet he encouraged Austria to take action and he gave the Austrian statesmen a free hand, fully conscious of the risk that a great European conflict might result. Bethmann-Hollweg was not simply bowing to the demands of the military who carried such a powerful weight in imperial Germany; he was himself among those who saw the growing Russian power as a threat to Germany's future, and he had an almost fatalistic belief that a world war was coming. In 1914 Germany's chances would be better than in later years. In the last critical days, when the prophesied world war threatened to become reality, Bethmann-Hollweg seems to have become frightened by his own courage and he made some desperate attempts to keep the conflict between Austria and Serbia localized, but in his heart he must have been aware that these efforts were condemned to failure.

If for no other reason, these last attempts could not succeed because the Austrians had wasted in an almost incredible manner the sympathy which the assassination had aroused. They sent their ultimatum to Serbia only on July 23—after more than three weeks—when the excitement about the murder of the archduke had begun to die down. The reason for the delay was Austrian dilatoriness (*Schlamperei*), although they rationalized these delays by maintaining that the harvest in Hungary had to be gathered in before they could call the men to arms. In the end, there was a further postponement of three days because the French president, Poincaré, was visiting the tsar and the Austrians did not want to present the ultimatum until Poincaré had left Russia, so that the Russian and French governments would not be able to agree immediately upon joint action.

Poincaré and the French prime minister, Viviani, were in St. Petersburg from July 20 to July 23, 1914. It is not known what they said in private to their Russian hosts about the course which ought to be pursued in the approaching crisis between Austria-Hungary and Serbia. The emphasis which in their public declarations the French and Russian statesmen placed on the close bonds uniting the Russian empire and the French republic must have strengthened the Russian will to oppose the Austrian action. And in the following critical week the French ambassador in Russia, Maurice

Nicholas II and Raymond Poincaré, the president of the French republic, in St. Petersburg on July 23, 1914.

Paléologue (1859–1944), certainly encouraged the Russian government to take a firm line. The Russians were in a better military position than they had been in 1908; their army had been built up and transport had been improved by the development of the railroad system in western Russia. Unquestionably, the Russian rulers, under the pressure of an excited public and of military men eager to avenge the defeat of 1905, felt unable to accept another diplomatic setback, and decided to prevent Austria from encroaching upon Serbian integrity and sovereignty. When, on July 24, they were informed of the contents of the Austrian ultimatum, they decided that if Austria took action against Serbia, they would institute partial mobilization —which meant mobilization of the military districts close to the Austrian border. But on July 30, after Austria had rejected the Serbian answers, had declared war against Serbia, and had mobilized part of its forces, the Russian government persuaded the tsar to declare general mobilization. The reasons for this change of plan were in part technical; the Russian general staff believed that, after a partial mobilization was under way, it would be difficult and slow to organize a general mobilization. It also seems clear, however, that this step must have been necessitated by Russian-French military agreements. The Russians and the French had some general knowledge of the German war plans. They were aware that at the outset most of the German military forces would be concentrated against France and that the possibility of successful French resistance depended on a quick advance of Russian troops into Germany.

After the Russians had ordered a general mobilization on July 30, the military timetables which the various general staffs had worked out began to dominate political action. The Russian mobilization impelled the German military leaders to demand immediate mobilization and to urge full mobilization on Austria. According to the military plans agreed upon by the German and Austrian chiefs of staff, the Austrian armies were to slow down the Russian advances toward Germany while the bulk of the German army, engaged in the attempt to knock France out of the war, would be unable to protect Germany's eastern frontier. With the Russians mobilizing, Austrian general mobilization, which would make possible quick counteraction, was required; but it was also necessary that the German campaign against France be started immediately and ended in time for German troops to be moved from the west to the east before the Austrian resistance against the superior Russian forces broke down. Thus, the German military leaders were anxious to terminate all further diplomatic negotiations so that they could invade France. Neither the monarchs of the three empires— Francis Joseph, Nicholas II, and William II—nor their chief civilian advisers had the courage to resist the military leaders who declared that without mobilization their campaign plans would be ruined and the existence of their nations would be endangered. Germany sent an ultimatum to Russia demanding immediate cessation of military preparations, and when no satisfactory answer had been received, declared war on Russia, on August 1. This move was followed on August 3 by a declaration of war against France, which the Germans justified with the palpably false statement that French forces had violated the German frontier.

The irrevocability of the military timetables condemned to failure the last-minute attempts of Sir Edward Grey, the British foreign secretary, to halt mobilization and convoke a conference. British diplomacy had worked hard to save the peace, but the question has been raised of whether it followed the right tactics. Could peace have been maintained if at an early state of the crisis Grey had declared that Great Britain would back France and Russia in case of war? An early British commitment might have gained time for a conference. Austria might have hesitated to take action against Serbia; and Russia, secure in the promise of British help, might have been less anxious to order general mobilization. Those who defend Grey's attitude argue that an assurance of British support might have had the contrary effect of encouraging Russia and France to assume an aggressive attitude. Moreover, Grey's defenders question whether a British declaration would have deterred Germany from its course, because the Germans did expect Britain to enter the war but not soon enough to save France from defeat.

Moreover, Grey might have hesitated to make any definite statement on what Britain would do in case of war because he could not be sure whether the British people would follow his lead. British public opinion was split on the issue. Decision was brought about only by the German invasion of Belgium on August 3. Belgium's neutrality had been guaranteed by an international treaty to which Germany was a party, and this violation of international law by Germany convinced both the British government and the British people of the necessity of entering the conflict. War was declared on August 4.

During the critical week before the German violation of Belgian neutrality, the Conservatives had favored the participation of Britain because of its ties with France and its interest in maintaining the balance of power. The Labor party opposed intervention. This view was shared by the radical wing of the Liberal party; thus the Liberals lacked any uniform policy on the issue. The Liberal government, like the Liberal party, was divided; even after the violation of Belgian neutrality two members of the government resigned to demonstrate their opposition to Britain's participation. In the debates and discussions on this issue Sir Edward Grey favored British entry into the war, but maintained that Britain had a free hand and was not obligated to support France and Russia. Formally, he was right, in that a binding political alliance had not been concluded. The agreements between the British and French general staff were purely military. Nevertheless, Grey's contention that Britain was free to choose its course was questionable. On the basis of the conversations between the two general staffs the French could expect the arrival of a British expeditionary force on French soil. No general staff would make such arrangements without informing its government and having its approval. In denying the existence of a commitment to France, Grey either was incredibly naïve about the possibility of separating political and military planning or was bending the truth in order to avoid arousing the resentment of the radicals in his party. The French ambassador in London, Paul Cambon, in demanding a British declaration of war against Germany, said that the British answer to this request would show whether "the word 'honor' will not have to be stricken out of the British vocabulary." Grey himself felt immensely relieved when, after the invasion of Belgium, the cabinet decided to enter the war. Waverers were won over by the argument that Britain's participation had now become a moral necessity.

The European Attitude Toward War in 1914

The First World War revealed the frightfulness of warfare in the industrial age. But the terrible losses in human life and material resources caused by the war have colored and distorted the interpretation of the events of July and August, 1914. The discussion of the origins of the First World War has been dominated by the question of guilt: historical research has been essentially an effort to determine the distribution of guilt among the individuals and nations involved. It should therefore be emphasized that in 1914 war was not considered to be a crime but was regarded as a legitimate though unpleasant and dangerous instrument of politics.

Certainly a few people did have some notion of the changes in warfare brought about by the enormously increased destructiveness of modern weapons. Courageous and farseeing individuals—such as Bertha von Suttner, author of the famous book *Lay Down Your Arms!* (1889)—had tried to arouse the public to the dangers of modern war by organizing pacifist movements. The destructiveness of war had also been underlined by the two International Peace Conferences held in The Hague in 1899 and 1907. But these conferences had been concerned with the limitation of armaments and with the humanizing of war rather than with its abolition. Up to 1914 no attempt had been made to prohibit war itself. Moreover, almost everyone was convinced that because the European economy had become a complex integrated structure, a war could last for only a few weeks or months and would be quickly decided in a few great battles. Nobody in 1914 was able to envisage the possibilities which would become stark reality in the next few years.

If government leaders hesitated to embark on the adventure of military conflict they were not deterred by fear of being stamped as criminals. Rather, after the experiences of the Franco-Prussian War and the Russo-Japanese War they saw lurking behind each war the danger of revolution. They were aware that they might unleash forces which the existing ruling group might be unable to control. The governments of the European nations had another equally weighty reason for refraining from obvious aggression. Their armies were based on conscription of the male population. It seemed difficult, if not impossible, to ask people to abandon civilian life and peaceful occupations when the necessity of war was not obvious. Separated by a deep rift from the bourgeois world, the workers were thought to be unwilling to accept war unless convinced that an attack had been made upon a peaceful country by external enemies.

Thus, in the summer of 1914, all the European governments were eager to appear as the innocent victims of aggression. In the course of the First World War this moralistic element, this insistence on the righteousness of one's own cause, grew steadily in emphasis; increasing hatred of the enemy bolstered internal strength. It helped stiffen the will to resist and minimized social and political friction. The war became a struggle of good against evil which had to be fought through until the enemy was completely destroyed.

The fear in government circles that the lower classes would resist mobilization had been primarily caused by the declaration of the Socialist Second International that the workers ought to respond to a call to arms with a general strike. Actually none of the European socialist parties heeded the recommendation of the Second International. Each of them backed the war policy of its government. Not only did opposition fail to materialize, the outbreak of war was greeted with an almost delirious enthusiasm. This astonishing response points to causes of war which went deeper than the calculations and miscalculations of foreign ministers and diplomats.

In most European countries the war seemed like a liberation from an unbearable situation. The feeling that political developments had reached a dead end was widespread among the ruling groups—not only in tsarist Russia and in Austria-Hungary, where the governments were involved in a desperate struggle to maintain outmoded forms of rule, but all over Europe. In Great Britain the reforms of the Liberal government did not mitigate social tensions; labor conflicts and strikes had been particularly vehement in the years immediately before the outbreak of the war. And although an attempt to solve the Irish question could no longer be postponed it endangered the authority of the government. In France politics had again become polarized between right and left, which opposed each other with renewed vehemence. In Italy impatience with the government's cautious policy of industrialization and democratization had stirred up extreme antiparliamentary movements on the right and left. And in Germany the elections to the Reichstag in 1912, from which the Social Democrats emerged as the strongest political party, had demonstrated that the masses could not be reconciled to their lack of political power by orderly administration and measures of social welfare.

The years before the First World War are usually regarded as having been full of sun and light in contrast to the darkness which descended on Europe in 1914. But actually the unrest in the years immediately preceding the outbreak of the war was great. This does not mean that the conflict was unavoidable. The war which began in 1914 was not an imperialist war in the sense that the economic interests of the various European nations were bound to clash; the economic expansion over the entire globe had increased both competition and cooperation among the financial and industrial companies of the various countries; in general, businessmen were no advocates of war. Also, despite strikes and violence, the possibility of an immediate revolution did not threaten the governments of those European states with enough reliable military and police forces to keep order—these included Great Britain, Germany, and France. Therefore, these nations did not need to take recourse to war to stave off their overthrow. But industrialization had created and was creating problems which steadily mounted, and which no form of government—neither authoritarianism nor parliamentarianism—seemed to be able to solve. There originated a longing for a turn of events which would make all these intractable problems disappear. To some politicians, weary of seeing their nation divided into hostile camps, war seemed to promise the restoration of a common purpose.

In the view of the German sociologist Max Weber rational organization and bureaucratization, which made man a cog in the wheel of a disciplined mass society, was the unavoidable future faced by the modern industrial world; to the people of the middle classes, immured in what was still a rather new phenomenon, the war came as an opportunity to break out of the monotonous uniformity of industrial society. The workers were in an ambiguous situation; they, or at least many of them, were gaining a greater share in a society from which they were alienated. But the revolution which was to make them the masters of the social order seemed far removed, certainly more distant than when the socialist parties had been founded.

In the minds of almost all classes the discontent with the existing social order made the war, with its sudden release from the bonds of daily routine and with its forging of new ties, the harbinger of a highly desirable new social order. Behind the obvious shock and fear there were also hope and expectation—this should not be forgotten in explaining the causes of the catastrophe which resulted in 37.5 million casualties, in the annihilation of nearly an entire male generation, and in the loss of European hegemony over the world.

CHAPTER 5

The First World War

THE NATURE OF TOTAL WAR

As TIME has passed since the days of August, 1914, it has become increasingly clear that the outbreak of the First World War meant the end of an age. To be sure, if we consider carefully the developments of the decades preceding the war we can distinguish trends and tendencies which were steering European politics and social life into new waters. But the First World War reinforced these trends and thus accelerated the tempo of change.

It would be a mistake to assume that the new era began only in 1918, with the end of hostilities. The First World War was not just a violent interlude separating the old era from the new. The new age came about during the war years, and what happened between 1914 and 1918 helps to make the period that followed comprehensible.

Most immediately apparent were the changes effected by the conflict itself, by innovations in the techniques and the conduct of the war. When the European powers mobilized in the radiant late-summer days of 1914, the troops marching through the streets to the railroad stations, accompanied by jubilant crowds, offered an impressive and colorful sight. Flowers were strewn before the men who were expected to return triumphant after a few weeks. Flags flew; bands played; and the soldiers went singing into the war. In the first months military action was conducted in a traditional manner. Extended columns of infantry marched along the roads. The cavalry scouted enemy positions; officers led their men to storm a town or village. But after the initial battles in the west the lines became weirdly silent. Soldiers dug themselves into deep trenches fortified by barbed wire; a no-man's-land between the opposing positions was illuminated at night by rockets, intended to reveal any enemy patrols trying to penetrate the lines. The graceful, elegant horses of the cavalry became superfluous. Reconnaissance was most efficient from the air, and sometimes these scouting planes armed with machine guns engaged in air battles. Pilots became the popular war heroes. The infantry soldier, clad in mud-colored gray or khaki, still had his rifle and bayonet but his most valuable weapons were the hand grenade and the machine gun. Before the war was over poison gas was being directed against enemy lines, and tanks moved clumsily over fields and trenches.

The changes in sea warfare were no less considerable. With one exception—the indecisive meeting of the British and German fleets at Jutland (1916)—no naval battles took place. Warships were used to protect convoys against the attacks of submarines, which became the supreme weapon in the struggle for control of the seas.

These changes indicate that in the twentieth century war was becoming more than the struggle of armed forces: not without reason does the term "total war" appear. To maintain a flow of the weapons which had become decisive, the continuous functioning of a sophisticated industrial complex was required. When the war broke out, only a very few had an inkling of the importance of a steady supply of raw materials and manpower, and it took some time for political and military leaders to be convinced of this fact.

The Home Front

In the question of manpower the crucial problem was to reconcile military and industrial needs. Miners and steelworkers might be perfectly suited for military service, but they possessed the skills and the physical abilities needed in mines and industry. Priorities had to be established. As the war dragged on and casualties became heavy, the tapping of new sources

War enthusiasm in 1914. *Young men, volunteering for military service, marching on "Unter den Linden," Berlin's main street.*

of manpower became a constant concern of the governments. The age limits for military service were extended; and women were employed in jobs previously reserved for men, working in offices and factories, as streetcar conductors and farmhands.

Every industry not immediately serving military ends had to be reduced to a minimum. One reason was the need for conserving manpower; another, the scarcity of raw materials. Before the conflict no European country had been self-sufficient. France, which had been less dependent on imports than other European powers, soon lost this advantageous position because a great part of its most industrialized regions was occupied by the Germans. International trade, through which raw materials had been obtained in peacetime, was interrupted by military action. Moreover, the importation of raw materials represented a drain on the gold reserves of each country because the manufacture of the exports which had brought in foreign currency was no longer possible. Strict control over raw materials—their conservation, collection, and distribution to factories according to military needs—became necessary.

Maintenance of the supply of food was the most burning problem, not only in great industrial countries like Great Britain and Germany which, in peacetime, had relied on imported wheat and other foodstuffs, but also in agrarian countries like Austria and France, where conscription denuded the land of agricultural workers. Moreover, the transportation of food to the urban centers was difficult because the railroads were overtaxed by military needs. All the governments resorted to rationing, which usually began with bread and meat, then extended to other foodstuffs, and finally included clothes, soap, and so on. Thus, manpower, raw materials, consumer goods, all were placed under government control.

Ministries for directing economic activities were established. Strikes were outlawed, working hours prolonged. Scarcity of goods drove prices upwards and price regulations became necessary in order to avoid a sharpening of the conflict between rich and poor with damaging consequences for civilian morale. Price regulations, however, were acceptable to employers only if they were supplemented by wage controls. In the planning and executing of such measures, governments sought the support of industrialists and trade union leaders, since their consent was necessary in carrying out these measures. Governments became deeply involved in the functioning of economic life in all its aspects. Certainly government intervention in economic affairs and government regulation of economic life were more thorough in some countries than in others—more complete in Germany and Great Britain than in Austria-Hungary, Russia, and Italy, with their ineffective bureaucracies. Nevertheless, the subjection of economic activities to government regulation all over Europe represented a radical break with the notion that the economy could function only when free from government intervention. Unquestionably, rationing and govern-

Because of the manpower shortage on the home front, women were employed in a gun factory.

ment regulations were the only possible means of assuring the existence of all the people. Even so, on the Continent, particularly in Russia, Austria, and Germany, these measures provided hardly a subsistence minimum; people were hungry and easily exhausted, and "black markets," from which the wealthy added to their rations, resulted in a spread of corruption and a decline in morale.

No longer confined to the battlefield, war became total as belligerent activities affected the entire life of the nation. To be sure, airplane construction was not yet advanced enough to permit mass bombing. A few raids by airplanes over enemy cities and a few flights of the big German airship, the Zeppelin, over the English east coast and London were more effective in inspiring terror than in inflicting serious damage. But they were signs of the form of wars to come.

The chief instrument used to throttle the economic life of the enemy was the blockade. The British controlled the North Sea and prevented Germany from receiving supplies from the other side of the Atlantic. The Germans suddenly recognized that their strongest weapon in sea warfare was the submarine and they declared the entire British Isles to be blockaded territory and claimed the right to search and sink all ships approaching British ports.

In the First World War the activities and the morale of the civilian population acquired crucial importance. There now existed not only a military front but also a home front. And to maintain the spirit of the home front became essential. In all countries censorship was used, both to prevent the spreading of news which might be helpful to the enemy and to control and direct all news media toward the strengthening of civilian morale. It was as a consequence of the First World War that "propaganda" came to be a pejorative term: all governments installed propaganda offices and all of them falsified news. One of the chief duties of the war propagandists was to discredit the enemy, to paint him in the darkest colors, so that the populace would become convinced that defeat would mean the destruction of all that was worth living for. The practice of viewing the war as a struggle against evil increased steadily. Anti-German propaganda was particularly effective because the conduct of the Germans provided a factual basis for reports of their atrocities. The brutal behavior of the German armies in Belgium was undeniable. Because they had expected to pass through unmolested, the Belgian resistance infuriated them. The suddenness of the German invasion made it impossible for the Belgians to mobilize and many fought in civilian clothes, identified as soldiers only by armbands. This practice was accepted in international law, but the Germans considered all those fighting out of uniform as *franc-tireurs*, to be shot when captured. The impression that the entire civilian population of Belgium was resisting made the Germans jittery; they took hostages and executed them when they found opposition. In the last week of August the London *Times* called the Germans "Huns," in reference to events in Louvain. There, in the belief that sniping had occurred and that Louvain was full of *franc-tireurs*, the Germans shot a large number of citizens and set the town on fire. The famous old library of the university was entirely destroyed. The "vandalism of Louvain" was soon aggravated by the "crime of Rheims." In September, 1914, the Germans, convinced that the tower of the cathedral of Rheims served as a French observation post, fired on the cathedral, severely damaging the roof and the nave. Even if the tower was being used, the destruction wrought on a great monument of European art was indefensible. The Germans provided further food for propaganda against them by their ruthless occupation policy in Belgium. They executed Edith Cavell, a nurse who had helped British and French soldiers to escape over the borders into the neutral Netherlands, ignoring the fact—recognized by some of their own occupation officers—that as head of a hospital she had selflessly worked to mitigate the sufferings of soldiers of all nations, and deserved mercy rather than justice. Another incident, called by President Wilson "one of the most distressing and I think one of the most unjustifiable incidents of the present war," was the deportation of more than 100,000 Belgian workers into Germany.

The War Aims

Nurtured by propaganda and publicly proclaimed by all governments, was the notion that the enemy was evil and that his defeat would create the foundation for a better world. This ideological and moralistic view made impossible a negotiated peace aimed at reestablishing a balance of power and restoring international collaboration. Each side was convinced that the war could end only with the complete defeat of the enemy, so that an entirely new world could be created. Each therefore attempted to present its war aims in generalized idealistic terms showing that victory would serve the interest of all mankind. Formulation of such war aims was relatively easy for Great Britain, France, and their allies in the last two years of the conflict. The war was declared to be a struggle for a new world order based on the principles of democracy and national self-determination, its purpose succinctly summarized in the famous slogan "to make the world safe for democracy." As long as Russia with its authoritarian government, was a member of the coalition against Germany, the assertion about fighting for democracy had a hollow sound. But after the overthrow of the tsar in March, 1917, the notion of a struggle between democracy and authoritarianism gained meaning, particularly since the overthrow coincided with the entrance into the war against Germany of the greatest democracy in the world, the United States. The fact that men and women of all classes contributed to the military effort gave force to

War enthusiasm in Great Britain. *A famous enlistment poster.*

the demand that they should have the right to decide the political fate of their country. Where before the First World War the demand for suffrage for women had been regarded as utopian and even ridiculous, and the request for women's suffrage had inspired a movement of some strength only in Great Britain, now this demand became more urgent and its justification was much more generally recognized. In Great Britain, Germany, and the United States, female suffrage was achieved soon after the war. In Italy and France its adversaries were able to delay giving women the vote until after the Second World War. But even there the final victory of female suffrage was never seriously in doubt.

It was difficult for Germany and its allies to place the war on a broad ideological level. The German Social Democratic party had been the largest and best organized of all socialist parties. Socialist approval of the money bills required for the financing of the war was the most striking and also the most surprising example of the abandonment of revolutionary internationalism by Social Democrats in favor of defense of the homeland. The German government gained the support of socialist and progressive forces without taking them into the government. Thus, during most of the war Germany continued to be ruled by the members of the conservative bureaucracy. Their innate resistance to liberal and democratic reforms was reinforced by the military, whose power now increased immensely. William II, who even in peacetime had failed to exercise steady leadership, did not dare to challenge the men of the hour. Thus the German military leaders Paul von Hindenburg (1847–1934) and Erich Ludendorff (1865–1937) began to exert—if not in form, at least in fact—a military dictatorship. As allies of the Conservatives they resisted political reforms, and the tensions which had existed in peacetime reemerged during the last two years of the war, expressing themselves in a bitter struggle about war aims. In the early weeks of the war, when the German advance in France appeared irreversible, industrialists and their Conservative allies insisted that the results of the war must be acquisition of a secure foundation for German world hegemony. Germany ought to keep Belgium and the valuable French steel and coal mines of the Longwy-Briey Basins. Later in the war, when the Germans occupied broad territorial stretches in the east, demands arose to annex these agricultural areas so that the German food supply would be secured for all time. Until almost the final months of the war, leaders of heavy industry and Conservatives supported by the military under Ludendorff asserted the need to fight for total victory so that Germany could attain these expansionist goals. When a quick victory proved elusive, however, those who opposed such war aims—whether they considered them unrealistic or immoral—began to raise their voices. Annexationists were confronted by those who believed that peace ought to be concluded on the basis of the status quo and that every effort should be made to reach a peace of understanding. Thus, in Germany from the second year of the war on the united front which had been established in August, 1914, began to show fissures, which became deeper month by month.

THE TIDES OF BATTLE

The Expanding Theater of War

The conflict that took place between 1914 and 1918 is rightly called a world war, for it assumed global dimensions. At the start, however, it was confined to the great European powers: Great Britain, France, Russia, Germany, and Austria-Hungary. Only two of the smaller European states participated from the outset in this struggle of the great powers: Serbia, whose conflict with Austria had led to the explosion; and Belgium, which had been forced to resist by the German violation of its internationally guaranteed neutrality. The first non-European power, Japan, entered the war in August. But its military contribution was limited to the conquest and occupation of the German colonial possessions in the Far East. A real enlargement of the theater of war took place with the entry of Turkey on the German side in November, 1914. Turkey occupied a key position. By allying itself with the western powers and Russia, it could have closed the ring around the Central Powers—as Austria and Germany were called—and ensured coordinated action against them from the west, east, and south. On the other hand, as an ally of Germany and Austria, Turkey could prevent the shipping of supplies to Russia through the Mediterranean and the Black Sea. Hence, a fierce diplomatic struggle for the favors of Turkey took place in Constantinople, but the hold which Germany had developed over Turkey through the building of the Baghdad Railway, reinforced by the appearance of two German naval ships in the Dardanelles, proved to be the stronger. The entry of Turkey extended the war into Mesopotamia and Persia, where British and Russian forces on the one hand and Turkish troops under German command on the other fought with alternating success. In order to relieve the pressure on Turkey, Germany and Austria became anxious to establish direct communication with the Ottoman Empire. Promising the cession of large parts of Macedonia, now in Serbian hands, they persuaded Bulgaria to enter the war in October, 1915. In counteraction, the Allies—France, Great Britain, and Russia—induced Rumania in August, 1916, and then Greece in June, 1917, to declare war on the Central Powers, although by that time Serbia had succumbed to the joint attacks from the west and the north, so that the Central Powers dominated a broad connected stretch of territory from the North Sea to

The German Military High Command. *Hindenburg, William II, Ludendorff.*

Mesopotamia and the Suez Canal. However, in 1915 the Allies had gained an important partner in Italy. Originally the Italians had declared themselves to be neutral because in their view the Austrians had started the war and had not acted in self-defense, requiring Italian assistance under the Triple Alliance. The Italians were courted by both sides, but the Central Powers could not make any promises that outweighed Italy's interest in using this war for the liberation of people of Italian nationality living under Austrian rule. The Allies in a secret agreement concluded in London in April, 1915, promised Italy, in addition to the Austrian provinces inhabited by Italians, a wide expanse on the eastern side of the Adriatic Sea, including northern Albania; the Dodecanese in the Aegean Sea; and—if Turkey was partitioned—a part of Asia Minor. Later, even Portugal and San Marino entered the war; by 1917, with exception of the Scandinavian countries, the Netherlands, Switzerland, and Spain, all the European nations were engaged on one side or the other. With the entry of the United States in April, 1917, the war finally took on a global character. Then a number of Latin-American states, among them Brazil, declared war on Germany, and others, such as Bolivia, Peru, and Ecuador, severed relations with Germany. In Asia, China and Siam and in Africa, Liberia joined the coalition against the Central Powers. In many of these cases the reason for participation was purely economic. The rupture with Germany served to tighten loopholes in the blockade, to prevent the transference of German capital, and to permit the confiscation of German assets. In any event, the war had become global.

The small size of the area occupied by the Central Powers in comparison with the vast extent of the territory represented by their enemies might lead

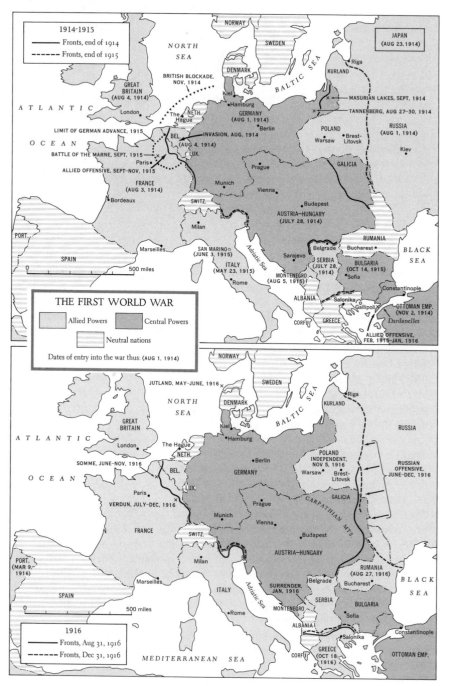

1914-1915
Fronts, end of 1914
Fronts, end of 1915

NORWAY

SWEDEN

JAPAN
(AUG 23, 1914)

NORTH
SEA

DENMARK

BALTIC SEA

Riga

KURLAND

BRITISH BLOCKADE,
NOV. 1914

GREAT
BRITAIN
(AUG 4, 1914)

MASURIAN LAKES, SEPT. 1914

TANNENBERG, AUG 27-30, 1914

ATLANTIC

London

Kiel

Hamburg

GERMANY
(AUG 1, 1914)

Berlin

POLAND

RUSSIA
(AUG 1, 1914)

The
Hague

NETH.

LIMIT OF GERMAN ADVANCE, 1915

OCEAN

BEL.
(AUG 4, 1914)

INVASION, AUG. 1914

Warsaw

Brest-
Litovsk

Kiev

BATTLE OF THE MARNE, SEPT., 1915

LUX.

ALLIED OFFENSIVE, SEPT-NOV, 1915

Paris

Prague

GALICIA

FRANCE
(AUG 3, 1914)

Munich

Vienna

Bordeaux

SWITZ.

Milan

Budapest

AUSTRIA-HUNGARY
(JULY 28, 1914)

PORT.

RUMANIA

BLACK
SEA

Marseilles

SAN MARINO
(JUNE 3, 1915)

Belgrade

Bucharest

SPAIN

Adriatic Sea

Sarajevo

SERBIA
(JULY 28,
1914)

BULGARIA
(OCT 14, 1915)

500 miles

ITALY
(MAY 23, 1915)

Rome

MONTENEGRO
(AUG 5, 1915)

Sofia

Constantinople

ALBANIA

Salonika

OTTOMAN EMP.
(NOV 2, 1914)

CORFU

GREECE

Gallipoli

Dardanelles

ALLIED OFFENSIVE,
FEB. 1915-JAN. 1916

THE FIRST WORLD WAR

Allied Powers   Central Powers

Neutral nations

Dates of entry into the war thus: (AUG 1, 1914)

NORWAY

JUTLAND, MAY-JUNE, 1916

SWEDEN

NORTH
SEA

DENMARK

BALTIC SEA

Riga

KURLAND

GREAT
BRITAIN

Kiel

RUSSIA

ATLANTIC

London

Hamburg

The Hague

NETH.

SOMME, JUNE-NOV, 1916

Berlin

POLAND
INDEPENDENT,
NOV 5, 1916

RUSSIAN
OFFENSIVE,
JUNE-DEC, 1916

OCEAN

BEL.

GERMANY

Warsaw

Brest-
Litovsk

LUX.

Paris

VERDUN, JULY-DEC, 1916

Prague

GALICIA

Munich

CARPATHIAN MTS

Vienna

FRANCE

SWITZ.

Budapest

PORT.
(MAR 9,
1916)

Milan

AUSTRIA-HUNGARY

BLACK
SEA

Marseilles

SURRENDER,
JAN, 1916

Belgrade

Bucharest

RUMANIA
(AUG 27, 1916)

SPAIN

Adriatic Sea

ITALY

SERBIA

BULGARIA

500 miles

Rome

MONTENEGRO

Sofia

ALBANIA

Constantinople

1916
Fronts, Aug 31, 1916
Fronts, Dec 31, 1916

CORFU

GREECE
(OCT 18,
1916)

Salonika

OTTOMAN EMP.

MEDITERRANEAN   SEA

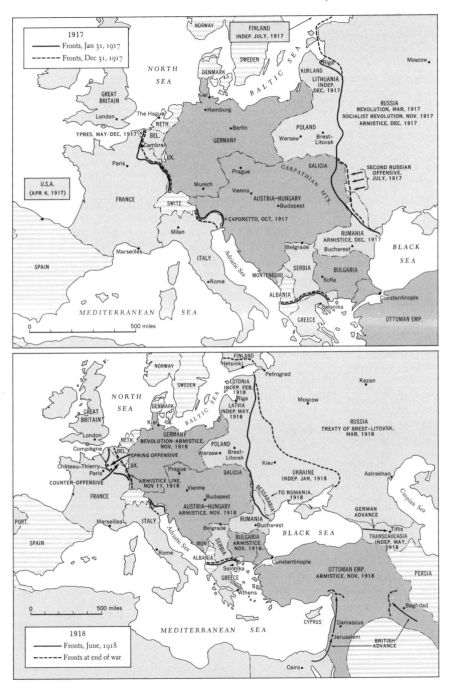

1917
— Fronts, Jan 31, 1917
- - - Fronts, Dec 31, 1917

NORWAY

FINLAND
INDEP. JULY, 1917

SWEDEN

NORTH SEA

DENMARK

BALTIC SEA

Riga

Moscow

KURLAND

LITHUANIA
INDEP.
DEC. 1917

RUSSIA
REVOLUTION, MAR, 1917
SOCIALIST REVOLUTION, NOV. 1917
ARMISTICE, DEC, 1917

GREAT BRITAIN

Kiel

•Hamburg

London

The Hague

NETH.

•Berlin

POLAND

Warsaw•

Brest-
Litovsk

YPRES, MAY-DEC, 1917✕

BEL.

Cambrai✕

GERMANY

Paris•

LUX.

Prague•

GALICIA

CARPATHIAN MTS.

SECOND RUSSIAN
OFFENSIVE,
JULY, 1917

U.S.A.
(APR 6, 1917)

FRANCE

SWITZ.

Munich•

Vienna•

AUSTRIA–HUNGARY
•Budapest

✕CAPORETTO, OCT. 1917

Milan•

RUMANIA
ARMISTICE, DEC, 1917

Marseilles•

ITALY

Adriatic Sea

Belgrade•

Bucharest•

BLACK SEA

SPAIN

•Rome

MONTENEGRO

SERBIA

BULGARIA

•Sofia

Constantinople

ALBANIA

Salonika•

MEDITERRANEAN SEA

GREECE

OTTOMAN EMP.

0 ⊢——————⊣ 500 miles

FINLAND

Helsinki•

Petrograd•

NORWAY

SWEDEN

ESTONIA
INDEP. FEB.
1918

Riga•

Kazan•

NORTH SEA

DENMARK

BALTIC SEA

LATVIA
INDEP. MAY,
1918

Moscow•

GREAT BRITAIN

Kiel•

GERMANY
REVOLUTION-ARMISTICE,
NOV., 1918

POLAND

RUSSIA
TREATY OF BREST-LITOVSK,
MAR. 1918

London•

NETH.

BEL.

Warsaw•

Brest-
Litovsk

Compiègne•

SPRING OFFENSIVE

LUX.

Château-Thierry•

Paris•

Prague•

Kiev•

UKRAINE
INDEP. JAN. 1918

Astrakhan•

COUNTER-OFFENSIVE

ARMISTICE LINE,
NOV 11, 1918

Vienna•

GALICIA

BESSARABIA

Caspian Sea

FRANCE

Budapest•

TO RUMANIA,
1918

GERMAN
ADVANCE

PORT.

AUSTRIA–HUNGARY
ARMISTICE, NOV. 1918

RUMANIA

Marseilles•

ITALY

Belgrade•

Bucharest•

BLACK SEA

•Tiflis

TRANSCAUCASIA
INDEP. MAY,
1918

SPAIN

Adriatic Sea

MONT.

SERBIA

BULGARIA
ARMISTICE,
NOV. 1918

•Rome

ALBANIA

Constantinople

PERSIA

Salonika•

GREECE

OTTOMAN EMP.
ARMISTICE, NOV. 1918

Athens•

CYPRUS

Baghdad•

Damascus•

MEDITERRANEAN SEA

Jerusalem•

BRITISH
ADVANCE

Cairo•

0 ⊢——————⊣ 500 miles

1918
— Fronts, June, 1918
- - - Fronts at end of war

one to believe that the defeat of the Central Powers was almost inevitable. But the actual fact is that many times Germany seemed near victory and the German collapse in 1918 was sudden and unexpected.

Stalemate in the West

When the war broke out, the German general staff planned to defeat France within six weeks and then to turn against Russia. A quick victory in the west was to be attained by concentrating almost all the German forces against France, most of them on the right wing, which was to advance in a great wheeling movement through Belgium and northern France and then turn south and finally east, trapping the French forces in a gigantic ring. The strategy used by Hannibal in his defeat of the Romans at Cannae was to be repeated on an immensely enlarged scale. This was the famous Schlieffen Plan, named after the German chief of staff who had conceived it about 1905. The plan failed; the German advances were halted in the Battle of the Marne, which takes its place as one of the decisive battles of history. There were many reasons for the failure. First, the Belgian resistance delayed the German advance. Also, the Germans had not counted on the appearance of a British expeditionary corps which, although thrown back in the battles of Mons and Le Cateau, seriously retarded their movement forward. Alexander von Kluck, the commander of the German First Army, operating on the extreme right, believed that the presence of the British forces made it impossible to include Paris in the wide encircling movement which had been envisaged. He ordered his troops to turn sharply to the south, leaving Paris at their right. And this gave the French their opportunity. Although forced to retreat throughout August, the French army had not disintegrated. The commander of the French forces, Joseph Joffre, was an adherent of the doctrine of continuous attack and had been less concerned with arranging a defensive position than with seizing an opportunity to attack. Kluck's move to the south made it possible for Joffre to attack the German flank and rear. A famous episode of the ensuing battle was that under orders from Gallieni, the commandant of Paris, the city's taxi drivers transported men directly from Paris to the front. On September 9, Kluck's army was ordered to retreat from the Marne to the Aisne. The German campaign plan had failed.

The German military command contributed to the defeat. It had watered down the original Schlieffen Plan; the right wing was weaker than it ought to have been. Moreover, the German army on the left had been engaged in a battle in Lorraine and could therefore spare no troops to reinforce the right wing at the decisive moment. Helmuth von Moltke, the German chief of staff, following the precepts of his uncle, the great strategist of the nineteenth century, gave his field commanders freedom of decision. But he followed this principle too literally and too slavishly. There was little leadership from above, nor was there much communication among the various German commanders. Thus, between the First German Army, operating on the extreme right, and the Second German Army, operating further left, a gap opened at the critical time when the French counterattack began. And Moltke, alarmed by the dangers which might result from French advances into this gap, ordered retreat.

Whatever responsibility for the outcome of the Battle of the Marne one assigns to the energy and courage of the French and British generals, or to the mistakes committed by the German military leaders, the entire Schlieffen Plan was probably not feasible; the distances involved in encircling the armed forces of an entire nation were too large to be covered by foot soldiers, at least with the speed and precision required for success. In the Second World War such gigantic encirclement maneuvers were frequently carried out with success but by then the armies were fully motorized, and communications more easily established and maintained.

The Battle of the Marne was followed by a race for the channel ports. Each side tried to regain freedom of movement by outflanking the other; but despite a bloody struggle along the seacoast in Flanders, neither was dislodged. The front now became stabilized: it began at the North Sea, in Flanders; then bulged out into France, with Germany retaining control of important French industrial areas; and then swung back to the Franco-German frontier along Alsace-Lorraine, ending at the Swiss border. The armies dug in. For the next four years, until the spring of 1918, the lines remained almost unchanged, although sporadic and bloody attempts were made to end the stalemate and break through the enemy's lines. In February, 1916, the Germans launched an attack on Verdun. This was intended to be a battle of attrition. The Germans wanted to draw the flower of the French army into this battle and destroy the morale of the French troops. But in June, when the battle was broken off, the German losses were hardly less great than the French and the German territorial gains were insignificant. In July, 1916, the French and the British attacked along the Somme; again, only small territorial gains had been made by November, when the battle at the Somme got stuck in the mud. The French and British attempted a breakthrough in the spring of 1917 by simultaneous attacks at two different points, Arras and along the Aisne; the general responsible for this offensive was the French commander in chief Nivelle. His main success was the conquering of the Chemin des Dames, a height in the center of the front line, but the losses were so terrible that mutiny broke out in the French army and General Henri Philippe Pétain (1856–1951), who was called in to replace Nivelle, decided on a purely defensive conduct of the war in the west. However the British commander, Douglas Haig, believed that Nivelle's offensive had failed because of tactical mistakes and that he, Haig could do better. Despite great doubts in the British cabinet, Haig ordered an offensive in Flanders, around Ypres, which began on July 31 and lasted until November. Again the territorial

The political and military leaders of Great Britain and France. *Haig, Joffre, Lloyd George are shown on the left. Foch, Haig, Clemenceau, and Weigand on the right.*

gains were small and the casualties staggering. The rain and mud of autumn slowed down every step so that the advancing troops offered easy targets. Passchendaele, as this battle is usually called, together "with the Somme and Verdun, will always rank as the most gigantic, tenacious, grim, futile and bloody fight ever waged in the history of war"[1]—an entirely useless slaughter. If any further proof was needed, Passchendaele showed that new weapons and new methods had to be introduced if the superiority of the defense over the offense was to be overcome.

German Success in the East

The failure at Verdun sufficiently proved to the Germans the futility of an offensive in the west. Those German military leaders who had believed since the failure in the Battle of the Marne that victory could be obtained only through defeat of Russia now gained the upper hand. The most influential and effective representatives of this view were Hindenburg and Ludendorff. They had acquired immense popularity in Germany because in August and September of 1914, in the battles of Tannenberg and the Masurian Lakes, they had defeated and annihilated two Russian armies advancing into East Prussia. Hindenburg's and Ludendorff's responsibility for these victories is somewhat diminished by the fact that they arrived— Hindenburg from retirement, Ludendorff from the west—when the German commanders on the spot had already made the arrangements for the battles. Nevertheless, Hindenburg and Ludendorff, as saviors of Germany

[1] David Lloyd George, *War Memoirs*, Vol. IV (London, 1934), p. 2110.

from the Russian barbarians, became popular heroes. In September, 1914, Hindenburg was made commander in chief of the German armies in the east and in 1916 he became chief of staff, with Ludendorff as his main assistant. The German conduct of the war in the east was brilliant. In 1915 a great offensive was started in Galicia, which the Russians had occupied, and soon the operations extended over the entire eastern frontier; by the time military activity halted in the fall the lines reached from the eastern part of Galicia straight to the north, with the Central Powers having conquered Poland, Lithuania, and Kurland.

These German victories were facilitated by the Russians' lack of munitions and equipment. At the beginning of 1915 the British had made an ingenious attempt to open a direct route to Russia through the Dardanelles. This operation—the Gallipoli campaign—failed mainly through lack of cooperation between the naval and the land forces. Thus, materials could be sent to the Russians only through Siberia; the Russians were forced to rely on their own resources for the 1916 summer campaign, which became the last military enterprise of tsarist Russia.

1917 : THE TURNING POINT OF THE WAR

From the end of 1915 on, the war assumed a new face. The expectation that it would end quickly had faded, and the patriotic fervor, with which news about the progress of military events had been greeted in all countries at the outset, was replaced by a questioning sobriety; heavy casualties and economic hardships had brought the reality of war into almost every home.

Living conditions of the civilian population in Germany plunged to their nadir in the winter of 1916–1917. There was a scarcity of coal and hence little heat. Rations of meat and butter were exiguous. In the memories of those who lived through those months, the winter was recalled as the turnip time, since this was the one abundantly available food. Turnips were publicly praised as an excellent substitute for potatoes, vegetables, and almost any kind of victual. The shock of this winter led to better planning in the following war winters, so that even if the situation did not fundamentally change, it appeared less desperate. In Austria lack of food in the big urban centers, primarily Vienna, was caused by inadequate transportation, since the railroads were needed to transfer troops from one theater of war to another. It was compounded by the unwillingness of Hungarian landowners and peasants to sell their products in Austria at low, controlled prices.

In almost all countries, radical groups were gaining in strength within the socialist parties. These groups opposed the support which the socialists were giving the war efforts of the governments. In Austria an event occurred which exemplified this phenomenon: On October 21, 1916, the Austrian prime minister, Count Stürgkh, was assassinated by Friedrich

Adler, son of the leader of the Austrian Social Democrats. Adler considered this deed a protest against the continuation of the war and against his father's leadership of the Socialist party which supported the war policy of the government. There is no doubt that Friedrich Adler was giving expression to a widespread feeling of war weariness. When Emperor Francis Joseph died in November, 1916, his successor, Emperor Charles, tried to negotiate a peace. His attempts were unsuccessful because Austria could not escape the encircling clasp of the German armies. But Austria became a less and less willing ally of Germany.

In England and France, shortages, although very noticeable, contributed less to a rising wave of discontent than the lack of military success, particularly the failure in the Battle of the Somme. In France this debacle, together with the heavy sacrifices in manpower during the defense of Verdun, produced a defeatist mood which expressed itself in local mutinies; a change in the high command, making Pétain commander in chief, sufficed to reestablish discipline, but political dissatisfaction continued to grow, until finally, in November, 1917, Clemenceau became prime minister—an appointment which meant, as was generally recognized, ruthless organization of all possible resources for complete victory.

Trench warfare. *This was taken during the Battle of the Somme, 1916.*

Before wireless communication had come into full use, communication on widely extended fronts was difficult; the French still used carrier pigeons in World War I.

In Great Britain the bad news about the Battle of the Somme had come after other disappointing reports: the Easter Rebellion in Ireland and the indecisive clash with the German high-seas fleet in the Battle of Jutland. These difficulties and failures were increasingly ascribed to the dilatoriness of the government in introducing conscription; its unwillingness to impose stringent, economic measures; and to Prime Minister Asquith's incapacity to accelerate production of weapons and munitions, and in general to mobilize the empire. In December, 1916, Asquith was replaced as prime minister by Lloyd George; like the appointment of Clemenceau in France ten months later, this meant that the war would be carried through to final victory. It also indicated that it had been realized in England too that the views about the nature of war, which had been heard in prewar days, had been erroneous, modern war was totalitarian and demanded extreme measures and efforts.

THE REVOLUTION IN RUSSIA

Developments in Russia were different from those in England. In Russia, too, the view began to develop that a successful outcome of war required measures which went beyond the purely military sphere, that the entire civilian life had to be organized and directed according to the needs of the war. But in Russia these demands for a new, more energetic leadership resulted in what was to become the most crucial and most important event of the First World War: the overthrow of tsarism and the Bolshevik conquest of power. The Somme offensive in the summer of 1916 formed part of a great strategic plan to subject Germany to allied attacks from all sides, west and east. The Russians took their share by attacking the southern section of the Austrian-German lines and succeeded in reaching the heights of the Carpathian Mountains. But there they were halted and forced to retreat—partly because of immense losses in manpower, and partly because of a breakdown in the transportation of supplies. Moreover, in this campaign, as in previous campaigns during the war, the Russians lacked ammunition. The failure of this offensive—called the Brusilov offensive, after the commander of the Russian troops—resulted in a general outcry that only a new government, which had the confidence of the Duma and contained leaders of the various political parties, would have the authority to take the necessary measures to increase industrial production and secure a food supply for the army and the workers in the industrial centers. Only a broadly based government would inspire enough confidence in the people to maintain their belief in a successful outcome of the war. Such demands ran counter to the deeply ingrained absolutist inclinations of the tsar and the tsarina, who considered the appointment of ministers as lying entirely in their hands. A personal motive for the resistance of the tsar and particularly also of the tsarina to any encroachment on the tsar's autocracy and to the formation of a more broadly based, liberal government, was their awareness that one of the first demands of such a government would be the removal of the corrupt Rasputin from the court; they believed his presence was needed to keep their hemophilic son alive.

Thus the tsarina insisted on maintaining the tsar's powers intact so that only men in favor of Rasputin would be members of the government. The result was a succession of incompetent and corrupt ministers, moreover, of men suspected to be germanophiles since it was well known that Rasputin opposed the entire war. People from different classes and of different political opinions—conservatives and liberals, grand dukes and foreign ambassadors—joined in attempts to persuade the tsar to install a parliamentary regime. Rasputin wsa assassinated by a member of the imperial family and a leading conservative politician, in the hopes that his removal would weaken the resistance of the tsar against the change in the government system. Actually, the opposite happened, the tsar closed himself in and became almost inaccessible to the influence of political circles; as the pressure grew, he went to the military headquarters where it was almost impossible to reach him. Thus, when bread riots broke out in Petrograd and the guard regiment joined the rebelling masses, the tsar found no defenders, not even among the military, and was forced to submit to the demands for abdication. He and his family were made prisoners, first in Tsarskoe Selo; from there they were brought to Siberia and then back to the Urals. In July, 1918, when monarchist troops approached the Urals, the tsar and tsarina and their children were executed. They had borne their fall from power with an astonishing fatalism; it seems almost as if they believed in the unavoidability of the fulfillment of one of Rasputin's prophecies—namely, that when he died tsarist Russia would also perish.

The tsar had abdicated in favor of his brother Michael. But Michael also resigned the throne, aware that support for a continuation of the dynasty was weak. Thus, the Duma established a provisional government composed of the chief leaders of all the bourgeois parties and tolerated by the moderate socialists, the Mensheviks, who were inclined to cooperate with the liberal bourgeoisie and to support the war for democracy.

The government came to power in a difficult situation, and from then on, throughout the next six months, events precipitated with confusing speed. For the members of the government the continuation and intensification of the war effort were paramount. But such policy needed the support of the masses and the overthrow of tsarism had raised their hopes: the workers expected the realization of socialism; the peasants, the acquisition of more land through partitioning the great estates. These demands had great weight, workers' councils had been formed in the factories and soldiers' councils in the armies, in which representatives of peasants were a crucial factor. Execution of the measures of the provisional government was widely dependent on these Soviets (councils) of workers and soldiers. Clearly, conservative and liberal members of the provisional government lacked enthusiasm for these radical demands. They declared that decisions about such fundamental changes should be left to a constituent assembly, elected on the basis of universal suffrage for men and women above eighteen years of age; war conditions, however, made such elections difficult. But the continuation of the war depended on intensified cooperation of workers and peasants, and these groups, disgruntled because of the postponement of socialization and land distribution, had to be assured that reforms would be coming. Kerensky, a socialist politician, who mainly by his rhetorical gifts had become vice-president of the Petrograd Soviet, was appointed minister of justice. A deep inner contrast was implanted in the provisional government. Unavoidably Kerensky's influence grew because he represented the main link to the increasingly restless and discontented mass of workers and peasants. In July Kerensky became prime minister. But the growing influence of the left in the government aroused resistance among conservatives and liberals and particularly generated indignation among officers and generals, because they saw army discipline disintegrating before their eyes. The result was military action on the part of Kornilov, the commander in chief of the army, in order to restore disci-

The Russian Revolution. *Street fighting in Petrograd.*

pline and order. He was opposed by Kerensky. A famous scene in the Russian film *October* (1927), by Sergei Eisenstein, which celebrated the Bolshevik Revolution, shows the workers of Petrograd destroying the railroad tracks on which Kornilov's troops were expected to arrive. It should be added that Kornilov's order to his troops to advance against Petrograd had found little obedience. But Kornilov's attempt, although abortive, undermined Kerensky's own position. It was considered an indication of the weakness and the half-heartedness of the provisional government that reactionary activities could have reached such a strength that counter-revolutionaries were able to attempt a coup. It had become clear that the adoption of a policy centering on continuation of the war left the former ruling group in a strong position, and revealed itself to be incompatible with the attainments of the goals of the workers and peasants. The hour of the Bolsheviks had come.

An event which occurred when Lenin arrived on the night of April 3, 1917, at Petrograd's Finland Station revealed itself now in its full significance. The Germans had permitted Lenin to travel from Switzerland, where he was in exile, through Germany to Russia, in the hopes that as leader of the radical Bolsheviks opposed to the war he would interfere with the work of the war-minded provisional government. When Lenin arrived, and was solemnly received in the waiting room formerly reserved for the imperial family, by the leaders of the Petrograd Soviet, the Mensheviks Chjeidze and Skobelev, he immediately rejected the invitation of these Menshevik leaders to cooperate in the defense of the revolution against enemies from within and from without. Addressing the assembled masses, Lenin declared that the revolution had not solved the fundamental problems of the Russian proletariat and that the task ahead was to turn the bourgeois revolution into a proletarian socialist revolution. Thus, at the outset, Lenin established the line which the Bolsheviks should follow and which separated them from all other parties. The real revolution that would give the proletariat monopoly of power was still to come, and every effort must be made to bring it about as soon as possible. This aim could not be attained in wartime, since war left power in the hands of the army and the bourgeoisie. The war therefore must be immediately ended. Peace and revolution were complementary to each other. But he also addressed the workers of other countries, reminding them of the Marxist tradition of international revolution and antimilitarism.

The demand for peace implied a propagandistic appeal to the Russian soldiers. And there can be no doubt that the soldiers were anxious to return home and participate in the expected land distribution. The Bolsheviks were also aware that the accomplishment of the task they had set themselves meant primarily gaining control over Russia's administrative and industrial center, Petrograd. Before the conquest of power, adherents of the Bolsheviks among the Russian population were not numerous. Even among the industrial workers, the Bolsheviks had less support than their socialist rivals, the Mensheviks. Petrograd was divided into a number of districts, each with its own workers' council. While the Mensheviks dominated the Petrograd municipal government, the Bolsheviks worked at the grass roots in the district Soviets and thus came to control certain sections of the city. This was their base for revolutionary action.

In the period from April, when Lenin returned to Russia and assumed leadership of the Bolshevik party, until October 24 (Russian calendar; November 9, Gregorian calendar), when the Bolsheviks seized power, Lenin's line of policy frequently seemed unrealistic. Even among prominent Bolsheviks, there were those who believed that it would be better to cooperate with the Mensheviks and to defend the gains which had been obtained through the overthrow of tsarism than to work for a dictatorship of the proletariat under Bolshevik control. Such considerations gained in strength when an attempt to seize power in July failed miserably. There were even temporary defections. But the turning point came when Kornilov's putsch revealed the weakness of Kerensky and his provisional government. Then doubts and hesitations disappeared, and a definite trend towards a more energetic and revolutionary government became noticeable even among those workers who were adherents of the Mensheviks.

Lenin—who, since the abortive Bolshevik putsch in July, was in hiding —urged immediate action. But those who were in closer touch with the mood of the Petrograd population decided to synchronize the renewed

ВЫСОКІЙ ПОСТЪ ДЛЯ ВОЖДЕЙ МЯТЕЖА

ЛЕНИНЪ ХОЧЕТЪ ЗАНЯТЬ ВЫСОКІЙ ПОСТЪ?.. ЧТО-ЖЪ? МѢСТО ДЛЯ НЕГО ГОТОВО!!!

Cartoon from *Petrogradskaia gazeta*, July 7, 1917. *Heading reads:* "A High Post for the Leaders of the Rebellion"; *caption says:* "Lenin wants a high post? Well? A position is ready for him."

attempt to seize power with the meeting of the all-Russian Congress of Soviets which was to assemble on October 25. Although the members of this Congress were by no means all Bolsheviks, they were all socialists and would approve of the demise of the Kerensky government and the taking over of power by a socialist government. Indeed, the Bolshevik *coup d'état*, brilliantly organized by Trotsky, met almost no serious resistance. Kerensky was unable to mount a military counteroffensive and the ministers of the provisional government who had remained in Petrograd were forced to surrender. On the next day the all-Russian Congress of Soviets met; under protest of a group of Mensheviks, the congress legitimized the creation of a revolutionary Bolshevik government.

Lenin's strategy appeared brilliantly justified. He possessed undisputed authority in the new government, whose members called themselves not ministers but People's Commissars. But Lenin needed all his authority to steer the government through the next months and years. The People's Commissars immediately took a number of steps which indicated that a new socialist era had come. One of their first decrees ordered the partition of the large estates and distribution of the land among the peasants without compensation for the former owners. All banks were nationalized, and control over the factories was given to the workers.

In order to underline the break with the bourgeois capitalist system, private bank accounts were confiscated, church property was seized, and secret diplomatic documents—among them agreements with the allies about territorial changes to be forced upon the enemies—were published.

The Bolshevik government was beset by more urgent problems, however, than those of internal reforms. For the allies were aware that the Bolshevik seizure of power meant Russia's withdrawal from the war; thus they gave their protection to the adversaries of the Bolsheviks—officers, monarchists, bourgeois politicians—who, at the fringes of the Russian empire, began to organize resistance. On the other hand, the conclusion of peace, the cornerstone of the policy of the new regime, could not come from a one-sided proclamation, but demanded negotiations with the Central Powers. Although the German and Austrian governments agreed with the Russian government that peace ought to be based on the principle of national self-determination, they gave this principle a peculiar interpretation. They insisted that Poland, Finland, and the Baltic states ought to be separated from Russia and remain under German and Austrian control, and that the Ukraine, almost the entire south of European Russia, become an independent state. The peace negotiations, which were conducted at Brest-Litovsk, offered a strange spectacle: on the one side were the delegations of the Central Powers, led by masters of the diplomatic craft, like von Kühlmann and Count Czernin, who were advised by high-ranking military officers; on the other side were the Russians, led by the

Russian Revolution, 1917. *Soldier has fixed a red flag to his bayonet.*

young revolutionary hero, Trotsky, and among whose delegates were a peasant and a sailor. Although Trotsky proclaimed the need for a peace without annexations and indemnities, and exposed the rulers of the Central Powers as ruthless annexationists, against whom he appealed to the solidarity of the workers of all countries, his rejection of the demands of the Central Powers was futile. Lenin was fully aware from the beginning that Russia had to give in, and, after a brief show of resistance, the Bolshevik government did so. The acceptance of this humiliating peace increased the indignation of all the bourgeois elements against the Bolsheviks, whose Russian antagonists were now augmented by the Social Revolutionaries, a radical party which represented the peasants. The Social Revolutionaries had so far cooperated with the Bolsheviks because of their policy of land distribution; but since a good part of the strength of the Social Revolutionaries lay in the Ukraine, they bitterly resented the handing over of this region to Germany. For Germany the war in the east seemed over. But for the Bolsheviks the end of the war with the Central Powers meant the beginning of civil war.

DECISION IN THE WEST

In the early spring of 1918 the Central Powers seemed in a brilliant position. They had freed themselves from the danger of a two-front war. Half a year later the German High Command was to declare to its government that the war must be considered lost. And in November, 1918, a Germany transformed by revolution into a republic agreed to an armistice which could only lead to a peace dictated by the western powers. What had happened to bring about this reversal of fortune?

All of Germany's successes in the east could not outweigh the fact that its strongest adversaries were in the west and that victory was impossible without defeating them. It seemed clear that action at sea would be required to subdue Great Britain, the most formidable of the western enemies. Early in the war, a naval blockade to deprive Germany of raw materials had been instituted by Britain and France. In international law a distinction is made between contraband—munitions and raw materials needed for the manufacture of military equipment—and noncontraband, notably food and clothing. Only contraband is subject to confiscation by a blockading power. But the British refused to recognize this distinction. No ships of any neutral power were permitted to go to a German port, and imports into the Scandinavian countries and the Netherlands were limited to quantities which assured that the goods would be used in the importing countries and not be reshipped to Germany.

A New Combatant: The United States

The British violation of recognized international law created serious trouble between the United States and Great Britain. But the United States finally sided with Great Britain against Germany because the Germans too violated international law—flagrantly and even more brutally than the British. The Germans felt that they could counterbalance the British blockade by a more effective form of economic warfare, a submarine blockade. Submarines could not remove goods or people from merchant ships; they could only sink the ships. The Germans declared the waters surrounding the British Isles to be a war zone in which all enemy vessels would be torpedoed and even those of neutral nations, if suspected of carrying goods, might be sunk. In May, 1915, a German submarine torpedoed the *Lusitania*, a British passenger liner; almost 1,200 people drowned, among them 118 American citizens. While it was true that the *Lusitania* carried ammunition, the death of more than a thousand civilians, many from neutral countries, seemed incredibly brutal. Indignation in the United States mounted. After a severe warning by President Wilson, the Germans relented and for two years they modified their conduct of submarine warfare. But pressure against Chancellor Bethmann-Hollweg and those of his advisers who advocated caution in using the submarine steadily mounted. It was difficult for the public to bear the hardships of the British blockade when Germany was believed to be in possession of a weapon with which it could retaliate. Moreover, the German navy had built many new submarines and the naval high command, supported by experts anxious to please the admirals, maintained that Great Britain could be starved out and forced to surrender in a short time. Hindenburg and Ludendorff gave full support to the demands of the navy. On January 31, 1917, the Germans proclaimed the resumption of unrestricted submarine warfare. President Wilson severed diplomatic relations with Germany, and provoked by the sinking of American ships, the United States declared war on Germany on April 6, 1917.

The effect of America's entry into the war was immense. British shipping losses, especially since the declaration of unrestricted submarine warfare, had risen dangerously. In April, 1917, alone, 875,000 tons of shipping were sunk. By organizing a convoy system, the British had tried to master this threat. But the entry of the United States into the war made the German submarine warfare an evident failure, because thereafter the number of ships convoyed and the number of ships protecting the convoys was increased steadily. Convoys of ships transporting food, war materials, and troops arrived safely in Britain, and the rate of shipping construction soon exceeded the rate of loss. Moreover, the entry of the United States into the war blunted the uplift in morale which the breakdown of Russia would otherwise have produced in Germany. Indeed, Wilson's insistence on a just and democratic peace increased internal tension in Germany and gave a particularly sharp edge to the debate on war aims. The demand grew for a guarantee that the war would not be fought to achieve the aims and ambitions of the ruling group but would be terminated as soon as the existence of the German people was no longer threatened. Both at home and abroad, distrust of the policy of the German leaders was reinforced by the impression created by the peace of Brest-Litovsk and its aftermath. In the areas separated from Russia the central powers established regimes controlled by small wealthy groups: German landowners in the Baltic States, a small pro-German clique in the Ukraine. German princes were placed on the thrones of such newly established states as Lithuania, Courland, and Finland. The behavior of the Germans in this area helped to give a wide echo to Trotsky's words during the peace negotiations that the Central Powers conducted the war not in the interest of the people but of a small exploitative ruling group.

Despite the apparent military advantage of the Central Powers at the beginning of 1918, their situation had grave weaknesses. The brutal German policy in the east kept the conquered areas restless and in revolt. Large military forces had to remain in the east, and the transportation of food, especially of wheat from the Ukraine, met many obstacles. Increasingly, the governments of the Central Powers were being criticized as overweening in their ambitions and unwilling or unable to terminate the war. The Allies had become strong enough to mount offensives at various fronts. In the fall of 1917 the British had thrown the Turks back from the Egyptian frontier and advanced into Palestine, taking Jerusalem on December 8, 1917.

War in the air. *German and British planes engage in a dogfight.*

Caporetto: *the result of ma-chine-gun fire on the south-ern front.*

Greece's entry into the war in June, 1917, had made possible an offensive against Bulgaria. On the other hand in October, 1917, Austrian and German troops had broken the Italian front in the Battle of Caporetto, brilliantly described by Ernest Hemingway in A *Farewell to Arms* (1929). To stem the panic among Italian troops, Italian military police were ordered to shoot every tenth man of any formation that was fleeing. Significantly, even the German victory at Caporetto did not eliminate Italy from the war. The British and French were able to send in enough reinforcements to re-construct an Italian front along the Piave.

Thus, at the beginning of 1918, despite the Treaty of Brest-Litovsk, Germany was not in an unassailable position, able to wait for the Allies to force the issue. The arrival of American troops and increasing disaffection within Germany necessitated action leading to a quick end to the war. The German military leaders responded with an offensive in the west which they believed, with the help of reinforcements from the east, would bring victory. But in its outcome this offensive, which started on March 21, 1918, was no different from previous ones in the west. Initially, territorial gains were large. But when the German soldiers advanced beyond the zone where they enjoyed protection from their artillery, they again found that in trench warfare defense was superior to attack, and the German offensive got stuck. German attacks in other areas of the front lacked even the force of the March offensive. The Germans were halted—by the French at Compiègne and by the Americans and the French at Château-Thierry. Starting in July, 1918, the Allies, now led by Ferdinand Foch, commander in chief of all the armies in France, began to attack. And their advances were powerfully supported by use of the tank—a new weapon which brought an element of movement into the war of position. At the same time, the Allied armies in Salonika and the Italians at the Piave began to advance and both the Bulgarian and the Austrian fronts collapsed; Bulgaria and Austria asked for peace.

At this point Ludendorff urged the German government to seek an armistice. German political leaders now lost all confidence in the German high command, and the German people and the troops were no longer willing to accept the leadership of the military or of the rulers who had supported them. Revolution spread from town to town. By November 9 all the German princes, William II included, had abdicated, and on November 11 the armistice was signed. The First World War was at an end.

CONSEQUENCES OF THE FIRST WORLD WAR

When the news of the armistice reached London Big Ben, silenced during the war, rang out again. In London and Paris people danced on the streets and embraced each other. It was as if people had suddenly awakened from an oppressive, terrifying nightmare and the world again appeared in its true colors and shapes. But the notion that one could now return to

British tanks on the western front in September, 1918.

the life which had existed before August 1914 was a deception. The world war had created burdens which perdured well into the post-war period.

The greatest changes, which created a grave problem for the European nations, had taken place in the economic sphere. The costs of the war had been enormously high. In 1917, for example, the German war expenditure amounted to two-thirds of the total German national income of prewar years. Only a small part of these vast sums had been obtained through taxation. In Germany the war had been financed through inflationary printing of paper money and internal loans (war loans); for the Allies a particularly important source of funds was the United States. By means of loans the European countries paid for the war materials which they bought from the United States; cash payments would have quickly exhausted their gold reserves.

Thus, in addition to the waste of capital and resources, there occurred a decline of the European economic position in comparison to that of the United States. The European powers were transformed from creditor nations into debtor nations. By the end of the war Great Britain's indebtedness to the United States government amounted to $3,696,000,000; that of France to $1,970,000,000; and that of Italy to $1,031,000,000. Altogether, the Allied powers of Europe owed the United States more than $7,000,000,000. In addition many loans were made in the period just after the end of the war; when the debt of the Allied nations to the United States was funded in 1922, the total indebtedness amounted to $11,656,932,900. The center of the world money market began to move from London to New York.

As a further consequence of the First World War, European investments in non-European countries diminished, and the opportunities of the European states for influencing economic development in other continents were lessened. Most German assets outside of Europe were confiscated by the governments of the countries in which they were located. Before the United States entered the war, loans were not easily obtainable, and Great Britain therefore paid for goods with gold and procured the necessary foreign exchange by mobilizing foreign securities held by British citizens. British and European holdings in non-European countries were thus considerably reduced. Moreover, because the European countries geared their industrial production to the war effort, their export trade ceased almost entirely, with the result that economic life in the non-European parts of the world was reoriented. For instance, before the First World War, the British and to a somewhat lesser degree the Germans dominated international trade with the states of Latin America. At that time agriculture was the economic mainstay of these countries, and manufactured goods were obtained from abroad. In the postwar period Latin-American trade with the United States, and investments by American firms in Latin America, increased steadily. The American economic influence accelerated industrial progress: the chief

American investments were in mining, and American capital played a leading part in the development of oil fields in Venezuela, Peru, Colombia, and Ecuador. Now these countries were set toward industrialization, and in the 1920's they achieved a remarkable prosperity. Economic development in India was similar. During the war the government actively promoted industrial growth so that India could supply equipment for the troops fighting in Mesopotamia and the Near East. The Tata Iron and Steel Company in Bihar became the largest steel works in the world, producing almost a million tons annually. Production figures around the world revealed the diminished economic role of the European continent. In 1925 the world output of manufactured goods was 20 per cent higher than in 1913; this rise can be attributed primarily to the expansion of production in the non-European world.

While the consequences of these structural shifts emerged only gradually, economic difficulties of a temporary character arose immediately. Industrial production, which had been geared to the war effort, had to be changed over to peaceful uses. This was necessarily a slow but urgent process, for as the armies demobilized soldiers returned home seeking work. In almost all European countries war was followed by a period of unemployment—an inappropriate reward for those who, a few months earlier, had been praised as the heroic defenders of their countries.

In the budgets of all European countries the payment of pensions to those who had been wounded in the war and to the widows and children of those who had been killed formed a significant part of governmental expenses. Instead of diminishing, taxes increased, and at the same time the possibilities of making changes in government expenses and of applying them to social or political purposes decreased.

Budgetary constraints occurred at a time when governments were expected to do more for the people than ever before. The war had shown that governments could direct economic life into the channels which served government interests. And it was hard to grasp why now, with war over, unemployment could not be prevented and the situation of the lower classes improved. Orators had proclaimed the end of the war a a victory for democracy; as a result of the sacrifices which total war had imposed on all elements of the population, the right of the lower classes to determine their own fates was generally recognized and had led to a broadening of suffrage all over Europe—although it varied in extent in different countries. It was an important aspect in the political situation of the postwar years that the expectations of what government could and ought to do had increased, whereas the governments had become more confined in the means which they had at their disposal for action.

The contrast between expectations and reality was a pervasive element in the entire intellectual atmosphere. The end of the war was believed to bring about a totally new era; the return to the routine of daily life, even more drab than it had been in the prewar era, seemed like a mockery of the sufferings which people had undergone. The British poet Siegfried Sassoon had written:

> You're quiet and peaceful, summering safe at home;
> You'd never think there was a bloody war on! . . .
> O yes, you would . . . why, you can hear the guns.
> Hark, Thud, thud, thud,—quite soft . . . they never cease
> Those whispering guns—

These lines reveal how the hard reality of war had raised doubts about the beliefs society had held before the war. War poetry shows the change of mind of the writers who wanted to communicate the war experience. If the poems and writings of the earlier years of the war were expressed in traditional patriotic terms, treating the soldier's craft as proper for young men and praising death on the battlefield as a fitting and beautiful end of life, the later poems and writings were—with their descriptions of horror, suffering, and destruction—an accusation against the war. For many writers traditional language and imagery were not only insufficient to express what they felt, they seemed to conceal reality and to lie by describing unheard of suffering and passion in mundane words and forms. In order to express the desperation of one's heart—whether aroused by the war or by the hopelessness of life—one must use words or images which arouse in the reader the same feelings which one has; this is not achieved with logically composed sentences or realistic and formal drawings which contain a moral meaning or prescription. Although their beginnings lie in the years before 1914, Expressionism in literature and non-representational art became the dominant intellectual trends with the First World War—a further sign of the break which the war represented in European life.

But if these changes and developments in the economic, political, and intellectual spheres made reconstruction of social life, adjusting the new to the old, extremely difficult, the task was immensely more complicated because the war had taken so dreadful a toll of human life. More than any other phenomenon the greatest problem of the situation after the First World War was that an entire generation was lost.

In western Europe the losses and casualties of the First World War were considerably larger than those suffered by the same states in the Second World War. Altogether, about 8.5 million men were dead. More than twice that number were wounded, many of them maimed for life. The total number of casualties, including killed, wounded, and missing, is figured as 37.5 million. The greatest number of war dead and wounded—about 6 million—was suffered by Germany. France's losses were 5.5 million,

War crimes. *The cathedral of Rheims after artillery bombardment.*

but with a population less than two thirds that of Germany, France suffered proportionately more in the First World War than any other belligerent. The losses in single battles were horrendous. In the Battle of Verdun the Germans and the French each lost more than 300,000 men. Passchendaele cost the British 245,000 men. An entire generation rotted on the battlefields. Modern warfare does not lead to a survival of the strongest or the best. Many who might have been leaders in the coming decade never returned from the war.

In considering the developments following the slaughter, it is important to remember that the usual transition from one generation to the next did not take place in the interwar period. It is true that at the end of the 1920's a few men of the war generation did advance to political leadership: Anthony Eden in Great Britain, Édouard Daladier in France, Heinrich Brüning in Germany. But the distinction which they enjoyed as members of the war generation emphasizes how few of those who could become national leaders survived. Benito Mussolini and Adolf Hitler made a great play over having been frontline soldiers fighting in the trenches. They pretended to be the representatives of the generation which the old men tried to keep down and to suffocate. Exaggerated as such claims were, the leading statesmen of Europe, far into the 1930's, almost up to the Second World War, were for the most part men who had come into positions before the First World War. Moreover, because the memory of the events and experiences of this war persisted long after 1918, people continued to look upon the wartime military leaders as father figures to whom they could entrust their fate. Instead of fading away, the generals, the Hindenburgs and the Pétains—whether victorious or defeated—remained important personages on the political scene. There was a strange incongruity between the new issues which the First World War had created and the aged political leaders whose task it was to grapple with these problems.

PART II

THE PEACE THAT FAILED

CHAPTER 6

Peacemaking

THE STATESMEN AND THEIR AIMS

THE TWO DECADES from 1919 to 1939 are frequently called the interwar years. It needs to be emphasized, however, that such a characterization is obviously the result of hindsight. When the statesmen of the victorious powers assembled in Paris in January, 1919 they expected, and were expected, to make a settlement which would establish peace for all time; moreover, the hope of them succeeding in what they had set out to do died only gradually. It became clear only in the thirties that what had been attained was not a lasting peace, that the threat of war still hung over the world. Though the peacemakers failed to achieve what the war-tired people of Europe yearned for, it must be said in their defense that they confronted a task of immeasurable complexity. The war had begun as a European conflict but had developed into a global war; consequently, although it was generally agreed that the settlement ought to be of a global character, some regarded the elimination of potentially explosive rivalries in Europe as the paramount task. This central difference was intensified by other differences. Some of the statesmen and diplomats—mainly those whose eyes were focused on the European part of the settlement—believed in reaching their goal by traditional methods; others believed in an entirely new approach to the problems of international relations. If we look at the personalities of the leaders assembled in Paris at the end of 1918 these differences become very evident.

Arthur Balfour, the British foreign secretary, had attended the Berlin Congress of 1878, and regarded the proceedings in Paris with the detachment of an old man; as a diplomat of the old school he was chiefly concerned with the reestablishment of a balance of power. But Balfour's attitude was an exception. The prevailing mood at the Paris Peace Conference was that of nineteenth-century nationalism. This emotion burned, for example, in the French prime minister, Clemenceau, for whom the French defeat in 1870–1871 was still a personal, unforgotten experience, so that his main concern now was to make a resumption of the Franco-German duel impossible. The principal representatives of nationalism, however, were the leaders and delegates of those nations which as a result of the war had emerged from the rule of—or dependence upon—other powers, and now

The leaders of the French army, Foch and Joffre, lead the victory parade along the Champs Elysees after signing the peace in 1919.

strove to establish independent national states. Nikola Pasic (c. 1845–1926), the Serbian Bismarck, and Eleutherios Venizelos (1864–1936), the popular and influential Greek statesman, worked for the fulfillment of Greek and Serbian national aims; they wanted to create a greater Serbia and a greater Greece. The Czech and Polish representatives, Eduard Beneš (1884–1948) and Ignace Paderewski (1860–1941), based the demands for their new states on the new principle that each nationality had the right to self-determination. But they could be obdurate and ruthless when the interests of their nations clashed with those of others.

At the same time, advocates of the "new diplomacy"—those who aimed at overcoming old conflicts and tensions by building a supranational organization and strengthening international law—were also strongly represented. They came chiefly from non-European countries, as did General Jan Christian Smuts (1870–1950), the influential South African statesman. The leader of these idealists was, of course, Woodrow Wilson (1856–1924). For the first time an American president went to Europe while in office. Wilson was enthusiastically and tumultuously received in Paris, in London, and in Rome. He was welcomed as the savior who would bring about a new and better age. And though many of the leaders of the European states may have been skeptical, Wilson had numerous adherents among the younger members of their delegations. However, the variety of views and approaches represented at the Paris Peace Conference made it unavoidable that the settlement which would result could not be a full realization of Wilsonian ideals, but a compromise in which the principles of a new diplomacy would be watered down by considerations of power politics and nationalist passions.

The Paris Peace Conference opened officially on January 18, 1919, and reached its highpoint with the signing of the peace treaty with Germany in the Hall of Mirrors in Versailles on June 28, 1919. Like the Congress of Vienna after the defeat of Napoleon, the Paris Peace Conference was not only a political but also a social event. Paris was crowded; the delegations of the various nations included politicians, military men, and experts in law, finance, geography, and history, and they mixed socially with the great French literary figures of this period.

A large number of committees were formed to discuss, negotiate, and finally to draft the articles settling the new frontiers, adjusting the legal and economic problems arising from these territorial changes, and determining the amounts and methods of payment of reparations. But the final decisions were made by the Big Four: Wilson, Lloyd George, Clemenceau, and Orlando—the president of the United States and the prime ministers of Great Britain, France, and Italy. They had difficulties in arriving at agreement. The chief contrast was between Wilson, proponent of a new diplomacy, and Clemenceau, concerned only about France's security, which in his opinion meant keeping Germany powerless. Orlando, in general inclined to follow Wilson's lead, was adamant where Italy's territorial demands were concerned. Lloyd George, after he had in his speeches before the British elections taken an extremely hard line toward Germany, was now less concerned about the issues than about obtaining agreements and results.

In the settlements which were arrived at in the end, each of the Big Four had to give in somewhat. Although their willingness to compromise secured the conclusion of peace treaties and the establishment of a League

The Big Four at the Paris Peace Conference: *Lloyd George, Orlando, Clemenceau, and Wilson.*

of Nations, their prestige in their own countries suffered greatly from the concessions they had to make and all were displaced as leaders of their governments.

THE SETTLEMENTS IN EASTERN EUROPE

The main business of the Paris Peace Conference was the conclusion of treaties with the enemy states: Turkey, Bulgaria, Austria-Hungary, and Germany. These settlements bear elegant-sounding and historic names because they were signed in various palaces in the suburbs of Paris. The short-lived Treaty of Sèvres (1920) terminated the war with Turkey. The Treaty of Neuilly (1919) established peace with Bulgaria. The situation resulting from the disintegration of the Habsburg empire was resolved by the Treaty of St. Germain (1919) with Austria and the Treaty of Trianon (1920) with Hungary. The most important of the peace settlements was the Treaty of Versailles (1919), ending the war with Germany.

These treaties dealt with two main issues, the one was political, the drawing of new frontiers on the basis of the principle of national self-determination; as those who formulated these treaties soon became aware, the application of the principle of national self-determination proved to be much more complex and difficult than it had been assumed. The other issue was of an economic nature: the reparations question, the fixing of sums to be paid in compensation for the damages and losses incurred during the war. This issue caused tension and friction in international relations throughout the entire next decade.

The Treaty of Sèvres and the Birth of Modern Turkey

The Treaty of Sèvres was the last treaty arranged at the Paris Peace Conference, being signed only on April 20, 1920. It is treated here first because in several respects it has a character very different from that of the other treaties. First of all, strictly speaking, it dealt not with Europe but with a non-European part of the world. Furthermore the principles which were supposed to determine the political settlement in Europe were not applied to the Ottoman Empire; the victors dealt with the Ottoman Empire as if it were a colony. But this high-handed treatment of an old nation conscious of its great past necessarily produced a strong reaction. Hence, this treaty—or, to be exact, the failure of this treaty—became closely connected with the rise of antiimperialism and anticolonialism in the Near East and with Russia's efforts to emancipate the nonwhite races from the tutelage of the great capitalist powers of the West. In the settlement of the peace with Turkey the last chapter of one story, that of the First World War, is immediately joined with the first chapter of a new story, that of the anti-European revolt.

During the war the western powers had made a number of agreements concerning the partitioning of the Ottoman Empire. There had been a general understanding that the Arab portions would be separated from Turkey, but the arrangements made by the Allies during the war also envisaged a partition of the Turkish heartland of Asia Minor. Even after the collapse of tsarism had made the details of this agreement obsolete, the notion of a partition was maintained. In April, 1919, the Italians appeared in Adalia, in southern Asia Minor, and a month later the Greeks landed in Smyrna. The Greek occupation bore, to quote from an official report of an investigating committee, "more resemblance to a conquest and a crusade than to any civilizing mission." An Allied force controlled Constantinople and its surrounding areas.

In the Treaty of Sèvres, Smyrna and Thrace were given to Greece, large areas in Asia Minor were assigned to Italy and France as their spheres of interest, and Constantinople was internationalized. The sultan, residing in occupied Constantinople, signed the treaty under protest. But the foreign advances into Asia Minor encountered a vehement Turkish reaction, and Turkish nationalism found a leader in a hero of the First World War, Mustafá Kemal Pasha (1881–1938), who began to organize resistance in the interior of the country. Kemal Pasha set up a countergovernment in Angora (now Ankara) and refused to recognize the treaty. To enforce the treaty, the Allies permitted the Greeks to advance from Smyrna into the interior. The Turco-Greek war, lasting from 1920 to 1922, ended with the complete defeat of Greece. The Turkish success was chiefly due to the brilliant military and political leadership of Kemal. But Turkey was also aided by supplies from Bolshevik Russia, which was glad to help this revolt against the dominance of the western powers. Most important, instead of rallying to the support of Greece, the Allies were competing against one another. Italy resented the increase of Greek power in Asia Minor, and France wanted to limit the British influence in the Near East. Hence, Italy and France were willing to withdraw from Asia Minor when they received the promise of economic concessions by the Turks. Only the British, particularly the prime minister, Lloyd George, remained passionate supporters of the Greeks. But although Lloyd George was inclined toward active intervention to assist the Greeks and to hold Constantinople, the British people were too tired of war to accept this policy. Left alone, the Greeks were defeated, and in the summer of 1923 the Treaty of Lausanne, replacing the Treaty of Sèvres, was concluded. The Turks lost most of the Aegean Islands, some to Italy, others to Greece. The Straits remained demilitarized and open to ships of all nations, but the Turks regained the strip of European territory, including Adrianople, which they had possessed before the First World War. They were again complete rulers all of Asia Minor, including Constantinople.

Kemal now became the creator of a modern state. Because the last sultan had opposed the nationalist movement, the sultanate was abolished and Turkey became a republic. The capital became Ankara, a city in the interior of Asia Minor, because Constantinople was too much imbued with

Kemal Atatürk in western dress.

the political and social institutions of the past and too close to the guns of the great powers. For a while the position of caliph, the spiritual head of all Muslims, was maintained and left in the hands of an Ottoman prince. But when the caliphate became a rallying point of all opposition forces it was also abolished. This was a crucial step in the modernization of Turkey—now all the habits, customs, and laws rooted in religious dogma could be abolished. One visible sign of this change was the abolition of the fez; Kemal justified it with the following statement:

It was necessary to abolish the fez which sat on the heads of our nation as an emblem of ignorance, negligence, fanaticism, hatred of progress and civilization, to accept in its place the hat, the headgear used by the whole civilized world and in this way to show that the Turkish nation in its mentality as in other respects in no way diverges from civilized social life.

The removal of the caliphate also made the adoption of a new legal code, no longer embodying the notions of the Muslim religion, possible: the Swiss legal code was taken as the model. Polygamy became illegal, the introduction of civil marriage, which also allowed divorce and gave equal rights to both parties, implied a complete change in the position of women. An important further step, made possible by the removal of the hold of the Muslim religion, was the introduction of the Latin alphabet and compulsory school attendance.

All these reforms were due to Kemal's initiative. Officially he was president of the Turkish republic, and adopted the name Kemal Atatürk. As such he had the right to appoint the prime minister, who was Ismet Pasha, one of Kemal's companions-in-arms (he took the name Inönü).

The various legislative measures passed through a parliament elected by universal suffrage, but since only one party, Kemal's People's party, existed, the parliament offered no resistance to Kemal's wishes and twice gave him emergency powers facilitating the execution of the reforms.

During Kemal's lifetime Turkey was hardly a parliamentary democracy in the Western pattern; in economic life the influence of Soviet Russia was strong. In the times of economic difficulties at the end of the twenties the foreign trade of the country was placed under government control, and in 1934 a five-year plan helped by a Russian loan and Russian advisors was introduced. This plan served the development of a basic industrial potential by building iron and steel works and the development of consumer industries by building paper, glass, and, most of all, textile factories. The problems which this emphasis on statism created came to the forefront only after Kemal's death.

The Treaties of Neuilly, Trianon, and St. Germain and Developments in Southeastern and Eastern Europe.

The immediate purpose of the treaties of Neuilly, Trianon, and St.-Germain was to conclude peace with Bulgaria, Hungary, and Austria. But these treaties involved the settlement of the entire area of eastern Europe, from the Aegean Sea in the south to the Baltic Sea in the north. The political, territorial, and economic questions with which the treaties had to deal were extremely complex. For one thing, the area was inhabited by a large number of different nationalities, with relations between some of them poisoned by the fact that before the First World War certain groups, such as the Magyars and the Germans, had dominated the others. Moreover, the reorganization of this area cut deeply into the existing economic structure. Austria-Hungary, which the treaties of Trianon and St.-Germain destroyed, had formed a natural economic unit that was now torn into parts. The various sovereign states among which the territory of the former Danube monarchy was divided needed financial resources, and the settlements therefore involved a distribution among them of the economic assets of the former Austria-Hungary.

The victors believed that the application of the principle of national self-determination would not only guarantee peace among the states of this region but would allow, in an area previously ruled by authoritarian governments, the functioning of democratic political institutions. After fifteen years, with the exception of Czechoslovakia, not one of the states created or reorganized at the Paris Peace Conference remained a democracy. What were the reasons for this situation? What were the weaknesses in the peace settlement which allowed developments so different from those envisaged at the end of the war?

It is easy to understand that democracy was a weak plant in those countries which, having been defeated, had to cede territories and pay

TERRITORIAL CHANGES AS
A RESULT OF WORLD WAR I

—— Line of Treaty of Brest–Litovsk

TERRITORIES LOST:

By Russia

By Austria–Hungary

By Germany

By Bulgaria

Plebiscite areas

·—·—· 1914 boundaries

Murmansk

White
Sea

BALTIC SEA

FINLAND

Helsinki

Petrograd

Oslo

NORWAY

Stockholm

SWEDEN

Moscow

NORTH
SEA

DENMARK

U.S.S.R.

Danzig

EAST
PRUSSIA

Hamburg

UNITED
KINGDOM

London

The
Hague

NETH.

Berlin

Warsaw

Brest–Litovsk

POLAND

Kiev

BELGIUM

GERMANY

Paris

LUX.

SAAR

Cracow

Lemberg

ALSACE

Prague

UKRAINE

FRANCE

LORRAINE

Munich

Vienna

SWITZ.

Budapest

Geneva

AUSTRIA–HUNGARY

RUMANIA

Milan

Venice

Trieste

Fiume

Bucharest

Belgrade

BLACK   SEA

Marseilles

ADRIATIC SEA

ITALY

SERBIA

BULGARIA

MONTENEGRO

Sofia

Barcelona

CORSICA

Rome

ALBANIA

Constantinople

Naples

GREECE

Aegean
Sea

TURKEY
(OTTOMAN EMPIRE)

SARDINIA

CORFU

Algiers

Tunis

SICILY

Athens

CRETE

ALGERIA

TUNISIA

MALTA (Br.)

MEDITERRANEAN   SEA

0   500 miles

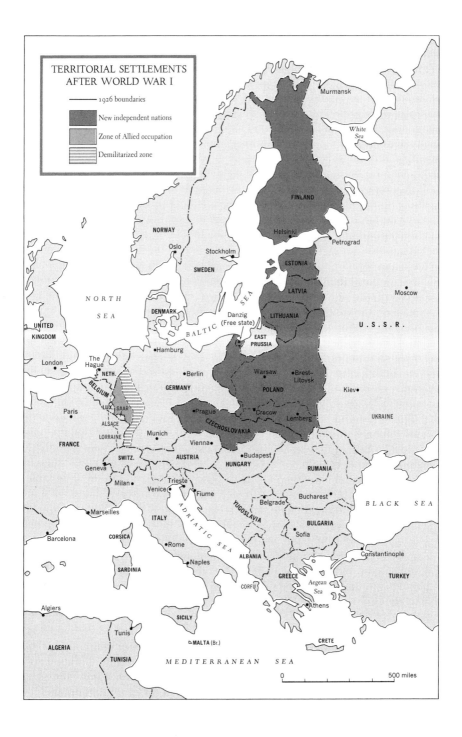

TERRITORIAL SETTLEMENTS
AFTER WORLD WAR I

——— 1926 boundaries

New independent nations

Zone of Allied occupation

Demilitarized zone

damages. Actually the conditions to which Bulgaria had to submit were not very harsh: some minor border revisions in favor of Serbia, Rumania, and Greece (see map); payment of reparations; and the reduction of her army to twenty thousand men. Although not crippling, these conditions were sufficiently hard to keep alive in the proud and ambitious Bulgarian nation a feeling of resentment against neighboring Rumania and Yugoslavia (the enlarged kingdom of Serbia). The officers of the diminished Bulgarian army were particularly eager for revenge. They kept a protecting hand over Macedonian nationalists who, dissatisfied because Macedonia had not been established as an independent state but had been divided between Yugoslavia and Greece, had fled to Bulgaria and operated from Bulgarian soil against Yugoslavia. Bulgarian officers allied to Macedonian nationalists vehemently opposed any policy which implied recognition of the peace settlement, and hence clashed with those who wanted to concentrate on domestic reforms.

Discredited by defeat, Bulgaria's leaders were replaced when the war ended. King Ferdinand abdicated in favor of his son Boris (ruled 1918–1943) and a new party, the Agrarian party, came into power. The Agrarian leader, Alexander Stamboliski, advocated cooperation among the peasants of southeastern Europe and aimed at a Balkan federation in which Serbians and Bulgarians would be reconciled. In Bulgaria, he introduced land reforms, dividing the extended agrarian estates. Although the number of large landowners hurt by these measures was small, Stamboliski's agrarian program was widely considered as a step toward Communism, especially since many members of his party expressed sympathy for the Bolshevik social and economic policy. Hence, the Bulgarian bourgeoisie, the military, and the king all became upset by Stamboliski's reforms. But since he had a firm grip over the peasants, who formed 80 per cent of the Bulgarian population, he could not be removed by democratic means. His enemies therefore resorted to violence. In the early summer of 1923 his government was overthrown by a military coup. Stamboliski was captured by Macedonian terrorists, cruelly mutilated, tortured, and finally killed. This military coup ended democracy in Bulgaria. Behind the façade of a series of impotent bourgeois governments, Macedonian nationalists and Bulgarian officers, sometimes in alliance, sometimes quarreling, maintained control and terrorized the country. Finally, in 1935, King Boris, who had played an important role behind the scenes all along, came into the foreground and established a dictatorship, supported by the army and the police.

In the peace settlements, Hungary suffered more extensive territorial losses than Bulgaria and Austria. The Treaty of Trianon provided that in addition to paying reparations and limiting its army to 35,000 men, Hungary would have to cede to Czechoslovakia, Yugoslavia, and Rumania, three quarters of its former territory, with two thirds of its population. These harsh conditions could hardly arouse in the defeated nation great enthusiasm for the principles, such as democracy, advocated by the victors. Moreover, through a change of regime in the last stages of the war the Hungarians had expected to gain the favor of the western democracies. Two weeks before the end of the war they had pronounced the union with Austria dissolved and had declared themselves independent. Power had been taken over by Count Mihely Károlyi, who as an enemy of Tisza and a sympathizer with democratic western ideas had been a lonely figure among the Hungarian aristocrats. Károlyi had immediately taken steps to initiate a radical land reform; he ceded himself his own vast land holdings —more than fifty thousand acres—to his peasants for distribution among them and his government began to arrange for the dissolution of large estates. Károlyi also supported the convocation of a constitutional assembly, to be elected by universal and secret suffrage of men and women. But the elections for this assembly never took place. Károlyi, who had opposed Austria-Hungary's participation in the war, was a sincere believer in Wilsonian principles, and his popularity declined when the victors treated Hungary not as a newly arisen nation, but as a defeated enemy, and supported the claims of Yugoslavia, Rumania, and Czechoslovakia to Hungarian territory. Under these circumstances Károlyi felt that he could no longer be useful, and in March, 1919, he resigned in favor of the radicals of the left. From March to August, 1919, Hungary was a Communist republic, with Béla Kun as the leading political figure. Although representing a small extremist minority, the government of Béla Kun originally enjoyed broad support. The Hungarians hoped and expected that with the help of Bolshevik Russia they might be able to repulse Rumanian and Czechoslovakian encroachments on what they regarded as Hungarian territory. Officers and soldiers of the old Habsburg army served under Kun, whose government was careful not to antagonize the non-Communist groups of society. The great landed estates were collectivized, but the management of these collectives was frequently entrusted to the former landowners or their administrators; thus, at first the old ruling group and the bourgeoisie were willing to tolerate the Communist government. However, after a few initial military successes, the Kun government was forced by Allied pressure to evacuate Slovakia, and Rumanian troops, backed by the French, advanced toward Budapest. Realizing that even the Communists were unable to save the territorial integrity of Hungary, the old ruling group and the bourgeoisie withdrew their support from Béla Kun and rallied around a former officer of the Austro-Hungarian navy, Admiral Nicholas Horthy (1868–1957). The Communists tried to retain power through terrorist measures, but under the pressure of external and internal foes their regime collapsed; Kun fled to Russia, where he was later executed in one of Stalin's purges. Horthy and his reactionary supporters took over; by the autumn of 1919, the old ruling group was in power again in Hungary, and Communists, those suspected of radical views, spokesmen for workers and peasants, and particularly Jews, were rounded up, tortured, and killed. After some months the terror ended and political life returned to its prewar pseudoconstitutionalism. Horthy reigned as regent. Legally the monarchy was restored, but Hungary's neighbors vetoed the return of the last Habsburg ruler as king, so the throne remained empty. Parliament was reestablished, but the right to vote remained limited and the elections were managed by the group in power. The landowners, large and small, were all-powerful in Hungary until the Second World War. Horthy and his group had bought the assistance of the Allies against the Communists by accepting the Treaty of Trianon, which was signed on June 4, 1920. Yet indignation about the treaty was immense. Hungarians resented the reduction of their nation to a minor power. Moreover, the loss of many of Hungary's former markets created great difficulties for industry and agriculture. The constant aim of Hungarian foreign policy was to change the peace settlement and to regain the areas which once had been under the crown of St. Stephen. During the interwar period, Hungary remained a constant factor of unrest and was the natural ally of any power seeking to revise the peace settlement.

In contrast to Bulgaria and Hungary—nations with strong national traditions—the Austria which emerged from the First World War had little relationship to the Austria of the Habsburgs. Since its territory was limited to the German-speaking part of the Habsburg empire, it became a small country, with about 6.5 million inhabitants. One German-speaking area, South Tyrol, was given to Italy. And the unwillingness of the South Tyroleans to adjust themselves to Italian rule created continual friction between Austria and Italy. In other respects, the Austrians had little cause to resent the manner in which their frontiers were drawn. The complaint which they could make against the Treaty of St.-Germain was that their nation was not permitted to join Germany, that it was deprived of the right of self-determination. This prohibition against *Anschluss* created a festering wound, for though the enthusiasm of the Austrians to become part of the German Reich may have been limited, there was doubt whether as a separate state Austria was economically viable. Vienna, formerly the capital of an empire, was one of the world's larger cities, much too large now for the small state of which it was the capital. After the war the inhabitants of Vienna formed a third of the entire population of Austria. This disproportion between the rural and the urban populations created constant economic difficulties and political tensions. In Vienna the socialists prevailed and established an effective municipal administration. The rest of the country was conservative and Catholic and this outlook dominated the government of the republic. Thus, the political situation was inherently unstable, and when in the 1930's economic difficulties and pressure from the north endangered Austrian independence, the rulers dared no longer trust the fate of Austria to the outcome of popular elections but turned to dictatorial forms of government.

Bulgaria, Hungary, and Austria had fought as allies of Germany. What was in store for the people on the victors' side? Serbia and Rumania had fought against the Central Powers, while Poles and Czechs, although not organized as independent political units before the war and suppressed under the authoritarian regimes of the Hohenzollerns and the Habsburgs, had gained the favor of the victors by forming volunteer brigades fighting on the allied side. The representatives of these nations—Serbia, Rumania, Poland, and Czechoslovakia—were admitted as full participants to the Paris Peace Conference. These countries are called the successor states because their territories, either entirely or partly, had formed part of the Habsburg Empire before the war (see map). Rumania and Poland received border extensions towards the east in order to keep Communism as far as possible away from Europe.

But while the principle of national self-determination formed the basic justification for establishing these nations as independent states, the population in this geographical area was strongly intermingled; the application of the principle of self-determination to this area was complicated and raised as many problems as it was assumed to solve.

A case in point is Yugoslavia, the enlarged kingdom of Serbia. The new name was intended to indicate that all the people living in this state were South Slavs—Yugoslavs—members of the various branches of the South Slav family. But though they were all South Slavs, the Serbs, Croatians, and Slovenes of Yugoslavia regarded themselves as distinct national groups, and this attitude created problems which impeded the working of democracy there. The Serbs and their leader, Pasic, considered themselves the creators of this new national state and were not ready to share power with the others. They clamored for a Greater Serbia, not for a federal state of several nationalities. Because a federal principle was rejected by the government, the Croatians refused to take seats in the constituent assembly elected in November, 1919, and in their absence a constitution was adopted which established a centralized state dominated by the Serbs. The consequent resentment of the Croatians and Slovenes was reinforced by religious contrasts and social friction. While the Serbs were Greek Orthodox, the Croatians and Slovenes were largely Roman Catholic. Moreover, the great majority of the Croatians were peasants, while the controlling element among the Serbs was a bourgeoisie favoring industrialization. When in 1928 the political leader of the Croatians, Stefan Radic, was assassinated, disintegration threatened and the king, relying on the support of the army, ended parliamentary rule and established a military dictatorship. The ensuing quiet in the political scene was deceiving, for although the Croatians were forcibly suppressed, they remained dissatisfied. Throughout the 1930's, the choice seemed to be between political disintegration and the continuation of a brutal dictatorship.

Democracy did not long survive either in Poland or in Rumania. There was no nationality problem in these countries, for the minority peoples (some Magyars and Germans in Transylvania) were powerless. A virulent anti-Semitism existed in both states; governments even tried to gain popularity by permitting and stimulating anti-Semitic disturbances. But the Jews carried little political weight and could defend themselves only by economic means. In Poland, as in many countries, a primary source of unrest and dissatisfaction was the agrarian problem. New regulations limited the maximum area which a single owner could hold to a hundred hectares (or well over two hundred acres), with a total of four hundred hectares permitted in the eastern border region. But the application of these laws encountered the obdurate resistance of the Polish nobility, who owned immense landed estates, and the laws remained chiefly on the books. The landowners found allies in the members of the bourgeoisie, who feared Communist influences among peasants and workers and were reluctant to allow them greater power. The deadlock resulting from this division of Polish political life into two hostile camps provided the opportunity for a *coup d'état* in 1926. Its leader was Józef Pilsudski (1867–1935), who was recognized as a patriot and military hero by all groups of society. He had struggled for Polish independence under tsarism; he had organized a Polish legion during the First World War; and with its help he had established an independent Polish government in the last phase of the war. In 1920, as leader of the Polish army, he had stopped the Russian advance before Warsaw and saved the country from Bolshevism. In his early years Pilsudski had been a socialist, and when he undertook the military coup of 1926 he was supported by the workers of Warsaw, who expected that he would reactivate the stalled movement toward democracy and social reform. But Pilsudski disappointed them. Once in power he allied himself with the bourgeoisie and the landowners, and the rule of these relatively small groups inevitably led to restrictions on liberty. In 1935 a constitution was forced upon the people which gave the president and the government unlimited powers. In the same year Pilsudski died, and power now remained in the hands of his confidants, chiefly men who had been officers in his Polish legion during the First World War. This group of colonels, less selfless than Pilsudski, and not beyond corruption, ruled in Poland in the years before the outbreak of the Second World War.

In Rumania a Liberal party, which represented the wealthy urban bourgeoisie, had ruled under the leadership of the Bratianu family since the latter part of the nineteenth century, and had been a determining factor in steering Rumania to the allied side. The end of the war saw democratic reforms: a widened suffrage and secret ballot. But the territorial acquisitions of Rumania after the war—Bessarabia and Transylvania, mainly agricultural regions—increased social tensions and sharpened the conflict between parties representing the interests of the peasants, anxious for agrarian reforms and protective tariffs, and the Liberal party, representing commercial and industrial interests that favored low tariffs so that Rumania's industrial products, particularly oil, could be easily sold on foreign markets. Thus, the Liberal party could keep power only by introducing an electoral change which provided that a party which received 40 per cent of the vote would get 50 per cent of the seats in Parliament. But even rigging elections could not keep the Liberals in power after their energetic leader, Jon Bratianu, died in 1927. With a deterioration of the economic situation the peasants became more radicalized and aggressive. Their leader, Maniu, who had succeeded in uniting the peasant parties of Bessarabia and Transylvania under his leadership, became prime minister in 1928. Maniu was a man of stubborn democratic honesty, but not much of a politician. In 1930, Maniu recalled King Carol to Rumania from exile. The king had abdicated in favor of his young son Michael, and gone into exile rather than give up his liaison with Magda Lupescu, a relationship which had begun before his marriage to a Greek princess, and which continued after his marriage, shocking his people. The condition for his return in 1930 was that Lupescu would not return with him. However, the king did not keep his promise and came into conflict with Maniu, who soon resigned. Maniu's intractable nature served a more admirable purpose after the Second World War, when he had come to power again and tried in vain to stave off the Communist takeover; he died in prison in 1953, having been condemned in 1947 to hard labor for life. But in 1930 the stubbornness which led him to resignation did damage; it began a period of political instability in which rigged elections became the chief means to securing power, as the government alternated between the Liberals and the peasant parties. Because the king had to give permission to dissolve Parliament, his power steadily increased; gradually the abolition of the Parliament and the establishment of a dictatorship appeared to be the simple solution for getting things done. But by the time the royal dictatorship was established in Rumania, Fascism and Nazism had already appeared on the scene; imitating the Italian and German leaders, Carol tried to establish a one-party system. He believed that he was riding the wave of the future, and certainly the Rumanian dictatorial regime was not far behind Fascism and Nazism in brutality and terror.

Only in Czechoslovakia did democracy continue to function throughout the entire interwar period. Like Yugoslavia, Czechoslovakia included people of several different nationalities: Czechs, Slovaks, Ruthenians, Germans. If in Czechoslovakia nationality conflicts were less sharp than in Yugoslavia, one reason may be found in the developments which preceded the foundation of the state. During the war, leaders of the Czechs and the Slovaks, among them Tomás Masaryk (1850–1937), an internationally known scholar of proved political courage and integrity, formed a committee which propagandized the cause of Czech independence and organized a military force fighting on the side of the Allies. Even before the war had ended the Allies recognized this committee as a provisional government. From the outset Czechs and Slovaks had worked together on this committee, and they were aware of the need for building a state based on cooperation among different nationalities. Thus, when parties were formed and parliamentary elections took place, the largest and most important political parties—the Social Democrats and the Agrarian party—included members of all nationalities, from all parts of the republic. One of the first measures of the new state, the dismemberment of the large landed estates, created among the peasants throughout the country a vested interest in the maintenance of the new republic. Furthermore, since Czechoslovakia had coal and iron mines and modern brewing and textile industries, its economy was better balanced between industry and agriculture than that of any other country in this area. Finally, as president of the republic, Masaryk, himself a Slovak, worked steadily for fairness toward all sections of the population. As a professor at the University of Prague before the war, Masaryk had educated the intellectual elite of the entire area, and he enjoyed immense respect and authority. Nonetheless, Czechoslovakia was by no means free of internal tensions. The Ruthenian and Slovak parts of the country were chiefly agrarian, and their inhabitants believed that the government neglected the agrarian sector of the economy in favor of the industrial parts in Bohemia. Moreover, most of the Ruthenians and Slovaks were Roman Catholic; their antagonism to the administration was sharpened by friction which developed between the anticlerical government and the Roman Catholic Church. Finally, many of the Germans living in Czechoslovakia, particularly in the Sudeten area, had before 1918 regarded themselves as the ruling element of the population; they accepted their sudden demotion with bad grace. But these centrifugal forces became dangerous and destructive to Czech democracy only when in the second part of the 1930's they were supported and stimulated by an outside power—Nazi Germany.

Thus, in the Balkans and in the former Habsburg empire two groups of powers developed as a result of the war: on the one hand were the defeated—Bulgaria and Hungary—both dissatisfied with the peace settlement; on the other were the victors—Rumania, Czechoslovakia, and Yugoslavia—who wished to maintain the *status quo* and formed a little entente to defend the situation created by the peace settlement. The antagonism between these two groups in foreign affairs increased the internal political instability of the various states because it prevented economic cooperation. An attempt to obtain through a Danube federation the economic cohesion formerly provided by the empire was in vain. The defeated saw in such an organization an effort to stabilize the *status quo*. The victors feared that it might be a first step toward the restoration of the Habsburg monarchy. In the end each country directed its economic policy toward autarky, in the hope that it could become independent of its neighbors. The artificial stimulation of industry resulted in stiff competition and low prices— a precarious and vulnerable economic situation.

The situation in the Balkans and eastern Europe held two particular dangers for the stability of Europe as a whole. Democracy there had succumbed because of contrasts between nationalities, conflicts between a radical peasantry and a bourgeoisie anxious to foster industrialization, resistance of a landowning class to agrarian reform, fear of revolution and of

Communism. The dictatorial or pseudodictatorial regimes which followed the democratic governments clamped the lid on these problems; they did not solve them. Thus, they were themselves unstable, and having come to power by force, they were threatened by force. They would rather take risks than endanger their position by retreat.

If the great powers of Europe had been united, they might have been able to work out a common policy for this area which would have improved the economic situation and relieved tension. But the great European powers were divided, and each side sought for support among the eastern European states, with the result that the antagonisms in eastern Europe deepened. On the other hand, the prestige of the great powers became tied up with the fortunes of their Balkan allies, and the conflicts over the Balkan area placed a severe handicap on all attempts to overcome tensions among the great powers.

THE TREATY OF VERSAILLES

Although the Paris Peace Conference reorganized the map in extensive areas of Europe, the main attention, then and subsequently, focused on that part of the settlement which arranged the peace with the western powers' principal enemy—Germany. This treaty was signed at Versailles on June 28, 1919, in the Hall of Mirrors, where in 1871 the German empire had been proclaimed. Its territorial provisions included the return of Alsace-Lorraine to France and the cession of areas with Polish populations —notably Poznán and the larger part of West Prussia—to Poland, so that a stretch of territory under Polish sovereignty, the so-called Polish Corridor, would separate East Prussia from the rest of Germany. Danzig, a German seaport at the northern end of the Polish Corridor, was established as a free city under supervision of the League of Nations; the intention was to guarantee Poland unimpeded access to the Baltic Sea. Memel, at the northern tip of East Prussia was also placed under the League of Nations; later it was seized by Lithuania. Plesbiscites were ordered in Schleswig and Upper Silesia and the southern part of East Prussia, and as a result of these, Germany had to give up some additional territory, although only the loss of the rich coal mines of Upper Silesia was of significance. Finally, Germany had to relinquish its colonies. Altogether, 13.1 per cent of Germany's prewar territory and 10 per cent of its population in 1910 were lost.

These territorial arrangements were complemented by clauses dealing with military and economic matters. The German army was limited to 100,000 officers and men. It was not to utilize aircraft, tanks, or aggressive weapons, and their production was prohibited. Artillery, aircraft, and tanks still in German possession were to be handed over to the victors. Also, the German navy was to be surrendered to the British; however, the Germans succeeded in scuttling most of their ships. In the future the German navy was to be restricted to twelve ships, none more than ten thousand tons; submarines were forbidden. The general staff and the officers' schools were to be abolished. Finally, as a guarantee for the fulfillment of the military clauses, the Rhineland would be occupied by Allied forces for up to fifteen years and would remain permanently demilitarized.

The Allies had great difficulty in reaching agreement about the economic aspects of the settlement. In the end, Article 231 of the Treaty of Versailles stated that the Germans must accept "responsibility of Germany and her allies for causing all the loss and damage to which the Allied and Associated Governments and their nationals have been subjected as a consequence of the war imposed upon them by the aggression of Germany and her allies." The far-reaching nature of this formulation was obvious. It might be interpreted as requiring Germany to finance pensions for officers, demobilization payments, and compensations for the wounded and maimed. The exact determination of how much, on the basis of this article, Germany would have to pay was difficult to reach, and no figure was specified in the treaty because the amount the experts believed Germany could pay was very different from the sum the people in the victorious countries had been led to expect. The treaty did state that in the next few years Germany was to pay five billion dollars, pending a definite settlement in 1921. However, the treaty included various provisions which weakened the German economy and hence reduced the nation's subsequent capacity to make payments. Germany had to hand over to the Allies most of its merchant marine, a quarter of its fishing fleet, and a good part of its railroad stock. For five years Germany had to build annually 200,000 tons of shipping for the victors. It had to make yearly deliveries of coal to France, Italy, and Belgium, and to pay the costs of the occupation of the Rhineland by the Allied armies. In addition, France received economic control over the Saar area, rich in coal and iron; for fifteen years this area was to be administered by the League of Nations; then a plebiscite was to decide its fate.

The strong moral condemnation of Germany and the German people that was contained in Article 231, with its statement that the war had been caused by German aggression, was also implied in other arrangements. Germany was not permitted to join the League of Nations; the Germans were to hand over their former political and military leaders to the Allies so that they could be judged by an international court for their crimes against international morality; the political union of Austria and Germany was prohibited, that is, the German-speaking people were not permitted to exert the principle of national self-determination. The impression that the Germans were treated as outcasts was reinforced by the manner in which the treaty was presented to them. The German delegation which had come to Versailles on April 29 was kept in isolation behind barbed wire. On May 7 the treaty was presented to the Germans without previous negotiations, and after they had received it, only an exchange of written notes took place.

On June 16 the Allies presented an ultimatum in which they declared that they would resume hostilities if the Germans had not agreed to sign the treaty within a week. They did so on June 23, and five days later the ceremony in the Hall of Mirrors took place.

The harshness of the Treaty of Versailles has been sharply criticized and is frequently mentioned as a reason for the rise of Nazism in Germany. It is probably more correct to say that the fault of the Treaty of Versailles was that it was a compromise, neither fully generous nor totally destructive. The French wanted to destroy German unity, or at least to separate the Rhineland from Germany, and to keep Germany disarmed and economically weak in the foreseeable future. Great Britain and the United States were opposed to these French aims, partly because they considered them to be immoral, partly because they regarded them as impossible to realize. All the victorious powers were agreed that if the conditions were unbearably harsh Germany might throw itself into the arms of the Bolsheviks and Communism might penetrate into the center of Europe. Thus the French aims were resisted by Great Britain and the United States. But in order to persuade the French to abandon their plans, the British and the Americans had to make concessions. The result was a treaty which appeared to be an attempt to cripple Germany permanently rather than to make possible its further existence in the society of states.

In view of the hatreds aroused in the war, perhaps nothing better than the Treaty of Versailles could have been arranged. By and large, it did establish frontiers according to the principle of national self-determination. And the necessity of revising and mitigating the military and economic clauses of the treaty was soon accepted. But the impression received by the Germans in the summer of 1919, when the treaty was presented to them, was that of unrelenting harshness. This impression was particularly strong because they believed that they had been assured generous treatment. The Germans thought that they had laid down their arms under the condition that the peace treaty would be concluded on the basis of Wilson's Fourteen Points. Actually, at the signing of the armistice, the Germans were hardly in a position to make conditions. Their armies were in full retreat, their people were in revolt, and further resistance was hopeless.

BEGINNINGS OF THE WEIMAR REPUBLIC

When in October, 1918, the German front in the west began to weaken, a new German government was formed, headed by Prince Max of Baden, a man of humane outlook and liberal principles whose activities on behalf of prisoners of war had earned him a high reputation even in the non-German world. His task as chancellor was to direct the political transition of Germany; the military failure had compromised the existing ruling group in the eyes of the German people. The constitutional changes made during October transformed Germany into a parliamentary democracy. Its government was made dependent on a vote of confidence in the Reichstag. The introduction of universal suffrage in Prussia meant that the dominating influence of the *Junkers* on the policy of the Reich was broken. Moreover, the leaders of the political parties of the center and left of center—the parties that had always urged a democratization of German political life—entered the government. Given time, perhaps the government could have persuaded the world that a new democratic Germany had arisen. But these changes and reforms took place under the shadow of imminent military catastrophe. When Prince Max of Baden formed his government, Ludendorff, despairing of the military situation, demanded the opening of negotiations which would lead to an immediate ending of hostilities. The government therefore informed President Wilson of its readiness for peace negotiations based on the Fourteen Points. An exchange of notes followed, lasting through October. Because the European allies distrusted the sincerity of this sudden conversion to democracy at the moment of defeat, Wilson demanded clear proof of the change in Germany. But meanwhile the government's appeal to Wilson was having an immense impact on the German people. They became suddenly aware of what had been concealed by optimistic military communiqués—the fact that the war was lost. The belief became widespread that the old leaders ought to give up power so that Wilson and his allies would have undeniable proof of the change in Germany. When William II hesitated to abdicate, mutinies—first in the navy—broke out. Unrest spread in the cities. Demonstrations and strikes indicated that the government could no longer rely on police or military force. On November 9, 1918, a republic for Germany was proclaimed in Berlin. Two days later the armistice was signed.

The revolution within Germany threw power into the laps of the socialists. But if they wanted to use the fall of the monarchy for a transformation of their country into a socialist state, the chaotic situation in Germany frustrated them. The socialists themselves were divided, and the next month saw a struggle between moderates and radicals. The moderate majority of the Social Democratic leaders, known as Majority Socialists to distinguish them from the dissident Independent Socialists, believed that radical social changes would result in the dissolution of the Reich, especially since separatist movements had begun to arise in Bavaria and the Rhineland. The Majority Socialists pushed the radicals out of the government, and the latter resumed revolutionary action. The driving force toward this revolutionary action was an extreme leftist organization, the Spartacus group, from which later the German Communist party developed. In the winter of 1918–1919 its leaders were Karl Liebknecht and Rosa Luxemburg, both of whom had been influential in the socialist movement before the First World War. There was fierce street fighting in Berlin, particularly vehement in the last weeks of 1918 and the first weeks of 1919. Uprisings spread in the Ruhr area and in Hamburg and in April a Soviet Republic was established in Bavaria. All these revolutionary movements were defeated.

Karl Liebknecht (center) and Rosa Luxemburg.

In order to fight off the radical left, the Majority Socialists felt constrained to accept help from the elements to their right. They were particularly anxious to gain control over an organized military force. Immediately after the proclamation of the republic in November, 1918, Friedrich Ebert (1871–1925), the leader of the socialists and head of the new federal government, approached Field Marshal von Hindenburg and General Groener, of the military high command—the latter having replaced Ludendorff—and the generals agreed to cooperate with the socialist leaders in order to maintain German unity.

The alliance between the Majority Socialists and the military high command had important consequences. Following Hindenburg's example the German civil servants recognized the legitimacy of the new government and placed their services at its disposal. The resulting administrative continuity helped to overcome the difficulties of demobilization and to ease the transition to a peacetime economy. But the support of the military high command for military action against the extremists on the left did not prevent the outbreak of Civil War, and had a fatal influence on future developments. When the troops returned to German soil from the occupied territories in the west and east, discipline dissolved; they left the ranks and went to their homes. This created a critical situation in the last months of 1918. The high command responded by starting to organize volunteer units (Freikorps) in which former officers had a leading role; these Freikorps played their part in the fight against the extremists. The weight of the conservative allies pushed the government strongly in the direction of ending the revolutionary situation in which Councils of

Workers and Soldiers interfered in the process of government. The government was urged to arrange as soon as possible elections through which the bourgeoisie and the more conservative part of the population could make their voices heard. At the end of January, 1919, when most of the revolutionary movements of the radical left had been defeated, elections to a constituent assembly took place. The new assembly met in Weimar on February 6, 1919.

However, the shotgun wedding between the socialists and the high command had consequences which extended far beyond the winter of 1918–1919, and stultified the development of democracy in Germany. Because the socialists relied on the old civil servants, the republic was obligated to preserve the rights which these functionaries had possessed under the empire. Thus, during the entire existence of the republic its administrative apparatus was in the hands of conservative, usually monarchist, civil servants who could not be dismissed and who exerted a controlling influence on the admission of new members to their ranks. Furthermore, when the new 100,000-man army was created, the task of selecting its officer corps remained in the hands of the officers of the old general staff. This reliance on conservative forces prevented the destruction or even the weakening of the powerful position of the landowners and industrialists. Promises of agrarian reform, made in the initial burst of revolutionary enthusiasm, were not kept. The industrialists fended off all attempts at socialization, although the trade unions did gain the assurance that employers would accept the principle of collective bargaining and refrain from obstructing the functioning of the unions in the factories. It has been argued that the socialists were unable to undertake a thorough transformation of German society because if they had acted against the bourgeoisie the resulting conflict would have destroyed the unity of the Reich. But the unity of the Reich withstood severe crises in the following years. The fact is that most of the leaders of the Majority Socialists were bureaucrats rather than revolutionaries and did not know what to do with the power which had fallen to them.

That in November, 1918, the German people were ready for far-reaching changes was shown by the elections which took place when reaction had already begun to set in. In the constituent assembly, those who advocated democratization of German political life obtained a striking majority: 328 deputies out of a total of 423. Within this republican group the moderate socialists, with 165 members, were strongest, but lacking a majority, they had to collaborate with the two bourgeois republican parties, the Catholic Center party and the left-liberal Democratic party, which together were not quite as strong as the socialists. Thus the constitution resulting from the deliberations of this assembly established not a socialist system, but a parliamentary democracy. All power was concentrated in the hands of a parliament (the Reichstag), elected through secret ballot by all men and women of at least twenty-one years of age, on the basis of proportional representation. The federal government of the republic was given more power than had been enjoyed by its counterpart in the empire; a provision for which a member of the Center party, Matthias Erzberger, was mainly responsible gave the right to raise direct taxes to the federal government, which then assigned funds to the various states. As in the United States, the president—the head of the republic—was to be elected directly by the people. The government, with a chancellor as its head, was responsible to the Reichstag. Thus, both the Reichstag and the president could claim to represent the people and to enjoy democratic legitimation. When they clashed, the door was opened for the overthrow of parliamentary democracy: in emergency situations the president had the right to rule by decree without previous approval of the parliament, and no law ever defined what an emergency situation was.

Despite internal conflicts and economic misery, the changes in the forms of political life and the emergence of new political leaders raised hopes in Germany. But when the draft of the peace treaty was handed to the German delegation in Versailles, these hopes turned into disappointment and vehement indignation. In the face of violent opposition, the treaty was accepted in the Reichstag by a small majority consisting of the moderate socialists and the Center party. A resumption of hostilities, as the military leaders admitted, was impossible. And it was feared that an occupation of Germany by the Allied armies might result in the disintegration of the Reich. The acceptance of the peace treaty led to a strengthening of the monarchical right and the radical left, the right accusing the republican government of a lack of feeling for national honor, the left advocating cooperation with Bolshevik Russia as a means of "liberation." After the summer of 1919 those parties that were the protagonists of a democratic republic and the true authors of the new constitution—the Center party, the Democratic party, and the Majority Socialists—did not again constitute a majority in the Reich. It has been said about the rise of the Nazis that, as long as there were free elections in Germany, the Nazis never gained a majority among the voters. And this is true. But it must also be said that after 1919, during the fourteen years of the Weimar Republic, those parties that were convinced supporters of the republican regime never had a clear majority either.

THE LEAGUE OF NATIONS

The fact that the war had been conducted in Europe, Africa, and Asia, and that, in its last phase, Latin American states had entered the war, implied that more was expected from the Paris Peace Conference than treaties drawing new frontiers in central and eastern Europe. People from all parts of the globe looked hopefully to the Paris Peace Conference; in their opinion the chief task of the statesmen assembled in Paris was the establishment of the principles, rules, and organization which—by recognizing the changes which the rise of non-European states had brought

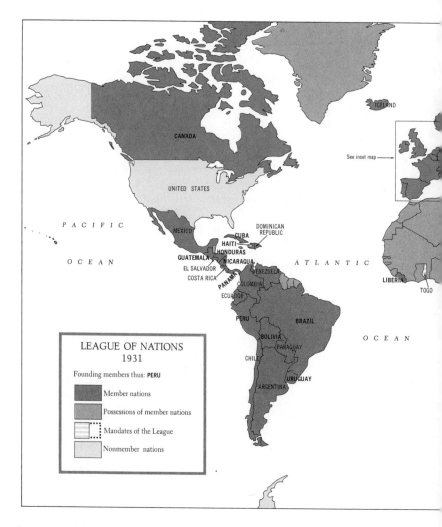

LEAGUE OF NATIONS
1931

Founding members thus: **PERU**

- Member nations
- Possessions of member nations
- Mandates of the League
- Nonmember nations

about—would guarantee a peaceful world order. This feeling for the need of a new world order expressed itself in the establishment of the League of Nations.

In contrast to the nineteenth-century concert of a few great European powers, the League was expected to embrace all the states of the world, and large and small were to have the same voice. The idea of the League owed its origin to a widespread rejection of prewar diplomacy, which with its concern for the balance of power, its eagerness for secret treaties and systems of alliances, and its insistence on strong armaments was considered to have been responsible for the outbreak of the First World War. During the war the need for a "new diplomacy" was particularly emphasized by writers and politicians of the Anglo-Saxon countries, and their

ideas found an eloquent advocate in President Woodrow Wilson who incorporated them in his peace program.

At the most critical time of the war, when Russia had made peace with the Central Powers, Wilson had given allied morale a great lift by providing a persuasive justification of the war. The allies were fighting for the creation of a new world. Boundaries should be drawn according to the principle of national self-determination, so that conflicts over expansion would not arise. Freedom of the seas and removal of economic restrictions should raise the level of economic well-being in all nations, and bind them together in cooperation. The single states should establish democratic forms of government so that the peaceful intentions of the people would prevail over the designs of small authoritarian militaristic groups.

Abolition of secret treaties and "open diplomacy" would further assure the coming of a peaceful era in international relations, and a world-embracing organization of nations would supervise the maintenance of this new order. Wilson summarized these democratic war aims in his so-called Fourteen Points that made a deep impression all over the world.

At the Paris Peace Conference, Wilson regarded the organization of the League of Nations as his most important task; in return for agreement to this project he was willing to make many concessions, for he was convinced that if the League were established it would be able in the course of time to rectify any errors in the peace treaties.

The life of the League was short. Its first meeting took place in 1920 and its last in 1939, although the official dissolution did not occur until April 18, 1946. Since the League did not succeed in preventing war, it can hardly be called a success; nevertheless, as the first attempt to create a world-embracing organization of states for the preservation of peace it represented a landmark. Its original members came from every part of the globe. Moreover, in the League Assembly, which met regularly every year, each member—whether great or small—had the same rights. The executive business was entrusted to a Council whose composition did preserve something of the old idea of the rule of the world by great powers: Great Britain, France, Italy, and Japan were its permanent members. But the Council also included a number of elected temporary members (originally four, later this number was steadily enlarged) and among them there regularly were representatives from Latin America, from Asia, and from the British dominions. Recognition of the equality of all nations and of their right to self-rule was also reflected in the fact that German and Ottoman territories in Asia and Africa which the victors had taken over were retained by them only as mandates, to be administered under supervision of the League of Nations with the aim of gradually preparing their inhabitants for full independence.

Nevertheless, the League failed to prevent aggression and to preserve peace. And the reasons can be traced back to its beginnings. Although it claimed to be a world-encompassing organization, it was not. President Wilson was unable to overcome American fears that membership in the League might lead to involvement in "foreign quarrels," and the United States remained outside the League.

But the failure of the League has to be explained by more than its lack of comprehensiveness. Even those states which had participated in the founding of this organization and belonged to it from the beginning were hesitant to agree to arrangements which would limit their sovereignty. Thus, from the outset the League's chances of success in preserving peace were limited, for it had no "teeth." Membership involved commitments to avoid war, to respect the territorial integrity of other powers, and to submit disputes to investigation, arbitration, and settlement by the Permanent Court of International Justice in The Hague or by the Council of the League. If a government refused to honor these commitments and became an aggressor, the members of the League were to apply economic sanctions: to sever all economic intercourse with the aggressor state. Clear presriptions for military action against the offender did not exist. Moreover, in questions of conflicts between states, decisions by the Council of the League required unanimity and were therefore almost impossible to obtain.

The most effective work of the League was done in promoting international cooperation in the technical and economic spheres. Its greatest successes were achieved by its health organization, which helped to control epidemics, to standardize drugs and vaccines, to promote worldwide studies on nutrition, and to improve health services in Asia. The Economic Section of the League provided valuable analyses and statistics. The League Organization on Communications and Transit furthered collaboration concerning such matters as electric power and inland navigation. The International Labor Organization, working under the League, had some success in improving working conditions.

SOVIET RUSSIA AND THE PEACE SETTLEMENT

The League lacked effectiveness not only because the United States—which had been expected to play a leading role—refused to participate, but also because Germany and Russia, two important powers, were excluded. Germany, as we shall discuss, was later permitted to join the League, but the exclusion of Russia, a country which covered such an immense amount of the globe, was of lasting significance. The events in Russia, from the time of the Bolshevik conquest of power in 1917 to the end of the Russo-Polish War in 1920, were an important factor, if only a negative one, in shaping the world which emerged from the Paris Peace Settlement.

Adherents of a Wilsonian peace were aware of the difficulties created by the absence of Russia, and several attempts were made—for instance, through a mission of the American diplomat William Bullitt—to get in contact with the leaders of Russia. But these efforts were not followed up energetically, for every attempt to come to an understanding with Russia immediately aroused the opposition of the influential groups in France and Great Britain which advocated intervention to overthrow the Bolshevik regime.

The Bolsheviks had started their rule with a number of startling and, to the rest of the world, shocking measures and decrees. They retained civil servants who accepted the new government, but they also gave positions in the bureaucracy to reliable party members without demanding examinations or special knowledge. Likewise, courts were staffed by judges who lacked legal training. Thus the obstacles which a conservative bureaucracy usually places in the path of a revolutionary regime were immediately removed—to the horror of the rest of Europe, which regarded civil servants as members of an exclusive higher order.

The economic measures which they instituted—confiscation of private accounts, nationalization of the banks, abolition of private trade, handing over the factories to the workers, making all land government property—were meant to signify the abolition of capitalism. Most of them, however, were soon somewhat modified. Larger estates were divided up, but the peasants remained in possession of their land, although they were forced to give certain quotas of their production to the government for distribution among other sectors of the population. The chaos which resulted when the workers directed the factories was soon replaced by planning. In 1921, after the civil war had ended, there was even an openly acknowledged change from the early Communism to a New Economic Policy (NEP), which permitted a remarkable amount of freedom of trade within the country. However, heavy industry, transportation, and the credit system remained nationalized, and foreign trade remained a government monopoly. Russia had abandoned the principles of capitalist economy, and the government's grip over economic life was firm enough to permit an enforcement of stricter controls at any time. Moreover, the original measures confiscating bank accounts, socializing factories, and nationalizing land had completely impoverished the middle classes and the nobility. The appropriation of industrial enterprises and the repudiation of state loans also hit foreigners—individuals, banks, governments—who had investments in Russia. And in all further negotiations with the Bolshevik leaders the claims of these foreign investors for compensation and for the repayment of debts contracted by tsarist Russia formed an insurmountable obstacle. In particular the French, because of the large loans which they had given to the tsarist government, for a long time remained adamant in refusing contact with the Bolshevik regime until they had received compensation for their losses.

But these conflicts over financial matters were only one aspect of the differences between Bolshevik Russia and the rest of the world. The Bolsheviks rejected all the liberal and democratic values for which the western powers had claimed to be fighting. Like the tsars, the Bolsheviks refused to permit freedom of the press and freedom of expression. The Russian leaders pursued a sharply antireligious policy, and church property was confiscated. Furthermore, attempts to establish a democratic basis for the regime were soon abandoned. After their seizure of power the Bolshevik leaders had been proclaimed to be the legitimate Russian government by a Congress of Soldiers' and Workers' Councils (Soviets). But the previous government had ordered elections to a constituent assembly which would create a final constitution, and before seizing power the Bolsheviks had accused the government of delaying these elections; they therefore felt constrained to let them take place. But the voting, on November 25, 1917, left the Bolsheviks still a minority. When the constituent assembly opened on January 18, 1918, they declared that, because the voter lists had been made out before the Bolshevik revolution, the constituent assembly "represented the old order." With the help of troops the assembly was dissolved. The soviets remained the popular basis of the regime. Within the soviets the Bolsheviks, who now had the support of the great majority of the industrial proletariat, shared power with the left-wing Social Revolutionaries, who represented the peasants.

The dissolution of the constituent assembly sharpened internal tensions. The Bolsheviks saw themselves as surrounded by enemies within the nation. In December, 1917, they had established the All-Russian Extraordinary Commission (Cheka) for the purpose of "combating counterrevolution and sabotage." With the organization of the Cheka, terror became a consciously used, openly recognized instrument of government. In the summer of 1918 the Bolshevik leaders broke with their only partner in government, the Social Revolutionaries. As representatives of the peasant population the Social Revolutionaries had opposed the acceptance of the Treaty of Brest-Litovsk, which deprived Russia of the Ukraine, one of its most important agricultural areas. In an effort to nullify this treaty and to effect a break with Germany, Social Revolutionaries on July 6, 1918, assassinated Count Wilhelm von Mirbach, the German ambassador in Moscow. There remain puzzling questions about this event. It is difficult to understand how the murderers could get easy access to Count Mirbach, and it has been suggested that the Bolsheviks themselves, who had received information about the plans of the Social Revolutionaries, made this possible. Lenin and

A Russian poster. *The Bolshevik knight slaying the capitalist dragon.*

the Bolsheviks were eager to effect a break with the Social Revolutionaries; the murder of the German ambassador would give justification for such a break. At the same time, the Bolsheviks would have gotten rid of an ambassador whom they knew had reported home that their regime was weak and near collapse. Even if not true, such rumors were indicative of the confused and desperate situation in Moscow at this time. The Bolsheviks succeeded, however, in defeating the attempt of the Social Revolutionaries to overthrow the government, to which the assassination of Mirbach had given the signal. But the struggle went on. Like the revolutionaries of tsarist times, the Social Revolutionaries tried to shake the regime through a series of assassinations. On August 30, 1918, Lenin himself was severely wounded. The Bolshevik answer was increased terror, directed by the Cheka. Exact figures about the number of victims of this Red Terror are lacking. From Bolshevik sources we know that at the beginning of September in Petrograd 512 "counterrevolutionaries and White guards" were shot in one day. Many were killed not for the commission of a specific crime, but because as members of the propertied classes they were regarded as enemies of the state. The indignation of the non-Russian world was great; representatives of foreign powers in Petrograd and Moscow protested, accusing the Bolsheviks of "barbarous oppression" and "unwarranted slaughter" which aroused "the indignation of the civilized world."

In the fall of 1918, when the weapon of terror was unleashed with utter ruthlessness, the Bolshevik position was precarious. The conflict with the Social Revolutionaries intensified the civil war. When the Peace of Brest-Litovsk was signed on March 3, 1918, British and French troops were sent to such harbors as Archangel and Vladivostok to prevent supplies and ammunitions which the allies had sent to Russia from falling into the hands of the Germans. In these areas occupied by the allies, and therefore beyond Bolshevik control, the enemies of the Bolsheviks had assembled and began to launch an attack against the Bolsheviks. From the north and from the east, later also from the Baltic states and from the Ukraine, tsarist generals advanced, half-heartedly supported by the Western powers. For two years, from 1918 to 1920, civil war raged. The Bolsheviks had the advantage of controlling the interior lines, which permitted them to move their troops rapidly from one threatened frontier to another. On the Bolshevik side the military hero of this civil war was Trotsky, the commissar of war. He succeeded in organizing an efficient and disciplined Red Army. He personally appeared at the most threatened points of the front, living in a railroad car which moved from one endangered sector to the other. Moreover, the leaders of the White Russians, as the opponents of the Bolsheviks were called, were disunited. Some, like Admiral Kolchak who advanced through Siberia into eastern Russia, wanted to restore the tsarist regime. Others realized the necessity for a more liberal and democratic program. Against the White Russians with their contradictory aims, the Bolsheviks were able

RUSSIA IN REVOLUTION
1917-1922

—··—··— 1914 boundaries

------- 1921 boundaries

——— Brest Litovsk Treaty Line, 1918

Territory lost by Russia in 1918

▲▲▲▲ 1918 } Limits of counterrevolu-
△ △ △ 1919 } tionary movements

MOVEMENTS OF
COUNTERREVOLUTIONARY FORCES

to keep the support of large parts of the population. The peasants feared that if reaction were victorious they would have to return the land which they had seized to its former owners. The assistance which the White Russians received from Great Britain and France, though minor and insufficient, made the Bolsheviks appear to be defenders of Russian national interest against foreign intervention. Officials of previous governments placed themselves at the service of the Bolsheviks and, strictly supervised by political commissars, were used by them as "technical experts." Bolshevik attempts—with the help of native Communist parties—to reconquer Finland, the Baltic states, and Poland failed. But in the rest of the former tsarist territories, the Bolsheviks gained control.

In the first two years of the civil war, however, the situation of the Soviet regime often seemed desperate. But the Bolshevik leaders were convinced time was on their side. For the European war was drawing to a close. The German government was tottering. Dissatisfaction was widespread in other countries and there was some reason to assume that the end of the war would be accompanied by revolution in several European states. At this time the Russian leaders could not imagine that Russia could become a socialist country while the rest of the world remained capitalist. As Lenin had proclaimed at the Finland Station, they supposed the Bolshevik revolution in Russia to be the first step of a revolutionary

Trotsky *(left)* in front of his armored train during the civil war.

process which would extend over the whole globe. They believed that their own position depended quite as much on the spread of the revolution into other countries as on their staying in power in Russia. Thus, while involved in a deadly struggle within Russia, they established a Communist International, intended to stimulate revolution elsewhere. The First Congress of the Communist International, or Comintern, took place in Moscow in March, 1919; it was a rather tame affair, for the only delegates from abroad were a few leaders of extremist groups that had split off from the socialist parties. More important was the Second Congress of the Communist International, which met in Moscow in August, 1920. Including representatives of the extreme left from a large number of countries, this congress gave a more definite form to the organization of the Communist International.

The establishment of the Communist International had far-reaching consequences. One of these was a definite split within the various Marxist-inspired workers' movements. Even before the First World War most of the socialist parties in Europe had included a left and a right—a revolutionary and a revisionist wing—but the unity of the socialist movement had been maintained. From 1919 on, there were two different Marxist parties: Socialists and Communists. Moreover, the structure of the Communist International was essentially different from that of the Second Socialist International. In the latter, the socialist parties of the various nations remained sovereign; the organization which included them all—the Second International—gave advice only. In the Communist International, supreme authority was held by the World Congress of the Communist Parties which met every year, or more precisely, by an executive committee which this congress elected. The decisions of this congress or its executive committee were binding upon all Communist parties; they had to follow the "line" laid down by the Communist International. The influence of the Russian Bolsheviks was predominant because the headquarters of the executive committee were in Moscow and its permanent secretary, Zinoviev, was a Bolshevik leader. One of the basic principles of the Communist International was that all Communist parties must regard the maintenance, defense, and strengthening of the Bolshevik regime in Russia as their paramount aim. The goal of the Communist International was world revolution, and the Communist parties in the various countries were to build up support for the revolutionary movement by forming special youth organizations, Communist trade unions, and the like, all subject to the same discipline as the Communist parties themselves. Whether these organizations would work openly and freely or secretly and illegally, or whether open and clandestine organizations would work side by side, was to be determined by the situation in each country.

At the time of its formation the Communist International had as its chief goal the overthrow of the governments in the great capitalist states of western Europe. From the beginning, however, the Communist leaders were aware that the European nations drew much of their strength from the control which they exerted over the non-European parts of the world. Therefore, the undermining of European rule over colonial areas was from the outset an openly declared aim of the Communist International. Its first manifesto, issued on April 6, 1919, already included the statement that "the colonial question in its fullest extent has been placed on the agenda.... Colonial slaves of Africa and Asia! The hour of proletariat dictatorship in Europe will also be the hour of your own liberation." This point was emphasized and elaborated in 1920, when special "theses on the national and colonial question" were presented. It was proclaimed that "our policy must be to bring into being a close alliance of all national and colonial liberation movements with Soviet Russia.... The task of the Communist International is to liberate the working people of the entire world. In its ranks the white, the yellow and the black-skinned peoples—the working people of the entire world—are fraternally united."

The existence of a government and of an organization like the Communist International, which stood not only outside the League of Nations, but was its bitter enemy, was a crucial factor in weakening the power of Europe in relation to the non-European world. As a result of the First World War, a change in the relationship between whites and nonwhites, between European rulers and colonial peoples, had taken place. Men of different races had fought side by side; the distance whites had kept from other races diminished. Where native movements for autonomy or independence had existed they gained a stronger impetus, and where nationalism had been sleeping, it was now awakened. The Bolshevik antagonism to the world established in the Paris Peace Conference strengthened these movements decisively; indigeneous peoples were aware that they were not the only ones who did not want to recognize the international order organized and controlled by the European powers. Although in the twenties these movements still seemed no serious threat to the great European colonial powers, they gradually gained in weight and, as we shall see, with the thirties, when the entire settlement of the Paris Peace Conference became threatened, they were a factor of significance in the consideration of the governments on the policy to be followed.

But when the Paris Peace Conference met, the increase in pressure against the colonial empires exerted by the Communist International appeared of small practical significance. Of much greater immediate importance was that just at the time of unofficial negotiations about the possibility of contacts with Russia, the threat of a Communist revolution in Europe did appear to have some reality behind it. Communist revolts broke out in various parts of eastern and central Europe. From March to August, 1919, the Communists, under Béla Kun, ruled in Hungary.

Lenin speaking to troops leaving Moscow for the front in the civil war, 1920. Trotsky is standing on the steps to the right of the podium. In later years, under Stalin, this picture was frequently reproduced, but on Stalin's orders, Trotsky was cut from the picture.

Throughout April, 1919, a Soviet republic existed in Bavaria. Communists were fought in Berlin and in the industrial Rhineland. The danger that the Bolsheviks would gain a foothold in central Europe, together with the Bolshevik repudiation of private enterprise, their use of terror, and their doubtful chances of survival against counterrevolutionary advances gave those who opposed all negotiations with the Communists easily the upper hand. Unavoidably, the settlement agreed upon in Paris took an anti-Russian aspect: the Paris Peace Conference adopted the policy of constructing a stout dam against the Bolsheviks in eastern Europe, a *cordon sanitaire* which would separate Bolshevik Russia from the democratic states. Finland had acquired independence by its own efforts. But the various Baltic nations—Estonia, Latvia, Lithuania—needed and received support in their resistance to Russian attempts at reconquest. Because it was believed that Poland and Rumania could become firm bulwarks against Communism, these states were given former Russian territory by the makers of the peace settlement, even in violation of the principle of national self-determination. Rumania received what had been Russian Bessarabia; Poland tried to push its eastern frontiers as far as possible into Russia and claimed the entire Ukraine. Although the Russo-Polish War of 1920 stemmed the Polish advance, western diplomatic help and economic aid gave the Poles a border extending far into Russian territory.

CHAPTER 7

The Era of Stabilization

DURING the First World War and in the arrangements of peace afterwards, France and Great Britain had been allies, and despite tensions and disputes over particular issues, had been close collaborators. Soon, however, differences in policy and outlook between the two nations became noticeable and exacerbated. These differences extended over the globe: for example, in the Near Eastern crisis of 1922, the British backed the Greeks, while the French favored the Turks. But the crucial issue in this deterioration of relations was a European issue, the divergences of Britain and France regarding the treatment of Germany; at the center of the dispute was the fulfillment of the arrangements made in the Treaty of Versailles —whether harsh or mild methods should be used. Lack of agreement between France and Britain had its impact on Germany, creating unrest and endangering the existence of the newly created republic. This unstable situation in the center of Europe had an unsettling effect on the entire continent.

UNREST AND CHAOS IN GERMANY: 1919–1924

Problems connected with the execution of the peace treaty dominated the policy of the Weimar Republic throughout its existence. In the first five years after the signing of the Treaty of Versailles the two principal issues concerned the reduction of the army to 100,000 men and the payment of reparations. These questions kept alive the conflicts which had developed over the acceptance of the peace treaty. Opponents of the treaty urged a purely negative obstructionist policy, suggesting that changes in the world situation would make enforcement of the terms impossible. The republican parties believed that a show of willingness to fulfill the clauses of the peace treaty was needed because it might help to embark on further negotiations and might gain sympathy for Germany in such negotiations.

German soldiers occupying government headquarters in Berlin during the Kapp Putsch; that they are in revolt against the republican government is shown in their display of the war flag of imperial Germany.

The most vehement opponents of adherence to the military clauses were the career officers, who had in the defense minister, the socialist Noske, an all too trusting chief. The general staff continued to function in disguised form as a section of the defense ministry. The military assisted the formation of unofficial, secret military organizations, provided them with weapons, and participated in their training. Among the men used by the army for keeping alive the military spirit was a corporal named Adolf Hitler, whose oratorical gifts seemed suited for this task.

The wave of military obstructionism reached its high point in March, 1920, when the reduction of the army to its accepted size could no longer be delayed. In a putsch organized by a former imperial civil servant, Wolfgang Kapp, the generals attempted to overthrow the government. Although the government had to flee Berlin, a general strike forced the putschists to surrender. The army was reduced to its prescribed strength and the illegal military organizations gradually disbanded. But the disorder of the Kapp Putsch led to Communist revolts, particularly in the Ruhr area, that could be suppressed only with the help of the military. The republican government, therefore, felt unable to take advantage of its victory over the rightists for a purge of the army of monarchist elements. The new 100,000-man army, the Reichswehr, remained firmly in the hands of the old officers' group.

The Treaty of Versailles had left determination of the exact amount of reparations and the details of their payment to later negotiations. These questions were thrashed out in a number of meetings and conferences which showed a wide gap between Allied demands and the Germans' estimate of their ability to pay; this disagreement served to maintain a poisoned atmosphere between the adversaries. An agreement that was submitted to Germany in the form of an ultimatum, and to which Germany felt forced to submit, was finally reached at a conference in London in May 1921: the amount of damages for which reparations were required was fixed at 132 billion marks (31.5 billion dollars), due in annual installments of 2 billion marks (close to 500 million dollars).

All the German political parties were convinced that their country could not pay this sum. But German politicians disagreed on how a reduction could be achieved. Once again the rightist parties advocated obstruction; the republican parties were in favor of making some payments and deliveries, in the hope that they would lead to the opening of negotiations and to economic cooperation. The most prominent protagonist of this fulfillment policy was Walter Rathenau (1867–1922). Rathenau was an uncommon figure: an aesthete who was close to many figures of modern art and literature, and a writer who in a number of widely read books had discussed the impact of modern technology on human existence, he was also a man of action who had proved his practical abilities as chairman of the great German electricity trust. And Rathenau was a good German patriot. At the beginning of the war he had suggested that the government inventory all raw materials—a most necessary measure—and had been entrusted with the task. In the difficult postwar situation Rathenau again put himself at the disposal of the government, serving as minister of reconstruction (May, 1921) and subsequently as foreign minister (February, 1922). His primary aim was to halt the inflationary trend of the German economy by substituting deliveries of goods for payments in gold; he hoped that economic cooperation, particularly between German and French industry, would gradually lead to a feasible reparations settlement. However, Rathenau was not master in his own foreign ministry, in which influential officials believed that western pressure on their nation would be weakened only if Germany exerted some counterpressure; they favored close connections with Soviet Russia. On April 16, 1922, when no improvement in the reparations arrangements seemed obtainable, Rathenau, the advocate of a western orientation in German foreign policy, was persuaded to conclude at Rapallo a treaty with Russia which provided for closer political and economic collaboration with the East. Nevertheless, because the German public regarded Rathenau as the embodiment of a policy of concessions to the victor, he became the chief target of the extremists of the right. On June 24, 1922, he was assassinated by members of a secret organization consisting chiefly of former officers who sought to eliminate as traitors the principal exponents of the fulfillment policy. Rathenau's assassination was only one in a long chain of political murders. Early in 1919, Karl Liebknecht and Rosa Luxemburg, who as leaders of the Spartacus group had been involved in the extremist revolt against the Majority Socialists, had been killed without trial after falling into the hands of the military. Matthias Erzberger, the leader of the Center party who had signed the armistice, had been assassinated in 1921, and in 1922 an attempt had been made on the life of the socialist Philipp Scheidemann, who in November, 1918, had proclaimed the republic in Berlin from the balcony of the Reichstag building. The members of the judiciary were conservative and nationalistic and refrained from probing the nationalistic organizations to which the murderers belonged.

With Rathenau's elimination, the pendulum swung to the side of those who favored a purely negative policy of refusal; even a complete collapse of the German currency should not be considered disastrous, since it would demonstrate Germany's inability to pay. In previous years the government, under the pressure of heavy industry, had not been averse to increasing the circulation of paper money because the depreciation of the mark helped the export trade and underlined the German inability to pay the demanded reparations. Now in early 1923, a government of experts under the business leader Heinrich Cuno, supported by the parties of the right, deliberately refused to make the deliveries to which Germany was obligated. The French reaction was quick and sharp. French troops moved into the Ruhr area, so that the mines of the district would now produce for France. But encouraged by the German government, the miners re-

The occupation of the Ruhr area in 1923. *French troops enter Essen.*

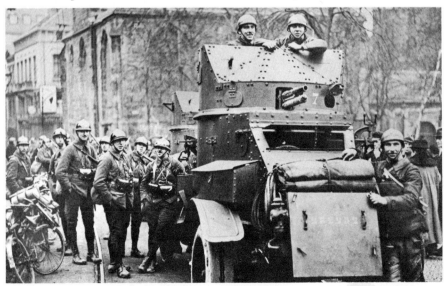

Inflation in Germany. A *kohlrabi* (*a type of turnip*) *cost fifty million marks in 1923.*

fused to work and embarked on a policy of passive resistance. To provide the money which the workers needed to live on, the German presses began to turn out currency with accelerated speed, and the mark plunged to unimaginable depths. At the beginning of 1923, the American dollar, which in 1914 had been the equivalent of 4.2 marks, brought 1,800 marks. By the fall of 1923 one American dollar was worth 4.2 trillion marks. Currency of this sort had no real value. When people received their wages they hastened to transform them into goods before their buying power diminished even further. Workers were hard hit because their wages, although steadily increased, did not keep up with the rising prices. Civil servants, with fixed salaries that only slowly adjusted to the upward trend, were in dire straits. Those dependent upon pensions, rents, or investment in government loans existed by selling whatever pieces of value they possessed. That the middle classes, usually a stabilizing social force, suffered most gravely and became embittered and increasingly radical was a fatal blow to the prestige of the republican regime. The inflation had a deeply demoralizing effect. While most people did not understand what was going on, those who did were able to make great amounts of money. Boys of seventeen and eighteen left school, turned to financial speculation, and quickly earned ten times as much as their fathers, who had been slowly working their way up through the bureaucratic hierarchy.

Conditions in Germany became chaotic. Separatist movements sprang up in the Rhineland. In Saxony, the radical left came into power. Bavaria was dominated by Bavarian monarchists and radical rightist organizations led by Ludendorff and Hitler. If a unified Reich and an ordered social life were to be maintained, the printing of money would have to be stopped, the passive resistance in the Ruhr would have to be abandoned, and Germany would have to resume reparations payments.

The necessity for admitting defeat was realized not only by those who had advocated the fulfillment policy but also by a leader of the rightist German People's party, Gustav Stresemann (1878–1929). Stresemann looked like a typical German petit bourgeois. Before 1914 he had been an enthusiastic admirer of William II and as a member of the Reichstag during the war years, he had been a rabid nationalist and annexationist and supported the high command in all its demands. But Stresemann had been deeply shaken by the way the military leaders had deceived themselves and the German people about their chances in the war. He became convinced that a reorganization of German political life on a democratic basis was unavoidable, and when the republican German Democratic party failed to accept him, he founded his own party, which aimed at the restoration of the monarchy but accepted the parliamentary system of government. In asserting the hopelessness of the contest over the Ruhr, Stresemann risked his popularity, but he was aware that by assuming leadership in this matter he was opening the door to a positive role for himself in the political life of the Weimar Republic. In a number of speeches made all over Germany during the early summer of 1923, he prepared the public for the necessity of abandoning the Ruhr struggle. And in August, 1923, he became chancellor, with the program of stabilizing the German currency and resuming the fulfillment policy. As a first step he ended the passive resistance in the Ruhr. He was helped by the fact that the chaotic situation which had developed in central Europe was having a damaging economic effect throughout the continent. All the great powers now recognized that for the sake of their own economic stability some compromise about German reparations payments had to be worked out; they agreed to the reopening of the question by a committee of experts headed by an American, Charles G. Dawes, and the formation of the Dawes Committee represents the beginning of a period of stabilization in European life.

THE ROAD TO THE REPARATIONS SETTLEMENT

The formation of the Dawes Committee, and even more, the acceptance of the Dawes Plan, did much to heal the rift between Great Britain and France which had steadily widened in the first five years after the Paris Peace Conference. But whereas France, in the years immediately following the war, at least insofar as European affairs were concerned, had been predominant, from the middle of the twenties on, Britain's role was decisive. Under British influence, after the unrest of the immediate postwar years, the second part of the twenties became an era of stabilization. In order to understand these developments, which include the formation of the Dawes Committee, the acceptance of the Dawes Plan, and the shift in political weight from France to England, we must turn our attention to the developments within these two countries in the years following the war.

France

The end of the First World War was a high point in French history. Alsace-Lorraine had been regained and the defeat in the Franco-Prussian War of 1870–1871 had been revenged. The First World War had been won by Allied forces under the command of a French general, Marshall Foch. The French army was looked upon as the first army of the world. Before the First World War the German army had formed the model for the military forces of many of the smaller states, but now French officers became instructors in the newly organized states, and the officers and soldiers in these new armies wore uniforms patterned after French uniforms.

It was in recognition of the role which France had played in the war that the peace conference met in Paris. With statesmen and politicians from all over the globe assembling there, Paris could claim, at least for the duration of the conference, to be capital of the world. Through their presence in Paris men from all over the world learned that, with Marcel Proust, Paul Claudel, André Gide, and Paul Valéry, a new generation of significant French writers had emerged and that French civilization was entering a new era of greatness.

But there was a reverse side to this picture of a France radiant in the joy of victory. The nation had lost 1,320,000 military men and 250,000 civilians in the war. Because the French birthrate was low these losses would be replaced only slowly and it was evident that in the number of males of military age France would remain inferior to Germany. Moreover, for four years the northern part of the country had been a theater of war and on their retreat in 1918 the Germans had devastated much of this area in which France's most important industries were situated. French finances, like those of other belligerents, had suffered from the war. Despite foreign loans, chiefly from the United States but also from Great Britain, France had been forced to print money; by the end of the war more than five times as much money was in circulation as in 1914, and prices were three and a half times as high as they had been before the war.

It is not astonishing that a country that had suffered as much as France would expect that its material losses would be paid for by the defeated opponent—Germany. The French were not overly concerned about the hardships which such demands would cause in German economic life. Inferior to Germany in manpower and in natural resources, France advocated the use of Germany's economic resources for rebuilding the economy of the victors, a measure that would weaken Germany's competitive capacities. And if the pressure on Germany also destroyed the unity of the Reich, this was not a development which the French would regret.

A military mentality was reflected in the elections which took place in

November, 1919: known as *horizon bleu* elections, after the color of French uniforms, they resulted in a great victory of the conservative *bloc national*, which obtained two thirds of the seats in the Chamber: 437 out of 613. The *cartel des gauches,* led by Édouard Herriot (1872–1957), and the Socialists lost heavily. This swing to the right was not purely the result of nationalist enthusiasm caused by victory; in France almost more than in any other country the coming to power of the Bolsheviks in Russia had aroused deep fears and hostility. The Bolshevik repudiation of the French prewar loans to Russia had provided the French bourgeoisie with some practical experience of what a revolution could involve. Alarm was reinforced by a change in the French economic system. The war had started a trend toward concentration in industry, with large corporations overshadowing the small family enter- prises characteristic of the prewar economy. The acquisition of Lorraine, with its rich iron-ore mines, strengthened the position of heavy industry within the industrial structure. A new social force in French political life emerged as membership in the Confédération Générale du Travail, the most important trade-union organization, soared from 600,000 in 1914 to 2,000,000 in 1920. In recognition of the strength of the workers the government under Clemenceau pushed through an eight-hour day and legal status for collective agreements before the 1919 elections. But this courting of labor appeared dangerous to the other strata of society because, in 1919, the French Socialist party was still in close contact with the Bolsheviks. Only in 1920, at the Socialist congress in Tours, did the party split: the larger group declared its adherence to the Communist International; the smaller, under Léon Blum, remained loyal to the Second Socialist Inter- national as it had been reconstructed after the war.

In the triumphant *bloc national* the most influential leader was Raymond Poincaré. His term as president of the republic ended in February, 1920, but he was elected to the Senate and continued political activities. As president he had supported Foch, who advocated separation of the Rhine- land from Germany, and he had been hostile to Clemenceau because of the latter's willingness to make concessions to the British and the United States and to content himself with a long-term occupation of the Rhineland. Poincaré favored the most adamant enforcement of the Treaty of Versailles. When the negotiations about reparations dragged on, he took over as prime minister and foreign minister, in 1922, and embarked on a policy which, disregarding the more accommodating approach of the British, was in- tended to force Germany to make the reparations payments which had been agreed upon—albeit under protest on Germany's part—in London in 1921. A strong motive for this policy was the difficult financial situation in which France found itself. The war had been financed with loans which demanded repayment. The French people resisted anything more than a small raise in taxation, so that government revenues amounted to a mere fraction of expenditures and the government was forced to finance its expenses by selling bonds. Reconstruction of the devastated and destroyed areas of the country placed a further burden on government finances. The money needed for this purpose was raised by loans, underwritten by the German reparations payments. When Germany balked at meeting the payments, the French deficit soared.

Poincaré's policy, designed to break down the German resistance to reparations payments, culminated in the invasion of the Ruhr. Poincaré's immediate aim was to have the coal and steel mines of the Ruhr working for the French government, so that, with the profits made from the sale of the Ruhr coal and steel, the cost of reconstruction of the destroyed areas could be paid. He also envisaged that this combination of military and economic pressure would strengthen the centrifugal forces in the Reich and perhaps lead to the foundation of a separate republic in the Rhineland.

The French occupation of the Ruhr proved to be a failure: the Reich remained unified and the passive resistance organized by the German government was so effective that all work in the mines ceased. It is true that the expenses involved in this passive resistance, i.e., paying miners for not working in the mines, led to bankruptcy. After nine months, in September, 1923, the Germans were forced to end the passive resistance and declare their intentions to resume payments and deliveries under the Versailles treaty. But the expenses involved in the Ruhr adventure had also deteriorated the French economic situation. The French franc declined rapidly in value, and speculators expected it to go the way of the German mark. A loan by American bankers, particularly J. P. Morgan and Company, stopped the run on the franc, but the French government had to accept the establishment of an international committee of experts who would assess the German economic situation and the possibilities for reparations: the Dawes Committee.

The result of all this was a reaction against Poincaré's policy in the French republic. Evidently the French became aware of the "painful impression of intransigence"—to quote from a note to the French government by the British foreign secretary, George Curzon—which French policy had made all over the world. In the elections of the year following the Ruhr occupation the *cartel des gauches* won: Poincaré resigned. The new prime minister was Herriot, and the foreign minister in the government of the left was Aristide Briand (1862–1932).

Briand remained foreign minister from 1925 to 1932. The early years of his political career, when he had been feared as a radical for his role in effecting the separation of church and state, were far behind him. He had subsequently served in many French cabinets, as minister of education, minister of justice, and prime minister. As prime minister during the German offensive against Verdun, Briand had experienced the horrors of this battle and his interests in the postwar years turned toward foreign affairs and the problems of peace. Briand was no less convinced than his predecessors that France needed guaranties against attack, but he hoped to achieve them through agreements and alliances embedded in a system of collective security which would automatically align the members of the League of Nations against any aggressor. Briand was a great orator and his speeches, always high points at meetings of the League of Nations in Geneva, created a great deal of international good will for France. Nevertheless, the acceptance of his foreign policy in France represented a resigned acknowledgment of the limitations of French power. Despite victory in war, and despite possession of the greatest European army, France was not able to go it alone in foreign policy during the postwar years.

Great Britain

Although Great Britain came to advocate a more lenient treatment of Germany than France, the British people did not have any sympathy for the Germans at the end of the war. Indeed, the hatred had grown so strong that it took years before personal contacts between the British and German people were resumed. The elections which took place in December 1918, and in which for the first time women were entitled to vote, were known as khaki elections, for the campaign and the voting both reflected the spirit of the khaki-clad soldier. In the campaign, the government promised to prosecute William II and all those Germans responsible for war atrocities and to make Germany pay the entire costs of war. With Lloyd George, the prime minister, assuring the people that he would "exact the last penny we can get out of Germany up to the limit of her capacity," the government gained an overwhelming victory, winning 478 seats while the opposition secured only 87. The government was a coalition of Conservatives (still called Unionists) and of Liberal adherents of Lloyd George and reflected the nationalist mood of this period in that the Conservatives, with 335 seats, were much stronger than their Liberal coalition partners.

Nevertheless, in Great Britain the expectations for the postwar world were different from those in France. The French had achieved concrete gains, such as the recovery of Alsace-Lorraine, and nurtured concrete aims, notably liberation from the incubus of German superiority and aggression. The British had much vaguer notions. They expected a peaceful world and a better life for all the people in the British Isles. The idea of a new order in international affairs went hand in hand with demands for reform in domestic life. The crucial importance of making the postwar world an era of social reforms was reflected in the address of the king at the opening of the postwar Parliament: "The aspirations for a better social order which have been quickened in the hearts of My people by the experience of the war must be encouraged by prompt and comprehensive

E nd

action.... since the outbreak of the war every party and every class have worked and fought together for a great ideal ... we must continue to manifest the same spirit. We must stop at no sacrifice of interest or prestige to stamp out unmerited poverty, to diminish unemployment, to provide decent homes, to improve the nation's health, and to raise the standard of well-being throughout the country." And these notions were underlined by Lloyd George in a speech in the House of Commons in February, 1919, in which he stated that there was no member in the House who was not pledged to the cause of social reform. "If we fail, history will condemn not merely the perfidy but the egregious folly of such failure."

The war effort had involved all classes of British society, and those who had participated in the war now expected fulfillment of their needs in peacetime. The government had given women of thirty and over the right to vote, and extended the male suffrage by removing property qualifications. But its record in instituting social reforms was unsatisfactory, despite such steps as the extension of unemployment insurance to almost all workers earning less than five pounds a week. The most important issue in postwar Britain was housing. Building had stopped during the war years, and it was estimated that at least 300,000 new houses were needed within one year after the war. But two years later the housing policy of the government had produced only 14,594 new houses, and when in 1923 budgetary cutbacks ended government subsidies for home construction, the shortage of houses was even worse than it had been in 1918. Slums remained an indelible and spreading blot on English industrial centers.

The disappointment of the expectations which victory and the promises of the government had aroused raised questions also about the past. It transformed enthusiasm for the wartime statesmen into doubts and criticism and aroused skepticism about the policy pursued toward Germany.

The failure to achieve social reform was partly a failure of the government, but also due in part to circumstances beyond its control. For one thing, the government was made up of prima donnas. Besides Lloyd George, who had acquired immense authority because of his war leadership, there were such formidable figures as the former prime minister Arthur Balfour, Alfred Milner of South African fame, and George Curzon, a former viceroy of India. Also included were the stars of a younger generation, among them the arrogant and witty F. E. Smith (later earl of Birkenhead), Winston Churchill, and Austen Chamberlain, Joseph Chamberlain's son and political heir. These and other leaders seemed more interested in maneuvering against one another for public favor than in carrying out a unified policy. Their ambitions and intrigues were fed by the press, particularly by the newspapers belonging to the press "Lords"—Northcliffe, Rothermere, Beaverbrook—who themselves were eager for a political role. As a coalition of Conservatives and Liberals the government was beset by conflicting principles whenever it strove to establish a definite line of policy.

The old conflict about free trade revived, with the Liberals eager to maintain an open trade policy and the Conservatives favoring preferential tariffs for the members of the British empire. There was also a conflict over the maintenance of government control over economic life within Great Britain. Without the possibility of some such control, the Liberals' demands for an active policy of social reforms could not be carried out. The Conservatives, however, used their strength in the House of Commons to force Lloyd George to abolish the economic restrictions and regulations introduced during wartime.

Other problems confronted the government as well. The turmoil which the war had raised did not easily subside; instead, unrest was widespread through the British empire. The peace conference, the question of the intervention in Russia, the struggle in the Near East absorbed much of the attention of British statesmen. Closer to home, a settlement of the Irish question, which had disturbed British political life for almost a century, could no longer be postponed. During the war the government had hesitated to take energetic steps toward the introduction of home rule in Ireland, and the result had been a rebellion at Easter time in 1916. It was quickly defeated, but the ruthlessness of its suppression destroyed the influence of the moderates in Ireland. The dominating force in Irish policy now became the Sinn Fein; the name, which means "we ourselves," indicated that the goal of this group was complete independence. The Sinn Fein engaged in guerilla warfare; British officers were attacked, manor houses belonging to those opposed to independence were burned, banks were robbed. To replace Irishmen who had resigned, the police force was strengthened by recruits from England, derisively called the Black and Tans, after the colors of their uniform. Their brutality aroused indignation even in England.

The Conservatives believed that dealings with the Sinn Fein should start only after the Black and Tans had reestablished order. But the Liberals wanted to enter upon negotiations immediately, and their view prevailed. In December, 1921, a treaty was signed which divided Ireland into a northern part, Ulster, which remained within the United Kingdom, and a southern part, the Irish Free State, with dominion status. Some members of the Sinn Fein, led by Eamon de Valera (born 1882), were not content with this arrangement; they fought bitterly against the moderate Irish government, and finally attained power. In 1937, they succeeded in gaining complete independence for the Irish Free State.

The most serious blow to all plans of social reform was an economic depression that engulfed Britain in 1921. The pent-up demand for goods that had not been available during the war had resulted in a boom which soon led to overexpansion and overspeculation. In consequence, a great rise in prices immediately after the war was suddenly followed by a decline, which led to a shrinking of production and a diminution of buying power.

In 1921 British exports to France fell by 65.2 per cent and to the United States by 42.6 per cent from the previous year's level. Altogether, British exports in 1921 were less than half of what they had been in 1920. The nadir of this depression was reached in June, 1921, with 23.1 per cent (2,185,000) of Britain's workers unemployed. The full extent of this misery was not reflected in this figure, however. Certain industries suffered more than others and in some localities unemployment climbed to 40 or 50 per cent of the labor force. After 1922 the situation improved, but not until the outbreak of the Second World War did the number of unemployed in Britain drop below a million. One of the permanent features in British economic life became the "dole," the benefits which the unemployed received under the Unemployment Insurance Act. They were strictly limited to two periods of sixteen weeks each and were paid only to those who proved to be in need. Unemployment and the dole seemed strange compensation for the hardships and sacrifices of a victorious war.

The 1920's in Great Britain became a time of disillusionment. The most flamboyant of the war leaders lost much of their appeal. Winston Churchill had to struggle hard to maintain his place in politics. Lloyd George aroused the greatest distrust. In 1922, in a famous speech in the Carleton Club, the very heart of the Conservative party, Stanley Baldwin, then president of the Board of Trade, said of Lloyd George that he was "a great dynamic force" but that a dynamic force could be "a very terrible thing." The Conservatives then voted against continuation of the coalition and Lloyd George never returned to a position in the government.

The view that no victory could compensate for the losses and damages of war became widespread. Pacifist organizations proliferated. Expenditure for the armed forces became unpopular. The government required the military services to base their budget estimates on the assumption that "the British Empire will not be engaged in any general war during the next ten years and that no expeditionary force will be required." Disarmament was regarded as the panacea.

The country which profited most from this change of view was Germany. It was believed that wartime propaganda had painted an exaggerated and false picture of Germany. Back in 1919 Keynes's *Economic Consequences of the Peace* had opened the attack upon the peace settlement, and now German demands for revision of the Treaty of Versailles began to find a hearing in Great Britain.

Because so many young men had been lost in the war, the older men remained in power much longer than their counterparts in the prewar days. It seemed impossible to make a dent in their closed ranks. Viewing the traditions and customs of political life with disgust young men turned away from politics. Rejection of accepted forms and values became characteristic of the most gifted writers and artists of the new generation. The great literary monument of the disillusionment and desperation of the postwar world in England was T. S. Eliot's *The Waste Land* (1922).

The abandonment, in pursuit of victory, of attitudes deeply rooted in liberal beliefs, and the disillusionment of the postwar era, aroused skepticism toward the traditions and the achievements of the past, and this changed political mood played a role in what, from the point of view of political history, might be regarded as the most striking event in the years after the war: the rise of the Labor party. In 1914 the replacement of the Liberal party by the Labor party would have been regarded as most improbable. The war had favored the chances of the Labor party. With the ousting of Asquith as prime minister in 1916, and his replacement by the dynamic Lloyd George, the Liberal party had been split into two hostile groups. Moreover, the war had strengthened the power of the Labor party. The shift of industries to war production, and the need for using all available manpower, required cooperation of the government with trade unions. Their power and therefore also their appeal had increased. By 1919 the membership of the trade unions had almost doubled, and amounted to more than eight million. In order to assure the support of the workers, two leading figures in the Labor party, Arthur Henderson and John Robert Clynes, had entered the war government and their activities disproved the thesis that Labor leaders were wild radicals who could not be entrusted with government responsibility. On the other hand, the kind of opposition to the war which had existed in the Liberal party in 1914 continued to dominate the thinking of some groups in the Labor party. Most prominent among the opponents of the war was Ramsay MacDonald (1866–1937).

An intellectual who looked like a peer of the realm, MacDonald was rather removed from the down-to-earth trade-union leaders who dominated the party organization. But MacDonald showed remarkable courage during the war, struggling against the tide of national hysteria and sponsoring meetings at which conscientious objectors expressed their pacifist views. MacDonald argued eloquently that the war would have meaning only if it was the beginning of a changed and better world. In 1917, he greeted the Russian Revolution as an inspiration for labor movements all over the globe and advocated the formation of workers' and soldiers' councils in Britain.

In the disillusionment of the postwar years Labor benefited from the fact that, in contrast to the Conservatives and Liberals, it represented the possibility of change and, at the same time, the war seemed to have proved that Labor was able to govern. This worked to Labor's advantage in the elections which were held in December, 1923. The coalition government under Lloyd George had been succeeded by a Conservative government, headed first by Bonar Law (1858–1923) and then by Stanley Baldwin (1867–1947). Baldwin decided on new elections in order to get a mandate for the realization of the old Conservative demand for protective tariffs, which he believed would alleviate unemployment. In the elections the Conservatives remained the strongest party, but they lost their majority. The Liberals and Labor combined had more votes than the Conservatives, and since Labor held more seats than the Liberals, Ramsay MacDonald was asked by King George V to form the government. Because this first Labor government lacked a majority and needed the support of the Liberals, its potential for action was strictly limited, and its accomplishments were meager. A housing act, providing state subsidies for the building of houses with controlled rents, was the main domestic achievement. In foreign affairs, the government established diplomatic relations with Soviet Russia and promptly signed a commercial treaty with the Russians. Storms of protest greeted these moves. On a minor issue—the somewhat questionable dropping of the prosecution of a Communist journalist—the Liberals voted against the government, and in the elections which followed, Labor was defeated. This loss was chiefly due to anti-Communist hysteria. The middle classes, who had been upset by MacDonald's negotiations with Soviet Russia, were turned decisively against Labor by the publication during the election campaign of a letter allegedly written by Zinoviev, the head of the Communist International, outlining a strategy for revolution in England. Although a clever falsification, the letter did compromise the Labor party. The Labor government lasted only ten months, but its tenure, though short, established Labor as the alternative to the Conservatives. Moreover, although Labor's domestic record had been unexciting, it could claim that in foreign affairs its rule had been an undisputed success—a success which had to be primarily attributed to Ramsay MacDonald. MacDonald had been foreign secretary as well as prime minister, and it was while he was foreign secretary that agreement on the reparations question was achieved.

When Labor came to power a committee of experts, the Dawes Committee, was examining the reparations question but it was still not settled whether the states involved, and particularly France, would consider the result of the committee's deliberations as binding on them. In a letter to Poincaré in February, 1924, MacDonald made a statement almost undiplomatic in its frankness: "It is widely felt in England that, contrary to the provisions of the Treaty of Versailles, France is endeavoring to create a situation which gains for it what it failed to get during the allied peace negotiations. . . . The people in this country regard with anxiety what appears to them to be the determination of France to ruin Germany and to dominate the continent without consideration of our reasonable interests and future consequences to European settlement." MacDonald clearly implied that England expected France to accept the report of the experts, and was not willing to bargain about this. The French people could have little doubt about the dangerous consequences of British hostility for French economic life in times of rising inflationary pressure. Fortunately for MacDonald, Herriot and the *cartel des gauches* came into

power in May, 1924, and the new government participated in a conference in London over which MacDonald presided. There were long and
difficult negotiations, but finally the liquidation of the Ruhr occupation
by a gradual withdrawal of French troops was conceded by Herriot. On the
basis of the report of the committee of experts, i.e., the Dawes Committee,
an agreement on reparations was signed on August 31 by all powers
concerned.

The policy of MacDonald was not very different from that of the
Conservative foreign secretaries who preceded and followed him. But Labor
and Conservatives arrived at the same policy from somewhat different
points of departure. MacDonald's approach was idealistic. He had been an
opponent of the war and he wanted to liquidate the consequences of the
war as quickly and as thoroughly as possible as a prerequisite for the
building of a peaceful international order. The Conservatives were more
realistic; in the main, they had become a party of businessmen. They
were concerned about the deterioration and the difficulties of the British
economic situation. They were unhappy about the weakness and the
collapse of the German mark, since the cheapness of the German goods
made them fierce competitors on the world market. They regarded a stabilization of the economic conditions in central Europe as necessary for
Britain's own recovery.

Moreover, financial circles in the United States, which had been exert-
ing a great influence on British economic policy since the war, were demanding a settlement of the reparations question. In the first months of
1923 Stanley Baldwin, then chancellor of the exchequer, had negotiated an
agreement with the American government on the repayment of the
loans which Britain had received from the United States during the war.
Officially the American government maintained that there was no connection between German reparations and the repayment of war loans
given to the Allies. But it was evident that the European states would not
repay their war debts until they received reparations from Germany. Thus,
a settlement of the reparations question which would allow an economic
recovery of Europe was in the American interest, and became a common
goal of the two English-speaking countries. American financial circles were
willing to assume a positive role. An American, Charles Dawes, chaired
the committee of experts, which was reexamining the reparations question, and American financial circles were ready to make the proposals of
the report work by giving a loan. It was this active interest and assistance
which gave Europe the possibility of a breathing space.

BRITAIN AS EUROPE'S LEADER: 1925–1929

The era of stabilization which Europe enjoyed in the second part of the
twenties was achieved in two steps. The first step to placing economic

The architects of the Locarno Treaties: *From left to right, Stresemann, Austen Chamberlain, and Briand.*

life on a firm basis was an agreement on reparations in accordance with the Dawes Plan. The next step was the conclusion of a political agreement among the principal European powers, embodied in the Locarno treaties, arranged in Locarno, Switzerland, in October, 1925, and signed in London on December 1, 1925.

After abandoning passive resistance in the Ruhr, Germany stabilized its currency by introducing a new basic unit, the *Rentenmark*, equivalent to a trillion of the old marks. This was an operation on paper, purely an elimination of a number of zeros. It assumed some reality because Hjalmar Schacht, president of the German Reichsbank since December, 1923, managed to obtain credits from British banks and a loan from Montagu Norman, the governor of the Bank of England. On the other hand he started a strictly deflationary policy by refusing to give any further credits to the German government or to German economic enterprises. The printing of money had ended. However, renewed pressure for reparations payments would have restored the inflationary trend if the stabilization of the German currency had not been complemented by the acceptance of the Dawes Plan.

The Dawes Plan fixed the German reparations payments for the next five years; the installments were then gradually to increase as Germany's economy recovered with the aid of a large foreign loan. An American commissioner was to make certain that Germany paid to the limits of its capacity. He was to control the remittance of reparations and to establish the transfer of payments in gold. It would be in his power to exert a far-reaching influence on German economic life, for he would supervise the policy of the Reichsbank and the financial administration of the railroads, as well as other state-run enterprises. The presence of this commissioner assured the Germans of a hearing if the payments envisaged in the Dawes Plan went beyond their capacity. Furthermore, the existence of the accompanying foreign loan meant that the financial interests of other nations were connected with German economic recovery and prosperity.

John Maynard Keynes (1883–1946) described the reparations settlement as follows: "Reparations and interallied debts are being mostly settled on paper and not in goods. The United States lends money to Germany, Germany transfers its equivalent to the allies, the allies pass it back to the United States government. Nothing real passes—no one is a pennyworse." In this brilliant satirical summary Keynes did not mention one issue which in the following years would become highly important. The loans had to be repaid with interest and the Germans had to earn this interest through exports. Because German wages had been low since the end of the war, and because the world economy was again expanding, after the economic nadir of 1921, the earnings of German exports were sufficient to pay the scheduled amount of reparations and the interest on the loans. The system functioned for a number of years, but it ran into trouble when the requisite combination of low German wages and world prosperity began to disappear.

With the establishment of international interest in the economic recovery of Germany it became important for the victors of the First World War to tie Germany also to the political settlement made at the Paris Peace Conference. To the Germans this meant a chance to regain a place among the great powers. These were the considerations which underlay the arrangements made at Locarno. The most important of them was a treaty concluded by Great Britain, Germany, France, Belgium, and Italy. Germany recognized that its western frontier, as defined in the Treaty of Versailles, was permanent. If there occurred an "unprovoked attack" by Germany against France or by France against Germany, the victim would be helped by Great Britain and Italy; especially noteworthy was the stipulation that not only a violation of the frontiers but also a "flagrant violation" of the demilitarization of the Rhineland was regarded as an act of aggression. This stipulation became important after the occupation of the Rhineland had ended in 1930, for six years later, when German troops marched into the Rhineland, the expressions "flagrant violation" and "unprovoked attack" became loopholes through which remilitarization of the Rhineland was condoned. Although nobody could deny that the Germans had broken the Locarno treaties, it was argued that this violation was neither "flagrant" nor "unprovoked." But in 1925 the general opinion was that the frontiers between Germany, France, and Belgium—and the permanent demilitarization of the Rhineland—were now recognized as final.

This treaty, the core of the Locarno arrangements, was complemented by a number of other agreements. Treaties concluded by Germany with France, Belgium, Poland, and Czechoslovakia established that all disputes which could not be resolved by diplomatic negotiations would be submitted to arbitration. Moreover, agreements between France and Poland and France and Czechoslovakia determined that if Germany refused arbitration, these states would assist one another against Germany, by force of arms, if necessary. Finally, Germany was to be admitted to the League of Nations and receive a permanent seat on the Council of the League. Germany declared, however, if the League imposed military sanctions on some state, Germany's participation would be limited by its military and geographical situation, because military clauses of the Treaty of Versailles had left the country too weak to join in military actions. Practically, this meant that Germany would not have to participate in military action against Soviet Russia.

To what extent did the Locarno agreements change the existing political situation, and to whose advantage were they? The admission to the League of Nations and the acquisition of a permanent seat on the Council meant that Germany was again recognized as an equal of other nations and as a great European power. For the Germans, abandonment of the claims to Alsace-Lorraine on their western frontier and the acknowledgment of restrictions on the exercise of sovereignty in the Rhineland were painful. However, there was no comparable acceptance of the permanence of the eastern borders; Germany abjured the use of force for revising these frontiers, but was not prevented from urging such revision. Moreover, Germany was able to maintain its special relationship with Russia, which had been established in 1922 with the Treaty of Rapallo; in April, 1926, in the Treaty of Berlin the two states confirmed the Treaty of Rapallo. Germany had not opted between east and west. It certainly was in no worse a bargaining position than before, perhaps in a better one.

France also had not lost. Ever since the end of the First World War, France had been insisting that its security demanded a firm alliance with the United States and Great Britain against Germany. Now it had finally obtained assurances of aid from Great Britain. To be sure, the Locarno treaty was not a special Franco-British alliance, just a guarantee of the existing frontiers of both France and Germany. But since nobody expected France to want to change the frontiers, it actually amounted to a promise of British support in case of a German attack. France would have liked a similar guarantee of the eastern frontiers of Germany. But the demilitarization of the Rhineland, coupled with France's military alliances with Poland and Czechoslovakia, had left Germany militarily powerless, unable to expand either to the east or to the west. Thus the Locarno treaties did not weaken the French position. If anything, they reinforced French military security.

For both France and Germany two ways were open. They could regard the Locarno arrangements as a new departure, the beginning of a cooperation which slowly and gradually might remove distrust and create a European community. Or they could fall back into antagonistic positions, their relative strength neither weakened nor increased.

The Locarno agreements were bitterly criticized in Germany and France. Briand and Stresemann, the foreign ministers who had concluded them, were accused of having abandoned essential national interests. Each of these men trusted the other and was convinced of the other's good will. But each had to demonstrate to his people that the treaties had advantages for their nation. To bring about a gradual recognition of these advantages, much could be done by Great Britain. If Britain cautiously balanced France against Germany and Germany against France by opposing every resurrection of German military power and every French attempt to use its military strength for keeping Germany economically weak, it might help to bring the old antagonists together. For a number of years Britain did indeed follow this course.

When the Locarno treaties were signed in London the portrait of Castlereagh was brought down from an attic in the British foreign office and hung in the room in which the solemn ceremony took place. The gesture was appropriate. Castlereagh had been banished to the attic because during the period of Britain's splendid isolation his policy of cooperation with the great European powers had seemed contradictory to the British tradition. But his aim of maintaining peace and stability in Europe by a diplomacy based upon conferences with the continent's leading statesmen appeared very similar to the policy which Austen Chamberlain, the British foreign secretary, was now pursuing. Indeed, the effect of the Locarno agreements was not limited to the mitigation of tensions between Germany and France. Their main effect was to reestablish a concert of the great European powers thereby restoring some order within Europe and extending the influence of the European powers through the entire world.

ITALY AND RUSSIA IN THE TWENTIES

The regulation of the reparations question and the political stabilization through the Locarno treaties implied a reaffirmation of those political values in the name of which the war had been conducted, most of all democracy; and a reaffirmation of the leadership of the two great European powers on which the chief burden of the victory had lain: France and Great Britain. The agreements of 1924 and 1925, of course, meant that Germany should be drawn into this constellation, although as we have indicated, it remained an open question to what extent and how completely this aim was attained. But there was still the further question how those powers which had remained excluded or had opposed the Paris Peace settlement would react to the establishment of a new concert of Europe and whether, even if they accepted the situation which the Locarno treaties had created, they would cooperate or would mainly tolerate it and wait for an opportunity to change it or overthrow it. This question refers to Italy and Russia.

The Rise of Fascism in Italy

Italy had fought in the First World War on the allied side; when the Paris Peace Conference convened, Orlando, the Italian prime minister, was one of the four men (the Big Four) who presided over the new organization of the globe—along with Wilson, Lloyd George, and Clemenceau. Nevertheless, in the postwar world Italy did not regard itself as a victorious power; it was anxious to see the peace treaties modified, and tended to support revisionist movements. This separation from the other Allies, already evident at the Paris Peace Conference, had its roots in the events accompanying Italy's entry into the war in 1915.

Unlike the other great powers, which were drawn into the hostilities in consequence of a chain of events over which they had lost control, Italy entered the war deliberately, with the aim of aggrandizement. In the secret Treaty of London of 1915, Great Britain, France, and Russia had promised Italy wide territorial gains. But the fulfillment of this treaty had encountered difficulties at the Paris Peace Conference, especially with regard to the extended Austrian territories which Italy was to receive: the Trentino and South Tyrol up to the Brenner Pass, Trieste, Istria, the islands along the Dalmatian coast, and a great part of Dalmatia. These acquisitions were intended to give Italy security against the Habsburg empire, which in 1915 nobody expected to disappear. But when the war ended, Austria-Hungary no longer existed and adherence to the arrangements of the Treaty of London was incompatible with the principle of self-determination for it would have placed more than a million Yugoslavs under Italian rule. Nevertheless, the Italians occupied Austrian territory up to the line assigned to them in the treaty of 1915, and when the Paris Peace Conference convened they insisted on their pound of flesh—the fulfillment of the treaty. Aware, however, of the obstacles which in these changed circumstances the execution of the early promises would encounter, the Italians intimated that they might be willing to accept less if they were given Fiume, which had not been assigned to them in the Treaty of London. But Fiume had a large Yugoslav population, and the Yugoslavs vehemently refused this Italian demand, since they did not want to see the two good ports on the eastern side of the

Adriatic Sea—Trieste and Fiume—in Italian hands. The question of Fiume became one of the stumbling blocks at the Paris Peace Conference. President Wilson's appeal to the Italian people to accept the principle of self-determination was rejected. For three weeks the Italian delegates absented themselves from the negotiations. Even after their return, the Fiume question remained undecided.

The Paris Peace Conference allowed Italy to extend its frontiers to the Brenner Pass and to take over the Istrian Peninsula, including the city of Trieste. Italy thus acquired all the Habsburg territories which had been regarded as *Italia irredenta* in the prewar years, but the government, in order to get backing for its additional claims, had whipped up nationalist excitement to such a degree that the joy over the fulfillment of these national aspirations was overshadowed by disappointment over the failure to obtain Fiume and Dalmatia. All over Italy, people spoke of "the mutilated victory."

In Italy the parliamentary system was in a serious crisis before 1914. The disappointing results of the war reanimated and reinforced contempt for the feebleness of parliamentary politics. The strong radical movements that had developed on the left and the right in response to the government's failure to address itself to the miseries of the South or to give reality to Italy's claim of being a great power, once again asserted themselves. Nationalist organizations of an antiparliamentary character sprang up everywhere. The fiery poet Gabriele d'Annunzio became an influential political leader in Italy. In the fall of 1919, while the negotiations over Fiume were still going on, he organized a troop of volunteers, who seized power in Fiume. There they remained until December, 1920. By then, Italy's foreign minister, Count Carlo Sforza (1873–1952), had negotiated a treaty according to which Fiume became an independent city-state and in compensation Italy received a number of islands on the Dalmatian coast. Now Italian troops turned d'Annunzio and his volunteers out of Fiume. But d'Annunzio had exposed the weak and vacillating character of the Italian government, which first made great demands and then hesitated to enforce them. Among the nationalist leaders of this period, the most efficient was the former Socialist leader Benito Mussolini (1883–1945), who had left the Socialist party because it had resisted Italian entry into the war. He had served in the war as a volunteer and was now seeking a platform from which to reenter political life. On March 23, 1919, in a building on the Piazza San Sepolcro in Milan, he founded his own organization, the *Fasci di Combattimento*, whose members came to be known as Fascists.

Resentment over thwarted nationalist aims was fed by economic misery and discontent. In Italy more than 50 per cent of the country's tax revenues came from consumer taxes, which fell off when the war caused a decrease in the production of consumer goods. An attempt was made to finance the Italian war effort through internal and foreign loans, and when these proved insufficient the government resorted to the printing of paper money. The consequence was inflation; in 1920 the lira had less than a fifth of its prewar value. The financial problems were increased by a growing deficit in the balance of trade.

During the war, when most of the male population was conscripted, agricultural production had been maintained on a satisfactory level through the efforts of women, children, and the elderly. But no work had been done for amelioration of the soil; the soil was exhausted. After the war Italy had to import not only coal and oil but also great quantities of grain.

Most directly hit by the inflation were the members of the middle classes: people with fixed incomes, such as civil servants, landlords prevented by law from raising rents, and rentiers who had invested their money in government bonds. But economic distress was also felt by the rural classes and the workers. After the war more than 50 per cent of all Italians were engaged in agriculture. Nine tenths of those who owned land possessed less than three acres, not nearly enough even for subsistence. And a great part of the rural population was entirely landless, working for wages on the great estates. During the war the government had promised a redistribution of the land; rumors—many exaggerated—about what had been done in Russia stimulated the impatience of the Italian peasants and raised their expectations. The war also increased unrest among the industrial workers. Hitherto industrial activity had largely taken the form of very small enterprises, employing less than ten workers. But during the war large-scale industrial establishments had become much more numerous. The wartime need for the production of guns, planes, cars, and ships led to the formation of great industrial complexes engaged in steel production, engineering, and shipping. Ansaldo employed more than 100,000 workers, but Iloa, Fiat, and others were also enterprises of remarkable size. These big industries were closely allied with the great Italian banks—the Banca Commerciale and the Banca di Sconto—and this combination of industrial and commercial interests developed into a powerful factor in Italian politics. The depreciation of the Italian currency facilitated the export of Italian industrial products and increased the wealth of the entrepreneur, whereas the wages of the workers could not keep up with the inflationary rise of prices. These economic difficulties, coupled with news about the workers' "paradise" in Russia, intensified the demand for social reform by the workers, and the long-standing influence of syndicalism and anarchism contributed to their radicalization. Dissatisfaction among the rural and industrial proletariat erupted in direct action. In dramatic fashion bands of peasants and agricultural workers, marching to the accompaniment of martial music and the pealing of church bells, occupied uncultivated land belonging to the great landowners. In cities and towns strikes increased. The strike wave reached its high point in the summer of 1920, when dismissals in the metallurgical industries led to an occupation of the factories by the workers in industrial regions. However, these demonstrations had no long-lasting effect. The police removed the peasants from the land which they had appropriated, and the workers, lacking raw materials, capital, and salesmen, were unable to keep the industries going and evacuated the factories. Nevertheless, the political activity of peasants and workers contributed significantly to the transformation of the Italian party system. Before the war the Italian political parties were rather loose in structure; the individual deputy owed his election to his reputation and his standing in his own district, not to his party label. After the war, the socialists, in close alliance with the trade unions, built an efficient, centrally directed organization. Furthermore, Pope Benedict XV gave permission for the foundation of a Catholic political party, and the Catholic People's party appeared on the scene. Eager for mass support, it looked beyond the Catholic bourgeoisie for adherents, seeking to attract the peasants of the south and the industrial workers, among whom Catholic trade unions began to compete with socialist trade unions. The guiding spirit of the Catholic People's party was a Sicilian priest, Don Luigi Sturzo, whose experience in the stagnant Italian south had made him aware of the need for social—particularly agrarian—reform. The influence of the two mass parties—the Socialists and the Catholic People's party— was strengthened by the adoption of the proportional voting system, which the government had introduced as a concession to the demands for reform: the number of deputies allowed each party was determined by the total number of votes received by the party throughout Italy. The bourgeois parties of the center and the left, Liberals and Democrats, were seriously threatened. This was the situation when the Fascists came to power in October, 1922.

Mussolini's claim that Fascism saved Italy from Bolshevism is palpably untrue. If there ever was danger of a successful Communist take-over in Italy after the First World War—and this is most doubtful—the revolutionary wave had certainly passed its crest by the spring of 1921. The new mass parties, now firmly entrenched, did not advocate revolution. However, they did agree on the need for far-reaching social and economic reform. Reform was deeply feared by the industrialists and landowners, still suffering from the shock of the occupation of factories and land by workers and peasants. In their anxiety they turned to the opponents of parliamentary democracy, hoping to gain support in their fight against reform. Mussolini's Fascists offered themselves as a most suitable instrument. Throughout Italy the party had formed paramilitary organizations, consisting chiefly of young unemployed war veterans. In the industrial centers of the north, these Fascist organizations made themselves popular with the bourgeoisie by protecting strikebreakers and disrupting socialist street demonstrations. In the rural areas they supported the landowners anxious to prevent the formation of unions of farm workers, or to break them up where they existed. The young Fascists were ruthless but effective. Moreover, Mussolini, their leader, inspired some confidence; he was a journalist of gifts and a remarkable orator. Although his boasts of intensive study of Marx and Nietzsche were consideraby exaggerated, his acquaintance with Marxist thought and modern philosophy was sufficient to give his writings and speeches intellectual respectability. Through his advocacy of Italy's entry into the war, and through his war service, he had demonstrated his patriotism, but Mussolini was too much of a Marxist to believe that the world could stand still and be satisfied with the same old ideas. He was therefore not only a nationalist but also a revolutionary activist. And this combination constituted his strength in the eyes of the Italian upper classes. On the one hand Mussolini seemed to have a hold over the masses which they had lost; on the other, he seemed to share their own nationalist ideals and their rejection of international socialism. They expected that Mussolini might develop his organization into a counterforce to the new mass parties. Leaders of the old political groups, such as Giolitti, regarded Mussolini's rise with benevolence. They believed that he would be useful and that cooperation with him would be feasible.

The test came with the Fascist seizure of power—the March on Rome on October 27, 1922. The version of this event which the Fascists later spread was that the Fascist organizations had converged on Rome and the government, faced by this revolutionary force, capitulated. Actually, negotiations about Fascist participation in the government had been going on for some time. Leaders of various political parties—Giolitti as well as the more conservative Antonio Salandra (1853–1931)—were willing to form a coalition government which included the Fascists. To clinch these negotiations Mussolini organized the March on Rome; his paramilitary organizations approached the capital from four directions. The government felt sure that it could defeat this Fascist revolt with the help of the army, and the king was willing to sign the order declaring a state of siege. But on the night of October 27, he changed his mind—it is not quite clear why—either because he had received an exaggerated report of the Fascist military strength, as he maintained after the fall of Mussolini, or because he had been informed about the unwillingness of the army to attack the Fascist squadrons. When Mussolini heard of the king's attitude he was no longer content with a subordinate partnership in a coalition government, and insisted that he be made prime minister. Only after this demand had been granted did he come to Rome; arriving on October 30 after traveling from Milan by sleeping car, he appeared before the king and was commissioned to form a government. The Fascist organizations now entered

Mussolini, in the back seat, leaves the Quirinale after being summoned by the king to form a government.

Rome and held a victory parade. The March on Rome shows all the features characteristic of Mussolini's policy in the first decade of Fascist rule: on the one hand, the dramatic gesture directed toward the outside world; on the other, cautious preparation and careful calculation.

In the first years of his regime Mussolini's policy was rather ambiguous. The Fascist paramilitary organizations became a militia paid by the state and were effectively used to eliminate opposition. Mussolini placed Fascists in key positions in his administration, and they controlled the police. However, his government included not only Fascists but also liberals, conservatives, and some members of the Catholic People's party, and the parliament continued to function. Mussolini's main difficulties at the beginning were created by the diversity, almost the contrasts, between his supporters. Conservatives and liberals cooperated with him because his government promised a "normalization" of Italian life, a reestablishment of stability, of social and political order, and tranquility. On the other hand, a good amount of the violence had been committed by the Fascist "squadri," the Fascist paramilitary organization; their aggressiveness and ruthlessness was a chief instrument in intimidating the farm workers and in breaking strikes, briefly, in achieving order and "normalization."

At the outset Mussolini's system of government seemed to be formed after the model of Giolitti's parliamentary dictatorship in the prewar years. However, because the mass of workers and peasants had become more vocal and better organized, such a parliamentary dictatorship was much more difficult to maintain. Accordingly the men in power had fewer hesitations to use ruthless and brutal methods. Moreover, Mussolini was determined to remain in power—not only because normalization required guarantees of stability at the top, but because of his love of power. The difficulty was that Mussolini had given repeated assurances that he would remain within the framework of the constitution in his conduct of affairs. Mussolini found a way around this difficulty by introducing a measure which provided a change in the electoral law: under the threat of a second wave of revolution he forced the parliament to accept the so-called Acerbo Law. This stated that the party with the largest number of votes would receive two-thirds of the seats in the Chamber of Deputies. The Acerbo Law of 1923, more than the "March of Rome" represented the end of parliamentary power, the forsaking of the constitution. It removed all obstacles in the way to a dictatorial regime. In the election of 1924 the government received a very strong vote which, by means of the Acerbo Law, was transformed into a two-thirds majority. The government had 356 of the 535 seats in the chamber.

The manner in which Mussolini had proceeded unified the opposition. Opponents of the government were still able to make themselves heard from the tribune of the parliament, and from there attacked Fascist brutality and the falsified election returns. Mussolini ordered his henchmen to beat up some of the prominent opposition leaders—for instance, the anti-Fascist liberal, Amendola—so that they would be unable to appear in parliament, or at least be intimidated. One of the main opponents of the Fascist regime was a young, highly respected socialist deputy, Giacomo Matteotti; in his writings and speeches Matteotti had presented extended proof of Fascist terrorist acts. In particular he had demonstrated how violence had been used to intimidate voters in the recent election, and Matteotti's revelations had been highly compromising to several members of the Fascist hierarchy. Matteotti suddenly disappeared; his body was later fished out of the Tiber. It soon became known that Matteotti had been assassinated, his abduction and murder instigated by prominent Fascists close to Mussolini.

Although there was no proof that Mussolini ordered Matteotti's death, the murder was a manifestation of the atmosphere of brutality and violence which had developed with the toleration and encouragement of government leaders. The excitement over these disclosures was immense. The parliamentary opposition—about a hundred deputies, among them the various socialist groups, some members of the Catholic People's party, and left-wing liberals—demanded the dissolution of the Fascist militia and refused to have any contact with the Fascists, members of a party including murderers. They therefore withdrew from the Chamber of Deputies and set up their own counterparliament on the Aventine. The demands of the opposition were strongly supported by the large Italian newspapers, which called for Mussolini's resignation. He seems to have thought of retirement, but the king, whom the opposition expected to take the initiative in dismissing Mussolini, did not act. Mussolini remained in power, and he now took the initiative. He said in a famous speech:

> I declare that I and I alone assume the political, moral, and historical responsibility for all that has happened. . . . If Fascism has been a criminal association, if all the acts of violence have been the result of a certain historical, political, and moral climate, the responsibility for this is mine.

Mussolini now steered energetically toward a one-party system and a totalitarian dictatorship.

The powers of parliament were increasingly curtailed and finally almost eliminated. It could no longer overthrow a government by a vote of lack of confidence. Its members could not propose a question for discussion, the head of the government determined the subjects to be debated in parliament. The position of the head of the government, or prime minister, was raised above that of other members of the cabinet. He was to appoint and dismiss the ministers and to direct their work. Neither individually nor collectively could the ministers remonstrate against his decisions. The prime minister also became almost independent of the crown, for if it should be necessary to appoint a new head of the government, the king was now obliged to choose him from a list of candidates put together by the Great Council of the Fascist party. Thus the Fascist party became an officially recognized institution and the decisive element in Italian political life. Soon it was the only legal political party; the other parties, having become entirely impotent, were forcibly dissolved. Since the list of candidates which the voters could accept or reject was put together by the Great Council of the Fascist party, only Fascists were elected to the Chamber of Deputies. The Fascist party was carefully organized at local and provincial levels as well as nationally; all party officials were appointed, not elected. The highest authority in the party was the Great Council, consisting of about thirty members selected by Mussolini as his most loyal followers. Mussolini was at once the prime minister—chief executive of the government—and the leader (*duce*) of the party. Through the channels of the party organization, local party officers reported to him about the efficiency and loyalty of government officials. By "supervising"—or informing on—administrative functionaries at all levels, the Fascists held a heavy club over the heads of civil servants, who soon saw the futility, if not the danger, of questioning the actions of party members. Little or nothing was done when members of the Fascist militia committed acts of violence. Terror became an instrument of rule. Many prominent political leaders of the pre-Fascist era went into exile. Some who remained in Italy were physically attacked and gravely wounded; some were imprisoned without trial, or banished to small islands in the Mediterranean or to isolated villages in the Calabrian mountains. Among the prominent political exiles were the brothers Carlo and Nello Rosselli, who in France founded a journal advocating liberal and socialist ideas. But the long arm of Mussolini reached even into France, and in 1937 the brothers Rosselli were assassinated by men hired by the Fascists.

Police supervision, reinforced by terror, was supplemented as a means of control by censorship, introduced immediately after the assassination of Matteotti. The censorship laws created so many obstacles in the way of privately owned and independent newspapers that these publications began to disappear. The owners were forced to sell them; some were taken over by the government; local papers were bought cheaply by local party officials. And censorship extended to every aspect of literature and scholarship. Writers and scholars were forced either to desist from writing on contemporary issues or to promote Fascist ideas. And the Fascists were very conscious of the importance and value of propaganda. They offered great spectacles to the masses; they embodied their doctrine in slogans, which appeared on posters all over the country; they impressed intellectuals by demonstrating interest in modern literary and artistic movements, such as Futurism; and by having the railroads run on time they showed foreigners that order had been restored.

Mussolini was aware that it was questionable how effective these instruments of control would be against unemployment and economic misery. Despite repeated assertions in his speeches that Fascism represented neither capitalism nor Marxian socialism, but rather a new social system, Mussolini kept close to the financial and industrial leaders who had helped him into power. Thus, after Fascist extremism had done its job, weakening and destroying possible centers of political opposition, Mussolini insisted on introducing stricter discipline among the *squadri* of the Fascist party, and it was decreed that party officers would be appointed, not elected. Moreover, Mussolini did not permit the party to infiltrate the bureaucracy. Although the party officers exercised political supervision over the civil servants, party and state were kept apart. This fundamentally conservative attitude was particularly noticeable in the regime's economic policy.

Mussolini's famous "corporate state," which was supposed to realize the new Fascist ideas in social and economic life, actually served the purposes of the wealthier classes. According to the charter which established this corporate state, the employers and employees of each branch of industry were to form a corporation; for each corporation, committees including representatives of the employers, the employees, and the government would decide questions of wages, working hours, and the like. The decisions of the committees were to be binding, and therefore strikes were forbidden. But since only Fascist trade unions were permitted to exist, the union leaders who represented the workers in the committees followed the line set by the government representatives, who usually sided with the industrialists. The economic recovery which took place all over Europe in the 1920's caused a reduction in unemployment and disguised the fact that the workers had become powerless. Moreover, impressed by Mussolini's claim to have saved his country from Bolshevism, both Italian and foreign bankers regarded Fascist Italy as trustworthy and stable and gave loans to the Fascist government which provided additional stimulus to Italian economic life.

The respectability of the regime and its popularity among the various groups of Italian society was also increased by the reconciliation, sealed in the Lateran Treaty of February 11, 1929, of the Italian state with the Roman Catholic Church. Mussolini had initiated negotiations with the Vatican almost immediately after coming to power. In the 1929 agreement the pope was recognized as the independent ruler of a small state—Vatican City—and the Church received a large financial sum as restitution for the expropriations at the time of Italy's unification. The relations between the Church and the state were regulated by a *concordate* which declared Roman Catholicism to be the official religion of the state, permitted the pope to appoint the Italian bishops after he had received the approval of the government for his candidates, guaranteed religious education in schools, and made a religious marriage ceremony mandatory. Two days after the conclusion of the Lateran Treaty, Pope Pius XI (pope from 1922 to 1939) declared that he regarded Mussolini as "a man sent by Providence."

Reconciliation with the Church may seem a strange step for one who in earlier years had flaunted his atheism and his contempt for the Church. But with the adoption of Fascism, Mussolini had accepted the view that the politician should not be bound by a system or principles. He emphasized the novelty of Fascist ideas, but when he came to power it was by no means clear what these new Fascist ideas actually were. In later years, when attempts were made to formulate the system of Fascism, this lack of a consistent framework of thought was justified by the assertion that thought independent from action did not exist.

It has always been easier to discover what Fascism rejected than what it stood for. In their statements about Fascist concepts of politics and government, Mussolini and his adherents emphasized that Fascism stood against the individualistic and rationalistic philosophy of the French Revolution. The law of politics, like the law of nature, was struggle; continued existence required continued growth and could be achieved only through action, not thought. Nations were living, viable units in politics, and man's function was to be an instrument in the hands of his nation's leader. Having turned from socialism and internationalism to nationalism, Mussolini preached the subordination of the individual to the nation with the excessive zeal of a convert. But he was also aware that the pursuit of a strictly nationalistic policy offered the best opportunity to conceal the contradictions of a regime which claimed to be revolutionary but actually defended and maintained the *status quo*. Thus personal inclination and political calculation combined to make the conduct of a forceful foreign policy, expressive of national egotism, the cornerstone of Mussolini's rule.

Mussolini disliked collective action and stabilization and wanted a fluid situation in which, by making use of the changing relations among various states, Italy could advance its own national interests. He stressed that Italy was not a satisfied nation, but "a nation hungry for land because we are prolific and intend to remain so." Mussolini always emphasized his disbelief in eternal peace and stressed that Italy must possess not only a powerful army and navy but also "an air force that dominates the skies." He set the new tone of Italian foreign policy as early as 1923, when he used the assassination of a group of Italian officers on the Greek-Albanian border as pretext for an ultimatum to Greece. He demanded an indemnity of fifty million lire, an inquiry with the assistance of the Italian military attaché, ceremonial apologies, and funeral honors. When the Greeks hesitated to comply he bombarded and occupied the island of Corfu, evacuating it only after the Greeks, on the advice of the great powers, had given in to the Italian demands. The tangible result of Mussolini's first adventure in foreign policy was small, and could have been obtained without force. But his aim had been to show the Italians that their state was no longer ruled by a weak, timid, internationally minded government, and he used every opportunity to demonstrate that Italy had embarked on a new active course in foreign policy. He was proud to have shown with his action in the Corfu incident that Italy had freed itself from the tutelage of Great Britain and France.

But in the 1920's the bark of Fascism was more threatening than its bite. Mussolini was careful to avoid moves which might lead to serious complications, such as a conflict with one of the great powers. He was aware that Italy was a much weaker state. Moreover, the Italian economy was in need of foreign loans. When Great Britain, France, and Germany initiated the negotiations which resulted in the Locarno treaties, Mussolini kept aloof of them because of his disapproval of the League of Nations and of collective action. But when these negotiations neared completion he rushed to Locarno and participated in the signing of the documents. He was not willing to arouse displeasure which might have repercussions on Italy's economic position. Moreover, he was anxious to demonstrate that Italy was one of the great European powers. One might add that one year after Matteotti's murder, Mussolini's position was still not secure enough to arouse further resentment in other countries by obstructing a policy of pacification. But if in the second half of the twenties he did not directly oppose the stabilization at which the other European powers were aiming, neither did he abandon his hostility to democracy and peace and his dreams of Italy as a great expansionist power. Still in the 1920's he took some concrete steps toward expansion through the establishment of an Italian protectorate over Albania. The fateful consequences of his emphasis on action and national prestige became apparent only in the 1930's, when the Nazis had come to power in Germany and pursued an aggressive course. Then Mussolini was hoisted with his own petard. He did not want to appear less virile and martial than the Fascist leader of Germany. By then the prosperity of the 1920's had passed and Italians had begun to notice how little the Fascist regime had changed the economic and social life of their nation. The only way out, it seemed to Mussolini, was to tie the fortunes of his country to the rising power of Nazi Germany.

The Stabilization of Communism in Russia

FROM LENIN TO STALIN

The main achievement of the Bolsheviks in the first three years of their rule was survival. Under the exigencies of the civil war many of the original measures intended to create the new socialist society in the economic and institutional field had to be abandoned. Under the high-sounding name of a New Economic Policy (NEP) a certain amount of freedom of trade in agrarian products, of personal ownership of land, of private entrepreneurship in industry and commerce had been restored—all, however, on a small scale. The question was how and when the march toward socialism could be taken up again. Lenin was aware that, because the proletariat had not come to power in a highly industrialized society, the introduction of socialism involved very special problems: it meant the construction of a completely new society in which socialism could function. But in addition to this most fundamental task, a variety of practical issues arose which demanded immediate answers: Was the foreign trade monopoly compatible with the need for foreign currency and for increased commerce? To what extent was it possible in Russia, which contained many different nationalities, to have both realization of the principle of national self-determination and a strong central government? What was the role of the trade unions? Could they, as representatives of the workers, be entrusted with the managing of the factories?

On all these questions vehement debates took place among the Bolshevik leaders, but in all of them Lenin's views prevailed. The trade unions were not subordinated to the economic administration of the government. They remained independent but mainly as "schools of communism," since the workers themselves could not yet run the economy. In the question of nationalities, the establishment of Soviet Russia as a federal state was crucial; although unity was maintained by means of cooperation among the Communist parties ruling in the different federal states, the federalist structure was meant to provide a guarantee against overt Russian chauvinism, which Lenin regarded as a detestable legacy of tsarism and as involving the danger of a purely bureaucratic rule. Despite economic disadvantages the government's foreign trade monopoly was strictly maintained, as requisite for avoiding inroads of capitalist behavior.

Until his death in 1924, Lenin had a decisive voice in Russian politics —not because he possessed any particular dictatorial powers but because of his intellectual authority and superiority. The reasons for Lenin's success in achieving and maintaining this paramount position are complex. Before he came to power, his study of Marxist theory had provided him with what he considered an infallible guide to the course to be followed, and his work as a part organizer had taught him to use men as instruments for definite purposes. Hence, after his return to Russia he was able to pursue the conquest of power, the secure establishment of his regime, and the social and political transformation of Russian life with ruthless single-mindedness and with a complete disregard for human life and legal restrictions. Furthermore, Lenin could count on a large number of followers who had studied his writings and accepted his leadership because they recognized his intellectual superiority. He demanded complete obedience only after a line of policy had been established; before any decision was made, he was willing to hear the views of his close followers and to discuss with them the various possibilities. Unlike Stalin, Lenin did not harbor resentment against those who gave advice contrary to the line finally adopted. However, after the decision had been made, opposition was no longer tolerated.

His hold over the masses of the workers is more difficult to understand than his eminent position among Bolshevik leaders. He was no great orator and his speeches, when read, seem monotonous. However, he never spoke down to the masses; he revealed to them with brutal frankness his views about the demands of the hour, explaining rather nakedly, but with strict logic, how he had arrived at his proposals; the masses had reason to believe that he took them into his confidence and that they could rely on him. They had no doubt of his selflessness; even as ruler of Russia he continued to live modestly, claiming no exceptions or privileges. Thus, the most powerful man of Russia wrote humbly to the director of the library and asked for permission to keep a book overnight, against the rules of the library, because he had no other time for reading.

Immediately after Lenin's death it was decided that his embalmed body be placed in a mausoleum on the square before the Kremlin so that contemporaries and later generations could show their respect. It was a decision which those who had been closest to Lenin considered as entirely contradictory to his ideas and character. His widow, Krupskaya, opposed the suggestion by saying: "If you want to honor the name of Vladimir Ilyich, build crèches, kindergartens, houses, schools, libraries, medical centers, hospitals, homes for the disabled, etc., and above all, let us put his precepts into practice." But the decision was made and the Lenin cult began. One of the originators and most active propagandists of the cult was the man who would succeed Lenin: Stalin.

Stalin's rise to supreme power in Soviet Russia owed much to luck. In May, 1922, Lenin suffered a stroke, and from that time until his death on January 21, 1924, he was able to work only intermittently. In his last years Lenin clashed with Stalin but was no longer able to follow up the orders by which he tried to curb him. He inserted in his last will a statement that Stalin was too ruthless and should be removed from office. But Lenin's suggestion was not carried out; many of the Bolshevik leaders were more in fear of Trotsky than of Stalin. They prefered to ally themselves with the solid and plodding Stalin against the brilliant but erratic Trotsky, whom they regarded as an unstable intellectual. Thus, when Lenin's will was read in a meeting of the Central Committee of the Communist party, a great majority—forty against ten—voted to suppress publication of the passage directed against Stalin.

In the early years of Bolshevik rule Stalin held a number of positions, highest in the official hierarchy being that of the people's commissar of nationalities. In this office he was instrumental in effecting the transformation of Russia into the federal Union of Soviet Socialist Republics; in 1922 the members of the Union were Russia, Byelorussia, the Ukraine, and Transcaucasia; to these, subsequently the Uzbek and Turkmen republics were added. The major fields of governmental activity—foreign policy, international trade, defense, economic planning, the organization of justice and education—were under federal control, but within this framework the governments of the various Soviet republics could adjust the school system, the administration of justice, the organization of agriculture, to the particular needs and demands of their regions and citizens.

Stalin was also the general secretary of the Central Committee of the Communist party; it was about this position that Lenin was primarily concerned, because Stalin's ruthlessness seemed to him to endanger the Communist party's coherence and enthusiasm. As general secretary of the Central Committee, Stalin, as Lenin wrote, "concentrated an enormous power in his hands." Understanding of the key role played by the general secretary of the Central Committee of the Communist party requires some acquaintance with the constitutional structure of Soviet Russia. The basic elements of the Bolshevik government were the Councils of the Workers and Peasants. Such councils existed on local, provincial, and regional levels, the higher councils consisting of members deputized by the lower councils. Every two years an all-union congress of councils elected a Central Executive Committee composed of two chambers, one representing the people, the other the governments of the member republics of the Soviet Union. This Central Executive Committee met every year, roughly fulfilling the role of a European parliament. It appointed the Council of People's Commissars, which exercised the highest executive power. The government thus appeared to be a pyramidal structure, rising from a broad base to a small peak. But the twelve people's commissars who directed policy were almost independent of the elected body which had appointed them. One reason was that the infrequent and relatively short meetings of the all-union congress of councils and the Central Executive Committee did not allow true supervision of the people's commissars, who had to make important decisions daily. Another reason was that the people's commissars drew their strength from their prominent position in the Communist party, for it was the party that was the controlling element within the Soviet structure. Legally, every man in the Soviet Union earning his livelihood through productive labor had the right to vote. But the lists of council candidates for whom the people could vote were assembled by the Communist party.

The Communist party was relatively small, comprising not more than 1 per cent of the population; in 1930 the party had 1,192,000 members. In sharp contrast to the pyramidal structure of the council system, the party was directed from above, by a Central Committee of about twenty of the most prominent Communists. While the most brilliant and active of these concentrated on work in a special committee—the Politburo—which laid down the general lines of Russian and Communist policy, Stalin immersed himself in the drudgery of party administration. As general secretary of the Central Committee of the Communist Party Stalin had a decisive voice in determining admission to the party and promotion within its ranks. Since the party determined who could be council candidates, he thus exerted control over personnel throughout the government. The result was that he knew intimately the rank-and-file Communists, and they, being dependent on him for promotion, were willing to accept his leadership.

The firm hold over the party organization represented Stalin's main strength in the struggle to succeed Lenin. But because of his role in the party organization Stalin could not only count on many adherents, he also knew well what the rank and file of the party were feeling and thinking. The great mass of party members were no longer the "old Bolsheviks" of tsarist times, well versed in Marxist thought and able to think independently about the problems of socialism. Since the Bolshevik seizure of power many young people had joined the party, frequently without substantial knowledge of the party's history, many of them only semi-literate. Stalin was aware that for them the Lenin cult fulfilled an important need, setting before them an example how a true socialist had acted. In 1924 Stalin himself published lectures on *The Foundations of Leninism* in which, using an endless number of quotations from Lenin, he summarized what he considered the essence of Lenin's teachings. Although pedestrian and certainly much less sophisticated than the writings on Leninism and revolutionary strategy by other Bolshevik leaders like

This picture of Lenin and Stalin is of great importance; under Stalin it was used to show his close relationship with Lenin. In fact, the photograph has been doctored.

Trotsky, Bukharin, or Zinoviev, Stalin's lectures made a great impact, because they codified Lenin's thought in a simple and clear system. Further, they were essential to Stalin's standing in the party, for he needed to prove that he was not only a Bolshevik fighter and organizer but also, like his competitors for Lenin's succession, a recognized theoretician.

The struggle for Lenin's succession dominated the Russian political scene in the years following Lenin's death. Although chiefly of a personal nature, the struggle was connected with a policy decision of crucial importance. When the Bolsheviks had come to power they had expected that their revolution would soon be followed by revolutions in the industrialized countries of Europe, first in Germany. All were convinced that the Bolshevik regime would not be able to remain in power if Russia was the only country in which the capitalist system was overthrown. It is by no means clear that Lenin ever changed his mind on the subject or ever lost hope that the revolution would also break out in the West. The year 1923, when it became clear that Lenin's death was imminent, was also the year when the end of inflation in Germany terminated the revolutionary ferment in central Europe; any hope that the revolution might spread beyond the Russian borders was crushed. Trotsky, as organizer of the 1917 revolt in Petrograd and as hero of the civil war, was much better known than Stalin and the latter's main rival to succeed Lenin. It seemed impossible to Trotsky to maintain an isolated socialist state within a capitalist world. Trotsky advanced the idea of the permanent revolution; that it was the chief function of Bolshevism in Russia even if, as a result, the Bolshevik regime in Russia might be destroyed, to organize and support revolutionary movements all over the world, because this would precipitate a new political and economic crisis which would end in a world revolution. At first Stalin shared this view. But when—after some hesitation—he had convinced himself of the solidity of the capitalist regimes in the face of Communist attacks, he set his course firmly toward the construction of a new Russian society able to stand on its own. During the Fourteenth Communist Party Congress, in March, 1925, Stalin obtained official approval of the doctrine of "socialism in one country."

Other Bolshevik leaders found abandonment of the idea of world revolution more difficult. Many of them, during long years in exile, had established close relations with extremists in other countries. Stalin had been outside of Russia just once—and then for a few weeks—and had no real acquaintance with social and industrial developments in other countries. Moreover, some of the Bolshevik leaders, such as Grigori Zinoviev, the head of the Communist International, and Karl Radek were motivated by ideological considerations in contrast to the empirical Stalin, who was aware that concentration on an economic transformation in Russia would strengthen his own position since an increasing number of party officials would be needed to direct and control the process.

Opposition to Stalin's policy of "socialism in one country" became pronounced only after it was evident that it resulted in the creation of an immense new bureaucracy. Trotsky, for instance, attacked Stalin because instead of leading to the disappearance of the state, in accordance with Marxist theory, his course of action resulted in an aggrandized bureaucratic machinery. But Stalin's views had become the accepted "line" of the Communist party, and Stalin stamped Trotsky's opposition as antirevolutionary and subversive. In 1927 Trotsky was divested of all his functions and expelled from the party, with seventy-five other leading members of the opposition. Exiled to Siberia, he continued his agitation there. In 1929 he was expelled from Russia, and found refuge in Mexico. Eleven years later he was assassinated by a man unquestionably acting on Stalin's orders.

"SOCIALISM IN ONE COUNTRY"

Pursuit of the policy of "socialism in one country" resulted in a major social upheaval accompanied by economic hardship and suffering. The golden age which theoretically was supposed to follow the defeat of capitalism seemed still far away, and the Bolshevik leaders were anxious to emphasize that a truly communist society could become reality only after the capitalist system had been overthrown all over the world; at the moment they were at work to create a system of transition, a socialist society.

The underlying aim of "socialism in one country" was to transform Russia into a highly industrialized state, able to compete with more advanced countries, such as Great Britain and the United States, and capable of putting up a good fight against aggression by capitalist nations. In Russia industrialization also involved a transformation of agriculture, which had to be made more efficient, so that the increasing number of industrial workers in the cities could be fed and a surplus could be produced for export, which alone could provide needed foreign currency. The vast changes had to be accomplished without impairment of the fundamental principle of a socialist regime—control of the state over economic life—and without the help of private or foreign capital. To achieve these aims the Russians devised a method that was entirely novel: the drafting of an economic plan which encompassed all fields of economic activity in all parts of the country. Thus, in the following years Russian life was dominated by the efforts to achieve the goals which were set in two Five-Year Plans. The first was initiated in 1928, but as the Russian leadership proudly proclaimed, it was carried out in four years, so the second Five-Year Plan could begin in 1932.

During the Second World War, Winston Churchill once asked Stalin whether he had found the stresses of the war as bad as those arising from carrying through the policy of the collective farms. " 'Oh, no,' he said, 'the Collective Farm policy was a terrible struggle.' "[1] The Russian economic planners ordered collectivization of agriculture primarily because it would facilitate the use of modern methods and machines which would increase production. But collectivization was expected also to strengthen the grip of the government over rural life. The somewhat wealthier peasants, the kulaks, who had been favored by Stolypin's reforms and later had flourished under the New Economic Policy, became disenchanted with the Bolshevik regime in the course of the 1920's. Because rationing and fixed food prices made agricultural production unremunerative, many peasants refused to deliver their produce to the cities and limited production to their own personal needs. When the government decided on collectivization, the kulaks regarded this policy as a direct attack on their property rights and on their very existence, and they resisted in all possible ways. They burned collective farms, they destroyed tractors and other agricultural machinery, and when integration into the collective-farm system finally became unavoidable, they slaughtered their animals; almost three million horses and cattle—nearly half of their entire stock—were killed. The government then decided to eliminate the kulaks as a class, and incited the poorer peasants against them, assisting this class warfare with police and military forces. The land owned by kulaks was confiscated; their houses were transformed into

---

[1] Winston S. Churchill, *The Second World War*, Vol. IV, *The Hinge of Fate* (Boston, 1950), p. 498.

clubs or schools, and an estimated two million were deported to remote areas, where they were used as forced labor.

The requirements for modernizing agriculture were important in determining the plans set up for industry. For example, the annual production of tractors increased from 6,000 at the beginning of the first Five-Year Plan to 150,000 at its end. Next to the needs of agriculture those of defense were most influential in shaping the industrialization program. The emphasis was on heavy industry. Large new cities sprang up in the vicinity of coal and iron mines; Magnitogorsk, in the midst of rich mineral deposits in the southern Urals, owed its existence to the Five-Year Plans; at the end of the first Five-Year Plan it had about 65,000 inhabitants; seven years later the population had grown to more than 150,000. The concentration on heavy industry necessarily limited the production of consumer goods; for instance, the Five-Year Plan envisaged a shoe industry which would give each person two new pairs every three years. This paucity of consumer goods meant that wages could be kept down and that the general standard of living remained low. From the point of view of the planners, the shortage in consumer goods had the advantage that workers were unable to spend all their wages and would place some of their earnings in the state bonds which helped to finance industrialization. The Five-Year Plans were also financed by the profits of the state stores and by taxes, notably a turnover tax, a form of sales tax.

Although Russian pronouncements and statistics tended to paint an exaggerated picture of the sucess of the Five-Year Plans, the main goals were undoubtedly achieved. Russia was transformed from an agrarian into an industrial country. In 1932, 70.7 per cent of the Russian national product came from industry. In addition, as a consequence of the centralized organization of Russian economic life, private enterprise disappeared almost completely.

The Soviet rulers, as firm believers in the theories of Marx, regarded intellectual achievements as a superstructure resting on the economic system; they attached great importance to intellectuals and their training. They were aware that an industrial society required a large corps of trained personnel—technicians, engineers, doctors, economists, teachers—and that the great bulk of the people ought to have an education which would enable them to handle modern machinery. Hence the Bolshevik regime established schools all over the country to eliminate illiteracy, which at the time of the revolution was widespread; in 1923, 27,000,000 people in Russia still could neither write nor read.

Workers took evening courses to prepare for university study; universities proliferated, emphasizing technical subjects and the natural sciences. With the reduction of illiteracy, publishing activities grew in extent and importance; newspapers and periodicals dispensed knowledge useful for increasing industrial and agricultural productivity, and they also spread propaganda.

The Russian rulers recognized that the work the masses were forced to do and the privations they were asked to undergo were made bearable only by the conviction that the end result would be a life safer and better than ever before. The Russian people had to be sure, however, that their leaders were steering toward this goal with utmost speed on the only possible route. Confidence in the state's leaders was emphasized; Stalin was shown to be omniscient and farseeing. What was later called the "personality cult" began to develop.

The years of the transformation into an industrial society have been called Russia's "iron age." In this period life in Russia was very different in spirit from what it had been for a brief time after the Bolsheviks came to power. Daring revolutionary intellectuals like Trotsky and Radek were now replaced by careful bureaucrats and technical experts. The experiments in avant-garde art and literature which had been promoted by Anatoli Lunacharski, commissar for education under Lenin, were now abandoned, and the government required artists to provide easily understandable, realistic representations of the achievements of the Five-Year Plans and of other events showing Russia's progress under Bolshevism. The fight of the militant atheists against religion was continued because the influence of the church formed an obstacle to the modernization of rural life. Free love and divorce, however, were no longer encouraged, as they had been in the first years of Bolshevik rule, and abortions were once again prohibited. It was hoped, however, that after the successful completion of the two Five-Year Plans, the production of consumer goods would be increased and the disciplined monotony which had become customary would gradually give way to an easier and more varied life. Furthermore, on June 12, 1936, there appeared in *Pravda* ("Truth"), the most widely distributed official newspaper, the draft of a new constitution, which seemed to indicate the beginning of a period in which the Soviet citizens would possess enlarged, well-defined rights.

THE AMBIGUITY OF THE WEIMAR REPUBLIC

Considering that even after Locarno resistance to the settlement created in Paris was muted rather than extinguished, the position of Germany was decisive for what the future might bring. We have explained that the treaties of Locarno must be viewed as providing a new starting point rather than a solution—that the question was whether Germany would consider the situation created at Locarno merely as a breathing space, intending to later embark on a policy aimed at overthrowing the existing order, or whether Germany now recognized the *status quo* and was willing to maintain it, or at least to rely for revisions on the mechanism which existed at the League of Nations for such a purpose. These are questions which are closely connected, almost identical with the question whether authoritarian Germany had been transformed into a democratic society.

Clearly there was a change in the German political climate after the acceptance of the Dawes Plan and the conference of Locarno. Until then events had crowded upon each other; a long procession of personalities had come forward and then disappeared from the scene after a short time: Liebknecht, Noske, Kapp, Rathenau, Erzberger, Cuno. There had been strikes and unrest, sometimes developing into civil war, in Berlin, in Bavaria, in the Rhineland, and in Saxony. There were moments when it seemed questionable whether the federal government could enforce its authority in all parts of the Reich, especially since the army and the judiciary kept their protecting hands over secret military organizations bitterly hostile to the republic. In critical situations, like that of the Ruhr occupation, hostility to the western powers created an alliance—called National Bolshevism—between the extreme right and the extreme left. The economic upheaval suddenly brought new economic leaders into the foreground. The most powerful of these was Hugo Stinnes (1870–1924), an owner of coal mines in the Ruhr, who built up a gigantic concern consisting of ironworks, banks, merchant ships, newspapers, and hotels, and who was one of the strongest adversaries of the fulfillment policy; however, Stinnes' phenomenal rise to economic power and political influence was quickly followed by the disintegration of his firm after the stabilization of the mark: the debts which he had contracted in building up his enterprises, easily repaid during inflation, became a stifling burden after stabilization.

These tumultuous events had taken place in a new political framework. Germany had become a republic, with a parliamentary system. The functions of the Reich had been enlarged at the expense of the members of the federation. General suffrage and the parliamentary system had also been introduced in the individual German states, so that, for instance, Prussia had a government headed by a Social Democrat until 1932. The position of the trade unions had been legally fortified, and as a result of the influence of the Social Democrats, governmental intervention and arbitration in labor conflicts secured a fair hearing for the cause of the trade unions.

But only after the years of continuous unrest and emergencies were over was it possible to test whether the changed constitutional forms would become a reality because they reflected a social transformation, the evolution of a democratic society and of a liberal spirit.

It should be emphasized that the parliamentary system never really functioned in Germany. Along with the Communists on the extreme left and some small parties on the extreme right there were five important political parties in Germany during the 1920's: three republican—the Social Democratic party, the Democratic party, and the Catholic Center party

—and two monarchist—the German People's party and the German Nationalist party. No single party ever had a majority. The governments changed frequently; several of them were minority governments or governments of experts, ruling with ever-shifting majorities. Those based on a parliamentary majority, such as the two governments of the Great Coalition, in 1923 and 1928, were possible only with right-wing support: these governments included—in addition to the three republican parties (Social Democrats, Democrats, Center party)—the monarchist German People's party. And the governments of Heinrich Brüning and Franz von Papen, preceding Hitler's rise to power, ruled by presidential emergency decrees, without a secure parliamentary basis. The tenuousness of the hold of the republican regime became evident in 1925, when Friedrich Ebert, the leader of the Social Democrats, died and popular elections for a new president of the republic were held. The people elected Field Marshal von Hindenburg, who received 800,000 votes more than Wilhelm Marx, the moderate Catholic who was the candidate of the republican parties. The Communist candidate, Ernst Thälmann, won almost 2 million votes. The republican center was weaker than the combined forces of the right and the left.

That—after many prosperous decades of monarchical authoritarianism —belief in the value of a monarchical form of government and distrust in parliaments and parliamentarianism had not completely waned in Germany is not astonishing. Inflation had impoverished the middle classes and many of them considered the failure of the new leaders to ward off economic catastrophe as clear proof of the inferiority of democracy and parliamentarianism. Antiparliamentary movements and attitudes found strong support in the bureaucracy and the army in which, as mentioned above, the men of the former ruling group remained dominant. They could not be deposed under the constitution, and they chose publicly to advocate a return to the traditional values of discipline, hierarchical order, and selfless state service, emphasizing not merely their differences from the new leaders but also the superiority of the old over the new.

However, changes in the economic situation of Germany played a decisive role in strengthening the antidemocratic and antiparliamentary right in Germany. During the twenties German economic life was on the rise. As devastating as the consequences of the inflation had been in many spheres of life, the loss of value of the currency also had an advantageous side. Export of German goods was facilitated because they would be sold at lower prices and many industrial enterprises could pay off their debts. With the profits from exports and new investments after the stabilization, the German industrial apparatus became thoroughly modernized. But the German economy also had weaknesses: one was agriculture.

Overseas competition, combined with modernization in the United States, had weakened the postwar agricultural situation all over Europe.

The situation in Germany was particularly bad, because even in the decades before the war German agrarians had been chiefly concerned with the production of grain and were unwilling or unable to change to a more specialized production of marketable goods, like fruits and vegetables; they had relied on protective tariffs and government support. After the war the situation became more critical. Wartime needs had exhausted the soil. Low profits and inflation prevented the formation of capital needed for modernization, and, without modernization, transition to a more specialized production was impossible. Moreover, the climate of the republic was less favorable to the demands of the agrarians than the Hohenzollern monarchy had been. Because the agrarian reform, which had been promised to the returning soldiers in the first weeks of the revolution, did not take place, the crisis in German agriculture continued and agricultural policy remained the subject of a bitter dispute. The *Junkers*, left in possession of their estates, demanded protective tariffs and government subventions. The socialists, who had become a powerful factor in the republic, as representatives of the workers, were interested in cheap food prices, and therefore had little sympathy for protective tariffs. The great landowners—mostly members of the high nobility, and, as such, monarchists—became the protectors and patrons of rightist and monarchical antiparliamentarian political parties and were inclined to give their support to antirepublican organizations.

The impact of agrarian opposition was immensely strengthened because the landowners had allies among an important group of German industrialists. Germany's share of world industrial production declined from its prewar level of 14.3 per cent to 11.6 per cent in the postwar period. But, considering the rise in industrial production in non-European countries like Japan and the United States, this decline was actually quite an achievement. Germany certainly did better than Great Britain. But a good part of German economic recovery had to be ascribed to the success of the electrical and chemical industries, particularly on the export market. German heavy industry lost ground to heavy industry in non-European countries. Since it could no longer manufacture armaments, heavy industry focused increasingly on the domestic market and joined the agrarians in the demand for high protective tariffs. The nationalistic inclinations of the industrialists were reinforced by their economic interests; they would reap great direct advantages from removal of the disarmament clauses of the Versailles treaty. The parties of the right, therefore, were no longer chiefly agrarian but also represented strong industrial interests; moreover, in appealing to times of past splendor, in contrast to the civilian drabness of the present, they exerted a powerful emotional appeal among wide groups of the bourgeoisie. After a slow and modest beginning immediately after the revolution, the nationalists soon became a factor which could not be left out of account. Almost all the coalition governments, therefore, which ruled in Germany—either in order to keep their right-wing partner, the German People's party, satisfied, or in order to draw some of the popular support away from the right—felt forced to make concessions to the nationalists. They publicly repudiated the war guilt clauses of the Versailles treaty; in a doubtful circumvention of the disarmament clauses they embarked on the building of pocket battleships, and soon after the Dawes Plan had begun functioning they demanded—probably prematurely—its revision. It is evident that these continued German demands made the French distrustful of German sincerity in concluding the Locarno treaties, and the French sharply opposed these revisionist aims. For several years the foreign ministers of Germany and France, Stresemann and Briand, succeeded in avoiding a serious break. But Franco-German relations remained precarious.

Although after 1920 the three republican parties never again had the majority in the Reichstag, they remained in the twenties the strongest bloc. But they were on the defensive. In the turmoil of defeat and under the threat of national disintegration, the chances for agrarian reform and for socialization had been missed; only a few had even recognized how necessary the end of the rule of the *Junkers* in the east and the curtailing of the power of the Ruhr industrialists was for the creation of a new democratic society. Further, the Dawes Plan presupposed the maintenance of the existing economic structure. Consequently, the left-wing parties, particularly the socialists, became primarily concerned with defending and improving the material interests of their constituencies. The vision of a new social order was lost in the bargaining over more wages and tariffs, social insurance payments, strikes, and arbitration.

However, German life did assume a new shape in one area—i.e., culture. Frustrated in more far-reaching plans, liberals and socialists were anxious to demonstrate that culturally, at least, a new era had begun. The municipal governments of many of the big German cities were in the hands of the socialists, who were responsible for building schools, hospitals, public offices, and, most of all, low-cost housing for workers and other low-income groups. This work was frequently entrusted to architects like Walter Gropius, the founder of the Bauhaus, who created a new functionalist style by subordinating architectural design to the building's purposes. Apartment houses in Frankfurt, Berlin, Düsseldorf, Stuttgart, and Dessau became showplaces of what was then considered daring modern architecture. The liberal or socialist ministers of education in federal states ruled by the left, most of all in Prussia, supported the modern tendencies in art and literature which had been fought by conservative ministers of education under the empire. The turmoil and the insecurity of these years created an excitement which was a spur to artistic and intellectual experiments. Furthermore, inflation had somehow shaken the belief in traditional values. And, as we have seen, some people profited considerably

Modern architecture in Germany. *The Bauhaus in Dessau.*

from speculations during the inflationary period. They put their money into things of lasting worth, such as works of art; they spent freely and quickly, anticipating the rapid depreciation of paper money. Thus, masking the grimness of the social reality there was a glittering façade, particularly in Berlin and other large cities. The amusement industry flourished. Art exhibitions, operas, theaters, and concerts were well attended. There was much experimentation in opera, drama, and art. In the early twenties, the first plays of the young Bertolt Brecht appeared on the German stage; the opera *Wozzeck*, by Alban Berg, had its first triumph; movies like *The Cabinet of Dr. Caligari* demonstrated the possibilities inherent in this new art form. The absence of social stability fostered cynicism, as well as sharpening social criticism—both evident in the drawings and paintings of George Grosz. Even after the economic crisis of the immediate postwar period had been overcome, a critical spirit remained alive, and eagerness for experimentation continued. Brecht's *Three-Penny Opera*, with a musical score by Kurt Weill, was notable not only for its new dramatic style, but also for its condemnation of corrupt bourgeois society and values. It proved an immense success, playing in Berlin continuously from 1928 until the rise of the Nazis. The intellectual atmosphere of Berlin after the First World War was electrifying; it attracted journalists, writers, and artists from all over the world. Such figures as Sinclair Lewis, Dorothy Thompson, Stephen Spender, Christopher Isherwood, and Ilya Ehrenburg were to look back nostalgically upon life in Berlin in the 1920's as one of their great experiences.

But because of their rejection of traditional forms of art, and because of their conscious cultivation of contacts with the most advanced intellectual movements in other countries, these cultural activities aroused opposition among many Germans. Conservatives regarded them as further proof that the Weimar regime represented a break with German tradition and was an alien element in German history. The monarchist and nationalist elite met annually in August in Bayreuth, where under the sharp eyes of that inexorable guardian of tradition, Richard Wagner's widow Cosima, they listened to *The Ring of the Nibelung* in the exact, and overdone, production which had first been seen in the nineteenth century. The distance widened between Berlin, the modern capital of the republic, and the rural areas, far removed from the rapid changes of modern life. This alienation of Berlin and other large urban centers from the rest of the country strengthened the appeal which in later years Nazi propaganda against the Weimar "system" would have among wide circles of the population.

BRAVE NEW WORLD

The revival of a spirit of enterprise and progress in the later part of the 1920's is not sufficiently described and explained by referring only to the somewhat precarious stabilization of the political situation. This revival occurred in the context of far-reaching developments in science and technology which transformed many aspects of human existence. The war had given powerful impetus to these developments, and they continued long after its end.

This change and progress is symbolized by an event which took place in the most prosperous year of the twenties. On May 21, 1927, after a daring and lonely flight, Charles Lindbergh arrived on the Paris airfield of Le Bourget—the first nonstop flight over the Atlantic in an eastward direction had been accomplished. No other event in the twenties caught the imagination of the world to the same extent. This is not difficult to explain. Lindbergh's feat touched the heart of the twentieth century in two ways: human pride in the continued existence of individual heroism and in advances in science and technology.

The use of the airplane as a regular means of transportation was the most visible evidence of the changes which technology had brought about. In the case of the airplane the war had been decisive in effecting a quick transition from the experimental stage to general use. Because of its role in the war, the great potential of aviation had been recognized. Passenger service was installed between London and Paris in 1919, and between Amsterdam and London a year later. Soon all larger European cities had airfields and were connected by scheduled commercial flights. While Lindbergh's achievement pointed towards the development of a regular transatlantic air service, this was delayed until more than ten years later, on the eve of the outbreak of the Second World War.

Lindbergh's plane, *The Spirit of St. Louis,* landing at Le Bourget, Paris, May 21, 1927.

The impact of the First World War on developments in the fields of transportation and communication was far-reaching in many ways. The First World War was not a motorized war: tanks appeared only in the final phase of the conflict; larger military units, if not marching on foot, were transported by rail. Smaller groups, however, particularly officers, moved around in automobiles; the resulting increase in automobile construction prepared for the postwar expansion of the auto industry, particularly the building of mass-produced, small, relatively inexpensive cars, which made it possible for a broad strata to own an automobile, although possession of a car was still the exception rather than the rule in Europe.

The use of wireless communication in the First World War opened the way for entirely new developments in this area. After the war, experiments in wireless communication were begun, financiers invested heavily, and the radio industry was established. The primitive earphones of wartime were replaced by sensitive receiving instruments; radio stations were equipped to present programs throughout the day. Each European state had a public broadcasting company working under government control; international conventions stipulated the wave lengths each country was entitled to use. In 1927, wireless telephone service was initiated between England and the United States.

The effects of the First World War on industrial life extended in a variety of directions. The war was of particular importance for the development of the chemical industry, which continued to grow in importance. The most significant consequence of wartime needs was probably the discovery that atmospheric nitrogen could be made into ammonia, which is an essential ingredient both for the manufacture of explosives and fertilizers. Their production was no longer dependent on imports from those countries—primarily Chile—which possessed deposits of natural sodium nitrates. Actually, without the industrial production of sodium nitrates, Germany could not have carried on the war for a great length of time. The chemical industry also benefited from the challenge to create substitutes for goods which could not be produced during wartime because of difficulties in obtaining raw materials.

Although a process for the manufacture of synthetic fibers was discovered in the nineteenth century and production of rayon had started before 1914, the war, by reducing the possibilities of importing silk and increasing the need for material to cover airplane wings, stimulated the output of a more durable viscose rayon. After the war the production of artificial silk became one of the most quickly developing industrial areas, increasing from 1920–1925 at the rate of 45 per cent per year. Rayon was economically cheaper than natural silk. It was used for a variety of purposes; for instance, as shorter skirts became the fashion in women's clothes, the sales of rayon stockings soared. Although in almost all European countries the chemical companies accelerated the manufacture of artificial fibers, their production was especially significant in Germany and Italy—in Germany because it helped regain for the German chemical industry the leading role it had played before the war; in Italy because this industry did not require the raw materials which Italy did not possess—coal and iron—but only electricity, which Italian waterpower could provide.

Technology and inventions which make scientific discoveries applicable to practical uses, frequently follow the original discoveries at a wide distance. The advances in transportation and communication and in the chemical industry were based on scientific discoveries which had been made a long time before, certainly before 1914. On the other hand the scientific discoveries of the twenties had their impact—an impact of revolutionary character—on the life of humanity only twenty years later, during and after the Second World War. But the 1920's were one of the great epochs in the history of science.

The "understanding of atomic physics ... had its origins at the turn of the century and its great synthesis and resolutions in the nineteen twenties."[2] Thus did J. Robert Oppenheimer, one of the principals in this scientific revolution, characterize the main stages of its development. Its great events at the turn of the century were Max Planck's publication in 1900 of "On the Theory of the Law of Energy Distribution in a Normal

Spectrum," which presented the thesis of the quantum theory, and Albert Einstein's publication in 1905 of the papers which set forth the special theory of relativity. By 1903 the need for a new theoretical outlook had been confirmed by experiments in the course of which Pierre and Marie Curie isolated radium and Antoine Henri Becquerel recognized the extent of radioactivity. After the First World War, the implications of these theories and discoveries were explored by a score of young scientists. The great centers of this absorbing intellectual adventure were Copenhagen, where Niels Bohr, the guiding spirit of the entire field of atomic reasearch, worked; Göttingen, where Max Born, James Franck, and David Hilbert maintained the tradition of this university as a center of mathematics and natural science; and Cambridge, where Ernest Rutherford continued his study of radioactivity and then, together with Sir James Chadwick, turned to the investigation of the composition of the atom. There was a lively exchange among all these groups, and the genesis of a new physical world view which, although it did not invalidate the classical Newtonian physics, limited its applicability, was the common achievement of scientists from many countries.

The creative excitement of these decades was caused by the necessity of revising the basic assumptions of classical physics, notably the supposition that through observation and experiments it is possible to establish the laws which demonstrate the causal connection determining the processes of nature. When Planck showed that certain incongruities in the radiation of energy is probable but it is not predetermined. Similarly, Einstein's demoncontinuous waves but in flashes, like a stream of bullets of fixed size ("quantum"), his theory suggested that the assumption of complete continuity in the process of nature was untenable. Nature is discontinuous; that a certain sequence of events will result from the release of a quantum of energy is probable but it is not predetermined. Similarly, Einstein's demonstration in his theory of relativity of the bonds between the dimensions of space and of time forced a reexamination of the value of the material provided by observation. It was found that when measurements of a small elementary particle like the electron focus on speed, those of its precise position become uncertain, while measurements of position reduce precision in the measurement of speed. The conclusion was that in the description of nature there remains an element of uncertainty.

The disclosure that discontinuity and uncertainty are inherent in nature nullified the expectation of earlier scientists that immutable laws would someday be discovered which could explain all known phenomena. The work of the physicist became limited to the exploration of relations among the phenomena. But this limitation actually gave the investigator scope for greater creative efforts.

The basis for this change in theoretical assumptions which was worked out in the 1920's and 1930's was concrete investigation; the intellectual speculations were accompaniments of the discoveries resulting from a study of the atom. Already in the nineteenth century there had been some research which showed that the atom did not form an indivisible basic unit of matter, as had been assumed. The investigations of the twentieth century gradually revealed that the atom is composed of a very small nucleus (usually consisting of positively charged protons and electrically neutral neutrons) which is surrounded by negatively charged electrons. The problem was that, despite the radioactivity of certain elements, which ought to have led to a loss of energy, their atoms remained stable. And the explanation of this fact with the help of the new theoretical insights led to the discovery of nuclear energy.

The general public understood as little, or perhaps even less, than we do today about the discoveries and advances in science. The terms "relativity" and the "principle of uncertainty" were used in everyday language and were often believed to have meanings of a philosophical nature, but such vague general associations as were connected with these terms only revealed that even the educated had no real conception of their exact scientific meaning. Still, the interest in these notions indicates something of the public's awareness of living in an age of great scientific advance. Scientific advances and innovations, however, arouse not only enthusiasm but also instill fear. The security which humans receive from feeling he or she lives in a well-known world begins to disappear and people become aware not only of new opportunities but also of new dangers, not only of widening horizons but also of new means of control. The fears which these great strides in science produced were not restricted to those segments who are generally opposed to change; others, too, raised questions about the consequences of the new inventions, and whether they would be beneficial.

The new means of communication had diminished the distance which in the previous century had separated private life and the world of politics and business. With voices from radio present in the home the individual was subjected to a constant barrage of demands from the world outside. Powerful propaganda efforts had been exerted during the First World War to keep spirits from sagging on the home front—the citizen was constantly encountering posters urging service in the army or the buying of war bonds, or warning about enemy spies. After the war, the technical devices of propaganda were taken up by advertisers in print, on billboards, in the cinema, and on the radio. The radio especially could be placed in the service of mass control—it was a powerful means of manipulating the emotions of the general public.

The changes wrought in the environment by science, technology, and industry created new possibilities for the conduct of public affairs. But these developments were not widely used in the political sphere until the 1930's; the extent to which their potential was realized depended upon the particular situation in each country, especially on the strength of its political tradition. For example, although the technique of radio "fireside chats" contributed to the popularity of Franklin Delano Roosevelt, its imitation by Doumergue, then French prime minister, was regarded as a sign of arrogance and authoritarianism and played a role in the downfall of the Doumergue government. It was natural that those political movements which arose in opposition to the established political structure were most ready to use new political techniques. Mussolini and Hitler both stressed that they were leaders of modern movements. Mussolini liked to be photographed piloting an airplane; Hitler was frequently seen in his Mercedes-Benz. In the western democracies there was much admiration for the courage of Neville Chamberlain, prime minister of Great Britain, when in September, 1938—in order to meet Hitler in Berchtesgaden—he entered an airplane for the first time in his life, with an umbrella on his arm. But the Nazis and Fascists considered Chamberlain's reluctance to use modern means of transportation contemptible—a sign of the backwardness of the democracies.

Since the eighteenth century, science has been connected with "enlightenment," with the hopes for the establishment of a better, i.e., more rational, world order. It was difficult, therefore, to realize that science could also be an oppressive force, serving to control human minds in whatever way was advantageous to those in whose hands the means of communication were. The first clear warning against a facile optimism that scientific progress would lead to a world which was rationally organized and in which life would be made happier, appeared in 1932, Aldous Huxley's *Brave New World*. This utopian novel is a powerful demonstration of the inner emptiness which might accompany a life completely organized and freed from emotional complexities and complications, and in which all right to choice or decision has been lost. But Huxley's novel appeared when a new mood had begun to develop in Europe, as it had become clear that the years of stability and prosperity were over.

CHAPTER 8

The Economic Crisis and the Rise of Nazism

THE WORLD ECONOMIC CRISIS

AFTER A FEW YEARS the stability achieved in 1925 was shattered by the world economic crisis. The impact of this crisis was all the more powerful because, as the 1920's passed, people had gradually become confident that the wounds left by the First World War could be healed, that the prosperity of the years before 1914 would again be reached, and that the march toward progress which the war had interrupted could be resumed. The economic crisis destroyed these expectations and hopes; the prewar world now appeared irretrievably lost, and many were convinced that the new course of events was leading inexorably downhill and would end in a holocaust more dangerous and devastating for the continuity of European life than the First World War had been. Thus the decade of the 1930's was a period full of anxiety and insecurity. A full recovery from the world economic crisis had still not occurred when the Second World War broke out in 1939.

The really acute phase of the economic breakdown lasted from 1929 to 1933; before its underlying causes are discussed, it might be well to recapitulate the dramatic events of these years. The actual beginning of the crisis was the collapse of the New York Stock Exchange under a wave of speculation in the last week of October, 1929, although some danger signs pointing to a decline in production had appeared earlier. In Europe the high point of the crisis occurred in the summer of 1931. In May, 1931, the most important Austrian bank, the *Kreditanstalt*, which was controlled by the Rothschilds, declared itself unable to fulfill its obligations. This failure shook confidence in the solvency of banks in Germany; there was an accelerated recall of money from them, and the main German banks soon found themselves insolvent and were forced to close. They were able to reopen only with the help of a government guarantee. In this critical economic situation the payment of international debts was clearly impossible, and the American president Herbert Hoover (1874–1964) suggested a

At the peak of the economic crisis in 1931, the British prime minister, Ramsay MacDonald, visited Berlin to strengthen the German government; this picture shows him seated between the two renowned German physicists Planck and Einstein, the three other men were members of the German cabinet.

one-year moratorium on reparations and war debts; after tedious negotiations, this was agreed upon in August. But the moratorium came too late to remedy the British financial situation, which had been seriously impaired by the economic collapse in central Europe. On September 21, 1931, Britain abandoned the gold standard; this event seemed to mark the end of an epoch, for hitherto the pound had enjoyed the reputation of being as good as gold. In the next years the level of economic activity remained low, although from 1934 on, slowly and gradually recovery began, especially in the industrial countries. Agricultural prices remained depressed, and the Balkan states, which were dependent on the export of agricultural products, continued to suffer severely. Moreover, France, which at the outset had seemed unaffected by the crisis, began to experience economic difficulties in 1932, and the French recession played its part in retarding recovery in the rest of Europe.

To understand the nature of this economic catastrophe—its severity, length, and spread—one must realize that two factors were at work. First, there was the decline in production, which led to a decrease in trade and created unemployment; second, there was the financial crisis.

The decline in production set in from what was a rather low plateau, for after the First World War production had remained sluggish. By 1929 the prewar level had indeed been reached, but the rate of economic growth ought to have been much larger in relation to the increased population, even though the rate of population growth was small. Moreover, the European share in world trade was less than it had been in 1914, as European nations faced competition from the rising economies of the non-European nations. To the diminished share of Europe in non-European markets the elimination of Russia from the world economic system must be added as a further restricting and damaging factor.

The economic boom in the second part of the 1920's was built on a narrow base. The limited amount of population growth restricted sales possibilities, especially since unemployment, which had been high in the years immediately after the war, was never entirely eliminated. Profits were attained through modernization of production rather than the result of new investments and market expansion. The boom lacked the strength to resist any serious blow.

Even before 1929 falling prices for agricultural goods indicated the onset of an unfavorable economic trend. This decline in prices immediately affected the peasant countries of southeastern Europe—especially Rumania, Bulgaria, and Yugoslavia, where—by tradition or as a result of agrarian reforms after the war—small farms with rather high production costs were the prevailing form of land ownership. For the farmers of these countries the falling agricultural prices made competition on the European market outside the Balkans impossible. Even within these Balkan states the price of wheat fell by almost half. Since the prices of industrial goods did not decline to the same degree, the people of these countries were caught in a disparity between industrial and agricultural prices—a "price scissor"—and they were unable to purchase manufactured goods from industrial countries. Hence a shrinking of industrial production throughout Europe took place, and it was aggravated by the widespread introduction of protective measures against foreign goods, by which each country tried to defend its own industries at the expense of all others.

This crisis in production took an extraordinary and dramatic form because its difficulties were compounded by a financial crisis. Its center was Wall Street, where in 1929 a speculative boom ended in a stock-market crash which ushered in a long depression. The American economic collapse had its immediate repercussions in Europe, particularly in Germany. American loans had been granted not only to the German government for the settlement of reparations but also to many private and semipublic enterprises within Germany—industrial companies, public utilities, and municipal governments. Foreign capital had been drawn into Germany by high interest rates, which the German economy had been able to sustain because labor costs were relatively low. With the stock-market crash the influx of

American money ended and American banks demanded the repayment of loans as soon as they became due. In a time of shrinking production and declining prices the abrupt withdrawal of American loans was a severe blow to the German economy; the situation was particularly critical because German businessmen, relying on the continuous availability of American capital, had used money borrowed on short terms for long-term investments. Despite the warnings of men like Schacht, the president of the Reichsbank, against this unsound practice, neither German businessmen nor foreign bankers had been able to resist the allure of easy gains.

With the withdrawal of American money from the German economy the liquid reserves of German banks and businesses came under steadily increasing pressure. In addition, because loans from abroad had to be repaid in foreign currency, the withdrawal endangered the German currency by absorbing the gold reserves of the Reichsbank; by 1931 they amounted to only 10 per cent of what they had been before the onset of the crisis. These developments reached their culmination in the summer of 1931 when the German public, becoming aware of the catastrophic financial situation, started a run on the banks. Because Germany had been the center for the investment of foreign money, the difficulties of the German banks meant great losses for the banks of other countries, particularly Great Britain and the United States. The result was a general restriction of credit, with capital for investments difficult or even impossible to obtain. The consequent lack of new investments prolonged the depression and slowed down recovery.

At this time the view of Keynes that in periods of depression new money ought to be pumped into the economy was regarded as a dangerous heresy by almost all economists. A deflationary policy marked by a balanced budget, with expenses limited to the absolute minimum, was the economists' prescription for the handling of both public and private finances in times of crisis; it was not realized that unemployment reinforced the depression because people without money could not buy goods. The generally sluggish economic development of the 1920's had created pockets of unemployment all over Europe; with the depression the numbers of unemployed increased rapidly. In Great Britain almost three million were jobless in 1931; in Germany at the beginning of 1933 industrial production was half of what it had been in 1929, while there were three times as many—six million—unemployed.

The economic crisis was a turning point in the interwar years because it changed the political climate and the political constellation in Europe. Even when economic life became less turbulent, there was no return to the situation which had existed before 1929.

With the end of the First World War the deep chasm, which before 1914 separated the workers from the ruling classes and the proponents of international socialism from the adherents of national states, seemed bridged. The workers had supported their governments during the war and in acknowledgment of this show of willingness to recognize the value of the national state, the political rights of the masses had been extended: the lowering of the voting age, suffrage for women, elimination of property qualifications, proportional representation—some, or all, of these measures had been adopted in every state of western and central Europe after the war. Most of the demands for political democratization which radicals had raised before the war were fulfilled.

But while political democratization had lowered the temperature of the class conflict between workers and bourgeoisie, this did not mean that divergent economic interests had been reconciled. In this area too the war opened new perspectives. The socialists had lost some of their enthusiasm for revolution—partly because they rejected vigorously the theories and actions of the leftist radicals who had come to power in Russia, partly because the introduction of economic controls and regulations by the various governments during the war had demonstrated that the change from a free economy to a controlled and planned economy could be obtained within the existing system. Correspondingly, the members of the bourgeoisie had become aware during the war of the beneficial consequences of smooth collaboration with the workers, and they were frightened by the specter of the Russian Revolution, which seemed to show what might happen if the workers were driven to desperation. Moreover, the economic decline which followed the war hit both workers and employers, two groups which were interested in giving impetus to economic life.

Hence the socialists and the bourgeoisie were willing to take some steps to meet each other. It was acknowledged that the workers were entitled to such concessions as the eight-hour day, increased unemployment benefits, rceognition of the right to strike, and the establishment of the closed shop, which made trade unions the only legitimate representatives of the workers in the factories. In exchange, the socialists toned down their revolutionary propaganda, emphasized the possibility of achieving their aims by democratic means, accepted some arbitration machinery in labor disputes, and acknowledged the need for the maintenance of national armed forces until disarmament was achieved.

Details about the advances achieved in the social legislation of the various European countries after the war varied; in Germany, where a revolution had taken place, the rights of the workers and trade unions were better secured than in France. Yet an improvement in labor conditions and in the relations between employers and workers had undoubtedly taken place.

However, the period of compromise was short-lived. The economic crisis again widened the gap between the classes. With governments drafting budgets in which, to save money, unemployment benefits were cut, and with industrial enterprises dismissing workers ruthlessly, the hope of achieving socialist goals through a gradual transformation of the capitalist system appeared increasingly illusory. There was a renewed trend toward revolutionary radicalism. At the same time industrial entrepreneurs tended to become more antilabor, regarding the trade unions as obstacles to retrenchment by means of lower wages and a reduced labor force. Reactionary and authoritarian notions received new impetus, and their resurgence was accompanied by a revival of nationalism. In the grim climate of depression each government thought first of its own people and introduced measures of economic protection to fend off foreign competition Concessions to other nations were condemned as signs of weakness.

Two areas of the European scene were particularly affected by intensified nationalist attitudes. In the Balkans hostilities among the various states sharpened and the exhortations of the greater powers for cooperation and toleration were no longer heeded, especially since they were no longer reinforced by loans. The French influence which had been predominant in this area lost ground and Italian and German influence increased. But tension also became more acute among the great powers of western Europe. Because the economic crisis had left Great Britain too weak to exert the role of intermediary and arbiter which it had assumed in the Locarno agreements, the resurgence of Franco-German hostility was almost unavoidable.

Thus all over Europe the economic crisis awakened and strengthened extremist tendencies on the left and on the right, and undermined the moderate center which clung to the ideals of democracy.

To understand the events of the 1930's, however, one must go beyond the effects of the economic crisis on the development of party politics. The entire political climate of the 1930's was different from that of the 1920's. One might say that only during the depression years did the full consequences of the shock represented by the First World War come to the surface. In large part this shock resulted from the collapse of assumptions once taken for granted. Before 1914 the steady progress of civilization had seemed assured, and the general principles of European morality were spread and accepted in widening areas of the world. The experience of the war, in which men ruthlessly attempted to create the most efficient machinery of death and destruction and to apply it against whole nations, disregarding conventions and morality when they stood in the way of national victory, could not easily be reconciled with the old principles, which with the return of peace were again proclaimed to be the acknowledged forms of civilized existence. Moreover, the young men who had been thrown straight from school into the conflict had learned that they had instincts and powers which the world of their parents seemed to have suppressed and which found no fulfillment or expression in the pattern of life to which their parents wished them to conform. The moving book by

Paul Fussell, *The Great War and Modern Memory*, registers well the intensity in emotional and ethical consciousness which the experience of the war had produced. It is no accident that after the war Lytton Strachey revealed the concealed hypocrisy of the Victorian age, that Freud's theories of repression and of the strength of the unconscious permeated art and literature. Nevertheless, in the period just after the coming of peace, the belief that the postwar years provided a chance for building a new and better democratic world prevailed over the mood whose essence was rejection of historical values and traditions. But when in the 1930's the disillusionment of the postwar world was combined with the miseries of the depression, it became much more difficult to deny the voices of those who preached that the forces which the experiences of the war had revealed—violence, ruthlessness, the drive for power—were the truly effective factors in society. In social and political life the use of war and warlike weapons seemed possible and permissible. With the strength of a delayed effect, the shock administered by the experiences of the First World War transformed the psychological approach to politics and social life.

This change in the European climate helps to explain a surprising and shocking development. Not much more than ten years after Great Britain and France had completed the arrangements which were meant to establish them safely as leaders of a democratic Europe, these two powers were in retreat; initiative had devolved to antidemocratic powers.

THE FIRST STIRRINGS OF REVOLT AGAINST
EUROPEAN CONTROL OF THE GLOBE

Although developments within the European state system were decisive for the events of the thirties, and ultimately for the outbreak of the Second World War, events outside Europe played their role in shifting the balance of power to the dictators. We have mentioned the decline of European economic power through the rise of industries outside Europe, through the sale of foreign assets in order to pay for the expenses of war. But the position of Great Britain and France, and therefore also their influence on the balance within Europe, also was weakened by the rise of nationalist movements aimed at ending the period of colonial rule and exploitation. The war, in which all races had fought side by side, had given impetus to movements for emancipation from colonial rule. By the beginning of the thirties these movements had become factors of considerable political relevance. The areas in which antagonism between the European ruler and settler and the native population began to play an increasingly important role were Africa and southern Asia.

Africa

In Africa one must distinguish between the Northern Arc, which the Arabs had conquered many centuries ago, and central and southern Africa. In central and southern Africa the British and French governments tried to establish in their colonies advisory councils which would gradually give the native population some part in the government. These measures had to be taken because British and French control over the former German colonies in Africa (Tanganyika, Togo, the Cameroons) was exercised in the form of a mandate, carried out under supervision of the League of Nations, with the purpose of educating the natives for self-government. Naturally, the concessions made to the natives in the former German colonies had to be extended to other areas as well. But in these parts self-government or even independence was a very distant goal.

In North Africa and the Near East the movement against European imperialism had much deeper roots. Since the Egyptian Jamal-ud-Din al-Afghani (1838–1897) had raised national and liberal claims for the Moslems in the nineteenth century, nationalist movements had taken hold in North Africa and the Near East. Even before the First World War the Arabs had begun to react against Ottoman rule. When the Turks entered the First World War this Arab nationalism received support from the British and the French, and with the encouragement of agents like T. E. Lawrence (1888–1935), the famous Lawrence of Arabia, hopes were high for the establishment of a larger Arab kingdom reaching from Arabia to Damascus and Baghdad. But these hopes were crushed in 1920—the year which the Arabs called *âm an-nakba* ("the year of the catastrophe"). The French drove the Arabs out of Damascus and took control in Lebanon and Syria, which were assigned to them as mandates. Anti-Jewish riots were crushed in Palestine which the British government in the so-called Balfour Declaration (1917) had promised as a national home for the Jewish people and which the British administered as a mandate. The British tried to reconcile the Arabs by creating a number of Arab states—Transjordania, Iraq, and Hejaz—but Arab hostility to European imperialism remained alive, and the British and French could maintain their control in this area only by playing upon religious and racial antagonisms, like those of the Christian Arabs toward the Mohammedans and the Druzes toward the Moslems, or by using force. Nationalism also reached the westernmost of the Arab settlements. Starting in the 1920's the "young Tunisians," as the Tunisian nationalists called themselves, exerted increasing pressure, and in the 1930's a nationalist movement became active in Morocco as well. Nevertheless, only slowly and gradually, during the 1920's and 1930's, did these anti-imperialist movements become a serious threat to the control of this part of Africa by Great Britain and France; there was only one area—Egypt—where Arab nationalism became politically significant immediately after the war.

Anti-British feeling in Egypt had intensified during the war when the British entirely took over Egyptian rule and interfered in Egyptian life, requisitioning cattle and foodstuffs and forcing Egyptians to work on railroads and other installations needed for the campaign in the Near East. The resentment created by these harsh measures promoted the emergence of the Wafd, a well-organized movement whose goal was complete Egyptian independence. Disorders were frequent from March, 1919, when Britain refused the demands of the Wafd, until 1922, and under the impact of these revolts the British were forced in 1921 to release the organizer and leader of the Wafd, Saad Zaghlul Pasha (c. 1860–1927), whom they had exiled to Malta. After his triumphal return a certain stabilization was finally achieved. The British recognized Egyptian sovereignty but retained the right to intervene in Egyptian affairs. They kept the Sudan under their control and assumed responsibility for the defense of Egypt and the protection of foreigners living there. Even after this compromise the situation remained precarious. Zaghlul continued to press for the abolition of all the special rights which the British had preserved, and the Wafd was regularly victorious in elections. The British, however, had the support of the Egyptian king, who disliked the democratic tendencies of the Wafd. Although the British were forced to make further concessions, their retreat was slow. Nevertheless, throughout the interwar years Egypt remained a serious political concern for Britain, and the maintenance of a position there absorbed part of Britain's military strength.

India

While Arab nationalism was gaining ground only slowly, a most serious challenge to the rule of the white man arose in India at just about the time the First World War came to an end. The events in India provided the most striking example of the mounting strength gained by the movements of non-European peoples for liberation from the rule of the white man. More than half a million Indians fought in the First World War, and both princes and commoners distinguished themselves by their bravery. Even before the war ended, the British government realized that this active participation in battle gave justification to the Indians' claims for participation in the government of their country. In August, 1917, Edwin Montagu, the secretary of state for India, announced in the House of Commons that the British government planned "not only the increasing association of Indians in every branch of the administration but also the granting of self-governing institutions with a view to the progressive realization of responsible government in India as an integral part of the British Empire."

The British believed that in effecting changes in the status of India they would be dealing chiefly with the British-educated upper classes and with the rulers of the princely states. They felt sure that they could proceed slowly and cautiously. But the movement toward Indian independence assumed a quick tempo and became a dramatic conflict because of the inspiring personality of its leader, Mohandas Gandhi (1869–1948).

For twenty years Gandhi had lived in South Africa, where he had been the acknowledged leader of the large number of Indian workers who had gone there as indentured laborers. Gandhi had brought about remarkable improvements in their legal and economic position. The methods he had employed in achieving these gains had involved strikes, demonstrations, and hunger marches; but he had kept his followers from committing any violence, and when the police took action he and his followers had gone to prison willingly, without offering resistance. Gandhi's struggle for the Indians in South Africa had made him a well-known and highly respected figure, and when he returned to India in 1916, leadership in the nationalist movement devolved upon him almost automatically.

Gandhi infused two crucial new ideas into the movement for independence. First, its basis had to be broadened. It was not to be limited to the educated upper classes, but was to include members of all social classes, particularly the poor agricultural and industrial workers. Second, the method to be employed in obtaining independence was to be the one which he had successfully used in South Africa—nonviolence.

The broadening of the social basis required a revolutionary step: the breaking down of the barriers between caste members and "untouchables." When Gandhi began to live among "untouchables" and adopted an "untouchable" girl as his daughter, his people were deeply shocked. But gradually his moral courage aroused admiration and reinforced his political leadership. His insistence on nonviolence gave the movement a strong moral basis. Gandhi himself stated that his campaign constituted "an attempt to revolutionize politics and restore moral force to its organic station. We hope by our action to show that physical force is nothing compared to moral force and that moral force never fails." The instrument through which Gandhi hoped to obtain a withdrawal of the British without using violence was noncooperation. Again, this idea was powerful because it contained a strong moral element. As Gandhi said: "Non-cooperation with evil is as much a duty as is cooperation with good."

Noncooperation also implied practical measures which greatly weakened the British hold over India. Lawyers, among them future leaders such as Nehru (1889–1964) and Patel (1875–1950), left the courts; students left the universities; and like the *Narodniki* in Russia in the nineteenth century, professional men and intellectuals went into the villages, to educate the people and to preach noncooperation. For the success of noncooperation the rejection of all imported goods was essential, and the symbol of autarky became the wearing of homespun cloth. Gandhi admonished every Indian to spin daily. He attributed particular value to this work because while spinning one had time for religious contemplation.

Organization of the movement for Indian independence was in the hands of the All-India Home Rule League, of which Gandhi became president in 1920. Under him a democratic mass organization was created, with village units, city districts, and provincial sections, all culminating in the All-Indian Congress Committee. The fight for Indian independence became a struggle between Congress and the British. Congress adopted the policy of noncooperation, declaring that "it is the duty of every Indian soldier and civilian to sever his connections with the government and find some other means of livelihood." Noncooperation, however, developed into civil disobedience, and the latter was frequently accompanied by riots and violence. Gandhi's response to the outbreaks of violence was a fast, which he ended only when the disturbances had stopped. Indicative of the religious veneration in which the Indians held Gandhi is the fact that he could almost always control them by means of a fast; the people accepted Gandhi's demands because a prolonged fast might endanger his life.

The British were rather insecure in their handling of Gandhi. In 1922 they arrested him as the author of a number of seditious articles, and condemned him to six years in prison, but they released him after two years in order to quiet the resentment which his imprisonment had caused.

A crisis occurred in 1930. Because the British government had refused to give a definite promise of independence, a new campaign of civil disobedience was started, and Gandhi, after some years of withdrawal from politics, agreed to lead it. He decided to dramatize this campaign by an action breaking the government's salt monopoly, and accordingly he organized and led a march to the sea, covering two hundred miles in twenty-four days. At the shore he picked up and ate some salt which the waves had left, as a demonstration that he did not feel bound by the regulations concerning it. Again, Gandhi was arrested. But the British government realized that some agreement had to be reached, and released him. In appreciation of this gesture Gandhi expressed the wish to see the viceroy, Lord Irwin, later earl of Halifax (1881–1959). In the course of this famous visit, the viceroy offered Gandhi a cup of tea and Gandhi, taking a paper bag out of his shawl, answered: "Thank you. I will put some salt into my tea to remind us of the famous Boston Tea Party." Gandhi's meeting with Lord Irwin resulted in the cessation of civil disobedience, the release of all political prisoners, the abandonment of the British salt monopoly, and the agreement of the Congress party to participate in a round-table conference in London. Gandhi himself went to London as a Congress representative. In London the immense difficulties which the internal situation of India put in the way of independence became strikingly apparent. The conference produced a dramatic split between Hindus and Moslems; the Moslems, a minority in India, demanded separate electorates, an arrangement which would prevent them from being outvoted; the Hindus insisted on a single electorate. The British government's decision for separate electorates inflamed the struggle anew, and it moved in a quickened tempo through the 1930's: campaigns of civil disobedience, arrests, fasts by Gandhi, British concessions, followed one upon the other. The solution—independence accompanied by the division of India into two states, one largely Hindu, the other largely Moslem, within the British Commonwealth of Nations—was achieved only after the Second World War.

The Change in the Far East: Japan and China

As a consequence of the First World War, two non-European powers—the United States and Japan—became equal in strength and importance to the European great powers; without their participation the affairs of the globe could no longer be decided. Indeed, developments in the Far East showed the extent to which in this particular area the United States and Japan now not only equaled the European great powers but even overshadowed them.

The involvement of the European nations and the United States in the European theater of war had given Japan opportunities of which it knew how to make full use. Japan was particularly anxious to strengthen its hold over China. China was forced to recognize Japan as the heir of Germany's rights in China and to give Japan extended economic privileges in Manchuria. Moreover, having taken over Germany's island possessions in the Pacific, Japan intended to keep them.

But Japanese policy ran counter to the interests of the United States. The occupied islands, particularly Yap, were so situated that control of them implied control of communications in the Pacific, and the Japanese hold over China nullified the American open-door policy. A naval armament race seemed unavoidable. But in the difficult economic circumstances after the First World War this aggravation of financial burdens seemed so senseless that the great naval powers were willing to make a serious attempt to settle their differences by negotiations. Accordingly, on December 12, 1921, they met in Washington, D.C. to discuss naval armament and the situation in the Pacific. In the opening speech, the American secretary of state, Charles Evans Hughes, made a number of concrete proposals for the limitation of naval armaments. On February 4, 1922, the conference ended with a settlement which in essence embodied these proposals in a series of complicated arrangements. One was the establishment of a definite ratio controlling the tonnage of the battleships of the great naval powers. Great Britain abandoned its claim to having the strongest navy in the world, and agreed to an American navy equal to its own. Britain and the United States were each allowed 525,000 tons of capital ships, Japan 350,000 tons, and

France and Italy 175,000 tons each. Moreover, during the next ten years no new capital ships, i.e., ships of 10,000 or more tons, were to be built. This naval agreement was supplemented by the Nine Power Treaty, signed by the United States, Great Britain, France, Italy, Japan, Belgium, the Netherlands, Portugal, and China, guaranteeing the integrity and sovereignty of China and promising maintenance of the open door. In consequence of this treaty, Japan returned the former German colony of Kiaochow to China. Finally, in another treaty—the Four Power Treaty—the United States, Great Britain, France, and Japan acknowledged one another's insular possessions in the Pacific and agreed to mutual consultation if their possessions were threatened. The Four Power Treaty is usually regarded as the most important diplomatic achievement of the Washington conference. At the time of the conference the old alliance between Japan and Great Britain was due for renewal. The United States looked with distrust upon this special bond between Great Britain and Japan, and the British were reluctant to retain a commitment which might place them in opposition to the United States. The Four Power Treaty was to replace the British-Japanese alliance and initiate an era of cooperation among all the powers interested in the Far East, preventing Japan from taking isolated action.

Taken together, these agreements reveal a remarkable shift of power in the Pacific. In that area Great Britain clearly had become secondary to the United States. It had bowed to American wishes in abandoning its old alliance with Japan, and because it could keep only a part of its navy in the Far East, the arrangements about naval strength made any unilateral involvement of Britain in a Far Eastern war an impossibility. Britain's efforts now had to be directed toward gaining cooperation, and if necessary common action, among all the powers interested in the Far East. But it is very doubtful whether the policy worked out at the Washington conference was suited to this goal and whether the consequences of the replacement of a British-Japanese alliance by the Four Power Treaty were beneficial.

The Japanese withdrew from China and for a number of years adhered scrupulously to the Washington agreements. But feeling became strong in Japan that the nation had gained little from its participation in the First World War, and the moderate Japanese statesmen anxious to cooperate with Great Britain, the European powers, and the United States, lost influence, while a militaristic group bent on imperialist expansion and opposed to the parliamentary regime gained in appeal.

These developments were furthered by events in China itself. The Revolution of 1911, brought about by the Chinese resentment against foreigners and indignation about the impotence of the imperial regime, was followed by a confused period of civil war, with the various provincial governors, the so-called warlords, fighting one another. The First World War gave events a new turn.

The handing over of the former German colonies in China to the

Japanese aroused national resentment in China, especially among intellectuals and students. On the other hand, the end of tsarism and the seizure of power in Russia by the Bolsheviks meant that China was no longer faced by a united front of powerful foreign states; on the contrary, China now had a defender among them, since the Communist International made the cause of colonial peoples and exploited races one of its main concerns. The Russian's also gave proof of their interest in China by giving up the privileges granted to tsarist Russia by the imperial Chinese governments. The intellectual leader of the Chinese revolution and protagonist of a united and socially reformed and modernized China, was Sun Yat-sen (1866–1925), who had been proclaimed president of the Chinese republic. But in 1922, China was divided by the feuds of warlords who ruled in the various provinces and Sun Yat-sen was almost powerless. He then turned to Russia and admitted Communists into his party, the Kuomintang. The alliance was not purely opportunistic: Sun Yat-sen saw in various measures of the Bolsheviks, mostly in their agrarian policy, models for what ought to be done in China. For a short time the Russians, since the chance for a revolution in central and western Europe seemed hopeless, believed that through the conquest of China by Communism a new impetus could be given to a forward march of the world revolution. With the help of Russian advisers, among whom Borodin was the outstanding figure, the Kuomintang was organized in a more effective way and the army was reformed. Sun Yat-sen died in 1925, but his successor, Chiang Kai-shek (1887–1975) succeeded in establishing Kuomintang rule over the principal parts of China. This consolidation, accomplished by another wave of anticapitalist strikes and demonstrations, induced the western powers to follow the Russian example, to give up their privileges and to evacuate the harbors which they had occupied in imperialist days; in this way they hoped to maintain trade with China and realize what was the officially proclaimed aim of their policy: open-door and independence of China. Encouraged by the support of the West, Chiang Kai-shek, who, more than Sun Yat-sen, considered cooperation with the Communists an emergency measure, broke with them. The Communists were driven out of the Kuomintang and of the government although, under the leadership of Mao Tse-tung (1893–1976) and Chu Teh (born 1886) they remained in control of some agrarian areas in northern China. The national government under Chiang Kai-shek proclaimed as its aim the establishment of a consititutional democracy, but announced this goal could only be reached after a transitional period in which all power was in the hands of the Kuomintang. National China became a one-party state. It was a period of centralization and organizational improvement: the currency was unified; the introduction of a budget brought some order into government financing; and the build-

Mao Tse-tung in 1933, when he was the leader of the radical left opposition to the Kuomintang under Chiang Kai-shek.

ing of railroads and highways furthered economic development and strengthened administrative control.

In contrast to the western powers, the Japanese did not consider a consolidation of the Chinese government as being in their interest. They feared that a politically strengthened China, pursuing a nationalistic economic policy, might exclude Japanese industrial goods from the Chinese market and make the Japanese economic situation critical. The Chinese, on the other hand, regarded the Japanese economic penetration into Manchuria with increasing distrust and Japan became the chief target of anti-imperialist movements and demonstrations; a boycott of Japanese goods was started. In September, 1931, the so-called Mukden incident—a railway explosion for which the Japanese blamed the Chinese—brought about a break. Japan invaded Manchuria and a war began, which ended only with the end of World War II. The European powers were unable to prevent the outbreak of this conflict, nor could the machinery of the League of Nations compose it. Japan refused to accept the recommendations of the League and withdrew from it in March, 1933.

The failure of the League during this crisis was one visible sign of the weakening of the system which had been established by the Paris Peace Conference; as such, it represented a serious blow to the authority of those powers considered to be the founders and chief defenders of the system: Britain and France. It became clear that, suffering from the effects of the economic crisis, they were unable to mobilize the necessary forces to stop the Japanese advance and impose a settlement. Those in Europe who were opposed to the political establishment also believed that the time had come for a change. Thus did the revolt against the settlement of Paris extend into Europe.

THE RISE OF NAZISM IN GERMANY

The event which decisively brought an end to the system established in Paris and also to the era of political stabilization was the rise of Nazism in Germany. The reasons for this rise were, of course, manifold. The economic crisis gave strong impetus to the Nazi movement; but this was not the only—and perhaps not even the most important—reason for its spread. To a large extent, Nazism was an inner German phenomenon, one which revived old political attitudes dominant in imperial Germany: authoritarianism and nationalism.

Decline of Parliamentary Government in the Weimar Republic

As we have seen, the leaders of the Weimar Republic had felt constrained to retain the monarchical civil servants, antagonistic to parliamentarianism and democracy, and to rely on an equally authoritarian officer corps which despised pacifism and internationalism. Thus a strongly antirepublican and antidemocratic influence emanated from men holding key positions in the republic, Furthermore, the popular support which the republic possessed at the outset was soon whittled down under the impact of the Treaty of Versailles.

Nevertheless, in the three or four years of increasing prosperity which followed the acceptance of the Dawes Plan and the conclusion of the Locarno agreements, the republican regime gained some ground and a slight swing to the republican left took place in the elections of 1928. It was a sign of the change in the political climate that the monarchist German People's party entered a coalition with the three republican parties. However, the situation changed quickly. One year after the elections the economic depression began to make itself felt. In September, 1929, Germany had 1,320,000 unemployed; one year later, 3,000,000; in September 1931, 4,350,000; and in 1932 the peak was reached with over 6,000,000. In Germany the widespread poverty and wretched conditions caused by the depression had an especially devastating psychological effect because they came so soon after the hardships of the inflation. Republican governments seemed unable to create a secure economic foundation for society. Left-wing and right-wing radicalism increased, with a resultant sharpening of tension between the left and right wings of the ruling coalition. The socialists, fearful that their adherents would go over to the Communists, became increasingly unwilling to agree to economic measures which might increase unemployment; and the German People's party tried to strengthen its appeal by adopting a more nationalist line in foreign policy. Particularly unfortunate was the death in October, 1929, of Gustav Stresemann, who had exerted a moderating influence in the German People's party. Shortly before his death he had achieved an important success: the acceptance of the Young Plan developed by a commission headed by the American Owen D. Young, which reduced the amount of the annual German reparations payments, eliminated the international controls over German economy, and brought to an immediate end the military occupation of the Rhineland. But because this agreement had been preceded by bitter diplomatic struggles, its acceptance aroused nationalist passions and resentment and weakened rather than helped the advocates of a policy of international understanding.

With Stresemann gone, the gap between the right and the left in the government widened steadily, and in March, 1930, the coalition disintegrated. The parties were unable to agree upon measures to overcome the accelerating economic crisis. The particular issue which led to the resignation of the government was very similar to one which brought about the fall of the Labor government in Great Britain a year later: payments to the unemployed. The socialists wanted to maintain unemployment benefits but in order to minimize the budget deficit they proposed raising the contributions. On the other hand, this seemed to the industrialists a unique opportunity to reduce the rights of the trade unions to participate in decisions on wages and dismissals and to become again masters in their own house.

Although never concealing his monarchist convictions, Hindenburg carried out his duties in accordance with the constitution during his first years as president. But he was surrounded by monarchist officers and friends who believed that the collapse of the coalition government might afford an opportunity for a change to a more authoritarian system, paving the way for a new monarchy. In 1930 they picked a rather nationalist member of the Center party, Heinrich Brüning (1885–1970), as chancellor. Brüning's political views had been formed by the experiences of the war. Despite physical disabilities he had volunteered for the army and served as an officer at the front; he preserved an almost childish adoration for officers and for military values and virtues. A strict Catholic, he lived ascetically, and tended toward obstinacy and self-righteousness. He was an administrator rather than a politician, an authoritarian rather than a democrat. Although at first Brüning impressed people as a new and interesting figure on the political scene, his lugubrious character did not inspire confidence and hope. He had made his career in the Center party as an expert in financial affairs and was a strict adherent of orthodox views on economics. He believed that the crisis could be overcome only by deflation and strict economies, including cuts in unemployment insurance. Fully aware that such a policy would never be approved by the socialists, he expected to draw his support from

During the elections to the Reichstag in 1932. *Parties distribute propaganda before a polling place.*

the center and the right; he was willing to woo the right by effecting a constitutional change which would result in a more authoritarian form of government. When the Reichstag refused to approve his financial proposals, Brüning dissolved that body and put his financial proposals into effect by emergency decrees.

The elections which took place on September 14, 1930, showed the expected shift to the right, but not to the German People's party and the German Nationalist party, which might have cooperated with Brüning; instead, gains were made by the extremist National Socialists, or Nazis, who increased their seats from 15 to 107. From this time until January 30, 1933, when their leader, Adolf Hitler (1889–1945), became chancellor, German politics was dominated by one issue: whether or not the National Socialists would come to power.

The outcome of the elections did not deter Brüning from his course; he rejected all suggestions that he resume cooperation with the socialists. The constitution in Paragraph 48 had provided that in emergency situations the president could rule by decree. It had hardly been envisaged that an emergency situation could last for several years, but Brüning, sure of presidential support, believed that if he could go on ruling by emergency decrees he would be able to demonstrate that the government would function much better with a less powerful parliament and a more independent executive. The ground would be prepared for a constitutional change in the direction of authoritarianism. He seems to have expected that such a fulfillment of demands of the right would take the wind out of the sails of the extremists and tame the National Socialists so that they would support his government. According to the constitution, emergency decrees became invalid if a majority of the Reichstag voted against them. However, Brüning anticipated correctly that although the socialists might not like this government they would regard it as a lesser evil than a government of the National Socialists. Thus, whenever the Reichstag voted on Brüning's emergency decrees the socialists abstained from voting, and the parties of the middle and the moderate right, which supported Brüning, defeated by a small margin the radicals of the right and left. A rather doubtful interpretation of the notion of emergency, combined with socialist tolerance, kept the Brüning government in power.

Brüning further ingratiated himself with the forces of the right by giving a nationalist turn to German foreign policy. In June, 1930, when the last French troops evacuated the Rhineland, official speeches celebrating this event expressed no appreciation of the French concessions, but instead raised demands for further revisions of the peace treaty. The British ambassador in Berlin wrote: "It is an unattractive feature of the German character to display little gratitude for favors received but when the receipt of favors is followed up by fresh demands there are grounds for feeling impatient." If the British government had followed the advice of its ambassador and had stood with France, the Germans might have become more cautious in making complaints and raising new demands. But Great Britain just tried to smooth things over without taking any definite stand and Germany went ahead with its policy of seeking revision.

The most disastrous German step in this campaign was the conclusion of a customs union with Austria in March, 1931. Such an agreement was hardly compatible with the 1919 prohibition against Anschluss, and it was in direct contradiction to stipulations which Austria had accepted in 1922 in order to receive financial support from France, Great Britain, and Italy. France brought the issue before the Permanent Court of International Justice in The Hague and the customs union was declared invalid. The prestige of the Brüning government waned in the face of nationalist resentment, of which the radical right made good use. Moreover, the political uncertainty created by the conflict over the customs union triggered in the summer of 1931 the dramatic explosion of the financial crisis which began in Vienna, then moved to Germany, and finally extended to London.

During that summer, Brüning and the president of the Reichsbank were forced to make desperate trips to London and Paris to plead for financial relief, and these appeals to former enemies further damaged the prestige of the government in the eyes of the nationalists. In the winter of 1931–1932, the nationalist opposition was still gaining in strength and unemployment reached frightening proportions.

Brüning was further handicapped by the fact that he could rule by emergency decrees only as long as he had the confidence of the president, to whom the power to issue the decrees actually belonged. In March, 1932, Hindenburg's first presidential term ended. In the subsequent election he received 53 per cent of the votes; Hitler received 36.8 per cent. Despite Hindenburg's imposing majority the result was a disappointment to him. The figures showed that right-wing radicalism had continued to grow; Brüning had failed to gain the cooperation of the rightist groups, and at the end of May, 1932, he was curtly dismissed by Hindenburg.

The details of what happened in Germany between Brüning's dismissal and Hitler's assumption of power in January, 1933, are intricate. There were intrigues centering around the president and the men who most influenced him: his son, Oskar, and his secretary, Otto Meissner. But the general pattern was constant. The continuing increase in popularity of nationalist extremism on the right made moderate conservatives less than ever inclined to resume cooperation with the socialists. Moreover, Hindenburg, getting old and dependent, decided against a return to parliamentarism. These authoritarian tendencies were strongly supported by the generals of the Reichswehr, particularly their representatives in the defense ministry, Kurt von Schleicher (1882–1934) and Kurt Freiherr von Hammerstein-Equord (1878–1943). They were sympathetic, if not to the National Socialist leaders, at least to the revival of nationalism and militarism which National Socialism preached. In their eyes the Nazis would be valuable material to be incorporated into the army when the hour arrived to break the chains of the disarmament clauses of Versailles. They were not willing to risk a serious political conflict in which the Reichswehr might have to fight the National Socialists with their paramilitary organizations. Indeed, they were not even sure that officers ordered to attack the Nazis would obey the command. Thus, all the men around the president wanted to cooperate with the National Socialists. The only stumbling block was the demand of their leader, Hitler, that he must be chancellor of any government supported by his party. Hindenburg's advisers wanted to use the National Socialists for their own purpose, but they did not want to get into a position in which the National Socialists might be able to call the tune. Brüning's successor, Papen, an ambitious and elegant former officer who through his great wealth had acquired newspapers and political influence, was disappointed in his lighthearted expectation that the National Socialists would cooperate with him. His successor, General Schleicher, was equally unsuccessful. By December, 1932, however, the situation began to change. Elections in November showed for the first time a slight decrease in the National Socialist vote; it became clear that the economic crisis had reached its peak. The conservatives and nationalists feared that if these trends continued, the occasion for the establishment of an authoritarian government and for a restoration of the monarchy might be missed. Likewise the National Socialist leaders began to feel that they might have waited too long. The masses might defect, having become convinced that National Socialism would never come to power. Under these circumstances, driven by ambition and stimulated by hatred of his successor Schleicher, Papen attempted once again to form a coalition with the National Socialists. He conceded to their leaders that Hitler should become chancellor, but only two other Nazis, Wilhelm Frick (1877–1946) and Hermann Göring (1893–1946), would become members of the cabinet, and Göring was to be minister without portfolio. The other members were to be either conservative politicians like Alfred Hugenberg (1865–1951), leader of the German Nationalist party, or experts. Papen himself, as vice-chancellor, would be present at all Hitler's audiences with the president. In such a government, Papen and his friends believed, Hitler's chancellorship would be of no danger. Completely surrounded by sound conservatives, Hitler would have no freedom of action. With these arguments Papen, supported by Hindenburg's son and by his secretary, overcame the president's resistance. On January 30, 1933, Hitler was appointed chancellor.

Adolf Hitler before the conquest of power. *With Hitler are his then most prominent lieutenants,* from left to right, G. Strasser, Roehm, Hitler, Göring, Brueckner.

Nazism in Germany

On the evening of January 30 the Nazis celebrated Hitler's appointment with a gigantic torch light parade in which they marched, along with organizations of military veterans, through the government quarter of Berlin. This demonstration was meant to emphasize that the formation of the Hitler government signified a new beginning and represented a revolution. The parallel with the rise of Fascism in Italy is striking. The formation of the government by Mussolini had been preceded by negotiations with other parties and by court intrigues; the outcome was a coalition. The traditional nature of the methods employed by Mussolini to gain office was concealed by the March on Rome, which made the seizure of power a conquest by force—a revolution. The torchlight parade on the evening of January 30 in Berlin was Hitler's "March on Rome." That the people around Hindenburg and the reactionary non-Nazi members of Hitler's government expected to control Hitler and to use the Nazis for their own purposes indicated that they had no understanding of Hitler's personality or of the reasons why so many people had been attracted to the National Socialist party. For though their final rise to power was due to the intrigues and subtle calculations of the military and the reactionaries, the Nazis had become a force in German politics because large masses of the German people approved of their radical demands for a new departure and saw in Hitler a messiah.

The rise of the Nazis reflected the disappearance of the bourgeois parties which had stood at the center in the German political scene. Among those who voted for the Nazis before 1933 were hardly any workers, at least not older workers. There had been some shift of votes from the Socialists to the Communists, but the sum of votes given to these two parties remained constant even during the depression. The Catholic Center party too kept most of its adherents, but the German Democratic party and the German People's party disintegrated. Certainly the Nazis had many kinds of supporters. With the help of Hjalmar Schacht, who had turned against the government because in his opinion the Young Plan was still too burdensome and ought not to have been accepted, they received money from industrialists, who expected that the Nazis would put an end to concessions to the workers. Members of the nobility and of the Wilhelminian ruling group lent their prestige and their support to the Nazis because they wanted to overthrow the despised republic. For the youth, particularly for students who believed they had little chance in the future and feared that they would become an academic proletariat, the Nazi demand for a new social order had great appeal; originally young people were the main adherents of the Nazis. Farmers and small-town residents were antagonistic to the big cities and the trend toward industrialization, which they believed were dominating the policy of the republic. Most of the Nazi votes came from the middle classes, particularly the lower middle classes. They had been hit hard by the inflation. Despite some improvement in the later 1920's the economic situation remained precarious for the owners of small industries faced with overwhelming competition from large-scale industries organized into trusts and cartels. Shopkeepers found their businesses suffering from the increasing popularity of department stores. Moreover, the depression fell heavily on the white-collar workers in factories, offices, and stores, who did not even enjoy the minimum protection afforded by the trade unions. Most members of the lower middle classes became convinced of the incompetence and corruption of those whom the republican form of government had brought into power. This view of the republican government had been fed by the monarchist parties of the right, particularly the German Nationalist party. But the gains were harvested not by the Nationalists, but by the Nazis. The National Socialist party had a strong appeal because it claimed that it was entirely different from other political parties and that it took part in elections only in order to overthrow the entire existing political setup.

The Structure of the Nazi Party

The character of Nazi propaganda and the form of the party organization emphasized the distinctiveness of National Socialism. At meetings, the paramilitary storm troopers first marched into the hall and flanked the podium; martial music was played until the main speaker appeared, greeting and being greeted by a raised right arm, the so-called Hitler salute. After an inflammatory speech he left immediately, again giving and receiving the Hitler salute. No questions were asked. Hecklers and people who tried to raise objections were thrown out of the meeting room by the storm troopers. The fact that such gatherings had the aspect of a religious revival meeting made them all the more appealing to Germans of the lower middle classes, who in their economic helplessness and isolation were drawn to a movement which seemed to make them part of a powerful world.

The structure of the party was hierarchical. At the top was the leader, Adolf Hitler. Below him was the *Gauleiter*, or subleader, having command of his own *Gau*, or region, and the *Gau* in turn divided into districts, each directed by a party official subordinate to the *Gauleiter*. The chain of command led strictly from above to below. Hitler gave the orders, and they were transmitted through the party hierarchy to the rank and file. From the beginning, Hitler considered this leadership principle to be crucial. Even in the 1920's, when the fortunes of the party were low, he refused to amalgamate with other small parties of nationalist extremism because such a move might threaten his position as the one and only leader. In the confusion of the German parliamentary system, with its numerous bour-

The Nazi Party Congress in Nuremberg in 1934. *In the middle, Hitler, between Himmler, the leader of the S.S. (left) and Lutze, leader of the S.A.*

geois parties and its many intrigues, the quality of decisiveness inherent in the leadership principle had attraction as promising a way out of chaos.

Resoluteness and decisiveness were communicated also by another feature peculiar to the National Socialist party: its paramilitary organizations, the *Sturmabteilung,* known as the S.A., or storm troopers, and the *Schutzstaffel,* or S.S. The S.S. gained importance only in later years, after Hitler's seizure of power; it began as a bodyguard for Hitler and his chief lieutenants. In earlier years the important and active military organization of the party was the S.A. Its original function was to protect Nazi speakers at open meetings. But this defensive role was soon superseded by an aggressive one, that of breaking up the meetings of Communists and other "enemies" of the nation. At first the S.A. men were given only uniforms and some food. Later, when the party became large and rich through membership dues and financial contributions, the storm troopers received regular wages. When unemployment was widespread, young men flocked to the S.A. The organization became strong enough to parade through the streets of the towns and to impede demonstrations of other groups and parties. Street fights, in which the S.A. excelled in roughness and violence, became frequent. The storm troopers committed a number of murders of political opponents, and their brutality—openly encouraged by Hitler—was one of the reasons why, until January, 1933, even nationalists who were sympathetic to Hitler's cause hesitated to entrust him with the government.

On the other hand, the ruthlessness of the S.A. helped to strengthen the Nazis. In many smaller towns the S.A. became all-powerful, and citizens found it easier and less dangerous to go along with the National Socialists than to oppose them. Moreover, through the violence of the S.A. a kind of undeclared civil war developed in Germany and the local governments which did not seem able to keep peace lost in prestige to the National Socialists who guaranteed that they would maintain order if they came to power.

Hitler's Political Technique

Hitler's originality lay in his understanding of the art of directing the minds of the masses. He explained his views about the techniques of propaganda at some length in *Mein Kampf* ("My Battle"), written in 1924: "The driving force of the most important changes in this world had been found less in scientific knowledge animating the masses but rather in a fanaticism dominating them and in a hysteria which drives them forward." Thus the intellectual content of political propaganda must be as simple as possible: "All effective propaganda has to limit itself to a very few points and to use them like slogans. . . . It has to confine itself to little and to repeat this eternally." A political leader should not discuss an issue in all facets and complications. Everything ought to be painted in either black or white: a "suggestively biased attitude. . . . towards the questions to be dealt with." Because the masses are not acting upon intellectual considerations, are not "thinking," a political leader need not fear to speak a lie if this might be effective. But the lie must be a "big lie." Small lies the people might recognize, for they themselves tell them, but "it would never come into their heads to fabricate colossal untruths and they would not believe that others could have the impudence to distort the truth so infamously." Thus the effectiveness of a message depends not on its truth, but only on the fanaticism and the passion with which it is conveyed; to a properly presented appeal the masses will respond by accepting what they are told.

Hitler followed these rules carefully in his speeches. His oratory was his strength, and the important stepping-stones in his rise to power were the great mass meetings at which, among flags and uniformed men, under a sharp spotlight in an otherwise darkened hall, the leader spoke. Deliberately he built up an image of himself as the embodiment of the mission of the German nation. He represented himself as a man with no family and no women, living ascetically so that he could devote himself exclusively to the German nation. But he did not want to appear inhuman either. He loved dogs; he smiled at children and gave them chocolate. All this was artfully fabricated—a "big lie." Actually, his sister conducted his household. For fifteen years he lived with a mistress, Eva Braun. He spent hours looking at movies in his own theatĕr. The photographs representing his private life which were published in German newspapers were carefully selected from the many taken by his official photographer.

Hitler's political ideas were crude and represented a mixture of Darwinism, Wagnerian romanticism, and Nietzschean philosophy, all simplified and vulgarized. "The whole work of nature is a mighty struggle between strength and weakness—an eternal victory of the strong over the weak," he said. Politics was to Hitler a struggle among races, but in his view the races were not equal; the "Aryan race"—and he never clearly defined this term—was superior to all others. Hitler believed in the importance of elites. Among the Aryans, the Germans were the elite. And among the Germans, the National Socialists were the elite, with the right and the duty to lead and to rule. Because struggle was the law of life, war was a necessity and the main task of a national leader was to make his state militarily strong so that it could win in battle and could expand.

In its political application this ideology resulted in certain concrete aims. Despite some shifts in his thought, Hitler always regarded France and Great Britain as Germany's enemies. However, he held them in contempt. As aging democracies they lacked the rule of an elite and were therefore weak and declining. The particular foe of the German nation, he believed, was Bolshevik Russia. For Russia was dangerous. It was not a democracy but a dictatorship. It showed no signs of age. Moreover, a military defeat of Russia would mean that its southwestern plains could provide the living space for which Germany had a great need. Finally, Hitler maintained that Communism was Jewish in origin, and to him the Jews were the most dangerous, the most fatal, enemies of the Aryans.

Anti-Semitism was central in Hitler's political thought. It was an effective propaganda device in Germany; the Jew could be blamed for those incomprehensible economic forces which destroyed the independence of small entrepreneurs and shop owners. But the usefulness of anti-Semitism as propaganda was secondary for Hitler; he was a convinced, passionate hater of the Jews. An admirer of Wagner's operas, Hitler was obsessed by the drama of Teutonic heroes, caught in a net by the dark dwarfs with their hoard of gold. There is no possibility of finding a rational explanation for such elements of Hitler's thought as anti-Semitism; it would be a mistake even to try to do so. As his whole career was to show, and as he himself frequently stated, in his crucial decisions he followed his intuition.

It is not difficult to determine where Hitler's ideas came from. He himself said in *Mein Kampf* that in his years in Vienna he "formed an image of the world and a view of life which became the granite foundation of my action. Vienna was and remained for me the hardest but also the most thorough school of my life." Adolf Hitler was born in Braunau, Austria, on April 20, 1889. His father, who had been a customs official, died when his son was fourteen. His mother spoiled him; he grew up undisciplined and with a very

An illustration of the anti-Semitic policy of the Nazis. *The sign reads, "Jews are not welcome in this town."*

uneven education. Hitler was unsuccessful at school, and left when he was sixteen. Always distrustful of people with learning, he imagined himself to be something "better," an artist. In 1907 he went to Vienna to study painting at the Academy of Arts but he failed the entrance examination. Apparently, the great tragedy of his early years was the death of his mother in 1908. He returned to Vienna after her death, where for some time he lived quite well, on the basis of the money left to him by his parents and on a government grant for orphan students which he received without really being entitled to it. But these financial resources were soon exhausted and he drifted through various menial jobs without ever setting out on a definite career. He slept on park benches and in flophouses and wore shabby and torn clothes which people gave him out of pity. His life later became somewhat more settled, although on a near-starvation level, when, following the advice of an acquaintance, Reinhold Hanisch, he began to paint postcards and posters which Hanisch peddled around. For several years Hitler and Hanisch lived together in a home for men in Vienna. But Hanisch seems to have been almost Hitler's only close acquaintance. Hitler later said that the Vienna years had been very lonely. He had contact only with tramps and drunkards; he never learned to discuss or to exchange thoughts with others. His way of expressing himself was to monologize, and as the transcripts of meetings with his ministers and advisers during the Second World War would show, he retained this mode of speech to the end. But monologizing provided good training for a public speaker.

As an outsider without any special trade Hitler found himself unable to compete for jobs with organized labor, and he developed an intense hatred of Marxism. Moreover, at this time the Germans in the Habsburg monarchy were vehement nationalists, using racist theories to justify their right to rule over the other nationalities. All the German nationalist parties in Austria-Hungary were passionately anti-Slavonic and anti-Semitic. Hitler's opposition to Marxism, his belief in the value of race and in the superiority of the Germanic race, his anti-Semitism were all echoes, and mostly pure repetitions, of notions that flourished in Vienna around the turn of the century.

The one further element important in the formation of Hitler's mind was the war experience. In 1913, he moved from Vienna to Munich. As he later said, he preferred a real German city to Vienna with its "promiscuous swarm of foreign people." But in Munich his existence was quite as uncertain and miserable as it had been in Vienna. When the war broke out he volunteered for a Bavarian regiment. Hitler was a good soldier and for the first time he found some recognition and felt himself to be a member of a community. Indeed, he met in his regiment men who later became his most devoted friends and followers: Rudolph Hess, who became party secretary, and Max Amann, who was the press chief in Nazi Germany. The war experience made Hitler an admirer of all things military; he was impressed by the hierarchical structure of an army, with its chain of command. After years of rootlessness, he found a home in the army. The collapse of Germany was a personal catastrophe for him. He could not admit that the defeat had been caused by the admired military leaders; in his view it was the result of a stab in the back by those dark forces which he had seen in Vienna—Marxists and Jews. He returned to Munich, and as we have seen, was employed by the army as a propaganda speaker to keep the military spirit alive in the disheartened and defeated German nation. In the course of this activity Hitler came into contact with a small group calling itself the National Socialist German Workers' party, which pursued a somewhat confused mixture of nationalist and socialist ideals. Hitler became a member, and was soon the leader of this group. He had found his calling.

In Hitler's system of values those social ideas for which he had no feeling were no less significant than those which he emphasized. Hitler had no sense of the importance of morality or law. He was willing to stand up for murderers. He closed his eyes to the sexual aberrations of many of his companions, but he did not hesitate to make use of his knowledge of their weaknesses when he wanted to get rid of them. In politics, and probably also in his personal life, Hitler knew only friends and foes—and those who were his friends became his foes when they did not offer him blind allegiance. He used every weapon to eliminate his enemies. When in the summer of 1934 the S.A. had become an obstacle, he had the leaders—his enthusiastic followers—executed without recourse to the regular courts, explaining that he was "the supreme justiciar" of the German people. He had people placed in "protective custody" without giving them any opportunity to defend themselves in the courts. The result was the establishment of the dreaded concentration camps, where many were kept without legal recourse for unlimited periods. He established special courts, like those of the S.S., which made their own laws, and he issued retroactive laws. The lack of sense of morality, the inability to grasp the value of a system of law, were deeply rooted in Hitler's personality; perhaps, as psychohistorians have written, the causes lay in his childhood, when his father—to the outside world the image of a strictly moral, righteous official—appears to have shown an irrational temper and uncontrollable sexual drives, and his mother protected her children against her husband by lies and deceit. Hitler's contempt for human beings showed itself early.

Almost inevitably Hitler's personality carried the seeds of his destruction. It has been debated why he could not be content with the success which he achieved. There were moments under his rule when Germany seemed to have obtained all that its people could have desired. But a halt would have meant the return to some legal order and the acceptance of some moral values permitting the existence of a stable communal life. In such a world neither the men who surrounded the leader, nor Hitler himself, would have fitted. Hence he drove restlessly on to new conquests until the chase ended in nothing. It is truly appropriate to call the Nazi revolution, as did Hermann Rauschning, at first Hitler's adherent and then his enemy, "the revolution of nihilism."

The Implementation of the Nazi Program

Hitler's aim was to obtain full power and then to launch Germany on a course of expansion, thereby fulfilling what he regarded as the natural law of politics. When he became chancellor in January, 1933, such an aim seemed far beyond his grasp. His government was a coalition in which the National Socialists were a minority. In foreign policy Germany's freedom of action was still restriced by the treaties of Versailles and Locarno. The size of the German army was limited and the Rhineland was demilitarized. One may reject Hitler's aims and detest his brutal methods, but still find remarkable the technical virtuosity with which he quickly freed himself from these internal and external restraints. A year and a half after he became chancellor, Hitler was the all-powerful dictator of Germany, and less than two years after that, in March, 1936, he made the treaties of Versailles and Locarno valueless pieces of paper.

At first, Hitler made use of the coalition with the German Nationalist party in order to stress the moderate and conservative character of his "national revolution." The black, white, and red of the German empire replaced the black, red, and gold of the national flag of the Weimar

Republic; carefully staged celebrations emphasized the continuity between the old imperial Germany and the new National Socialist state. In March, 1933, the artfully contrived climax of the opening of the Reichstag in the Hohenzollern residence at Potsdam was Hitler's bow before President Hindenburg.

Hitler and the National Socialists had several reasons for the temporary adoption of a conservative line. First of all, Hitler had to win the confidence of old Hindenburg, who by refusing to sign emergency decrees could still bring about the fall of the government. Also, the new chancellor was anxious to avoid any obstruction by the bureaucracy and to make sure that the military leadership would not turn against him. Moreover, popular support of National Socialism would be strengthened if the members of the various conservative and nationalist parties and organizations, who had stayed away from the Nazis, could be lured into enrolling in the Nazi party. The conservative line also helped to secure the continuation of financial support for the Nazi party from the leaders of industrial trusts and banks, such as the Krupp steel works and the I. G. Farben chemical works.

When the government was formed, Hitler insisted that the Reichstag be dissolved and new elections take place. The National Socialists entered the election campaign with immense advantages. They enjoyed the prestige of having their leader as head of the government. They could use the government machinery for propaganda, and on the basis of Paragraph 48 of the constitution they issued emergency decrees which limited the right of

The burning of the Reichstag on February 28, 1933.

assembly of opposition parties and suppressed their newspapers and political publications. However, the decisive turn in the election campaign was brought about on the night of February 27, 1933, when the building in which the Reichstag met went up in flames. Though Marinus van der Lubbe, the young Dutchman who was caught in the building, never denied the deed, it was immediately assumed that he alone could not have caused the immense fire.

The Nazi leaders immediately accused the Communists, maintaining that the Reichstag fire was intended as the signal for a Communist revolt; but they never produced any proof, and it is certain that the Communists were not involved. We do know that the Nazis were only waiting for a Communist provocation which would give them the opportunity to suppress the Communist party and impose further restrictions on the other opposition parties. It has been suggested, therefore, that the National Socialists themselves used Lubbe as a cat's paw and were responsible for the Reichstag fire. Whether this is true or not, the Nazi leaders welcomed the fire and utilized it most efficiently.

On February 28, the day after the burning of the Reichstag, the government issued a number of emergency decrees which were not rescinded until the end of Hitler's Third Reich in 1945. As a "defensive measure against Communist acts of violence," the government rescinded the guarantees of such basic rights as personal freedom, the free expression of opinion, the freedom of assembly and association, the privacy of postal and telephone communications, and the inviolability of property. In addition the number of crimes to which the death penalty could be applied was increased, and the spreading of rumors or false news was classified as treason. Finally, the Reich government was empowered to take over the government of the various federal states if necessary.

The elections, a week after the Reichstag fire, gave the National Socialists 43.9 per cent of the vote. It has been argued in favor of the political maturity of the German people that although the elections took place under severe pressure and restrictions, the National Socialists did not receive a clear majority. It is perhaps more significant that even after the dictatorial character of the Hitler regime had revealed itself, almost 44 per cent of the German people voted for the Nazis. Together with the German National-ist party, with 8 per cent of the vote, the National Socialist party had the majority.

But application of the emergency decrees soon made this alliance unnecessary. The Communist deputies, representing 12.2 per cent of the vote, were arrested and not permitted to enter the Reichstag. Now even without the German Nationalist party the Nazis had a majority.

For Hitler this was only a first step. He wanted to eliminate entirely both parliament and elections. His government therefore proposed an Enabling Law, which would transfer the legislative power from the Reichstag to the government for four years; as a change in the constitution, such a law had to be approved by two thirds of the Reichstag. Hitler obtained the support of the Catholic Center party by threatening to use the emergency decrees against this party as he had used them against the Communists. The members of the Center party reasoned that by agreeing to the Enabling Law they might save their party and retain some influence. The Enabling Law was accepted on March 23; only the Social Democrats voted against it, while outside the hall the storm troopers shouted, "We want the bill or fire and murder."

With the emergency decrees of February 28 and the Enabling Law of March 23 all legislative and executive power was concentrated in the hands of the Hitler government, and all guarantees against transgressions by the executive had been removed. This was the "legal" framework for Hitler's dictatorship from 1933 to 1945.

However, the possession of the legal instruments for establishing a dictatorship did not overcome all obstacles to Hitler's unlimited control. Although his party now constituted a majority in the Reichstag, he was committed to retaining the coalition government. The prestige of the president, Hindenburg, was superior to his. Opposition parties and newspapers, though hampered, continued to exist. And the traditional spokesmen for educated public opinion—civil servants, professors, clergymen—could still make themselves heard. Hitler's technique for weakening and finally eliminating these remaining centers of independence was masterly. His approach was always the same. Instead of moving against all his opponents at once, he attacked one at a time, in each case proceeding gradually.

Characteristic was the way in which he ended the multiparty system. After the Communist party had been eliminated, Hitler's first target was the Social Democratic party. In this effort his coalition partners were willing helpers, and few objections were raised by the other bourgeois parties. The strength of the Social Democrats lay in their close relation to the trade unions, whose strikes could severely handicap the work of the government. Hence, Hitler's first move was to separate the trade unions from the Social Democrats; he did so by promising the unions undisturbed, continued existence if they abandoned political activities and concentrated exclusively on economic goals. Timid and bureaucratic, the union leaders fell into this trap and accepted the restrictions. Next, the Nazis declared that independent trade unions were unnecessary. The unions ought to become part of a great comprehensive organization which would include employers as well as workers. With a great celebration on May 1, which was declared to be a national holiday, a German labor front was founded. The next day the buildings of the unions were occupied, their funds were confiscated, and some of their leaders were arrested. With the elimination of the trade unions the Social Democrats lost all their remaining power to exert pressure. And when some important socialists, threatened by imprisonment, left

Germany and attacked the regime from outside, the Nazis used their conduct as an excuse to declare Social Democratic activities treasonous; they prohibited the party and imprisoned many of its leaders.

Next, Hitler proceeded against the bourgeois parties outside his government. Most important among them was the Catholic Center party. Hitler again applied the tactics which he had used against the socialists: he destroyed his antagonist's source of power. A basic reason for the existence of the Center party was the need to maintain and protect the position of the Roman Catholic Church and its members. Hitler sent Papen to Rome to negotiate a concordat; for many years the Vatican had been eager for such an agreement, which would secure the legal status of the Catholic Church in Germany and would guarantee the bishops freedom of communication with the Vatican. But no previous federal government had been willing to conclude a concordat. The Vatican accepted Hitler's offer, probably as a result of the authoritarian inclinations of Pope Pius XI and the pro-German bias of his secretary of state Eugenio Pacelli, later Pope Pius XII. It was a fatal mistake. The concordat gave the first international approval to the Nazi regime and raised its prestige. It did not secure the position of Roman Catholicism in Germany, which Hitler went on to attack and undermine as soon as his immediate aim, the dissolution of the Center party, had been achieved. At the time, however, German Catholics, assured by the concordat that their religion would not suffer under the Nazi regime, abandoned membership in the Center party, and under pressure from the Vatican the party's leaders on July 8 agreed to its dissolution.

Hitler still had to dispose of his coalition partner—the German Nationalist party. When he became chancellor, he had promised not to change the composition of the government, which was to include, besides himself, only two National Socialists. However, he managed to increase the influence of his own party in the coalition by creating new departments headed by Nazis: Göring, who had distinguished himself in the war as pilot and was the most respectable of Hitler's close collaborators, became air minister; Joseph Goebbels (1897–1945), who had been head of the Nazi party in Berlin and was the most intellectual and also the most cynical of the Nazi leaders, became minister of propaganda. Moreover, members of the German Nationalist party who went over to the National Socialists were rewarded with advantageous positions in the administration and in the party. Those who refused, encountered endless difficulties. Therefore, strong pressure developed within the German Nationalist party to assure its members of continued influence in the government and administration by amalgamating with the Nazi party. Thus the party began to disintegrate and was finally dissolved. On July 14 a government enactment proclaimed that "the National Socialist German Workers' Party constitutes the only political party in Germany"; to attempt to maintain or organize any other political party became a crime. Germany was a one-party state. The elimination of

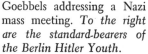

Goebbels addressing a Nazi mass meeting. *To the right are the standard-bearers of the Berlin Hitler Youth.*

the multiparty system was certainly Germany's most decisive step toward totalitarianism. But it was only one among many. Nazi commissars were placed at the head of the various federal states and appointed state governments dominated by Nazis. The press and the publishing houses were coordinated by the formation of a comprehensive Nazi-controlled association. Only members of this association were permitted to own, edit, or work on newspapers. A similar take-over occurred in the universities. New chairs were created for fields like racial science, and these were filled by National Socialists. The politically oriented newcomers were supported by the rectors of the universities, now not elected, but appointed by the Nazi minister of education. The expression of pronounced Nazi views became the prerequisite for obtaining tenure and promotion. No excuse is possible for the lack of resistance shown by the German intellectual community to the abolition of academic freedom. But because the Nazi infiltration of the universities happened gradually, many professors became aware of the systematic destruction of their independence only after it had been lost.

Similarly, the full aims of Hitler's anti-Semitic policy were only gradually apparent. It is certain that from the outset his mind was set on what during the Second World War became the "final solution"—the annihilation of the Jews. But at the beginning of the Nazi regime, Hitler created the impression that Jews would be permitted to continue their activities in economic life and in the professions; they were to be excluded from government service except for those who had done military service during the First World War. Soon, however, the screws were tightened. The exemption of war veterans from dismissal was rescinded. Doctors, lawyers, journalists, writers were organized in associations from which Jews were excluded; those who did not belong to these associations met increasing difficulties in the exercise of their professions. Admission to schools and universities was denied to Jewish youth. Gradually the same method was applied to business and economic life. Such activities required membership in organizations from which Jews were excluded. At the same time currency regulations and export restrictions made immigration a way of escape only for those who were still at the beginning of their careers, for middle-aged and older persons immigration seemed hardly feasible; most hesitated until it was too late.

The anti-Semitic policy reached a climax in the Nuremberg Laws of September 15, 1935, which deprived Jews and people with Jewish blood of German citizenship, prohibited marriage and sexual intercourse between people with Jewish blood and non-Jewish Germans, and denied Jews the right to employ non-Jewish female servants. Jews were forced to wear a yellow Star of David on their clothing whenever they went into the streets. They were pushed back into the ghetto. Protests against these measures were of no avail. As a matter of fact, few dared to endanger themselves by indicating disapproval.

All these changes were accompanied by a systematic policy of terror. When the Nazis came to power one of their first moves was to obtain control of the police. Since the ministers of the interior in the federal states were in command of the police the Nazis made sure that these posts were filled by reliable party members. Nazis also were appointed as police presidents in the larger urban centers. These officials arranged for the storm troopers to serve as an auxiliary police force. The emergency decrees passed after the Reichstag fire gave the police the right to arrest and keep in custody anyone suspected of disloyalty to the state. Nobody was secure; an incautious remark or the personal hostility of a storm trooper might result in imprisonment. People disappeared and were never heard of again. The police refused to interfere with Nazi demonstrations, as on April 1, 1933, when the Nazis marched unhindered through the streets of the center of Berlin, throwing stones into the windows of department stores and shops owned by Jews. Similar outbreaks by Nazi students in the universities forced professors regarded as unfriendly to the new regime to abandon their courses. In the atmosphere of terror, made more nightmarish by the official silence about these dark happenings, people gave up asking questions and closed their eyes and ears to what was going on around them. Moreover, the terror did not recede after the first few months; instead, it was embodied in an organization—the Secret State Police, or Gestapo—that developed into a large institution with headquarters in Berlin and offices all over Germany.

Kristallnacht: smashed windows of a Jewish shop on the morning after
November 9, 1938.

The Gestapo devoted itself to the task of ferreting out the enemies of
Nazism, who were arrested, interrogated, tortured, and placed in detention
camps, without any legal recourse.

Under these circumstances the only serious threat to Hitler's leadership
came from within—from the Nazi party itself. Many of those prominent in
the party, like the fanatic but colorless Heinrich Himmler (1900–1945), the
leader of the S.S., and the intelligent but generally despised Goebbels, the
minister of propaganda, were aware that they had little personal following
and were entirely dependent on Hitler. Göring, whose primitive enjoyment
of luxury and power gave him a certain human appeal, was entirely satisfied
with the power and riches he obtained as second in command and as
Hitler's designated heir. But many of the early party members sincerely
believed that the Nazi assumption of power would bring about a social
revolution and that they would be the leaders of a new society very different
from the old. A center of such aspirations was the S.A., and the main
advocate of these ideas was the leader of the S.A., Ernst Röhm (1887–
1934). His concrete aim was to have the S.A. become part of the army,
with the S.A. leaders receiving officers' ranks. Such demands disquieted the
generals of the Reichswehr, who did not want to see their control of the
training and organization of the army disturbed by the "wild men" of the
S.A. Hitler was anxious not to arouse the distrust of the military leaders
because he anticipated needing army support for his plan to combine the
position of president with that of chancellor after the death of Hindenburg,

which in 1934 was imminent. The situation was further complicated by the activities of the conservatives, who were fully aware that without Hindenburg they would lack the power to halt a second revolution and were therefore trying to put a stop to Nazi radicalism before Hindenburg's death. Out of this tangle of motives arose the blood bath of June 30, 1934. Hitler himself led the action against Röhm and other leaders of the S.A. whom he surprised in a small summer resort in Bavaria. Röhm and his associates were executed without trial; in his speech of justification Hitler emphasized his having discovered them in bed with young S.A. men. Actually he had known for a long time of the prevalence of homosexuality within the S.A. In Berlin, Göring proceeded not only against the leaders of the S.A. but also against other adversaries of the Nazis, like Schleicher, the former chancellor; he also arranged the execution of two of vice-chancellor Papen's secretaries, who had acted as spokesmen of the conservatives. Papen himself was placed under house arrest. Thus, Hitler shook off the radical wing of his party and earned the gratitude of the military leaders; he also demonstrated that he had not become a prisoner of the conservatives. The events of June 30 were both an expression of Hitler's utter disregard for law and morality and a sign of the omnipotence which he had reached. When Hindenburg died on August 2, Hitler combined the offices of president and chancellor without encountering objections.

In two sectors of social life—in economic affairs and in military affairs—the changes brought about by the Nazi dictatorship were less pronounced than in others. From the beginning the interests of the economic and military leaders harmonized with Hitler's aims. Economic life became strictly organized and controlled; industrial and commercial activities were coordinated by the trade associations to which all the entrepreneurs had to belong and from which, as we have seen, Jews—and also Freemasons—were excluded. The intermediary between the government and business was Hjalmar Schacht, who served Hitler as president of the Reichsbank and as minister of economics. Schacht abandoned the deflationary policy of previous governments; he pumped new money into the economy by initiating public works, such as the construction of the system of Autobahns, and by providing industry with armament contracts. The inflationary consequences of this policy were kept to a minimum by strict currency controls and import restrictions. Moreover, the secrecy with which German rearmament was surrounded kept the public in the dark about the extent of government expenditures and pump priming.

As the entire world has now learned, government support of economic activity—pump priming—can prove an effective means of overcoming economic depression. However, there are limits to the successful pursuit of an inflationary policy. Schacht himself believed that they had been reached by 1938, and he left the government because Hitler insisted on continuing this course. The damaging consequences did not come out into the open before the outbreak of the war in 1939. By then Germany was faced by the alternative of either a recession or a war and the Nazi leaders were entirely aware of this problem.

Once the danger of S.A. interference had been removed, the military leaders were quite content with Hitler's rule. In Hitler, Germany had a head of state who not only approved of rearmament but was anxious to accelerate the process. Thus, the military leaders no longer encountered government opposition to their desire for rearmament. However, their independence of the Nazi control was more apparent than real. The air force, created only after 1933, was under the command of Göring, and its officers were enthusiastic Nazis. Moreover, the quick promotions resulting from the expansion of the army made the younger officers favorably inclined toward the Nazi regime. In 1938, when the old army leaders began to fear that Hitler's foreign policy might be too risky, Hitler had no difficulty in replacing with more subservient generals those whom he regarded as obstructionists.

By 1936, Hitler could claim with justification that he had established a totalitarian state; with the exception of some pockets of resistance by small groups in the Roman Catholic and Protestant churches, all activities, organizations, and institutions had been adjusted (*gleichgeschaltet*) to the Nazi regime and were subject to the direction by the Nazi leader. But was there equal justification for the claim—which Hitler and the party chiefs made with still greater emphasis—that the Nazi conquest of power represented a revolution? "Revolution" may be understood as the overthrow of a ruling class and its replacement by another; in what respects, and to what extent, did the Nazi regime transform the basic structure of German social life?

The Nazi movement cannot be identified with a particular class or stratum of German society. Farmers and members of the lower middle class formed its backbone. But in the period of economic misery the unemployed swelled the Nazi ranks, and civil servants and white-collar workers joined them. Within these groups the younger generation in particular became Nazis; in 1930, the year of the party's first great electoral victory, more than two thirds of its members were under forty and more than one third under thirty years of age. Those who saw before them only a hard and bleak future were enticed by the Nazi promise of a complete change; the varied membership of the party was united only by common disaffection with the present.

Consequently, when the Nazis came to power they had no economic or social program aimed at changing the German social structure. They had promised their middle-class adherents protection against the absorption of small businesses by department and chain stores, and indeed they issued decrees which restricted the kinds of merchandise which these stores might sell and subjected them to a special tax. But the opposition of banks and other credit institutions which had invested in these enterprises led gradually to mitigation of the measures against chain and department stores. Beyond this somewhat ephemeral concession to the small middle-class businessman, the Nazis when they came to power had no concrete economic or social plans. Their "revolution" consisted in infusing a new "spirit" into the entire social body. Their apparently revolutionary actions were primarily propagandistic. They aimed at showing that a new nation had arisen in which all groups and classes harmoniously cooperated for the common good. The first of May became a national holiday intended to recognize the importance of the workers; this was only one of the many holidays created to emphasize the solidarity of the German nation. With the establishment of comradeship among the classes, "German Socialism," it was proclaimed, would become a reality. Organizations like the Hitler Youth and the Labor Service were meant to serve this purpose. The Hitler Youth consisted of boys and girls in their early years. The Labor Service was obligatory for students, voluntary for others; its disciplinary and educational effects were more highly appreciated by visiting foreigners than by those who had to undergo this training.

For Hitler the dividing lines in modern society were created not by differing education, differing professions, differing economic status, but by race. However, even within a superior race like the Germans there was an elite which alone had the right to rule; those few who came from the right stock and had excelled in their activities in the Hitler Youth were prepared for their tasks of leadership in special training schools, housed in buildings modeled after the castles of the knightly orders of the Middle Ages; the training—and these surroundings—were intended to awaken in the trainees the qualities of obedience, physical prowess, instinctivity, and will power.

The mixture of propaganda and racial romanticism in the social policy of the Nazis reflected the absence of concrete ideas about desirable changes in the German social structure. But this lack had its advantages for the Nazi regime. Since no revolution had occurred which changed the German class structure, and no ruling class had been toppled and replaced, each group of society seemed to have kept the position which it had held before the Nazis had obtained power. Except for the obvious victims of the change of regime—Jews, and politicians who had fought the Nazis—the individual did not experience an immediate diminution of status; the tenor of his life was not perceptibly changed, and this apparent stability was one reason for the lack of resistance to the Nazi regime in all levels of society.

The emphasis which Nazi propaganda placed on the establishment of a new national community was to a large extent directed toward mitigating the resentment arising from the realization of political powerlessness. The Nazi rulers took particular care to keep the industrial workers content. The labor front gave much attention to conditions in the factories, secured regular vacations for the workers, and through a special organization, called

"Strength Through Joy," subsidized travel for the workers and their families during these vacations.

Nevertheless, it might be doubted whether propagandistic flattery and handouts would have been effective if employers and employees had not been consoled for their loss of political influence by economic prosperity. At the time the Nazis took over, recovery from the depression was beginning, and this trend the Nazis aided by their policy of military rearmament. In 1938 the federal budget was seven times as large as it had been before the Nazis came to power, and 74 per cent of this budget was used for military purposes. Enterprises carrying out government contracts were given credit or were assured of orders for a fixed number of years. For example, in December, 1933, the government contracted to buy motor fuel from the large German chemical concern of I.G. Farben for ten years at fixed prices. By such arrangements, industry gradually surrendered its independence and granted the government control over production and prices. But as a collaborator with the regime, industry—and particularly the large companies—began to flourish.

The spurt in economic life which resulted from rearmament also transformed the situation on the labor market. In 1936–1937 the number of employed was greater than the number of employed and unemployed together had been in 1933. Soon there was a labor shortage in Germany. Although on the average, wages were even lower than they had been in the 1920's, the unskilled worker in Nazi Germany in the 1930's had the advantage of being sure of finding a job, and the skilled worker was so much sought after that his wages were kept high. After the haunting experiences of the depression, economic security seemed to both employers and employees a benefit worth paying for.

The question was, however, how long the prosperity produced by rearmament could last. Necessarily, this economic policy was accompanied by currency restrictions and limitations on imports, and the Nazi rulers were all the more willing to utilize such measures because they cut off the German people from the outside world. Nevertheless, because rearmament is economically unproductive, the inflationary consequences of the extension of credit which this policy required could not remain concealed indefinitely. Hitler had little fear that an end of economic prosperity would disrupt the new spirit of national community which the Nazi revolution claimed to have created; he was not concerned with stabilizing the situation which existed. His economic measures were never intended to provide a lasting solution. They were aimed at a change through territorial expansion, for which the rearmament policy was the requisite.

For Hitler the establishment of a totalitarian dictatorship was a means to a greater end: the expansion of Germany by war. In *Mein Kampf* he had written that along with the abrogation of the Treaty of Versailles and the restoration of the pre-1914 frontiers, Germany required additional "living space"; these goals were to be achieved, if necessary, by war. The rise to power of a man with such a program of expansion aroused fears in the non-German world. Yet Hitler succeeded in preventing common action, utilizing tactics very similar to those he had employed in domestic policy: proceeding slowly and gradually and dividing his enemies.

The Beginning of Nazi Foreign Policy

Hitler began his conduct of foreign policy with loud protestations of peaceful intentions: he was willing to disarm if Germany received equal treatment. Nevertheless, in October, 1933, he declared that the plans for disarmament discussed in the Disarmament Conference, which had been meeting at Geneva since 1932, discriminated against Germany; Germany withdrew from the Conference and the League of Nations. This was the first step toward a new foreign policy. Hitler softened this blow by declaring that his nation would be willing to reenter if its claims to equality in armament were recognized. The British government, occupied with the pursuit of economic recovery, refused to participate in any strong counteraction and began to explore the possibility of coming to some agreement on armament limitations. The British felt encouraged in these attempts to bring Germany back to international cooperation when on January 26, 1934, in a sudden reversal of foreign policy, Hitler concluded a nonaggression pact with Poland. The German demands for a return of Danzig and the Polish Corridor had always been regarded as a serious danger to European peace. In coming to an agreement with Poland the new ruler of Germany, however brutal his domestic policy might be, seemed to show that he was aware that methods of violence were inappropriate in international relations. The first year of Hitler's conduct of foreign policy ended with a great plus for the Reich. Germany had indicated that it no longer felt bound by the military clauses of the Treaty of Versailles, and yet was still courted as a participant in international negotiations.

In 1934 the skies darkened for Germany. Himself an Austrian, Hitler felt emotional about the *Anschluss*. He reacted sharply to measures of the Austrian chancellor, Engelbert Dollfuss, who established a Catholic authoritarian regime with the purpose of keeping Austria independent. By prohibiting Germans from traveling to Austria Hitler ruined the Austrian tourist industry, and he gave active support to the Austrian Nazi party, which Dollfuss had outlawed. Austrian Nazis who fled to Germany were organized into a military legion stationed near the border. On July 25, 1934, the Austrian Nazis tried to seize power by force. They succeeded in assassinating Dollfuss, but the putsch failed. Another Catholic chancellor, Kurt von Schuschnigg (born 1897) took over and continued Dollfus' anti-Nazi policy. The German government tried to shake off responsibility for the putsch and dissolved the Austrian legion, but the disclaimers were not believed and the image of Hitler as a man of peace was severely damaged.

The revelation of Hitler's aggressiveness had two important consequences. France strengthened its bonds with the eastern neighbors of Germany and began to cooperate with Soviet Russia, which was thoroughly alarmed by Hitler's vehement anti-Communism and suspected that his pact with Poland might mean the preparation of a Polish German war against Russia. Sponsored by the French, the Russians entered the League of Nations in September, 1934, and eight months later a Franco-Russian alliance was concluded in which each promised to come to the other's aid against unprovoked aggression.

Hitler's Austrian policy also brought about a change in Italy's attitude. Mussolini had regarded the rise of Hitler with satisfaction, and in the first months of 1933 had done his best to calm the fears which the Nazi seizure of power had raised in Europe and to dissuade France and Great Britain from taking action. Mussolini, with his antagonism against democracy and pacifism, his contempt for disarmament and the League of Nations, sympathized with Hitler's very similar attitude towards foreign policy. Mussolini saw definite advantages in a strengthened Germany, envisaging Italy as a balance wheel between Britain and France on one side and Germany on the other, and hoping that by acting as a broker Italy would gain increased power. But he recognized that the absorption of Austria by Germany would be counter to Italy's interests. Germany might then interfere in Italy's sphere of interest in the Danube Valley and the Balkans. Moreover, with a greater Germany on the other side of the Brenner Pass, the Germans under Italian rule in South Tyrol would become entirely intractable. Mussolini therefore helped Dollfuss to establish his anti-Nazi dictatorship, and when the news of Dollfuss' assassination came, he sent troops to the Brenner frontier, in order to show what he would not permit the *Anschluss*. From cautious support of Hitler, Mussolini had moved into the anti-Nazi camp. In January, 1935, negotiations in Rome with the French foreign minister, Pierre Laval (1883–1945), led to an agreement which even envisaged conversations between the French and Italian military staffs with the purpose of arranging for concerted action in case of war with Germany. The deterioration of the German position became evident when Hitler made his next move. In March, 1935, he declared the disarmament clauses of the Treaty of Versailles abolished, and announced a great augmentation of the German army and the introduction of general conscription. In a conference at Stresa, Great Britain, France, and Italy agreed to a sharp condemnation of this unilateral violation of an international treaty, declared their interest in the maintenance of Austrian independence, and threatened that further aggressive actions would evoke not only protests but counteraction. At this time Germany, except for the understanding with Poland, was isolated and seemed unable to move.

But the situation changed rapidly. Two months later, in June, Great Britain and Germany signed a naval agreement which defined the relative strength of their navies. Germany was permitted to have as many submarines as Britain, while the strength of the rest of the German fleet was to be restricted to one third that of the British fleet. Among the many mistakes of British foreign policy with respect to Nazi Germany the conclusion of the Anglo-German naval agreement is the most incomprehensible. The practical advantages for Britain were slight, for Germany was more interested in building a strong force of submarines than in creating a high-seas navy. The political disadvantages were immense, since by recognizing this departure from the military provisions of the Treaty of Versailles, Britain undermined the basis on which the Stresa front had been formed. Strangely enough, the British government seems not to have foreseen the implications of this naval agreement with Germany, and was apparently guided by purely technical considerations, notably the belief that the fixed strength of the German navy would facilitate negotiations with other powers about naval limitations.

The Italian Conquest of Ethiopia

Hitler, however, was encouraged to continue an aggressive foreign policy, and Mussolini felt himself confirmed in his view that democracies were unable to act vigorously, and, therefore, cooperation with Hitler could produce more concrete results than cooperation with Britain and France. Military conversations between the French and Italian staffs were postponed. Moreover, although Mussolini had found cooperation with France and Great Britain useful for the preservation of Austrian independence, he expected to be paid for his support, and he decided to cash in as quickly as possible. The result was the Italo-Ethiopian War. The Italian conquest of Ethiopia, completed in May, 1936, in a sense constituted revenge for the old defeat at Adua, a visible demonstration that Fascist Italy had become a great imperial power, stronger and more influential than democratic and parliamentary Italy had been. Also, Mussolini hoped to settle some of Italy's surplus population in Ethiopia. In his negotiations with Mussolini in January, 1935, Laval had indicated that France would have no objection to extension of the Italian influence over Ethiopia, and Mussolini expected a similar attitude from Great Britain. But strangely enough, while Hitler's actions had always found defenders in Britain, Mussolini's invasion of Ethiopia met vehement indignation. To the British people this seemed the occasion to set in motion the machinery of the League of Nations against aggression. When in December, 1935, it appeared that the British foreign secretary, Sir Samuel Hoare (1880–1959), was willing to make a bargain with Mussolini, popular excitement in Britain was so great that Hoare was dismissed and replaced by

Anthony Eden (1897–1977), a strong advocate of the League of Nations and of collective security. But this did not mean that, after the rejection of the bargain with Mussolini by the British public, the government had now decided to carry out a policy of collective security even if it should result in war. The British continued to pursue an ineffectual middle course; they were not too unhappy when the French tried to slow down their attempts to use sanctions against Italy, and they hesitated to insist on the application of the one effective sanction—the cutting off of Italy's oil supplies. The result was that in the League of Nations the British demanded only halfhearted measures, which embittered the Italians against Great Britain and France without preventing their advance in Ethiopia.

The Reoccupation of the Rhineland

It was in this situation, on March 7, 1936, that Hitler ended the demilitarization of the Rhineland by ordering his troops to march into the region, and thus violated not only the Treaty of Versailles but also the Locarno pact. Hitler counted on the disarray into which the Ethiopian war had put the Stresa front to prevent action by the western powers. Nevertheless, he was aware that he was gambling. As he later stated, the twenty-four hours while he was waiting for the reaction of the French were the most exciting and nerve-racking of his life. If the French had answered by sending troops into the Rhineland, the German forces would have been withdrawn to the right bank of the Rhine. This was the condition which the

German troops advance to occupy the Rhineland, March 7, 1936.

German military leaders had forced upon Hitler before agreeing to this move. But there was no French military response. Hitler's gamble had come off, and the political balance in Europe was entirely altered. As long as the Rhineland had been demilitarized and the important industrial areas of the Ruhr had remained unprotected, France had held the military advantage and had been in no real danger of attack. Now, with German troops near the French border and the Ruhr area in the hinterland, a conflict with Germany would mean bitter and serious war. Germany was again the strongest military power on the European continent.

CHAPTER 9

Toward the Inevitable Conflict

THE YEARS OF APPEASEMENT

How DID the western powers, Great Britain and France, react to the threat which the rise of Nazi Germany represented to the system established after the First World War? Or, as we might ask with the wisdom of hindsight, why for almost a decade was their response so very weak? The obvious answer is, of course, that they too were hard hit by the economic crisis and that their forces and resources were absorbed in the struggle to overcome their economic difficulties. But although this answer is correct, it does not go far below the surface. The economic crisis had such a powerful effect in Great Britain and in France because, after the First World War, neither had adjusted their economic activities and institutional structures to the new developments and the new constellation of forces which had arisen during the war, or whose emergence the First World War had accelerated. In order to understand the hesitation of the British and French governments to take up the challenge which the rise of Nazism represented we will have to go back beyond the thirties to the economic situation and the social problems with which Great Britain and France were faced ever since the end of the First World War.

Great Britain

The economic world crisis did not create Great Britain's economic vulnerability; it only made people aware of it. During the First World War the diminution of foreign assets as a result of the overseas procurement of war materials had sapped the strength of an economy in which imports exceeded exports. Furthermore, after the war, the British government adopted two courses of action which, though they seemed safe and appropriate in the relatively prosperous period of the middle 1920's, turned out in the subsequent depression to have the effect of severely aggravating the economic crisis and retarding recovery: one was the industrial policy which centered in the handling of the general strike in 1926; the other was the return to the gold standard in 1925.

The general strike of 1926 developed out of a crisis in the British coal industry, which had been lagging behind its German and American competitors even before the First World War and was now also hit severely by the increasing use of oil. During the war, coal mining had been controlled by the government; the return of the mines to private ownership led, unavoidably, to a crisis. The miners' trade union demanded guarantees that a general wage level would be maintained. The owners were not willing to give these guarantees because some of the mines were considerably less profitable than others and many were not profitable at all. Three fourths of all British coal was produced at a loss. With the help of government subsidies a showdown was postponed, and the French occupation of the Ruhr, which temporarily eliminated the competition of German coal, gave relief to the British coal industry. But in 1923, after the German passive resistance in the Ruhr had ended, a crisis could no longer be avoided. When wage contracts had to be renegotiated, the owners and the miners' trade union were at loggerheads about a reduction of wages, an extension of working hours, and so on. A commission established by the government under Sir Herbert Samuel, sided with the workers rather than the owners in its report and recommended a thorough reorganization of the coal-mining industry. But though in its general tenor the Samuel report was favorable to the workers, it did suggest that they accept wage reductions pending reorganization. On this issue negotiations broke down. The miners were backed by all the British trade unions and the consequence was a general strike lasting ten days, in May, 1926. Prime Minister Baldwin had probably been anxious to avoid this gigantic industrial conflict. But some members of his government, eager to put labor in its place, considered a showdown desirable.

The government was well prepared for a general strike. A state of emergency was declared; the country was divided into districts under civil commissioners supported by civil servants; and a force of volunteers trained for such an emergency was mobilized. The most urgently needed services were maintained and food supplies reached the cities. Thus the government gradually neutralized the major effects of the work stoppage, and some members of the cabinet, among them Neville Chamberlain and Winston Churchill, urged that the strike be declared illegal, its instigators imprisoned, and the funds of the trade unions confiscated. The union leaders feared that when the financial reserves of the unions were depleted, either the strike would peter out or the workers in their desperation would resort to force, perhaps causing civil war. Therefore, relying on a compromise formula which Sir Herbert Samuel had worked out and which envisaged wage reductions only after measures of reorganization in the coal industry had been effectively adopted, they called off the general strike. It was a defeat for the workers, all the more humiliating because the miners, infuriated by the suggestion of wage reductions in the compromise formula, continued to strike throughout the summer. But then their powers of

The general strike of 1926. A *street in London shows the impact of the lack of public transportation.*

resistance were exhausted. Increasingly discouraged, they returned to work. They had no national contract, only local and regional contracts; the overall result was that they had to work longer hours for lower wages.

In the prosperity of the second part of the 1920's English life took on something of the glamor of the prewar years, and the general strike soon seemed a thing of the past. But its consequences were far-reaching. The opportunity for a thorough overhauling of the coal industry had been missed; it continued to ail and the mining regions remained centers of low wages and unemployment. The bleakness, hardships, and dangers of life among British coal miners have found literary expression in George Orwell's realistic and moving *Road to Wigan Pier* (1937).

Moreover, the general strike increased distrust between the working class and the rest of the population. The failure of the government to force upon the employers concessions which would have prevented the stoppage raised suspicions about the intentions of the ruling group, and they were reinforced by the intransigent and vehement pronouncements of some of its members while the strike was in progress. After its collapse Baldwin took a conciliatory attitude, urging that industry reinstate the workers without reducing wages. But he lacked energy in the pursuit of this policy and was not able to restrain his antilabor colleagues. In 1927 the Conservative majority in Parliament struck a blow against the trade unions by passing a bill which limited the right to strike to trade disputes; sympathy strikes became illegal. Furthermore the unions were no longer allowed to collect money for political purposes. The intransigence of the government stiffened the resistance of the workers against all measures which might involve a temporary reduction in wages or a temporary increase in unemployment through the closing of unprofitable enterprises. To compete effectively on the world market British industry required modernization, but this was not feasible without the workers' cooperation, which was unobtainable after the general strike.

Equally fatal for Britain's economy was the return to the gold standard which Winston Churchill, Conservative chancellor of the exchequer, announced in his first budget speech, in April, 1925. At this time nobody questioned the principle that the basic unit in a currency must be defined as equivalent to a stated quantity of gold. The mistake of Churchill's measure was not so much that the pound was tied again to a fixed weight of gold, but that the ratio chosen, namely the prewar parity, was too high. Churchill was acting on the advice of the governor of the Bank of England, Montagu Norman, who hoped that by returning to the prewar standard London would regain the dominating position in the money market which it had lost to New York during the First World War. However, the result of this step was an increase in the price of British goods on the world market and hence a weakening of Britain's position in international trade. This effect was the more dangerous because of Great Britain's adverse balance of trade. Financiers would now view every further widening of the gap between exports and imports as seriously endangering British economic life. Furthermore, lulled into false security by the prosperity of the nineteenth century, British industrialists had been remiss in renewing and modernizing their

British unemployment during the Great Depression. *Workers wait for news of job possibilities at the labor exchange at Wigan Pier.*

equipment; now the decline in profits made investments for these purposes impossible. Keynes was one of the few who realized that the return to prewar parity represented a further "competitive handicap." In general, these difficulties were fully recognized only after it was too late, when the prosperity of the later 1920's had ended in depression.

From 1924 to 1929, a Conservative government was in power, headed by Stanley Baldwin. He had risen to a leading position in the Conservative party only after the war. He was very different from the great aristocrats, Salisbury and Balfour, who had been Conservative prime ministers earlier in the century and who might have had a sharper understanding of the change in the distribution of political and economic power brought about by the war. Baldwin was a rich industrialist, and his assumption of the Conservative leadership indicates the importance which businessmen had gained in the party. However, Baldwin was not the conventional businessman—unsentimental, purposeful and efficient; he was lazy and had no clear program nor plans. He acted only when action was unavoidable, and then his conduct was determined by intuition rather than cold reason. In his expressions of longing for a quiet and peaceful life, remote from the turbulence of industrial society, he reflected perfectly the nostalgic mood of the middle classes, which were frightened by the size of the problems of the postwar world and constructed an idealized picture of the stability and prosperity of Victorian and Edwardian England. Thus, Baldwin was con-

The leaders of the British national government: Baldwin (*left*) and Mac-Donald.

tent to see some of the splendor of prewar England return in the later 1920's without questioning how firm and deep-rooted the prosperity of this period was. Moreover, Baldwin's easygoing attitude permitted his cabinet a free hand; energetic ministers were able to make their own policy. The tenure of Austen Chamberlain as foreign secretary was a success. His half brother Neville Chamberlain (1869–1940), minister of health, enlarged the system of social security by gaining passage of an old-age-pension bill. Churchill, chancellor of the exchequer, tried to stimulate industry by lowering income taxes and increasing death duties. But the manner in which, against Baldwin's expressed desire, Churchill and Chamberlain insisted on making use of the defeat of the general strike to obtain passage of legislation curtailing the power of labor showed the tension which existed below the surface during these few fat years.

When signs of an incipient depression appeared, the popularity of the Conservatives was immediately reduced, and as a result of elections held in June, 1929, another Labor government under Ramsay MacDonald came into power. Actually, the Conservatives still remained the strongest in the popular vote; but the boundaries of the electoral districts were drawn in such a way that Labor received 280 seats in the House of Commons and the Conservatives only 261; the 59 Liberal members turned the scales. Because, as in 1924, the Labor government relied on Liberal support, radical measures involving socialization were precluded, but Labor had no real program for solving the unemployment problem within the existing economic system. The government's freedom of action was further limited because MacDonald had given the chancellorship of the exchequer to Philip Snowden (1864–1937), an old member of the Labor party and a convinced adherent of free trade and economic orthodoxy. Meanwhile, with the spread of the depression unemployment increased until in December, 1930, it reached 2.5 million, about 1.5 million more than when Labor had come into power eighteen months previously. With income from taxation declining and payments to the unemployed rising, the budget became unbalanced. A committee which investigated the economic situation took a very gloomy view. Its report recommended economies in government and particularly a reduction in unemployment benefits. This pessimistic evaluation of the British economy coincided with the financial crisis in Germany, in which British banking interests were deeply involved. A panic followed, and the consequence was that those who owned pounds transformed them into other currencies: a flight from the pound set in; a currency crisis was added to the budget crisis. Because Labor had no majority in the House of Commons, negotiations with the leaders of the other parties became necessary; urged on by British and American bankers, these leaders made their further support contingent upon a reduction in unemployment benefits. This was a bitter pill, hard to swallow for members of a Labor government. When the members of the government could come to no agreement on whether to accept such a cut, resignation seemed inevitable; a coalition of Conservatives and Liberals was expected to take over. But instead of submitting his resignation, MacDonald astonished his party with the announcement that he had agreed to remain as prime minister, heading a national government which would include the leaders of all three parties. Most members of the Labor party refused to follow him; only two Labor politicians of reputation—Snowden and J. H. Thomas (1874–1949) —accepted positions in the new government. A national Labor party which MacDonald founded remained insignificant. Nevertheless, MacDonald's "treason"—as his action was regarded by his former party associates—was a blow from which the Labor party began to recover only at the end of the 1930's.

MacDonald's behavior in this crisis is a puzzle. Many ascribe it to defects in his character, particularly to his vanity and social snobbery. When after the formation of the national government MacDonald was told that he would find himself popular in unfamiliar circles, he is reported to have exclaimed, "Yes, tomorrow every duchess in London will be wanting to kiss me." But it should not be forgotten that his socialist beliefs arose from a vague political idealism. He had never been a Marxist, and had never concerned himself with economic analysis. In economic questions he was accustomed to follow the views of experts, and he was probably honestly persuaded that he was placing country before party.

FROM RAMSAY MACDONALD TO NEVILLE CHAMBERLAIN

The new government began by introducing severe measures of economy: a reduction in the salaries of civil servants and a cut in unemployment benefits, which were now limited to twenty-six weeks a year and given only after a means test. Wage reductions in the armed services led to a mutiny in the British navy at Invergordon, Scotland, and although the mutiny ended quickly, it triggered a new financial panic. The government reacted with a step which a few months before would have been considered out of the question: taking the pound off the gold standard. As a result the share of British exports in world trade remained relatively stable. Elections held on October 27, 1931, to provide a popular mandate for the government resulted in its overwhelming triumph; Labor received 46 seats, while the parties in the national government now had 556, of which 472 were Conservative. Although the label of national government was retained and MacDonald ended his tenure only in 1935, actually the Conservative party ruled in Britain until the Second World War.

Stanley Baldwin remained leader of the Conservative party and as such was the most powerful figure in the national government, even while MacDonald was prime minister. After MacDonald's withdrawal, Baldwin took over the prime ministership. He resigned two years later, in 1937, at the height of his influence and fame. These had been immensely increased by his skillful handling of the crisis brought about by King Edward VIII's insistence on marrying a divorcee, a matter that ended with the abdication of the King. Baldwin's successor as prime minister was Neville Chamberlain, a son of Joseph Chamberlain. In his family Neville had been regarded as inferior in political talent to his older brother Austen; Neville therefore had been destined for a business career. When he finally entered political life, he became concerned primarily with affairs of economic policy. After he had been minister of health in the Conservative government of the 1920's, he served as chancellor of the exchequer in the national government; as such he was chiefly responsible for the manner in which the national government tried to lift Great Britain out of the depression.

The economic policy of the national government was strictly orthodox. The main aim was to keep the budget balanced and, as far as was compatible with this aim, to stimulate industry by keeping taxes low. Under the shield of a national government, the Conservatives were able to carry through a measure that symbolized the death of the liberal England of the nineteenth century: they introduced protective tariffs. For the party of Joseph Chamberlain, and especially for his son, this was a unique opportunity to establish closer economic ties between Great Britain and its empire by means of preferential tariffs. To do so seemed the more desirable because, in the course of the twentieth century, the cohesion of the British Empire had steadily weakened. The bond between Great Britain and the dominions (Australia, Canada, New Zealand, the Union of South Africa, and the Irish Free State) had become tenuous, sentimental rather than legal. A formula accepted by Great Britain and the dominions at a conference in 1926 stated that the dominions were "autonomous communities within the British Empire, equal in status, in no way subordinate one to another in any aspect of their domestic or external affairs, though united by a common allegiance to the Crown, and freely associated as members of the British Commonwealth of Nations." In 1931 the Statute of Westminster defined this new notion of a "British Commonwealth of Nations" in contractual constitutional terms. Because the dominions regarded themselves as fully independent in domestic and foreign policy, they gave a cool reception to the British government's suggestion to improve the economic situation by preferential tariffs among the members of the empire. The negotiations in Ottawa during the summer of 1932 were difficult, and the results fell far short of Joseph Chamberlain's dream of free trade within the empire; essentially, it was agreed that the dominions would retain their existing duties on industrial products from Great Britain but would raise duties on industrial products from other countries.

Thus the economic policy of the British government remained cautious. Neville Chamberlain himself called the course which he pursued a "pegging away." Indeed, a gradual but slow economic recovery, assisted by a general improvement in the world economic situation, took place in Britain. But the industrial apparatus was never thoroughly overhauled, and in the severely depressed areas, people continued to live close to starvation. Unemployment never went below a million.

The issues the British government had to handle in the 1930's— independence of the dominions, unrest in India, shocks like the abdication crisis, and, most importantly, the economic difficulties of Great Britain— were diverse and complex. Since a balanced budget was the cornerstone of British economic policy, the government shied away from new, additional burdens that could easily unbalance the budget and might halt the march toward recovery. There was great reluctance, therefore, to embark on a policy of rearmament or to pursue a foreign policy that demanded a strengthening of Britain's military forces. To justify this reluctance, most members of the ruling Conservative party tended to minimize the dangers which threatened from the dictators, particularly from the rise of Hitler, and to take an overly optimistic view of the possibility of coming to peaceful terms with them. Churchill, almost alone among the Conservatives, raised a warning voice against Hitler's aggressive tendencies. But at this time his political influence was at its lowest. While Labor's opposition to the dictators was clear and definite, the pacifist tradition in the party made the Laborites unwilling to accept the necessity of military rearmament; their recommendation of relying on collective security was rather unrealistic.

There was an influential group in the British ruling class, however, which regarded the rise of Nazism with a favorable eye. To this group belonged Dawson, the influential editor of the London *Times* who since the early 1920's had been fighting a pretended pro-French orientation of British foreign policy; and empire-minded politicians like Lord Lothian, who wanted to free England from bonds to the continent; and Germanophile aristocrats like the Astors who saw Hitler as a restorer of the good German society of imperial days. The benevolent attitude of this group toward Hitler arose from a variety of sources. The members of the group accepted the revisionist thesis that Germany had been unfairly treated in the Treaty of Versailles and that Germany would be a satisfied and peaceful power if these injustices were removed. They had a certain admiration for the disciplined and orderly German ways which Hitler was supposed to have reintroduced; moreover, because Germany was the strongest nation in Europe, they believed that Germany was entitled to hegemony on the European continent and would then keep that restless continent orderly and quiet. They were inclined to believe the Nazi propaganda thesis which held that, before the Nazi seizure of power, Germany had been in danger of becoming Communist; and they were anxious to have on the European continent a powerful force that would form a dam against the spread of Communism. The importance of this group—the Cliveden set, as it has been called after the country place of the Astors—lies in the fact that it influenced, almost prescribed, the policy Neville Chamberlain followed after he became prime minister in 1937.

Neville Chamberlain turned his particular attention to foreign policy because he was impatient with the disturbances of economic life by political crises. He possessed a naïve arrogance that considered all other peoples inferior to the British, so that there was not much difference whether they were democracies or dictatorships. He saw no reason, therefore, why Britain should not come to an understanding with the dictators, and, lacking in imagination, he had no inkling of the dynamic expansionism inherent in Nazism. Neville Chamberlain approached the negotiations with Hitler as a businessman approaches a deal with other businessmen, trusting that among men of property and common sense a bargain to reciprocal advantage should always be possible. If Great Britain showed Hitler goodwill by a number of concessions, he assumed, Hitler would be willing to cooperate with Great Britain in maintaining peace. With such misconceptions, Neville Chamberlain embarked hopefully on a policy of appeasement. The original view of the Chamberlain family that Neville lacked political talents proved fully justified.

France

Although the French reaction to Nazi expansion was as weak as that of Great Britain the weakness of French foreign policy had very different origins. In the 1930's a net drop in population and a shift in the French economic structure contributed to a sense of national decline, unrest, and tension.

Although France had acquired Alsace-Lorraine as a result of the war, its losses had been so heavy that in 1921, when the first postwar census was taken, its population—39,210,000 people—was smaller than in 1914. During the First World War, and for many years after, the French government never dared to make an official statement about the number of men killed in the war. More than a quarter of the 1,400,000 dead or missing would have been between twenty and twenty-five years of age by the end of the war; this necessarily resulted in a decline in birth, and in the middle of the 1930's the number of births became smaller than the number of deaths. The following year the population began to increase again, but only because of the immigration of foreigners into France. The lack of manpower and the need for using the available manpower in economic life led the French to reduce conscription to one year; France was less formidable than it might have appeared after the victory in the First World War.

While the demographic statistics presented a somber picture, the tension which accompanied the shift in the French economic structure might be regarded as a kind of growing pains. At the beginning of the decade, in

1931, 45.1 per cent of the labor force was employed in industry, in contrast to 36.1 per cent twenty-five years before; clearly there had been a shift from agriculture to industry. Particularly noticeable was the growth of heavy industry, such as mining, iron and steel production, and the manufacture of machinery; for instance, in 1931 the iron and steel industry employed over 100,000 more men than in 1906. Accompanying this development, during the interwar years, was a trend toward industrial concentration. The increasing importance of the workers led to demands for an active social policy, while the French bourgeoisie, frightened by the Russian Revolution, the loss of Russian investments, and the inflation of the early 1920's, tended to regard labor's claims as the beginning of a dangerous revolutionary development.

During the 1930's these tensions were sharpened by a deterioration of the economic and financial situation. Throughout the preceding decade French economic development had been favorable. Reconstruction of the destroyed areas, completed by 1926, had resulted in a modernization of industrial installations. Poincaré, who in 1926 had returned as prime minister, though without influence on foreign policy, had quickly ended the inflation by drastic economies which balanced the budget. The nation entered the depression period in an economically strong position, and because France was more self-sufficient than other highly industrialized powers it remained, at least at first, relatively immune to the effects of the depression. The French government made use of this economic strength in the critical political and financial negotiations about the *Anschluss* and the Hoover moratorium during the hectic summer of 1931. In the following years, however, the general weakness of the international markets had repercussions on France. Exports declined rapidly. If those of 1912 are taken as a base and represented by 100, they had risen to 125 in 1929, but declined to 59 in 1936. The decrease in exports resulted in a steadily widening deficit in the balance of trade, reaching 64 per cent in 1936, and was accompanied by a lower rate of industrial production, which in 1935 was back at the prewar level. Because of the demographic situation unemployment was a less serious problem in France than in Germany or Great Britain; nevertheless, in 1935 the number of unemployed had reached half a million. A degree of waste in government spending, of slight consequence in the days of prosperity, now resulted in budget deficits. Fear of inflation led to a flight from the franc. The parties of the left regarded these problems chiefly as the result of the selfish attempts of the rich to save their own fortunes; economic difficulties would end if the flight from the franc could be stopped. Thus it was difficult, if not impossible, for the government to get parliament to accept measures of economy and tax increases. Because only stopgap actions were taken the situation continued to deteriorate, and the politicians were accused of incompetence and corruption. By the end of 1934 both Poincaré and Briand were dead, and the political leaders of this period—Édouard Herriot, Édouard Daladier, André Tardieu—lacked the prestige and the authority enjoyed by their predecessors—the heroes of the Dreyfus Affair and the French victory.

A striking indication of the tension which was developing in French society was the Stavisky affair of 1934. In comparison to the Dreyfus Affair, which had involved great questions of principle, this was a murky business, a small financial swindle revealing some corruption. But the Stavisky scandal has its place in history because it showed that the old conflict between right and left—existing since the French Revolution, surfacing in the Dreyfus Affair but seemingly overcome by the national revival brought on by the First World War—had broken out again, in renewed strength. The eagerness with which the scandal was blown up into a crisis of republican and democratic institutions was an expression of the desperate feeling of the French middle classes that they were losing out against the forces of big business and labor. The explosion caused by the Stavisky affair must also be regarded as a sign of the malaise arising from the impression that the successive French governments had wasted the brilliant position which France had gained with its victory in the First World War.

Serge Alexander Stavisky was a financial swindler of tremendous charm and ingenuity. He had managed to make many acquaintances among politicians, and because he had served as an informer, his relations with the police were good. If not for these contacts the fraudulence of his financial dealings would have been discovered earlier. When finally his enterprise collapsed, puzzling things happened. The police surrounded his house, but reached Stavisky only after he had shot himself. One of the judges investigating the scandal was found dead on the railroad tracks. Rumors spread that Stavisky had not committed suicide but had been shot by the police because he knew too much and that the investigating judge had been eliminated for the same reason. A high official, a brother-in-law of Camille Chautemps, one of the most influential leaders of the Radical Socialists, was suspected of responsibility for silencing the scandal. The rightists boiled over in indignation about the corruption among the parliamentary leaders of the left. When the prime minister, Daladier, dismissed the president of the Paris police, who with little justification was regarded as an embodiment of energy and integrity, war veterans and other organizations of the right arranged demonstrations, marched to the parliament building, and tried to storm it. The police fired, but Marshal Lyautey, one of France's most distinguished military leaders, announced that on the following day he himself would march at the head of the demonstrators. Unable or unwilling to face this outburst, Daladier resigned, and a new government of national unity was formed.

The head of the new government was Gaston Doumergue (1863–1937), who had been president of the republic from 1924 to 1931, and it included all the surviving former prime ministers as well as military heroes such as

Marshal Pétain. It was a last—rather ephemeral—attempt to hold together the divergent forces of French society by an appeal to national solidarity, and to infuse new life into French foreign policy. Louis Barthou (1862–1934), the foreign minister under Doumergue, tried to make full use of the decline in Hitler's prestige in the summer of 1934 which had resulted from the purge of the S.A. and the murder by Nazis of the Austrian chancellor Engelbert Dollfuss. Barthou cold-shouldered British attempts to resume negotiations about armament limitations with Germany and visited the capitals of Czechoslovakia, Yugoslavia, and Rumania—which were allied in the so-called Little Entente—and of Russia in order to forge a firm alliance between these powers and France. An "eastern" Locarno, which would prevent German expansion toward the east, was to supplement the "western" Locarno, with its guarantee of the permanence of the Franco-German frontier. But on October 9, 1934, King Alexander of Yugoslavia, on a visit to strengthen his nation's ties with France, was assassinated in Marseilles by a Macedonian nationalist; another victim was Barthou himself, who was seated in the car next to the king. With Barthou's death French foreign policy returned quickly to a dependence on Great Britain.

The Doumergue government made an attempt to overcome the most evident weaknesses of French political life. It concentrated on plans to strengthen the executive at the expense of the legislative, chiefly by facilitating the dissolution of parliament and by depriving deputies of the right to augment suggested financial legislation. But Doumergue overplayed his hand; he tried to overcome resistance by appealing through radio addresses directly to the people. This authoritarian technique went against all republican tradition and the parliamentarians gained broad support as defenders of democracy against the penetration of "Fascist" ideas into French political life. The Doumergue government fell and the succeeding governments mainly marked time until the elections scheduled for the spring of 1936. In this period of weak transitional governments Hitler marched into the Rhineland. The French government in power was not strong enough to make a decision which would have demanded an abandonment of the dogma that France could not march alone, that she had to keep in line with England. So instead of ordering its troops into the Rhineland the French government acceded to the urging of England that the issue ought to be solved by negotiations.

The election campaign of 1936 was entirely a struggle between the right and the left. And the left fought the election as a Popular Front which reached from the middle-class Radical Socialists to the Communists. The Popular Front won an impressive victory. While the Communists agreed to support the government without actively participating in it, the Socialists, for the first time in French history, entered the government as a party, and their leader, Léon Blum (1872–1950), became prime minister. Blum was a strange figure to be leader of the Socialist party. He was neither a tough politician nor a Marxist. He was an intellectual, a man of wide culture, and a humanitarian. His sympathies with the underprivileged had brought him into the Socialist camp. His human qualities would shine brilliantly in his courageous stand against the Nazis during the German occupation of France. After the Second World War he would be prime minister again, and at the end of his life he was recognized to be as a major national figure. But when Blum became prime minister for the first time in June, 1936, his particular qualities were little suited to the situation. He was a pacifist, an internationalist, with little interest in the details of foreign policy. His main concern was social reform; he expected to improve the situation of the poorer classes by modernizing French life. A wave of strikes underlining the urgent need for social reform accompanied the formation of the Popular Front government. These strikes were of a new type—the sit-down: the workers refused to work but remained in the factories, making the use of strikebreakers impossible. Removal of the strikers would have required force, which the Popular Front government did not want to employ against its own supporters. Hence the industrialists were forced to make a number of concessions, granting the workers rights which their counterparts in most other European industrial countries already possessed—compulsory collective bargaining, the forty-hour week, paid holidays—and also wage increases of from 12 to 15 per cent. These arrangements were negotiated under government auspices and were supplemented by legislative measures intended to restrict the influence of high finance and big business on French policy. The Bank of France was brought under government control; its credit policy could no longer obstruct the financial measures of the government. The armament industry was nationalized, and the government inaugurated a series of public works to fight unemployment. Such reforms were long overdue. Thus, if France was to develop a strong air force, the nationalization of the armament industry was necessary, since it would make possible concentration on a few types of mass-produced airplanes.

Léon Blum, French prime minister, addressing a meeting.

Even so, because time was needed to harvest the advantages of the change, airplane production in France remained dangerously weak for some years.

Meanwhile, the direct consequences of the measures taken by the Blum government were a sharpening of internal conflicts and then also a weakening of the coherence of the Popular Front. Industrialists and bankers, deeply resentful of the concessions to which they had been forced, continued the flight from the franc and sharply attacked the government policy of spending freely without attempting to balance the budget. The government had promised to maintain the value of the franc, but was soon forced to devaluate. This measure spurred fear of inflation among the middle classes, and the Radical Socialists, their representatives in the government, became doubtful about continued cooperation with the parties on the left. First Blum had to declare a "breathing spell" in social reforms, in order to restore confidence among the bourgeois partners in his coalition; then he was replaced as prime minister by a Radical Socialist, although the Socialists still remained members of the government. Then the Socialists left the government, although they continued to support it in parliament. But in 1938 Daladier, the Radical Socialist prime minister, turned to the right, and the Communists and Socialists resumed their old roles as members of the opposition.

One reason for the formation of the Popular Front, and the main motive underlying the Communist participation in it, had been to establish a firm stand against the advance of Nazism and Fascism. Unavoidably, many of those who resisted the social program of the Popular Front also opposed its ideas on foreign policy; they complained that both the domestic reforms and the international action against Fascism served the aims of international Communism rather than the national interests of France. "Better Hitler than Blum" was a slogan which spread among the rightists. Only a few organizations, although rather noisy ones, favored a Fascist regime in France, but many adherents of the right believed that because of its terrible losses in the First World War their nation should avoid involvement in another conflict at almost any cost; they saw no reason why France should obstruct Germany's ambitions in the east. France had built along the German frontier a strong defense line, called the Maginot Line after the politician responsible for its construction. Its conception shows clearly the dilemma which faced French policy. In case of a war against Germany the French troops under arms would not be strong enough to embark immediately on offensive action. This would become possible only after full mobilization and would take time: the Maginot Line was intended to provide the shield behind which the mobilization would take place. But on the other hand the fortified region was limited to the area opposite the German border, from Switzerland to Luxembourg; the more northern part of the frontier was hardly fortified. This was meant to show that the French were able and willing to act energetically in case of a crisis, that they were able to take the offensive, to advance into Germany through Belgium. It was to indicate that they were not willing to give Germany a free hand in Eastern Europe. But this concession to the political concepts of the past began to become doubtful in the face of the military realties of the present.

Officially no French government ever admitted that it was willing to write off the alliances with the eastern European states. But the governments of the right which succeeded the Popular Front were inclined to minimize French commitments rather than to reinforce them. French foreign policy remained strong in words but timid in deeds. Its only serious concern was to avoid separation from Great Britain.

THE DEMOCRACIES IN RETREAT

The militarization of the Rhineland upset the assumptions on which European statesmen had based their foreign policy. Germany was no longer open to French attack, and the great industrial area of the Ruhr was no longer exposed to the fire of French guns. The weakening of the French position had immediate repercussions in eastern and southeastern Europe. Except for Czechoslovakia, which continued to rely on the support of Great Britain and France, the states of this region began to drift into the German orbit; this development was assisted by the German economic policy under the clever direction of Hjalmar Schacht. The eastern European countries, suffering acutely from the slump in agricultural prices, welcomed the opportunity offered by Germany to conclude barter agreements by which they could exchange agricultural products for German manufactured goods. Moreover, the German success in the Rhineland and the Italian triumph in Ethiopia had increased the prestige and appeal of the totalitarian systems. Mussolini, who in the 1920's had declared that Fascism was not an export article, was now proudly proclaiming that the democracies were obsolete and decaying and that Fascism represented the wave of the future. The various dictatorial regimes in Poland, Yugoslavia, Hungary, Rumania, and Bulgaria, now began to imitate Fascist or National Socialist forms and methods, and claimed that their systems of government embodied a new political spirit, appropriate to the twentieth century.

Mussolini's praise of Fascism as a young international force which would triumph over the dying world of the democracies indicated that he had moved into the German camp. Close cooperation between Italy and Nazi Germany was established by October, 1936, after the trip to Germany of Count Galeazzo Ciano (1903–1944)—Mussolini's foreign minister and son-in-law. The so-called Rome-Berlin Axis was then confirmed by an exchange of visits, with Mussolini going to Berlin in September, 1937, and Hitler to Rome in May, 1938. The meetings of the two dictators were accompanied by immense military reviews, which were recorded on film so that the world would be impressed with the might of the Fascist powers. The western democracies were confronted by the alternatives of opposition by force and negotiations ending in concessions. Appeasement began.

The Spanish Civil War

The event in which the Axis powers first tested the democracies' will to resist was the Spanish Civil War. The contest in Spain was bitter, vehement, and long because it represented the clash of forces deeply rooted in Spanish social and intellectual life. Essentially a struggle of modern industrial and democratic forces against the continued existence of agrarian feudalism, it became enmeshed with the traditional movements for regional independence against Castilian centralism and with the age-old dispute about the position of the Church in Spanish social life.

In 1931 the inability of the Spanish army to put down a Moroccan uprising compromised the monarchy and the ruling group; revolt followed, and a republic was established in which full power was held by a democratically elected parliament. From the beginning the republican regime led a precarious existence. The new constitution separated church and state, but attempts to remove the Church from all activities which were not strictly religious aroused the resistance of the Catholic hierarchy and of many Catholics among the population. The workers, by tradition radical and anarchist, were dissatisfied by the failure of the republican government to

Nationalist troops in Madrid, 1936.

put through anticapitalist measures. Riots, strikes, burnings of churches occurred in various parts of the country; violence led to a resurgence of rightist parties, and the counterrevolutionaries organized themselves into a movement on the Fascist pattern—the Falange. To fight reaction, all the parties from the center to the extreme left joined together in a Popular Front, which triumphed in the elections of February, 1936, more than two months before the victory of the French Popular Front.

The victors regarded their success as a mandate to purge the administration of reactionaries and to go ahead with a program of modernization and social reform. The Popular Front government took steps to divide up the great estates; it forced industrialists to take back workers who had been dismissed because of participation in strikes; and it closed Catholic schools. But the far-reaching nature of these measures spurred the rightist opposition to action. The military had been considering a *coup d'état* for a long time; now the Spanish antirepublicans received encouragement from Mussolini, who promised money and weapons. A putsch was planned for the middle of July, 1936. On July 12, 1936, the murder of the monarchist leader José Calvo Sotelo by a republican who was captain of the police played right into the hands of the conspirators. This crime seemed to show that the government was unable to guarantee order and security, and gave some justification for the rebellion, which erupted on July 17. Although the revolt was popular among upper- and middle-class groups and had the active support of organizations like the Falange, it began primarily as an officers' conspiracy. The officers ordered their troops to occupy government buildings and took over the administration of various towns, or entrusted it to rightist political leaders.

The course of the Spanish Civil War was long and confused. Originally the military coup was not a success. The generals seized power in extended areas of northern and northwestern Spain and in North Africa, where the best-trained units of the army were stationed under General Francisco Franco (1892–1975). But the entire southwest (except for a few small isolated areas), the center of Spain, and the Basque coast in the north, remained loyal to the republic. By the end of July the ground forces of the two opposing camps were numerically roughly equal. To strengthen their forces, the republican leaders, after some hesitation, distributed weapons to the workers. The resulting dependence on the masses led to a government shift toward the left, with the socialists, Communists, and anarchists becoming increasingly influential.

After the incomplete success of the military putsch both sides appealed for foreign aid: the republicans to France and Russia, the military to Italy and Germany. The Fascist powers were quick to respond. Mussolini sent bombing planes; Hitler authorized the immediate dispatch of some twenty transport planes. The acquisition of these airplanes was crucial; the Spanish

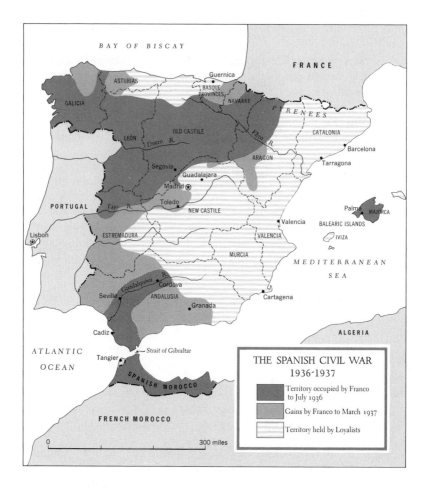

THE SPANISH CIVIL WAR
1936-1937

Territory occupied by Franco
to July 1936

Gains by Franco to March 1937

Territory held by Loyalists

navy had remained loyal to the republican government, and air transport was the only means for bringing the well-disciplined Moroccan troops from Africa into Spain. Hitler said correctly, some years later: "Franco ought to erect a monument to the glory of the German transport aircraft. The Spanish Revolution of Franco has to thank this aircraft for its victory." By means of the Moroccan troops led by Franco, the Spanish Fascists succeeded in extending their rule over the south of Spain and in establishing a bridge to the territory which they controlled in the north. By the end of September the republicans no longer had a common frontier with Portugal. But even though the Fascists advanced in four columns into the suburbs of Madrid and had a "fifth column" of adherents within the city, their attempt to take the capital failed as the Spanish republicans rose heroically to its defense in the winter 1936–1937. The Fascists halted outside Madrid, and from there extended their rule toward the west. Only three regions remained under republican control. One of these stretched from Madrid to southeastern Spain. It was connected by a small coastal strip with the second center of republican power, Catalonia. Finally, the Basque country in the north, along the Atlantic coast, remained republican. Isolated as they were, these centers of republican strength were no match for the Fascists, who conquered one after the other. The anti-Fascist regime in the Basque area fell in the summer of 1937. Then the war dragged on. Barcelona, the chief city of Catalonia, was taken in January, 1939; and thousands of freezing and starving Spanish republicans along with the remaining republican troops—altogether almost 400,000 people —crossed the frontiers to France, where on open land, fenced in by wires, lacking shelter and food, they dragged on their lives. Two months later, in March, 1939, Madrid surrendered. By then Spain was no longer a center of international politics.

The Spanish Civil War and European Diplomacy

The war was not just an internal Spanish affair. It was a struggle in which directly or indirectly the whole of Europe was involved. If the dispatch of German and Italian planes had been crucial in revitalizing the military revolt after its initial setback, the arrival of Russian tanks and aircraft in the fall of 1936 decisively helped the republican defense of Madrid against the renewed attack of the Fascists; moreover, Russian advisers gave coherence to the somewhat disorganized military effort of the republicans. Germany and Italy responded by boosting the Spanish Fascist regime with diplomatic recognition. But they also gave concrete assistance. The Germans sent more aircraft, and pilots as well—bomber squadrons of the so-called Condor Legion. The most famous—or infamous—exploit of the German fliers was the attack on Guernica during Franco's campaign against the Basque country (April, 1937). First they bombed the small rural town, then they machine-gunned the streets, killing and wounding about 2,500 of the 7,000 inhabitants. Later, the Germans would admit that this assault had been an experiment to test the effects of terror bombing.

Mussolini concluded a secret treaty with Franco in November, 1936 which secured Italy against the possibility of French-Spanish cooperation, promised Spanish benevolent neutrality in case of a war, and if necessary, the establishment of Italian bases on Majorca and Spanish territory. Mussolini now ordered the transportation of volunteer blackshirt brigades, under the command of Italian officers, to Spain; by February, 1937, 48,000 Italians were fighting there. But they were badly trained and disciplined; driven into an offensive by Mussolini's expectation that Italian help would quickly end the war in Franco's favor, they received a severe setback at Guadalajara, near Madrid (March, 1937). This loss of prestige impelled Mussolini to continue sending troops, and now, most important, airplanes to Spain.

Undoubtedly the German and the Italian assistance to the Fascists was more effective than the Russian aid to the republicans, especially since the long route through the Mediterranean from the Black Sea was threatened by German and Italian submarines and warships. A balance could have been struck if the republicans had received airplanes, tanks, and supplies from the north, from France. But though Léon Blum, the French prime minister, was willing to send assistance, he was opposed by the British leaders and the nonsocialist members of his own government, who feared international complications, particularly the strengthening of Communism. Blum yielded to these pressures despite the indignation of the Communists and of many members of his own Socialist party.

Disagreement concerning the Spanish Civil War was an important factor in breaking up the French Popular Front. Hoping to localize the conflict, France and Great Britain suggested to the other powers a policy of nonintervention. The negotiations to implement this policy were long and drawn-out, and even after Russia, Germany, and Italy had been won over and a committee entrusted with the supervision of nonintervention had been established, Germany and Italy raised endless difficulties; they finally withdrew their troops only when they felt sure that doing so would not endanger the victory of Fascism in Spain.

For Hitler and Mussolini the Spanish Civil War was heartening proof of the weakness of their adversaries; they learned that although Russia, France, and Great Britain might be opposed to any disturbance of the *status quo*, they did not agree about how to control Fascist aggression. Evidently the main concern of the western powers was to avoid war.

But the Spanish Civil War did more than reveal the immense strength

Francisco Franco enjoys dinner at the front during the Spanish Civil War.

which the Fascist powers had gained. With the failure of the democracies, the opposition to Fascism lost its drive. When the Spanish Civil War began it had seemed evident that the democratic forces had right on their side and that democracy and Fascism met in Spain in a situation of equality—not prejudiced in favor of Fascism. It had appeared that if Fascism received a check in Spain the myth of its inevitable progress would be destroyed. After this one great effort the Fascist nightmare under which Europe lived might disappear.

> Tomorrow for the young the poets exploding like bombs,
> The walks by the lake, the weeks of perfect communion;
> Tomorrow the bicycle races
> Through the suburbs on summer evenings. But today the struggle.[1]

Men from all over the globe volunteered to fight for the Spanish republic. One of the most efficient of the republican military units was the International Brigade, in which Communists, socialists, and liberals served. Writers of many nationalities—George Orwell, who was British; Ernest Hemingway, an American; André Malraux, of France; Arthur Koestler, a Hungarian—came to Spain, fought with the republicans, and advocated their cause in their writings. Their hour of triumph was the heroic defense of Madrid. But they also experienced the dissension which broke out with the approach of defeat—particularly a bitter struggle between Communists and anarchists in which many sincere fighters against Fascism were brutally killed.

In the years of appeasement that followed, those who had served in defense of the Spanish republic had a hard time. The governments of the western democracies looked with disfavor on these freedom fighters— "premature anti-Fascists," they were later termed by American officials. In Russia, after Stalin had turned away from the idea of a Communist-democratic alliance against Fascism, many of the participants in the Spanish Civil War were treated as criminals. However, some of the fighters for the Spanish republic survived, and were able to begin new political careers after the Second World War. Among the Communists, Ernö Gerö became one of the political leaders of Hungary. Palmiro Togliatti and Luigi Longo gained prominence in the Communist party in Italy. Of the non-Communists Pietro Nenni and Randolfo Pacciardi became ministers in Italy; André Malraux, in France. But in the years immediately following the Spanish Civil War the spirit of the fight against Fascism in Spain seemed to remain alive only in works of art; the painting "Guernica" (1937) by Pablo Picasso and Ernest Hemingway's novel *For Whom the Bell Tolls* (1940) expressed the tragic hopelessness of man's struggle against inhuman forces.

[1] W. H. Auden, "Spain 1937," quoted by Hugh Thomas, *The Spanish Civil War* (New York, 1961), p. 221.

Anschluss *and the Invasion of Czechoslovakia*

The weakness which the western democracies had shown—first in the Rhineland crisis and then in the Spanish Civil War—gave Hitler the green light to proceed with his aggressive and expansionist foreign policy. In a meeting with his chief military and civilian advisers in November, 1937, he announced that Germany needed more living space, which could be secured only through war; such a war ought to take place in the early 1940's because German rearmament would then reach its peak. Preconditions for a successful war were the elimination of Czechoslovakia and the achievement of the *Anschluss*. Hitler also intimated that the situation which had developed in the Mediterranean as a result of the Spanish Civil War might afford an opportunity for quick action. Although subsequently he adjusted his tactics to changing circumstances, and the actual sequence of events was different from the one envisaged at this meeting, this speech did reveal his fundamental aims. When his chief military advisers expressed some reservations and doubts, they paid for their hesitation with loss of their positions. One of them, Werner von Fritsch, was charged with homosexuality; by the time the groundlessness of this accusation was proved it was too late to reinstate him. The other, Werner von Blomberg, the minister of war, was

Anschluss: Hitler announces the incorporation of Austria into greater Germany at a mass meeting in the center of Vienna.

declared to have violated the officers' code of honor by marrying a former prostitute, even though Hitler had approved of the marriage and attended the wedding. The dismissal of these two generals demonstrated that the army had lost its independence. At the same time the foreign minister, Konstantin von Neurath (1873–1956), a professional diplomat who had been a compliant servant of the Nazis but was somewhat too cautious in Hitler's views, was replaced by a Nazi, Joachim von Ribbentrop (1893–1946). All obstacles to action had been removed.

Hitler's first victim was Austria. Stepped-up Nazi propaganda in Austria for *Anschluss* with Germany had led to increased measures of suppression by the Austrian government. In an interview with Chancellor Schuschnigg on February 4, 1938, Hitler demanded that these measures be lifted and that some of the Austrian Nazis be included in the government. Intimidated by Hitler's vehemence and by the threat of German troop movements toward the Austrian border, Schuschnigg gave in. But he soon realized that once the Nazis had entered the government they would take complete control. On March 9, in desperation, he announced a plebiscite in which the people were asked to vote on whether they wanted to keep Austrian independence. On March 11, Hitler sent an ultimatum demanding postponement of the plebiscite, and on March 12, dispatched his troops into Austria under the pretext that Schuschnigg's government was unable to maintain order. On March 14, 1938, Vienna, where Hitler in his youth had lived in utter misery, saw him return in triumph: the *Anschluss* creating a greater Germany had been achieved. The western powers did nothing except protest feebly on paper; Mussolini, who in 1934, when the first Nazi putsch took place in Austria, had moved his troops to the Brenner frontier, now declared that he was uninterested in the fate of Austria; he had gone too far to deviate from his pro-German course. Overjoyed, Hitler told Mussolini that he would never forget what he had done for him.

The next victim was Czechoslovakia. Hitler wanted the incorporation into Germany of the Sudeten region, a broad stretch of northern Czechoslovakia populated chiefly by Germans. Because this area was south of the mountains separating Germany from Czechoslovakia and included the Czechoslovakian line of fortifications, its loss would mean the end of Czechoslovakia as an independent factor in European power politics. Here again, the western powers put up only weak resistance against Hitler's expansionist policy. The crisis first erupted in the spring of 1938, and several times in the months that followed Europe seemed to be on the brink of war. Although the British government of Neville Chamberlain was little concerned about the fate of the Sudeten Germans and of Czechoslovakia—the affair being, in Chamberlain's words, "a quarrel in a faraway country between people of whom we know nothing"—the British were aware that they could not remain on the sidelines of a European conflict developing from Hitler's demands on Czechoslovakia. This danger was great, for since 1924 France had been tied to Czechoslovakia through a clear and definite defensive alliance, and Soviet Russia was obligated to support France and Czechoslovakia if they had to defend themselves against German aggression. Hence, the British government's main concern was to prevent a clash by force which would make fulfillment of the alliance commitments by France and Russia an automatic consequence. The British tried to persuade Hitler to be content with autonomy for the Sudeten Germans within the Czechoslovak state, and pressed Czechoslovakia to agree to this concession. But Hitler spurred the Nazis in the Sudeten area to demonstrations which led to clashes with the police; he then declared that Czechoslovakian brutality made further existence of the Sudeten Germans under Czechoslovak rule impossible and demanded complete separation of this region from Czechoslovakia, threatening to back his demand by military action.

At this critical moment Chamberlain decided to fly to Berchtesgaden, where he met Hitler on September 15, 1938. There Chamberlain gave Hitler what he wanted, the Sudeten area, in return for a promise that Germany would refrain from immediate military action. The British and French governments forced the Czechs to accept this solution by threatening to withdraw all support if they refused. But Hitler was still not satisfied; in a second meeting between Hitler and Chamberlain, in Bad Godesberg on September 22, Hitler declared that the procedure envisaged at Berchtesgaden for the German take-over was too slow. The transfer would have to be completed by October 1—if necessary, by military invasion. The deadlock seemed complete, and Chamberlain returned to London with little hope that peace could be maintained. But Mussolini, anxious to avoid war and eager to increase his prestige by appearing as Europe's arbiter, intervened, persuading Hitler to convene a conference at Munich on September 29.

The Munich Conference was a shocking demonstration of the extent to which the methods of international politics had deviated from those envisioned for the new world order at the end of the First World War. Then, the expectation had been that the great and the small nations would have an equal voice. But at Munich, the leaders of the four great European powers—Hitler, Mussolini, Daladier, and Chamberlain—conferred alone; only after all decisions had been made were the representatives of Czechoslovakia, the state most concerned, informed of the agreement by a yawning Chamberlain and a nervous Daladier. Hitler had made one concession; the deadline for the complete occupation of the Sudeten area was postponed to October 10. One may wonder what would have happened if the Czechoslovaks had rejected the Munich agreement and fought, whether then public opinion in Britain and France might have forced these powers to come to the rescue. But the Czechoslovaks and their president, Beneš exhausted from endless negotiations and broken promises, felt that they

Neville Chamberlain and Hitler after the Munich Conference, 1938.

could not risk such a gamble. They gave in; Benes abdicated, leaving the government of the country to men he believed might get along better with the triumphant Nazis.

In an eloquent attack on British foreign policy in the House of Commons, Winston Churchill characterized the Munich Conference as "a disaster of the first magnitude." But his was a lonely voice. Returning from Munich, Chamberlain was received like a victorious conquerer. To the enthusiastic crowds he said, "This is the second time in our history that there has come back from Germany to Downing Street, peace with honour. I believe it is peace for our time." Perhaps no remark shows more clearly the erroneous assumptions of Chamberlain's appeasement policy. Later he tried to defend the Munich agreement by explaining that it gave Great Britain and France time to rearm. But this justification was palpably false. In the year between Munich and the outbreak of the Second World War the gap in armed strength between Germany and the western powers did not narrow; it widened. The elimination of Czechoslovakia freed numerous German forces for service elsewhere, and the substantial military equipment installed in the fortifications of the Sudeten area now fell into German hands. Chamberlain did not put enough energy into the drive for British rearmament to compensate for this increase in German military strength. He regarded Hitler as a great German patriot who wanted only to complete Bismarck's work by uniting all Germans in one national state and would then rule happily and peacefully ever after. Defending the Munich settlement in the House of Commons, Chamberlain said, "There is sincerity and goodwill on both sides."

During the winter of 1938–1939 European politicians were in a euphoric mood. The French signed a pact which provided for consultation in all questions of dispute with Germany and indicated that the Germans could have a free hand in southeastern Europe. The British also expressed their willingness to regard southeastern Europe as a German sphere of interest. The harmony between the western democracies and the Axis powers was somewhat disturbed by Mussolini, who suddenly made loud claims for Nice, Savoy, and Tunisia, but the British recognized the Italian conquest of Ethiopia and hoped to act as mediators between the French and the Italians.

None of the men in control in France and Great Britain was very much bothered by events in Germany showing that Nazi brutality had not abated; in one night all the synagogues were burned and destroyed; the Jews were eliminated from German economic life and deprived of their property. At the beginning of 1939 the British government was convinced that political appeasement could now be strengthened by close economic cooperation between Germany and Great Britain. Chamberlain stated on March 10 that Europe was settling down to a period of tranquillity. Six months later Great Britain and France were at war with Germany.

The End of Appeasement

The event which changed British policy from appeasement to resistance was the incorporation of what had been left of Czechoslovakia into Greater Germany. The Nazis stimulated agitation for independence of the Slovakian region of the Czechoslovak state, and when the Czechoslovakian government took measures to suppress this movement Hitler ordered Emil Hácha (1872–1945), Benes̆' successor as president of the republic, to Berlin and forced him to recognize a German protectorate over Czechoslovakia. The next morning, on March 16, 1939, German troops poured over the borders and Hitler entered Prague.

Suddenly British public opinion turned against Germany. This abrupt explosion of British anger—after so many retreats—is difficult to understand. It has been said that British indignation was aroused because with this action Hitler demonstrated that he was not content with uniting Germans under his rule, and showed that his previous appeals for national self-determination had been hollow pretense disguising a brutal policy of expansion. It is true that the occupation of Czechoslovakia showed up the misconception of those who had presented Hitler as a great German patriot. It is more likely, however, that many people in Great Britain were simply tired of being faced by one crisis after the other, of being bullied. And it appeared unlikely that a Hitler dominating Europe would leave the British empire undisturbed.

Chamberlain now reversed his policy, but because of the pressure of public opinion rather than because he had changed his mind. Indeed, he tried until the last moment to renew contacts with Hitler. Publicly, however, he gave the impression of having abandoned appeasement, and

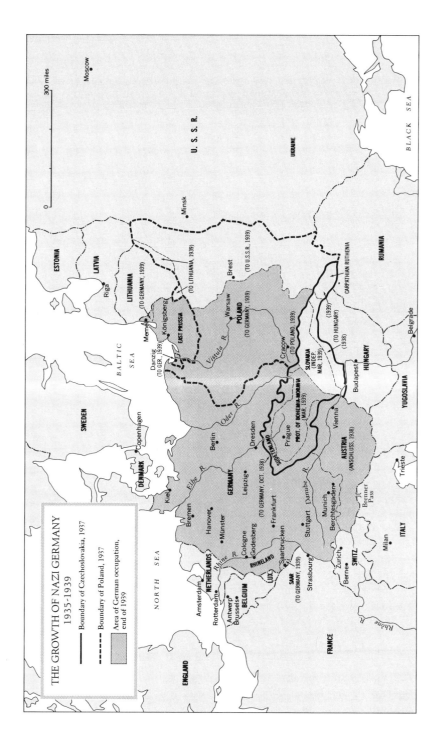

THE GROWTH OF NAZI GERMANY
1935-1939

—— Boundary of Czechoslovakia, 1937

- - - Boundary of Poland, 1937

Area of German occupation, end of 1939

300 miles

Moscow

U. S. S. R.

UKRAINE

BLACK SEA

Minsk

ESTONIA

LATVIA

Riga

LITHUANIA

(TO GERMANY, 1939)

(TO LITHUANIA, 1939)

Brest

(TO U.S.S.R, 1939)

RUMANIA

Memel

Königsberg

EAST PRUSSIA

Danzig

(TO GER., 1939)

Warsaw

POLAND

(TO GERMANY, 1939)

Vistula R.

Cracow

(TO POLAND, 1939)

SLOVAKIA

(INDEP.

MAR. 1939)

CARPATHIAN RUTHENIA

(1939)

(TO HUNGARY)

(1938)

Belgrade

BALTIC SEA

Oder R.

PROT. OF BOHEMIA-MORAVIA

(MAR. 1939)

Prague

Budapest

HUNGARY

YUGOSLAVIA

SWEDEN

Copenhagen

DENMARK

Kiel

Berlin

Dresden

SUDETENLAND

(TO GERMANY, OCT. 1938)

Vienna

AUSTRIA

(ANSCHLUSS, 1938)

Trieste

Elbe R.

Bremen

Hanover

Leipzig

Munster

Frankfurt

GERMANY

Cologne

Godesberg

Danube R.

Stuttgart

Munich

Berchtesgaden

Bremner

Pass

Milan

ITALY

NORTH SEA

Amsterdam

NETHERLANDS

Rotterdam

Antwerp

Brussels

BELGIUM

LUX.

Rhine R.

RHINELAND

Saarbrucken

SAR

(TO GERMANY, 1935)

Strasbourg

Zurich

Berne

SWITZ.

Rhône R.

FRANCE

ENGLAND

dramatized this shift with a spectacular diplomatic move. His government gave guarantees to the two states which were now most directly in the way of further German expansion and therefore most immediately threatened—Poland and Rumania. Many Frenchmen might have preferred to evade their obligations to Poland, behaving as they had toward Czechoslovakia, but the British support of Poland meant that French retreat was impossible. When Hitler marched his troops into Poland, on the pretext that the Poles had not accepted his demands for restoration to the Reich of Danzig and the Polish Corridor, Great Britain and then France declared war on Germany, on September 3, 1939.

Hitler does not seem to have expected that his action against Poland would result in war with Great Britain and France. Lacking all sense of moral values he had no appreciation of the revulsion which his march into Prague had aroused, nor did he understand why powers which had refused to fight for strategically important and relatively accessible Czechoslovakia would undertake war for distant and indefensible Poland. On the other hand, it appears that in his quarrel with Poland, Hitler was not willing to agree to another peaceful settlement. Hitler was convinced that to restore German prestige, damaged by the defeat in the First World War, a successful military campaign was needed. Instead of being exhilarated by the results of the Munich Conference, he had been depressed. He had felt that in yielding to Mussolini's demands for a conference he had let slip the opportunity for a victorious war. Nevertheless, although he did not fear war if his actions against Poland involved him in a conflict with Great Britain and France, he would have preferred these powers to remain neutral, so that the campaign against Poland could be kept localized. He had a trump card which in his opinion would secure British and French neutrality. On August 23, 1939, a week before the attack on Poland, Germany had signed a nonaggression pact with Soviet Russia.

The surprise was great because in all the calculations of the policy makers the insuperability of the contrast between Nazi Germany and Communist Russia had been taken for granted. When after the German march into Prague, Great Britain gave guarantees to Poland and Rumania, the British and French governments felt sure that they would also be able to gain Soviet Russia's help in stemming further German expansion. British and French missions were sent to Moscow, but after a period of fruitless negotiations they heard the news that instead of tying Russia to the western powers, Stalin had made a pact with Nazi Germany.

SOVIET RUSSIA DURING THE INTERWAR YEARS

It is a strange reversal of fortunes that in the weeks preceding the outbreak of the Second World War, Soviet Russia's friendship and assistance were eagerly sought by the great European powers. History seemed to have turned full circle. Twenty years before, the statesmen arranging in Paris the future of Europe and of the world had been anxious to move Russia out of Europe. And indeed, during most of the interwar years Russia had remained on the periphery of international events. In the 1930's, with Hitler gaining increasing power, Russia gradually took a more active role in European affairs; but still in 1938 it had been allowed no voice in the arrangements for settling the Czech crisis.

If now in 1939 Russia's support was eagerly sought by both of the antagonistic groups, this was proof of the breakdown of the principles on which the settlements reached at the Paris Peace Conference had been based: the notion that the exercise of democracy, and obedience to international law were requisites for acceptance as an equal partner in international life. With the return to power politics implied in the breakdown of the international system established at Versailles, it became increasingly obvious that, in the eventuality of war, Russia's wealth in natural resources, foodstuffs, and minerals, and Russia's military strength would be important.

During the interwar years European intellectual and scholarly circles had never lacked an interest in the developments in Russia, and the chances of success or failure of the Soviet experiment had been the object of vehement, rather partisan, discussion. But the answer to the puzzling question of the extent to which industrialization had created a new modern society in Russia was made immensely more complex and difficult by the violent methods with which the Bolsheviks had established themselves and had carried through the policy of collectivization and industrialization. How strong was Soviet Russia, and to what degree was it possible to rely on it? These uncertainties, which had contributed to make Russia an outsider for so long during the interwar years, had deepened by events in Russia in the second part of the thirties.

Stalinism and the Purge Trials

The publication in June, 1936 of the draft of a constitution had raised the hopes that Russia was now entering a period of liberalization, but these hopes were soon destroyed by Stalin's purges, which made him a dreaded absolute ruler, with the secret police his most important and most feared instrument of government. The number of people who became victims of these purges—who were imprisoned, exiled, or executed —runs into the millions. The most prominent among them were condemned in "show trials," the first of which took place in August, 1936, two months after the publication of the new constitution. Best known among the sixteen defendants in this trial were Grigori Zinoviev and Lev B. Kamenev, both former members of the Politburo. The second great trial was staged in 1937. Among the seventeen defendants was Karl Radek,

Soviet Russia's leading political writer. Between the second and the third trials there occurred a secret purge of the Russian general staff; its victims included Mikhail Tukhachevski, a hero of the civil war and the Russo-Polish War, and a number of generals. The third and last trial, in March, 1938, was the most sensational; among its twenty-one defendants were Nikolai Bukharin, who had edited the newspaper *Izvestia* ("News") and was recognized as a leading Bolshevik theoretician; Aleksei Rykov, who had been chairman of the Council of People's Commissars; H. G. Yagoda, a former head of the secret police; N. M. Krestinski, a deputy commissar for foreign affairs; and a number of high diplomats. At all these trials the defendants made "confessions," perhaps obtained through pressure. Most of the defendants were condemned to death and executed, and even those, like Radek, who received only prison sentences never reappeared in public life.

In the light of revelations made after the death of Stalin, the purges have usually been ascribed to his abnormal psychology. Undoubtedly Stalin's pathological distrust and suspicion did play a role in the organization of these trials and the cruelty of the punishments meted out to the defendants. Before 1936, and then again after Stalin's death, Bolshevik leaders who recommended a line of policy which the majority rejected were demoted or removed from power; but they were not killed. The use of the death penalty for political opposition was limited to the time of Stalin's reign. Although the manner of procedure against the defendants in the purge trials was determined by Stalin's abnormal mentality, he did have rational cause to fear the influence of these men.

Some of them, like Bukharin, had opposed Stalin's agrarian policy and maintained that agricultural production could have been increased more effectively by working with the kulaks than by eliminating them. These men were probably more popular than the strict bureaucrats and experts —Stalin's loyal followers—who imposed the hardships of the Five-Year Plans.

Most of those who doubted or opposed Stalin's economic policy recommended a change toward greater production of consumer goods, and the occurrence of such a change might have been expected to promote their chances for a successful political comeback. Stalin was unwilling to permit any loosening of controls or any alterations in economic policy, anticipating that the result would be a threat to his position.

But there was still another element in Stalin's campaign. Those against whom the purges were particularly directed were the "old Bolsheviks." In the purges the old leadership of the Bolshevik party from top to bottom was destroyed. Having been trained in discussions of Marxist theory, the old Bolsheviks were not willing to accept orders from above without question, and it has been reliably reported that behind the closed doors of the Politbureau and of party committees, vehement debates took place.

Moreover, many of the old Bolsheviks were internationalists, with a strong belief in the common interest of workers all over the world; in the years of rising Fascism and Nazism they wanted to transform the Communist International into an organization comprising all workers' parties and operating independently from dictates by Moscow. The old Bolsheviks expected a more liberal course, which would realize some of the old socialist ideals of a free and progressive way of life; for example, they were anxious to see a slowdown of the policy of forced collectivization which had begun in 1932 and 1933. The main representative of this liberalism was the leader of the Bolshevik party in Leningrad, Kirov; he was assassinated in 1934, as we now know, by Stalin's orders—although at the purge trials one of the main accusations against the defendants was that they had been responsible for Kirov's death.

Stalin undoubtedly saw a threat to his power in the attitude of the old Bolsheviks working for relaxation in the drive towards industrialization and for an improvement of economic and social life of the masses. But with the rise of the Nazis in Germany the possibility of international war had been greatly increased. Armament production had to be augmented and accelerated, not slowed down: a continued emphasis on heavy industry, not a shift toward consumer goods, was needed.

On the diplomatic front prudence indicated that all options ought to be held open and no premature decision made in favor of the democracies against the Axis powers. Every possible obstacle to a uniform direction of policy appropriate to the dangerous situation had to be removed. This

Stalin in his office in the Kremlin; note portrait of Karl Marx.

consideration was probably a motive in one of the most astounding purges: the execution of Tukhachevski and other military leaders. Under Tukhachevski the army had developed into an almost independent power factor and Stalin may have wondered to what extent he would be able to rely on the army if his policy was contradictory to the views of the military leaders. Stalin's distrust of Tukhachevski seems to have been fomented by the Nazis, who expected that Tukhachevski's fall would weaken the Russian military organization. Through Eduard Beneš, the president of Czechoslovakia, they succeeded in placing before Stalin cleverly falsified documents compromising Tukhachevski. Significantly, the elimination of Tukhachevski and his followers was accompanied by the reintroduction of political commissars into the army.

The ruthlessness with which Stalin pursued a policy of continued economic austerity and tightened the reins of government may have been a means of giving Russia greater strength in the critical years of the thirties, but these explanations for the purges do not mean that anyone who was not as suspicious and brutal, not as jealous of power and autocratic as Stalin was would have found it necessary to proceed in this inhuman manner.

Stalin's Foreign Policy

In the threatening atmosphere of the middle 1930's, continued economic austerity and a tightening of the reins of government seemed appropriate. But the ruthlessness with which these policies were pursued had a dubious effect on Russia's relations with other powers.

When the Russian leaders had embarked on a policy of "socialism in one country" they were naturally anxious to remain undisturbed by the outside world. They had normalized diplomatic relations with their neighbors in the west and participated in international efforts toward securing peace, including the Kellogg-Briand pact and the Disarmament Conference. Because of Hitler's emphatically pronounced anti-Communism, his rise to power was disquieting to the rulers of Soviet Russia and they began to seek closer ties with countries that might be equally interested in checking Nazi expansionism. After Russia joined the League of Nations in September, 1934, the Soviet foreign minister, Maxim Litvinov (1876–1952), became a chief advocate of strict sanctions against aggressors. In 1935 Soviet Russia concluded with France and Czechoslovakia agreements promising mutual assistance in case of unprovoked aggression. Correspondingly, on orders from Moscow the policies of the Communist parties in western Europe began to change. At the Seventh Congress of the Comintern, in the summer of 1935, the formula was proclaimed which initiated the new policy of the Popular Front: Communists were now willing to cooperate with the leaders of any group—socialist or rightist—which took a line of resistance to the Nazis.

Just when these broad movements of opposition to Nazism and Fascism seemed to be gaining impetus and the Popular Front obtained electoral victories in Spain and France, the occurrence of the Russian purges resulted in renewed doubts among the democratic forces about the possibility of cooperation with the Bolsheviks. The Russians even extended the purges to the various Communist parties outside of the Soviet Union, attempting to eliminate from power those whom they considered allies of the purge victims and to establish as leaders of the Communist parties men of proven loyalty to Stalin. Russia intervened in the Spanish Civil War not only to defeat Franco but also to eliminate the leaders of the left who were not Stalinists. Such developments strengthened the hands of those politicians in Great Britain and France who from the outset—for ideological and economic reasons—had opposed cooperation with the Soviet Union. It was said that a regime which had to take recourse to terroristic measures could hardly be regarded as a stable and reliable ally, and the question was raised of whether the Russian government was any more humane or civilized than the Nazi and Fascist dictatorships. In the negotiations on the Czechoslovakian crisis during the summer of 1938 Great Britain and France cold-shouldered Russia as they steered openly toward appeasement with Nazi Germany.

We do not know whether Stalin ever had much interest or confidence in an alliance with the western democracies. It is certain, however, that the Munich Conference and the appeasement policy of the western powers increased his fear that these states might come to an agreement with Germany at the expense of the Soviet Union, perhaps giving Hitler a free hand to attack Russia. Moreover, Stalin was enough of a Marxist to regard as negligible the difference between capitalist Nazi Germany and the capitalist democracies of the west. Thus, when in the summer of 1939 British and French missions appeared in Moscow, and at the same time the Nazis expressed eager interest in a pact with Russia, Stalin's main interest was to make sure that these various powers did not unite against the Soviet Union. An agreement with Nazi Germany had the advantage that the Nazis were willing to hand over to Russia the Baltic states and parts of Poland, which Britain and France refused to do. Stalin may also have found the single-minded, ruthless Hitler more attractive than the vacillating western statesmen, who until recently had embraced appeasement. Everything points to the conclusion that Stalin favored an agreement with Hitler. If he continued the negotiations with Great Britain and France, the chief reason was that otherwise the western powers, despairing of Russian support, might drop Poland; Russia would then be faced alone by a Nazi Germany strengthened by victory over Poland. In short, the purpose of Stalin's diplomacy was to bring about war between Germany and the West.

Like all the other statesmen of the time, Stalin miscalculated. If Great Britain and France were slow and not very forthright in their approach to

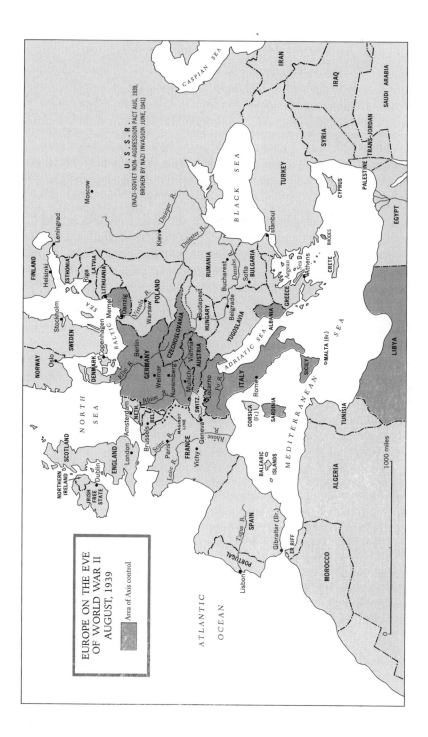

EUROPE ON THE EVE
OF WORLD WAR II
AUGUST, 1939

Area of Axis control

1000 miles

ATLANTIC

OCEAN

NORTH

SEA

NORTHERN
IRELAND
SCOTLAND
ENGLAND
IRISH
FREE
STATE
Dublin
London
Amsterdam
Brussels
NETH.
BEL.
Paris
Seine R.
Loire R.
FRANCE
Vichy
Geneva
SWITZ.
MAGINOT
LINE
Rhine R.
Rhone R.
SPAIN
PORTUGAL
Lisbon
Tagus R.
Gibraltar (Br.)
ER RIFF
MOROCCO
ALGERIA
TUNISIA

FINLAND
Helsinki
NORWAY
Oslo
SWEDEN
Stockholm
Copenhagen
DENMARK
BALTIC SEA
Leningrad
Moscow
ESTHONIA
LATVIA
Riga
LITHUANIA
Memel
Danzig
Vistula R.
Warsaw
POLAND
Kiev
Dnieper R.
Dniester R.

GERMANY
Berlin
Weimar
Elbe R.
Nuremberg
Munich
Locarno
Po R.

CZECHOSLOVAKIA
Vienna
AUSTRIA
Budapest
HUNGARY
Danube
Belgrade
YUGOSLAVIA
RUMANIA
Bucharest
Sofia
BULGARIA
ALBANIA
GREECE
Athens
Aegean Sea
CRETE
RHODES

ITALY
Rome
SARDINIA
CORSICA
(Fr.)
BALEARIC
ISLANDS
ADRIATIC SEA
SICILY
MALTA (Br.)
MEDITERRANEAN SEA

LIBYA

U. S. S. R.
(NAZI-SOVIET NON-AGGRESSION PACT AUG, 1939,
BROKEN BY NAZI INVASION JUNE, 1941)

CASPIAN SEA

BLACK SEA

Istanbul
TURKEY
IRAN
IRAQ
SYRIA
CYPRUS
PALESTINE
TRANS-JORDAN
SAUDI ARABIA
EGYPT

Russia the reason was that they believed erroneously that Soviet Russia and Nazi Germany could never come to an understanding. Meanwhile, Hitler had been persuaded by his foreign minister, Ribbentrop, that a German agreement with Russia would intimidate Great Britain and France into abandoning Poland, so that his forces would have a quick and easy victory. And Stalin believed that the western democracies and Nazi Germany were almost equal in strength and would exhaust themselves in a long and bitter war; Russia—remaining at peace—would emerge as the strongest power on the European continent. The tragedy of the Second World War began with a comedy of errors.

If the war had not broken out over Poland in the summer of 1939, it probably would have been triggered by some other issue. Hitler was straining for control of the continent, and from 1933 on, Europe had been disturbed by crisis after crisis, each more serious than the one before. With everyone living under the threat of an imminent war, the situation had become almost unbearable. Yet when hostilities finally erupted over the German invasion of Poland on September 1, 1939, the public reaction was very different from what it had been at the outbreak of the First World War twenty-five years before. In 1939 there was no enthusiasm, no feeling of liberation. The dreary procession of democratic retreats and defeats, the demonstrated inability to subordinate social conflicts and divergent class interests to the common aim of preserving the basis of freedom had weakened confidence in the strength of the western powers. There seemed validity in the claim of the totalitarian states that they were the wave of the future. Behind the acceptance of the necessity of the war by the people in democratic countries there was a feeling of doom. In the face of terrible defeats, it would require the awakening of a primitive feeling of national pride to shake off this fatalism and to restore hope and confidence.

CHAPTER 10

The Second World War

THE SECOND WORLD WAR began as a war of Poland, Great Britain, and France against Nazi Germany and for the next two years remained primarily a European war. It became a global conflict in December, 1941, when the Japanese attacked Pearl Harbor and provoked the United States into the war. The fifteen months following the entry of the United States were decisive. Winston Churchill, in the fourth volume of his history of the Second World War, saw this period as "the turning point" of the war.[1] Until the end of the summer of 1942 Germany attacked and advanced. Thereafter, the initiative was held by the opponents of Fascism.

Within this general trend of events—the Fascists first on the offensive, then on the defensive—there were movements and countermovements. Thus although the Fascists seemed overwhelmingly superior in the first half of the war, even then their power did receive certain checks, without which the subsequent attack against them could not have been mounted.

THE EUROPEAN WAR

Germany in Command

Until the autumn of 1940 the Germans marched from triumph to triumph. Poland, whose resistance to Hitler's demands had ended the period of appeasement, was eliminated in a campaign of just one month, which provided the first glimpse of the military weapons and tactics which would dominate the conduct of the war. The Germans used their tremendous air superiority to destroy the Polish air force on the ground and then to bomb roads and railroads and interrupt communications so that the Polish

---

[1] Winston S. Churchill, *The Second World War*, Vol. IV, *The Hinge of Fate* (Boston, 1950), p. 830.

troops lost any possibility of movement. There was no such thing as a relatively safe rear. By concentrating an overwhelming force of tanks at certain points the Germans broke through the Polish lines; they then secured their flanks at the breakthrough points and sent the tanks, followed by motorized infantry, streaming into the open countryside, where they turned to the right or left, dividing the enemy forces into isolated segments which were encircled and annihilated one after the other. In the confusion created by this lightning attack, or *Blitzkrieg*, only the big cities maintained organized resistance. Warsaw was heroically defended, the German answer was a bombardment from the air which reduced it to ruins—the first example of the destruction of a large city by air attack.

On September 27, hardly four weeks after the outbreak of the war, Polish resistance was at an end; and Poland was partitioned between Germany and Soviet Russia. The Russians quickly occupied the eastern half of Poland, which had been promised to them in the German-Soviet treaty, and they also advanced into the Baltic states—Lithuania, Estonia, and Latvia. Thus they gained control of a long stretch of the southern coast of the Baltic Sea. The Germans annexed a large part of Poland and for the remainder created a Polish protectorate ruled by a German government. The delimitation of the German and Russian spheres was settled in Moscow on September 28 in what was called the German-Soviet Boundary and Friendship Treaty.

The beginning of the Second World War. *German motorized troops driving into Poland. Note the boundary sign with the Polish eagle which the Germans removed and took along.*

The "Phony War"

French and British military leaders were slow to learn the lessons of the Polish campaign. They believed that the *Blitzkrieg* tactics had been effective only because of Poland's military weakness and could not be applied against armies of greater power. Although German strength in the west was limited, the British and French had not supported the Poles by an attack on Germany, being satisfied to gain time for building up their forces.

What followed was the period of the "phony war." In the west the enemies confronted each other without engaging in serious fighting. German inactivity lulled the French and British into false security. They placed unjustifiably high hopes on the effects of economic warfare; from the outset they set up a tight blockade to prevent Germany from getting goods from abroad. Because they doubted that the Germans would dare to attack in the west, their measures for strengthening the defenses in France lacked the necessary energy. The Maginot Line was not extended along the Belgian frontier to the coast. The French and British governments felt so secure in the west that their attention focused on other areas. When the Russians invaded Finland in November, 1939, in order to improve their military defense line in the north, the French and British decided to assemble an expeditionary force to aid the Finns. But before this assistance could be sent, the war ended, in March, 1940, with the Finns conceding to the Russians the demanded frontier revision.

Concerned by the British and French interest in this northern area Hitler decided to eliminate the possibility of military action by the western Allies from the north. On April 9 German troops drove over the Danish frontier and occupied Denmark; at the same time they attacked Norway. The Norwegians resisted but were overwhelmed. The German success was due to a brilliantly executed combination of action by naval and air forces and paratroops. The British and French countermeasures were fumbling; troops

French troops manning the Maginot Line.

were thrown in without antiaircraft protection and artillery and were quickly destroyed by the Germans.

From the British point of view the Norwegian defeat had one favorable consequence. A dramatic session of the House of Commons showed that Neville Chamberlain had lost the confidence of his countrymen. He resigned on May 10 and was succeeded by Winston Churchill, who formed a government in which all three parties—Conservative, Liberal, and Labor —participated. Churchill writes that he went to bed that night with "a profound sense of relief. At last I had the authority to give directions over the whole scene. I felt as if I were walking with Destiny, and that all my past life had been but a preparation for this hour and for this trial."[2]

The Opening of the Western Offensive

On the very day this change of government took place, the German offensive in the west began. While the Maginot Line remained quiet, the northern wing of the German armies advanced on a broad front, invading the Netherlands and Belgium. German paratroops seized the Dutch airfields and bridges and made an orderly defense of the country impossible. An air raid on Rotterdam obliterated the center of the city, and on May 14 the Dutch army capitulated after Queen Wilhelmina (ruled 1890–1948) and the government had succeeded in escaping to England. Belgian resistance lasted longer, thanks to British and French support. But the Germans, utilizing the same tactics as in Poland, achieved a breakthrough in the Ardennes and their tanks raced ahead into France, toward Amiens and Abbeville, splitting the defending forces into two parts. The northern part, including the entire Belgian army, most of the British troops in France, and a portion of the French army, was then enclosed in a steadily contracting ring. On May 27 the Belgian King Leopold III (ruled 1934–1951) capitulated with his army. British and French troops were pushed back to the beaches of Dunkirk and evacuated from there. Waiting on the beaches, the Allied forces were subjected to steady bombing from the air. A German tank attack probably would have been disastrous, but Hitler evidently believed that the destruction of the exposed troops could be left to the air force, and kept his tanks back. Nevertheless, the saving of these forces required an immense effort; the miracle of Dunkirk was made possible by the strength of the British navy, under whose protection an endless number of small craft brought the soldiers over the Channel. Between May 27 and June 4, 338,226 men reached England.

The tanks which Hitler did not employ at Dunkirk were used in the attack against the other half of the Allied forces, consisting of the bulk of the French army, which had formed a front along the Somme. Again, the German tanks succeeded in breaking through the defenders' lines. Roads

[2] *Ibid*, Vol. I, *The Gathering Storm* (Boston, 1948), p. 667.

were clogged with refugees; German airplanes strafed people scurrying along, creating panic and confusion. The collapse of communications prevented French airplanes and antitank guns from reaching the front, and the enemy was able to advance rapidly.

On June 14 the Germans entered Paris. The French government had fled southward. In hurried visits, Churchill tried to persuade the French to remain in the war. Prime Minister Paul Reynaud (1878–1966) was willing to do so. But with Germans advancing over the Loire and attacking from the rear the Maginot Line, where the last well-organized French military force was stationed, the military leaders declared all further resistance useless and demanded that the government end the war. Reynaud resigned and was succeeded by Marshall Pétain, who on June 17 asked for an armistice. Most of the country was occupied by the Germans; only southeastern France and North Africa remained under French control. In the unoccupied part of France, with Vichy as capital, a French government under Pétain as head of state was established; in the later parts of the war, starting in April, 1942, the directing spirit of this government was Pierre Laval, who expected a German victory and regarded close cooperation with the Nazis as the only possible French policy.

North Africa's freedom from German occupation subsequently proved of great value to the Allied forces, but in the spring and summer of 1940 the French surrender appeared an unmitigated disaster. This impression was reinforced by the establishment under Pétain of a new authoritarian government in Vichy, so that even unoccupied France was absorbed into the antidemocratic camp. There is no doubt that in the shock of defeat

After the French defeat in 1940. *Motorized German S.S. troops at the Place de la Bastille in Paris.*

many Frenchman shared Pétain's belief that an abondonment of the ideas of the Third Republic, and a new hierarchical organization of society, were desirable. Few remained convinced, with Charles de Gaulle, that France had lost a battle but not the war. "The outcome of the struggle has not been decided by the Battle of France. This is a world war."[3] This statement was part of De Gaulle's first appeal from London, in June, 1940, to form a movement for the liberation of France. De Gaulle had made a name for himself through writings in which he had stressed the importance of tanks and motorized forces in future wars. In the campaign of 1940 he had proved himself as a tank commander against the Germans; he was named under secretary of war by Reynaud on June 6 because he could be relied on to support the prime minister's efforts to keep France in the war. When these proved abortive, De Gaulle escaped in a British plane to London. There he organized the Free French movement, insisting that he alone spoke for France and that France was still a great power. He kept a proud distance from the various governments-in-exile which, after the German occupation of their countries, were set up in London.

The Battle of Britain

On June 10, before the French campaign had ended, Italy entered the war. The Italians had been resentful that Hitler had gone ahead even though they had told him that Italy was not ready for war in 1939. As long as the "phony war" lasted, neutrality seemed appropriate, since it might give Italy a chance to act as a mediator. But as Germany progressed unchecked, Mussolini became increasingly restless. His proud claims of having created a new disciplined and powerful state would seem idle boasts if Italy remained outside the war. For the outcome of the campaign in France, Italy's entry into the conflict was irrelevant. But it presented a serious threat to British communication through the Mediterranean and to the British position in the Near East.

Great Britain was dangerously alone. The German high command was sure that "the final German victory over England is only a question of time,"[4] and plans were made for invading England. But German strategy had always centered on land warfare and the military leaders, including Hitler, felt insecure in planning for a campaign combining naval and land operations. According to the German military leaders a successful invasion first required air attacks to eliminate all serious British resistance. And Göring, the commander of the German air force, gave assurances that his bombers and fighter planes could force Great Britain to its knees.

The German air fleet was superior to the British, although antiaircraft

---

[3] Quoted in *The Complete War Memoirs of Charles De Gaulle*, Vol. I, *The Call to Honour*, trans. by Jonathan Griffins (New York, 1955), p. 84.

[4] From entry dated June 30, 1940, *War Diary of General Jodl*.

Petain, head of the French government after the surrender, addressing the citizens of Vichy.

artillery and the concentration of air squadrons in southern England compensated somewhat for the difference in numbers. The Germans began in July with an attack on airfields and military installations, forcing the British into air battles in order to destroy the Royal Air Force. And indeed the R.A.F. did lose continuously in strength. Then, at the beginning of September—in a change which is generally considered to have been a crucial mistake—the Germans switched to bombing attacks on London. The decisive days of the "Battle of Britain" were in the middle of September, when the British had to put their reserves into the defense of London. The British inflicted heavy losses on the German air fleet. These blows made the Germans aware that full air protection for a landing operation was unobtainable, and they abandoned their invasion plans. However, they continued night raids on London until November, averaging two hundred bombers on each mission. These had no direct strategic purpose; they were intended to weaken British morale and will to resist. The *Blitz* on London was followed by attacks on other cities; the most devastating being the raid on Coventry on November 14, in which four hundred people were killed and the center of the city, including its historic cathedral, was completely destroyed. At the end of the year London again became the target of an air attack; incendiary bombs were used and many of the city's most ancient monuments, including Guildhall and numerous churches designed by Sir Christopher Wren, were badly damaged or destroyed. But the morale of the people was not broken nor was the production of war materials interrupted. Britain actually managed to produce more airplanes than Germany in 1940. In the Battle of Britain, Hitler had received his first check; he was forced to abandon the plan to achieve quick victory through a direct attack on Great Britain. As Churchill said of the British pilots who were instrumental in this triumph: "Never in the field of human conflict was so much owed by so many to so few."

THE SHIFT OF THE THEATER OF WAR
FROM THE WEST TO THE EAST

England's Chances of Survival

The victory in the Battle of Britain gave an immense lift to the morale of the opponents of the Nazis because, after the almost clocklike precision of the campaigns in Poland, Norway, and France, it demonstrated that even Nazi plans could go awry. Still, the British situation seemed hopeless. Churchill himself later confessed that, whereas "normally I wake up buoyant to face the new day," in 1940 "I woke with dread in my heart."

Churchill saw little chance that England could win the war alone, but believed that if England could hold out long enough the United States

After the air raids in London. *Tumbling ruins with St. Paul Cathedral in the background.*

would enter the war against the Nazis. When Churchill became a member of the government on the outbreak of the war he began a correspondence with President Roosevelt, informing the president about the developing war scene. Roosevelt's antagonism to Nazi despotism was well known. Moreover, it was his basic axiom, which he had held since the First World War, that it was of vital importance for the security of the United States to have the command over the Atlantic in friendly hands. He fully sympathized with the English, whom he was most eager to help. But he certainly preferred that the Nazis be held in check without the United States taking an active part in the war. Roosevelt also felt that the United States could enter the war only with the full backing of Congress and the American people and that they had not yet been awakened to the dangers which democracy and their way of life would face if the Nazis ruled Europe. Roosevelt knew that before the United States took any action which might lead to war, it had to be better prepared militarily; only in 1940 was the military budget increased and conscription introduced.

Churchill's demands for concrete action of support became urgent in the summer of 1940; Britain's losses in small ships and destroyers during the evacuation at Dunkirk were so great that Britain's shipping lanes had become extremely vulnerable to attack by German submarines. The maintenance of the shipping lanes not only for the provision of food but for import of raw materials needed to manufacture war equipment and airplanes was vital. Thus, Churchill wrote to Roosevelt: "We must ask, therefore, as a matter of life or death, to be reinforced with these [American] destroyers." On the American side the difficulties—constitutional as well as practical—of such a move were very great, but after long and complicated negotiations, on September 2, 1940, an agreement was reached which helped to increase the security of both countries. Britain would receive fifty overage destroyers from the United States; in exchange, it would lease naval and air bases in the West Indies for ninety-nine years to the United States. This deal did not represent a violation of American neutrality, but it certainly gave strong public expression to the community of interests between the United States and Britain. Churchill was not wrong in thinking that after this first step was made other steps would follow, which would bring American participation in the war nearer and nearer. Indeed, in a broadcast on December 29, 1940, Roosevelt declared formally that it was the task of the United States to serve as "the arsenal of democracy," and Congress responded by passing in March, 1941, the Lend-Lease Act, which permitted the president to provide war materials to those states whose survival was vital to the security of the United States; after the Nazi invasion of Russia this act was applied also to Soviet Russia. The identity of American and British interests was publicly announced in the Atlantic Charter, a document issued after a meeting between Roosevelt and Churchill on a warship off the coast of Newfoundland in August, 1941. In the Atlantic Charter, the two leaders emphasized that the war must result in freedom, independence, and an improvement in living standards for all peoples. Thus, although Churchill remained impatient for the United States to become a full participant in the war, his expectation that this would happen—which in the summer of 1940 seemed a wild gamble—appeared more and more a correct calculation.

Hopeful signs for Britain could be found not only in the diplomatic field. In modern military operations information and intelligence, an area which in previous times held only a rather subordinate role in comparison to strategy and tactics, had become vitally important. And it was in this field that the English had a great asset. They had been able to get hold of a "complete, new, electrically operated" cipher machine, fabricated in Germany under the manufacturing name of Enigma; it was by means of this machine that Hitler and the German High Command exchanged signals with the various chiefs of the army, air, and navy staffs and with the army group commanders. It was possible, therefore, to receive these signals in England. Of course, they were given in code and the decoding required mathematical skill of the highest order. But the fact is that by means of Ultra—the code name for this intelligence operation —the British gained a good amount of advance information about military movements planned by the Germans. Ultra proved its value first in the Battle of Britain: information about the areas which the Lüftwaffe was to attack and knowledge of the direction from which the planes came made it possible to intercept them before they reached their goal or to concentrate planes from various regions in the threatened areas. Ultra, together with radar, which, in contrast to the Germans, the British had fully developed, contributed importantly to the outcome of the Battle of Britain. Ultra played its role in all further campaigns in which British and American troops were involved: in the earlier years, when the Germans were superior and on the offensive, frequently by indicating where and when the attack would come, so that retreat from untenable positions could be arranged in time—this happened in North Africa when Rommel opened his general offensive; or later in revealing the distribution of German tank divisions in France—information which had great importance for the success of the Normandy invasion in June 1944.

The British had also broken the code of the "Abwehr," the German secret service. In consequence they knew about the spies the Germans had in England and began to "control" them, offering them the alternative either to disappear in prison or to continue their activities but to tell their employers in Germany what the English wanted them to know. This "doublecross system" had little risks for the English because, in possession of the code of the Abwehr, they knew exactly what these agents reported to Germany. The result was the establishment of an elaborate system of deception, which had some success in keeping the German troops dispersed—either by threatening landings in France long before it was feasible, or by giving the Germans incorrect information about the locale where the invasion on the continent would take place.

During the winter of 1940–1941, British scientists also established that the rapid development of an atomic bomb was possible, although continuation of work on this project was then transferred to Canada and the United States.

However, even if Britain could hold out, would there be any chance to regain a foothold on the continent from which a counteroffensive could be started? The struggle which took place in the Mediterranean area in the winter of 1940–1941 and the spring of 1941 was England's attempt to keep the door open for a later invasion of Europe; for Hitler it was a campaign to ensure complete control of the European continent.

The Mediterranean Campaign

After the triumphant French campaign the Germans had forced Hungary and Rumania into the German orbit; they had even sent troops into Rumania to guard the oil fields against possible attacks by enemies. Mussolini had always considered the Balkans his own domain, and was not pleased to see the Germans extending into this area. Moreover, he was dissatisfied with the minor role his country was playing in the European conflict, and decided to gain military laurels by attacking Greece. But the Italian troops which moved from Albania toward Greece were not prepared for the valiant resistance they encountered. Instead of the Italians occupying Greece, the Greeks conquered a fourth of Italian-controlled Albania.

The Italian plight in the winter of 1940–1941 was made even worse by defeats inflicted by the British in North Africa, where Hitler finally felt that he had to come to the assistance of his fellow dictator by sending German tanks, under one of the best German tank commanders, Erwin Rommel. But Hitler's main attention was directed toward the Balkans. The Italian difficulties gave him the opportunity to firmly establish the German hegemony over this area. While Hungary, Rumania, and Bulgaria accepted close ties with the Axis, assuming the role of satellites, Yugoslavia refused a similar arrangement; Hitler overwhelmed the country in a quick campaign which he continued into Greece. The Greeks were unable to hold off the Germans, and their country was occupied in a few weeks. Finally, through the daring use of paratroops, even Crete was conquered and in German hands by May 31, 1941. In vain had the British sent support to Greece from Africa.

It had been a rather desperate move on the part of the British, since the chances of resisting the German onslaught were small. But Churchill and Anthony Eden, who had again become secretary of foreign affairs, were convinced that the possibilities of mobilizing the European peoples at a later, more favorable time, against the Nazis would end if they could not point out that they had tried to help the one country which had been willing to take up arms against the Fascist powers.

The resultant weakening of their forces in Africa left the British unable to resist Rommel, who drove them back to the Egyptian frontier. The entire area seemed helpless and open to a German onslaught, and it is difficult to imagine what would have happened if Hitler had moved into Egypt, Turkey, and other states of the Near East. But Hitler's target was the Soviet Union. Although the Balkan campaign had caused delays in his plans for an attack against Russia, Hitler now ordered them carried out; on June 22, 1941, German troops marched over the borders of Russia. At the same time the Finns resumed military operations against Russia.

The Eastern Offensive

After the failure to achieve a quick decision against Great Britain, Hitler seems to have been somewhat uncertain what his next move ought to be. It was then that the plan of a campaign against Russia began to take definite form. German expansion toward the east had always been Hitler's aim, but he had intended to postpone this enterprise until the western nations had been defeated. However, after the victory in France, Great Britain's aggressive potential seemed negligible, and Hitler concluded that the subjection of Russia could be achieved while the war against Great Britain continued. His hostility toward Russia had been reinforced by the energy with which the Bolshevik leaders had acted after the defeat of Poland, taking immediate possession of those areas which had been defined in the German-Soviet treaty as belonging to the Russian sphere of interest. In a visit to Berlin in November, 1940, the Soviet foreign minister, Vyacheslav Molotov (born 1890), showed that the Russians were by no means willing to give the Germans a free hand in the Balkans. Even earlier, Hitler had ordered the German general staff to work out plans for an attack against Russia; after Molotov's visit he decided to carry out these plans in 1941.

The Soviet rulers had received warnings of what was coming, but up to the last moment they made desperate attempts to avoid a break with Germany. They had no illusions about how precarious their situation would be in case of war with Germany.

At first, the campaign against Russia seemed to lead to a quick and complete triumph, even discounting Nazi exaggeration of the number of Russian prisoners of war taken in the early weeks of the campaign. The Russians conceded after the war that "Soviet strategic theory as propounded by the Draft Field Regulations of 1939 and other documents did not prove to be entirely realistic. For one thing, they denied the effectiveness of the

Blitzkrieg which tended to be dismissed as a lopsided bourgeois theory."[5] The Russians were surprised by the German use of tank formations for breakthroughs and encirclement. The Germans' air superiority enabled their air force to attack Russian airfields and destroy Russian planes on the ground. The Russian debacle was magnified by orders ascribed to Stalin to hold out in advance positions, causing the troops to miss opportunities to retreat before the ring of encirclement was closed. At Kiev, in one such encirclement of Russian forces, the Germans took 175,000 prisoners of war.

By October the Germans were before Moscow and Leningrad, and in a speech on October 2 Hitler announced a "final drive" against Moscow. People began to flee the city. Trains were packed; officials set out in their cars; and although some factories worked day and night to produce anti-tank defenses, or "hedgehogs," which were immediately placed in the roads around Moscow, other factories were evacuated. Doubts grew that the capital could be held.

The official will to defend the city was underlined by an announcement that Stalin was in Moscow. In the first weeks of the war he seems to have been near a nervous collapse and to have almost lost control. But Stalin's firmness in the desperate situation when the Germans were beleaguering Leningrad and approaching Moscow muted all criticism and established him in undisputed authority as the supreme military leader. He began to be presented as a second Peter the Great. In newspapers and literature there was a deliberate stimulation of interest in the Russian past, even in tsarist history, and the war came to be called the "Great Patriot War." The Bolshevik leaders wanted the struggle to be seen as an event which concerned not only Communists, but all the Russian people. At the beginning of November, in two great speeches, Stalin invoked Russian nationalism as the inspiration for resistance to the hordes of invading barbarians. By then, the German offensive had lost its impetus, probably less because of the strength of the Russian stand than because of logistical difficulties: the necessary supplies for the tanks, artillery, and men had not kept up with the rapid advance. When the Germans started a second push in November, the Russians were prepared; their embittered resistance, together with an early onset of winter, which severely hurt the insufficiently clad German troops, caused this second offensive against Moscow to fail.

Nevertheless, the Russian situation remained serious. By the end of the campaign of 1941 the Germans had conquered most of the Ukraine, were close to Moscow, and had surrounded Leningrad, which remained under siege for eighteen months. These advances had been bought with very heavy losses—between 700,000 and 800,000 men. The Russians were quick to

[5] This citation is from the Russian official *History of the War* (1960). Quoted by Alexander Werth, *Russia at War, 1941–1945* (New York, 1964), p. 133.

**AXIS EXPANSION IN THE WEST
1942**

Greatest extent of Axis occupation
or control

Areas controlled by Vichy France

ARCTIC   OCEAN

Petsamo

FINLAND

Helsinki

NORWAY

Oslo   Stockholm   ESTONIA

SWEDEN   LATVIA

SCOTLAND   LITHUANIA

NORTH   DENMARK   EAST
SEA   Copenhagen   PRUSSIA

IRELAND   Hamburg   Warsaw

ENGLAND   Berlin   POLAND
Coventry   Rotterdam
London   NETH.   GERMANY   CARPATHIAN MTS.
Brussels   Lidice
Abbeville   BEL.   Prague
ATLANTIC   Dunkirk   LUX.   CZECHOSLOVAKIA
Amiens   Rhine R.
OCEAN   Paris   Munich   Vienna   Budapest
Loire R.   FRANCE   AUSTRIA   HUNGARY   RUMANIA
Oradour-sur-Glane   Vichy   SWITZ.
Bordeaux   Belgrade   BULGARIA
ITALY   YUGOSLAVIA
Marseilles   ADRIATIC SEA
CORSICA   Rome   ALBANIA
Madrid   Barcelona   Naples   GREECE
Lisbon   SARDINIA
SPAIN
Seville   MEDITERRANEAN

ER RIFF   SICILY

Casablanca   MALTA   SEA
TUNISIA   (Br.)

MOROCCO   ALGERIA

IFNI

LIBYA

0   500 miles

BALTIC SEA

ATLANTIC

PORTUGAL

learn from their defeats. Generals who had been promoted because of their political merits were replaced by brilliant professionals, such as Georgi Zhukov, Semion Timoshenko, and Boris Shaposhnikov. The Russians showed great ingenuity in transporting factories from threatened areas into the safe hinterland of the Urals and Siberia. They were able to accelerate the production of tanks, airplanes, and artillery; and the Russian heavy artillery proved to be superior to that of the Germans. Moreover, supplies from Great Britain and the United States began to arrive on convoys that traveled on hazardous sea lanes to Murmansk. These supplies filled the gaps in production that occurred while factories were being moved to safe areas. In contrast to what had happened in Poland, France, and the Balkans, victory in one quick campaign escaped the Germans in Russia.

THE WAR AT ITS HEIGHT

The Global War

At the beginning of 1942 the entire war changed in character. It ceased to be a purely European conflict, and became global. To Japanese advocates of expansionism the European struggle seemed to offer a unique opportunity for establishing a Japanese empire in the Far East. Great Britain was unable to intervene, and the German occupation of the Netherlands and France made the Far Eastern possessions of these countries an easy prey. From French Indochina, which they occupied in 1940, the Japanese prepared to move against Burma, the East Indies, and Singapore. The United States, which wanted to help Britain, and in addition had a vital interest in preventing the domination of this area by a single power, opposed these Japanese moves by diplomatic representations and economic pressures. Negotiations conducted in Washington between the two states were unsuccessful, however, and were near collapse when, on December 7, 1941, the Japanese made a surprise attack on the United States fleet in Pearl Harbor, sinking three battleships and severely damaging five others. The next day the United States formally declared war on Japan.

The outbreak of hostilities between Japan and the United States was followed on December 11, by declarations of war on the United States by Germany and Italy. The Axis powers were bound by a treaty concluded in 1940 to assist Japan in case of attack by a state not involved in the European war; it remains strange, however, that Hitler, who had few inclinations to honor treaty obligations, believed that he had to fulfill this one. To declare war on the United States was his personal decision, and his hatred of President Roosevelt, the protagonist of the democratic world, was probably a prime motive. Most of all, Hitler's decision showed that despite the setbacks in Russia he felt supremely confident. His lack of knowledge of American politics also played its role. He seems never to have considered that without this declaration of war, American military action might have focused on the Far East rather than Europe.

There can be no doubt also that the German declaration of war on the United States solved the dilemma by which Roosevelt had been faced in the preceding months. The United States and Great Britain had moved closer and closer together and American protection of a neutrality zone far into the Atlantic Ocean had considerably diminished the effects of the German submarine war. Yet Roosevelt and his advisers had become increasingly convinced that direct participation of the United States in the war was needed for defeating Nazi Germany. But Roosevelt also believed that, although the American people approved a policy of giving strong support to Great Britain, they would still have to be shown that they were directly threatened in order to accept the necessity of participation in the war unhesitatingly; but so far the Germans had avoided all direct provocation. After the German declaration of war it was now possible to coordinate British and American war efforts in a much more systematic and effective fashion.

On December 22, Churchill and a number of his military advisors arrived in Washington, and except for a trip to Canada he stayed in the United States until January 14, 1942. In the meetings in Washington two important decisions were made, one strategical, the other organizational. It was agreed that a defeat of Hitler was the first goal; the European theater of war was given precedence over the Far East. In addition, a unified command was created: within each of the various theaters of war the British and American troops were placed under a single commander, either British or American. The direction of the strategy of the war was entrusted to a committee, the Combined Chiefs of Staff, in which the outstanding figures were General George C. Marshall (1880–1959), the chief of staff of the army on the American side, and Sir John Dill (1881–1944) on the British side.

There was never close cooperation in military planning between the Combined Chiefs of Staff and the Russian general staff. On the contrary, the Russians were most reluctant to give information to the British and American military representatives in Moscow. The organizational unification of British and American military effort helped to prevent the delays, frictions, and disorders which usually occur in the conduct of a coalition war; even so, some decisions were reached only after long debates. It was the bond of friendship and respect which existed between Roosevelt and Churchill—together with their interest in and understanding of military affairs—that served to smooth out the difficulties which arose from differences among the generals.

The main issue under dispute throughout the war years was the timing of the invasion of France. The Americans were eager to embark on this enterprise in 1942, the British were probably right in considering such an undertaking premature at a time when the Germans were at the height of their power and the American troops were inexperienced. The British idea of abandoning the plan of a continental invasion in 1942 and substituting a landing in North Africa was appropriate, just as at a later stage the Americans were probably justified in opposing British plans to extend operation in the Mediterranean area by an attack through the Balkan Peninsula—the "soft underbelly of the Axis"—and in insisting instead on invasion of France across the English Channel.

Total War

In becoming global the war also had become total, at least in the sense that in all countries the needs of war were accepted to be controlling all spheres and activities of life, although, according to geography, wealth, and closeness to war, the degree of control and regulation varied.

Britain's insular position and its dependence on other countries for food had quickly led to controls of imports and exports, allocation of raw material, and, in order to prevent a lowering of morale, limitations on profits. Rationing of food and clothes was efficiently organized. The main problem for Britain as well as for all the European belligerents was manpower; the British National Service Act of December 1941 established that men and women—men from 18–50, women from 20–30—were subject to either military or essential civilian war service. The manpower needs became so great that in the final year of the war a "grandmother category" had to be added, i.e., the conscription of women was extended to age 50.

The most severe manpower regulations, however, were those in Russia. There all men from 16–55 and all women from 16–45 were mobilized. The reason for the almost unbelievable extent of this mobilization was the catastrophic effect of the German victories in the early months of the war: the occupation of Russia's industrially most advanced regions, the loss of about 2.5 million men and immense amounts of equipment, most importantly 14,000 tanks, more than 90 per cent of what the Russians had originally possessed. Industries now had to be constructed in the security of the remote Ural region to which workers had to be transported; more than 50 per cent of the labor force employed in these factories were women. By 1943 the Russians were producing 2,000 tanks and 3,000 airplanes per month.

The greatest change brought about by the transformation of the European war into a global war took place in Germany. This may seem astounding because the expansionist and aggressive policy which the Nazis had conducted could be expected to have prepared from the outset for total war. But Nazi leaders were thinking in terms of *Blitzkrieg*. Their aim was to have a limited military production which provided a supply of weapons and equipment adequate for a *Blitzkrieg*. A material reservoir of this size would be maintained; after a *Blitzkrieg* campaign was over the loss of material would soon be replaced, especially since the material taken from the enemy would compensate for part of the losses. This approach to military production had the advantage of flexibility so that changes could be easily made, suited to the particularities of a planned campaign. Moreover, this method left the working of a great part of the German industrial machine quite undisturbed. The continuation of a peace economy in war time was also secured by partial demobilization after each campaign.

The failure of the *Blitzkrieg* in the east changed this situation. Supplies of equipment and weapons lasting for a limited number of months would no longer suffice. An increase in armaments and an expansion of the army was necessary, which meant that Germany had to convert to total mobilization, with allocation of war materials, standardization of weapons, and reduction of plane production to a few types. A Ministry of Armaments and Production provided centralized direction; indeed, under its minister, Albert Speer, it trebled German armaments production within two years. In its handling of manpower mobilization, however, Germany differed from the other countries; the number of women employed in industry and agriculture did not increase. Nazi ideology considered the maintenance of the race as the main function of women. The activities of women should be confined to the house; after the Nazis had come to power they dismissed all married women who were public employees; they denied women the right to be a judge or prosecutor, reduced the number of women teachers and made every possible effort to eliminate women from the labor force. Men ought not to be subordinated to women as might happen if they were employed in factories. The needs of wartime did not effect any change in this policy. Hitler insisted on the maintenance of these principles to the end.

Europe Under the Nazis

The adjustment of economic and civil life to the needs of total war had its bearing not only on Germany but had repercussions in all the countries occupied by the Nazis, i.e., throughout Europe. Soon after the conquest the occupied areas were organized according to Nazi aims. In the occupied territories of the East the Germans acted as if they were permanent rulers. Many of the inhabitants were removed and resettled, and large landed estates were given to German generals and Nazi leaders. Yugoslavia was divided, with one part forming the kingdom of Croatia, ruled by an Italian prince, and the rest remaining under direct German administration. Bulgaria, Rumania, and Hungary, being Nazi allies, retained their old rulers but were dominated by German-supported parties patterned after the Nazis. Norway, the Netherlands, Belgium, and part of France were under German occupation. The Germans used puppet governments as instruments for their rule, which came to be known as Quisling governments, after the Norwegian Nazi leader, Vidkun Quisling.

One of the chief aims of German occupation policy was economic exploitation. All the occupied countries had to pay for the costs of German occupation and these costs were set extremely high. A good part of business profits were swallowed up in taxes which went to Germany, mostly in form of deliveries of raw material and food. Moreover, rationing was introduced in the occupied countries but on levels very different from those in Germany. An industrial worker in Germany received twice as much bread, three times as much meat, seven times as much fats as an industrial worker in France. And although the difference in rations which the general consumer received was not quite as striking, it was considerable. Almost until the last year of the war it was possible to maintain a fairly high standard of living in Germany; meanwhile people in many occupied areas were starving. Regular economic activities and personal lives were further interrupted by the conscription and transportation of men of captive countries to Germany to work there in factories and labor battalions. The propaganda intended to justify these measures emphasized that German arms were defending Europe against Communism and that German domination would usher in a new period in which Europe would be unified. In all the subject countries parties organized in the pattern of the German Nazi party were established, and military units were formed to join in the fight against Communism. Thus in the campaign against Russian, Rumanian, Hungarian, and Italian armies, as well as legions of volunteers from all over Europe—even from Spain—fought under the German command.

With the tightening of German controls over Europe, resistance movements arose in almost all of the occupied countries. Originally these movements consisted of isolated groups, such as the remnants of the former political parties, among which the Socialists and Communists had particularly kept some cohesion, or of groups of nationalists, Catholics, and Protestants, who felt that they dishonored themselves if they allowed the brutal and un-Christian behavior of the Nazis to go on without taking some action. In the course of time these various units began to cooperate with one another and combine into coordinated resistance organizations. All these movements worked underground; for several years their activities consisted mainly of giving help and protection to those who, for political or racial reasons, were persecuted by the Nazis; *Anne Frank: The Diary of a Young Girl* (1947) gives a moving portrayal of the existence of a Jewish family hidden by Dutch friends, but in the end found by the Nazis.

Another function of the resistance was the transmission of intelligence, particularly about German military movements; the French were able to maintain secret contacts with Great Britain, and the headquarters of De Gaulle's Free French movement in London were extremely well informed

AXIS EXPANSION IN THE EAST
1942

Greatest extent of Axis control

about developments in France. The various resistance groups kept in contact through secretly printed newspapers, many of a very high intellectual level. They contained not only uncensored news but also lively debates on what the political structure of the occupied countries should be after liberation. The generally accepted aim was a thorough reorganization of political and social life. This demand for radical changes was only partly the result of the importance of Socialists and Communists in the resistance; repudiation of the prewar ruling groups, whose policies had led to defeat and occupation, was general, and contempt for the men of the former ruling circles was intensified by the willingness of many financial and industrial leaders to collaborate with the Germans.

Throughout the occupation, the men of the resistance undertook single acts of sabotage, but the introduction of more elaborate guerilla operations depended on circumstances. The Germans never succeeded in completely controlling the wild and inaccessible mountain regions of Yugoslavia; Yugoslav military organizations—the Communists under Marshal Tito (born 1892), the royalists under Draza Mihajlovic—remained active, usually fighting the Germans but sometimes fighting each other. In the wide forests and swamps of Russia, units composed of peasants and of soldiers who had escaped German encirclements operated behind the front, substantially damaging the German lines of communications. Resistance armies in Italy and France went into action when the invasion by American and British forces was imminent, contributing considerably to the collapse of German rule in the occupied areas.

Those participating in the resistance constituted a relatively small part of the populations, and they were exposed to great danger up to the end. The German secret police ruthlessly tortured people believed to possess information about underground activities, and the German troops, particularly the fanatic members of the S.S., tried to stamp out sabotage and resistance by brute force. They made arrests in the middle of the night, took hostages and killed them on the smallest provocation, and shot people for the slightest suspicious moves.

The names of Lidice and Oradour are testimonies of Nazi terrorism. In revenge for the assassination of the Gestapo leader Reinhard Heydrich in 1942, the Czech village of Lidice was destroyed; its entire adult male population was killed, the women were placed in camps, and the children, separated from their families and nameless, were dispersed. In the French town of Oradour, in punishment for presumed support of partisans, the men were shot and the women and the children were herded into the church and burned. Because the conqueror's controls were so thorough and brutal, the resistance movement could exert effective pressure on the Nazis only when their reserves became strained and their grip started to loosen.

It is frequently said of the Germans that they are a systematic people. In confirmation of what admittedly is a somewhat doubtful generalization

German soldiers arresting Jews in Budapest for deportation to concentration camps.

it can be pointed out that when the Germans systematized the war effort by total mobilization, the Nazis thought the time had also come for what they called "the final solution" to the Jewish question. On January 20, 1942, in Wannsee, near Berlin, a conference was held under the chairmanship of Reinhard Heydrich, then the chief of the dreaded Security Service of the S.S. Along with delegates of the chief organizations of the Nazi party, representatives of the Ministries of the Interior, of Justice, and of the Foreign Office took part; other participants were high officials of the civil administrations of all the occupied territories. The presence of this last category was particularly important because, as Heydrich stated in presenting the agenda of the conference, the main purpose was to arrange for the particular measures needed so that Europe could "be combed through from west to east" for Jews who would be evacuated "group by group, into so-called transit ghettos, to be transported from there farther to the east." An exception was made for Jews over sixty-five or those wounded or decorated in the First World War; they would be herded into a ghetto in Theresienstadt in Bohemia. All others would be transported to the east; indeed, now began the tragic spectacle of long trains coming from all parts of Europe, even as far as Rome, carrying Jews packed in cattle cars to the east. And the east, of course, meant the extermination camps of Chelmno, Belsek, Majdanek, Treblinka, and Auschwitz, where gradually, often after having been forced to labor for the Nazis, nearly six million Jews were annihilated in the gas chambers.

It has been said that what made Hitler and Nazism unacceptable to

German concentration camp at Sachsenhausen, near Berlin. *In 10° F. weather the thinly clad inmates of the camp were forced to stand at attention for over six hours as guards searched outside the camp for an escaped prisoner. This was usual procedure in case of an escape, and often lasted much longer; many died from the cruel exposure and others dropped from exhaustion.*

the civilized world was the persecution of the Jews; otherwise, cooperation, and even approval of certain features of his regime, would have been possible. This is entirely wrong. The entire regime, in all its aspects, was brutal, amoral, lawless. The Jewish policy was the most terrifying, the most tragic, and the most extreme aspect of the barbarianism which animated the Nazi regime throughout.

THE HINGE OF FATE

After the check which the Germans had received before Moscow in the winter of 1941, it was evident that the war would last long and that superiority in resources and materials would become increasingly decisive for victory. The entry of the United States into the war provided the Allies with a productive capacity which assured them material superiority. But it required time until American industrial potential was fully realized and American troops could effectively intervene in the war. The situation in the year 1942, therefore, was still precarious for the opponents of the Axis powers who still possessed the initiative. It seemed by no means impossible that the Japanese might gain full control in the Far East and the Axis in Europe might drive the British from the Mediterranean and knock Russia out of the war, thereby attaining an almost invincible position before the United States could make its weight felt.

In the first months of 1942, the advance of the Japanese in the Far East was awesome. They took the Philippines from the Americans; they conquered British forces on the Malay Peninsula and by February 15 were in Singapore, where they took sixty thousand prisoners. In combined land and sea operations they overran the Netherlands East Indies, reaching Batavia in March. They occupied Burma, and took Mandalay on May 2. The road to India seemed open to them, and the barriers against their advance into Australia appeared to have fallen.

In Europe the campaigns of 1942 were of crucial importance. A German offensive in the east was undertaken at a time when, despite the failure before Moscow, German power was still at its peak. Hitler counted on accomplishing in a second Russian campaign what he had not succeeded in doing in 1941. The offensive began in June. It was mainly directed toward the southern half of the Russian front, its purpose being to deprive the Russians of the agricultural areas of the Ukraine, the industrial areas of the Donets Basin, and the oil fields of the Caucasus. The Nazis expected that Moscow and Leningrad, cut off from supplies, would be taken from the rear by encircling movements. The German armies succeeded in penetrating into the Caucasus, but their advance to the Volga was stopped at Stalingrad, and the battle for Stalingrad developed into one of the decisive battles of the war. Stalingrad was strategically important because its conquest would have cut communications between Moscow and the south. Moreover, the name had great symbolic value to both Germans and Russians.

At the beginning of the winter, except for a few buildings on the right bank of the Volga, all of Stalingrad had been taken, and Hitler announced on November 9 that the city was "firmly in German hands." But the Russians resisted obstinately, using heavy artillery from the other side of the river. Then they succeeded in breaking through the front north and south of Stalingrad, and by the end of November the Germans, led by General Friedrich Paulus, were no longer attacking the Russians but defending themselves; the army before Stalingrad, 300,000 men strong, was encircled. Hitler forbade any attempt at withdrawal by a breakthrough toward the west, assuring Paulus of provisions by air. But this proved impossible, and slowly but steadily the ring around Paulus' army was drawn closer, until the German forces were reduced to a few isolated groups. On January 31, 1943, Paulus surrendered, with the 123,000 men who were left of his army. Hitler's reaction was an emotional outburst of reproach that Paulus had not committed suicide.

The hole torn in the German front through the encirclement of the army

The battle for Stalingrad. *One of the last German airplanes to take off from Paulus' encircled army.*

before Stalingrad made the Germans' situation in southern Russia untenable and forced them to draw back. By the spring of 1943 the lines on the eastern front were roughly the same as they had been one year earlier.

In the fall of 1942, while the German military situation was deteriorating in Russia, there was a reversal of fortune in the Mediterranean area as well. In the winter of 1941–1942 the British had succeeded in forcing their opponents back from the Egyptian frontier, but in 1942 Rommel, commander of the German-Italian forces, had pushed the British back into Egypt, where overextended supply lines forced him to a halt. A lull permitted the British to strengthen their position through reinforcements sent by sea around Africa; at the end of October the British Eighth Army under a new commander, Bernard Montgomery, was able to take the offensive. The Battle of El Alamein became the first victory of British troops over a German army in the Second World War. The fighting began on October 23, 1942, with a heavy artillery barrage which opened some holes in the German lines; British tanks penetrated these gaps and forced the Germans to withdraw. The front was small, consisting of hardly forty miles between sea and desert; because of British air superiority and control of the sea, the German supply lines, which ran along this narrow stretch between sea and desert, became unusable, and Rommel's troops were forced back from one position to another, finally from Libya into Tunisia.

While the British were exploiting their victory at El Alamein, a combined force of British and American troops under General Dwight D.

Eisenhower landed in French North Africa on November 8. The Americans had yielded to the British insistence that an invasion of the European continent was not feasible in 1942, but some action which would divert German forces from the Russian front seemed necessary, and North Africa was chosen as the site for a surprise invasion. The operation was entirely successful. The French in Morocco offered only token resistance and then transferred their support to the British and Americans. The Germans in Tunisia had to fight not only Montgomery's Eighth Army coming from the south but also the British-American forces coming from the west. Encircled, the German beachhead in Tunisia was eliminated by the middle of May, 1943.

During this same period, the summer of 1943, the Allies were also beginning to make gains in the Pacific theater. In three great sea and air battles—of the Coral Sea in May, of Midway in June, and of the Solomon Islands in August—the Japanese fleet was crippled, and further advances toward the south were checked. The British succeeded in bolstering the defenses of India, and Chinese resistance on the Asian mainland remained alive. Despite amazing conquests, Japan was still enclosed in a ring of hostile forces. By the end of the summer the offensives of Japan and the Axis forces had been halted and the initiative was held by the anti-Fascist coalition.

Germany Before Surrender

Now the outcome of the war was inevitable. The American industrial machine was in full gear and was producing planes, ships, and tanks at a rate which would have seemed impossible at the beginning of the war. The Russian factories which had been transported into the Urals and Siberia were working to capacity. British war production increased steadily because air superiority gained with American help meant protection from sustained German air attacks. Now it was Germany that suffered from steady bombings; by the end of the war most of the larger German cities were in ruins. Clearly the decisive factor in warfare had become superiority in weapons and equipment, based on industrial mass production. Even Hitler recognized this fact and in the final stages of the war expected a favorable outcome only from new miracle weapons. But the guided missiles, the V-1 and the V-2 rockets which Germany was able to put into use in 1944, were of limited effectiveness, and work on jet engines had not been completed when the war ended.

For the Germans, the sole rational hope for victory lay in the possibility of breaking up the coalition which was closing in on them from all sides. The relations of the United States and Great Britain with their Russian ally had been troubled from the start. When the Germans invaded Russia in 1941, Britain and the United States promised to give the Soviet Union all possible support, and indeed the supplies sent there were of crucial

Werner von Braun among German officers at Peenemuende, center of construction of German V-weapons.

importance in maintaining Russian resistance in the critical first years of the German-Russian struggle. But the Russian leaders did little to publicize this outside help among their people; in their public statements about their allies they blew hot and cold. Their main interest was to promote a "second front," an Allied invasion of western Europe. Sometimes the Russians accused Britain and the United States of timidity and lack of energy in their pursuit of the anti-Fascist war; sometimes they praised them—depending on what approach seemed more likely at the moment to accelerate the opening of this second front.

Relations were further troubled because the Russians were unwilling to recognize the governments-in-exile, particularly the Polish government. They wanted to avoid any commitments which might affect the settlement of frontiers after the war. In eastern Europe they supported only the resistance movements led by Communists. When in January, 1943, after the successful landing in North Africa, Churchill and Roosevelt met in Casablanca, one of their purposes in demanding from Germany "unconditional surrender" was to dispel Russian fears that the western powers might make a "deal" with Nazi Germany at the expense of the Soviet Union. At the meetings of Roosevelt and Churchill with Stalin in December, 1943, in Teheran and in February, 1945, in Yalta in the Crimea, military questions stood in the foreground. But at Yalta the approaching end of the war made the consideration of the postwar settlement a necessity, although the decisions remained rather vague and general. The liberated and the defeated countries were to become democracies. Germany and Austria were to be occupied, with each of the victorious powers receiving a zone of occupation, although in the capitals—Berlin and Vienna—a central administration assuring uniformity of occupation policies was to be established. With regard to postwar boundaries and compensation for war damages general principles were laid down rather than that they were settled in detail. There was no real reason for the Nazis to hope that the anti-Fascist coalition could be broken up before Germany was completely defeated. Neither the Russians nor the western powers were willing to negotiate as long as Hitler was in power. Germans with political insight believed that better peace terms or a separate settlement with either the West or the East might be obtained if Hitler was removed. The result was a conspiracy by socialists and liberals, high civil servants and generals, which culminated on July 20, 1944, in an attempt on Hitler's life. But the attempt failed; just a moment too soon, Hitler moved away from the place where a bomb exploded. The war was thus destined to last for almost another year.

Why did the German people go on fighting though their situation was clearly hopeless? Obviously the Allies were unwilling to negotiate with Hitler and the men around him, so for the Nazi leaders there was no alternative to struggling on. German troops on the eastern front fought willingly and obstinately until the surrender because Nazi propaganda had drummed into them a passionate hatred of Bolshevism, and they feared the retribution which might be exacted for what had been done to the Russian people; a Russian invasion and occupation of German soil seemed worse than death.

Although the decline in the German fortunes after 1942 weakened the hold of Hitler and of Nazism over the minds of the German people, a corps of loyal Nazis survived until the end. Members of the S.S. particularly stayed firmly tied to the Nazi regime and their military units remained a valuable fighting force, which was thrown into combat at critical points until the final weeks of the war. Moreover, many of the teen-age members of the Nazi youth organization, who were conscripted in the last winter of the war, continued to regard Hitler as a man of destiny. The fanaticism of the S.S. guaranteed to the Nazi rulers an instrument for control by terror, and toward the end it was primarily fear and terror that kept the German people in the war. Himmler and his police imprisoned and tortured everyone suspected of holding anti-Nazi opinions or defeatist views. Such crimes—judged in Nazi-staffed People's Courts from which there was no appeal—were punished by death. The ruthlessness of the S.S. police increased after the attempt on Hitler's life. Entire families of persons suspected of political crimes were placed in custody. There was a grisly report in the last days of the war about corpses of soldiers by the hundreds dangling from the trees of one of Berlin's streets because they had absented themselves from their military units.

Organization of resistance to the Nazi rule was impeded not only by the thoroughness and the terror methods of the police but ironically also by Allied bombing attacks. The saturation bombing of German cities disrupted communications and thereby strengthened the control of the Nazi rulers, who had priority use of roads, railroads, telegraph, and telephone. In coping with civil disasters, the Nazis made certain that water and food were given only to those who had appropriate identification papers. The Nazis were in charge of evacuating people from bombed quarters, and for weeks the whereabouts of the evacuees might be unknown even to close relatives and friends. The Nazi leaders and the Nazi apparatus alone maintained awareness of the situation as a whole; for the rest of the population life became atomized.

Even though the end seemed in sight in the spring of 1943, after the victories at Stalingrad and in North Africa, the military operations of the last two years of the Second World War were bitterly fought. Severely mauled, the German war machine was still formidable, and the Japanese still controlled a vast area of great natural resources and great defensive strength. A serious Allied defeat might have raised a cry for negotiations with the enemy, which would inevitably have been accompanied by all the difficulties involved in gaining cooperation among members of a coalition.

The Overthrow of Mussolini

The first of the Axis powers to collapse was Italy. After the defeat of the Germans in Tunisia the American-British forces, now in control of air and sea in the Mediterranean, landed in Sicily, and soon conquered the island. During the Sicilian invasion, on July 25, 1943, Mussolini was overthrown by a group which included leaders of the anti-Fascist underground, some prominent Fascists, and the military high command. Although the new government under Pietro Badoglio (1871–1956), a military man, officially declared it would continue the war, secret negotiations for an armistice were started immediately. The Nazi leaders were prepared for such an event. When the armistice was announced on September 8, German tank divisions closed in on Rome and plans for an Allied landing on the beaches near Rome had to be abandoned as too risky. During the winter the fronts stabilized between Rome and Naples; even the landing of Allied troops in Anzio did not lead beyond the formation of a beachhead. Central and northern Italy remained under Axis control.

After being overthrown Mussolini had been imprisoned, but German paratroopers succeeded in liberating him. He was induced by the Germans to establish a Fascist government in northern Italy, where he proclaimed that, free from conservative and monarchist restraints, he could now pursue the original Fascist ideas of social reform. But actually his government called the Republic of Salò after the small town where some of its offices were installed, was controlled by the Germans. It was the Germans who insisted on holding trials at Verona for six Fascist leaders who had participated in the overthrow of Mussolini, among them his son-in-law Count Ciano. They were condemned to death and executed.

The End of the War in Europe

The collapse of Fascism did not end the fighting in Italy, but it had a great moral effect, spurring anti-German activities all over Europe, and in addition was of military significance for all the theaters of war. The Allies could give more effective support to the partisans fighting in Yugoslavia; German manpower resources became severely strained because the Italian occupation troops in the Balkans now had to be replaced by German forces. Moreover, the necessity of sending German tank divisions from the Russian front to Italy in July, at the time of the overthrow of the Fascist regime, had its impact on the eastern theater. The Germans were then undertaking another offensive, their last in the east, in the center of the Russian front. But the Russians, in a counteroffensive, forced them back on a broad front, reaching the Dnieper and reconquering Kiev in November, 1943.

From this time on, the Allies held the initiative entirely, and in 1944 they advanced everywhere. The Russians continued to attack throughout the winter and by the beginning of the summer of 1944 were driving on to the borders of Poland and Rumania. By the end of the summer they had reached East Prussia, forced Finland out of the war, and shifted the chief weight of their attack to the southern part of the front, where they brought about the surrender of Rumania and Bulgaria. The Russian armies thus were approaching the frontiers of Nazi Germany from the southeast as well as from the east, their advances facilitated by the increasing pressure which Great Britain and the United States were able to exert.

The stalemate on the Italian front was broken; Rome and Florence were taken, so only northern Italy remained in German hands. And Greece was liberated.

The decisive accomplishment, however, of the United States and Great Britain in 1944 was the invasion of western Europe. On June 6, 1944, American and British forces crossed the English Channel and established beachheads on the Normandy coast. The success of this daring operation was primarily due to the complete Allied domination of the air, which frustrated German efforts to reinforce and supply their front lines. Moreover, the landings were protected by the heavy guns of the British and American ships, their fire directed in accordance with the excellent information about the German positions provided by the French underground. Artificial harbors brought over from England solved the problem of establishing a continuous stream of supplies for the invading troops—a problem which had appeared to stand in the way of any landing on a great scale. Nevertheless, it was a difficult operation which had been meticulously planned and

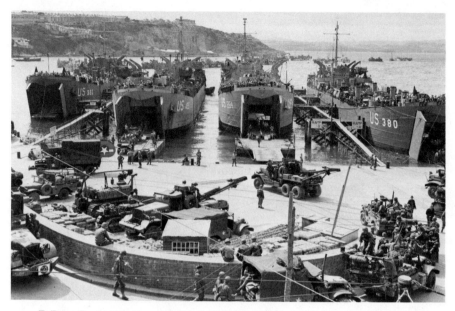

D-Day. *In preparation for the invasion, artillery is loaded aboard American transport ships on the southern coast of England.*

brilliantly executed under the supreme command of General Eisenhower, with the British General Montgomery and the American General Omar Bradley as field commanders.

The hours after the initial waves of American and British troops had landed on the beaches were critical. But the German military leadership proved to be uncertain and faulty. The German generals could not agree on whether to defend the entire coastline or to permit the Allies to move into the interior and draw them into a battle while they were still relatively weak. Moreover, at the crucial moment Hitler refused to allow the employment of the German tank reserves because he was convinced that the landing in Normandy was a feint and that a stronger force would attack elsewhere on the coast. Once landed in strength, the Allies were able to effect a breakthrough with their tanks and to fan out in the rear, driving the Germans to retreat. By September, the liberation of France and Belgium was nearing completion, and the Allied armies were establishing themselves along the former German frontiers, where they were forced to stop because supplies were running short. A question which has been raised but can never be answered is whether the war might have been ended in 1944, if the Allies, instead of advancing on a broad front had kept their northern wing back and given all their supplies to the advancing tank forces of Patton on their southern wing, which then might have crossed the Rhine and penetrated into southern Germany.

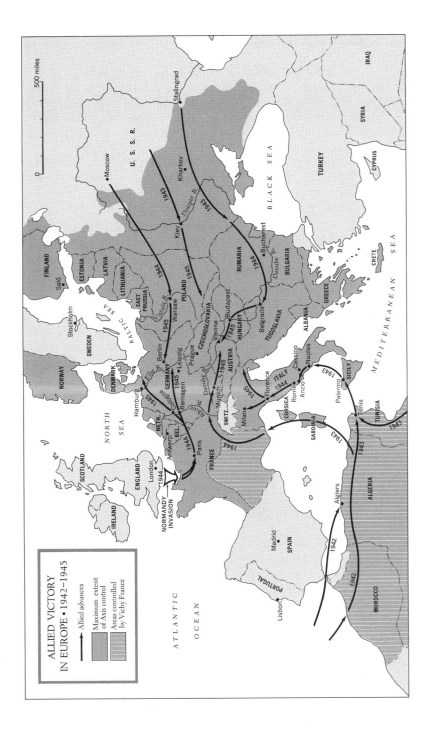

ALLIED VICTORY
IN EUROPE • 1942–1945

→ Allied advances

Maximum extent
of Axis control

Areas controlled
by Vichy France

500 miles

IRAQ

SYRIA

CYPRUS

TURKEY

BLACK SEA

Stalingrad

Kharkov

Moscow

U. S. S. R.

1943

Dnieper R.

1943

Kiev

FINLAND

Saló

ESTONIA

LATVIA

LITHUANIA

EAST
PRUSSIA

1944

BALTIC SEA

Stockholm

SWEDEN

NORWAY

DENMARK

Hamburg

1945

Berlin

1945

Elbe

Leipzig

Prague

Warsaw

POLAND

1945

CZECHOSLOVAKIA

Vistula R.

Vienna

1945

Budapest

HUNGARY

AUSTRIA

Danube

1945

Munich

Rhine

Milan

SWITZ.

1944

Florence

1944

Rome

Cassino

Anzio

Naples

ITALY

CORSICA

SARDINIA

1943

Palermo

SICILY

1943

Tunis

TUNISIA

1943

Belgrade

YUGOSLAVIA

RUMANIA

Bucharest

Danube

1944

BULGARIA

ALBANIA

GREECE

CRETE

MEDITERRANEAN SEA

Cologne

Remagen

GERMANY

1945

NETH.

Antwerp

BEL.

1944

Paris

FRANCE

NORMANDY
INVASION

1944

London

ENGLAND

SCOTLAND

IRELAND

NORTH
SEA

ATLANTIC
OCEAN

SPAIN

Madrid

PORTUGAL

Lisbon

Algiers

ALGERIA

1942

1942

MOROCCO

As it was, a further campaign in 1945 was needed. Before the Allies could resume their advance in the west, Hitler ordered a last German offensive, with troops and tanks brought together from all parts of the front. In December, 1944, the Germans attempted to break through the center of the American-British line in the Ardennes. This last German offensive was so secretly prepared that even Ultra had given no indication to the allies of what was coming. On the first two days of their attack the Germans advanced quickly and inflicted heavy losses upon the Americans. Moreover, the initial German success shook Anglo-American morale because it seemed to demonstrate the illusory nature of the assumption that the war was almost over; the alliance with Russia rose in value. But after moving forward two days the Germans were halted; the western allies were able to regain the initiative, and in two weeks of fighting the German armies were pushed back to the line from which they had started. German losses in men and particularly in tanks were so severe that probably the effect of the "Battle of the Bulge" was to shorten the war. To relieve the pressure on the Allies on the western front, the Russians resumed the offensive in Poland early in January, and by the end of February they had driven the Germans out of Poland and were within fifty miles of Berlin. The British and American forces were able to mount an offensive in February, and on March 8 the American First Army crossed the Rhine at Remagen, south of Bonn. While the Germans were still fighting desperately in the east, the Allies in the west were mainly conducting mopping-up operations. On April 26 Russian and Allied forces met at the Elbe River. Three days later the German troops in Italy surrendered. On April 30, with Russian troops converging on Berlin from all sides, Hitler committed suicide in his bunker in the center of the city. With Hitler's death, German resistance ended. The German military commanders surrendered unconditionally on May 7 in Rheims to Eisenhower and one day later in Berlin to Zhukov, the Russian conqueror of Berlin.

The complete defeat of the German military forces after their series of stunning victories has raised many questions about the nature of Hitler's military talents and leadership. German generals, anxious to maintain the prestige of the German general staff, have claimed for themselves the credit for all the successes, while putting the blame for the defeats on Hitler. Their explanation is too simple. Hitler rightly emphasized, contrary to traditional military thought, the importance of tanks and airplanes in modern warfare. He made certain that due attention was given to the construction of these weapons and to training in their use. Unlike many of his generals, Hitler was aware of the daring ways in which these new weapons could be employed, and he took an active part in the planning of the successful Norwegian and French campaigns of 1940, which showed the possibilities of the modern *Blitzkrieg*. And Hitler's strategic judgment was

A Russian soldier raises the Soviet flag on the Reichstag after the conquest of Berlin, May, 1945.

not much worse than that of his generals. He was undoubtedly right when, against their advice, he insisted on defending an advanced front line in Russia during the winter of 1941–1942; retreat would have brought certain disaster. But Hitler lacked technical training and the patience for logistic details; he was inclined to plan and order operations without taking such factors as supplies and communications fully into account. He relied on his intuition, particularly after the early successes of the German army had confirmed his own and his followers' faith in his supreme military talents. His intuition, however, played him false at two critical moments: in 1940, when he refused to use his tanks against the encircled British army at Dunkirk; and in 1944, when he believed that the invasion in Normandy was a feint and reserves had to be kept back to repulse a landing elsewhere. But there were other signs of deterioration in Hitler's military leadership during the last three years of the war. Confident of his intuition and unable to grasp fully the technical difficulties involved in fighting in Russia or in the desert, he regarded each reverse as the fault of cowardly or treasonous subordinates; he denied his generals any freedom of action and reserved all decisions, even at the local level, for himself. By prohibiting withdrawals he sacrificed troops which could have been saved. He lived shut off in his headquarters, avoiding all encounters which might deter him from indulging in his strategic daydreams. Because he seldom visited the front and the bombed German cities, he lost contact with the crude reality of totalitarian war. In the final months he gave orders to armies which did not exist or existed only on paper. It seems that not until April 22, when he was informed of the failure of S.S. troops to attack the Russians, did he realize the hopelessness of the situation and decide to stay in Berlin to the end.

One of the last scraps of news Hitler received was of the end of his fellow dictator, Mussolini, on April 28. When the German army in Italy surrendered, Mussolini and his mistress had tried to escape to Switzerland, but at Lake Como, near the Swiss border, Italian resistance fighters caught and shot them. Then their bodies were brought to Milan, and hung head downward in the Piazza Loreto. The news of Mussolini's death confirmed Hitler in his decision to commit suicide. At this last moment he married his mistress, Eva Braun, and then dictated a long verbose testament which repeated the usual accusations against "international Jewry"; having poisoned his favorite dog so that it would not have to live with another master, he shot himself and together with Eva Braun, who had taken poison, was burned. The facts of Hitler's melodramatic end are well proven.

The bodies of Mussolini (*third from left*) and his mistress Clara Petacci (*third from right*), placed on show in the Piazza Loreto in Milan, where in August, 1944, Italian hostages had been shot by German military orders.

The Fall of Japan

The German surrender made it possible for the British and Americans to concentrate their final effort on the Far East. In May, 1945, when the war in Europe ended, Japan found itself in roughly the same position in which Germany had been five months before; the initiative was in the hands of the allies. By the beginning of May, just before the monsoon season would have forced a halt in military operations, British, Indian, and Chinese troops under the command of Lord Louis Mountbatten, reconquered Burma in a difficult and risky operation; most of the supplies had to be brought in by air, and more than 200,000 engineers and laborers were employed in building the airfields and roads needed to maintain the impetus of the advance.

A similar success was registered by the Americans in the Philippines. Their operations to recover these islands had started in October, 1944. In a brilliant strategic stroke the Americans passed up the most southern Philippine island, Mindanao and began their offensive with an operation against the central Philippine island of Leyte. The landing there on October 20 was made possible by a naval victory in Leyte Gulf, which severely crippled the Japanese air force and eliminated the Japanese fleet as a factor of military importance. The battle was of great significance for naval history, demonstrating that the time had passed when victory at sea could be decided by encounters among heavy battleships. At Leyte Gulf aircraft carriers, airplanes, destroyers, and torpedo boats were the chief instruments of destruction. The defeat of their navy prevented the Japanese from getting supplies to their troops in the Philippines, and the American forces under General Douglas MacArthur (1880–1964) proceeded without setback to victory in the islands.

Having gained control of the Philippines, the Americans could advance to Iwo Jima and Okinawa, islands closer to Japan, which might serve as bases for a direct attack on the Japanese mainland. Well aware of the strategic importance of these two islands, which formed their homeland's outer line of defense, the Japanese resisted tenaciously, and the fighting was sharp and bloody. However, in the middle of March, Iwo Jima was conquered, and on May 21, two weeks after the surrender of Germany, Sugar Loaf Hill, the key to the Japanese position on Okinawa, was taken.

Japan was now subjected to continuous intensive bombing by American planes. The loss of shipping resulting from these air attacks was fatal to the Japanese war effort, for Japan was dependent on imported coal, oil, and food. Recognizing that their situation was hopeless, the Japanese were ready to surrender; their decision was accelerated on August 6 and 8 by the dropping of two atomic bombs, one on Hiroshima and one on Nagasaki, which burned out more than half of these cities, killed 130,000 people, and injured an equal number. Japan accepted the Allied terms of surrender on August 14. On September 2, 1945, the Second World War officially came to an end on the deck of the battleship *Missouri* in Tokyo Bay, as the Japanese signed the articles of surrender in the presence of General MacArthur.

The decision to drop the atomic bomb aroused a dispute which is still going on. Scientists had counseled against its use because of its terrifying destructive power. An initial explosion of the bomb on a deserted island, which would have demonstrated its efficacy to the Japanese, would have been more in line with American ideas about morality and law in international relations. Yet, when the decision was made American leaders were not aware of how near Japan was to surrender, and believed that heavy fighting was still ahead. It is perhaps instructive that the last military action in the Second World War demonstrated that, as devastating as the war had been, the limits of destruction which modern technology could achieve had not yet been reached.

PART III

A "NEW" EUROPE

CHAPTER 11

Postwar Uncertainties

FROM WARTIME COOPERATION TO CONFLICTS OVER THE PEACE SETTLEMENT

Europe at the End of Hostilities

The most visible imprint left by the Second World War was physical destruction. Except for the university towns of Oxford, Cambridge, and Heidelberg, which out of consideration for their historic value had been left intact, all the larger towns of England and Germany had suffered extensive damage, with many areas, particularly in their centers, completely razed. Warsaw, Vienna, Budapest, Rotterdam were in ruins. In France most of the harbors along the channel coast had been hit severely.

In contrast, the European countryside, except where it had been the site of military operations, was untouched. But communications between rural and urban areas had been severed, and the various parts of a country existed almost in isolation. Roads, bridges, and railroad lines had been demolished or damaged. Locomotives and railroad equipment had been broken or stalled at the military fronts or had so deteriorated that they were almost unusable. The factories which produced the equipment needed for reconstruction had been wrecked, and manpower was not immediately available. Roads were clogged with people trying either to return to their own countries or to find new homes. To those who saw the European continent in the spring and early summer of 1945 it seemed incredible that within a few years life might again become normal.

The Germans had been adequately fed during most of the war, but they had been supplied at the expense of the Nazi-occupied countries. Hence, in most of Europe people were near starvation and their capacity for work was small. The inhabitants of the Nazi-occupied countries, having served as forced laborers, were dispersed in labor camps all over Europe. Civilians who had been imprisoned and tortured because of participation in the resistance or because they had been held as hostages, came back from

De Gaulle marching through the Arc de Triomphe in Paris after the German retreat. *Left of De Gaulle, in the center of the picture is Georges Bidault, influential French politician of the 1950's.*

their prison camps. A reporter described the arrival of a train with such women prisoners in Paris: "All the women looked alike; their faces were gray-green, with reddish-brown circles around their eyes, which seemed to see but not to take in. They were dressed like scarecrows, in what had been given them at camp, clothes taken from the dead of all nationalities." [1]

During the war the populations of entire regions had been moved; thus the Nazis had transferred the inhabitants out of parts of Poland and the Ukraine so that Germans could be settled there. At the end of the war an analogous policy was carried out by Hungarians, Yugoslavs, and Czechs who were unwilling to tolerate troublesome German minorities within their borders. In addition, Germans of East Prussia and Silesia, in fear of the approaching Russian armies, fled toward the west.

Impoverishment, scarcity, physical destruction, and social disintegra-

[1] Janet Flanner (Genêt), *Paris Journal: 1944–1965* (New York, 1965), p. 26.

tion were not confined to Germany, Austria, and Italy; all of Europe, not only the defeated countries, was undergoing suffering and privation. The most urgent need was to bring back some order and stability; initially this task fell upon the victors, whose troops were stationed all over Europe, since occupation of the defeated countries required secure lines of communication. Only the victors—mainly the Americans—could supply food and the basic resources needed for rebuilding roads and houses. It was in the victors' own interest to restore tolerable conditions of life; the morale and discipline of the occupying troops would suffer if they were surrounded by a starving, desperate population. But economic help could not be separated from the reorganization of an administrative apparatus, and this in turn was clearly tied to the reestablishment of some political order and authority. In most of the liberated countries the political situation was tense, almost revolutionary. The leading politicians of the prewar era, who had withdrawn or gone into exile during the period of Nazi rule, came forward in the expectation that they would again play a leading role. Their aim was restoration of the prewar situation in their respective states. But quite new ideas had been developed in the resistance movements, which envisaged a united Europe and a society in which the powers of big business would be curtailed and opportunities would be more equally distributed. Thus, the returning politicians were confronted by new leaders who had come to prominence through their activities in the resistance movements and now wanted social and political changes which would weaken the influence of the previously ruling circles. Because of the omnipresence of their military forces, it was inevitable that the victors would exert a certain amount of political influence even in areas over which they had less than complete control. All over Europe the Americans, the British, and the Russians became involved in the revival of political and social life.

Would it be possible to maintain unity among the victorious powers in peacetime and undertake the reorganization and rebuilding of Europe as a common enterprise?

Wartime Preparations for Postwar Europe

During the war a somewhat idealized picture of one's companions-in-arms had been constructed. Probably the United States and Great Britain had emphasized the heroism of the Russian soldiers and the steadfastness of the Russian leadership more than the Soviets, who had praised the virtues of their Western allies intermingled with severe reproaches. But behind the picture painted in wartime there remained the image formed in previous decades. For the Americans Russia remained the country of Communism and the protagonist of world revolution. For the Russians the United States and Great Britain, but chiefly the United States, were the prototypes of capitalism and the advocates of Russian encirclement. It must be added that on both sides the notions about the nature of the other country were hardly based on concrete knowledge. The Russians certainly had no clear idea about the working of the American Constitution and the limitations on the power of the American president; the Americans —partly because even in wartime the Soviets had prevented foreigners' access to information and severely limited their travel within Russia—had no concrete notion of the staggering losses in manpower and industrial installations which Russia had suffered, and probably overestimated Russian strength.

The leaders of the various allied countries were certainly aware of the difficulties of cooperation among powers so differently constituted, and expected that fundamental divergences might emerge in discussions about the organization of postwar Europe. As long as the war against the Nazis was being fought, the appearance of tensions and conflict was undesirable, and wartime conferences among the Big Three—Churchill, Stalin, and Roosevelt—at Teheran and Yalta were chiefly concerned with plans of military strategy. The issue of a peace settlement had been agreed upon only in very general terms. Russian agreement to the foundation of a United Nations Organization was taken as a sign, particularly in the American delegation, of Soviet willingness to cooperate in the postwar era. It was accepted that Russian national security required friendly governments along Russia's western borders; in this context an expansion of Russian territory towards the West into Poland was envisaged, while Poland was to receive compensation from German territory. The main principle on which the German settlement was to be based was "to ensure that Germany would never again be able to disturb the peace of the world." Hence, the powers agreed that leading Nazis were to be punished and Germany was to be demilitarized. The question of reparations created great difficulties at Yalta. The Russians were firmly determined to get compensation by the Germans for the immense damages they had suffered. The British were adamantly opposed to reparations. Roosevelt finally agreed to a figure of $20 billion of which one-half would go to the Russians, but in order to avoid the economic disorder and disruption which occurred after the First World War, reparations would be made in goods, production and equipment, not gold. This would have to be arranged by a central administration—the assumption being that Gemany would remain united.

There was one concrete question about which agreement was reached during wartime: the question of occupation. In general the armies of Russia and the western powers occupied those areas into which they had advanced, but in Germany and in Austria specified zones were assigned to each of them. Thus, at the end of the war the following picture emerged.

Russian troops were stationed in the Balkans, with the exception of

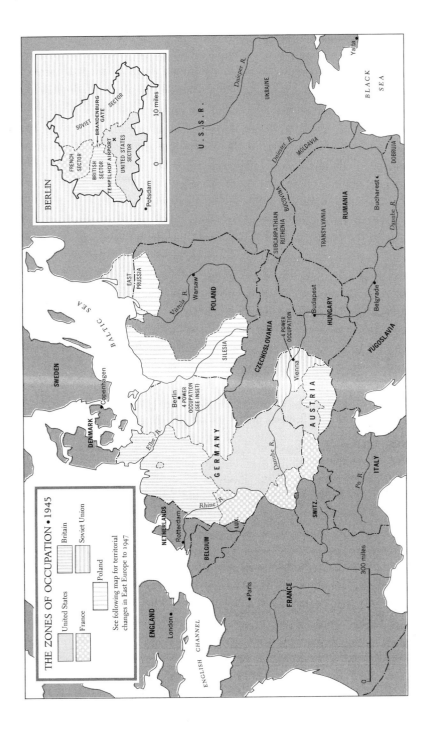

THE ZONES OF OCCUPATION • 1945

United States
France

Britain
Soviet Union

Poland

See following map for territorial
changes in East Europe to 1947

BERLIN

SOVIET SECTOR

BRANDENBURG GATE

FRENCH SECTOR

BRITISH SECTOR

TEMPELHOF AIRPORT

UNITED STATES SECTOR

0   10 miles

• Potsdam

ENGLAND

London •

ENGLISH CHANNEL

NETHERLANDS

Rotterdam •

BELGIUM

Lux.

FRANCE

• Paris

Rhine R.

GERMANY

Elbe R.

Berlin
4 POWER
OCCUPATION
(SEE INSET)

DENMARK

Copenhagen •

SWEDEN

BALTIC SEA

EAST PRUSSIA

SILESIA

POLAND

Vistula R.

Warsaw •

CZECHOSLOVAKIA

SUBCARPATHIAN RUTHENIA

Danube R.

AUSTRIA

Vienna •

4 POWER
OCCUPATION

Budapest •

HUNGARY

SWITZ.

Po R.

ITALY

YUGOSLAVIA

Belgrade •

BUCOVINA

MOLDAVIA

TRANSYLVANIA

RUMANIA

Bucharest •

Danube R.

DOBRUJA

U. S. S. R.

UKRAINE

Dnieper R.

Dniester R.

Yalta •

BLACK SEA

0   300 miles

Greece and Yugoslavia, where the partisans, under Tito, had succeeded in driving out the Germans without any Russian military support. The Russians also occupied Poland, Czechoslovakia, and an eastern section of Austria; in Germany American troops had advanced to the Elbe, but were withdrawn in accordance with an agreement to give the Russians an occupation zone that extended beyond the Elbe into central Germany, including Thuringia. The western parts of Austria were divided into three zones—American, British, and French—and the same was done with the non-Russian occupied area of Germany. The American zone in Germany was the largest of the three; and it had about 17 million inhabitants. The British zone was smaller but had 5 million more people because it included the densely populated Ruhr area. The French zone was the smallest in size and population (5 million). The line drawn between the Russian zone, on the one hand, and the three zones of the western powers, on the other, has remained the boundary which today separates East Germany, the German Democratic Republic, from West Germany, the Federal Republic of Germany. But when the zones were established no permanent political division of Germany was foreseen. A sign of this was that Berlin, the German capital, was intended to be occupied and administered by the United States, Britain, France, and Russia in common.

It is evident that the issues over which agreement had been reached during the war—basic principles and division of occupation zones—were either so general or so technical that all practical questions were left open. They were to be decided at a postwar conference of the Big Three in Potsdam.

In the last months of the war some of the difficulties which the Big Three would encounter had emerged, and it had become clear that the political composition of the governments in the areas of eastern Europe which the Russians had occupied would form a stumbling block. The establishment of a government in liberated Poland became the object of a sharp dispute in the early months of 1945. There were two Polish governments in exile, a Communist one in Russia and another in London, composed of leaders of prewar Poland. Both governments had organized resistance groups and had frequently clashed. After the Russians had occupied Poland, they established the Polish Communist group in power and prevented the return of the Poles from England. In Britain and the United States this action raised doubts whether the Russians were willing to permit democratic systems in the liberated countries under their control. Confronted by this issue immediately upon his becoming president, Truman reacted sharply: without warning he suddenly ended Lend-Lease, and the Russian application for a reconstruction loan was intentionally "mislaid" in the Department of State. This particular crisis was overcome when Stalin conceded that a few moderate Poles should be admitted to the Polish government. The Big Three then could meet in Potsdam, in Germany, throughout the second half of July, 1945.

The Potsdam Conference

The fact that the meeting took place in Potsdam emphasized the equality in status among the three powers. If the conference had taken place in the United States, in Great Britain, or in the Soviet Union, this might have implied superiority of the power which acted as host. Thus Berlin—about which it had been agreed that it should be ruled by the United States, Great Britain, and Russia in common—was a natural choice. However, air attacks, and at the end fighting, had wreaked such destruction in the city that it seemed simpler to go into the suburbs and accommodate the statesmen and the accompanying diplomats and military personnel among the palaces and villas around the lakes of Potsdam. But undoubtedly a consideration of historical nature also played its part. It seemed appropriate to seal the end of Prussianism and militarism at Potsdam which, since the eighteenth century, counted as the embodiment of the Prussian militaristic spirit.

When the Big Three assembled in Potsdam, they approached the settlement with widely different ideas. Churchill and Stalin were inclined to divide the globe into spheres of influence; insofar as they had concrete areas in mind, such a division would have meant that Russia would have had eastern Europe and the Balkans in its sphere, Great Britain the Mediterranean with Italy and Greece. In the American delegation such spheres of influence were unpopular because the term smacked of *ancien*

After the war. *The Krupp works in ruins.*

The Potsdam Conference. *Churchill, a cigar in his mouth, is seated in the back to the left; Stalin is at the right; Truman is seated with his back to the camera.*

regime diplomacy. The view about the postwar world held by the great majority of the American people and strongly represented in the American delegation was less power-conscious, more idealistic. It was that the spread of democracy an self-determination all over the world; the establishment of basic human rights and freedom of economic exchange underpinned by international cooperation; the easing of inequalities in the economic and social sphere would be the best, almost the only possible guarantees of peace. Although Roosevelt himself was tinged by this idealistic globalism to which their eighteenth-century tradition made the American people strongly inclined, he had also been very much aware of the importance of the power factor and had made no commitment which would have made adjustment to a settlement based on the principle of balance of power impossible. His successor, Harry S. Truman, had not been clearly informed about the diplomatic negotiations and approached his task with the view generally held by the American public: an idealistic, one-world view. Actually, at Potsdam the weight of the United States and Soviet Russia was greater than that of an exhausted and financially weak Great Britain. Moreover, during the conference elections took place in Great Britain, and Churchill, who was in Potsdam at the opening of the conference, and who, despite the losses of the war was firmly decided to maintain Britain's imperial position, was replaced as prime minister and British representative by the leader of the Labor party, Clement Attlee, who was convinced that only a reorganization of political, economic, and social institutions could secure a continued influential position in the world for Britain. Thus, the main contrast at the conference was that between Truman, representing an idealistic, global view, and Stalin, aiming at concrete gains and hardly enamored of a spread of parliamentary democracy.

The chairman of the Potsdam Conference was Truman. Truman's conduct of his chairmanship has been praised because of his decisiveness, but there is some question whether this attitude did not arise from a certain insecurity, and whether Truman's eagerness for quick results had the consequence that the really knotty problems were not thoroughly discussed and solved. Truman had some reason in rushing the conference because, while at Potsdam, he received news that the atomic bomb had been successfully tested. In the American delegation the view was widely held that when American possession of the atomic bomb became generally known, many of the questions now under dispute would be decided in ways the United States wanted. Briefly, it was to American advantage to establish methods of procedure but to postpone decisions of substance. At the conference Truman informed Stalin of the existence of the atomic bomb, but the off-hand manner in which he offered this information might have increased Stalin's distrust of the United States, since it could be taken to indicate that the United States wanted to keep possession of this weapon for itself.

The Potsdam Conference ended with a communique which seemed to indicate success, but the agreements arrived at referred to principles and methods rather than substance. The one concrete result, Russian assurance to enter the war against Japan, was really futile since the atomic bomb eliminated the need for Russian support against Japan. There was some agreement over the reparations question: the Russians would take their reparations out of their zone and would receive 25 per cent of the industrial equipment removed from western zones; 15 per cent would be counted as payment for food brought from the agricultural eastern zone to the industrial western zone. These provisions were rather in contradiction to the principle of treating Germany as an economic unit, which was again proclaimed to be fundamental. It was also stated that peace treaties should be prepared with "recognized democratic governments" of former enemy states—i.e., Italy, Rumania, Bulgaria, Hungary. But since one of the disputed issues was whether the governments Russia had established in the eastern countries were democratic governments, this formulation concealed the continued existence of divergences. There was agreement about the mechanism to which the solution of these questions ought to be entrusted. A Council of Foreign Ministers, in which France and China should also be members, would handle the peace treaties and general political questions. A Four-Power Allied Control Council, composed of the United States, Great Britain, Russia, and France would handle the German questions.

There were some areas in which final decisions were made and successfully carried out. One was the punishment of major war crimes. A trial before an international tribunal at Nuremberg between November, 1945, and October, 1946, resulted in the death sentence, and subsequent hanging, of ten Nazi leaders, among them Foreign Minister Joachim von Ribbentrop, Hitler's military advisers Wilhelm Keitel and Alfred Jodl, Minister of the Interior Wilhelm Frick, and the Jew-baiter Julius Streicher. Göring committed suicide in prison. Himmler had killed himself after capture.

Also, the issue which traditionally formed a main center of dispute in peace negotiations—the question of the drawing of new boundaries—caused no great difficulties. Readjustments were relatively minor and the victorious powers took care that in the areas which they controlled serious conflicts did not arise. In the east Rumania had to cede northern Bucovina and Bessarabia to Soviet Russia, and part of Dobruja to Bulgaria. But Rumania received northern Transylvania from Hungary, which also had

The Nuremberg Trials. *Among the Nazi leaders in the front row are Göring (at the extreme left), Hess (second from left), Ribbentrop (third from left), and Schacht (at the extreme right). In the second row Papen is third from left and Speer third from right.*

to relinquish some land to Czechoslovakia. Finland lost to Russia the territory of Petsamo in the north and the Karelian Isthmus in the south. Russia kept the Baltic states and extended its dominance southward along the Baltic Sea by annexing the northern part of what had been East Prussia; Poland recognized the frontiers which Russia had established in 1939 as a result of the Nazi-Soviet pact, but was promised extension of its frontiers in the west as compensation.

The boundary changes in the areas controlled by the United States and Great Britain were still less significant. It was recognized that the former frontiers of France had to be restored, and after some negotiations it was agreed that the Saar region would be economically attached to France so that France would have priority in the use of Saar coal; the territory itself would remain under German sovereignty. Slight frontier revisions in favor of Belgium and Denmark were arranged at the expense of Germany. Italy ceded some border territory to France, lost all of its overseas possessions, and returned the Dodecanese islands to Greece.

When the two councils established for the conclusion of peace treaties and for the problems arising out of the occupation of Germany began their work they were immediately faced by two issues that eventually would cause the wartime alliances to break down: the stumbling block in the negotiations about the conclusion of the peace treaties was the composition of the governments of countries under Russian occupation; the one relating to the occupation of Germany was the question of German reparations.

THE UNITED STATES AND SOVIET RUSSIA
CONFRONT EACH OTHER IN EUROPE

The Problem of the Peace Treaties and the
Development of East-West Conflict

Ostensibly the efforts of the Council of Foreign Ministers to draft peace treaties were successful. After negotiations extending over almost one and a half years, peace treaties with Italy, Bulgaria, Rumania, Hungary, and Finland were signed in February, 1947. But the negotiations— conducted in a number of meetings of the Council of Foreign Ministers in London, Moscow, and Paris—had revealed the Russian unwillingness to accept the formula proposed by the United States that these states ought to have a "government broadly representative of all democratic elements in the population and pledged to the earliest possible establishment through free elections of a government responsive to the will of the people." The discussions were sharp and breakdowns sometimes seemed unavoidable. By the end some compromise was obtained by allowing some representatives of non-Communist parties into the govern-

Winston Churchill delivers a famous address. *On March 5, 1946, in a speech delivered in Fulton, Missouri, the former British prime minister warned that an "iron curtain" separated eastern Europe from the rest of the continent. The phrase "iron curtain" was to be often repeated during the Cold War years.*

ments of the eastern states. But this was only a token, avoiding the impression of capitulation to Russian demands rather than a real loosening of the Communist grasp over this area. The result of these meetings was a deterioration of the political atmosphere. The American delegation was aware that they had failed to open up eastern Europe to western influence: The Russians wanted the area which they controlled to be separated from the west by an "iron curtain"—a term which Churchill had coined in a speech in Fulton, Missouri on March 5, 1946.

In the United States now the conviction grew that the Russian resistance to the demand of allowing truly democratic forms of government in these countries was an indication that after having been saved from defeat the Russians returned to the idea of world revolution and were planning Communist expansion all over Europe. There were a variety of reasons which led American public opinion to conclude that Russia was pursuing an aggressive expansionist policy which might soon provoke another war. The Russians had been highly admired during the war and great hopes had been placed on establishing a new, peaceful world in cooperation with them. The emergence of difficulties and friction had a strongly disillusioning effect. The Russians seemed to have been deceptive. The dictatorial character of their regime and the brutality of Stalinism had been somewhat underplayed during wartime. It came now almost as a revelation that Russia was not a democracy. An incitement of public opinion against Russia to increase the armament budget and to maintain a strong military posture also played a role in producing anti-Soviet feeling.

The interpretation that Russia planned an aggressive policy seemed confirmed by events in several areas. Early in 1947 it had become clear that the Soviet Union was not willing to accept the American plan for the control of atomic energy; it must be admitted that the Russian objections to the plan, which would have secured American monopoly in atomic weapons for a number of years and which called for an international inspection system that the Russians felt encroached on their sovereignty, were not entirely unjustified. But at the time Russian obstructionism was primarily considered as a further indication of their unwillingness to subordinate themselves to an international order. At the same time it was believed that Russia was expanding by aggressive action in the Balkans. In Greece the government seemed unable to defeat Communist guerillas operating in the north of the country. The guerillas were able to continue the fight because of the support they received from their Communist neighbors in the north. Great Britain, which had assisted the non-Communist forces in Greece since the war, no longer felt able to do so and the United States decided to take Britain's place. The American government acted in the belief that only by direct participation could they prevent Russian domination over Greece and Turkey. This was the occasion of the announcement of the Truman Doctrine in March, 1947, in which the president stated "that it must be the policy of the United States to support free people who are resisting attempted subjugation by armed minorities or by outside pressures." The Truman Doctrine became crucial in European politics during the following decade.

In the American view it was necessary to build a dam against further Russian advances. It was assumed that the Russians had been encouraged to embark on their aggressive and expansionist course because they believed it would be easy to establish Communist regimes all over Europe: economic misery had created great dissatisfaction and Communist parties of great strength had been formed. In France and Italy elections had taken place soon after the war and, within a somewhat changed and modernized constitutional framework—Italy, for instance, had become a

Scene from the Greek civil war. *Mules carrying munitions into the mountains.*

republic—parliamentary regimes were functioning again. The great role which the Communists had played in the resistance movements in both countries had given them a strong popular appeal. They had become mass parties whose leaders participated in the government. The American leaders decided that preventing Europe from falling into Russian hands required measures of two kinds: in the political field and in the economic field. In the spring of 1947, under discreet prompting by the United States, the Communist ministers were removed from the governments in France and Italy. The United States had indicated that the elimination of the Communists from the governments would smooth the way for economic help from the United States and indeed, on June 5, 1947, General George Marshall, then American secretary of state, announced that if the European nations would work out a comprehensive plan describing the requirements for their economic recovery, the United States would respond with loans and technical assistance. Ten months later, in April, 1948, the Marshall Plan began to function.

The Problem of German Reparations and the
Break Between Russia and the West

In 1947 American and Russian policy were so much set on a course of confrontation that there was probably little chance for returning to any kind of cooperation. But if there was such a possibility a conflict on German reparations extinguished all such chances. The American government was convinced that attempts to make western Europe secure against Communist penetration or domination could be successful only if Germany could revive economically and if its economic resources could be used for the needs of western Europe. In a foreign ministers conference in Moscow in the spring of 1947, which was meant to prepare the draft for a peace treaty with Germany, the Russians insisted on receiving $10 billion in reparations from current German industrial production. The United States and Great Britain saw in this insistence more than an emphatic bid for compensation for war damages; it appeared to them an attempt to prolong misery and chaos in Germany, also damaging the economic life in western Europe. The Russian reparations policy seemed a clear sign that the Russians were preparing the ground for a spread of Communism all over the west. Thus, the American and British governments did not only refuse the Russian demand but took measures in the later part of 1947 and the early part of 1948 to rebuild the economic life of West Germany and to prepare Germany's participation in the European Recovery Plan. The English and American occupation zones became economically united and one German administration for the two zones was established. Right after the war, only a very limited amount of German industrial production had been allowed, in order to prevent the possibility of future German rearmament; in the summer of 1947 the level was raised to prewar heights. These economic measures were sustained by a currency reform which extended to all three western zones of occupation; the Russians had to respond with a currency reform of their own. Then German political life was revived; local elections had taken place in the various provinces and federal states in all three zones. Obviously the next step was the establishment of a parliament and a government for the whole of West Germany. The Russians could have no illusions that West Germany, which was much more powerful in population and mineral resources than the Russian-occupied East Germany, was being constituted as an independent power and slipping out of their grasp.

This policy aggravated the tension with Soviet Russia. It was clear that it would nullify whatever still remained from the wartime agreements because a condition for German economic revival was the abandonment of reparations. The execution of such a policy against Russian opposition meant the end of four-power control.

The Beginning of the Cold War: The Berlin Blockade
There can be no doubt that most of those who made American policy were seriously convinced that they faced a dangerous threat which might at any time lead to war. But it is now also clear that this was a misconception. The Russians had no serious plans to take over western Europe nor were they able or willing to undertake a war which would involve the United States, and it was erroneous to assume that movements like the guerilla war in Greece, or, later, the attack of North Korea against South Korea, were directed by Moscow and part of a broad political design.

On the other hand it must also be said that the Russians were no less guided by misconceptions about American policy than the Americans about Russian policy. As Zhdanov (1896–1948), one of Stalin's most trusted lieutenants, said about the Truman Doctrine in 1947; "The United States proclaimed a new, frankly predatory and expansionist course. The purpose of this new, frankly expansionist course is to establish the world supremacy of American imperialism." This view of the world situation clearly had its usefulness for Stalin, because it justified continued emphasis on heavy industry and a rigidly disciplined life. Dictatorial measures could be presented as national necessity. This view also hit a responsive chord, however, because it agreed with what the Russians had been told in theoretical writings and had experienced in the first years of the regime. That is, the Russians saw themselves still threatened by the same danger which they had feared throughout the interwar years: a capitalist encirclement aiming at the overthrow of their regime. They were unable to conceive that American interest in truly representative regimes in Poland, Hungary, and Czechoslovakia had no ulterior motive; they believed it would be an attempt to move the jumping-off place from which operations could be launched as close as possible

TERRITORIAL CHANGES IN
EASTERN EUROPE TO 1947

—·—·— 1947 boundaries

——— 1939 boundaries

•••••• Nazi–Soviet boundary, 1939

Territorial changes resulting from
pre- and post-war settlements

0   500 miles

Petsamo
Murmansk
(TO U.S.S.R.)

WHITE
SEA

(TO U.S.S.R.)

GULF OF BOTHNIA

FINLAND

NORWAY

Oslo

Stockholm

SWEDEN

Helsinki

Leningrad

KARELIAN ISTHMUS
(TO U.S.S.R.)

Moscow

NORTH
SEA

DENMARK

Copenhagen

BALTIC SEA

ESTONIA
(TO U.S.S.R.)

LATVIA
(TO U.S.S.R.)

LITHUANIA
(TO U.S.S.R.)

Königsberg
(TO U.S.S.R.)

EAST
PRUSSIA
(TO POLAND)

Danzig
(TO POLAND)

Minsk

Berlin

(TO POLAND)

POLAND

Warsaw

EASTERN
POLAND
(TO U.S.S.R.)

U.S.S.R.

GERMANY

Prague

Cracow

Kiev

CZECHOSLOVAKIA

NORTHERN
BUCOVINA
(TO U.S.S.R.)

Vienna

Bratislava

(TO U.S.S.R.)

SWITZ.

AUSTRIA

Budapest

SUBCARPATHIAN
RUTHENIA
(TO U.S.S.R.)

BESSARABIA

Odessa

HUNGARY

RUMANIA

Trieste
(FREE CITY)

(TO YUGOSLAVIA)

Bucharest

BLACK
SEA

ITALY

ADRIATIC SEA

Belgrade

YUGOSLAVIA

DOBRUJA
(TO BULGARIA)

BULGARIA

Rome

Tirana

ALBANIA

Sofia

GREECE

Istanbul

TURKEY

to the center of Russia. On the basis of this misconception of American intentions they acted in these countries with a ruthlessness which seemed only to confirm the American view of the dangerous character of Russian policy. When Communists were eliminated from the governments in Italy and France, the Russians forced leaders of non-Communist parties in the eastern satellites out of the government. Some were also put on trial with trumped-up charges of treason. Maniu, the revered leader of the Rumanian Peasant party, ended his life in solitary confinement. Purges and trials were accompanied by loud accusations against the aggressive intentions of the capitalist world and further poisoned the atmosphere. The last and also the most brutal coup to eliminate possible political opposition took place in Czechoslovakia in February, 1948. By clever use of an opportunity given by a government crisis the Communists established themselves as sole rulers. This event was the more shocking because during the interwar years Czechoslovakia had stood out as a democratic western-oriented country, and its leaders had enjoyed a high reputation in the west. Now Beneš, the president, resigned and the foreign minister, Jan Masaryk (1886–1948), the son of the founder of the state, died in circumstances which were suspicious enough to raise serious doubts about the official explanation of suicide.

These purges coincided with the reconstruction of an international Communist organization in September, 1947. The Communist International had been dissolved during the war as a concession to the western allies. The new organization was called Cominform because its center was an "information bureau" charged "with the organization of interchange of experience and, if need be, coordination of the activities of the Communist parties on the basis of mutual agreement." The latter task soon became paramount. The Cominform determined the line which the various Communist parties were to follow. One of the first developments to show the Communist powers in action as a bloc was their decline of the invitation to participate in the deliberations about Secretary Marshall's suggestion to work out a plan for European recovery; they instead formed a counterpart to the western economic recovery program in a Council for Mutual Economic Assistance.

While the Russian goal of creating a wide glacis on their western front as protection against attacks by enemies was clear, their policy concerning Germany was more complex. Considering the thorough devastation of Russian industrial installations in the war there is no reason to doubt that the Russians were passionately concerned with receiving reparations from Germany. Such demands were presented to their allies by the Russians from the earliest wartime conferences on and they placed great value on Roosevelt's agreement with the figure of ten billion dollars for Russia. But it must also be said that the Russians—with some justification as two world wars had shown—had great fears of Germany and believed that a recovered and remilitarized Germany would be the natural spearhead of an attack against Russia. The Russians were undoubtedly aware that reparations from current production would postpone German economic recovery and also retain for Russia a voice in the handling of German affairs. They saw, therefore, in America's plan for putting Germany on its feet again, proof of American aggressive plans against Russia, and resented the creation of a western Germany, the development of which they were unable to influence.

The Russians now decided on a step, the purposes of which are even now unclear. On July 24, 1948, they halted all rail and road traffic between Berlin and the West. While all other cooperation in German affairs between Russia and the western powers had broken down, the occupation and administration of Berlin was still under the common control of the United States, Great Britain, France, and Russia. There are two possibilities for explaining what the Russians intended by their move: they might have wanted to lock up their zone by driving the United States, Great Britain, and France out of Berlin; or they might have wanted to provoke a crisis in order to achieve new negotiations about a German settlement —the latter interpretation now seems more likely. The fact is that the Berlin Blockade terminated any lingering notions of postwar cooperation: the Cold War had begun.

What the Russians seemed to have been sure of is that the western powers, particularly the British and French, would be most reluctant to take measures which would invoke a risk of war; they clearly believed that the West would have to agree to negotiations. Actually, war was a greater possibility than the Russians thought. General Lucius Clay, who headed the American occupation in Germany, suggested that a train containing American troops should force its way into Berlin with orders to shoot if they encountered resistance. This proposal was rejected but the Russians were wrong in their conviction that if no military clash occurred, the blockade would force Berlin into starvation and surrender. They overlooked the possibility that the two million people of West Berlin might be supplied by air. But that is what happened. An airlift broke the blockade, negotiations were started, and on May 12, 1949, the Russians removed the restrictions on communications between western Germany and West Berlin.

Berlin was to remain a ticklish spot. Western and eastern Berlin had entirely separate administrations, and in order to make economic life in western Berlin possible, it received financial support from western Germany. West Berlin became a western showcase in Russian-dominated eastern Europe. In contrast to the rather bleak East Berlin, life in West Berlin appeared rather splendid.

The blockade was over but the Cold War continued. The importance

The Berlin Blockade. *An American airplane arrives with supplies.*

of Europe as a central theater of the Cold War soon waned. The Far East became the main theater of this strange war.

EXTENSION OF THE COLD WAR TO THE FAR EAST
Asia at the End of Hostilities

The Second World War had been a global war. It is somewhat misleading, therefore, to focus solely on European issues in discussing the problems of the postwar world. The tensions which arose in Europe were closely connected with the developments which had taken place in the Far East and the Cold War was as much an event in the Far East as in Europe.

When Japan surrendered on August 14, 1945, friction between Russia and the West in this area seemed unlikely. During the war Russia had been anxious to concentrate all its military efforts upon Germany and had carefully avoided embroilment with Japan. However, at the Yalta conference, Stalin had promised that his nation would enter the war against Japan after the termination of military operations in Europe. Accordingly, Russian forces were assembled near the Manchurian border and Russia declared war on Japan on August 8. Since the Japanese military situation had become hopeless by then, and the atomic bomb dropped on Hiroshima on August 6 had broken the Japanese will to resist, Russia's entry into the war played no part in the Japanese defeat. The procedures followed by the Americans in negotiating and accepting the Japanese surrender showed clearly that they regarded the settlement with Japan exclusively as their own. And during the following years, the United States remained the only outside force to exert control and influence over the reconstruction of Japan as a political power.

But Japanese troops had penetrated far into China and had occupied most of southeast Asia. The Japanese surrender had wide repercussions in these regions. In these areas not only the United States but also China and Great Britain had fought, and America's allies were unprepared for Japan's sudden collapse.

The size of the area, the number of inhabitants, the variety of peoples, made the handling of the problems of southeast Asia a complex task. These inherent difficulties were aggravated by revolutionary ferment resulting from Japanese rule and occupation.

Japan had treated the nations of southeast Asia in various ways. For instance, Thailand had been considered an ally, and had been permitted to enlarge its frontiers at the expense of its neighbor, French Indochina. In other areas, in Malaya and in the islands of Indonesia—Java, Sumatra, Borneo, Celebes—the Japanese had ruled through military administrations. In China, in the Philippines, and in Burma they had established puppet governments. French Indochina was a special case. As long as France was in the Nazi orbit, the French administrators of Indochina had collaborated with Japan. But after the liberation of France, the French turned against Japan and the Japanese established a puppet government.

Japan exploited all these areas brutally. Yet the Japanese occupation had revolutionary and lasting consequences. The Japanese invasion of this area demonstrated that Asian people were able to shake off the yoke of European rulers; nationalism had received a powerful impetus. The attitude of the nationalist leaders of these peoples to the Japanese rule was rather ambiguous. Some regarded the formation of a national government, even if limited in its freedom of action by Japanese power, as a first step toward independence, and were willing to cooperate with the Japanese in setting up the puppet regimes. Others considered Japanese rule to be quite as oppressive as that of the western powers, and organized resistance movements. In the course of these developments indigenous leaders gained a strong hold over the masses. The nationalist leader in Indochina, Ho Chi Minh (1890–1969), fought against the Japanese; in Indonesia, Achmed Sukarno (born 1901) cooperated with the Japanese, but held out against their plans to divide the region into independent units, championing a united Indonesia.

The Retreat from Colonialism

Since the Allied forces in southeast Asia were under British command during the war, the British took charge of the area after hostilities ended. The first task of the British was to organize the surrender of the Japanese forces which were stationed in this area and burdened its economy. The presence of large armies, the disturbances of war, the flight of people from their homes, and the interruption of communications had restricted cultivation of the land, and in many regions people were starving Therefore, a foremost concern of the British authorities was to increase the production of food, particularly rice, and to arrange for its distribution. In attempting to accomplish this task the British were confronted with an unpleasant political dilemma. Undoubtedly cooperation with the indigenous governments and forces would have been most effective. But this would have strengthened the governments which the French and the Dutch, who had formerly been the rulers in these regions and were anxious to resume control, wanted to eliminate. The French and the Dutch were Britain's allies and Britain itself had colonies in southeast Asia. This contradiction between short-range and long-range interests prevented the development of a uniform policy for the entire area. Settlements were difficult to arrive at, and they varied from one region to the other. The Dutch were unable to reinstate themselves and were forced to recognize the independent Republic of Indonesia in 1946. The French reestablished their rule in Indochina, but fighting against them never ceased and after long and costly campaigns, climaxed by the defeat at Dien Bien Phu in 1954, the French withdrew and left three independent states: Laos, Cambodia, and Vietnam. The British returned to Malaya and Singapore and promoted a political evolution through which Malaya became independent but remained part of the British empire. In southeast Asia the Japanese defeat started a process of revolution which has not yet been completed.

The first manifestoes of the Communist International had stated that the liberation of the peoples of Asia and Africa from colonial rule formed an integral part of the Communist fight against capitalism. Thus, the Russians, although not directly involved in the struggle in southeast Asia, clearly favored nationalist movements in this region, and they had close contacts with some of the nationalist leaders. For instance, Ho Chi Minh was trained in Moscow and worked in the Communist movements in Europe before returning to his native Indochina.

Since American foreign policy too had an anticolonial tradition, the rise of nationalist movements in southeast Asia did not necessarily place Russia and America on opposite sides. However, the United States acted in close cooperation with Great Britain and France in Europe, and there was danger, therefore, that the United States would be stamped as an ally of traditional European imperialism, and that because the United States was more powerful, American imperialism would appear as the most sinister force. This actually did happen in China, the nation which presented the most difficult problems of the Asian postwar situation.

A Chain of Open Conflicts
THE STRUGGLE IN CHINA

That China would be a source of conflict between Russia and the United States was not apparent at the end of the war. Here again the most urgent task was to effect the disarmament and withdrawal of the Japanese armies, stationed in the vast regions along the Yangtze and the Yellow rivers. The fact that much time had to be spent arranging the removal of these troops proved to be a disadvantage to the Chinese Nationalist government under Chiang Kai-shek. In the interim period the Communist armies of Mao Tse-tung in the north had the opportunity to expand their power. In August, 1945, Russia had recognized Chiang Kai-shek's regime as the central government of China, so it seemed justifiable to assume that the Russians were anxious to establish cooperation between the Communists in the north and Chiang Kai-shek's government in the south. The United States had a similar aim. The Chiang Kai-shek government had been frequently criticized in the United States for its lack of energy in pursuing the war against the Japanese, and many Americans hoped and believed that cooperation with the Communists would stimulate the Nationalists and provide an impetus to social and agricultural reform which would be highly desirable for China. But protracted negotiations failed to settle the differences between the Nationalist government of Chiang Kai-shek and Mao Tse-tung's Communist forces. Instead, there developed a sharp contest between the two opposing Chinese governments for the control of Manchuria, and in this conflict the Russians decided to back Mao. At the time of the Japanese surrender, the Russians had occupied Manchuria—temporarily, they declared. In the next months, they made no effort to evacuate the area, but in April, 1946, when the struggle over German reparations became critical, they removed their troops from Manchuria very suddenly, and the rapidity of their retreat gave the Chinese Communists the opportunity to move in.

The American government continued its efforts to establish peace in China, but neither of the warring factions really wanted an agreement, because each believed that it could win over the entire country. When General Marshall, who had been sent to China in December, 1945, abandoned his peace efforts in January, 1947, he assigned responsibility for the failure of his mission to both sides: the "dominant group of reactionaries" in Chiang Kai-shek's government and the "dyed in the wool"[2] Communists in the other camp. The final result was an open confrontation and civil war between Chiang Kai-shek's forces, somewhat reluctantly and halfheartedly backed by the United States, and Mao Tse-tung's Communists, supported by Russia.

THE KOREAN WAR

By the beginning of 1949 the victory of the Chinese Communists under Mao Tse-tung was a certainty, and by the end of the year the Nationalist government under Chiang Kai-shek had withdrawn to Formosa (Taiwan). The United States refused to recognize the Communists as the legitimate rulers of China and continued to give recognition and protection to the Nationalist government. The tension between the United States and Communist China became the crucial element in the next dangerous crisis of the Cold War, that of Korea.

After the Second World War the area of Korea north of the thirty-eighth parallel, had been occupied by the Russians, that south of it by the Americans. As in Germany, agreement on a single government for the entire country had been impossible to reach. Eventually, the occupying forces were withdrawn, the Russians leaving a Communist regime in North Korea, the Americans a western-oriented democracy in South Korea. On June 25, 1950, North Korean troops began to invade South Korea, attempting to unify their divided nation. American military leaders had gradually become convinced that a non-Communist South Korea was indispensable for the defense of Japan, and the United States government ordered American troops into South Korea to support the faltering South Korean government. The matter was brought before the United Nations at a time when the Russians were boycotting the Security Council, and a resolution was passed condemning the North Korean aggression. A United Nations Command was set up, headed by General Douglas MacArthur, and although most of the troops were American they were supported by contingents from many other countries. The U.N. military operations were conducted with wavering success. Having succeeded in driving the North Koreans out of the south, the Americans advanced beyond the thirty-eighth parallel, but there they encountered opposition by strong North Korean forces aided by Communist Chinese armies, and were driven back into South Korea. Finally a front along the thirty-eighth parallel was established and armistice negotiations were initiated. In July, 1953, after almost two years of negotiations, an armistice was concluded which ended the war and virtually restored the *status quo ante*: Korea remained divided along the thirty-eighth parallel.

[2] These phrases are from General Marshall's statement on China on February 7, 1947.

THE FRENCH DEFEAT IN INDOCHINA AND THE END OF THE COLD WAR

While the Korean War slowly petered out, another dangerous military clash developed on the southern frontier of China. There, a nationalist and Communist-led movement known as the Viet Minh, under the leadership of Ho Chi-Minh, was fighting the French for greater autonomy in that part of Indochina which, after the separation of Laos and Cambodia, was called Vietnam.

The Viet Minh received recognition and aid from Communist China and Soviet Russia, while France and the puppet regime which it had established were supported by Great Britain and the United States. Modern weapons and bombing from the air were unable to destroy the guerrilla forces fighting in millet fields and rice paddies, and when the French advanced into the north, a part of their forces were cut off and finally forced to surrender at Dien Bien Phu, in May, 1954; ten thousand French soldiers became prisoners. At this point mediation by Russia, the United States, and Great Britain resulted in an armistice; among its terms were provisions for an election to be held in 1956, to unify Vietnam. Until then Vietnam was to be divided along the seventeenth parallel, with the northern half Communist-controlled and the southern half western-oriented. This was not a solution that would last. Tensions smoldered on until the explosion happened, but this was in a different situation. With the agreement on Vietnam the most acute phase of the Cold War had ended.

CHAPTER 12

Reconstruction in Europe: 1950-1956

THE BASIC TASKS OF RECONSTRUCTION

SIMULTANEOUSLY with the struggle between the superpowers, the rebuilding of a political order had begun in the various European countries. Because their revival and continued existence depended on the protection of either the United States or Soviet Russia, these nations could not develop exclusively according to their own inherent tendencies; rather, they had to follow the leadership, and to a certain extent the prescriptions, of Soviet Russia in the East and of the United States in the West. Unavoidably the forms which reconstruction took in the West and in the East were widely different. In the countries in the Soviet sphere—East Germany, Poland, Czechoslovakia, Hungary, Rumania, Bulgaria—the organization of government which existed in the Soviet Union became the model: an executive elected and controlled by the Communist party or its leadership. In the Western bloc no direct imitation of the Constitution of the United States took place but all the states of the Western bloc became parliamentary democracies—a constitutional form considered as the European equivalent of American democracy. Despite these fundamental differences in form and principles the foremost task of reconstruction was the same in all European countries, both of the West and of the East, which meant that frequently they encountered rather similar difficulties.

Of necessity all governmental activities centered on the revival of economic life; thus, economic issues shaped and dominated political reconstruction. This order of priorities was taken for granted in the Eastern bloc, since Marxist philosophy has always viewed the organization of economic life as controlling the political and social order. Of course, the importance of economic prosperity for political stability was also recognized in the non-Marxian world, especially since the economic crisis of 1929, which had opened the door to Nazism and to the catastrophe of the Second World War. Nevertheless, it may be doubted whether before the war concern with the economic situation would have been considered as the almost all-absorbing task of government. By assigning government an active role in economic reconstruction the lines between politics and economics in western-oriented nations became more obfuscated than ever before; governments had not only the right but the duty to play an active role in the reorganization of economic life, and to exert a directing and controlling influence on economics. Of course, in the Western bloc the views to what extent and by what means a government should influence economic life differed; therefore, the measures adopted in the countries of western Europe varied. But it has become a basic assumption in European political life since the Second World War that the main task of a government is the creation of favorable economic conditions; it has a right to intervene in economic affairs. It is no longer possible to write political history without being centrally concerned with economic developments, plans, and measures.

The paramount importance of the economic issue for the reconstruction of Europe encouraged the tendency to enter into plans and actions beyond national boundaries and to organize on supranational regional levels. This approach was strongly supported by the superpowers not only because it seemed more practical and efficient but also because it solidified the bloc under their leadership. Cooperative procedure was also favored by various individual governments because it might make projects possible which went beyond the financial means of an individual state. Such cooperation led, for example, to the establishment of CERN, the European Research Center for High Energy Particle Physics in Northern Italy, and of ESRO, the European Center for Space Research in Paris.

It would be wrong, however, to see at work in these efforts for supranational cooperation and integration only motives of a practical, political, and financial nature. They corresponded to feelings which had developed among the European peoples during the war, to a subtle shift which had taken place in the attitude towards nationalism. During the war a reaction against the strident nationalism embodied in Hitler's doctrine of the superiority of the German race had set in. This did not mean that nationalism was replaced by cosmopolitanism: The individual heroics of a young Yugoslav partisan shouting defiance at German soldiers as they executed him, or of a French resistance leader who took poison in order to avoid betraying his comrades under torture, were certainly inspired by deep national feeling. It would seem, however, that the nationalism which emerged from the Second World War was no longer the nationalism of the early twentieth century, which had been intensely competitive and had placed one's own nation above all others. The nationalism of the Second World War was inspired by the belief that in the nation and through that nation higher, more general eternal values could be realized.

Catholics, Socialists, and Communists were all convinced that their ideas drew strength from being rooted in the requirements of a national existence. The two greatest poets of the French resistance, Louis Aragon and Paul Éluard, were Communists, protagonists of a new social order and devoted internationalists, but in their poems these themes were interwoven with a passionate praise of French life and customs, landscape and history. The manner in which nationalism as a reaction to Hitlerian tyranny had become tied to and permeated by supranational values is reflected in the fact that in the postwar years the political parties which had the widest political appeal were the Catholic party and the Communist party—both wedded to supranational ideologies.

THE CONTEXT OF RECONSTRUCTION:
SCIENCE, TECHNOLOGY, AND ECONOMICS

Notions of European unity or of organization on a regional basis could hardly have been put into practice if, after the Second World War, science and technology had not created conditions which facilitated cooperation and integration.

The impetus military needs had given to scientific and technical developments continued into the period following the war; and it gained in strength and speed. The application of new discoveries and inventions to economic life had an impact on the forms of economic organization and on both public and individual life. It is important to be aware that the context in which reconstruction of Europe took place was a steadily progressing and accelerating transformation extending into all spheres of human activity.

The explosion of atomic bombs over Hiroshima and Nagasaki is usually viewed as the beginning of the nuclear age. The harnessing of atomic energy was so dramatic an event that the fact has often been overlooked that in a variety of other fields the war gave a powerful impetus to scientific discoveries and technological inventions. The importance, for the conduct of war, of transportation and communication brought about—as the First World War—new inventions and discoveries which resulted in great changes in these areas after the war.

Transport planes used in the war opened the way for air mass transportation, which brought the continents closer together; the jet engine, invented during the war, accelerated air travel over large spaces. The motorization of the military forces created the basis for a rapid development of the automobile industry, for business firms as well as private individuals.

Whereas before 1939 only the most affluent had traveled abroad, the revolution in transportation gave the middle classes the possibility of moving easily beyond the frontiers which separated one country from another.

Widened horizons were also provided by radio and television. Radio had already been in use before the war. In wartime it had become the main source of information about the state of the world, the approach of enemy airplanes, or, as in occupied countries, a secret source of moral support. With improved instruments and enlarged programs radio almost took on the aspect of a necessity of life. Television was first displayed at the New York World's Fair of 1939 but remained expensive for several years after the war, with extremely limited programming. It became lower priced in the fifties; by 1975 every fourth person in western Europe, every tenth person in eastern Europe, and every fifth person in Russia, had a television set. The area in which people moved, and about which they acquired some knowledge had widened beyond their own country to the entire continent, and the world.

Reconstruction was not limited to the restoration of previously existing industrial installations; the exploitation of scientific and technological innovations made in wartime meant that certain industries expanded, and that for some new products new industrial enterprises had to be established. Previously existing enterprises like Fiat in Italy or Volkswagen in Germany became new industrial giants; on the other hand, a small tool manufacturer like Max Grundig, recognizing the possibilities of radio and television, built up the largest radio factory in Europe. Of the industries which had stimulated the second industrial revolution the chemical industry retained a leading role after the Second World War. In the fifties its output trebled. This expansion was due partly to a remarkable increase in synthetic products, which replaced metals, wood, glass, and partly to the marketing of numerous new pharmaceutical products, the result of medical research stimulated by the war. However, competition in the field of the chemical industry was keen and much capital investment was needed, with the result that only large enterprises could work profitably. The largest chemical firm on the continent was the Italian Montecatini; another giant was the West German Bayer. Bayer had been part of I. G. Farben but had become independent after the war when I. G. Farben, because of its monopolistic character, had been dissolved by order of the allies. Of equal if not greater importance were developments in the electrical industry, which widely expanded because of the manufacture of products using electronics. The age of the computer had begun, radio began to be superseded by television; movies and television became color movies and color television. After the Marshall Plan had provided a spark, the rise in industrial productivity was astounding. By 1956 industrial production in Germany and Italy was more than double of what it had been in the last normal peace year of 1937. In France and Great Britain, although somewhat less, production had also advanced by more than 50 per cent.

There was a variety of reasons why industrial growth was an interconnected process advancing on a broad front over a wide area: the influence of the superpowers stimulated planning for the entire region; many wartime patents were of an international character; and advances in transportation and communication facilitated marketing across national borders, so that production of one good in various factories was frequently uneconomical.

A further crucial factor in overcoming national separation and isolation was the employment situation. In the later part of the fifties, when the industrial machine was again in full swing, neither Germany nor France had enough workers to keep it going, so they added workers from other countries to their labor force; in the middle of the sixties the number of foreign workers in Germany amounted to 1.3 million, in France to 1.8 million. Most came from the Mediterranean area, a great number from Italy, where, in the agrarian south, unemployment was very high. Although not without influence on the integration of Europe, this was a temporary situation because in the later sixties the effects of a population increase and a beginning recession made the employment of foreign workers less desirable.

Reconstruction, particularly economic reconstruction, required experts, and there perhaps a further point needs to be made: Issues of great importance in wartime—for instance, distribution of food supply and of raw materials—had made many people interested in the possibilities of centralized planning. Moreover, the war had promoted thinking on a wide scale, disregarding national boundaries. Thus, centralized planning and planning on a great scale were wartime legacies most appropriate for reconstruction, and there developed a great need for experts in these activities. Thus, a new powerful figure appears on the political scene: the technocrat. A political consequence was a decline in the importance of the parliaments. In a democracy the parliament, because its aim is to represent the will of the people, is supposed to make decisions. In the early twentieth century the will of parliament frequently was hindered or deviated by professional bureaucrats or members of the old ruling group, who claimed to have better judgment on the basis that they possessed what many parliamentarians lacked: practical experience. In modern society access to the most varied sources of information is possible. The argument of administrative experience no longer has great weight. But in modern society the will of parliament also becomes restricted and obstructed: by the planners and technocrats who think not only on a wide scale but also in the long-term, so that when a plan is adopted and set to work there is no possibility of cutting off financial support for developments which are expected to come to fruition only after years of investment; the channels, once they have been entered, cannot be abandoned.

RECONSTRUCTION IN THE EASTERN BLOC

Reconstruction in Soviet Russia

A peculiar and unique feature of the situation in eastern Europe was that Soviet Russia, which dominated the states in the East and gave them leadership, was itself one of the countries in need of reconstruction. Actually, Russian reconstruction presented more extended, more serious, more difficult problems than reconstruction in any other part of the world. The Soviet Union is estimated to have lost sixteen to twenty million citizens in the Second World War, more than central and western Europe together. Other statistics are equally startling: 1,700 towns and cities and 70,000 villages were devastated, primarily in western Russia, which in pre-war times had been the Soviet Union's most highly developed area. Russian industrial installations and transportation facilities in this area had been entirely destroyed and masses of human beings had been forced to move to other parts.

Russian reluctance to finance the rebuilding of its economic life by American loans was probably equaled by American hesitancy to grant them. But the financing of reconstruction by means of the labors of the Soviet people meant that the iron age of the first Five-Year Plan was now followed by another iron age: the production of consumer goods remained rigidly curtailed, and a housing shortage forced large families often consisting of several adults to live in a single room. The losses suffered in the war also produced a shortage of labor; in order to exploit fully all available resources, labor camps were formed in which prisoners of war, displaced persons, and all those whom the regime mistrusted were assembled and put to work.

Thus life in Russia remained carefully planned, strictly regulated, and sharply disciplined. During the Second World War the restrictions and controls which had existed in the thirties had been somewhat relaxed; because it was hoped to increase and intensify agricultural production, the government had closed its eyes during wartime to the formation of small, privately owned peasant farms. The postwar situation, therefore, demanded not only maintenance of the controls which had existed before the war, but also a crackdown on the relaxation and transgressions which the war had brought about.

Concentration on heavy industry and expansion of the collective farm system remained the economic program. Moreover, the prospects for an increase in production of consumer goods diminished because the rising tension with the United States led to an expenditure on military weapons greater than ever before. It was unavoidable that, after the immense efforts of the war, the imposition of continued hardships and the reinforcement of controls were hard to accept and aroused a certain degree of

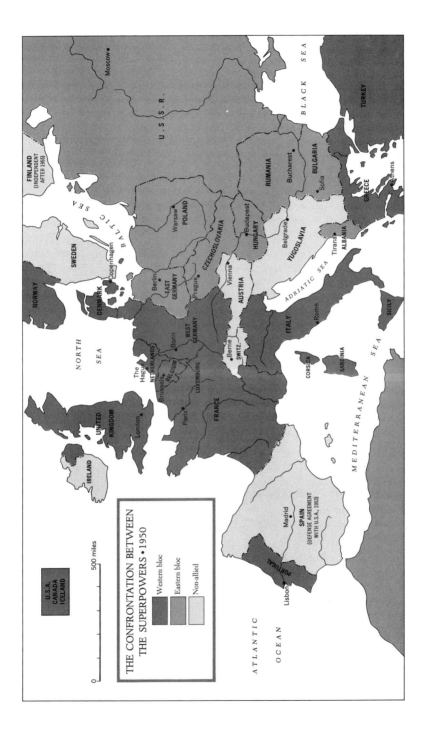

THE CONFRONTATION BETWEEN
THE SUPERPOWERS · 1950

Western bloc

Eastern bloc

Non-allied

U.S.A.
CANADA
ICELAND

0   500 miles

ATLANTIC
OCEAN

NORTH
SEA

BALTIC SEA

BLACK
SEA

U. S. S. R.

Moscow •

FINLAND
(INDEPENDENT
AFTER 1955)

SWEDEN

NORWAY

DENMARK

Copenhagen •

POLAND

Warsaw •

EAST
GERMANY
Berlin •

WEST
GERMANY
Bonn •

CZECHOSLOVAKIA

Prague •

AUSTRIA
Vienna •

HUNGARY
Budapest •

RUMANIA
Bucharest •

BULGARIA
Sofia •

YUGOSLAVIA
Belgrade •

ALBANIA
Tirana •

GREECE
Athens •

TURKEY

NETHERLANDS
The Hague •

Brussels •
BELGIUM

LUXEMBURG

FRANCE

Paris •

SWITZ.
Berne •

ITALY
Rome •

CORSICA

SARDINIA

SICILY

ADRIATIC SEA

MEDITERRANEAN
SEA

UNITED
KINGDOM
London •

IRELAND

SPAIN
(DEFENSE AGREEMENT
WITH U.S.A., 1953)
Madrid •

PORTUGAL
Lisbon •

discontent. Perhaps such dissatisfaction could not be entirely disregarded because the victory in war had given the army and its leaders a reputation and prestige not unequal to that enjoyed by the leaders of the Communist party. There was danger that the army might become a state within the state; that with resentment against the government's repressive measures growing, the military might try to influence policy decisions.

Stalin, deeply suspicious by nature, regarded it necessary to reassert the authority of the Communist party and, still more, his own dictatorship by taking brutal action against all possible nuclei of opposition. The outward sign of Stalin's policy to reduce the prestige of the army was to remove its most famous general, Marshal Zhukov, from his prominent position as commander of the Russian forces in Berlin to an obscure command post in Russia. Soviet writers and scientists had gained some freedom during the war and showed in their writings some knowledge of western literature and even a certain admiration for it. Andre Zhdanov, the Communist party leader in the successful defense of Leningrad, and, till his death in 1948, Stalin's greatest collaborator, reminded writers and scholars in a famous speech in August 1946 that, despite being "outwardly beautiful" bourgeois "culture is putrid and baneful in its moral foundations;" writers ought to be "engineers of human souls" and had "an enormous responsibility for the education of the people and for the education of Soviet youth." Zhadanov reorganized the literary and scientific organizations by excluding those who had shown signs of admiration for the West and laid down the correct line which the organizations ought to follow. But Stalin himself, not Zhdanov, was responsible for the most grotesque application of dictatorial methods to scientific research; he forced Russian scientists to accept as correct the theories of the geneticist Trofim Lysenko. Lysenko's theory, which implied inheritance of acquired characteristics, might have pleased Stalin since it seemed to indicate the possibility of effecting fundamental changes by forceful measures from above. At first open resistance to, and later surreptitious criticism of, Lysenko's theories by Russian scientists indicated that Lysenko never provided sufficient scientific proof for his thesis. Briefly, his case is a most extraordinary example of validating scientific theories by political dictation.

The weapon, however, which Stalin most thoroughly and most effectively used to eradicate opposition and to enforce absolute obedience was the police; he was particularly close to the people's commissar for state security, i.e., the head of the secret police, Beria. Whenever Stalin found, or only suspected, opposition to his authority, or even a possibility of opposition, Beria would act as if a conspiracy had taken place and would execute the conspirators. There is no doubt that in the last years of Stalin's life the pathological aspects of his character—his paranoia that he was surrounded by rivals and enemies, his constant fear of losing power, his megalomania and ruthlessness, his complete disregard for human life —dominated him so completely that even those who ruled with him lived in terror of him and felt freed when he died on March 9, 1953. There were bitter fights for the succession until, three years later, Nikita Khrushchev emerged as the leading figure, and in a closed session of the Twentieth Communist party Congress ended the Stalinist era by revealing the criminal features of Stalin's regime.

Stalin left to his successors no easy legacy. Although he had succeeded in organizing the various states of eastern Europe according to the Soviet pattern, the brutal repressiveness of his procedure and his unwillingness to accept any adjustments to special circumstances had created tensions which endangered the coherence of the Eastern bloc.

Reconstruction in the Satellite Countries

TREATY BONDS BETWEEN SOVIET RUSSIA AND THE SATELLITES

The fundamental basis for the pursuit of a common line by the Communist powers was provided by the Communist Information Bureau (Cominform). However, the Cominform comprised representatives of the Communist parties of all European states and its activities were chiefly propagandistic. In addition, Soviet Russia created particular ties with all the Communist-controlled states. During the war Russia had concluded mutual-assistance treaties with the governments-in-exile which guaranteed help in case of future German aggression and provided for close economic, cultural, and political cooperation with Yugoslavia, Czechoslovakia, and Poland. Similar pacts were negotiated in 1948 with Bulgaria, Rumania, Hungary, and Finland, the former Axis satellites. A comparable treaty, assuring assistance against attack by Japan or by powers allied to Japan, was signed with China in 1950. Chinese agreements with North Korea and North Vietnam tied these countries to the Russian bloc. Finally, in 1955 the relation of the Communist states in Europe to one another and to Soviet Russia was redefined by a pact concluded in Warsaw; in addition to the partners of previous mutual-assistance agreements—Soviet Russia, Albania, Bulgaria, Hungary, Poland, Rumania, Czechoslovakia—the treaty included East Germany, which now advanced to full membership in the Soviet alliance system. The Warsaw Pact precluded participation of its members in any other coalition or alliance and assured members of immediate assistance, including the use of armed force, in the event of armed aggression, establishing for this purpose a joint command for the armed forces of the members, as well as a consultative committee to harmonize political action. The stationing of Russian troops in eastern European countries, notably in Rumania, Hungary, Poland, and East Germany, which until then had been justified by the need to maintain communications with the Russian occupation zones in Germany and Austria, was now guaranteed by bilateral treaties.

The instrument by which these political bonds were economically fortified was the Council of Mutual Assistance, established, as has been mentioned, in reaction to the Marshall Plan.

THE ESTABLISHMENT OF A NEW ORDER IN THE SATELLITE COUNTRIES

The precondition of the establishment of a Communist political and social order in eastern Europe was the elimination of all bourgeois and non-Communist parties and elements from political power. Socialists, members of the middle classes, and peasants had participated in the last phases of the struggle against the Fascist regimes in Hungary, Czechoslovakia, and the Balkans, and the demand of the United States and Great Britain for the formation of democratic governments in these countries had assured representatives of these groups of some hold in the governments. We have discussed that in 1947–1948, in connection with the increase in tension between Russia and the United States, the Communists in all the eastern European countries became the sole possessors of power. In towns, villages, factories, and business enterprises committees of the Communist party were established and acquired undisputed authority, which guaranteed that all aspects of life would be handled in accordance with the principles of the Communist party and the orders of the state; the hold of these party committees over the organizations they supervised was also secured by the favors they could distribute.

With the ending of the influence of any bourgeois, non-Communist elements in the government the construction of a new economic order was to begin. Bulgaria and Czechoslovakia were the first to act, drafting four-year plans in 1949; in 1950 Hungary followed with a five-year plan and Poland with a six-year plan; the last countries were Rumania and East Germany, both issuing five-year plans in 1951—the primary aims of all these plans were identical. The Soviet model was to be introduced in all these countries: i.e., industrialization which placed emphasis on heavy industry and collectivization of agriculture. It has been said that the adoption of the Soviet model was hardly suited for these areas; their real strength lay in agriculture, and in some of these states—Czechoslovakia, Rumania, Bulgaria—agricultural reforms, which broke up great landed estates and created small peasant holdings, had taken place after the First World War. However, the adoption of a policy of industrialization and collectivization in the satellite countries was not solely a blind imitation of the Russian model. In the past these areas had been oriented towards the West; they exported agricultural products to the West and received from the West machinery and industrial products. The economic reorganization of these states after the Second World War was therefore aimed at breaking their ties with the West, i.e., making them industrially independent and orienting their trade towards Russia.

If one takes an overall view, these goals were attained. By 1951, 92 per cent of Bulgaria's trade was with Soviet Russia. Even Poland's trade with Russia, which before the war amounted to only 7 per cent of the country's foreign trade, had reached 58 per cent by 1951. At the same time, industrial production increased remarkably. By 1952, annual production in Poland and Czechoslovakia, the two most industrialized countries of the bloc, was double its prewar level, and the total steel production in eastern Europe was then roughly equal to that of West Germany, and twice what it had been before the war. The labor force employed in industry in eastern Europe increased about 33 per cent by the early 1950's.

It is evident that this immense transformation—the creation of a new social and economic order, the change from a primarily agrarian to a strongly industrial society—created tensions and aroused criticism, opposition, and also obstructionism. Moreover, in addition to the unrest which such a social revolution must generate there were particular reasons for dissatisfaction. The Soviet leaders, regarding the economic recovery of their own country as their foremost target, pursued a policy of direct exploitation in these areas. Hungary and Rumania, even after the Communists were in full power, were forced to continue to pay reparations to Russia. Moreover, the Russians seized all German property in these countries and dismantled all German industrial installations, which they then transferred to Russia. The Russians also participated in a number of joint companies controlling such enterprises as the Rumanian merchant marine and the Hungarian bauxite mines. Thus, a portion of the earnings of these companies went directly to Russia. Moreover, the Russians imposed upon these countries agreements to deliver certain goods, such as coal, at extremely low prices. For decades under bourgeois or Fascist regimes, these countries were ideologically unprepared for Communist rule. Thus, after the Communist seizure of power, measures of indoctrination were begun and pursued with ruthless energy. The Communist youth organizations, backed by the power of the ministers of education, promoted an educational system propagating a strictly Marxist ideology. In many countries in the East, however—Poland, Czechoslovakia, and Hungary—the Catholic Church had a stronghold and a clash with the Church was therefore unavoidable, and indeed in every satellite country with a strong Roman Catholic population sensational proceedings against the leaders of the Roman Catholic Church were instigated: in 1946 against Archbishop Stepinac in Yugoslavia, in 1949 against Cardinal Mindszenty in Hungary, and in 1951 against Archbishop Beran in Czechoslovakia.

These factors—Russian exploitation and anti-Church action—exacerbated the tensions over what was the most unpopular and most hotly resisted part of the Sovietization of this area: the collectivization of agriculture. By tradition and also by the more recent agrarian reforms mentioned above, small peasant farms were numerous; collectivization meant loss of cherished values without any visible advantage. Some of the Communist leaders of these countries had doubts that collectivization was appropriate to their areas, or at least were in favor of a slow and cautious procedure. This issue brought about the first big crisis in the Eastern bloc.

THE DEFECTION OF TITO AND THE STALINIST PURGES

Immediately after the war Yugoslavia appeared to become more quickly and more thoroughly a replica of the Soviet model than any other of the eastern European states. Because the Yugoslavs themselves, rather than foreign armies, had thrown off the Nazi rule, and because this liberation was chiefly the work of the Yugoslav Communist party under Tito, no bourgeois or socialist elements had to be taken into the Yugoslav postwar government. It was therefore a purely Communist government and, in accordance with the Soviet model, began immediately a program of industrialization and collectivization.

But because it was composed of different nationalities, and because of the old rivalries and conflicts among these nationalities—Serbs, Croats, Slovenes—circumspection had to be used in proceeding toward the new socialist society in order not to provoke friction and to endanger the unity of Yugoslavia. Since Yugoslavia lay on the borders between the East and the West, Stalin regarded delays and deviation with particular distrust; he wanted to keep the situation there under sharp control. But Russia had no strong lever within Yugoslavia, for Yugoslavia was the only country of eastern Europe which had not been liberated by Russian armies. When Stalin demanded that Russia be given control over the Yugoslavian army and the secret police, Tito refused. Thus, in June 1948, in reaction to Tito's disobedience, at a Cominform meeting which Yugoslav representatives did not attend, Yugoslavia was excluded from the Cominform.

The Russians evidently expected that this measure would force Tito to submit but, as the military leader of the partisans during the war, Tito had become a national hero with a very strong hold over the people. His popularity, together with some economic help from the West, made it possible for him to retain power, and the Russians resigned themselves to this situation although they continued vehement vocal attacks against Tito and maintained an economic blockade of Yugoslavia. Under Tito, Yugoslavia developed a special form of Communism—a mixed economy. There was no overall economic planning for the entire country. In agriculture, collective farms coexisted with privately owned farms. Industry was nationalized, but control was exercised by the workers in the individual factories and there was a free market for the sale of many consumer goods.

Tito's defection aroused fears in Stalin and the Russian leaders that other eastern European countries might follow the Yugoslav example, with each country forging its own individual type of Communism. Consequently, under pressure from the Russians, widespread purges took place in the eastern states. Whereas the purges of 1947–1948 had been chiefly directed against politicians from the bourgeois camp, this new wave of purges was directed against Communists.

One aim of the purges was to make the Communist party an absolutely reliable instrument for execution of directives given from above. In every eastern European country the size of the Communist party had increased considerably, since many former members of the dissolved and suppressed non-Communist parties thought it useful to enter the Communist ranks; this influx of incompletely trained and untested members was considered especially dangerous for the efficiency of the party because even the upper strata contained discordant elements—on the one hand, those who had taken refuge in Moscow during the war, and on the other hand, those who had remained at home working in the underground. These two groups now competed for control of the party. In danger of becoming unwieldy and divided, the Communist parties in eastern Europe instituted mass purges. Hundreds of thousands were deprived of membership in the party as "alien" or "hostile" elements. Another aim of the purges was to eliminate those Communist leaders who might be inclined to follow the example of Tito, and the consequence was a substantial change in the composition of the Central Committees of the Communist parties in the various states. Leaders who might be inclined toward Titoist deviations were brought before tribunals in sensational procedures patterned after the Russian purge trials of the 1930's, complete with accusations of treason, confessions, and finally the imposition of the death penalty. The most outstanding victims of these trials, starting in 1949, were Traicho Kostov, the vice premier of the Bulgarian government; Laszlo Rajk, the minister of the interior in Hungary; and in Czechoslovakia, Vladimir Clementis, the foreign minister, and Rudolf Slansky, general secretary of the Communist party and deputy prime minister. Wladyslaw Gomulka, the general secretary of the Polish Communist party, was deposed and later imprisoned, but he escaped execution.

The purges and trials of the leadership in the Russian satellite countries continued until 1953, and in the course of time their purposes went beyond those of party discipline and the elimination of Titoists. The motives for the persecution of individuals are frequently obscure. These were the years when Stalin's suspiciousness had clearly become pathological and when anticipation of his approaching death sharpened the conflicts among Russian Communist leaders anxious to eliminate possible rivals. The trials in the satellite countries appear to have been repercussions of the struggles in the Russian leadership group, as is suggested by the fact that some of these trials, like some of those in Russia, had anti-Semitic overtones. In his dealings with the various eastern European nations Stalin preferred to work through one person entirely devoted and obedient to him. And the purges served to concentrate power in each country in the hands of one entirely pro-Stalin Communist leader: Mátyás Rákosi in Hungary; Walter Ulbricht in East Germany; Klement Gottwald in Czechoslovakia; Boleslav Bierut in Poland. Like Stalin himself, though to a slighter extent, each of these leaders became the center of a cult of personality. By the time Stalin died in 1953, the various means which had been applied to unify the Russian-controlled areas of Europe—ideological uniformity, institutional identity, economic integration, force—appeared to have transformed them into a monolithic bloc ruled and directed by Russia.

As we have mentioned before, the price which had been paid was high; dissatisfaction and tension were pushed below the surface only by means of force. How tense the situation was became clear in the summer of 1953, after Stalin's death, when the introduction of a new wage policy led to a revolt of workers in East Berlin, suppressed only by intervention of Russian military forces. All over the Eastern bloc this was taken as a sign that a dangerpoint had been reached, and that a change of course in economic policy was urgent and had to be undertaken as quickly as possible. The state which embarked on the changes with greatest energy was Hungary; Rákosi, who had risen to the prime ministership of Hungary as a loyal Stalinist, remained general secretary of the party but lost the prime ministership to Imre Nagy, an advocate of the new course. In other eastern European countries the shift in direction was more moderate. In Poland the all-powerful Stalinist Boleslav Bierut prevented any radical change.

Obviously, the establishment of a new leadership and a new political line could proceed more easily in an atmosphere of lowered international tension. This was one reason why the Russians were in favor of ending the acute phase of the Cold War by a compromise over Indochina, and why in the spring of 1955, to almost everyone's surprise, they agreed to a treaty which terminated the occupation of Austria and restored Austrian sovereignty, thus removing one of the sources of friction along the line where American and Russian spheres of interest touched. The various facets of the new Russian policy were clearly indicated by Khrushchev in his speech to the Twentieth Congress of the Communist party. He admitted the possibility of different "forms of transition of various countries to socialism" and he revised the traditional Marxist thesis that "war is inevitable so long as imperialism exists."

The Russian leaders were not unaware that the relaxation of tensions between East and West, combined with an economic policy which permitted the eastern European states considerable variation within the prescribed general framework, might endanger Russian domination. The Warsaw Pact of 1955 had not only the purpose of strengthening military cooperation against the West, the Russians were anxious to counteract the dangers of a lessening of tension and the centrifugal consequences of greater economic autonomy in the satellite countries by reinforcing political and military bonds. The formation early in 1956 of a Joint Nuclear Research Institute including all the Communist states also reflected this trend. There can be little doubt that the uniformity which Stalin had pressed upon the European Communist world had brought things almost to a breaking point; the attempt of the new Russian leaders to modify his policy was almost unavoidable, but because of the explosive tensions which had accumulated under Stalin, "controlled transition" proved to be a complicated process full of dangers for the coherence of the Russian alliance system.

RECONSTRUCTION IN THE WEST

Treaty Bonds in the Western Bloc

Originally when the war ended there was a great difference between the situation in the East and the situation in the West. Russia, the superpower in the East was a European power. It had contiguous frontiers with the states of eastern Europe. The United States, the superpower in the West, was far removed from Europe and it was generally expected, although this soon proved to be erroneous, that it would withdraw from Europe after hostilities had ended. The peoples in western Europe living under the threatening shadow of Russia were naturally anxious to acquire greater strength by forming a bloc; moreover, in western Europe the tendency to supranational cooperation, which had developed during the war, had found a particularly strong echo. The first step toward a closer tie among the nations of western Europe was the Pact of Brussels, concluded on March 17, 1948: Great Britain, France, and the so-called Benelux countries, Belgium, the Netherlands, and Luxembourg) promised to come to each other's help in the case of a military attack and agreed to the formation of a permanent council which would advise on common interests and common action. Simultaneously delegates from most of the non-Communist European countries met in Brussels to make plans for European cooperation and integration of a more comprehensive character. From this initiative developed both a regularly meeting council, of which the foreign ministers of all the western European states were members, and a Council of Europe, which included delegates from western European parliaments. Their unwillingness to have their sovereignty limited, strongly emphasized by Great Britain and later also by France and other powers, restricted the practical efficacy of these institutions and enthusiasm for them declined. But they continued to exist and were significant in keeping the trend toward European integration alive.

These developments took place in circumstances greatly changed from those which had existed at the end of the war. It had become clear that the United States, feeling threatened by a Russian expansion, would not fall back into isolation but remain interested in the maintenance of an independent western Europe. The crucial indication of this change in the American attitude had been Secretary Marshall's speech of June 6, 1947; it is significant that the Pact of Brussels was concluded in April, 1948, one month before the European Recovery Program (ERP), through which Marshall's offer of American economic help for European reconstruction was carried out, began to function.

It was also obvious that, as important as the Pact of Brussels was as an expression of European willingness to resist Russian pressure, even the combined forces of the states which had concluded the pact were not strong enough to resist the Russians in case of war. Thus, almost immediately after the conclusion of the Pact of Brussels, attempts were made to include the Americans in military arrangements to defend western Europe. The outcome was the North Atlantic Treaty Organization—NATO. It comprised—next to the members of the Pact of Brussels—the United States, Canada, and five other European powers: Italy, Portugal, Denmark, Iceland, and Norway. The most important practical consequence of this agreement lay in the military field: the military forces of the European partners of the treaty and the American-Canadian forces stationed in Europe were integrated and placed under an international command. But NATO was also a political alliance, with the participating powers promising to defend each other against any attack on "the freedom, common heritage, and civilization of their people." Thus, by 1950, most of western Europe was tied together with the United States by close military and economic bonds.

Closer cooperation in the West had a problem, however, which Soviet Russia had not encountered. The Russians had been able to integrate their German occupation zone by establishing a Communist regime in East Germany. Reliability and obedience was guaranteed by the complete dependence of this regime on Soviet Russia. But the establishment of parliamentary democracy in West Germany did not exclude the possibility of political changes which might bring nationalistic forces back into power. Moreover, the German mineral riches might make a resurrection of German military power possible. Thus, the defeat of Nazism did not end all fear of German aggressiveness among Germany's western neighbors. It was clear that German partnership in the Western bloc implied that in the course of time Germany would again become a fully sovereign power, but the problem was to make sure that this freedom of action would not result in another German attempt to gain hegemony and domination.

These difficulties were removed by a number of further agreements reached after long and difficult negotiations. The issue which was first resolved concerned an economic question. Although it had been recognized that it was necessary to eliminate the danger that Germany might use its mineral resources for rearmament, it was also necessary to make German steel and coal available to European economic reconstruction. This problem was solved by the creation of a European Coal and Steel Community (ECSC) in 1951. The French foreign minister, Robert Schuman, made a courageous proposal to place the coal and steel production of Germany, France, and the Benelux countries under common administration. This agency, the so-called High Authority, composed of experts from the various participating countries, had the right to set and regulate prices, to increase or limit production, and to levy fees which would finance the organization. Great Britain did not participate because of the belief that this organization would hamper the English coal industry and was incompatible with its relations to the countries of the Commonwealth; thus began a long-lasting separation of Great Britain from economic cooperation with the countries of the western European continent, since the coal and steel community proved to be the first step in the gradual process of European economic integration.

One of the aims of the Second World War had been the eradication of German militarism; to persuade Germany's neighbors to revise this policy and allow German rearmament was much more difficult than agreement on economic collaboration with Germany. The proposal for a revision of policy came from the United States. Because of the outbreak of the Korean War, the American government feared that its military resources might become overstrained, and it demanded that Germany be permitted to rearm to strengthen the western military posture in Europe; for some time a positive outcome seemed to be lost in a maze of negotiations. America's allies, particularly the French, responded with a remarkable lack of enthusiasm to this American eagerness to forget the past. But unable to resist the request of their powerful ally, the French suggested an integrated European army, in which they hoped the German contribution would be kept to a minimum. After lengthy negotiations, a treaty for a European Defense Community was concluded in May, 1952. But most of the signatory powers felt doubtful about the abandonment of sovereignty over their military forces implied in an integrated army. The French themselves in August, 1954, rejected ratification of the treaty, and suddenly a different and much simpler solution was obtained. West

Germany became a member of NATO; foreign troops stationed on German soil could now be regarded not as occupation forces but as allies, present on the basis of NATO membership. The French were reconciled to German rearmament by a British promise to leave several divisions on the Continent; thus, the French felt, if war did break out the British would be immediately involved. This is a striking example how the future is frequently seen in terms of the past because, as things have developed, a war between Germany and France is highly unlikely.

In contrast to the situation in the Eastern bloc integration in the western part of Europe could not be attained exclusively by pressure from above. The feeling for common values above national interests which had developed in the times of resistance against the Nazis was an important factor in fomenting an impetus for integration. It is significant that in building the Western bloc, the leaders of the Catholic parties in France, Italy, and Germany played principal roles.

But it should also not be overlooked that in bringing closer cooperation about, the threat to security and military consideration and needs played a decisive role. This had its influence on the course which the rebuilding of political order took in the different countries of western Europe. The war had ended with the expectation among the great mass of peoples of Europe that a new era was beginning. It was commonly held that, considering the extreme sufferings which people had undergone and the endurance which they had shown, they deserved to have full employment, to have full protection in the case of illness, and to receive pensions which provided them with material security in their old age. Insofar as the interests of private entrepreneurs, large banks, and big industrial enterprises were contradictory to such aims and placed obstacles in their way, the government should take them over and exercise all the power necessary to insure that economic affairs would be conducted in the interest of all citizens and not of a wealthy elite. In the postwar situation all the European governments moved somewhat in this direction. But it is also evident that a quick reconstitution of industrial activity, which could allow the build-up of a strong military apparatus, and long-range economic and social reforms were difficult to pursue simultaneously. Moreover, the American inclination to identify democracy with a free enterprise system lent support to the opponents of fundamental structural changes. The demands and needs of military security took much wind out of the sails of reformism, which had been very strong in the immediate postwar period. Certainly the manner in which the political order in the western European states was constructed pointed in the direction that political freedom was possible only if an individual had economic security, that political freedom and economic security of the individual were complementary to each other. But the countertrend which set in was strong enough to break the full force of these trends. The result was that in most European states a precarious balance between old and new emerged.

Internal Developments in Western Bloc Nations

As we have seen, during the first decade after the end of the Second World War parties of very similar political aims and outlook were in power, namely, political parties which emphasized Christianity and Roman Catholicism as a common feature. In Italy the party was called *Democrazia Cristiana* (Christian Democracy), and from 1948 to 1953 it had the absolute majority in parliament. In West Germany the name of the party was *Christlich-Demokratische Union* (Christian Democratic Union) and it became the largest German political party in the parliamentary elections of 1949, the first elections held after the war; the Christian Democratic Union obtained an absolute majority in 1953. In France the M.R.P. (for *Mouvement Républicain Populaire*), as the Catholic party was called, had its greatest strength immediately after the war and then declined, first slowly, later rather rapidly; in 1946 the M.R.P. received one vote in four; five years later, only one in eight. Nevertheless, no government in France was formed in this period without the participation of the M.R.P. Among members of these parties the idea of a unified Europe,

Konrad Adenauer, the German chancellor, with the Israeli prime minister, David Ben-Gurion.

of building a Christian fortress against the attack of barbarians, had strong historical roots, and the leaders of these parties enthusiastically pursued a policy of European collaboration. The men chiefly responsible for the European direction of French, Italian, and West German foreign policy in these critical years were Robert Schuman, between 1947–1953, French prime minister and later foreign minister, who initiated the creation of the Coal and Steel Community; Alcide de Gasperi, Italian prime minister from 1945–1953; and Konrad Adenauer, German chancellor from 1949–1963.

The Recovery of the Defeated Powers

De Gasperi and Adenauer impressed themselves upon the history of their countries by charting the political course of postwar Italy and Germany. Both leaders were very different from the idealistic statesmen of the early years of the twentieth century, with their passionate commitment to the great causes of social reform or national expansion. Their speeches emphasized concrete points and justified their policies with practical, commonsense reasons. What they wrote or said tended to be monotonous and pedestrian—Adenauer's chief saving grace was a dry wit which revealed his sharp eye for the weaknesses of his fellow men. De Gasperi and Adenauer appeared disinclined to embark on a discussion of broad principles and seemed to consider a good style and beautiful phrases as unnecessary embroidery. They gave the impression of being always in a rush, always exclusively concerned with settling the business at hand. The matter-of-factness of these two may have been rooted in their feeling that they no longer had much time to accomplish what they felt destined to do. De Gasperi had been at the beginning of a promising political career when Fascism came to power in Italy; he spent the next twenty years partly in prison, partly as an employee in the library of the Vatican. He was in his sixties when he reentered politics as a leader of the Italian resistance. Adenauer was close to seventy when, after twelve years in a political wilderness during the Nazi regime, he was reinstituted as lord mayor of Cologne by the occupying American forces and could resume a political career.

The situation in Italy and Germany when De Gasperi and Adenauer took over was hardly suited for men of great plans and imagination. For the leaders of the two defeated nations the targets were prescribed: setting economic life in motion and achieving membership in the society of sovereign states.

ITALY

These prosaic aims somewhat contradicted the political atmosphere of Italy after the defeat of Fascism: the experiences in the resistance in the fina' phase of the war seemed to have broken down barriers between classes. It was widely expected that Italy after Fascism would be a new, more democratic, and more equalitarian state. This explains why Socialists and Communists emerged in great strength, but the Christian Democratic party, an amalgam of Catholicism and political moderation, emerged as the strongest party in the elections of 1946. As a result of the work of this constituent assembly, Italy changed from a monarchy to a republic; in other respects, however, the constitution adopted by the assembly was very similar to the one which had existed before Fascism. Only the anti-clerical emphasis of the nineteenth-century liberal constitution was eliminated: Mussolini's Concordat with the Pope became an integral part of the new constitution and Roman Catholicism remained in Italy "the sole religion of the state."

The Italian economic situation was so miserable that, inevitably, wider claims for reform had to take a back seat to the problems of economic recovery. In this area De Gasperi had an extremely capable helper: Luigi Einaudi, Italy's leading economist, first as director of the Bank of Italy and then as minister of the budget, balanced the Italian budget by rigorous means; in 1948 he became the first president of the Italian republic.

Thanks to the rapid progress of the Allied armies into the Italian industrial north, and thanks to the activities of the partisans, the damage done by the war to industrial installations was a relatively low 15 per cent. Italy therefore was able quickly to restore industrial production and to export consumer goods to the rest of Europe. But as other countries set their own industrial machinery in motion, the demand for Italian goods decreased. Then the Marshall Plan provided a new stimulus, and the Italian government used the industrial and financial holdings inherited from the Fascist government to provide capital for industrial modernization. The results were startling indeed. The index of industrial production in 1954 was 71 per cent above that of 1938, the last prewar year. And electric-power production—because of Italy's lack of coal, probably the most important of the country's industries—had increased in 1953 by more than 100 per cent over 1938. By 1954 real wages were more than five times what they had been at the end of the war and almost 50 per cent higher than they had been in 1938. Nevertheless, the Italian economic situation still had great weaknesses. The domestic market remained rather undeveloped because of the poverty of the agrarian south. Although in 1954, 40 per cent of the national income came from industrial activities and only 26 per cent from agriculture, 42.4 per cent of the working population were engaged in agriculture. These figures show that the rural population had remained utterly poor, unable to buy any manufactured goods.

In 1951, five million Italians were still illiterate. Many of these people tried to leave the land and to find work in the industrial centers of the north where they swelled the labor market; some made use of opportunities, which by then had opened up, to work in Germany and France. Although unemployment had decreased, Italy still had more than four million jobless in 1954. This problem could be solved only by land reform in the agrarian south which would give more land to the peasants, but would also bring industry into· this region. In dealing with this issue, the De Gasperi regime failed. Land reform had been promised at the end of the war, but the government proceeded with this task only slowly and hesitatingly. The industrial revival neither destroyed nor changed the previously existing social structure; the members of the old ruling group —industrialists allied with landowners—remained powerful throughout the early years of reconstruction. They were willing to support the Christian Democratic government because it controlled the financial resources needed by industry; they were willing to raise the wages of the workers in order to ease industrial recovery; they even accepted the introduction of an income tax, which had not previously existed in Italy—although it should be remarked that the tax law permitted declarations which had only a very remote relation to actuality. But the old ruling group opposed changes—such as land reform—which would fundamentally alter the social structure.

The pressure of the poor and unemployed from the south coming to the industrial north in the hope for work kept radicalism among the workers alive; the Communists and their left socialist allies continued to exercise strong appeal among the workers and made gains among the peasants and rural workers in the south. The trade unions in Italy were, and remained, Communist controlled. The Christian Democrats themselves split into a right wing which was willing to cooperate even with monarchists and former Fascists to prevent any change in the social structure, and a left wing which believed in the necessity of cooperation with the leftists to effect thorough social reforms. This split, together with discontent about the inertia of the government, resulted in elections in 1953 which denied De Gasperi his desired absolute majority, and he was forced to retire. But the hopes that his withdrawal would give a new impetus to structural reforms were deceived. Right and left in the Christian Democratic party were so balanced that the policy of the government became standing-still rather than action and reform.

WEST GERMANY

In many respects the task which Adenauer had in West Germany was easier than that of De Gasperi. In West Germany, the break with the past, not only with Nazism but also with the pre-Nazi past, was more thorough than in Italy. The severance of eastern Germany meant the disappearance of the *Junkers*, the owners of large estates east of the Elbe, who had

Alcide de Gasperi addresses a crowd before the 1948 elections.

continuously pressed for protective tariffs and government subsidies and opposed democratic reform. The creation of the Coal and Steel Community kept the industrial barons of the Ruhr in check. Thus the German ruling group was freed of its socially most reactionary and politically most aggressive elements. One result was a change in the composition of the German civil service, since the classes from which its members had been recruited no longer existed; although still a power within the state, the civil service became less authoritarian.

Germany's situation also differed from Italy's in that its cities and industries had been thoroughly destroyed. The huge task of reconstruction required the cooperation of all strata of the population—of government, employers, and employees, of capitalists and workers. At the same time, the scarcity of goods of all kinds made production, once begun, highly profitable; in the first years the Germans themselves eagerly bought all they could produce. Workers were therefore in great demand, and unemployment disappeared almost completely. The economy of West Germany was able to absorb the refugees from the eastern part of Germany, and even benefited from their presence.

They turned out to be less of a discontented nationalist pressure group than had been expected and feared. The shortage of workers made employers willing to accept improvements in the status of labor. Maintenance of full employment was recognized as legitimate government function, an extended social security system which provided pensions in adjustment to changes in standard of living was adopted, and "co-determination," which gave the workers a share in the management of industry, was established by law. After the dictatorial handling of social questions by the Nazis, such government intervention in labor relations was considered entirely compatible with the principles of the "free market policy" advocated by Erhard, Adenauer's minister of economic affairs. If employers shared a willingness to improve the status of labor, the workers too were in a cooperative mood. They were anxious to work, so that with their earnings, they could begin to obtain the necessities of life. Thus although wages at the outset were low, the attitude of the trade unions in wage negotiations was conciliatory and no strikes of significance occurred in Germany in the first years after the war. Consequently German goods quickly reconquered a position on foreign markets.

The prevailing eagerness to prevent conflicts which might delay reconstruction and economic recovery goes far to explain the popularity of the majority party, the Christian Democratic Union, in Germany. Another reason, of course, was that the loss of the eastern part of Germany meant a great increase in the percentage of Catholics in the population, since the south and west of Germany had always been predominantly Catholic (in 1933 Catholics constituted 32.5 per cent of the German population; in West Germany in 1950 the figure was 43.8 per cent). However, the Christian Democratic Union was strong even in the northern, predominantly Protestant areas. The predecessor of the Christian Democratic Union, the old Center party, had always included a variety of social groups, ranging from the workers in the Catholic trade unions to industrialists and landowners. After the Nazi collapse, when external circumstances as well as emotional needs required a new beginning through common action, the appeal of a party which could be regarded as a microcosm of the entire population was obviously great; the German Christian Democratic Union could be characterized as an organized consensus.

The position of Chancellor Adenauer, the leader of the Christian Democratic Union, was strong also for constitutional reasons. In an effort to avoid the instability characteristic of the Weimar Republic, the constitution of West Germany had sharply restricted the rights of parliament. Once a chancellor had been appointed and had received a vote of confidence, the vote of a majority against him could force him to resign only if his opponents had agreed on who would replace him. The only two other parties were the Free Democratic party, a small bourgeois party, which, although it later changed course, was then on the right of the Christian Democratic Union, and a Socialist party on the left, and it seemed most unlikely that these two extremes would come together and agree on a candidate for the chancellorship.

The opposition was ineffective, also because it had no clear alternative policy to offer. The Socialist demand for socialization of key industries aroused little enthusiasm even among the workers—because the swollen bureaucracy of the Nazi dictatorship had produced a deep dislike of the red tape connected with all government-controlled enterprises, because the trade unions were concentrating on the immediate problem of getting the economy moving again, and were not bothering about an ideal society in a distant future, and also because the social security system and co-determination protected the basic interests of the workers. Party rivalry also took a less bitter form because West Germany had retained a federal structure and in some of the states a coalition between Socialists and Christian Democrats was in power.

For the Socialists the chief target of criticism was Adenauer's foreign policy. The chancellor was said to toe the American line, destroying all possibilities for agreement with the east and all chances for German reunification by adopting an anti-Russian course. Yet, to the majority of the German people these objections against the foreign policy of Adenauer's government seemed rather theoretical. Still numbed by defeat and conscious of the immense military strength of the two superpowers, the German people in these early years had little interest in resuming a role in international affairs. They were content to devote themselves, under American protection, to the tasks of material improvement. After Germany's position had become more secure and more powerful, alternative politics began to develop and a fluidity which undermined the monopoly of power of the Christian Democrats entered into party political life.

It is ironic that, as a result of the Cold War, which made the economic and military strengthening of western Europe a necessity, the two European countries which most quickly returned to prosperity were those which had lost the war. Germany and Italy were able to draw strength out of weakness. They were the countries of the *"Wirtschaftswunder"* (economic miracle).

Postwar Strains in France and Britain

FRANCE

France was deeply divided: geographically France had been separated into German-occupied France and Vichy France; ideologically into resisters and resistance sympathizers versus collaborators and those who had tolerated collaboration. These divisions were not class divisions. The resistance movements had included men and women from the entire political spectrum—from nationalists on the right to Communists on the extreme left. The members of the resistance felt that the reorganization of French political life was their right and their duty. They wanted something better than what had existed before, but they had not worked out how this new world should look. They were united in their hatred of Nazi collaborators and in their rejection of the prewar political system.

It was not difficult to settle accounts with individual traitors; in all of the formerly occupied countries trials against Nazi collaborators and war criminals took place. In France members of the Vichy government were brought before a high court. Laval was executed; Pétain was sentenced to prison and died there. Most of the Nazi collaborators and sympathizers in

France were tried before special courts; in the first year 40,000 out of 125,000 defendants received more or less severe punishment. But the men of the resistance, or at least most of them, attributed responsibility for the surrender to Fascism and Nazism not only to individuals but to a system which had allowed a determining political influence to industrialists and bankers. Democracy, it was believed, could not flourish where economic power was concentrated in the hands of a few big capitalists. The successful functioning of a parliamentary democracy was thought to be predicated upon social and economic reforms which would strengthen the position of the great masses of the population against the rich upper group. In the last months of the war, and in the liberation period, resistance groups tried in many areas to assume executive power and constitute themselves as governments. They were balked by the military leaders of the victorious American and British armies, who were primarily interested in smoothly functioning supply and communication lines, and feared disorder and chaos. Furthermore, De Gaulle, the acknowledged head of the French resistance, opposed the encroachment of individual groups on what he considered to be the paramount authority of the state.

Yet despite the failure of the resistance to effect changes and reforms during the fluid situation at the war's end, it was generally recognized that France could not just reactivate its former constitution. A plebiscite determined that it was necessary, as DeGaulle declared in a broadcast in September, 1945, "to adopt a different system in order to revive the spirit of clarity, justice and efficiency which is the true spirit of the republic." Most of the members of the constituent assembly which was elected in 1945 to draft a new constitution agreed that government instability had been the chief weakness of the Third Republic. De Gaulle, who returned to France with immense prestige, emphasized the necessity of strengthening the power and independence of the executive branch. But the left wing—the Communists and Socialists—which dominated the constituent assembly attempted to ensure stability in the government by means of a complete subordination of the executive to the legislative branch; the Chamber of Deputies became all-powerful. De Gaulle saw in this arrangement a disturbing sign that the period of party squabbles was returning, and he resigned as head of the Provisional Government in January, 1946.

He was right, in that government stability turned out to be no greater in the Fourth Republic than it had been in the Third. There were prolonged government crises and an endless succession of ministries. In 1946 the Communists had emerged as the strongest political party. But after they had been eliminated from the government in May, 1947, they never received much more than 25 per cent of the vote. The majority was formed by a left-center coalition of Catholic democrats, the M.R.P.,

Socialists, and left-liberal groups; almost every French government under the Fourth Republic obtained its support from these parties. Frequent changes in administration were caused less by political conflicts and disagreement over issues than by the maneuverings of ambitious politicians eager to become ministers and inclined to intrigue against one another. In the 1950's French political life found itself in a depressing rut. When the same men or groups remain in power for a very long time opposition tends to increase in strength and shrillness. Majorities for the existing government became increasingly precarious; but no alternative was in sight. Extremists, particularly of the right, were gaining in popular appeal; for a short time demagogues like Pierre Poujade, who preached tax reduction as remedy for all social ills, gained a considerable number of votes; the left and right wings of the coalition began to pull in opposite directions in their efforts to pacify the radicals on their fringes.

Yet, the troubles of the Fourth Republic cannot be blamed just on the resentment of the "outs" against the "ins" or on the bickering of the politicians, who in truth did not quite deserve the harsh criticism which they received. Obviously, it was very difficult to work simultaneously for two different goals: to achieve transition from a wartime to a peacetime economy, and also to fulfill demands for social change. In actuality important measures of social reform were carried through. Work committees in all establishments with more than one hundred workers were introduced to give the employees some part in the organization of work in factories, and a number of key industries—fuel and power, insurance and large financial concerns, air transport and the merchant marine—were nationalized. But with a drift of the parties away from the center to the right and to the left the reform impetus waned. Moreover, the problem was really more fundamental. It was how to renew the outmoded French industrial apparatus which, with its numerous small family enterprises, was resistant to modern technology. The Fourth Republic did handle this matter well. It set up a special office under Jean Monnet (born 1888) to draw up a comprehensive scheme of economic modernization. The Monnet plan established voluntary programs for updating the basic industries, for improving farming methods, and for furthering reconstruction and new building. The government was to provide advice by experts, facilitate the procurement of the necessary labor, and make available the capital needed for investments. Marshall Plan aid, coming at a very opportune moment, was used to help carry out this policy of modernization. Nevertheless, time was needed for the results to become evident, since—as in the Russian Five-Year Plans—the emphasis was placed on heavy industry and the production of machinery. The plan gave priority to coal, electricity, transport, steel, cement, and agricultural machinery. And it would be the Fifth Republic, of Charles de Gaulle, that would harvest much of what the Fourth Republic planted in the field of economic improvement and modernization.

By 1956 French industrial production was 50 per cent higher than it had been in 1929, France's best year during the interwar period, and 87 per cent higher than in 1938, the last year before the war. But this progress in modernizing industry went relatively unnoticed, while the failure of the French government to handle urgent pocketbook issues was all too obvious. The development which hurt the French people most was inflation, produced by the scarcity of goods after the war, by large government loans to industry, and by a series of budgetary deficits. The rapid course of inflation was marked by a steep rise in prices. Wages, although rising, did not keep step, and the purchasing power of both the workers and the middle classes was low; in 1951 the average working-class family spent a third of its weekly budget on meat. Attempts to stem the inflation were futile because the government was unable to get along without a rising deficit. The nationalized industries were unprofitable at this time: the introduction of new forms of management had been costly; the government lacked the courage to brave the indignation which dismissal of superfluous personnel would arouse; and in view of the inflation, the government felt unable to burden the populace further by increases in the costs of railroads and electricity. The social-security system also showed a high deficit because its funds came from a percentage of the workers' wages, but the size of its benefits was determined in relation to prices. In addition the French system of taxation was unsatisfactory, and the left and right wings of the governments were unable to agree on reform.

But even without these many difficulties, it is unlikely that the budget could have been balanced, for funds spent in the effort to preserve French colonial power seemed to pour into a bottomless hole. During the war the French empire had been thrown into confusion. The colonial administrators, possessing a freedom of action which had been lost by the inhabitants of Axis-controlled Europe, were torn between Vichy France and the Free France of De Gaulle. Some segments of the French empire, such as Indochina, were taken by the Japanese; others, such as Madagascar, Syria, and North Africa, were occupied by British and American forces. The loosening of ties with France during the war revealed widespread dissatisfaction with the French colonial system: the chief targets were the authoritarianism with which the colonies were ruled from Paris and the economic exploitation which had cut off the colonies from trade with all countries but France. In all the colonies dissatisfaction was fed by the nationalist movements which had been active since the First World War and received new impetus during the Second World War.

The members of the French constituent assembly realized the necessity of redefining the relationship between France and its overseas possessions. But the arrangements which resulted were a compromise and lacked clarity:

the new constitution provided for a French Union, to consist of metropolitan France, its overseas departments (that is, the administrative units of Algeria, which was regarded as part of France proper), protectorates (Tunisia and Morocco), its colonies (primarily in West Africa), and its associate states (Vietnam, Cambodia, Laos—together constituting Indochina). The president of the French republic was also to be the president of this French Union, and he was assisted by an assembly. But the assembly had only advisory functions, and half of its members represented metropolitan France, so real power remained with the Paris government. A promise for elected assemblies in each of the overseas territories was also rather deceptive, since the composition and the powers of these assemblies were to be determined by the French parliament. Certainly the influence of the natives remained carefully hedged in, and the very limited concessions to the desire for self-rule could not stem the colonial movements toward nationalism and independence.

Yet preservation of the empire bore not only upon French financial interests and economic power but upon the most sensitive nerve of the French political body: the army. The French army had never been entirely integrated into the life of the republic. Against the anticlerical and individualistic spirit of the French Revolution it had regarded itself as the guardian of discipline and of national tradition. With the victory in the First World War the contrasts between the army and the republic had receded into the background, and in the 1920's one of France's greatest soldiers, the monarchist Marshal Lyautey, pacified Morocco and accomplished in the service of the Third Republic what has been characterized as "the masterpiece of French colonization." Lyautey, in whose school many of the officers of the two world wars were trained, composed a famous essay "On the Colonial Role of the Army" (1900). If the spirit of the republic was not very favorable toward the ideas of the army, outside the republic—in the colonies—the army could play a great role in the service of France. Moreover, there were a number of elite regiments, with distinguished military records, consisting of Africans.

Postwar developments strengthened the ties between the officer corps and the French colonial empire. In 1940 the military had suffered a crushing loss of prestige, and at the end of the Second World War cadres of the French resistance demanded a place in the army; for the regular officers they were intruders, an alien and unpalatable element. And the entire atmosphere of postwar France was antagonistic to the traditions of the army. The political climate in which socialists were regarded as a moderating force and the intellectual climate in which the value of revolution was accepted by the most prominent intellectual leaders of postwar France whatever their political views might be—by the Communist Jean-Paul Sartre (born 1905) or the anti-Communist Albert Camus (1913–1960)—were contrary to the ideas in which French officers were trained. The close military collaboration in Europe with officers of other nationalities, particularly with Americans, resulted in an emphasis on new weapons and the technological aspects of warfare and a tendency to overlook the values of the past; and the joint European military organization did not grant French officers that prominent place to which they felt entitled by the great military history of France. But in the colonies the army could be what it had always been; it could maintain—or regain—its identity.

Thus, the army embarked with enthusiasm on the task of asserting France's claim to regain its former possessions in Indochina. It must be said also that many civilian politicians supported the army, since they perceived that a gain in French international prestige might earn them the popular appeal they lost by their handling of domestic affairs. After this enterprise ended in the ignominious defeat of Dien Bien Phu, and in bitter recriminations between civilian and military leaders, the latter tried to regain prestige for the army by eager support of other enterprises which would show that France was still an imperial power: for example, the cooperation with Great Britain and Israel against Egypt in the Suez Affair.

BRITAIN

The people of Great Britain, under siege since 1940, also expected the end of the war to usher in a better world. Their longing for an escape from the dark and anxious years of the war, and for a new life, revealed itself almost immediately. Even before Japan's surrender, the British electorate overthrew Churchill. The Labor party received just 100,000 more votes than the other parties, but they were so distributed that Labor emerged with a majority of 250 over the Conservatives and Liberals in the House of Commons. There were several reasons for this change in government. The Conservatives had been in power since 1931, and if elections had not been postponed because of the war, the usual swing away from the party in power would probably have occurred five years earlier. The credit which Churchill's war leadership had gained could not be transferred to the Conservative party. The slowness with which the Conservatives had enacted measures to overcome depression before the war, the failure of Chamberlain's appeasement policy, the lack of energy in pursuing rearmament, which had left Great Britain open to Nazi aggression —all these were still in the minds of the people. Greater enthusiasm and greater effort for social reform could be expected from Labor than from the Conservatives. An important factor was that Labor had been a coalition partner in the Churchill government, and some of Labor's leaders—Clement Attlee, Ernest Bevin, Sir Stafford Cripps—had played distinguished roles in the war.

The government now formed by Clement Attlee (1883–1967) became one of Britain's great reform ministries. Building on the foundation laid by Asquith's Liberal government before the First World War, Labor established the "welfare state." The National Insurance Act, which became law in 1946, provided for almost complete coverage in cases of sickness, old age, and unemployment. It is characteristic of the connection between Labor and the pre-1914 Liberals that this act grew out of a report by the Liberal economist William Beveridge. The National Insurance Act was complemented by a National Health Service Act which assured complete medical care to all residents of Britain; it aroused the bitter resistance of physicians and was carried through by the energy of Aneurin Bevan (1897–1960), probably the one Labor leader who somewhat resembled Churchill in imagination, charm, and rhetorical power. Like the Liberals before the First World War, the Labor party encountered resistance in the House of Lords. The result was further curtailment of the power of the upper chamber with respect to legislation; henceforth it could only impose a veto effecting a brief delay.

In economic policy Labor went far beyond anything the Liberals had ever envisaged, undertaking to create a socialist society, although the term used was "nationalization" rather than "socialization." The Bank of England, the road-transport system, coal mines, civil aviation, canals and docks, the electrical supply industry, and the iron industry were placed under state control and managed by government-appointed boards. The previous owners received compensation.

Through such measures Labor expected to provide a new impetus to British economic life and increased opportunity to the masses. However, these reforms did not provide the expected stimulus to society because the British people were exhausted after the tensions of the long war. Moreover, the beneficial effects of these reforms were counteracted by their coincidence with a severe economic crisis.

The developments of the Second World War had aggravated the long-standing difficulties of British economic life, particularly the problem of its unfavorable balance of trade. British foreign assets had disappeared and foreign debts had increased. Some temporary relief and some improvement in the competitive position of British goods on foreign markets was achieved through loans from the United States and a devaluation of the currency in September, 1949. But a lasting remedy could come only from a limitation of imports and an increase in exports—restriction of the production of consumer goods for the home market and forced production of goods for foreign markets. The Labor government, whose socialist ideology justified a controlled economy, continued rationing of food, fuel, and clothing, and restricted the amount of currency which a traveler might take out of the country. The architect of this austerity policy was Sir Stafford Cripps (1889–1952), a brilliantly gifted technocrat, also an ascetic, who was little inclined to acknowledge the need for human amenities. The time of Labor rule was constraining rather than liberating, gloomy rather than exhilarating.

The economic situation was further aggravated by the expense involved in maintaining Britain's empire. Colonies facilitated access to raw materials such as oil, rubber, and cotton and to foodstuffs such as coffee, tea, and rice. But they also burdened the mother country with the need to maintain a strong military posture all over the globe. Indeed, of the many justifications for colonial rule produced by the Victorians, the one which still had some validity was that only a modern industrial power could adequately defend a colony against attack. The preservation of an empire required an extended military establishment, with all the expenses necessary for the equipment of a modern army, navy, and air force. And in a time of shrinking distances successful military protection also involved participation in the politics of the entire area in which the colonial territory was situated. Indeed, at the end of the war British troops were distributed all over the world; they were to be found in Germany, Italy, and Greece; in the Near East, Egypt, and Africa; and in the extended regions of southeast Asia. There was no conflict on the globe in which Britain was not involved. Unquestionably the occupation forces in Germany, expensive as they were, had to be maintained if Great Britain was to continue to play a role in Europe. But in the nation's straitened economic circumstances, an increase of the working force at home and a reduction in military expenses were evidently desirable, and the Labor government became anxious to decrease non-European military obligations as far as possible.

Abandonment of Britain's colonies was entirely compatible with Labor's fundamental principles. The party had always opposed imperialism and its concomitant, power politics. Although in the wartime conferences Churchill had emphasized the special interest of Great Britain in the eastern Mediterranean, the Labor government in 1948 declared itself unable to defend Greece and Turkey against Communism and left this task to the United States. The result was the Truman Doctrine. Moreover, the Labor government was anxious to give independence to those British colonies and dependencies which had fully developed political institutions and to introduce self-government for those which were still ruled by British governors because they were believed to be unready for independence. The most spectacular result of this policy was the granting of independence to India. The Labor government offered full freedom to India in March, 1946, but implementation was delayed by difficulties chiefly of an internal nature, caused by the differences between Hindus and Moslems. After long negotiations, the only feasible solution appeared to be the establishment of two states, one Hindu and one Moslem. The creation of India

Fuel shortage in Great Britain. *During the bitterly cold winter of 1948, the British people stood in long queues to draw their meager coal rations.*

and Pakistan involved an exchange of population, the moving of millions of refugees, accompanied by terrible hardships. Moreover, the delineation of the frontiers did not cleanly separate Hindus from Moslems, and some controversies, such as the dispute over the control of Kashmir, led to bitter and long-lasting tension between the two states. The most distinguished victim of the hatred aroused by the division of India and Gandhi, the founder of the modern Indian nationalist movement; in 1948 he was assassinated by a fanatic Hindu who resented his agreement to the establishment of two states. Nevertheless, the creation of an independent India and Pakistan ended an explosive situation which had troubled the British empire for decades, and Labor had the added satisfaction that India decided to remain a member of the British Commonwealth. The granting of independence to India led unavoidably to the same change in status for the other states of this area: Burma and Ceylon, with Burma leaving, Ceylon remaining in the Commonwealth.

However, the continued restrictions on economic life at home were diminishing the government's popularity, and Labor began to lose ground. Elections in 1950 resulted in a Labor majority so small that it was almost unmanageable. In October, 1951, the Conservatives were returned to power and Churchill again became prime minister. Some Labor measures —the nationalization of the iron and steel industries and of road transport —were revoked. But the Conservatives were aware that they had received no mandate to eliminate the main features of the welfare state. Moreover, the possibilities for initiating a new economic policy were limited because payments of pensions, compensation for war damage, expenses for the welfare state, and interest on public loans formed large, irremovable items in the budget. Nor were the Conservatives able to solve the basic problem of the deficit in the balance of trade. Yet life in Britain did become less constricted. The Conservatives were helped by the general prosperity of the 1950's; they succeeded in cutting red tape and in accelerating housing construction. The Conservatives only improved upon the domestic policy of the Labor government; they did not alter it.

But the Conservatives differed basically from Labor in their view about Britain's position in the world. Churchill declared in a famous speech that he had not become the king's prime minister to preside over the dissolution of the British Empire. The Conservatives were decided to take a more aggressive stand in foreign affairs. This was one of the motives for the British joining the French and Israelis in what became the Suez crisis.

CHAPTER 13

The Crises of 1956 and
Their Impact on International Relations

THE GROWTH OF TENSIONS WITHIN THE EASTERN
AND WESTERN BLOCS

IT IS A STRANGE coincidence that in the fall of 1956 in the East and West the leading powers of the two blocs—the United States and Soviet Russia—took action against members of their own alliance: Russia against Hungary, the United States against France and Britain. The strangeness of this coincidence, however, consists less in the fact itself than in the simultaneity of the events. It was not unnatural that the bonds of the two alliances, which had been very tightly knit under the pressure of postwar events, began to loosen, especially when, as after the settlement in Indochina, the world situation looked less threatening. We have mentioned that the Russians had become aware that their demands for rapid industrialization and collectivization created dangerous social tensions in the satellite countries: thus they were modifying their policy; the Hungarian Revolt arose out of the ticklish situation which such a change in policy can create. In the West political and economic bonds had been forged simultaneously, but although their effects were long-lasting, the active phase of the European Recovery Program had ended by 1952. The weight of the alliance shifted to diplomatic and military cooperation; insofar as further assistance was given by the United States, it was channeled through the Mutual Security Agency, which was concerned with military needs. As a result the ideological bond—the notion of defending the traditions and values of western civilization—which had helped to cement the western alliance, began to lose its significance. The alliance seemed more and more an instrument of American power politics; this aspect emerged strongly in the question of the treatment of the Spanish dictatorship of Francisco Franco.

During the Second World War, Spanish volunteers had fought on the side of the Axis against Russia, although Franco, emphasizing the poverty of his country, avoided direct participation; after the war the victorious governments seriously considered taking steps to overthrow the Franco regime. But in 1953, after vainly trying to overcome the resistance of its European allies to the admission of Spain to NATO, the United States made agreements with Spain by which in return for assistance to the Spanish army, navy, and air force, it obtained military bases in Spain. This was a decisive step in stimulating industrial activity in Spain, which in the following years gained increasing power and speed. When in 1955, after a visit to Spain, the American secretary of state, John Foster Dulles, joined Franco to issue a communiqué stating that they "found themselves in mutual understanding" with regard to "the principal problems that affected the peace and security of free nations," the term "free world," which western statesmen liked to apply to the American alliance system, acquired a somewhat hollow sound. If the United States could act in this way on its own, the western European leaders felt they had the right to do likewise.

CRISIS IN THE EAST

Unrest in Poland and Hungary

Although the basic reasons for discontent—forced and rapid collectivization—were the same in Hungary as in other satellite countries, the Hungarian situation had its peculiar complicating features. The possibility of a revolt arose from a struggle between Stalinists and the adherents of the new Communist line. When Nagy became prime minister, his Stalinist predecessor, Rákosi, remained party secretary. In the first year of Nagy's regime, 51 per cent of the collective-farm members left the collective system, and 12 per cent of the collective farms had to be dissolved; Nagy intended to continue the policy of abandoning concentration on heavy industry and instead strengthening the development of the other sectors of the economy. Since the war, the working classes in Hungary had increased by almost 50 per cent, and a thorough training of these masses in Communist doctrine had not been possible. With the slowing down of collectivization in agriculture, Communist control of the rural population also became weakened. Accordingly, the Communist party regarded the measures introduced by Nagy with suspicion and feared that it might be losing its grip over the workers and peasants.

When Khrushchev accused Malenkov, his rival for Stalin's succession, of mistakes in the direction of industrial and agricultural policy, Rákosi, who controlled the Central Committee of the Hungarian Communist party, incriminated Nagy as a follower of Malenkov. Taking advantage of Nagy's temporary illness, he succeeded in deposing him as prime minister and expelling him from the party. Rákosi returned to power as prime minister in the spring of 1955. But the clock could not be turned back. In the meetings of clubs named for the poet Sandor Petöfi, which had been set up by the government for intellectual improvement, students and intellectuals debated political issues; both industrial workers and the rural population remained critical and suspicious of the Rákosi government. When in the summer of 1956 Rákosi moved to arrest Nagy and four hundred of his associates, he encountered opposition in the Central Committee, and some members of this opposition turned to the Soviet embassy for help. Perturbed by the revolutionary ferment in Hungary, the Russians decided to drop Rákosi and install a new prime minister, Ernö Gerö, who was expected to steer a middle line between Rákosi's Stalinism and Nagy's new course.

That this attempt at "controlled transition" failed was to a large extent the result of external events. Just at this time, Khrushchev moved to improve relations with Yugoslavia. The rejection of Stalin's policy, which early in 1956 had been publicly proclaimed at the Twentieth Congress of the Communist party, included a condemnation of Stalin's treatment of Tito, and in consequence meetings between the Russian and Yugoslav leaders took place, which resulted on June 20, 1956, in a communiqué declaring "that the ways of socialist development vary in different countries and conditions," and "that the wealth of the forms of socialist development contributes to its strength." Naturally, the Russian satellites in eastern Europe asked why they should not have that freedom of choice in the form of socialist development which had been granted to Yugoslavia.

The first country in which demands for autonomy in domestic affairs were raised was Poland. There, the changed Russian attitude after Stalin's death had not resulted in any great shift in leadership or any dramatic reversal in economic policy; it had largely meant a general relaxation which curtailed the power of the secret police and permitted greater freedom in intellectual expression. In March, 1956, the sudden death of Bierut, who had dominated the Polish Communist party since the war, gave new impetus to the liberalizing trend. In April, amnesty was granted to thirty thousand prisoners, among them nine thousand political offenders. And it became evident that demands for a change had spread widely among the workers. In June, a strike in Poznán had to be suppressed by military forces. Impressed by the amount of dissatisfaction which had come to the fore in the Poznán strike, the majority of the government, including Bierut's successor as party secretary, accepted the need to accelerate liberalization. Wladyslaw Gomulka (born 1905), who had been released from prison, was permitted to participate in the deliberations of the Central Committee and became a member of the Polish Politburo, while Marshal Konstantin Rokossovski, the commander of the Russian troops in Poland, was relieved of his membership in the Polish Politburo. The great question was whether the Soviet leaders would regard these actions as provocative. However, in negotiations with the Russians, Gomulka was able to overcome their distrust. Though he had always been critical of the precipitate collectivization of agriculture which the Russians had imposed on the satellites, he was a loyal Marxist-Leninist, convinced of the need for the Communist party to keep control and exert leadership, and persuaded that Russia and Poland had to stand together. Briefly, he assured the Russians that Poland would remain a reliable member of the Warsaw Pact. Assured of Polish loyalty in foreign policy, the Russian leaders were willing to permit Poland autonomy in seeking its "ways of socialist development." On October 21, 1956, Gomulka was elected general secretary of the Polish Communist party.

The Revolt in Hungary

The Russian concessions to Yugoslavia and Poland provided the spark for events in Hungary. When the Hungarians heard of the success of the Polish move, they felt that they too should try to gain greater independence. At the universities of Budapest, Pécs, and Szeged, in the Budapest technical college, and in other public buildings, heated debates took place about the means to force the government into greater activity; it was agreed to hold a "silent sympathy demonstration" before the Polish embassy on October 23. It is estimated that more than fifty thousand people participated in this demonstration. In the evening Prime Minister Gerö made a broadcast. He had been expected to accept the need for a more independent and liberal policy, but instead, surprisingly, Gerö took a hard Stalinist line in his speech. In response, the public demonstrations assumed a sharply antigovernment character. The gigantic statue of Stalin in the city park was demolished, and students attempted to take over the radio station, in order to broadcast the demands of the opposition. To protect the building, the police began to shoot. Troops were sent against the crowds surrounding the station, but instead of dispersing the demonstrators they fraternized with them. The government proved powerless to control the opposition.

The distinguishing feature of the Hungarian revolution was that, in contrast to the Polish events of the same month, it did not remain limited to a struggle within the party between the Stalinists and the adherents of a new course, but developed into a movement against Communist rule in general. Encouraging broadcasts from the West, which seemed to promise outside support, played their role in transforming the intraparty conflict into an anti-Communist revolt. But the reasons for the broadening impact of the revolt were manifold. On the night of October 23 the government, in panicky desperation, appealed to the Russian troops for help and announced at the same time that Imre Nagy had become prime minister. Nagy's appointment was expected to appease the demonstrators, but he was also expected to share the powers of government with Gerö and other Stalinists. The Russian military forces in Hungary were weak and their advance into

Budapest resulted in bitter, indecisive fighting, while in the countryside, now free of troops, revolutionary committees were formed. The frontier between Hungary and Austria was opened.

Nagy, whose appointment had been announced without his own approval, was in a thoroughly untenable position. Because of the government appeal for help to Russian troops, and his presumed cooperation with Gerö, the opposition leaders regarded Nagy with the greatest distrust. They believed that his assumption of office could not be considered a guarantee of the beginning of a new course, and that therefore this was not the time to relax pressure on the government. Complying with the demands of the anti-Stalinists, Nagy got rid of Gerö and formed a government composed chiefly of members of the Communist opposition; György Lukács, the famous Marxist scholar, became minister of education. But by then many non-Communists had joined the opposition movement, and they were not content to abandon the struggle without further liberation measures. For instance, Cardinal Mindszenty, who was freed from prison and whose courageous stand against the government gave him great authority, demanded the formation of a Christian Democratic party similar to Adenauer's party in Germany. He stated that he "rejected *en bloc* everything Hungary had done since 1945, not only since 1949, and the establishment of dictatorship." And he came out in favor of "private ownership."

Nagy was rightly afraid that the Russians might interfere if order were not quickly reestablished. He tried to appease the non-Communist opposition by taking into the government leaders of the former Social Democratic,

The Hungarian revolution. *The Stalin statue is pulled down and destroyed.*

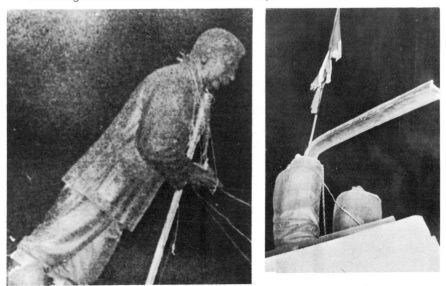

Small Holder, and National Peasant parties. But they were willing to cooperate with him and the Communists only if he made further concessions. On October 30 Nagy announced the restoration of a multiparty system, and on October 31 he declared that Hungary proposed to withdraw from the Warsaw Pact.

It is evident that the Russians could not permit a break in their bloc. They had been waiting and vacillating in their attitude to the events in Hungary. Probably they would have followed the kind of policy they adopted toward Poland, permitting Nagy freedom to undertake economic and cultural changes, if there had been no doubt of Hungary's adherence to the basic principles of Communism and of its loyalty to the Warsaw Pact. The Russians had agreed to withdraw their troops from Hungary on October 30, but at the same time they began to assemble strong forces along the Hungarian frontier, preparing for any eventuality. When Nagy announced Hungary's secession from the Warsaw Pact, they decided to intervene. In the early morning of November 4, Russian troops entered Budapest, and by nightfall the revolt had ended. Mindszenty found asylum in the American embassy. Nagy sought refuge in the Yugoslav embassy, but was handed over to the Hungarians, and he and other leaders of the liberating movement were executed. Some of the participants managed to escape over the Austrian frontier, and there, as along the Franco-Spanish border seventeen years before, camps were established to house the disillusioned and impoverished refugees whose desperate stand for freedom had been crushed by the pitilessly functioning machines of totalitarian dictatorship.

THE SUEZ AFFAIR

An underlying motive of the British Conservative government in taking action in Suez was its concern with the decline of the British imperial power; it was an attempt to restore British authority in the Near East. But the occasion for action arose out of long, involved negotiations about the independence of Egypt which had started immediately after the war. The Labor ministry had not been able to resolve the issues in dispute between Great Britain and Egypt. Labor had declared its readiness to withdraw British forces from Egypt, as desired by the Egyptian government, but had refused to let the Sudan come under Egyptian rule against the wishes of the Sudanese people. Egypt's pride had been further hurt by the failure of its army to crush the state of Israel, which had arisen after the British mandate ended in 1948. The United States and Soviet Russia granted immediate recognition to Israel and after a successful defense against the surrounding Arab states Israel was taken into the United Nations. The withdrawal of British troops from Palestine weakened Britain's military posture in the Near East and this stimulated Egyptian nationalist demands. Nationalist students and an aroused populace engaged in fierce demonstrations against foreigners and put the Egyptian government under pressure to force the withdrawal of British troops from Egypt, the Sudan, and Suez. Clashes between British troops and Egyptian volunteers, the looting and burning of buildings and shops in Cairo by the excited masses, and the power struggle between a discredited government and a luxury-loving king brought Egypt to the brink of chaos. In 1952 a revolution by nationalist army officers deposed the king, ended the rule of the old party politicians, and established an authoritarian republic. The new regime was anxious for a success in foreign relations; the Conservatives now in power in Britain used this opportunity to arrive at a settlement. They agreed to a complete withdrawal of British forces from Egypt and the Suez Canal, in exchange for guarantees that free passage through the canal and its control through the international Suez Canal Company would be maintained. Moreover, in case of war the British received the right to reenter the canal area with their troops. The Sudan became an independent state. Opposition to this agreement came from Conservative dichards who regarded the treaty as a British defeat. But the government explained that with the growing importance of air transport and air warfare, the Suez Canal had lost its strategic significance.

It is evident, however, that the British policy makers had still other reasons for seeking an understanding with the new Egyptian rulers. No longer burdened with the mandate over Palestine which had poisoned British relations with the Arab states, Britain's Conservative rulers were anxious again to establish Great Britain as the great ally of the Arab nations and the leading power in the Near East. The wealth of this area—notably oil, with pipelines running to the Mediterranean—and its geographical situation as a link between the Mediterranean and India, meant that the power controlling it was an important force in world politics. Gamal Abdel Nasser (1918–1970), who had emerged as the leader of the new Egypt, was trying to combine the Arab nations in a unified bloc, and the British regarded their agreement with him as a step toward strengthening their nation's hold in the entire region. But they seem to have been too confident of Arab backing. When in 1955 Britain made a defense pact with Turkey and Iraq, the so-called Baghdad Pact, Egypt reacted sharply against this western interference in Near Eastern policy, particularly in the plans for a common Arab defense league. And Nasser showed his independence from the West by recognizing Communist China and ordering armaments from Czechoslovakia. This Egyptian flirtation with the East was taken amiss by the United States, which on July 19, 1956, withdrew its offer to help finance the building of a dam at Aswan. A week later, on July 26, Nasser declared that Egypt was nationalizing the Suez Canal Company and would use the revenue for the building of the Aswan Dam.

The Suez affair of October, 1956, must be seen against this background. The Conservative government wanted to maintain a strong British position in the Near East and had agreed to a troop withdrawal from Egypt and the Suez area because it expected to gain Arab cooperation. When Nasser showed more independence than had been expected, the British saw in his breach of the agreement on the Suez Canal an opportunity to crush him. Anthony Eden, who had followed Churchill as prime minister in 1955, joined the leaders of Israel and France in secretly preparing a military operation which would begin with a clash between Israel and Egypt and then lead to the intervention of French and British troops, which would occupy the Suez Canal to separate the Egyptian and Israeli forces. Militarily the operation was executed as planned, but diplomatically the plot failed. The British miscalculated the American attitude. An explanation of the zig-zag course of American policy in the Suez affair, if an explanation is possible, must be left to specialists in the history of American diplomacy. The fact is that the United States and Soviet Russia, cooperating in the United Nations, forced the British and French to accept a ceasefire on November 3, 1956, and to evacuate the canal area. Instead of restoring Britain's old influence in the Near East the affair marked the end of a chapter in British imperial history.

In 1958 a *coup d'état* overthrew the pro-British regime in Iraq, killing King Faisal II, his heir, and the prime minister, Nuri as-Said. Britain had lost its most reliable ally in the Near East. When the pro-western president of Lebanon felt threatened, his position was upheld by the landing not of British but of American troops. In 1959, Britain conceded independence to Cyprus, thereby abandoning its last important military stronghold in this region. Henceforth, if outside powers played a role in the rivalries and maneuverings of the Arab countries, they were Soviet Russia and the United States; they no longer included Great Britain.

THE CRISES OF 1956 IN RETROSPECT

It has frequently been said that the Suez affair, which began on October 30 and therefore coincided with the events in Hungary, caused the failure of the Hungarian revolt. Perhaps the developments in the Near East did hasten the Russians' decision to intervene, for surely they did not want to have an exposed flank in southeastern Europe in the event of a serious international crisis; without Suez there might have been a chance for the Hungarians to negotiate a less brutal surrender. But there can be no doubt that as soon as the opposition movement had developed into an anti-Communist revolt, the Russians were forced to reestablish their authority over Hungary. And it is certainly nonsense to maintain that if the West had been united, the uprising might have succeeded. Neither the United States nor any western European power was willing at this moment to undertake war with Russia, and since the Russians could not tolerate Hungary's defection to the West, active support of the revolt by the West would have meant war. Actually, the American government owed a certain amount of gratitude to the British and French because the Suez affair provided a justification for America's inactivity in Hungary. The Suez affair concealed the fact that the Russians had called the bluff of the American liberation policy.

The events of October–November, 1956, despite the upheaval which they caused in international relations, ultimately had the effect of reducing tension between the United States and Russia. The unwillingness of the western powers to give more than vocal support to the Hungarian revolt could be taken by Russia as a sign that although they had refused officially to acknowledge that eastern Europe was a Soviet sphere of interest, they did actually recognize Russia's control over this area. In the handling of the Suez affair—in forcing the British and French to evacuate the area which they had occupied—the United States cooperated with the Soviet Union, and although an underlying American motive may have been to prevent the Arab nations from throwing themselves into Russia's arms, the Russians must have regarded the American attitude as a sign of the weakening of imperialist aggression. The tone of American-Soviet diplomatic exchanges did not improve, but there seemed to be less danger of action behind the threats.

The Development of Independent States in Africa

Whereas the movement for the establishment of the rule of indigenous people in the Far East received its decisive impetus from the collapse of Japanese power at the end of the Second World War, for the end of colonial rule in Africa the Suez affair was of decisive importance. The British Labor government had cautiously begun to promote self-government in Britain's colonies in Africa by establishing legislative assemblies in the Gold Coast and Nigeria and by increasing the number of nonwhite members in the legislative council of Kenya. After Suez, Britain accelerated the termination of its responsibilities in Africa; also the Conservatives now admitted that the maintenance of a colonial empire involved Britain in difficult military struggles and was too heavy a burden.

In 1957 Ghana, the former Gold Coast, became independent; at the celebration the duchess of Kent, the queen's cousin, danced the fox-trot with President Kwame Nkrumah under the admiring gaze of the American vice president, Richard Nixon. Nigeria gained independence in 1960; Sierra Leone and Tanganyika, in 1961; Uganda, in 1962: Kenya, in 1963. All these new republics remained members of the Commonwealth. Only British Somaliland, which in 1960 united with Italian Somaliland, became an independent state outside the Commonwealth. The Conserva-

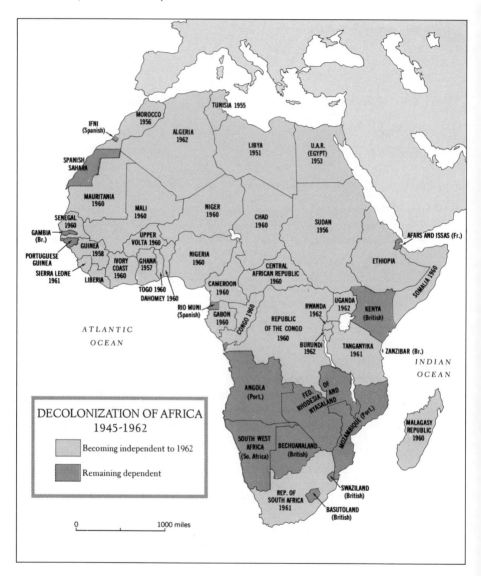

TUNISIA 1955

MOROCCO
1956

IFNI
(Spanish)

ALGERIA
1962

LIBYA
1951

U.A.R.
(EGYPT)
1953

SPANISH
SAHARA

MAURITANIA
1960

MALI
1960

NIGER
1960

CHAD
1960

SUDAN
1956

AFARS AND ISSAS (Fr.)

SENEGAL
1960

GAMBIA
(Br.)

GUINEA
1958

UPPER
VOLTA 1960

PORTUGUESE
GUINEA

SIERRA LEONE
1961

IVORY
COAST
1960

GHANA
1957

NIGERIA
1960

CENTRAL
AFRICAN REPUBLIC
1960

ETHIOPIA

LIBERIA

TOGO 1960

DAHOMEY 1960

CAMEROON
1960

SOMALIA 1960

RIO MUNI
(Spanish)

GABON
1960

CONGO 1960

RWANDA
1962

UGANDA
1962

KENYA
(British)

ATLANTIC
OCEAN

REPUBLIC
OF THE CONGO
1960

BURUNDI
1962

TANGANYIKA
1961

ZANZIBAR (Br.)

INDIAN
OCEAN

ANGOLA
(Port.)

FED.
OF
RHODESIA AND
NYASALAND

MOZAMBIQUE (Port.)

MALAGASY
REPUBLIC
1960

DECOLONIZATION OF AFRICA
1945-1962

Becoming independent to 1962

Remaining dependent

SOUTH WEST
AFRICA
(So. Africa)

BECHUANALAND
(British)

SWAZILAND
(British)

REP. OF
SOUTH AFRICA
1961

BASUTOLAND
(British)

0   1000 miles

tive conversion to anticolonialism was dramatically underlined by a speech made in Cape Town, South Africa, by Harold Macmillan (born 1894), who had replaced Anthony Eden as prime minister after the Suez debacle. Macmillan spoke of the "wind of change" sweeping through the African continent, unmistakably dissociating himself from the white man's belief in his superiority over the black.

The movements for emancipation in the various colonial territories of Africa affected one another. Ghana's achievement of sovereignty in 1957 strengthened and accelerated nationalism all over central Africa. In this political climate Belgium felt unable to keep control over its large colonial empire. In 1960, in a precipitate move, Belgium granted independence to the Congo, and in the same year the Republic of the Congo was admitted to the United Nations. During their rule in the Congo, the Belgians were frequently criticized for exploiting the people, and indeed they cared little about educating or giving rights to their colonial subjects. When the Belgian administration withdrew, the Congolese were insufficiently prepared to take over. The country had rich mineral resources; its mines yielded copper, diamonds, and 90 per cent of the world's supply of uranium. Coffee and cotton were the major products of its agriculture. But the people of this economically important and wealthy region still lived in a tribal society. The sudden relinquishment of power by the Belgian rulers led to outbreaks against the whites, to turmoil and internal war. The central government in Leopoldville was opposed by separatist movements, backed by white businessmen who wanted to protect their lives, their properties, and their investments and were assisted in their struggle by white mercenaries. The central government appealed to Soviet Russia for help against the white capitalists, and the Congo conflict threatened to cause a serious crisis between East and West. Its course was punctuated by bitter debates in the United Nations. By 1963 the struggle had died down, and with the help of the United Nations a settled state was obtained. The Russians had lost their most prominent adherent, Patrice Lumumba, who in 1961 had been murdered, but the United States also abandoned support of the prowhite separatist regime in Katanga.

The Congo crisis strikingly illustrated the fact that in central Africa, the struggle was not just between colonials and their foreign rulers but between black men and white. The conflict had a strongly racial element. The racial issue has become decisive in the most southern regions of Africa—South Africa and Rhodesia—where the whites, although their number is not inconsiderable, form a small minority within the total population. In Rhodesia, attempts to create a more stable regime by bringing the blacks into the government, unavoidably kept Great Britian, because of former ties and economic interests, involved as intermediary trying to effect a non-violent transition from white to black rule. These British attempts were supported by the United States, fearing that without peaceful transition to indigenous rule, the blacks would look for support to Soviet Russia. Competitions among the newly established indigenous states as well as their economic importance invites interference from outside and makes this area a target for rivalry among the superpowers.

The End of French Colonial Rule in Africa

The longest, most complex, and most bitterly fought struggle developed over the termination of French colonial rule in Africa; the beginnings of this struggle go back to the years before the Suez affair and the end was reached only in 1962, six years after Suez.

In November, 1954, four months after the settlement of the hostilities in Indochina negotiated by Prime Minister Pierre Mendès-France (born 1907) in Geneva, an outbreak of terrorism occurred in Algeria; it was the beginning of a long and devastating war. The French army looked upon the situation in Algeria with a certain satisfaction; it was sure that now it had the opportunity of avenging its defeat in the Far East and of proving its value for France. Moslem nationalists had become increasingly active in French North Africa: Morocco, Tunisia, and Algeria. In Morocco and Tunisia the French government decided to yield to the movements for independence. Arrangements were initiated by Mendès-France immediately after the settlement in Indochina, and although French rightists, with the support of the army, succeeded in overthrowing Mendès-France and delaying the conclusion of the necessary agreements, Morocco received independence on March 2, 1956, and Tunisia on March 20, 1956. The defenders of French colonial interests found some justification for the abandonment of Morocco and Tunisia in the expectation that these two countries would now refrain from supporting the Algerian nationalists.

There was no intention of giving up Algeria, where the situation was judged to be fundamentally different from that in Tunisia and Morocco. Algeria had been a French possession for more than a hundred years. Many Frenchmen had settled there, and administratively Algeria, which was divided into the departments of Algiers, Oran, and Constantine, formed part of continental France. Dissatisfaction with French rule arose from the fact that the role of the Moslems was subordinate to that of the *colons*, or European settlers. There were two electoral colleges, each choosing the same number of deputies, but the electorate of one consisted of 1.2 million settlers, that of the other of 8.5 million Moslems. Because Algeria essentially formed part of France, the granting· of independence was vehemently opposed not only by the army and the extreme right but also by many adherents of the government parties. The government therefore jogged a weary course. Together with Israel and Great Britain, France engineered the action against Egypt after the nationalization of the Suez

Canal, hoping that this blow to Arab nationalism would discourage the Moslems in Algeria. However, when the Suez affair ended in a fiasco, the movement for Algerian independence grew in strength. Guerilla warfare, which the Moslems conducted with great skill, absorbed more than 400,000 French soldiers, who were unable to put an end to terroristic acts or to restore safety in the hinterland. The mounting costs of the war increased the French budgetary deficit and accelerated inflation.

The barbaric cruelty with which the war was pursued aroused sharp criticism among French intellectuals and men of the church. A left-wing opposition to the war began to develop. The various governments tried to restore peace by offering the Moslems increased political influence but fearing the strength of the French opposition to surrender, they did not go very far in their concessions; and the Frenchmen in Algiers, with the full backing of the officers in command there, were adamant in refusing to accept any diminution of their power. Orders of the French government which ran against the wishes of the *colons* and the army were barely obeyed.

In the spring of 1958 the crisis came to a head. Weak and frequently changing governments slowly moved in the direction of further concessions to the nationalists. On May 13, 1958, during a government crisis in Paris, in the course of a demonstration by the *colons* against the vacillations of Paris the government building in Algiers was occupied, and the army agreed to spearhead the move against further concessions. A new government quickly established in Paris proved unable to assert its authority over the military in Algiers. On the contrary, the rebelling French officers in Algeria were in direct contact with officers and deputies in metropolitan France; to show the helplessness of the government, troops under order of the generals in Algiers occupied Corsica. Without means to suppress the rebellion the parliamentary politicians gave in, and on May 29, 1958, Charles de Gaulle was installed as prime minister.

The Rise of Charles de Gaulle

Those who brought De Gaulle into power—army officers in Algiers and metropolitan France, *colons* in North Africa, politicians of the right and center such as Jacques Soustelle and Georges Bidault—later had reason to regret what they had done. But in 1958, De Gaulle, who was both an officer and the leader of a popular movement, seemed the only person who might be able to inspire the French people to the efforts required to bring the Algerian war to a victorious end. Much psychological insight would have been needed to realize that he was not the man to serve a movement, that he was accustomed to stand for himself and to chart his own course.

In his first measures as prime minister in 1958 De Gaulle acted according to expectations. He accepted office on condition that he be permitted to rule by decree for the next six months and to draft a new constitution, which would be submitted to the people for approval in a referendum. As could be foreseen, the constitution, which was adopted by a clear majority in September, 1958, strengthened the executive branch of the government. The president was to be elected for seven years by the members of the parliament (consisting of a Senate and a National Assembly) and by representatives of the local and regional councils. But a few years later, in 1962, this law was changed, and by a referendum, popular election was introduced. The president was a powerful figure. He had the right to appoint the prime minister and to dissolve the National Assembly. The powers of parliament were weakened in that a vote to overthrow the government required a majority of the total membership of the National Assembly, not just of the members present. Moreover, with the approval of the Assembly the government could, for a limited time, rule by decree; only after this period had ended, which would frequently be after the decrees had fulfilled their purpose, did they have to be ratified by parliament. Assured of being able to carry out what he had in mind, De Gaulle, in January, 1959, assumed the presidency of the Fifth Republic, to which he had been elected late in December.

Independence for Algeria

De Gaulle's constitution also provided a settlement of the colonial question. And this aspect of his constitution showed an unexpected adventurousness. It envisaged a French community in which the various colonies would be autonomous, although in matters of defense, foreign affairs, and overall economic policy, they would act jointly. Actually, this plan for a French community never fully materialized. De Gaulle permitted the colonies to vote on whether they wanted to become members of the community or to enjoy complete independence. In 1960 the French colonies (Dahomey, Cameroun, Ubangi-Shari, Chad, Gabon, Ivory Coast, Mali, Niger, Senegal, Upper Volta) achieved full independence; but cultural and economic ties with France remained close. Algeria, however, was excluded from these arrangements, and the war there dragged on. While De Gaulle continued to insist that Algeria had to remain French, he cautiously and gradually moved into a more flexible position, and on September 16, 1959, announced that self-determination for Algeria was the only dignified method by which France could discharge its obligations toward North Africa. In a referendum, the Algerians were to be given the choice of assimilation, full independence, or—as a middle way—close association with France. De Gaulle tried to placate the opposition by stating that such a referendum could be held only after the area had been pacified. Nevertheless, his acceptance of self-determination opened the floodgates. The movement toward the separation of Algeria from France became irresistible. On July 8, 1961, the French people approved in a referendum the principle of self-determination for Algeria. The army officers there, in a

Charles de Gaulle in a characteristic pose during a campaign rally.

last desperate move, tried to repeat the game which they had played in 1958. But now they received no support from France, and their own soldiers began to refuse to obey them. The insurrection collapsed; prominent generals, among them Raoul Salan and Maurice Challe, who had led the rebellion, and politicians such as Jacques Soustelle and George Bidault, who were passionate protagonists of a French Algeria, fled and were condemned *in absentia.* Negotiations with Algerian nationalist leaders now began, and although they were interrupted by recurrent crises, a settlement was reached in March, 1962. Algeria was officially named independent on July 3, 1962.

In terminating the Algerian war De Gaulle succeeded in doing what no other French government had been able to do. He did it by turning the eyes of the French army away from the past and toward the future. He proclaimed that the real opportunities for French greatness were in Europe. For this reason the break with the leadership of the army was less dangerous than it might appear; in a France oriented exclusively toward Europe an army based on the traditions of colonial warfare was of little relevance. A modernized force equipped with atomic weapons was appropriate to the goals which De Gaulle had set and De Gaulle spared no expense to make France a nuclear power. For France, the abandonment of the colonies made possible full concentration on Europe. The loss of the empire was a definite end and a new beginning.

CHAPTER 14

Europe Recovered: The Abundant Decade

THERE WAS A TIME when wars were regarded as the most memorable events about which historians reported to later generations. This is no longer our attitude, and in perspective, other factors and forces seem to have exerted greater influence on the course of history. Still, it cannot be denied that the existence of those who lived in the first half of the twentieth century was decisively affected by the two wars which extended over the entire globe and shook the foundations of European life. There is a sharp distinction between prewar and postwar situations, and this is relevant for the First as well as for the Second World War; something of this division underlies the organization of this book and is justified by the importance and the impact of the two world wars. Nevertheless, there comes a time when the problems which a war has created no longer determine the course of events, when a situation has come about which creates a new impetus and gives history a new direction. The postwar period has ended and a new era has begun. This is a gradual process, the result of a variety of factors, and cannot be tied to any particular event or any definite year. But probably it can be said that in the late fifties and the early sixties the shadow of the Second World War began to recede and a new political landscape began to become visible.

A NEW EUROPE

Changes on the International Scene

Changes in the international scene and developments on the European continent combined to set European politics on a new course. On the level of international politics the relations between the United States and Soviet Russia began to take on a new form in the years between 1956 and 1962. The cooperation between the two powers in the Suez crisis and, more importantly, the Hungarian crisis, which revealed American unwillingness to undertake an active policy of liberation, created a somewhat relaxed atmosphere, although this improvement in the political world soon seemed to be only temporary. A new beginning to clear up differences seemed to be made when in November, 1958, Khrushchev, now the acknowledged leader in the Soviet hierarchy, declared that the situation in Berlin represented a serious and acute threat to peace and was no longer tolerable. Probably the presence of the West in Berlin appeared to the Russians increasingly undesirable because the relatively luxurious life of West Berliners nourished the discontent of the East Germans with their regime. Lengthy negotiations between the United States and Russia seemed to introduce a period of détente, with Khrushchev visiting the United States and a visit of President Eisenhower to Moscow in the offing. An agreement was reached that the problem of Berlin ought to be discussed and settled in a summit conference to be held in Paris in May 1960. But when the conference met, the Russian delegation, which had arrived early in Paris, refused to attend because they had just received proof that the Americans were sending high-altitude spy planes over Russia. The consequence of this was a rapid deterioration of relations between the United States and the Soviet Union.

The situation became explosive when, in August, 1961, under the protection of Russian soldiers, a wall was built separating the western and eastern sectors of Berlin. This procedure aroused indignation and violent protests all over the western world. A breach of the wall by American tanks was considered, but in the end no military action was taken. The Russians, on the other hand, stopped interfering with air traffic and communications to West Berlin. As serious as the crisis over the Berlin Wall had appeared at the beginning, its result was actually a diminution of the tension between Soviet Russia and the West over Germany. The lines between East and West Germany were now firmly drawn. The United States, by refraining from taking action, had indirectly conceded a sphere of interest to the Russians, in which they could do what they wanted. On the other hand, a visit by President Kennedy to West Berlin two years later underlined that any Russian interference in affairs outside East Germany would be regarded as an attack.

Although the outcome of the crisis over the building of the Berlin Wall was to defuse a potentially dangerous situation, it must also be considered an American retreat. During the Cuban Missile Crisis, which occurred in the fall of 1962, one year after the Berlin Wall, the Americans did not back down: withdrawal of Russian ballistic missiles from Cuba was made under the pressure of an American naval blockade. Both events —the Berlin Wall and the Cuban Missile Crisis—revealed that a stalemate had been reached between the United States and Russia, and that both were aware of the dreadful consequences, and therefore impossibility, of nuclear war between them.

There was a further reason why the United States and Soviet Russia became less inclined to let their differences evolve in a serious confronta-

Part of the Berlin Wall.

tion: both regarded with great suspicion developments in the Far East.

Since the late fifties disputes over Communist tactics had arisen between Mao's China and Khrushchev's Russia; the Chinese were no longer willing to regard Russia as a model for the construction of a socialist society and believed that the aim of a world revolution ought to be pursued more aggressively. What had been a theoretical dispute became an open break in the early sixties, when the Russians believed the Chinese wanted to entangle them in war in the West and the Chinese thought that Russian negotiations with the West about a nuclear armistice foreshadowed a surrender to the capitalist world.

On the other hand the United States also felt threatened by the Chinese and their attempt to dominate the Far East. Consequently the American policy aimed at containing the Chinese by supporting Taiwan and by defending the offshore islands of Quemoy and Matsu: The United States also became involved in supporting the prowestern regime in South Vietnam against Communist North Vietnam. The development which led to the long and costly Vietnam War had begun.

The strongest indication that both the United States and Russia recognized that a balance of power had been established between them, was the signing in 1963 of a Nuclear Test Ban Treaty. Although the treaty was rather limited in its effects regarding the creation of new atomic weapons, it at least acknowledged a responsibility for human well-being, whether friend or foe.

With this tendency toward relaxation and the shift of attention to the Far East, Europe was no longer the chief battleground for the superpowers. Military security was no longer their exclusive concern, and it was possible to set different priorities. It must be added that, for many Europeans, America's involvement in the Far East, and its support of some rather corrupt regimes seemed to indicate that the United States placed power politics over the pursuit of democratic ideals. The ideological cement of the Western bloc crumbled, although this aspect of the relations of western Europe to the United States became important only later, in the 1960's.

Population Growth and Economic Revival:
The Basis for the Abundant Decade

At the end of the fifties and the beginning of the sixties a new situation was created in Europe, which was in part the result of postwar reconstruction.

A determining factor in the development of a new European society was the growth of population. After the rapid rise in population in the period before the First World War, the interwar years had been a period of stagnation; some countries—for example, France and Ireland—even had an absolute decline of population. This trend was reversed after the Second World War: excluding Soviet Russia, which is believed to have increased by 18 million, the European population increased from 380 to 421 million, an increase of more than 10 per cent from 1940 to 1959. A closer look at these figures shows some remarkable features. The tempo in population growth in eastern Europe was slower than in the West because of the unsettling effects of industrialization and urbanization, which led to late marriages and greater application of birth control. In western Europe the increase was 12 per cent and was particularly astounding in France, which gained 3 million people in the fifties; from the middle of the fifties on, however, the French birthrate declined again. The demographic development in France—so very different from the decline in French population after the First World War—gave a strong foundation to the prominent role which France played in European politics under De Gaulle. The population growth altered the political climate because of the change in age structure which was involved. Whereas the population of the interwar years was predominantly old or middle-aged, from the end of the sixties on the young became the most important element in the composition of the population.

The rise in population had an important impact on economic developments also. In the first years after the war industrial production in Europe was far below the prewar level—with exception of a few countries like Sweden and Spain, which had remained outside the war. Then, under the stimulus of the Marshall Plan, a surge began which, in the course of the fifties, raised industrial production in most of western Europe by 80 per cent; in some countries, like Germany and Italy, even by over 100 per cent. The impetus continued in the 1960s, so that a further rise of 60 to 70 per cent took place, although the statistics show that in the later part of the 1960's the increase began to flatten out. The figures of industrial growth in eastern Europe are even more startling, but they mean less because industrial production started there on such a low level. One country, however, which did not share in this development was Great Britain. At the end of the fifties the increase amounted only to 25 per cent; even at the end of the sixties industrial production had grown since 1950 only by 75 per cent.

The reason for Britain being left behind in the industrial surge was partly psychological: fatigue after having been under siege for five years; and the traditionalism which made Britain slow to adapt to new economic trends. Moreover, an important change in the industrial structure, which affected Great Britain, took place after the war: Coal, which had been the foundation of Britain's industrial predominance, steadily declined in importance. Liquid fuel was cheaper and took its place, particularly since the discovery of vast oil reserves in the Middle East in the 1940s and 1950s. Large oil refineries were built in the great harbor cities of western Europe and an extended network of pipelines brought oil to the various parts of the continent.

One of the significant features of the revival of industrial activity in western Europe was a definite turn towards mass production: entrepreneurs was interested in having expanding markets for their products, especially since modern means of communication facilitated the transportation of manufactured goods. Mass production as well as wide sales distribution could best be achieved by big firms; many smaller firms closed down while the larger ones formed combines. This trend towards bigness in industrial enterprises was furthered also by the struggle against the invasion of the European market by American firms; American capital strength as well as American know-how in fields like electronics made them powerful competitors.

The natural result of this situation was the expansion of European economic cooperation, which had begun with the coal and steel community, into other fields. These negotiations had a successful conclusion in the Treaty of Rome of March 26, 1957. The signers were the same six countries which had formed the European Coal and Steel Community: France, Germany, Italy, Belgium, Holland, and Luxembourg. These countries established in Rome a European Atomic Energy Community

After signing the agreements which established the European Common Market; in the center are Adenauer and De Gaulle.

(EURATOM), which would make the uses of atomic energy available to all the participating countries. More important, they agreed on the establishment of a Common Market (European Economic Community). Its aims were to abolish all trade barriers among the six, to establish a common external tariff, to permit the free movement of labor and capital among the member states, and—by equalizing wage rates and social-security systems—to bring about uniform working conditions in the Common Market area without creating unemployment. Clearly, these goals could not be achieved in a single stroke; for instance, in some of the participating countries agriculture was highly protected and would collapse if customs barriers were removed suddenly. The Rome agreement therefore envisaged a development in stages, to be completed within fifteen years. A European Commission with headquarters in Brussels, acting under the instructions of a regularly meeting council of ministers, was entrusted with the administration of the Common Market and the guidance of its development. On January 1, 1959, the Common Market began to function by lowering tariffs 10 per cent among the member countries, and thereafter, despite difficult negotiations and crises, progress was made in realizing its program.

One of the most significant effects of the Common Market was the impetus that it gave to trade among the six participants. Between 1958 and 1962 intracommunity trade rose by 97 per cent; by contrast, imports from outside the Common Market grew only 38 per cent, and exports to non-Market countries increased by 29 per cent. This "little Europe" began to form a vital and stable basis for the economic life of its six members.

Great Britain remained outside the Common Market. When the negotiations opened Britain had hesitated to join, since the British regarded a European free trade zone as incompatible with the system of preferences existing between them and Commonwealth countries; also, British trade unions feared that adjustment to the wages and the social security system of the continent would curtail the benefits of the British welfare state. After the Common Market had been established and proved successful, Great Britain tried to counter by founding a free trade association which comprised seven "outsiders," those countries which had remained outside the Common Market: Denmark, Norway, Sweden, Portugal, Switzerland, and Austria. But this association was limited to a lowering of tariffs; none of the wider aims of the Common Market was attempted or feasible for this somewhat disparate group of states. Although these countries took part in the rise of economic activities of the fifties, the driving force was provided by the Common Market countries.

This discussion of the European economic developments in the fifties to the beginning of the sixties has been almost exclusively concerned with the Western bloc. The reason is not that there was no economic growth in the Eastern bloc; on the contrary, as we have mentioned, the increase in industrial activity was rapid and great, with the emphasis still placed on heavy industry and machinery and not consumer goods; in this respect it is rather revealing that the share of the chemical industry in industrial production in Russia was 6 per cent, whereas in the West it amounted to 12 per cent. Although in the East changes in economic and social circumstances might be the further outcome of industrialization, such changes had not taken place in the fifties; it was only in the West that, with the beginning of the sixties, life had not only revived but had profoundly altered. In the West the emergence of a new Europe was visible. Not only had towns been rebuilt with the help of the governments, they had been renovated. The houses in the older parts of London were repainted and repaired; in Paris the century-old grime, which had made the Louvre and the facades of the houses around the Louvre a dirty grey was removed and they emerged white and gilded. Steel and glass office buildings and high-rise hotels rose around the centers of the cities; modern settlements for the middle and working classes were built on the outside of the towns. Even the countryside, although retaining much of its old ways, was drawn into the new life through the numerous freeways which connected not only the regions of a country but also the various European states. Individual countries became much smaller; Europe was no longer merely an idea, but a concrete geographical space.

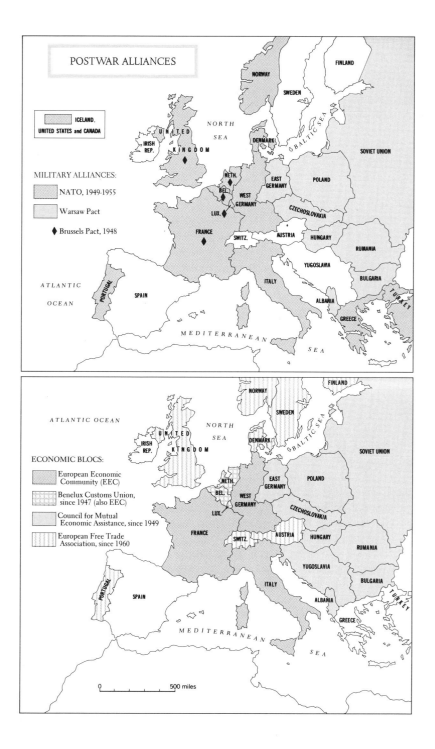

POSTWAR ALLIANCES

ICELAND,
UNITED STATES and CANADA

MILITARY ALLIANCES:

NATO, 1949-1955

Warsaw Pact

◆ Brussels Pact, 1948

ATLANTIC OCEAN

NORTH SEA

MEDITERRANEAN SEA

BALTIC SEA

NORWAY
SWEDEN
FINLAND
IRISH REP.
UNITED KINGDOM
DENMARK
SOVIET UNION
NETH.
BEL.
LUX.
WEST GERMANY
EAST GERMANY
POLAND
CZECHOSLOVAKIA
FRANCE
SWITZ.
AUSTRIA
HUNGARY
RUMANIA
YUGOSLAVIA
BULGARIA
ITALY
ALBANIA
GREECE
TURKEY
PORTUGAL
SPAIN

ECONOMIC BLOCS:

European Economic
Community (EEC)

Benelux Customs Union,
since 1947 (also EEC)

Council for Mutual
Economic Assistance, since 1949

European Free Trade
Association, since 1960

ATLANTIC OCEAN

NORTH SEA

MEDITERRANEAN SEA

BALTIC SEA

NORWAY
SWEDEN
FINLAND
IRISH REP.
UNITED KINGDOM
DENMARK
SOVIET UNION
NETH.
BEL.
LUX.
WEST GERMANY
EAST GERMANY
POLAND
CZECHOSLOVAKIA
FRANCE
SWITZ.
AUSTRIA
HUNGARY
RUMANIA
YUGOSLAVIA
BULGARIA
ITALY
ALBANIA
GREECE
TURKEY
PORTUGAL
SPAIN

0   500 miles

A DECADE OF DÉTENTE IN FOREIGN POLICY

De Gaulle's "Europe of the Fatherlands"

Relaxation of international tensions and economic prosperity created the possibility for greater independence in European foreign policy. Thus, western Europe saw a new departure in foreign policy, the driving force behind which was Charles de Gaulle, who was the dominating figure among the European statesmen of the 1960's.

At first it might seem strange to associate De Gaulle's name with a new departure, he certainly appears to be a figure of an old rather than a new Europe. De Gaulle came from an aristocratic Roman Catholic family; his father—not wealthy enough to follow the usual career of a French aristocrat, that of an officer or a landowner—taught philosophy and history at a Jesuit college. The De Gaulles did not belong to the ruling group of the Third Republic but stood very much alone; and an inflexible independence was deeply rooted in Charles de Gaulle's character. He demonstrated this proud independence throughout his entire career. During the interwar years he had differed from the overwhelming majority of his military colleagues in advocating a highly motorized professional army. In the dark days of the spring of 1940 he had been stamped as a traitor by his comrades because he refused to accept Marshal Pétain's verdict of the necessity for surrender. During the war—photographs showing De Gaulle in friendly colloquy with Churchill and Roosevelt notwithstanding —the Anglo-Saxon leaders had found cooperation with him extremely difficult. Even when De Gaulle had no real power he had insisted on the inviolability of every right that France possessed, and could not be deflected from what he regarded as the appropriate course. When, walking to the Thanksgiving Mass at Notre Dame, he was deliriously received in the liberated Paris and unanimously elected president of the provisional government by the constituent assembly, this general approval had little effect. He did not become more pliable, and resigned four months later, in January, 1946.

This independence was combined with a fierce French patriotism, in accordance with his aristocratic family tradition, but Charles de Gaulle's feeling for the greatness of France and for France as a leader of Europe had little to do with the ideology created by the French Revolution. It reached back into deeper, more mystical source. In his memoirs De Gaulle wrote that he imagined France "like the princess in the fairy stories or the Madonna in the frescoes, as dedicated to an exalted and exceptional destiny. . . . Providence had created her either for complete successes or for exemplary misfortunes. If, in spite of this, mediocrity shows in her âcts," this is "an absurd anomaly. . . . France is not really herself unless in the front rank. . . . In short, to my mind, France cannot be France without greatness." [1]

This romantic, almost religious patriotism had nothing to do with the aggressive nationalism of the nineteenth century which aimed at elevating one nation at the cost of all others. De Gaulle's concern was with preserving the integrity of France—the inviolability of its territory, the uniqueness of its spirit.

Because De Gaulle viewed France as an individual he had an understanding also for the individuality of other nations. While rejecting a united Europe which would submerge individual nations, he favored a closer alliance among all the nations of the continent so that Europe would mean the "Europe of the Fatherlands."

The course of De Gaulle's foreign policy was based on these concepts. He steered France away from the Anglo-Saxon powers. In his antagonism to the United States and Great Britain there may have been a residue of personal resentment at the coolness he had experienced from Roosevelt and Churchill during the war. But there were more basic reasons. De Gaulle saw in the cooperation of the United States and Great Britain the danger of Anglo-American rule over the globe or over wide parts of the globe —a Pax Americana; he feared in particular the ideological and institutional uniformity which these Anglo-Saxon protagonists of democracy and world government might want to impose. He felt that such internationalism might suffocate the individual character of a nation. De Gaulle's eagerness to restrict and diminish Anglo-Saxon influence showed itself in many ways. For example, he made a strong stand to secure the maintenance of French as a language of diplomacy. More important was his resistance to the attempts of England to enter the Common Market. When, after lengthy negotiations, the way seemed free for Great Britain to enter the European Common Market, De Gaulle vetoed this move, first in 1963, and then again in 1967. De Gaulle used every opportunity to regain independence for France by emancipating it from bonds which the western alliance had placed on French freedom of action. In gradual steps De Gaulle withdrew French forces from the NATO Command: in 1959 he withdrew the Mediterranean Fleet; in 1963 the Atlantic Fleet; and in 1966 he ended all French participation in NATO. Its headquarters were transferred from Paris to Brussels. Whereas De Gaulle evidently feared that the French might be seduced by the Anglo-Saxon ideology, he did not think that Soviet Russia represented a similar threat. Soviet Russia was for him a traditional great power rather than center and protagonist of a world-

[1] *The Complete War Memoirs of Charles de Gaulle,* Vol. 1, *The Call to Honour,* trans. by Jonathan Griffin (New York, 1955), p. 72.

encompassing international movement. During the war De Gaulle had concluded a treaty with Soviet Russia. In 1964 he negotiated a commercial agreement with Soviet Russia, and in June 1963, three months after France left NATO, De Gaulle visited Moscow where he received the welcome of a hero. But the fact that De Gaulle regarded Communism as less dangerous than Anglo-Saxon imperialism did not mean that he was not suspicious of further increases in Russian power and was anxious to prevent the possibility of Russian expansion into the heart of Europe. In this context it is significant that, although De Gaulle had withdrawn the French forces from the NATO Command, France still remained a member of the Atlantic alliance. Moreover, his opposition to Russian expansion was also a crucial reason for his policy of Franco-German cooperation.

Although De Gaulle had fought the Nazis in their attempt to dominate Europe, he saw Germany as similar to France—a "fatherland," a country with its own culture, one of the constituent elements of the Europe of independent nations he wanted to recreate. Moreover, Germany could serve as a dam against Russian expansion. Thus, De Gaulle backed West Germany against the Russian attempts to drive the West out of Berlin, he established close contacts with German Chancellor Adenauer, and in 1962, he made a successful tour through West Germany, thus initiating a new era in the relations between the two countries.

Although in his emphasis on the sovereignty of the national state De Gaulle was a traditionalist, he was cool and realistic in his considerations of practical political actions. He was aware that in order to be independent a nation must be strong and therefore in possession of modern military weapons. It seemed to him of central importance to set an end to the French military inferiority which was created by lack of nuclear weapons. France ought to possess a *force de frappe*—as nuclear armor was called. The French governments before De Gaulle had already initiated nuclear research, somewhat resentful because of the American lack of support in this enterprise. De Gaulle extended the work, and in 1960 the first French atomic bomb was exploded; in 1966 the French exploded a hydrogen bomb; and two years later a variety of nuclear weapons was tried out by the French in the Pacific.

Atomic weapons, however, form only part of the sophisticated equipment needed by a modern army. A modernized military force can exist only in the framework of a modern industrial society. The work of modernization of the French economy had been started with the Monnet Plan, and De Gaulle could reap the fruits which then had been planted. Under De Gaulle the tempo was accelerated and perhaps even overextended. The results and consequences of this hectic expansion were very visible in France. Tall buildings with all modern comforts were erected for the population drawn into the towns but they were constructed around urban centers in which people still lived and worked under the conditions of preindustrial times. It is rather typical for the entire French situation that after some stretches of broad modern highways roads suddenly narrow down to two lanes. In France, it has been said, there are two economies that uneasily co-exist: a modern one, most of it implanted since the war by the technocrats and a few big state and private firms; and below it, an old creaking infrastructure, based on artisanship, low turnover with high profits, and the ideal of the small family business. The De Gaulle regime increased the sharpness of this contrast which was a reason for the crisis of the regime at the end of the sixties.

Great Britain as an Outsider

In former times one could have expected that England would have contested France for the role of leadership on the European continent. But Great Britain was in a particularly weak and uncertain position in the crucial years of De Gaulle's ascent.

The Suez affair had been conceived as an attempted assertion of Britain's influence in the Middle East, a demonstration that Britain was still an imperial power. Britain's failure necessarily led to a painful reexamination and reevaluation of its international position. The abandonment of the Suez enterprise under pressure by the United States left little doubt that the members of the Commonwealth—particularly the self-governing dominions of Canada, Australia, and New Zealand—would increasingly lean toward the United States on which they had to rely for military protection, and that Britain, if it wanted to remain the center of the Commonwealth, had to establish a "special relation" with the United States and harmonize its policy with that of Washington. This retreat from the assertion of imperial power was not limited to the Commonwealth but extended over the entire globe. The speech which early in 1960 the British Prime Minister Macmillan made in Johannesburg and in which he mentioned the "winds of change" which were blowing over the continent, indicated the end of British support for white rule in Africa and thereby a separation of ties and a possibility of conflicts with the ruling groups in its former colonies.

Recognition of a changed situation in economic affairs was as difficult, if not more difficult, for Great Britain than adjustment to an altered international situation. If anything had kept courage and energy alive in the war years it was the hope and expectation that at the end there would be a better life. The welfare state which the Labor government established fulfilled some of these expectations. But it was paid for with very high taxes, and as a result of pressure by the trade unions, wages rose steeply and steadily. The outlook for profits was not encouraging; in the period between 1955 and 1964 Britain had the lowest investment rate of all European countries.

Britain's standard of living made British goods costly and limited the possibilities for selling them on foreign markets. Exports fell especially since Britain's one great mineral resource—coal—had lost much in importance. But as an industrial and nonagrarian country the need for import of raw material and foodstuffs remained constant and high. The indicator of these economic difficulties—despite the reduction of political and military commitments through the abandonment of Britain's imperial role— was an unfavorable balance of payments which not only resisted all attempts at improvement but widened from year to year.

There was no easy solution. There was awareness that the instruction given at the prestigious universities of Oxford and Cambridge and which provided intensive intellectual training to fit people for any kind of managerial job, was no longer effective in this age of specialized technical knowledge. Measures were taken to build a large number of polytechnical institutes and new universities and to introduce in the schools a system of examinations which would pick out the gifted pupils and make it possible for them by means of government grants to attend the universities.

These were reforms which might bear fruit in the future. They did not improve the situation existing in the 1960's. In the first years of this decade the Conservatives were in power under Macmillan and then, from 1964 to 1970, Labor took over under Harold Wilson. But although the parties in control changed, the manner in which the economic problems were handled did not greatly alter. Both parties were aware that the British people would not permit a dismantling of the welfare state. It is true that the Conservatives denationalized steel, which Labor had nationalized, and that, when Labor came into power again they renationalized it. But essentially both political parties, Conservative and Labor, worked with temporary expedients like currency restrictions, foreign loans, devaluation, export incentives.

In this steadily deteriorating economic situation the Common Market seemed to offer some prospects for improving the export-import situation, and Great Britain applied for admission. It was twice vetoed by De Gaulle, who justified his refusal because in order to maintain its standard of living Britain had demanded special provisoes. Actually De Gaulle continued to consider Britain too closely tied to the United States. Britain's entry in the Common Market came about only in 1973, after the death of De Gaulle.

Italy and Germany: New Initiatives in Foreign Policy

While Britain's weakness can be considered as a kind of negative support for De Gaulle's attempt to regain a preeminent position for the

European nations, Italy and Germany, the two most important members of the Common Market, gave him some positive support. The two statesmen who had directed the resurgence of their defeated countries after the Second World War—De Gasperi and Adenauer—had both disappeared from the political scene: De Gasperi died in 1954; Adenauer resigned as Chancellor in 1963. With their departure Italian and German policy lost something of its rigidity. Both Adenauer and De Gasperi had regarded hostility to Soviet Russia and alliance with the United States as the unshakable foundation of their foreign policy. Their successors, even if they did not want to change course, were inclined to be more flexible. Greater flexibility was also appropriate because of new developments on the domestic scene. In the first decades of reconstruction people had concentrated on the necessities of life; their paramount interests, beyond having employment, had been to obtain housing, furniture, food, and, after these basic needs had been satisfied, to improve gradually the external conditions of life. But, with increasing prosperity, demands unavoidably rose. It also became evident that in the course of reconstruction great wealth had been acquired, so that internal tensions and class conflicts began to re-emerge. The trade unions became more vocal in pressing for higher wages and extended social security, and accordingly increased membership. Political parties to the left of the ruling Catholic parties gained in votes in the 1960's. In Italy the Christian Democrats lost slightly, the Socialists gained somewhat, and the Communists increased considerably. In Germany the losses of the Christian Democrats also were only slight but the gains of the Socialists were remarkable; by the end of the sixties they had become almost even with the Christian Democrats.

The Christian Democrats in Italy had always been split into different groups; in accordance with the voting trend the leftist group within the party won out and it was therefore decided to undertake an "opening to the left," i.e., the formation of a coalition with the Socialists. Even the propaganda of the left for allowing divorce and finally the acceptance of a plebiscite allowing divorce—strenuously opposed by the Christian Democrats—did not interrupt the search for a left-wing coalition. De Gaulle's initiative for a more flexible foreign policy was welcomed, since one of the conditions of the Socialists was to avoid blind adherence to the American line. Although there was agreement that agrarian reform and industrialization in the south ought to be energetically attacked and take priority, agreement about the details of the planned reforms was so difficult to reach that one government crisis followed the other and during the sixties the political effects of the "opening to the left" were minimal.

In Germany the Christian Democrats hoped to cut off a further trend towards the left by forming a coalition government with the Socialists. It was clear to the Socialist leaders that as long as the Christian Democrats headed the government, no far-reaching measures of reform could be expected. Therefore, the leader of the Socialists, Willy Brandt, who had gained reputation and popularity as mayor of Berlin during the blockade, became foreign minister, convinced that in this area it was possible to take action which would show that the participation of the Socialists in the government represented a new departure. Brandt, in accordance with De Gaulle's example, sought to establish normal relations with the countries of the Eastern bloc. By resuming diplomatic relations with Yugoslavia Brandt tacitly disregarded the principle which had guided the foreign policy of preceding West German governments, and which after its originator was called the "Hallstein Doctrine": namely, that West Germany would have no diplomatic relations with any power which had recognized eastern Germany. Brandt not only began negotiations with the other countries of the Eastern bloc, through intermediaries he also contacted the East German government. The progress was slow and results were visible only in 1970, when the Socialists overtook the Christian Democrats and Brandt became chancellor.

A "Wind of Change" in Eastern Europe

The tendency to deemphasize the division separating East from West was not only pursued in western Europe; it was also supported by events in the Eastern bloc. Since the Hungarian Revolt Khrushchev had many critics who were anxious to see him stumble, and he tried to confound them by success in foreign policy. The consequences, as we have seen, were a number of spectacular but also erratic moves; with the defeat in the Cuban Missile Crisis Khrushchev lost his hold over the government, although officially he was "retired" only in 1964. The men who now became the leaders of Soviet Russia—Alexei Kosygin and Leonid Brezhnev—moved cautiously. They were aware that because of the scarcity of bread resulting from failures in the agrarian sector of the economy popular discontent had developed, which they were anxious to erase. They placed greater emphasis on the production of consumer goods and attempted to raise the living standard of the population by increasing trade with the capitalist world. In the first five years of the sixties trade with the West had more than doubled; foreign firms were permitted to enter the Russian market, for instance, the Italian Fiat Works constructed a huge automobile factory in Russia. The Russian leaders had their reasons for welcoming De Gaulle's visit to Moscow in 1966 and to make it an occasion of remarkable enthusiasm. Moreover, like Khrushchev in his last years of power, Kosygin and Brezhnev were primarily concerned with developments in the Far East, where Chinese construction of an atomic bomb and increasing American involvement in Vietnam threatened to eliminate Soviet influence.

With the memory of the Hungarian Revolt fresh in their minds this was not a time to tighten the reins on their allies in the Eastern bloc. On the contrary, demands for deliveries for the Russian economy ended, and although the thesis that there were "different ways to socialism" had proved so dangerous in the fifties when it provided the spark for the movements in Poland and Hungary, the Russians did not put up strong resistance when the governments of the satellites continued to attempt, cautiously but consistently, the establishment of a political line suited to their own particular situations and needs.

As stated above, one of the policies which had been forced upon these countries by Stalinist Russia, and which had aroused the strongest amount of resentment was the rapid collectivization of agriculture. It is indicative of the differences which developed among the states in the Eastern bloc that in the sixties the proportion of collectivized arable land varied greatly. Rumania, in contrast to what Soviet Russia regarded as an appropriate division of labor, placed all its emphasis on the development of heavy industry and maintained extended trade with the capitalist countries. The Rumanian leaders were inclined to emphasize their independence from Russian policy at every opportunity. In Poland resistance against agricultural collectivization had been strong, and even in the sixties it only amounted to about 13 per cent of all arable land, much less than in its neighboring states. Collectivization was most advanced in Czechoslovakia and East Germany. In Czechoslovakia it amounted to 82.6 per cent, in East Germany, the former land of the *Junkers*, to 96 per cent, though East Germany deviated somewhat from the Russian model by placing emphasis on consumer goods in the process of industrialization. Yet the great advance in the collectivization of agriculture in Germany and Czechoslovakia must be attributed to the leaders in these countries, Ulbricht in East Germany and Novotny in Czechoslovakia, the only leading personalities in the Eastern bloc who had been personally close to Stalin. Undoubtedly, the autocratic rigidity with which they continued the Stalinist line led to tension in their countries.

The movements towards increased political and economic contacts were supplemented by attempts to effect some intellectual co-existence. The decade of the sixties opened with the Second Vatican Council, which had been convoked by Pope John XXIII in order to adjust the Church's outlook to the situation which had developed after the Second World War. The council brought the Church closer to the people by permitting the use of local languages in the mass, and diminished papal autocracy by giving a greater voice to the bishops and cooperating with Christian churches all over the world. These notions were also emphasized in John XXIII's encyclica, *Mater et Magistra* and *Pacem in Terris*, which emphasized the need for social justice and for greater rights of the workers.

Walter Ulbricht, chairman of the council of state of East Germany, at the microphones, surrounded by Communist leaders.

John XXIII's successor, Paul VI (pope 1964–1978) was less inclined to follow his predecessor's modernizing tendency. He disappointed many liberal members of the Church by strictly maintaining the prohibition of artificial birth control. But he allowed and encouraged the priests in countries behind the Iron Curtain to cooperate with their governments. Marxists were no longer automatically excommunicated, and when Nicholas Podgorny, who as president of the Soviet Union, was the Russian head of state, visited Rome in 1966, he was received by the pope. Uncertain as the outlook was, the division of Europe into two parts seemed less final, less permanent than it had appeared ten years ago.

CHAPTER 15

Crises and Stability

THE END OF ILLUSIONS: 1968-1973

If during the sixties developments in Europe seemed to take a hopeful course it did not follow that these were peaceful or prosperous years for the entire world. On the contrary, in the Far East the Vietnamese War intensified and took increasingly brutal forms. Internal war in the liberated Congo between radicals and moderates showed that the African continent was becoming the center of a new power struggle. And the Israeli victory over Arab forces in the Six-Day War of June 1967, ending with the occupation of the Gaza Strip and the West Bank of the Jordan, indicated that the situation in the Near East remained unsettled. It soon became clear that in Europe also, behind what appeared a smooth facade, great tensions had remained alive which would explode in various crises.

During the five years from 1968 to 1973 there were three great crises in Europe: first in 1968 the "Spring of Prague"—a term designating a weakening of Communist control in Czechoslovakia; then, in the same year, a student revolt in Paris which, in cooperation with a workers' strike, endangered the regime of De Gaulle; and finally, in 1973, the cutting off of oil supplies by the Arab states in revenge for support given to Israel. Although these crises, certainly the crisis in Czechoslovakia and the unrest in France, had local reasons, they all had an impact which went far beyond a limited regime and extended all over Europe. They influenced economic life, leading to changes in the balance of economic strength between East and West. They gave impetus to new developments in the alignment of political parties, and most of all they showed that the tendency towards an independent foreign policy which had appeared on the horizon in the abundant 1960's went beyond what was obtainable in the existing world constellation.

The "Spring of Prague"

In Czechoslovakia the autocratic rule of Stalin's friend Novotny was increasingly resented; dissatisfaction was nourished by the multinational character of the state—the differences between Czechs and Slovaks. A policy of centralization, which gave no room to regional and national autonomy, aroused opposition all over the country and created such a dangerous situation that through a coup within the Presidium of the Communist party Novotny was removed from power and Alexander Dubcek was made secretary of the party in January 1968. The intention of Dubcek and those who came into power with him was not to eliminate the rule of the Communist party. Their aim was to decentralize the administration, a measure expected to quiet the Slovaks, who felt dominated by the Czechs, to gain a broader popular basis by introducing democratic procedures into the organization of the party, and to give life in a socialist society a less regulated, oppressive character. The latter was particularly important in Czechoslovakia, which had a strong intellectual middle class; this group soon began demands for intellectual freedom. Indeed, during several months, vital and brilliant intellectual discussions were conducted in newspapers, periodicals, and books. This was the so-called Spring of Prague, and the extent to which this outburst of intellectal life formed an essential part of the movement is perhaps best indicated by the suicide of a student, who, when the movement was suppressed by the Russians, set himself on fire as a demonstration against the reinstitution of censorship and the information monopoly of an official, pro-Russian newspaper. Actually the Russians acted much more slowly and cautiously than they had in Hungary twelve years earlier; Dubcek also tried not to provoke them by remaining in steady contact with them. But the concessions which he made to the Russians weakened his position in Czechoslovakia and alienated him from a good part of the reformist movement. Under these circumstances the Russians believed that the time had come to end a movement on which they looked with a certain anxiety because of the strategic importance of Czechoslovakia—i.e., its closeness to the West. Thus, Russian tanks and troops, which had been poised at the border of Czechoslovakia, moved in and occupied Prague.

Slowly but inexorably the Russians eased the Czechoslovak leaders of the reform movement out of power. In this policy they were supported by the Communist rulers of Hungary, Poland, and East Germany, who, whatever sympathies they might have had for Dubcek's attempt to chart his own way to socialism, were prompted by concern for the stability of their own regime and by the fear that by leaving the Czechoslovak reform movement in power the West might get a foothold in the Eastern bloc.

In the West the indignation over the Russian suppression of the Czechoslovak reform movement was great. A measure of its strength was the statement of Jean-Paul Sartre, the French existentialist philosopher, and

Prague, August 21, 1968, the day of the Russian invasion. *The two buses had been used in vain as barricades to stop the advance of the invading troops; note the Russian tank behind the buses.*

a member of the Communist party since the Second World War; he called the Russian move "pure aggression, such as is defined in terms of international law as war crime." At the time of the Hungarian Revolt, intellectuals who had been members of the Communist party, particularly in Italy and France withdrew; the same happened after the Russian intervention in Czechoslovakia. This did not mean that they became supporters of the existing parliamentary system, but it meant that the Soviet regime was no longer considered as above criticism and that Russia was no longer the model for a society which would be freed from the injustice and the misery inherent in the capitalist system.

The Student Revolt

The excitement which the events in Czechoslovakia aroused spread to western Europe and contributed to the student revolts which broke out on the Continent and changed the political atmosphere, creating sharp tensions and stimulating political extremism.

Student dissatisfaction and unrest, although noticeable all over the western world in the later half of the sixties, became a center of political concern through events in Paris in May 1968. The revolt began at the University of Nanterre near Paris, where students protested against deficiencies which had developed at almost all continental universities: overcrowded lecture halls, insufficient space in laboratories, diminished attention to individuals by professors. A sympathy strike took place at the Sorbonne, and when in the course of demonstrations the students occupied some buildings, the police were called in to remove them. A struggle followed in which hundreds of people were wounded and arrested. The police acted with unnecessary brutality and many of the inhabitants of the houses in the Quartier Latin, indignant over the behavior of the police, took the side of the students and the students soon dominated this section of the city. But the movement became a threat to the French government because it coincided with a struggle of workers for higher wages. The workers declared a sympathy strike for the student movement; this strike developed into a general strike and gave the movement a revolutionary character: by the middle of May ten million people were on strike in France. But the development of the student revolt into a serious social conflict also worked against the students. They lost the support of the middle classes, who turned on the side of the authorities, and the government managed to bring the workers back to the factories in early June by concessions on the issue of wages. Great demonstrations in support of the government and De Gaulle showed how the situation had changed. The students were isolated; their strike ended.

The events in Paris made evident what actually was always known: that students, without an alliance with stronger forces, cannot hope to overthrow a government. Yet, the Paris student revolt was more than an episode; student unrest has unsettled university life all over Europe and has continued; it seems to reflect an uneasiness about a political and social structure which, although particularly strong and widespread among the younger generation, is also shared by other parts of the population. Its reasons, therefore, deserve closer consideration.

The Intellectual Revolt Against Modern Society

On May 14, at the height of the crisis, the French prime minister, Georges Pompidou, said in the National Assembly: "The events which we have just experienced are not just a flash of fire . . . our civilization is being questioned, not the government, not the institutions, not even France, but the materialistic and soulless modern society." Pompidou saw correctly that the practical difficulties which the overcrowding of universities had created for students all over Europe, and about which they rightly complained, were not decisive for the discontent of the young, that their alienation from existing society had more profound causes.

These causes are closely linked to particular issues of the ending sixties and beginning seventies.

The student revolt in Paris took place when Russian opposition to the Hungarian Revolt and, more recently, the Czechoslovak reform movement had greatly damaged the prestige and the attraction of Soviet Communism. It was also a time when American interference in Vietnam had made it a hard task to continue to defend and admire American democracy. Political thought and political action had previously revolved around the contrast between Communism and democracy; when both were failing a vacuum was created. It is not by accident that when the students occupied the Sorbonne the black flag of anarchism appeared above the building.

The contrast between ideological claims and practical behavior, which the actions of the leading Communist and democratic countries made strikingly evident, exacerbated a generation crisis which in itself was particularly intense in these years. The large number of young people who were now becoming adults felt widely separated from their elders, not only because the most important experiences of their parents—the rise of Fascism and Nazism, the Second World War—had by then become history and thus many attitudes of their elders seemed no longer comprehensible, but also because the young were used to continual change in the external conditions of life brought about by science and technology, whereas their elders had difficulties in overcoming a feeling of strangeness in the rapidly altering world. Continually changing circumstances seemed to diminish the value of experience; the authority of age was questioned and no longer accepted. There were two closely connected areas in which the loss of authoritative traditions was very striking: religion and morality. The issue which revealed this contrast most clearly was the dispute over birth control: the possibility of sexual intercourse without the risk of pregnancy brought into question all the accepted views about matrimony, family, the church and the role of women. Since traditional morality could no longer be applied to the possibilities which existed for the development of the human personality, it was a lack of courage to follow conventional attitudes; it was moral duty to live according to the new realities.

Of course, the problem of the incompatibility of modernism with traditional religious and moral assumptions can be traced far back. It had been a topic of constant discussion since the nineteenth century. A crucial issue in almost all of Ibsen's plays was the bourgeois hypocrisy, which presented to the outside a picture of strict, conventional morality but lived and acted under different rules: Freud had discovered that the suppression of instinctual drives in favor of conventions was a main reason for the mental illness of modern man. But during the Second World War some of these accusations against bourgeois society seemed rather hollow.

The heroism with which the resistance movements—composed of people of all classes and opinions—countered the brutality of Nazism and Fascism, showed humanity's willingness to fight against evil, disregarding self-interest and individual well-being. In his novel, *The Plague*, which appeared two years after the end of the war, Albert Camus commemorated the experience of the war and the resistance in an artistic vision, which described how men behaved in a town isolated from the rest of the world, devastated by a plague which inexorably decimated the population. The doctrine which Camus' novel was to communicate was that "what you learn in the midst of torture and oppression is that in men there are more things to admire than to despise." In 1957, Camus received the Nobel Prize for Literature.

But when it emerged that, despite the heroism of the war years, no new morality had emerged after the war, disappointment intensified the sharpness and bitterness of the accusations against conventional moral attitudes. Camus had written *The Plague* when he was involved in a conflict with Sartre with whom he had closely worked during the resistance. Sartre believed that Camus' trust in the inner qualities of humans was illusionary and that a revolutionary change of society was needed to bring about a life that was good in all its aspects. The issue was whether membership in the Communist party was necessary or appropriate to overcome the injustices of the existing society.

Sartre, a party member, took the position previous critics of the bourgeois order and morality had also taken: radical political movements and parties had to be joined and supported in order to bring about a change. A novel and unique feature of the late 1960's was the belief of radicals that political action in the old style was increasingly futile. In the period before the First World War and also before the Second World War, opposition to the existing system usually could depend on the mass support of the workers. In the postwar reconstruction period, however, the interests of workers and employers were parallel. Trade unions were not only legalized all over the West, they were consulted by those in power and had become part of the existing system. Policy decisions were frequently no longer achieved by a struggle between political parties, they were the result of agreement between organizations. In consequence the difference over whether right or left ruled was no longer great within western political structures. The possibilities of bringing about fundamental changes in a democratic way were slight. The individual seemed powerless in the hands of forces over which he had no control. Moreover, it appeared to many that not only individuals were powerless but that also the European nations were losing their individual physiognomy. Europe was becoming "Americanized." American words penetrated European languages, corrupting even the French language, as De Gaulle noted with disgust. American products, like Coca-Cola or blue jeans, acquired popularity in Europe. Americanization, and perhaps even more, the opposition to Americanization, had its roots in American activities and influence in economic life. The economic upswing had attracted foreign capital, and American investments in Europe had increased particularly. Until 1956 European holdings in the United States were greater than American holdings in Europe, but from then on the situation began to change rapidly; by 1969 American investments in Europe were 2.5 times as large as European investments in the States. This meant that some industrial activities, like the computer industry, were very largely—up to 80 per cent—in American hands; in others, like the automobile industry, the percentage of American capital was lower (25 per cent) but still substantial. The form which this American participation in European industries took was frequently that of a multinational corporation, composed of companies working in various countries, but under a global strategy for the entire combine. In both the totalitarian states and the democracies the question of control moved further and further away from the individual.

One may doubt that many of the younger generation who were restless and dissatisfied were inclined to undertake a precise analysis of the shifts in the political and economic structure which caused their dissatisfaction; but there can be no doubt about the existence of a widespread feeling of powerlessness. It was clearly reflected in the fields of art and literature. These were years in which exhibitions honored the great masters of the earlier part of the century: Picasso and Braque, and when even those who decades ago had considered them as destroyers of true art now queued up

The events of May 1968 in Paris. *Students throwing pavement stones at the police on the Boulevard St. Michel.*

for hours to admire their paintings. But the monumental character of their paintings, which focused on the line and form behind a confused surface of color and motion, was almost diametrically opposed to the formless restlessness which dominated the mobiles and the kaleidoscopes, the pop art and the rock music, of the younger generation. Some of the same developments might be found in film, which immediately after the Second World War had sought—in a number of impressive, particularly Italian movies—to reveal the social reality, the poverty and danger, of life. In the sixties, in films like Alain Resnais's *Last Year at Marienbad* and Michelangelo Antonioni's *Blow-up* the medium turned away from reality to presentation of a dreamlike existence. But the most direct expression of the absurdity of life in which the words of one have no meaning for the other and men take actions which have no purpose was found in the theater. Probably the most famous of these plays was Samuel Beckett's *Waiting for Godot*, where people eagerly work and compete to placate a power which they have never seen and of which they know not even whether it exists. This was a work of art which deeply touched the spirit of these years. In recognition of this, twenty-two years after Camus, Samuel Beckett received the Nobel Prize for Literature.

The Oil Crisis: 1973

The original motives of student unrest were real and, to a large extent, justified complaints about the traditional nature of university education in Europe. However, the intellectual milieu and psychological background of the student revolts explain why the movement did not end with university reforms and abolition of particular abuses but had an impact beyond the university and a part in creating a disturbed and disturbing political atmosphere in Europe.

This might not have happened if soon after the explosion of student discontent western Europe had not received another shock: the oil crisis. It had its origins in the Arab-Israeli war of October 1973 and in Arab resentment over the support given by the United States and western European countries to Israel: A blockade, cutting off the oil supply, was imposed by the oil-producing Arab countries on the United States, though it was not inflicted on the European states—with exception of the Netherlands, which had most openly given support to Israel. But the Arab states, partly because they claimed that for military reasons they needed the oil themselves, partly because they wanted to prevent oil going via Europe to the United States, reduced the amount of oil delivered to the European countries and raised the price. Certain temporary measures, like prohibition of automobile driving on Sundays and holidays, were put in force in Europe until negotiations of the individual European nations with the Arab states restored a sufficient influx of oil. But the oil crisis had a long-lasting impact. First of all it showed the fragility and precariousness of the bond which had been created by the Common Market; the various states negotiated individually with the Arab states and did not make common cause with the Netherlands, as could have rightly been expected. And the oil crisis led to a deterioration of the general economic situation of western Europe: the replacement of coal by oil, and accordingly, the import of great amounts of oil from the Middle East had led to a steadily increasing negative balance of payments of western Europe with the Arab states, and this development was accelerated by the rise in oil prices; Europe's need for enlarging its exports was intensified. Finally, the oil crisis had strikingly shown the dependent relationship of Europe with other powers; western Europe was drawn into the oil crisis because of outside conflicts and tensions between Arab countries, Israel, and the United States. The oil crisis meant an awakening from illusions of an independent Europe and a return to reality. The oil crisis represented a clear warning that there were limits to European freedom and action, that advance in economic prosperity was not continuous, and that not only in the east and west but also in the south, western Europe was surrounded by powerful neighbors. It was a strong reminder of the fact which every geographic map showed that, despite great riches in resources and a densely populated area, western Europe was only a slim promontory hanging out precariously on the eastern shore of the Atlantic Ocean.

THE 1970'S: SEARCHING FOR THE MIDDLE ROAD

The impact of the oil crisis on western Europe was particularly striking because it played a role in transforming a slowdown in economic advance which had set in at the end of the sixties into a recession. A striking, almost startling aspect of the years since 1973 has been that economically the roles between the Western and the Eastern blocs have almost reversed. The countries of the Eastern bloc have shown definite signs of prosperity and economic advance, while in the West the economy has been in a recession. Statistics of the increase of industrial production in the countries of eastern and western Europe make this very clear. In the six years from 1969 to 1975, the increase in industrial production in the countries of the Eastern bloc was steady, and amounted in most of them to almost 50 per cent. In western Europe a few countries showed a rise of 25 per cent, but in most countries of the West the increase was not much beyond 10 per cent. What kept these figures in the West low was that in some of these years a decrease rather than an increase in industrial production took place. A comparison of the figures of the two Germanys is instructive: in eastern Germany the increase in industrial production amounted to 43 per cent, in West Germany to 11 per cent. These developments in the economic sphere had a decisive influence on the course of events in Europe in the 1970's.

The Eastern Bloc
THE PROBLEMS OF RISING PROSPERITY

The favorable economic situation in the East might be considered as the outcome of two developments. On one hand, the emphasis on the development of heavy industry which Stalin had forced upon his satellites, and which for two decades had produced a life of hardships and scarcity, now bore fruit; from this basis other industries—primarily consumer goods —were developing. For instance, it is characteristic that in all these countries the increase in production of chemical, coal, and petroleum products —i.e., products used in clothing, building, transportation—was far in advance of the growth rate in the other areas of industrial production. On the other hand, the pressure of Soviet Russia on the economy of these countries relaxed. At the beginning of the sixties Soviet Russia had attempted to impose a unified plan on the entire area which would divide it between countries supplying raw materials and others producing finished goods. But with this proposal Soviet Russia had overreached itself. The protests were vehement and Rumania simply refused to follow the Russian guidelines. This was a turning point; Russia gradually permitted each of the countries to follow its own path in building a socialist society.

Increasing prosperity also raised new problems. Agriculture had difficulty in fulfilling the needs of the expanding industrial sector; this became an urgent concern of the governments which set the prices in these socialist countries. In Czechoslovakia, and more so in Poland, where, because of the resistance to collectivization, most of the land was in the hands of small farmers and was worked in uneconomic, old-fashioned ways, scarcity led to a rise in the price of bread which encountered vehement opposition by the industrial workers. Demonstrations and strikes occurred and the government had to retreat. This forced the retirement of Gomulka, the Polish Communist leader, in 1970; his successor, Gierek, encountered the same difficulties a few years later but was able to hold on to power.

In general the governments of the satellite countries tried to eliminate deficiencies and to comply with the demands for more consumer goods by imports, particularly imports from the West; in this respect they followed the example which Soviet Russia had set in the sixties. The eastern-western trade more than doubled in the first half of the 1970's, partly based on credits which western financial institutions were now willing to give. Inevitably the attitude to the western world became more moderate. The situation of the Catholic Church in Poland and Hungary improved, and in Hungary in 1976 permission to the installation of a new primate, Laszlo Lekai was given.

To what extent trading contacts with the West expanded into the cultural sphere and lowered the barriers impeding travel and intellectual

Dresden, one of East Germany's most splendid baroque cities, had almost been entirely destroyed by an air raid during the Second World War. This picture, of the reconstructed main center, is an example of the way in which other East German towns and cities have been rebuilt.

exchange depended on the governments of the various countries, each of which handled this question in its own way. Poland and Czechoslovakia did not favor closer contacts and their governments continue to keep their people under sharp control. Hungary took a different course. Janos Kadar, who had come to power in 1956 with the support of Russian military forces during the Hungarian revolt, did not install a harsh and oppressive regime as had been expected but followed a rather moderate course, introducing decentralization in the economic sphere, which permitted economic enterprises greater freedom in planning and producing. This moderation, combined with increasing prosperity, seems to have provided broad support for the regime on the part of the population: In Hungary foreign books can be found in the bookshops, traveling to the West is not difficult. It is amusing but also revealing that after the summer of 1976, the Hungarian government proudly announced that of the Hungarians who had traveled to the West in the summer, over 90 per cent did not use this opportunity to defect but returned to Hungary.

The degree to which a western presence is allowed in the Eastern bloc and is visible varies, but unquestionably there has been an intensification of contacts; a clear indication is the exchange of numerous official visits which have brought the leaders of the eastern countries to the West and the leaders of the western countries to the East, among them two American presidents.

It does not appear that the Russians regarded the intensification of economic relations with the West as a danger to their control over the states of the Eastern bloc. They did not consider a dissolution of their alliance with these states as a serious possibility. Their troops were still in some of these states; and, despite the development of economic relations with the capitalist West, the trade of the states of the Eastern bloc with Russia remained much more important. Military cooperation and economic integration had gone too far to allow a breaking of the bonds. Moreover, all the governments of the countries in the Eastern bloc assured the Russians of their loyalty to the Soviet Union and they were certainly aware—as they had learned from the experiences of Hungary in 1956 and Czechoslovakia in 1968—that the entire system, and therefore also their own position, would collapse if they separated from the Russians.

THE MAINTENANCE OF IDEOLOGICAL ORTHODOXY

The Russians were concerned with the possible intellectual consequences of closer contact with the western world. It is comprehensible that in the more relaxed atmosphere which had developed in the Eastern bloc demands would be raised, particularly by intellectuals, to lift restrictions on intellectual freedom. What the Russians considered as a possible danger was disintegration of Communism as the only intellectual system—a development which would undermine the leadership of Soviet Russia among the Communist parties of the world. They had already been attacked by the Chinese as having falsified the true precepts of Marxism; increased contacts with the West might reinforce theoretical doubts, revisionist notions, and sectarianism. Fearing an intellectual movement which would impair their own position as leader of the Communist movement, the Russians wanted to call a meeting of all the Communist parties which, as past Communist congresses had done, would issue a joint declaration confirming Soviet Russia in its leadership role. Since the various Communist parties were well aware that such a meeting might reduce the freedom which they had painfully gained for pursuing their own course towards socialism, they were less than enthusiastic about the Russian suggestion. But in the end their reluctance, very strong in the West but noticeable also in the East, was overcome. In June 1976 a conference of European Communist parties assembled in East Berlin. At the end of the conference a document was published that established a common position, which confirmed the Russian policy "of peaceful co-existence, active cooperation between states irrespective of their social systems, and international détente"—the Chinese had rejected the latter as a contradiction of the ideas of Marxism. But on the other hand the Russians had to concede that these aims could be attained in different countries in different ways so that each Communist party was equal and possessed "sovereign independence," and that there should be "no interference in its internal affairs"; on the contrary, there would be "respect for their free choice of different roads in the struggle for social change of a progressive nature and for socialism."

Up to this point the declaration seemed to express not much more than what—admittedly after tensions, retreats, and advances—the states of the Eastern bloc had achieved, and what now defined the relationship between Russia and the states of the Eastern bloc. But another voice was also heard: the voice of the Communist parties in western Europe. They believed that the Russians, and probably also the leaders of the countries of the Eastern bloc, were unaware of the extent to which even among those who might be inclined to Communism the Russian intervention in Hungary and Czechoslovakia had aroused indignation and identified Communism with oppression. In their view it was necessary to draw a clear line, stating that the policy which the Communist parties in western Europe would follow would be appropriate to the situation which existed in western Europe and would not take Russia as a model. In order to gain the approval of these western European Communists, the declaration stated that a "dialogue and cooperation between Communists and all other democratic and peace-loving forces" might be necessary, and this might include "broader Catholic forces, members of other Christian communities and adherents to other faiths." What was implied in these sentences had been expressed in a speech by the Spanish Communist leader, Santiago Carillo:

In former years Moscow, where dream began to take on reality, was our Rome. We talked of the great socialist October Revolution as the day of our birth. Those were the times of our childhood. . . . The existence of new problems has made our differences apparent, has made us realize the divergent opinions among us that could not be solved otherwise but through discussion, in a spirit of criticism and self-criticism, in the recognition of the diversity of views and of national forms of socialism and of socialist politics. . . . We, the Communists of today have no center that gives us directives, have no international discipline imposed upon us. What unites us today are the bonds of affinity based on the theory of scientific socialism.

At this congress Carillo and other leaders of Communist parties in western Europe introduced a movement that came to be called Eurocommunism. We shall hear more about it in its appropriate context, that of the developments in western Europe during the seventies. But its impact on Russia and the states of the Eastern bloc might be briefly touched upon here. The appearance of Eurocommunism has not impinged on relations with the West insofar as political or economic contacts and negotiations are concerned. But restrictions and pressures on intellectual life have continued with unabated, if not increased, strength; the harassment and persecutions of those who advocate greater freedom in the intellectual and cultural sphere and defend those who have not bowed to restrictions on freedom of thought have been intensified. In the intellectual and cultural sphere the curtain has again descended between the West and Russia and the Eastern bloc.

The Western Bloc

The economic recession dominated the developments in the states of the Western bloc. It expressed itself particularly in the steady rise of unemployment and inflation. Unemployment hit the young particularly hard; even after years of training or study they might not find a job. The question of which problem—inflation or unemployment—should have priority exacerbated internal tensions, since the restrictions involved in fighting inflation increased unemployment, whereas wiping out unemployment meant pouring new money into the economy, which increased inflation.

It ought to be emphasized, however, that, very differently from what had happened in the great depression of 1929, the recession of the 1970's did not lead to a sharp movement towards extremism or towards the right in any of the western European countries.

THE POLICY OF CONSENSUS: SWEDEN, GREAT BRITAIN, WEST GERMANY

The countries which, inspired by the British model of the welfare state, had gone furthest in providing social services to their citizens were the Scandinavian countries, particularly Sweden: Social insurance covered all spheres of life; pensions, amounting to 65 per cent of the highest salary earned during a person's working years, gave financial security after retirement. Within this framework free enterprise continued to prevail, even though the government set wages and intensive consultation, particularly with the trade unions, took place before any new legislation was brought before parliament; the trade unions had almost a veto power. High taxes were the basis for the functioning of this system. Representing 40 per cent of the gross national income, Swedish taxes were the highest in the world. As long as the European economy flourished Sweden's wealth in timber and iron ore, and its long experience in industries like shipbuilding, made it one of the wealthiest countries of Europe. But with the onset of the recession exports began to lag and the high taxes became increasingly burdensome. After thirty years of rule by the Social Democratic party the conservatives, called the Center party, came into power in 1976. But this was not the beginning of a sharp reaction. It soon became clear that the changes which they intended to make were chiefly minor adjustments, particularly in the tax rate. The welfare state was far too entrenched in the society for any party to dare to demolish it.

The same can be said about Great Britain. There a Conservative, Edward Heath, who had successfully conducted negotiations about Great Britain's entry into the Common Market, had become prime minister. Heath believed that to obtain the full advantages which entry in the Common Market offered, it was necessary to stop the continuous process of the rises in wages, which, in adjustment to inflation, the trade unions demanded and usually obtained. Heath introduced an antiinflationary law meant to freeze wages and prices; it met strong opposition from Labor and the trade unions. The question of wage rises became critical in the coal industry; the miners went on strike and were supported by workers in other industries. These strikes coincided with the Arab oil boycott and severe restrictions had to be placed on the use of electricity, airplane and railroad schedules were cut, etc. The Christmas of 1973 was dark and gloomy. This demonstration of the chaotic situation which could develop when workers unite to oppose measures of the government ended Heath's policy of confrontation with the trade unions. Elections held in 1974 brought a victory of Labor; the new prime minister, Harold Wilson, or particularly his chancellor of the exchequer, Denis Healy, succeeded in persuading the trade unions that the entire existence of industrial life, including also the existence of the workers, would be jeopardized if British goods could not compete on the world market because of demands for wage rises. The trade unions voluntarily agreed to keep demands for wages below a certain level which would keep British goods competitive on the world market. The economic situation was also eased by an improvement in the balance of payments; oil from the North Sea had begun to come in quantities, making reductions in imports of oil from the Near East possible. But the main consequence of the crisis was the realization of the need to abandon a policy of confrontation and to use a policy of consensus. The principal aim of recent Labor policy has been to promote legislation which would make consultation of the representatives of workers in questions of factory policy obligatory, so that tests of strength between employers and employees would be replaced by cooperation.

In drawing up this proposal the British government clearly had looked over to the other side of the channel, to Germany. Germany, which had flourished more than other continental countries in the sixties and was recognized again to have become a great power, withstood the recession relatively well, although the appearance of unemployment, unknown in Germany since the 1930's, had a disturbing effect. In 1970, the Socialist party had come into power with Willy Brandt as chancellor. Brandt's behavior and actions during the Nazi period and the Second World War provided the basis from which he rose to leadership in the postwar world.

Chancellor Willy Brandt, during a visit to Poland in 1970, kneels before a memorial to the victims of the Warsaw Ghetto. Brandt's trip culminated with the signing of a German-Polish treaty, part of his policy of *Ostpolitik*.

When the Nazis came to power Brandt was twenty years of age, a minor employee in a firm of ship brokers. Since his early years he had been an active and prominent member of the Socialist youth; fearing reprisals by the Nazis, he left Germany and went to Norway. When the Germans occupied Norway he became an active member of the Norwegian resistance, and was naturalized as a Norwegian. But after the Nazi defeat he returned to Berlin, where he soon played a leading role in the Social Democratic party. As mayor of the city, he showed courage and steadfastness during the building of the wall, and gained great popularity. Thus the way was opened for a national career which carried him to the chancellorship as leader of the Socialist party. But his views on foreign policy and domestic policy were formed in the times of his struggle against the Nazis. He was always aware of the immensity of the crimes which Germany had committed, and did not believe that the fall of the Nazis had wiped the German slate clean. Germany had to work to regain the good-will of its neighbors. It did not behoove the Germans to maintain hostility to the East by taking a rigidly legalistic attitude. They ought to be willing to take the first steps to arrive at some kind of relationship with the states of the Eastern bloc. Brandt, when he was foreign minister, had taken up contacts with the countries of the Eastern bloc. Now as chancellor Brandt concluded treaties with Soviet Russia and Poland in which Germany recognized existing frontiers, and he made an agreement with eastern Germany in which it was stated that changes of the status quo could and should be made only by peaceful means.

His participation in the Norwegian resistance had taught him the value of cooperation with people from all classes and groups. Probably a decisive factor in the success of the Social Democrats was the program which they had given themselves in 1959, the so-called Godesberg Program, in which they took some distance from Marxism by proclaiming that economic planning ought to take place only insofar as it was necessary and that there should be as much freedom left in economic development as was possible. The Godesberg Program represented an abandonment of the notion of class struggle. It was emphatically a program of reform and not revolution and was directed towards cooperation in economic life among all those who had a stake in it. Strikes, although some occurred, were relatively rare in Germany. The trade unions were involved in all stages of the policy-making process. What the Socialists demanded when they had come to power in 1970, was that this practice, which had been customary, should now become law, so that in changed circumstances workers and trade unions could not again be excluded and forced into an inferior position, with the possible consequence a rise of revolutionary extremism. In 1974, Brandt proposed legislation which, after long discussion, was adopted by the parliament; the new law assured representatives of the workers in large enterprises half the seats on the board of directors, and, by obligating the firms to place some percentage of their profits in shares held for the workers, made the workers co-owners. The workers or their trade unions had become an integral element of the economic and political order. Decisions were to be reached not by one party winning out over the other but by consensus. The lack of serious economic conflicts and strikes was one of the reasons why Germany weathered the storm of the recession rather well.

The execution of the consensus policy was no longer in the hands of Brandt. He had to resign as chancellor in 1974 because he felt forced to assume responsibility for bureaucratic failures in his administration. With him the last leading statesman, whose career rested on his actions during the Second World War, disappeared. Of course, Brandt did not have the influence and power of the great war leaders who had determined policy after the Second World War—Churchill, De Gaulle, Stalin—but in Brandt's policy there was still an element of that courage and idealism which had inspired those who took up the struggle against the Nazis against what seemed insuperable odds. Brandt's successor, Helmut Schmidt, was a very different personality: an expert in economics, almost a technocrat, he is a realist concerned with attainable improvements in the economic situation and the removal of friction in foreign policy, rather than the pursuit of idealistic principles. Schmidt as a political type is similar to the men who in the seventies have come to power in France and Italy: Giscard d'Estaing, the successor of De Gaulle and Pompidou as French president, who, in contrast to De Gaulle's emphasis on foreign policy places the modernization of French economic life in the foreground; and Andreotti, who has been head of the Italian cabinet longer than any prime minister since De Gasperi, not only because he is a politician of unusual tactical cleverness but because of his having been able to bring an unusual amount of administrative efficiency into the Italian government apparatus. All of them are primarily concerned with economic issues which they want to solve through compromise and negotiations. They are representatives of a policy of consensus and the popularity which they undoubtedly enjoy is a sign to what extent this policy corresponds to the wishes of a great part of the population of western Europe.

But if the oil crisis and the difficulties of the recession have resulted in far-reaching acceptance of a policy of consensus, it has also created new problems in domestic policy. The enlarged possibilities for influence which consensus policy gives to those who want to work within the system has the opposite effect of diminishing the possibilities of those who oppose the system to make themselves heard. The rise of the consensus policy has led to the emergence of two phenomena which have come into the foreground in the seventies: Eurocommunism and terrorism.

EUROCOMMUNISM AND TERRORISM: FRANCE, ITALY, SPAIN

In the emergence of Eurocommunism two factors have played a crucial role: the impossibility, after Hungary and Czechoslovakia, of maintaining the Soviet state as a political model, and the view that under the conditions of consensus policy more could be achieved by working within than by working outside the existing system. But it is no accident that the appearance of Eurocommunism was almost simultaneous to that of terrorism. If Eurocommunism means that Communism rejects the notion of trying to overthrow an existing regime by revolution and wants to work within the system for a thorough social change, it also means that those who do not believe that the system can be reformed but that it has to be overthrown by revolution can no longer work in the Communist party and have no place to go. Their main instrument to reach their goal becomes direct action: bringing disorder into the system by violence.

Germany was the western country in which twentieth-century terrorism made its first appearance. Germany, with a strong Marxist tradition among intellectuals and a large student population which the universities could not accommodate, and for which particularly in the times of recession the employment situation was difficult, had an extreme fringe. Although diminished in numbers with the disappearance of the heady prospects

Paris in the 1970's. *Note contrast of the Eiffel Tower and older buildings and bridges with the newly constructed radio and television center on the left, and the very modern bridge in the foreground.*

of the student revolt, and increasingly isolated, the extremists did not want to give up and resorted to violence against a system which appeared so impermeable. Nevertheless, in Germany the terrorists were a closely knit and only very small group; since a Communist party never existed in Germany a terrorist attitude was not fed, therefore, by members of the Communist party who were dissatisfied with the abandonment of a policy of revolutionary overthrow and were opposed to the acceptance of Eurocommunism.

The countries in which Eurocommunism became an important political force are Spain and Italy. While it looked for a while that the French Communist party would also adopt this course this possibility has receded into the background. France seems to be content in a rather suspended political position. Although immediately after the student revolt De Gaulle was greeted with demonstrations of loyalty, his prestige had actually suffered a serious blow and, not unaware of this, he relinquished power. His two successors—first Georges Pompidou, who died in 1974, and then Giscard d'Estaing—were probably inclined to move to the center and to the left but their freedom of action was impeded by the fact that their chief parliamentary support was the Gaullist party which was far to the right. The acceptance of a Eurocommunist policy by the French Communist party was therefore of doubtful value because Communism might have lost the particular attraction of radical appeal without any practical or concrete effects, since the door to power might have remained closed. The elections of 1978, in which the left Socialists and Communists again failed to achieve a majority, confirmed only that there was no need now to decide on adoption of a Eurocommunist line.

The Communist leaders in Spain and Italy operated under very different conditions. After the Second World War Spain under Franco had been placed under quarantine by the other European powers; as we have mentioned, only the United States, in need of military bases in Spain, had maintained contacts and given economic support. But since the end of the war Spain had entered a period of rapid industrialization. The population engaged in industrial activities doubled between 1950 and 1970; while those active in agriculture declined by 50 per cent. These figures are significant in that this was a period of remarkable population growth. Industrialization meant an increase in the middle classes and workers whose dissatisfaction with Franco's autocratic regime became widespread: there were strikes, student revolts, antigovernment demonstrations; when Franco died in 1974, his regime was in crisis. What the Spaniards feared most was another civil war. Thus they willingly accepted the restoration of the monarchy under Franco's chosen heir, King Juan Carlos. He initiated a gradual but steady return to democracy, but just because this process evoked the opposition of the adherents of Franco, some of whom were still powerful, a Communist party which advocated revolution, and that means increased political disorder, would have committed suicide; a further weakening of the democratic forces would have had no appeal among the great masses fearing a return of the civil war. But Carillo, the leader of the Spanish Communists, the main representative of Eurocommunism, has also given a more general justification of the Eurocommunist position. In a society in which there is a mixed economy—i.e., where extensive industrial enterprises belong to the government, and in which the economy is controlled and widely directed by the government—it makes no sense to overthrow the regime. It makes more sense to try to get a share in the government to extend the sphere of government control until a socialist society evolves. The situation which Marx had analyzed, even the situation which had existed when the Bolsheviks took over in Russia, was simply very different from the one which existed now in western Europe.

The Communist party in Spain was relatively small. The country in which Eurocommunism is really of crucial political importance is Italy. Radicalism and revolutionism have deep roots in Italy. In contrast to northern Europe, where the chief problem has been to persuade the middle classes to recognize the trade unions as legitimate partners in the policy-making process, the main problem in Italy is to persuade the members of the Communist party to abandon the idea of a revolutionary overthrow of the system and to cooperate within the system. Italian Communist leaders have strong reasons for seeking a more direct involvement in the government. The Communist party had grown steadily but it was rather doubtful whether people would continue to vote for it if they never harvested any concrete advantages. Communists controlled the municipal governments of many great cities—Rome, Bologna, Milan—and their administration was considered to represent an improvement over the preceding Christian Democratic administrations. But there were limits what they could do if they did not get support from the central government in Rome.

Finally, there remained the great question of the misery in the south. These areas might be the origin of a resurgence of Fascism; clearly they could only be secured if industrialization and agrarian reform would be pushed forward with great energy. Moreover, in Italian Communism, since the time of its first leaders, Gramsci and Togliatti, there has always been a strong feeling of the urgent need for bettering the life of the terribly poor peasant population in the south—a feeling that it is more important to do something for these people now than to wait for the uncertain future brought by a revolution. Thus, the Communists pressed for, and in 1978 achieved, a firm agreement with the Christian Democrats about supporting them in the execution of a thorough and wide-ranging reform program. But there is no doubt that the opposition in the party is strong and will change leaders if the hoped-for results do not occur. Moreover, there were many who regarded this line of policy as treason to all the traditions of Italian radicalism. We have said that the simultaneous appearance of Eurocommunism and terrorism is not accidental; they act upon each other at least as far as the increase in terrorism has reinforced the Communist cooperation with Christian Democracy and produced a certain amount of consensus even in Italy.

EPILOGUE: *1984*

In surveying the contours of the European political landscape at the end of the 1970's, the overwhelming impression is that a complete change has occurred since the beginning of this century: a change in boundaries, forms of government, social and economic structure, the conduct of life.

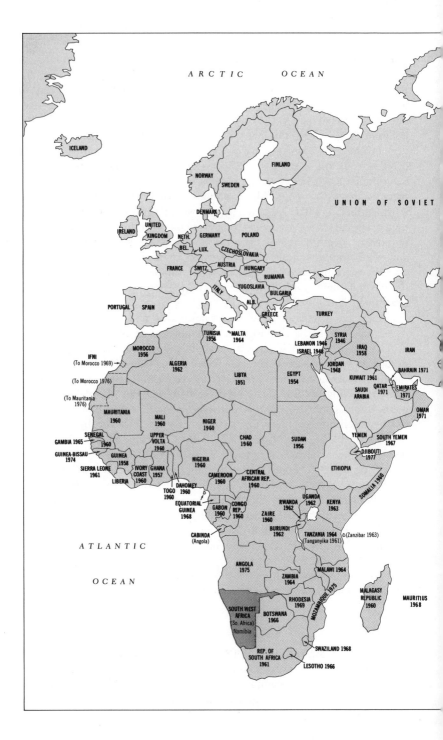

ARCTIC   OCEAN

UNION OF SOVIET

ICELAND

FINLAND

NORWAY
SWEDEN

DENMARK

IRELAND   UNITED
           KINGDOM   NETH.   GERMANY   POLAND
                     BEL.   LUX.   CZECHOSLOVAKIA
           FRANCE   SWITZ. AUSTRIA   HUNGARY
                                      RUMANIA
                            YUGOSLAVIA
PORTUGAL   SPAIN   BULGARIA
                              ITALY   ALB.
                                    GREECE   TURKEY

                     TUNISIA   MALTA   SYRIA
                     1956   1964   1946
MOROCCO   LEBANON 1946   IRAQ
IFNI   1956   ISRAEL 1948   1958   IRAN
(To Morocco 1969)→   ALGERIA   JORDAN
                     1962   1948   KUWAIT 1961   BAHRAIN 1971
(To Morocco 1976)   LIBYA   EGYPT   QATAR   EMIRATES
                               1951   1954   SAUDI   1971   1971
(To Mauritania   ARABIA   OMAN
1976)   1971
        MAURITANIA   MALI
        1960   1960   NIGER   YEMEN   SOUTH YEMEN
    SENEGAL   1960   1967
GAMBIA 1965 1960   UPPER   CHAD   SUDAN   DJIBOUTI
GUINEA-BISSAU   VOLTA   1960   1956   1977
1974   GUINEA 1960
SIERRA LEONE 1958   IVORY GHANA NIGERIA   ETHIOPIA
1961   LIBERIA COAST 1957   1960   CAMEROON CENTRAL
                    1960   TOGO   1960   AFRICAN REP.
                          DAHOMEY 1960   1960   SOMALIA 1960
                          1960   EQUATORIAL   RWANDA UGANDA
                                        GUINEA   GABON 1962   1962   KENYA
                                        1968   1960   CONGO   1963
                                                        REP.   ZAIRE
                                        CABINDA 1960   1960   BURUNDI
                                        (Angola)   1962   TANZANIA 1964 ◌(Zanzibar 1963)
                                                                      (Tanganyika 1961)

ATLANTIC

OCEAN   ANGOLA   MALAWI 1964
                         1975   ZAMBIA
                                      1964   MALAGASY   MAURITIUS
                                              RHODESIA   REPUBLIC   1968
                                              1969   1960
                         SOUTH WEST
                         AFRICA   BOTSWANA
                         (So. Africa) 1966   SWAZILAND 1968
                         Namibia
                                REP. OF
                                SOUTH AFRICA
                                1961   LESOTHO 1966

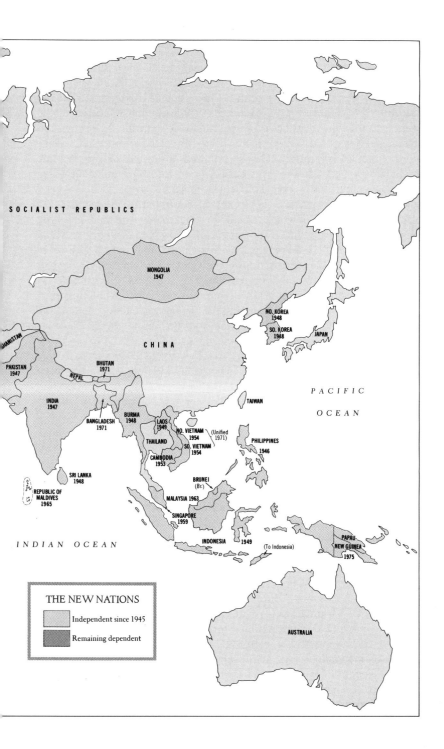

SOCIALIST REPUBLICS

MONGOLIA
1947

NO. KOREA
1948

SO. KOREA
1948

JAPAN

CHINA

PACIFIC

OCEAN

AFGHANISTAN

PAKISTAN
1947

BHUTAN
1971

NEPAL

INDIA
1947

TAIWAN

BURMA
1948

BANGLADESH
1971

LAOS
1949

NO. VIETNAM
1954

(Unified
1971)

THAILAND

SO. VIETNAM
1954

PHILIPPINES
1946

CAMBODIA
1953

SRI LANKA
1948

REPUBLIC OF
MALDIVES
1965

BRUNEI
(Br.)

MALAYSIA 1963

SINGAPORE
1959

INDONESIA   1949

(To Indonesia)

PAPAU-
NEW GUINEA
1975

INDIAN OCEAN

AUSTRALIA

THE NEW NATIONS

Independent since 1945

Remaining dependent

In 1949, George Orwell published a utopian novel called *1984*, suggesting how the world might look in that remote year. Like H. G. Wells had done in the beginning of the century, like Aldous Huxley had done in the early thirties, Orwell too considered as the main characteristics of the future features which had been brought about by scientific discoveries and technology. But whereas Wells had expected from the advances of science the abolition of all misery, Orwell followed the more pessimistic line which Huxley had pursued: the possibility of directing and controlling the human mind and action by scientific means. Orwell even darkened Huxley's picture by placing the means of control into the hands of a totalitarian dictatorship which would be able to regulate and supervise every minute of man's life, and deprive man of the possibility to think for himself. Orwell's *1984* was meant to be a warning not to give in to totalitarianism. It was written during the Cold War and is a product of its atmosphere—that explains its popularity; it has been widely read and still is an interesting document of the mind of this period—but this time-bound purpose also explains its defects: a certain crudeness, a certain unwillingness to give serious consideration and analysis to things to come. However, there is a remarkable thesis in Orwell's novel: In order to have full control over man's mind it is necessary to erase the past. We might find in this assumption an echo of a question which has been asked frequently in our time, and with particular urgency since the Second World War. What really does the past mean in a period in which life in its entirety seems to have been transformed?

Certainly an answer to this question requires greater distance than a survey of one decade can give; it demands looking upon the century as a whole. From this perspective the past emerges as more relevant than it appears when placed in relation to the events of the day. Even that development which appears as the greatest, the most thorough separation from the past—i.e., the loss of European hegemony over the globe and the rise of non-European powers to world leadership—appears less as a break than as an evolution. Within Europe two superpowers confront each other, and prevent the whole of Europe from being subjected to the other. This confirms that, although the European powers do not rule the globe any longer, Europe still has enough weight to be decisive in the competition of the superpowers; Europe still exists as a factor in the international system. Within Europe—and within the two blocs created by the two great rivals—the various national formations are still alive, each acting in ways which appear appropriate to its interests and character. Even the fall of monarchies, the disappearance of the glamor of the courts, and the splendor of an army led by aristocrats belong to a wider development which has been going on for centuries, and in the twentieth century is reaching its conclusion: the breakdown and removal of the privileges of a feudal society, with consequences, ranging over all fields of life which are involved in the establishment of equality. If the existence of these privileges and rights gave rulers the strength to keep other classes out of power, the breakdown of these privileges must be viewed as the complement to the solution of what we have called the greatest problem of this century: the elimination of the barriers between industrial workers and the rest of society, the integration of the workers into society. Whatever one thinks about the forms and the results of this process, which is still not complete, if one looks upon the situation which existed at the beginning of the century great strides have been made.

History usually is regarded as the record of changes, but there is not only change but also continuity in the historical process. The twentieth century has been a century of rapid, revolutionary, breathtaking changes, but in Europe these changes have had their roots in the past, and thus despite the differences between present-day Europe and the Europe of earlier times continuity has been preserved—this is not only a historical fact, it is also an achievement.

SUGGESTIONS
FOR FURTHER READING

(Books marked * are available in paperback.)

The printed material on the history of the twentieth century—documentary publications, memoirs, comprehensive histories, historical monographs—would fill a library; the following bibliography is severely selective. It is limited to works published in English, with the emphasis on titles of recent date. Included are books providing a general orientation, as well as those describing in detail events which were treated only briefly in the text, because of limitations of space. Special attention has been given to books which permit insight into the conditions of life and to writings which contain interpretations different from those presented in the text.

Printed collections of documentary sources are not listed, but most of the works mentioned contain detailed bibliographies which indicate source material and may serve as guides for further reading.

GENERAL

Contemporary history poses particular problems for both research and presentation. These are well outlined in *Geoffrey Barraclough, *An Introduction to Contemporary History* (New York, 1964) (Penguin). There are few comprehensive treatments of the entire period from 1890 to the present or to the end of the Second World War; A rapid survey of political and cultural developments is given by George Lichtheim, *Europe in the Twentieth Century* (London, 1972), and a more detailed analysis is found in the *New Cambridge Modern History*, but the relevant Vol. XII exists in both an original and a revised version—*The Era of Violence*, ed. by David Thomson (Cambridge, Eng., 1960) and *The Shifting Balance of World Forces, 1898–1945*, ed. by C. L. Mowat (Cambridge, Eng., 1968)—and since these versions are not identical both of them must be considered. The basic factors determining the economic developments are analyzed in the *Cambridge Economic History of Europe*, Vol. VI, *The Industrial Revolutions and After*, ed. by M. M. Postan and H. J. Habakkuk (Cambridge, Eng., 1965), which contains also a consideration of demographic development and a valuable account of the transformation of society after the Industrial Revolution will be found in David Landes, *The*

Unbound Prometheus: Technological Change and Industrial Development in Western Europe from 1750 to the Present (Cambridge, Mass., 1972). Volumes V and VI of *Propylaen Geschichte Europas* are of interest to those who do not read German because of unusually rich, well selected illustrative and statistical material.

FROM 1890 TO THE BEGINNING OF THE FIRST WORLD WAR

A lively description of the political scene in Europe before the First World War is given in *Barbara W. Tuchman, *The Proud Tower* (New York, 1966) (Bantam); the reader should be aware, however, that although the general picture stands up well, details are not always correct and the author has an anti-German bias. Less personally engaged and more comprehensive is Oron J. Hale, *The Great Illusion: 1900–1914* (New York, 1971). Much discussion has been aroused by the question of the extent to which intellectual developments in this period prepared the way for the new intellectual trends in the postwar world; for perceptive descriptions of the intellectual climate of this period see *H. Stuart Hughes, *Consciousness and Society* (New York, 1958) (Vintage) and *Gerhard Masur, *Prophets of Yesterday* (New York, 1961) (Harper Colophon); Christopher Caudwell, *Studies in a Dying Culture* (New York, 1938) is also pertinent, although it is concerned exclusively with the literary scene. A brilliant analysis, limited to the intellectual antecedents of later developments, is *Hannah Arendt, *The Origins of Totalitarianism* (New York, 1951) (Meridian). The facts concerning the economic influence of Europe in the non-European parts of the world can be learned from *Herbert Feis, *Europe: The World's Banker, 1870–1914* (New Haven, 1930) (Norton). The two most important works concerning the development of the concept of imperialism are *John A. Hobson, *Imperialism: A Study* (London, 1902) (Ann Arbor) and *V. I. Lenin, *Imperialism, the Highest Stage of Capitalism* (written 1916) (China Books; also International Publishers); for the crisis in Marxism brought about by the economic progress of this period, see Peter Gay, *The Dilemma of Democratic Socialism: Eduard Bernstein's Challenge to Marx* (New York, 1952) (Collier).

For all the great European powers there exist national histories covering this period, some of them reaching up to the Second World War or to the present. For Great Britain, see R. C. K. Ensor, *England, 1817–1914* (Oxford, 1936) and *Robert K. Webb, *Modern England: From the Eighteenth Century to the Present* (New York, 1968) (Dodd, Mead); for France, *D. W. Brogan, *France Under the Republic, 1870–1939* (New York, 1940) (Harper Torchbook, in two volumes), also published under the title *The Development of Modern France*, and *Modern France: Problems of the Third and Fourth Republics*, ed. by Edward Mead Earle (Princeton, N.J., 1951); for Spain, Raymond Carr, *Spain, 1808–1939* (Oxford, 1966); for Italy, Christopher Seton-Watson, *Italy from Liberalism to Fascism, 1870–1925* (London, 1967); for Germany, Hajo Holborn, *A History of Modern Germany*, Vol. III (New York, 1969), on the years 1840–1945 and now Gordon A. Craig, *Germany: 1870–1945* (Oxford, 1978); for Austria, *A. J. P. Taylor, *The Habsburg Monarchy, 1809–1918*

(London, 1948) (Harper Torchbook); for Russia, *Sir Bernard Pares, A History of Russia, revised ed. (New York, 1953) (Vintage).

In addition, for an understanding of particular aspects of British history during this period one may turn to a number of illuminating biographies and autobiographies. *Roy Jenkins, Asquith: Portrait of a Man and an Era (New York, 1965) (Dutton), is the biography of the leading British statesman of the period by a prominent member of the Labor party who describes the problem of political leadership in a parliamentary system with deep understanding. The first volumes of Winston S. Churchill, the standard biography, begun by Randolph Churchill and continued by Martin J. Gilbert—Youth, 1874–1900 (Boston, 1966) and Young Statesman, 1901–1914 (Boston, 1967)—deserve attention not only because of their significance in explaining Churchill's early development but also because of the light which they shed on the English ruling group. The power of the British monarch was limited, but Sir Harold Nicolson, in King George the Fifth: His Life and Reign (London, 1952), contributes to the analysis of important political developments in his account of the crisis over the House of Lords. Samuel Hynes, The Edwardian Turn of Mind (Princeton, 1968) is full of interesting details throwing light on unknown or forgotten aspects of the world before the First World War. The contrast between the autobiographies of two women prominent in politics, Margot Asquith, Autobiography, ed. by Mark Bonham Carter (Boston, 1962) and Beatrice Webb, Our Partnership (New York, London, and Toronto, 1948), is highly amusing. Among the many good British autobiographies the best is the five-volume series by Leonard Sidney Woolf, consisting of Sowing (New York, 1960), covering the years 1880–1904; Growing (New York, 1961), on 1904–1911; Beginning Again (New York, 1963, 1964), on 1911–1918; Downhill All the Way (New York, 1967), on 1919–1939; and The Journey Not the Arrival Matters (New York, 1969). It reaches from the beginning of the twentieth century to the present and is a moving commentary on the decline of the English liberal tradition.

For the two leading French statesmen we have good biographical treatments, Geoffrey Bruun, Clemenceau (Cambridge, Mass., 1943) and Gordon Wright, Raymond Poincaré and the French Presidency (Stanford, 1942). On the details of the Dreyfus case and the present evaluation of the importance of this affair, see Douglas Johnson, France and the Dreyfus Affair (London, 1966) and Guy Chapman, The Dreyfus Case: A Reassessment (London, 1955). For the background of the affair and some of its consequences see David B. Ralston, The Army of the Republic: The Place of the Military in the Political Evolution of France, 1871–1914 (Cambridge, Mass., and London, 1967) and Eugen Joseph Weber, The Nationalist Revival in France, 1905–1914 (Berkeley, Calif., 1959). Roger Henry Soltau, French Political Thought in the Nineteenth Century (New Haven, 1931), although not a recent book, is distinguished by its understanding of the tension which led to the separation of church and state.

For Spain, see Joan Connelly Ullman, The Tragic Week: A Study of Anticlericalism in Spain, 1875–1912 (Cambridge, Mass., 1968), which describes in detail the crisis which frustrated attempts at reform.

The particular character of the Italian parliamentary system is well presented in A. William Salomone, *Italy in the Giolittian Era: Italian Democracy in the Making* (Philadelphia, 1960). R. A. Webster, *Industrial Imperialism in Italy: 1908–1915* (Berkeley, Calif., 1975) breaks new ground by showing the economic aspects of Giolitti's political course. For the concrete issues involved in the problem of the Italian south, see Denis Mack Smith, *A History of Sicily: Modern Sicily after 1713* (New York, 1968).

Germany under William II has been investigated from different points of view in recent years. The best biography of the emperor himself is probably Michael Balfour, *The Kaiser and His Times* (London, 1964). There are several treatments in English of leading personalities of the period: Norman Rich, *Friedrich von Holstein: Politics and Diplomacy in the Era of Bismarck and Wilhelm II* (Cambridge, England, 1965); Lamar Cecil, *Albert Ballin: Business and Politics in Imperial Germany* (Princeton, N.J., 1967); John G. Williamson, *Karl Helfferich, 1872–1924: Economist, Financier, Politician* (Princeton, N.J., 1971). For the political consequences of the problems connected with the German industrialization, see the essays collected in *Imperial Germany*, ed. by James J. Sheehan (New York, 1976), and the collection of articles by Eckart Kehr, published in English translation under the title, *Economic Interest, Militarism, and Foreign Policy* (Berkeley, Calif., 1977). For an understanding of the mentality of the German bourgeoisie in this period one turns best to a novel, Heinrich Mann, *Little Superman* (*Der Untertan*, 1918; originally trans. as *The Patrioteer*). For the impact of German industrial development on attitudes in the social democracy, see *Carl E. Schorske, *German Social Democracy, 1905–1917: The Development of the Great Schism* (Cambridge, Mass., 1955) (Wiley), and Peter Gay, *The Dilemma of Democratic Socialism* (New York, 1962).

On Austria-Hungary, see Robert A. Kann, *The Habsburg Empire: A Study in Integration and Disintegration* (New York, 1957) and C. A. Macartney, *Hungary: A Short History* (Chicago, 1962), which provide details on the complex structure of the Habsburg monarchy.

In Russia, personal factors played a decisive role in the fall of tsarism. For a picture of the relevant political personalities of this period, see *Sir Bernard Pares, *The Fall of the Russian Monarchy* (London, 1939) (Vintage), and for the origin of the ideas dominating the rulers, see Robert F. Byrnes, *Pobedonostsev: His Life and Thought* (Bloomington, Ind., and London, 1968). The description of industrial life given in the first chapters of *I. Deutscher, *Stalin: A Political Biography* (New York and London, 1949) (Oxford Galaxy) and the discussion of *Theodore H. von Laue, *Why Lenin? Why Stalin? A Reappraisal of the Russian Revolution, 1900–1930* (Philadelphia and New York, 1964) (Lippincott) rightly stress the immense difficulties in the way of solving Russian economic and social problems.

DIPLOMATIC EVENTS AND THE FIRST WORLD WAR

The diplomatic history of the thirty-five years before the First World War has been examined in minute detail because archives of the foreign offices became accessible soon after 1918. The decisive years for the formation of new constellations among the powers are treated in William L. Langer, *The Diplomacy of Imperialism, 1890–1902*, 2 vols. (New York, 1935), which contains a discussion of the literature and concept of imperialism; articles by the same author collected in *Explorations in Crisis: Papers on International History* (Cambridge, Mass., 1969) study main events in the following decade. The methods and techniques of prewar diplomacy emerge clearly from Sir Harold Nicolson, *Portrait of a Diplomatist* (Boston and New York, 1930). The most comprehensive description of the events leading to the outbreak of the First World War will be found in Luigi Albertini, *The Origins of the War of 1914*, 3 vols. (London, New York, and Toronto, 1952–1957). For those who find these three volumes heavy going, *Laurence Lafore, *The Long Fuse* (Philadelphia and New York, 1965) (Lippincott) can be recommended as a brief and reliable account which also reviews previous literature. Vladimir Dedijer, *The Road to Sarajevo* (New York, 1966) has interest as a very detailed investigation of a special problem, that of responsibility for the events in Sarajevo. *Fritz Fischer, *Germany's Aims in the First World War* (New York, 1967) (Norton) is a study of German war aims but also throws much light on German responsibility for the outbreak of the war. The history of the war itself has been treated in many memoirs, among them those of Lloyd George and Churchill, and also in studies of military history. A valuable analysis of the connection between military planning and political necessities is Paul Guinn, *British Strategy and Politics, 1914–1918* (London, 1965), and the relationship between war and economic developments is investigated in Gerald D. Feldman, *Army Industry and Labor in Germany, 1914–1918* (Princeton, N.J., 1966), which deals with Germany but is of general interest because similar situations existed in other countries. The First World War is placed in a wider historical context in Hajo Holborn, *The Political Collapse of Europe* (New York, 1951).

THE INTERWAR PERIOD

A number of works supply good general views of important aspects of these decades. Raymond J. Sontag, *A Broken World: 1919–1939* (New York, 1971) is a competent survey, although not without idiosyncrasies. The connections which linked the two world wars are emphasized in *Raymond Aron, *The Century of Total War* (New York, 1954) (Beacon). The great divide in the interwar years affecting the role of Europe was the depression which began in 1929; for a review of its effects see *Survey of International Affairs, 1931*, ed. by Arnold J. Toynbee (London, 1932), and for a more detailed analysis of its impact in the various European countries see "The Great Depression," *Journal of Contemporary History*, Vol. IV, No. 4 (1969). Fascism is examined as a general European phenomenon in *European Fascism*, ed. by S. J. Woolf (New York, 1968) (Vintage). *E. H. Carr, *The Twenty Years' Crisis, 1919–1939* (London, 1939) (Harper Torchbook) is noteworthy as a document of the time rather than as a valid statement of the significance of these years. Those novels of André Malraux which have the crucial political events of this period as background suggest something of the revolutionary radicalism which the hesitating and wavering policy of the ruling groups produced.

The ideas and interests which influenced and determined the peace settlement have been thoroughly discussed and analyzed by Arno J. Mayer in *Political Origins of the New Diplomacy, 1917–1918* (New Haven, 1959) (Meridian) and *Politics and Diplomacy of Peacemaking. Containment and Counterrevolution at Versailles, 1918–1919* (New York, 1967) (Vintage). *Sir Harold Nicolson, *Peacemaking, 1919* (New York, 1939) (Universal Library) gives a report of the peace conference from a human angle. The results of all the peace negotiations are succinctly summarized in Arnold J. Toynbee, *The World after the Peace Conference* (London, 1925), and throughout the entire following period the yearly volumes of the *Survey of International Affairs*, to which the preceding Toynbee book is a prologue, are a helpful guide. The role of the Russian problem in the politics of the postwar years is clarified in Richard H. Ullman, *Britain and the Russian Civil War* (Princeton, N.J., 1968), at least insofar as Great Britain is concerned.

For a comprehensive treatment of the conduct of foreign affairs during the interwar years see *The Diplomats, 1919–1939*, ed. by Gordon Craig and Felix Gilbert (Princeton, N.J., 1953) (Atheneum). Sir Harold Nicolson, *Curzon: The Last Phase, 1919–1925* (New York, 1939) demonstrates the possibilities and advantages of traditional diplomacy in the settlement of the postwar world. For a brilliant summarization of the failure of diplomacy in the 1930's see *Winston S. Churchill, *The Second World War*, Vol. I, *The Gathering Storm* (Boston, 1948) (Bantam). Charles S. Mayer, *Recasting Bourgeois Europe: Stabilization of France, Germany, and Italy* (Princeton, N.J., 1975) connects the general European situation with the economic and social problems of the chief continental powers; likewise Stephen A. Schuker, *The End of French Predominance in Europe: The Financial Crisis of 1924 and the Adoption of the Dawes Plan* (Chapel Hill, N.C., 1976) connects developments in European foreign policy with issues of international finance. In general, the events of foreign policy in the 1930's cannot be separated from the internal history of the various European countries, extensively treated in books listed in the following paragraphs.

The two states on which we have an overabundance of historical literature are Germany and Great Britain. This is natural because their policies were crucial for the development of the interwar years.

For the Weimar Republic, see Peter Gay, *Weimar Culture* (New York, 1968) and Walter Laqueur, *Weimar* (New York, 1974). Two leading statesmen of the Weimar Republic are treated in Klaus Epstein, *Matthias Erzberger and the Dilemma of German Democracy* (Princeton, N.J., 1959) and *Henry Ashby Turner, Jr., *Stresemann and the Politics of the Weimar Republic* (Princeton, N.J., 1963) (Princeton); these books indicate how precarious the hold of the democratic forces was. This is underlined by Christoph M. Kimmich, *Germany and the League of Nations* (Chicago, 1976), who shows the impact of the enemies of the republic in foreign policy. The strength of the opponents of the republic is delineated in *Gordon Craig, *The Politics of the Prussian Army, 1640–1945* (New York, 1955) (Oxford Galaxy) and also in Andreas Dorpalen, *Hindenburg and the Weimar Republic* (Princeton, N.J., 1964), which portrays the surrender of power to the Nazis. For intellectual trends which contributed to the rise of the Nazis see *George L. Mosse. *The*

Crisis of German Ideology (New York, 1964) (Universal Library). On Germany under the Nazis only a few books will be mentioned, works which throw light on the diverse aspects of the regime. Of books on Hitler *Alan Bullock, *Hitler: A Study in Tyranny* (London, 1952) (Harper Torchbook) long held first place, but Joachim C. Fest, *Hitler* must now be considered as the most authoritative biography; Robert G. L. Waite, *The Psychopathic God: Adolf Hitler* (New York, 1977), though somewhat questionable in its psychology, has some important insights. These works, of course, use sources like the memoirs of Albert Speer or the diaries of Josef Goebbels. An example of the establishment and functioning of Nazi control is presented in Oron J. Hale, *The Captive Press in the Third Reich* (Princeton, N.J., 1964). For the cultural policy of the Nazis see Barbara Miller Lane, *Architecture and Politics in Germany, 1918–1945* (Cambridge, Mass., 1968). The impact of the Nazi regime on the German social structure is carefully analyzed in *David Schoenbaum, *Hitler's Social Revolution: Class and Status in Nazi Germany, 1933–1939* (New York, 1966) (Doubleday Anchor). The best survey of the Nazi regime in all its various aspects is *Karl Dietrich Bracher, *The German Dictatorship* (New York, 1970) (Praeger). A colorful but rather simplified account of the Nazi years, with a very full bibliography, is *William L. Shirer, *The Rise and Fall of the Third Reich: A History of Nazi Germany* (New York, 1960) (Fawcett Crest, also Simon and Schuster, in two volumes).

On Great Britain, a lively, amusingly prejudiced history of the interwar years is A. J. P. Taylor, *English History, 1914–1945* (New York and Oxford, 1965); the impact of the First World War on the intellectual postwar world is analyzed by Paul Fussell, *The Great War and Modern Memory* (New York, 1975); the social problems of this period are well presented in *Robert Graves and Alan Hodge, *The Long Week-End: A Social History of Great Britain, 1918–1939* (New York, 1941) (Norton), and for a discussion of British policy from the point of view of Labor see Alan Bullock, *The Life and Times of Ernest Bevin*, Vol. I, *Trade Union Leader, 1881–1940* (London, Melbourne, and Toronto, 1960). An important biography is David Marquand, *Ramsay MacDonald* (London, 1977), which tries to place the personality and policy of this statesman in a more favorable light. Robert R. James, *Churchill: A Study in Failure, 1900–1939* (New York, 1970) gives an interesting, unorthodox point of view. A central issue of historical discussion is the appeasement policy of the 1930's. For the problems of decision making in British policy, see D. C. Watt, *Personalities and Policies: Studies in the Formulation of British Foreign Policy in the Twentieth Century* (Notre Dame, Ind., 1965). The attitude of the entire group of appeasers emerges brilliantly from *A. L. Rowse, *Appeasement: A Study in Political Decline, 1933–1939* (New York, 1961) (Norton). For biographies of two of the main appeasers see Andrew Boyle, *Montagu Norman: A Biography* (London, 1967) and William R. Rock, *Neville Chamberlain* (New York, 1969). The latter book discusses the entire dispute about the appeasement policy and tries hard to be fair to the appeasers—too hard, in my opinion. The desperation among the young produced by the policy of the ruling group is movingly evoked in *Peter Stansky and William Abrahams, *Journey to the Frontier: Two Roads to the Spanish Civil War* (Boston,

1966) (Norton). Hugh Dalton, *The Fateful Years: Memoirs, 1931–1945* (London, 1957) must be mentioned as the best book of political memoirs on this period.

To gain an understanding of the policy of France in the interwar years, see the reports of one of the best-informed journalists of the time, collected in Alexander Werth, *The Twilight of France, 1933–1940* (New York, 1942). Joel G. Colton, *Léon Blum: Humanist in Politics* (New York, 1966) gives a good picture of the most interesting French statesman of this period. Next to the above-mentioned book by Stephen A. Schuker, Judith M. Hughes, *To the Maginot Line: The Politics of French Military Preparation in the 1920's* (Cambridge, Mass., 1971), depicts the contrast between French claims and actual strength. Geoffrey Warner, *Pierre Laval and the Eclipse of France* (New York, 1968) represents a very substantial contribution to our understanding of the evolution of French appeasement and defeatism.

The rise of the Bolsheviks in Russia is described in remarkable detail and with great clarity in Alexander Rabinowitch, *The Bolsheviks Come to Power: The Revolution of 1917 in Petrograd* (New York, 1976). For the rise of Stalin, see Robert C. Tucker, *Stalin as Revolutionary, 1879–1929: A Study in History and Personality* (New York, 1973); and for the opposition to him, Stephen F. Cohen, *Bukharin and the Bolshevik Revolution: A Political Biography* (New York, 1974). *Ilya Ehrenburg, *Memoirs, 1921–1941* (Cleveland and New York, 1964) (Universal Library) shows the conditions of intellectual work in Stalin's time. The aspects of oppression are sharply revealed in the writings of *Aleksandr I. Solzhenitsyn, particularly in his *The Gulag Archipelago* (New York, 1974–75) (Harper & Row).

The rise of Fascism in Italy is fully described and analyzed by Adrian Lyttelton, *The Seizure of Power: Fascism in Italy, 1919–1929* (London, 1973). *H. Stuart Hughes, *The United States and Italy* (Cambridge, Mass., 1953) (Norton) places this development in a broader context, and Charles F. Delzell, *Mussolini's Enemies: The Italian Anti-Fascist Resistance* (Princeton, N.J., 1961) gives details about the oppressive nature of the regime.

The Spanish Civil War was an international event, but also the climax of the internal developments in Spain during the 1920's and 1930's; as such it is presented in *Gabriel Jackson, *The Spanish Republic and the Civil War, 1931–1939* (Princeton, N.J., 1965) (Princeton) and in *Stanley Payne, *The Spanish Revolution* (New York, 1970) (Norton). A clear, general account of the war will be found in *Hugh Thomas, *The Spanish Civil War* (New York, 1961) (Harper Colophon).

For an exposition of developments in the Balkan countries and their dependence on the policy of the great European powers, see *Hugh Seton-Watson, *Eastern Europe Between the Wars, 1918–1941* (Cambridge, Eng., 1945) (Harper Torchbook). This dependence emerged clearly in the Czech crisis. *John W. Wheeler-Bennett, *Munich: Prologue to Tragedy* (London, 1948) (Viking Compass), although no longer quite up-to-date, remains valuable as a testimony of the emotional atmosphere surrounding the Czech crisis and Munich.

THE SECOND WORLD WAR

The events of the Second World War are fully described in *Gordon Wright, *The Ordeal of Total War, 1939–1945* (New York, Evanston, Ill., and London, 1968) (Harper Torchbook); this book has an excellent bibliography. John Lukacs, *The Last European War: September 1939–December 1941* (New York, 1976) deserves particular mention, especially the "description of the lives of the people" in the second part. It should be mentioned that two of the main actors in the Second World War have written memoirs that not only have great historical interest but are also remarkable literary achievements: *Winston S. Churchill, *The Second World War*, 6 vols. (Boston, 1948–1953) (Bantam) and *Charles de Gaulle, *The Comlete War Memoirs of Charles de Gaulle, 1940–1946*, 3 vols. in one, Vol. I trans. by Jonathan Griffin, Vols. II–III trans. by Richard Howard (New York, 1955–1960) (Simon and Schuster). Sir Llewellyn Woodward, *British Foreign Policy in the Second World War* (London, 1962) provides an illustration of the interaction of political and military events, and one of the decisive developments—the emergence of close cooperation between Great Britain and the United States—is narrated in Joseph P. Lash, *Roosevelt and Churchill, 1939–1941: The Partnership That Saved the West* (New York, 1976). The economic aspects of the war are analyzed in Alan S. Milward, *War, Economy, and Society 1939–1945* (Berkeley, Calif., 1977). There has been a rash of books on the role of intelligence operations, not always reliable, but F. W. Winterbotham, *The Ultra Secret* (New York, 1974) and J. C. Masterman, *The Double-Cross System in the War of 1939 to 1945* (New Haven, Conn., 1972) are revealing. For the German side of the war see Harold C. Deutsch, *The Conspiracy Against Hitler in the Twilight War* (Minneapolis, 1968); F. H. Hinsley, *Hitler's Strategy* (Cambridge, Eng., 1951); and *Hugh R. Trevor-Roper, *The Last Days of Hitler* (New York, 1947) (Collier). For the grimmest aspect of the Second World War—the Holocaust—see *Lucy S. Dawidowicz, *The War Against the Jews: 1933–1945* (New York, 1975) (Bantam).

AFTER THE SECOND WORLD WAR

Historical treatment of the last thirty years is either concerned with providing surveys or with discussing single events. The available source material is spotty although the Statistical Yearbooks edited by the Department of Economic and Social Affairs of the United Nations provide the material needed to establish the main features of the postwar economic development.

As an introduction to the basic problems of global diplomacy Raymond Aron, *Peace and War: A Theory of International Relations* (New York, 1966) remains unsurpassed. A helpful survey of the postwar period is Walter Laqueur, *Europe Since Hitler* (Harmondsworth, England, 1972). Adam Ulan, *Expansion and Coexistence: The History of Soviet Foreign Policy* (New York, 1968) traces Russian foreign policy throughout the entire postwar period. Alastair Buchan, *The End of the Postwar Era: A New Balance of World Power* (New

York, 1974) also attempts an evaluation of the developments of the entire period. For a general discussion of the postwar intellectual atmosphere, see H. Stuart Hughes, *The Sea Change* (New York, 1975).

With regard to particular events, the years of the Cold War have been discussed passionately; Louis J. Halle, *The Cold War as History* (New York, 1967) gives the facts. Two recent books, based on much new material, have made much of the preceding discussion obsolete: Martin J. Sherwin, *A World Destroyed: The Atomic Bomb and the Grand Alliance* (New York, 1975), and Daniel Yergin, *Shattered Peace: The Origins of the Cold War and the National Security State* (Boston, 1977). Robert J. Donovan, *Conflict and Crisis: The Presidency of Harry S. Truman, 1945–1948* (New York, 1977) although perhaps less critical, adds some valuable material. Regarding eastern Europe the manner in which the Bolsheviks established control in eastern Europe has been described in Hugh Seton-Watson, *The Pattern of Communist Revolution* (London, 1953). For a more detailed discussion of the events in the Balkans see *Robert Lee Wolff, *The Balkans in Our Time* (Cambridge, Mass., 1967) (Norton). An informative description of the situation within the eastern bloc is Zbigniew K. Brzezinski, *The Soviet Bloc: Unity and Conflict* (Cambridge, Mass., 1960); and for the events in Czechoslovakia, see H. Gordon Skilling, *Czechoslovakia's Interrupted Revolution* (Princeton, N.J., 1976).

Regarding western Europe, the changes in France since the Second World War have been startling; some picture evolves from the articles collected in *France Since 1930*, ed. by John E. Talbott (New York, 1972). A novel by *Simone de Beauvoir, *The Mandarins* (1954) (Popular Library; also Meridian), is an interesting reproduction of the intellectual atmosphere in France at the time of the end of the war; the principal figures of the novel, although under disguised names, are Sartre and Camus. For a general survey of the economic and political development in France after the war, see Donald C. McKay, *The United States and France* (Cambridge, Mass., 1951). An outstanding analysis of the entire French situation is *John Ardagh, *The New French Revolution* (New York, 1968) (Harper Colophon).

For Great Britain it might be well to refer to the above-mentioned book by *Robert K. Webb, *Modern England: From the Eighteenth Century to the Present* (New York, 1968) (Dodd, Mead), which uses the somewhat dispersed literature in a critical way. A very thorough and reliable survey is *Peter Calvocarossi, *The British Experience: 1945–1975* (New York, 1978) (Pantheon). Richard Crossman, *The Diaries of a Cabinet Minister: 1964–1968* (New York, 1976/77) place the reader in the middle of British parliamentary life.

Writings in English on postwar Germany are less satisfactory. For German foreign policy in the post war period see *Gordon Craig, *From Bismarck to Adenauer: Aspects of German Statecraft* (Baltimore, 1958) (Harper Torchbook). Lewis J. Edinger, *Kurt Schumacher: A Study in Personality and Political Behavior* (Stanford, 1965) provides a good introduction to the party struggles of the years immediately after the war, although since then a somewhat new situation has developed. But *Postwar German Culture*, an anthology ed. by Charles E. McClelland and Steven P. Scher gives a very broad and comprehensive picture of the tendencies in German intellectual life. The astounding Italian recovery has been carefully studied; see *H. Stuart Hughes, *The United States and Italy* (Cambridge, Mass., 1953 (Norton) and *Muriel Grindrod, *The Rebuilding of Italy: Politics and Economics, 1945–1955* (London and New York, 1955) (Oxford). For more recent developments on the domestic scene, see *Communism in Italy and France*, ed. by Donald L. M. Blackmer and Sidney Tarrow (Princeton, N.J., 1975). See *Santiago Carrillo, *Eurocommunism and the State* (New York, 1978) (Lawrence Hill), for an account of that phenomenon by a leading proponent. For a thorough study of terrorism see Walter Laqueur, *Terrorism* (Boston, 1977).

Index